Lecture Notes in Computer Science

Edited by G. Goos, Karlsruhe and J. Hartmanis, Ithaca

10

Computing Methods in Applied Sciences and Engineering

Part 1

International Symposium, Versailles, December 17–21, 1973

IRIA LABORIA
Institut de Recherche d'Informatique et d'Automatique

Edited by R. Glowinski and J. L. Lions

Springer-Verlag
Berlin · Heidelberg · New York 1974

Dr. R. Glowinski
Dr. J. L. Lions

IRIA LABORIA
Domaine de Voluceau – Rocquencourt
F-78150 Le Chesnay/France

AMS Subject Classifications (1970): 65-02, 65K05, 65Lxx, 65Mxx, 65Nxx, 65P05, 76-04, 93E10, 93E25
CR Subject Classifications (1974): 3.1, 3.2, 5.1

ISBN 3-540-06768-X Springer-Verlag Berlin · Heidelberg · New York
ISBN 0-387-06768-X Springer-Verlag New York · Heidelberg · Berlin

Offsetdruck: Julius Beltz, Hemsbach/Bergstr.

PREFACE

Le présent volume rassemble les travaux présentés au Colloque "International sur les Méthodes de Calcul Scientifique et Technique", organisé par l'IRIA-LABORIA ♦ du 17 au 21 Décembre 1973, sous le patronage de l'IFIP.

Ce Colloque a réuni à Versailles près de 400 chercheurs et ingénieurs de tous les pays du monde. L'originalité des travaux présentés, la qualité de l'auditoire et des questions posées tout au long du Colloque, attestent de l'extrême intérêt scientifique et technique, qui s'attache à l'usage des ordinateurs pour le calcul scientifique.

Les organisateurs tiennent à remercier tout particulièrement :

Monsieur André DANZIN, Directeur de l'IRIA

Monsieur Michel MONPETIT, Directeur Adjoint de l'IRIA

Le Service des Relations Extérieures de l'IRIA

qui ont permis l'organisation de ce Colloque.

Nos remerciements vont, également, à tous les conférenciers et aux différents présidents de séance :

MM. J.H. ARGYRIS
A.V. BALAKRISHNAN
P. BROUSSE
J. DOUGLAS
D. FEINGOLD
B. FRAEIJS de VEUBEKE
P. MOREL
W. PRAGER
E. ROUBINE
O.C. ZIENKIEWICZ

qui ont animé d'intéressantes discussions.

R. GLOWINSKI et J.L. LIONS

♦ Institut de Recherche d'Informatique et d'Automatique
Laboratoire de Recherche de l'IRIA.

PREFACE

This book contains the lectures which have been presented during the " International Symposium on Computing Methods in Applied Sciences and Engineering " organised by IRIA - LABORIA ♦ under the sponsorship of IFIP. (December 17, 21, 1973)

400 people, scientists and engineers coming from many countries attended this meeting in Versailles. The originality of the work presented, the high quality of the audience and the pertinent questions raised during the symposium show how important is, at the present time, the scientific and technical interest for the use of computers in applied science and engineering.

The organisers wish to express their gratitude to :

Monsieur André DANZIN, Director of IRIA,

Monsieur Michel MONPETIT, Deputy Director of IRIA

The IRIA Public Relations Office
who have contributed to the organisation of this Symposium.

They also address their thanks to all the speakers and to the chairmen of sessions :

MM. J.H. ARGYRIS
A. V. BALAKRISHNAN
P. BROUSSE
J. DOUGLAS
D. FEINGOLD
B. FRAEIJS de VEUBEKE
P. MOREL
W. PRAGER
E. ROUBINE
O. C. ZIENKIEWICZ

who have directed interesting discussions.

R. GLOWINSKI J. L. LIONS

♦ Institut de Recherche d'Informatique et d'Automatique
Laboratoire de Recherche de l'IRIA

textes des communications

Ce colloque est organisé par l'IRIA sous le patronage de l'International Federation for Information Processing.

This symposium is organised by IRIA under the sponsorship of the International Federation for Information Processing.

Organisateurs
Organizers

R. Glowinski
J.L. Lions

TABLE DES MATIERES
TABLE OF CONTENTS

TOME I
PART I

GENERALITES
GENERALITIES

Methods of stuctural optimization -
W. Prager 1

Optimisation des systèmes portants
et propulsifs par la méthode des
singularités -
L. Malavard 20

Some contributions to non-linear
solid mechanics -
J.H. Argyris, P.C. Dunne 42

ELEMENTS FINIS
FINITE ELEMENTS

One-sided approximation and
plate bending -
G. Strang 140

Quelques méthodes d'éléments finis
pour le problème d'une plaque encastrée -
P.G. Ciarlet 156

Un nouvel élément de coques générales -
B.M. Irons 177

Numerical solution of the stationary
Navier-Stokes equations by finite element
methods -
P. Jamet, P.A. Raviart 193

Finite elements method in aerospace
engineering problems
B. Fraeijs de Veubeke 224

Visco-plasticity and plasticity
An alternative for finite element
solution of material nonlinearities -
O.C. Zienkiewicz 259

Some superconvergence results for an H^1 - Galerkin procedure for the heat equation -
J. Douglas, T. Dupont, M.F. Wheeler 288

Application de la méthode des éléments finis - Un procédé de sous-assemblage -
J.M. Boisserie 312

PROBLEMES NON-LINEAIRES
NON-LINEAR PROBLEMS

Formulation and application of certain primal and mixed finite element models of finite deformations of elastic bodies -
J.T. Oden 334

Méthodes numériques pour le projet d'appareillages industriels avancés -
S. Albertoni 366

Etude numérique du champ magnétique dans un alternateur tétrapolaire par la méthode des éléments finis -
R. Glowinski, A. Marrocco 392

Une nouvelle méthode d'analyse numérique des problèmes de filtration dans les matériaux poreux -
C. Baiocchi 410

CIRCUITS ET TRANSISTORS
NETWORKS AND SEMI-CONDUCTORS

Numerical methods for stiff systems of differential equations related with transistors, tunnel diodes, etc. -
W. Miranker, F. Hoppensteadt 416

Conception, simulation, optimisation d'un filtre à l'aide d'un ordinateur -
A. Guerard 433

Computing methods in semiconductor problems -
M. Reiser 441

Simulation numérique de la fabrication et du comportement des dispositifs semiconducteurs
D. Vandorpe 467

TABLE DES MATIERES
TABLE OF CONTENTS

TOME II
PART II

MECANIQUES DES FLUIDES
FLUIDS MECHANICS

Recent advances in computational fluid dynamics - T.D. Butler 1

Méthodes et techniques d'intégration numérique adaptées à l'étude des écoulements planétaires - R. Sadourny 22

Flow computations with accurate space derivative methods - J. Gazdag 37

Numerical simulation of the Taylor-Green vortex - S.A. Orszag 50

Problèmes et méthodes numériques en physique des plasmas à très haute température - C. Mercier, J.C. Adam, Soubbaramayer, J.L. Soule 65

Problèmes de contrôle optimal en physique des plasmas - J.P. Boujot, J.P. Morera, R. Temam 107

Problèmes de stabilité numérique posés par les systèmes hyperboliques avec conditions aux limites - J.J. Smolderen 135

Résolution numérique des équations de Navier-Stokes pour les fluides compressibles - R. Peyret 160

PROBLEMES D'ONDES
WAVES PROBLEMS

Three dimensional flows around airfoils with shocks - A. Jameson 185

Lage amplitude wave propagation in arteries and veins - Y. Kivity, R. Collins 213

Increase of accuracy of projective-difference schemes -
G.I. Marchuk, V.V. Shaydourov 240

Méthodes numériques en électro-magnétisme -
J.Ch. Bolomey 261

CONTROLE OPTIMAL
OPTIMAL CONTROL

Time-optimal control synthesis for non-linear systems
A flight dynamic example -
A.V. Balakrishnan 289

Numerical analysis of problems arising in biochemistry -
J.P. Kernevez 312

Sur l'approximation numérique d'inéquations quasi-variationnelles stationnaires -
A. Bensoussan, J.L. Lions 325

Gestion optimale des réservoirs d'une vallée hydraulique -
A. Breton, F. Falgarone 339

FILTRAGE ET IDENTIFICATION
FILTERING AND IDENTIFICATION

Algorithmes de calcul de modèles markoviens pour fonctions aléatoires -
P. Faurre 352

Estimation de paramètres distribués dans les equations aux dérivées partielles -
G. Chavent 361

Adaption de la méthode du gradient à un problème d'identification de domaine -
J. Cea, A. Gioan, J. Michel 391

Application de la méthode des éléments finis à la résolution d'un problème de domaine optimal -
D. Bégis, R. Glowinski 403

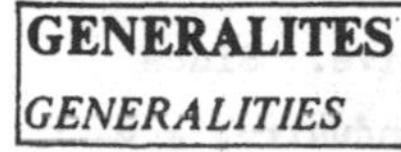

METHODS OF STRUCTURAL OPTIMIZATION*

William Prager

Professor Emeritus, Brown University, Providence, R. I., USA

ABSTRACT

The paper is concerned with methods of optimal structural design. Typical ingredients of structural optimization problems are discussed in Sect. 1. The basic problem is identified as one in mathematical programming, in general nonlinear programming, and the difficulties are indicated that are experienced in the application of standard methods of nonlinear programming. The following three sections deal with optimal plastic design, which is the most developed area of structural optimization because linear programming is applicable to it. Sections 2 and 3 are respectively concerned with the optimal plastic design of a truss of given layout and the determination of the optimal layout of a truss that has to transmit given loads to a given foundation. Optimal plastic design of beams and grillages is discussed in Sect. 4. Section 5 is devoted to optimal design of elastic trusses and beams. Computational aspects of structural optimization are discussed in Sect. 6, and some new ideas are mentioned in Sect. 7.

1. INTRODUCTION

To be well-posed, a problem of optimal structural design requires specification of the purpose of the structure, the design constraints, and the design objective. The general purpose of a structure is to carry given loads. In general, a structure will have to carry several alternative sets of loads, but it may happen that the design of the structure is governed by only one of them. Design constraints may concern the geometry of the structure or its behavior under the given loads. Geometric constraints specify at least the space that is available for the structure, but may go much further in restricting the shape of the structure and the dimensions of its members. Behavioral constraints set bounds on quantities that characterize the response of the structure to the loads for which it is being designed. Examples of behavioral constraints are upper bounds on stresses and deflections, and lower bounds on fundamental natural frequencies or on the ratio in which the given loads would have to be increased before they would cause failure by buckling or plastic flow. The general design objective is minimization of the combined costs of the manufacture of the structure and its operation over the expected lifetime. It is typical for aerospace structures that the cost of the fuel that would be needed to carry additional structural weight and the accompanying reduction in payload are much more important considerations than the manufacturing cost. In these circum-

* Research supported by the U. S. Army Research Office - Durham.

stances, minimization of structural weight becomes the design objective. Since structural optimization is particularly important in the aerospace industry, a vast majority of papers on structural optimization is concerned with design for minimal weight.

Naturally discrete or artificially discretized problems of structural optimization are essentially problems of mathematical programming, usually nonlinear programming. The development of powerful methods of nonlinear programming, and the availability of computers with large immediate-access memories therefore raised hopes for automated optimal design of practical structures by direct application of these programming methods. Except for optimal plastic design, which may be treated by linear programming, these hopes have not so far been fulfilled. Automated design procedures were in fact developed that solve the basic nonlinear programming problem by gradient or feasible directions methods, or treat it by a sequence of linear programs, or transform it into an unconstrained problem by the introduction of penalty functions (for a survey, see Pope and Schmit, 1971). According to Gellatly and Berke, 1971, however, the use of these direct methods entails a prohibitive number of design iterations for structures with more than about 150 design variables. Even for much smaller numbers of design variables, the possibility is troublesome that the procedure may converge towards a local optimum. To get some assurance that a global optimum has been achieved, it may be necessary to start the procedure from quite different initial designs and choose from the corresponding final designs the one with the smallest weight.

Sved and Ginos, 1968, have pointed out another reason why direct search techniques may not be satisfactory. Consider, for example, the minimum-weight design of a truss for given loads. One way of approaching the problem of optimal layout is to start with a lattice of possible nodes and consider the truss in which any two of these nodes are connected by a bar. The bar forces of this highly redundant basic truss must satisfy conditions of equilibrium and compatibility, which will be incorporated in the formulation of the problem, and the search will be conducted over "feasible" trusses for which these conditions are satisfied. The optimal truss, however, may be a subtruss of the basic truss obtained from the latter by the omission of certain bars. In this case, the bar forces of the optimal truss together with zero forces in the omitted bars will not satisfy all compatibility conditions of the basic truss. Accordingly, the optimal truss is not a member of the set over which the search is extended. Sved and Ginos concluded that it would be necessary to supplement the search described above by a similar search of the feasible designs of each statically stable subtruss of the basic truss. Since each of these subtrusses has a different set of compatibility conditions, this would be an enormous task. Sheu and Schmit, 1972, have shown how it can be reduced to manageable size, at least for the comparatively small example trusses they considered. (The largest of their basic trusses has eight nodes and twenty-two bars.)

In recent years, attention has turned from the direct application of the search techniques of nonlinear programming to the derivation of optimality conditions and their use in design procedures. Some of this work is surveyed in the following. Various problems of optimal plastic design and optimal elastic design are discussed in Sects. 2-4 and 5, respectively. Section 6 treats computational aspects of structural optimization, and some new ideas are mentioned in Sect. 7.

2. OPTIMAL PLASTIC DESIGN OF TRUSS OF GIVEN LAYOUT

By far the most developed area of structural optimization is optimal plastic design. Here, the structural material is treated as rigid, perfectly plastic, and the structure is to use the smallest possible amount of material subject to the condition that a given state of loading should represent the load-carrying capacity of the structure.

It was recognized quite early (Foulkes, 1954) that the optimal plastic design of a structure of given layout may be formulated as a linear program. Consider, for instance, the minimum-volume design of a truss with the layout shown in Fig. 1. The bars of the truss are to be made of a rigid, perfectly plastic material with the

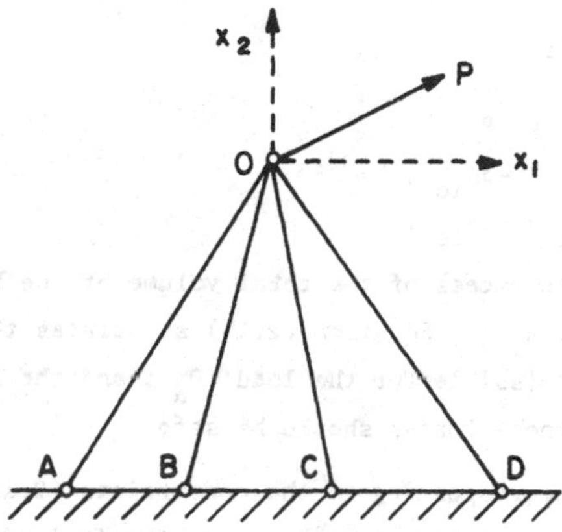

Fig. 1: Optimization of truss of given layout

tensile and compressive yield limits $\pm\sigma$, and the possibility of buckling is to be disregarded in the analysis. The foundation, which supports the truss, is assumed to be rigid. To exclude degenerate cases, in which some of the four bars are missing in the optimal truss, we prescribe a minimum cross-sectional area A_{io} for bar i, $(i=1,\ldots,4)$, and write the actual cross-sectional area of this bar as $A_{io} + A_i$, where $A_i \geq 0$. At the joint O, which is taken as the origin of the coordinates

x_α , (α = 1,2) , a load with components P_α is to act. The length of bar i will be denoted by ℓ_i , and the direction cosines of the axis of this bar (oriented from the foundation towards 0) by $c_{i\alpha}$.

The following concepts will be useful in the discussion of this problem. For generality, they will be defined without reference to the particularly simple example in Fig. 1. A system of axial forces in the bars of a truss that equilibrates given loads acting at the joints of the truss will be called "statically admissible" for these loads. For specified cross-sectional areas of the bars, a statically admissible system of bar forces will be called "safe" if the corresponding axial stress in each bar does not have an absolute value in excess of σ . A system of rates of extension of the bars of the truss will be called "kinematically admissible" if it is derived from velocities of the joints of the truss that do not violate the kinematic constraints at the supports.

Let us now return to the problem in Fig. 1. According to the static theorem of limit analysis (see, for instance, Prager, 1959), the load P_α will not exceed the load-carrying capacity of the truss if there exists a safe, statically admissible system of bar forces F_i for this load. Accordingly, an optimal design is characterized by the following linear program*:

Minimize

$$\sigma\varepsilon_o \Sigma_i \ell_i A_i \tag{2.1a}$$

subject to

$$\Sigma_i c_{i\alpha} F_i = P_\alpha , \tag{2.1b}$$

$$F_i + \sigma A_i \geq -\sigma A_{io} , \tag{2.1c}$$

$$-F_i + \sigma A_i \geq -\sigma A_{io} . \tag{2.1d}$$

The sum in (2.1a) is the excess of the total volume of the bars of the truss over the minimal volume $\Sigma_i \ell_i A_{io}$. Equation (2.1b) stipulates that the bar forces F_i should be statically admissible for the load P_α , and the inequalities (2.1c) and (2.1d) stipulate that these forces should be safe.

If the dual variables corresponding to the constraints (2.1b) through (2.1d) are denoted by v_α , $\hat{\mu}_i$, μ_i , the dual program has the following form:

Maximize

$$\Sigma_\alpha P_\alpha v_\alpha - \sigma\Sigma_i A_{io}(\hat{\mu}_i + \mu_i) \tag{2.2a}$$

subject to

$$\mu_i - \hat{\mu}_i = \Sigma_\alpha c_{i\alpha} v_\alpha , \tag{2.2b}$$

$$\mu_i + \hat{\mu}_i \leq \varepsilon_o \ell_i . \tag{2.2c}$$

* To facilitate the mechanical interpretation of the dual program, the factor $\sigma\varepsilon_o$ has been introduced in the objective function, where ε_o is a reference rate of extension.

Note that the variables v_α are not restricted in sign, and that the equality sign applies in (2.2c) if $A_i > 0$. Note further that $\hat{\mu}_i > 0$ only if the stress $F_i/(A_{io} + A_i)$ has the value $-\sigma$, and that $\mu_i > 0$ only if this stress has the value σ. Accordingly, either $\hat{\mu}_i$ or μ_i or both vanish.

The dual problem may be given a mechanical interpretation by identifying $v_\alpha,(\alpha=1,2)$, as the velocity components of the joint 0 in a collapse mechanism under the load P_α, and $\mu_i - \hat{\mu}_i$ as the corresponding rate of elongation λ_i of bar i. Now, $\hat{\mu}_i > 0$ only if the equality sign holds in (2.1c), i.e. if the bar i is at the compressive yield limit; in this case, $\mu_i = 0$, $\lambda_i = \mu_i - \hat{\mu}_i < 0$, and

$$\mu_i + \hat{\mu}_i = |\lambda_i| . \tag{2.3}$$

The same relation is obtained for $\mu_i > 0$, in which case $\hat{\mu}_i = 0$ and $\lambda_i > 0$. Accordingly, the constraint (2.2c) may be written as

$$|\varepsilon_i| \leq \varepsilon_o , \text{ with equality sign for } A_i > 0 , \tag{2.4}$$

where ε_i is the axial strain rate of bar i in the considered collapse mechanism. Note that the signs of ε_i and F_i are coupled by the relation

$$F_i \varepsilon_i \geq 0 . \tag{2.5}$$

If a truss of the given layout is at all capable of carrying the load P_α, there exists at least one statically admissible system of bar forces, and the cross-sectional areas $A_{io} + A_i$ may be chosen sufficiently large to fulfill the constraints (2.1c) and (2.1d). According to the existence theorem of linear programming, this fact assures the existence of solutions of both the primal and the dual problems. There exists therefore a joint velocity that entails rates of extension satisfying (2.4) and (2.5).

Note that the linear programming formulation of our problem is readily adapted to the case where none of several alternative loads P'_α, P''_α, ... is to exceed the load-carrying capacity of the truss. For each load, we then have equilibrium equations of the form (2.1b) and yield constraints of the forms (2.1c) and (2.1d). The mechanical interpretation of the dual yields the optimality condition

$$|\varepsilon'_i| + |\varepsilon''_i| + \ldots \leq \varepsilon_o , \text{ with equality sign for } A_i > 0 , \tag{2.6}$$

where ε'_i, ε''_i, ... are axial strain rates in collapse mechanisms under the loads P'_α, P''_α, ... If one of these loads is too small to influence the optimal design, the corresponding rates of extension vanish.

3. OPTIMAL LAYOUT OF A TRUSS

The preceding discussion of the optimal design of the truss in Fig. 1 obviously remains valid if the joint 0 is connected to the foundation by more than four bars. This remark enables us to attack the problem of optimal layout by starting from a "basic" layout that comprises, in addition to the joint 0, a large number of potential joints at the foundation, and setting $A_{io} = 0$ for all bars of this layout to allow for the possibility that some of them may be omitted in the optimal truss. In the limiting case, where any point of the horizontal foundation is a potential joint, the optimality condition (2.4) calls for a homogeneous strain rate field in the strip between the foundation and the horizontal through O that has strain rates ε satisfying the following conditions:

$$|\varepsilon| \begin{cases} = 0 & \text{for the horizontal direction,} & (3.1a) \\ = \varepsilon_o & \text{for the direction of any bar of the optimal truss,} & (3.1b) \\ \leq \varepsilon_o & \text{for any other direction.} & (3.1c) \end{cases}$$

It follows from (3.1) that the bars of the optimal truss are along the principal directions of the considered strain rate field. Depending on whether one or both principal rates of extension have the absolute value ε_o, we have the cases shown in Figs. 2a and b. In the first case, the optimal truss is degenerate and consists

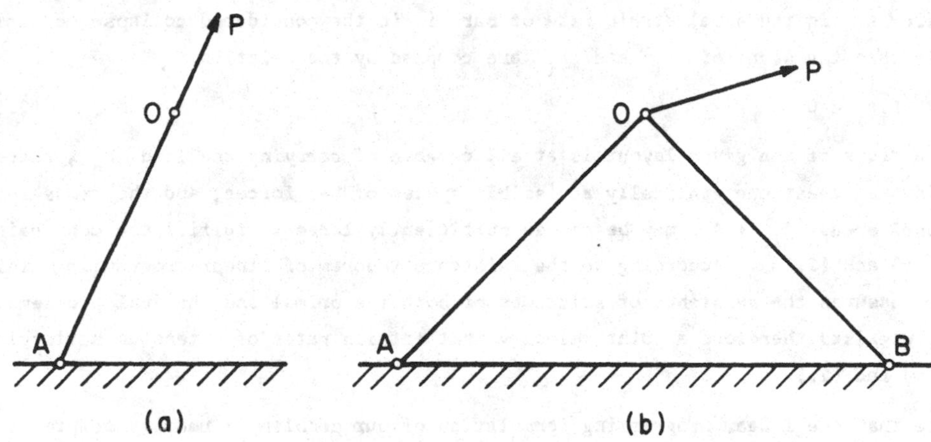

Fig. 2: (a) Degenerate optimal truss for load inclined by 45° or less against vertical

(b) Optimal truss for load inclined by more than 45° against vertical

of a single bar OA along the line of action of the load, which forms an angle of 45° or less with the vertical. In the second case, the optimal truss consists of the bars OA and OB that form angles of 45° with the vertical, while the angle between load and vertical exceeds 45°.

The conditions (3.1b) and (3.1c) quite generally govern the optimal layout of trusses for a single state of loading (Michell, 1904). Figure 3a shows the optimal truss for the transmission of the load P at O to a rigid, horizontal foundation of the limited width AB. The bars of the truss follow the principal lines of a strain rate field with principal strain rates $\pm\varepsilon_o$; along the foundation, this field has vanishing strain rate. The bars of the optimal truss form a dense orthogonal net in the region OCDE ; in the figure, only a few of these curved bars are shown. In the circular sectors ACD and BDE , there are dense systems of radial bars. Along the contour bars OCA and OEB , the axial forces are constant, and the curvature of these bars causes small axial forces in the bars of the other family. Accordingly, the interior bars of the truss are light in comparison to the contour bars. There is a substantial body of literature on trusses of this kind, which are known as Michell trusses (see, for instance, Hemp, 1966). While Michell trusses with their infinity of bars are not practical, they provide the smallest

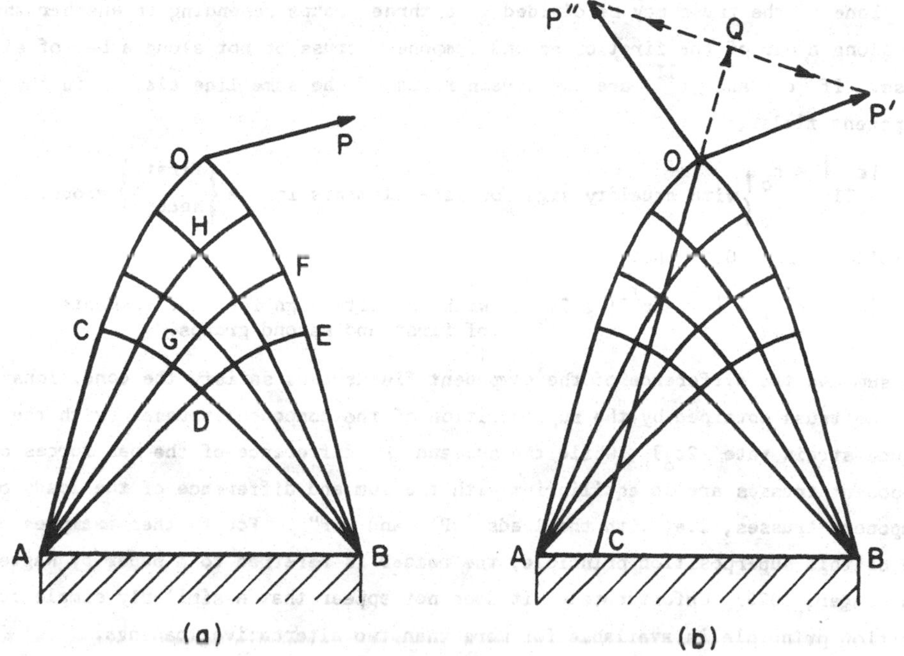

Fig. 3: (a) Optimal transmission of load P to foundation AB
(b) Optimal transmission of alternative loads P' and P" to foundation AB

possible structural weight, which is used in assessing the efficiency of more practical designs. The Michell efficiency of a truss is defined as the inverse ratio of the weights of this truss and the Michell truss for the same loading.

To formulate an optimization problem that leads to more realistic designs, one might enforce a finite number of bars by including the weight of the connections at the joints in the structural weight that is to be minimized, for instance by adding, for each joint, a fixed weight corresponding to the average weight of a connection. As is well known, fixed cost problems of this kind create considerable algorithmic difficulties.

An interesting superposition principle that furnishes the optimal truss for two alternative loadings is due to Hemp, 1968. The illustrative problem in Fig. 3b concerns the transmission of the alternative loads represented by the vectors OP' and OP" to a rigid foundation of the limited width AB. With Q as the center of the segment P'P", the given loads are written as OQ ± QP', and the optimal trusses ("component trusses") are determined for the single loads OQ and QP'. The first consists of the single bar OC, while the second has the layout in Fig. 3a. The strain rate fields for the collapse mechanisms of the component trusses, which satisfy the conditions (3.1), will be called "component fields". The line elements of the plane of the truss may be divided into three groups depending on whether they are along a bar of the first or second component truss or not along a bar of either truss. If ε^{I} and ε^{II} are the strain rates of the same line element in the two component fields,

$$\left.\begin{array}{l}|\varepsilon^{I}| \le \varepsilon_o \\ |\varepsilon^{II}| \le \varepsilon_o\end{array}\right\} \text{with equality sign for line elements in the } \left\{\begin{array}{l}\text{first} \\ \text{second}\end{array}\right\} \text{group.} \tag{3.2}$$

It follows from (3.2) that

$$|\varepsilon^{I} + \varepsilon^{II}| + |\varepsilon^{I} - \varepsilon^{II}| \le 2\varepsilon_o \,, \quad \text{with equality sign for line elements of first and second groups.} \tag{3.3}$$

The sum and the difference of the component fields thus satisfy the conditions (3.1) for the truss obtained by the superposition of the component trusses (with the reference strain rate $2\varepsilon_o$), while the sum and the difference of the bar forces of the component trusses are in equilibrium with the sum and difference of the loads on the component trusses, i.e. with the loads OP' and OP". For further examples of the use of this superposition principle, the reader is referred to a paper by Nagtegaal and Prager, 1973. Unfortunately, it does not appear that a similarly simple superposition principle is available for more than two alternative loadings.

Returning to the optimal design of a truss for a single loading, we mention the use of dynamic programming by Palmer and Sheppard, 1970. Figure 4a shows a symmetric transmission tower that carries a horizontal load 2P at the top. The uniform height h of the panels is given, as is the width $2y_3$ at the base, but the widths $2y_1$ and $2y_2$ at the bottoms of the two top panels are to be optimally chosen from a discrete set of given values, say 0.2h, 0.4h, 0.6h, 0.8h. Figure 4b shows the typical panel with the forces acting on it. Starting with the bottom panel, for which y_3 has a given value, say $y_3 = 0.6h$, we compute the weight W_3 of this panel for each possible value of y_2 and select the value $y_2 = y_2^*$ that minimizes W_3. A similar computation is carried out for the next higher panel using $y_2 = y_2^*$, and so on. The optimal truss found in this way has $y_2 = 0.6h$, $y_1 = 0.4h$ (Fig. 5a). Although this truss has the high Michell efficiency of 0.91, the method is open

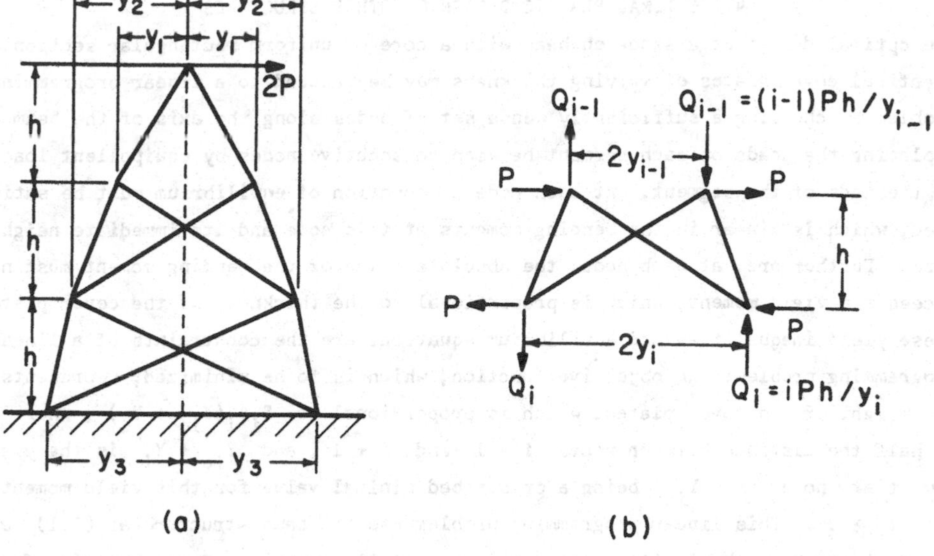

Fig. 4: (a) General layout of transmission tower: h and y_3 are given, y_1 and y_2 are to be optimally chosen
(b) Equilibrium of typical panel

to the criticism that the general layout of the truss has been chosen in advance, whereas the optimal truss is likely to have the general layout in Fig. 5b, which does not lend itself to optimization by dynamic programming.

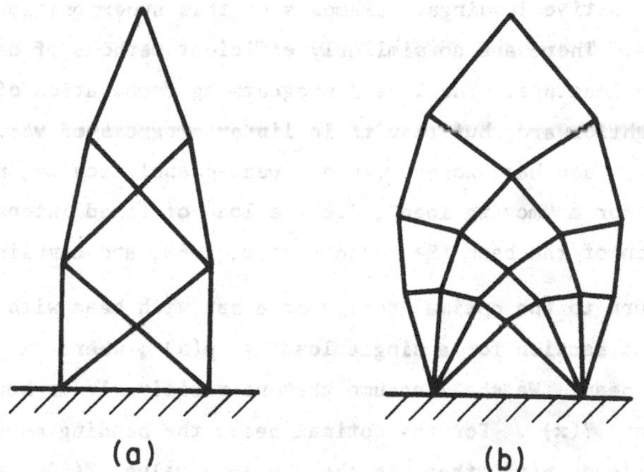

Fig. 5: (a) Optimal layout by dynamic programming
(b) Likely optimal layout

4. OPTIMAL PLASTIC DESIGN OF OTHER STRUCTURES

The optimal design of a sandwich beam with a core of uniform rectangular section and identical cover plates of varying thickness may be reduced to a linear programming problem by choosing a sufficiently dense set of nodes along the axis of the beam and replacing the loads on each segment between consecutive nodes by equipollent loads at the ends of the segment. At each node an equation of equilibrium must be satisfied, which is linear in the bending moments at this node and its immediate neighbors. Furthermore, at each node, the absolute value of the bending moment must not exceed the yield moment, which is proportional to the thickness of the cover plates. These yield inequalities and equilibrium equations are the constraints of a linear programming problem; the objective function, which is to be minimized, represents the weight of the cover plates, which is proportional to $\Sigma_i \ell_i (Y_{io} + Y_i)$, where ℓ_i is half the distance between nodes $i - 1$ and $i + 1$, and $Y_{io} + Y_i$ is the yield moment at node i , Y_{io} being a prescribed minimal value for this yield moment, and $Y_i \geq 0$. This linear programming problem has the same structure as (2.1), and its dual may be mechanically interpreted in a similar manner. For a building frame with many floors and bays, this formulation obviously results in a linear programming problem of considerable size, particularly when several states of loading must be considered. To reduce the problem to a manageable size, special methods were developed (see, for instance, Livesley, 1956, and Heyman and Prager, 1958). With the large core memories of modern computers, the need for such methods, which require special programming, has disappeared.

It follows from the analogy between the problems of optimal plastic design of trusses and beams that the superposition principle of Hemp, 1968, applies also to beams subject to two alternative loadings. Examples of this superposition have been given by Nagtegaal, 1973a. There are no similarly efficient methods of dealing with three or more alternative loadings. The linear programming formulation of problems of this kind is straightforward but results in linear programs of very large size. An interesting limiting case has, however, been treated analytically, namely the optimal plastic design for a "moving load", i.e., a load of fixed intensity that may act at any cross section of the beam (Save and Prager, 1963, and Lamblin and Save,1971).

Let us briefly return to the optimal design of a sandwich beam with prismatic core of rectangular cross section for a single loading $p(x)$, where x denotes distance measured along the beam. We shall assume that no positive lower bound is prescribed for the yield moment $Y(x)$. For the optimal beam, the bending moment $M(x)$ at collapse under the load $p(x)$ then has the absolute value $Y(x)$, and we have the following continuous problem of linear programming:

Minimize

$$\int |M| \, dx \tag{4.1}$$

subject to

$$d^2M/dx^2 = p \ . \tag{4.2}$$

The integration in (4.1) is extended over the entire beam; (4.2) expresses the fact that the bending moment $M(x)$ must be statically admissible for the load $p(x)$. In analogy with the discussion leading to (2.4) and (2.5), it can be shown that a beam is optimal, if there exist statically admissible bending moments $M(x)$ and kinematically admissible rates of deflection $v(x)$ such that the rates of curvature $\kappa = -d^2v/dx^2$ satisfy the conditions

$$|\kappa| \le \kappa_0 \ , \text{ with equality for } M \ne 0 \ , \tag{4.3}$$

$$M\kappa \ge 0 \ , \tag{4.4}$$

where κ_0 is an arbitrary reference rate of curvature. Examples for the use of this optimality condition were given by Heyman, 1951. Figure 6a shows a propped cantilever beam carrying a uniform load p. The kinematic constraints at the supports call for the vanishing of the rate of deflection v at both ends and the vanishing of dv/dx at the clamped end. Since $v(x)$ must be in class C^1, these conditions together with the optimality condition (4.3) determine $v(x)$ when κ_0 has been chosen (Fig. 6b). It is found that $\kappa(x)$ and hence $M(x)$ change sign at

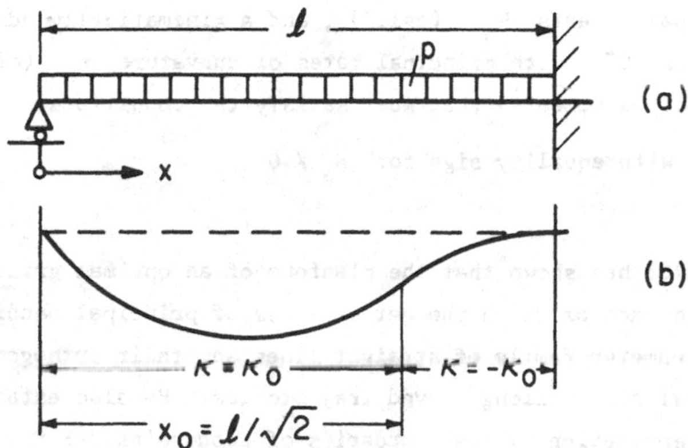

Fig. 6: (a) Uniformly loaded, propped cantilever beam
(b) Rates of deflection at collapse of optimal design

$x = x_0 = \ell/\sqrt{2}$. With the conditions $M(0) = M(x_0) = 0$, the differential equation (4.2) uniquely determines $M(x)$ and hence the yield moment $Y(x) = |M(x)|$ of the optimal beam.

The optimal plastic design of a <u>dense</u> grillage of sandwich beams with uniform core dimensions but variable thickness of cover plates (Rozvany, 1972) leads to a continuous problem of linear programming that is a two-dimensional analog of the problem indicated by (4.1) and (4.2). Denote by M_x, M_y the bending moments, and by M_{xy} the twisting moment in the grillage with respect to rectangular Cartesian coordinates x,y in the median plane of the grillage, and let $p(x,y)$ be the distributed load. The beams of the grillage follow the lines of the principal bending moments

$$M_{1,2} = \tfrac{1}{2}(M_x + M_y) \pm [\tfrac{1}{4}(M_x - M_y)^2 + M_{xy}^2]^{1/2} \qquad (4.5)$$

and have the yield moments $|M_1|$ and $|M_2|$. The optimal grillage is characterized by the following continuous problem of linear programming:

Minimize

$$\int(|M_1| + |M_2|)\, dA \qquad (4.6)$$

subject to

$$\partial^2 M_x/\partial x^2 + \partial^2 M_y/\partial y^2 + 2\partial^2 M_{xy}/\partial x\partial y = p . \qquad (4.7)$$

In (4.6), dA is the area element of the planform of the grillage, the integration is extended over this planform, and M_1 and M_2 are defined by (4.5). The constraint (4.7) is the equation of equilibrium.

At collapse of an optimal grillage, we must have a statically admissible moment field with principal moments M_α, $(\alpha=1,2)$, and a kinematically admissible rate of deflection field in C^1, with principal rates of curvature κ_α (of the same directions as the principal moments) that must satisfy the conditions

$$|\kappa_\alpha| \leq \kappa_o , \text{ with equality sign for } M_\alpha \neq 0 , \qquad (4.8)$$

$$M_\alpha \kappa_\alpha \geq 0 . \qquad (4.9)$$

Rozvany (1972, 1973) has shown that the planform of an optimal grillage is divided into subdomains in each of which the net of lines of principal bending moments consists of a one-parameter family of straight lines and their orthogonal trajectories, with zero principal moment along curved trajectories. He also established a set of rules for the determination of the boundaries of subdomains. For a summary of this work, see Rozvany, 1974.

Figure 7a shows an optimal layout of a square grillage that is simply supported along the edges and subjected to a distributed load of varying intensity but constant sign. For a downward load on a horizontal grillage, the directions of positive or negative principal moments are indicated by full or dashed lines. The principal moments have opposite signs in the corner regions (e.g. OAB) but the same sign in the central square ABCD . Figure 7b shows an optimal layout of a square grillage that is clamped along the edges. Only in the central square BCEF does this layout correspond to the idea evoked by the term grillage; outside this square, one of the principal bending moments vanishes. A load at a point in the central square

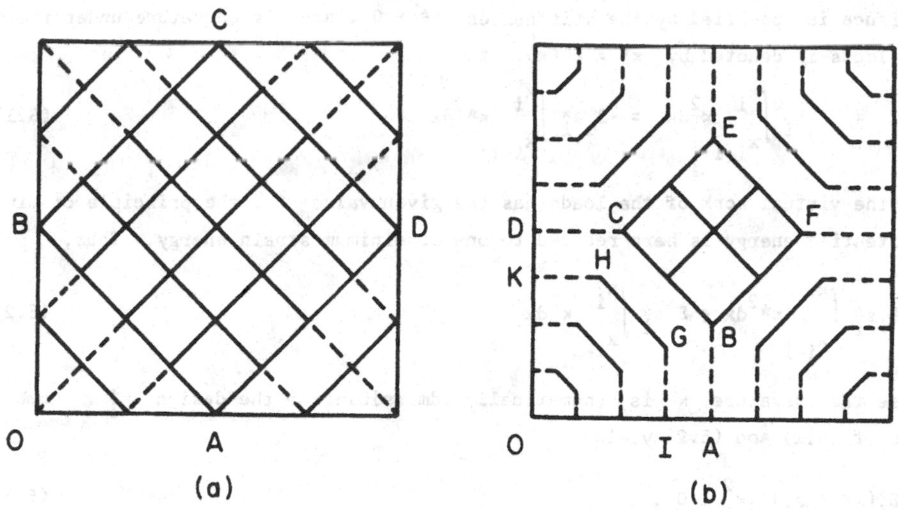

Fig. 7: (a) Optimal grillage simply supported along edge
(b) Optimal "grillage" built in along edge

is transmitted to the edge beams of this square and, by them, to cantilevers such as AB or DC . A beam such as GH is simply supported by the cantilevers IG and KH .

Hemp's superposition principle may also be applied to the optimal design of a grillage for two alternative loadings (Rozvany, 1974).

5. OPTIMAL ELASTIC DESIGN

The compliance of an elastic structure to a given system of loads is defined as the virtual work of these loads on the elastic displacements caused by them. Alternatively, the compliance may be evaluated as twice the strain energy stored in the structure when it is carrying the given loads. Prescribing an upper bound for the compliance of an elastic structure thus amounts to introducing an overall constraint on its deformations.

As an example of optimal design with a compliance constraint, consider the design of a sandwich beam with constant core dimensions and <u>segmentwise constant</u> cross-sectional areas of the identical cover plates. The beam is to have a prescribed compliance C to a given loading. Let $s_i \geq 0$ be the bending stiffness of the optimal beam in the segment (x_{i-1}, x_i) , and denote by $\kappa = \kappa(x)$ the curvature of the optimal beam produced by the given loads. If a second design with the same compliance is specified by the stiffnesses $s_i^* \geq 0$, and its curvature under the given loads is denoted by $\kappa^* = \kappa^*(x)$, then

$$C = \Sigma_i s_i \int_{x_{i-1}}^{x_i} \kappa^2 dx = \Sigma_i s_i^* \int_{x_{i-1}}^{x_i} \kappa^{*2} dx . \tag{5.1}$$

Since the virtual work of the loads has the given value C , the principle of minimum potential energy is here reduced to one of minimum strain energy. Thus,

$$\Sigma_i s_i^* \int_{x_{i-1}}^{x_i} \kappa^{*2} dx \leq \Sigma_i s_i^* \int_{x_{i-1}}^{x_i} \kappa^2 dx , \tag{5.2}$$

because the curvature κ is kinematically admissible for the design s_i^* . Combination of (5.1) and (5.2) yields

$$\Sigma_i (s_i^* - s_i) \ell_i \kappa_i^2 \geq 0 , \tag{5.3}$$

where

$$\kappa_i = \left\{ \ell_i^{-1} \int_{x_{i-1}}^{x_i} \kappa^2 dx \right\}^{1/2} \tag{5.4}$$

is the mean square curvature for the segment (x_{i-1}, x_i) and ℓ_i is the length of this segment.

It is possible that some segments of the optimal beam have vanishing stiffnesses. For example, a beam may be conceived as a propped cantilever. If, however, it only has to carry a load close to the built-in end, the optimal design will be a cantilever that extends only from this end to the point of application of the load. If the segment (x_{i-1}, x_i) has vanishing stiffness, we have

$$s_i^* - s_i \geq 0 , \quad s_i = 0 . \tag{5.5}$$

Finally, because the weight per unit length of a sandwich beam of this kind is proportional to its stiffness, the optimality of the design s_i is expressed by the inequality

$$\Sigma_i (s_i^* - s_i) \ell_i \geq 0 . \tag{5.6}$$

According to a theorem of Farkas, 1902, the inequality (5.6) will follow from the inequalities (5.3) and (5.5) if and only if it is a nonnegative linear combination of these inequalities. Let the coefficients of this linear combination be $1/\kappa_o^2$ and μ_i/κ_o^2, where κ_o is a reference curvature, and $\mu_i = 0$ for $s_i > 0$. Farkas' theorem then yields the optimality condition

$$\kappa_i^2 \leq \kappa_o^2 \text{, with equality sign for } s_i > 0 . \tag{5.7}$$

By the introduction of the mean square bending moments

$$M_i = \left\{ \ell_i^{-1} \int_{x_{i-1}}^{x_i} M^2 dx \right\}^{1/2} , \tag{5.8}$$

the optimality condition (5.7) may be given the alternative form

$$M_i/s_i \leq \kappa_o \text{ , with equality sign for } s_i > 0 \text{ .} \tag{5.9}$$

Note that the compliance C may be written as

$$C = \Sigma_i \ell_i M_i^2/s_i \text{ .} \tag{5.10}$$

It follows from (5.9) and (5.10) that the reference curvature is given by

$$\kappa_o = C/\Sigma_i \ell_i M_i \text{ .} \tag{5.11}$$

When the compliance is not to exceed a prescribed value C for either one of two alternative loadings, an inequality of the form (5.3) is valid for the mean square curvatures κ_i' under the first loading as well as for the mean square curvatures κ_i'' under the second loading. Application of Farkas' theorem to these inequalities and (5.5) and (5.6) then yields the optimality condition

$$\mu'\kappa_i'^2 + \mu''\kappa_i''^2 \leq \kappa_o^2 \text{ , with equality sign for } s_i > 0 \text{ ,} \tag{5.12}$$

where μ' and μ'' are dimensionless, nonnegative Lagrangian multipliers satisfying

$$\mu' + \mu'' = 1 \text{ .} \tag{5.13}$$

For $\mu' = 0$ or $\mu'' = 0$, the first or second loading does not influence the optimal design. In this case, (5.12) reduces to (5.7) applied to the other loading, and κ_o is found from (5.11). For other values of μ' , μ'' , the compliance to either one of the loadings has the value C , and κ_o is again found from (5.11), where the mean square bending moments M_i may be taken from either loading.

Because the optimality condition (5.12) contains the squares of κ_i' , κ_i'' , it cannot be stated in the form of a superposition principle similar to Hemp's principle for optimal plastic design for two alternative loadings.

As was pointed out by Prager and Taylor, 1968, the way in which the optimality conditions (5.7) and (5.12) were derived may be used for other problems of optimal design, provided that the behavioral constraints concern quantities that are characterized by minimum principles in the manner in which the compliance is characterized by the principle of minimum potential energy. Constraints that have been treated in this manner concern not only static elastic compliance but also dynamic elastic compliance under harmonically varying loads (Icerman, 1969; Mroz, 1970; Plaut, 1971), fundamental frequency (Taylor, 1967a & 1968; Sheu, 1968), elastic buckling load (Taylor, 1967b; Taylor and Liu, 1968), static deflection at a specified point (Shield and Prager, 1970; Chern, 1971), and rate of deflection in stationary creep (Prager, 1968). Much earlier, essentially the same technique was used by Drucker and Shield, 1957, for optimal plastic design.

6. COMPUTATIONAL ASPECTS

For the problems in Figs. 3, 6, and 7, the optimality condition directly led to the optimal designs. Problems of this kind are exceptional. As a rule, optimality conditions are used as guides in the iterative improvement of an initial design. To indicate some basic ideas used in procedures of this kind, we consider a very simple example. Let a single set of loads be carried by a sandwich beam with segmentwise constant cross section, which is to be designed for a given compliance to these loads. The optimality condition (5.9) remains valid if the total volume of the cover plates is prescribed (or, what amounts to the same, the value of $S = \Sigma_i \ell_i s_i$) and the compliance is to be minimized. Starting with an arbitrary design s_i', for instance the uniform design $s_i' = S/\Sigma_i \ell_i$, we compute its mean square bending moments M_i', which will not, in general, satisfy the optimality condition (5.9). The compliance C'' of a second design s_i'' with mean square bending moments M_i'' satisfies the relations

$$C'' = \Sigma_i \ell_i M_i''^2/s_i'' \leq \Sigma_i \ell_i M_i'^2/s_i'' , \tag{6.1}$$

where the inequality follows from the principle of minimum complementary energy because the mean square bending moments M_i' are computed from bending moments that are statically admissible for the second design. Since (6.1) gives an upper bound for C'', and since a design of minimal compliance is sought, it is natural to determine the stiffnesses s_i'' that furnish the least upper bound subject to the condition that $\Sigma_i \ell_i s_i'' = S$. These stiffnesses are found to be

$$s_i'' = M_i'/\kappa_o \quad \text{where} \quad \kappa_o = \Sigma_i \ell_i M_i'/S . \tag{6.2}$$

Note that the use of the redesign formula (6.2) amounts to using the optimality condition (5.9) with the assumption that the redesign does not change the mean square bending moments. This is strictly true for a statically determinate beam. For an indeterminate beam, we can only assert that the mean square bending moments will not change materially if the stiffness changes are sufficiently small. Accordingly, the redesign formula (6.2) will have to be used iteratively. Experience with many problems has shown that this iterative method furnishes excellent results when the number of redesign steps is made to equal the number of segments. For large numbers of segments, it has been found that the ε-algorithm of Wynn, 1961, may be used advantageously to speed convergence, though no theoretical justification has as yet been offered for this.

Another means of speeding up convergence is as follows. Using the condition $\Sigma_i \ell_i s_i = S$ to find $\kappa_o = \Sigma_i \ell_i M_i / S$ in (5.9), we write this optimality condition in the form

$$s_i = [\lambda + (1-\lambda) M_i S / (s_i \Sigma_i \ell_i M_i)] s_i , \qquad (6.3)$$

where λ is an arbitrary constant. We then transform (6.3) into an iteration formula by writing the left side as s_i'' but using the values of M_i' and s_i' on the right. Experience has shown that with, say, $\lambda = -0.9$, this kind of iteration works extremely well in the neighborhood of the optimal design. For example, for a beam with five segments and starting from a uniform design, a single use of the redesign formula (6.2) followed by a single iteration based on (6.3) typically furnish as good results as five successive uses of (6.2). On the other hand, the immediate application of iterations based on (6.3) to the uniform initial design is less satisfactory than the iterations (6.2).

In connection with iterative optimal design, it is important to note that the analysis of a design furnishes information that may be used to evaluate upper and lower bounds for the compliance of the optimal design (Nagtegaal, 1973b). This enables the designer to decide whether it is worthwhile to continue the iterations.

The treatment of multiple constraints is much more difficult. Martin, 1970, discussed the case of prescribed upper bounds C', C'' on the compliance to two alternative loadings. When both constraints are active, the equations expressing C', C'' in terms of the bending moments M', M'' and the Lagrangian multipliers μ', μ'' are linear in C', C'' but nonlinear in μ', μ''. Martin therefore suggests that μ', μ'' be treated as the independent variables, and that the mapping of the μ', μ''-plane on the C', C''-plane be explored. While this approach can be extended to three or more constraints, it rapidly becomes awkward as the number of constraints increases.

Gellatly and Berke, 1971, discuss the combination of stress constraints with several displacement constraints. In each redesign step, the stress constraints and one displacement constraint at a time are treated as the constraints of a separate optimization problem, and, for each member, the largest of the resulting member sizes is adopted for the next design. When the design obtained in this manner is analyzed, it will, in general, be found that none of the constraints is satisfied as an equality. Before the next redesign is initiated, the member sizes are uniformly scaled so that at least one constraint is satisfied as equality. For details of the procedure, the reader is referred to the original paper and its discussion by Kiusalaas, 1972.

7. CONCLUDING REMARKS

There are numerous ideas that could not be taken up in this survey. A few will be briefly mentioned in this section.

For a sandwich beam with segmentwise constant cross section, the segment boundaries x_i may be at the choice of the designer (Sheu and Prager, 1968). At the same time, the cross-sectional areas A_i of the cover plates may be restricted to the members of a discrete set of standard sections. This kind of condition has long been regarded as difficult because it transforms the problem into one of integer programming. Masur, 1974, has recently shown that the problem is not as difficult as had been assumed.

Pickett, Rubinstein, and Nelson, 1973, have suggested to reduce the dimensionality of the optimization problem by restricting the search to the linear combinations of a number of trial designs, the choice of which may be guided by experience with similar problems. Moreover, if the trial designs are scaled to have equal structural weights, the one with the smallest coefficient in the optimal linear combination may be replaced by a new trial design, and a new optimal linear combination may be sought.

A somewhat related idea is to simplify the analyses of subsequent designs by a Ritz approach. This is, of course, done anyhow when finite element methods are used for the analysis (Dupuis, 1972; Maier, Zavelani-Rossi, and Benedetti, 1972), but non-localized coordinate functions might be more advantageous for the optimization problem.

Discussing the optimal design of an elastic plate, Mroz, 1973, has used linear combinations of coordinate functions for both the plate thickness and the deflection. If both combinations have the same number of terms, this approach leads to a system of non-linear equations for the deflection coefficients. After these equations have been solved, the thickness coefficients are found from a system of linear equations.

The limited space does not permit the discussion of further problems. It is hoped, however, that those that were discussed will have conveyed the idea that optimal structural design is a field that merits the attention of numerical analysts.

REFERENCES

Chern, J.-M., Int. J. Solids & Structs. 7, 373 (1971).

Dupuis, G., Int. J. Num. Meth. Engg. 4, 331 (1972).

Drucker, D. C., & Shield, R. T., Proc. 9th Int. Congr. Appl. Mech. (Brussels) 5, 212 (1957).

Farkas, J., J. reine & angew. Math. 124, 1 (1902).

Foulkes, J., Proc. Roy. Soc. (London) A 223, 482 (1954).

Gellatly, R. A., & Berke, L., Wright-Patterson Air Force Base, Tech. Rep. AFFDL-TR-165 (1971).

Hegemier, G. A., & Prager, W., Int. J. Mech. Scis. 11, 209 (1969).

Hemp, W. S., Proc. Int. Congr. Appl. Mech. (Munich) 621 (1966).

- - , Abstract of Lect. Course "Optimal Structures", Oxford, 15 (1968).

Heyman, J., Quart. Appl. Math. 8, 373 (1951).

- - , & Prager, W., J. Franklin Inst. 266, 339 (1958).

Icerman, L. J., Int. J. Solids & Structs. 5, 473 (1969).

Kiusalaas, J., NASA Tech. Note D-7115 (1972).

Lamblin, D. O., & Save, M., Meccanica 6, 151 (1971).

Livesley, R. K., Quart. J. Mech. & Appl. Math. 9, 257 (1956).

Maier, G., Zavelani-Rossi, A., & Benedetti, D., Int. J. Num. Meth. Engg. 4, 455 (1973).

Martin, J. B., J. Optim. Theory & Appls. 6, 22 (1970).

Masur, E. F., Computer Meth. Appl. Mech. & Engg. (1974), to appear.

Michell, A. G., Phil. Mag. 8, 859 (1904).

Mroz, Z., J. Struct. Mech. 1, 371 (1973).

Nagtegaal, J. C., Int. J. Solids & Structs. (1973a), to appear.

- - , SIAM J. Appl. Math. 25 (1973b), to appear.

- - , & Prager, W., Int. J. Mech. Scis. 15, [illegible] (197[illegible]).

Palmer, A. C., & Sheppard, D., Proc. Instn. Civ. Engrs. 47, 363 (1970).

Pickett, R. M., Rubinstein, M. F., & Nelson, R. B., AIAA J. 11, 489 (1973).

Plaut, R. H., Quart. Appl. Math. 29, 315 (1971).

Pope, G. C., & Schmit, L. A., AGARDograph AG-149 (1971).

Prager, W., An Introduction to Plasticity, Reading, Mass., 1959.

- - , J. Appl. Math. & Phys. 19, 252 (1968).

- - , & Taylor, J. E., J. Appl. Mech. 35, 102 (1968).

Rozvany, G. I. N., Computer Meth. Appl. Mech. & Engg. 1, 253 (1972).

- - , J. Struct. Mech. 2 (1973), to appear.

- - , Proc. IUTAM Sympos. Optim. Struct. Design (Warsaw) (1974), to appear.

Save, M., & Prager, W., J. Mech. & Phys. Solids 20, 255 (1963).

Sheu, C. Y., Int. J. Solids & Structs. 4, 953 (1968).

- - , & Prager, W., J. Opt. Theory & Appls. 2, 179 (1968).

- - , & Schmit, L. A., AIAA J. 10, 155 (1972).

Shield, R. T., & Prager, W., J. Appl. Math. & Phys. 21, 513 (1970).

Sved, G., & Ginos, Z., Int. J. Mech. Scis. 10, 803 (1968).

Taylor, J. E., AIAA J. 5, 1911 (1967a) & 6, 1379 (1968).

- - , J. Appl. Mech. 34, 486 (1967b).

- - , & Liu, C. Y., AIAA J. 6, 1497 (1968).

Wynn, P., Math. of Computation 15, 151 (1961).

OPTIMISATION DES SYSTEMES PORTANTS ET PROPULSIFS PAR LA METHODE DES SINGULARITES

L. MALAVARD

Université Paris VI et LIMSI* - CNRS

INTRODUCTION

La méthode des singularités à répartition discrétisée est utilisée depuis de nombreuses années pour résoudre numériquement des problèmes de potentiel des vitesses d'écoulements aéro-hydrodynamiques. Exploitée d'abord par une équipe d'aérodynamiciens de Douglas Aircraf Company, J.L. Hess, A.M. Smith, J.P. Giesing, en utilisant des distributions de sources sur la surface d'un obstacle pour définir le mouvement du fluide qui l'entoure, elle fut reprise par divers auteurs et en particulier au LIMSI par T.S. Luu, G. Coulmy, J. Corniglion et al. qui la développèrent avec succès en faisant intervenir des singularités de types très variés et dont la nature pouvait être la mieux appropriée au problème aux limites considéré.

Cette communication a pour objet de montrer que cette méthode est particulièrement bien adaptée à la résolution numérique d'un important problème d'aéro-hydrodynamique : celui de la recherche de la répartition optimale de circulation des éléments actifs d'un système portant ou propulsif animés d'un mouvement donné. Bien qu'il ne s'agisse ici que de la résolution d'équations de Laplace, on verra qu'en général la complexité de la géométrie des surfaces frontières et de certaines conditions aux limites rendrait inopérantes la plupart des autres méthodes classiques.

La position du problème aéro-hydrodynamique est présentée dans la première partie : modèle théorique du fonctionnement des systèmes portants et/ou propulsifs et la condition d'optimum qui traduit une perte d'énergie minimum pour un effet portant ou propulsif imposé.

Les bases de la méthode des singularités, telle qu'elle est exploitée par Luu, Coulmy et al., sont reprises dans la seconde partie pour en marquer certains aspects importants : non-unicité de la nature des singularités dans la création d'un potentiel, leur choix pour réaliser au mieux le type de conditions aux

---

* LIMSI - CNRS : Laboratoire d'Informatique pour la Mécanique et les Sciences de l'Ingénieur du Centre National de la Recherche Scientifique (France).

limites à imposer, le cas particulier de distributions périodiques de singularités, etc.

La dernière partie est consacrée aux applications de la méthode pour le traitement des systèmes cycliques bi et tridimensionnels : ailes oscillantes, ailes battantes, voilures tournantes ; détermination des lois optimales de circulation et recherche des mouvements propres à donner aux éléments actifs pour satisfaire la condition d'optimum.

1. POSITION DU PROBLEME

1.1. - Définition et hypothèses de base.

Un système portant ou/et propulsif est un ensemble mécanique formé d'éléments actifs, de types ailes ou pales, animés de mouvements appropriés afin d'assurer à l'ensemble une portance ou/et une propulsion.

Outre les ailes et hélices de formes diverses, entrent dans cette définition aussi bien les voilures tournantes des hélicoptères, des gyroplanes, des autogyres que les ailes battantes et les propulseurs à voilure oscillante.

Pour effectuer l'étude du fonctionnement aéro-hydrodynamique de ces systèmes on considère, en première étape, que le fluide est parfait et incompressible. Dans le cas général le mouvement d'un élément (d'une pale par exemple) dans un fluide illimité et au repos à l'infini engendre à partir de sa ligne du bord de fuite une surface Σ' de discontinuité des vitesses tangentielles, habituellement désigné par "sillage tourbillonnaire". Cette surface Σ' est caractérisée par la valeur de la circulation $\Gamma(M)$ en chacun de ses points M : la circulation étant prise sur un lacet passant à l'extérieur de Σ' et partant du point M sur l'une des faces de Σ' pour y revenir sur l'autre face. La valeur de $\Gamma(M)$ est fixée au moment de la formation de Σ' au bord de fuite par les conditions classiques de Kutta-Joukowsky et de la constance de la circulation avec le temps t.

La forme géométrique de Σ' évolue avec le temps ; il est cependant possible d'en obtenir une première approximation en admettant l'hypothèse usuelle des faibles perturbations : si les éléments du système sont très minces et, par exemple, réduits à des surfaces matérielles dont les sections (profils) sont en outre très peu courbées et inclinées sur le vent relatif, les vitesses $\vec{V}$ des particules fluides sont très petites vis-à-vis de la vitesse $\vec{V_0}$ qui caractérise le déplacement général du système, $|\vec{V}| / |\vec{V_0}| \ll 1$. Il est alors loisible de confondre le sillage Σ' avec la surface Σ engendrée au cours du temps par le déplacement de la ligne du bord de fuite. Cette approche est conforme aux méthodes adoptées dans les théories classiques des surfaces sustentatrices et des hélices.

Le mouvement du fluide peut être défini, à tout instant t, par un potentiel des vitesses φ satisfaisant l'équation de Laplace. Les conditions aux limites sont les suivantes :

- à l'infini, fluide au repos, $\overrightarrow{grad}\,\varphi\big|_\infty = 0$
- en chaque point M de la surface S d'un élément (aile ou pale), dont la vitesse d'entrainement est $\vec{W}(M)$, la condition de glissement exige que la dérivée normale $\varphi'_n = \vec{W}.\vec{n}$
- en chaque point M du sillage Σ la différence entre la valeur du potentiel φ^+ sur la face supérieure et la valeur φ^- sur la face inférieure correspond à la circulation Γ en ce point : $\varphi^+ - \varphi^- = \Gamma$
  et cette circulation Γ est celle autour du profil au moment t où son bord de fuite passait au point M. Enfin la dérivée normale demeure continue à la traversée de Σ.

Dans le cas général et tel qu'il est posé la résolution pratique de ce problème soulève encore beaucoup de difficultés, sauf dans le cas bidimensionnel d'un profil animé d'un mouvement arbitrairement donné. On se bornera donc ici à rechercher des conditions d'optimisation des systèmes à fonctionnement cyclique.

1.2. - Energie communiquée au fluide ; effort moyen.

Lorsque le fonctionnement du système est cyclique le sillage Σ est formé de surfaces à géométrie périodique. En se plaçant suffisamment loin à l'aval du système on peut considérer que dans chaque tranche de fluide, correspondant à une période, l'écoulement présente les mêmes propriétés de périodicité que si le nombre de tranches était infini dans les deux sens.

Si l'on désigne par ρ la masse volumique du fluide, par dv un élément de volume et par φ'_x, φ'_y, φ'_z les composantes de la vitesse, l'énergie cinétique E du fluide contenu dans le domaine D défini par une telle tranche est donnée par :

$$E = \frac{\rho}{2}\iiint_D \left(\varphi'^2_x + \varphi'^2_y + \varphi'^2_z\right) dv$$

que l'on peut encore écrire, compte-tenu de la définition du potentiel des vitesses φ :

$$E = -\frac{\rho}{2}\iint_{\Sigma_0} \Gamma\,\varphi'_n\, d\Sigma$$

où Σ_0 est la portion de surface de Σ correspondant à une période.

Quand les cordes des éléments (ailes, pales, etc.) du système sont petites par rapport à une longueur de référence de celui-ci, telle que son envergure, ou la longueur de la pale, ou l'amplitude de Σ_0 ou le déplacement du système pour une période T_0, on peut admettre l'approximation de la ligne portante. La surface sustentatrice formant un élément est ainsi réduite à une ligne portante confondue avec la ligne $\widehat{AB}$ du bord de fuite.

Désignons par $\vec{\tau}$ le vecteur unitaire tangent en un point de cette ligne et par $\vec{W}$ la vitesse d'entrainement de ce point. Puisque le déplacement de cette ligne de bord de fuite $\widehat{AB}$ génère la surface Σ on peut définir la normale à Σ en prenant le vecteur unitaire déduit du produit vectoriel $\vec{\tau}\wedge\vec{W}$. Avec les approximations admises on peut alors montrer que l'effort aérodynamique qui supporte l'élément $\vec{\tau}\,ds$ de la ligne portante est donné par :

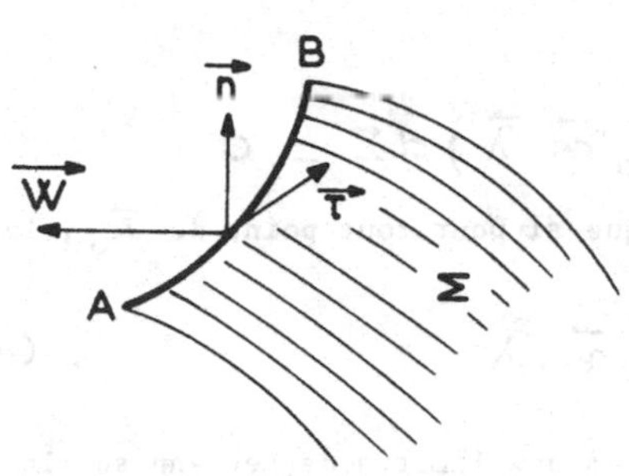

$$\rho(\varphi^+-\varphi^-)(\vec{\tau}\wedge\vec{W})ds$$

soit encore :

$$\rho\,\Gamma\,\vec{n}\,\frac{d\Sigma}{dt}$$

Ainsi la force moyenne supportée par la ligne portante $\widehat{AB}$ pendant une période T_o de fonctionnement est donnée par :

$$\frac{1}{T_o}\int_{t_o}^{t_o+T_o}\int_A^B \rho\,\Gamma\,(\vec{\tau}\wedge\vec{W})\,ds\,dt = \frac{1}{T_o}\int_{\Sigma_o}\rho\,\Gamma\,\vec{n}\,d\Sigma \qquad (1.1)$$

1.3. - Condition optimale.

Pour une direction fixée par le vecteur unitaire $\vec{\lambda}$ on peut imposer que la projection suivant λ de la force moyenne ait une valeur constante et rechercher quelle est la condition à respecter pour que l'énergie cinétique E communiquée au fluide soit minimale. Ce qui revient encore à imposer que le travail

$$\mathcal{T} = V_o\,\rho\int_{\Sigma_o}\Gamma\,(\vec{n}.\vec{\lambda})\,d\Sigma = \text{Cons}^t$$

(où V_o est la vitesse de référence) de sorte que

$$E = -\frac{\rho}{2}\int_{\Sigma_o}\Gamma\,\varphi'_n\,d\Sigma \qquad (1.2)$$

soit minimale.

Dans ce but, supposons que l'on donne à Γ, pris comme variable indépendante une variation $\delta\Gamma$; on a

$$\delta\mathcal{T} = V_o\,\rho\int_{\Sigma_o}\delta\Gamma\,(n.\lambda)\,d\Sigma$$

et

$$\delta E = -\frac{\rho}{2}\int_{\Sigma_o}(\delta\Gamma\,\varphi'_n + \Gamma\,\delta\varphi'_n)\,d\Sigma$$

à partir de la définition du potentiel φ il est aisé de vérifier que les deux intégrales $\int\delta\Gamma\,\varphi'_n\,d\Sigma$ et $\int\Gamma\,\delta\varphi'_n\,d\Sigma$ sont égales ; on pourra donc, en particulier, écrire :

$$\delta E = -\rho\int_{\Sigma_o}\delta\Gamma\,\varphi'_n\,d\Sigma$$

D'après le calcul des variations l'extremum sera atteint pour les fonctions Γ telles que la différence

$$\delta E - c\,\delta\mathcal{T} = 0$$

où c est une constante arbitraire. Soit encore :

$$\int_{\Sigma_0} \delta\Gamma \left(\varphi'_n + c V_0 \vec{n}.\vec{\lambda} \right) d\Sigma = 0$$

ce qui ne peut avoir lieu quel que soit $\delta\Gamma$ que si pour tout point de Σ_0, la condition suivante est satisfaite :

$$\frac{\varphi'_n}{V_0} = - c\, \vec{n}.\vec{\lambda} \qquad (1.3)$$

Cette condition correspond à des données aux limites de Neumann sur la surface Σ_0 ; la résolution du problème permet alors d'atteindre la répartition sur cette surface de la différence du potentiel $(\varphi^+ - \varphi^-)$ et donc, finalement, la loi optimale de distribution de la circulation Γ pour le mouvement du système considéré. La condition (1.3) est classique et son usage est familier dans l'étude du fonctionnement stationnaire des ailes ordinaires et des hélices usuelles ; il était bon d'en rappéler le caractère général et notamment pour les applications aux systèmes à fonctionnement instationnaire ou cyclique.

2. LA METHODE DES SINGULARITES A REPARTITION DISCRETISEE

2.1. - Généralités et choix des singularités.

Bien que le principe de la méthode des singularités soit classique, certains de ses aspects, importants pour les résolutions numériques, restent mal connus. Aussi, avant d'appliquer cette méthode aux problèmes énoncés précédemment, n'est-il pas inutile de revenir sur quelques considérations générales qui précisent ses possibilités pour traiter les champs Laplaciens ou Poissonniens avec une diversité portant aussi bien sur la géométrie des frontières que sur les données aux limites.

Considérons, par exemple, dans un domaine D^+ illimité à l'extérieur d'une enveloppe fermée C, un potentiel φ solution de l'équation de Poisson $\nabla^2\varphi = Q_p$ et remplissant les données aux limites sur C. Dans le domaine D^- intérieur à C, le prolongement du potentiel φ reste arbitraire et on peut considérer qu'il est régi par l'équation de Laplace. Il est alors bien connu que l'application du théorème de Green permet d'exprimer le potentiel φ dans D^+ par :

$$\varphi(M) = \iint_C \left[\left(\varphi'^+_n - \varphi'^-_n\right)_P G(P,M) - \left(\varphi^+ - \varphi^-\right)_P \frac{\partial G(P,M)}{\partial n} \right] ds + \int_{D^+} Q_p\, G(P,M)\, dv \qquad (2.1)$$

où $G(M,P) = G(P,M) = \begin{cases} \dfrac{1}{4\pi r} & \text{pour } \mathbb{R}^3 \\ \dfrac{1}{2\pi}\log r & \mathbb{R}^2 \end{cases}$ et $r = |\overrightarrow{PM}|$

($\vec{n}$ étant la direction de la normale extérieure à C).

On peut donc considérer que φ est engendré par une répartition de source dans l'espace D^+ avec une intensité définie par le second membre de l'équation de Poisson et une répartition de source et de doublet sur la frontière C. La densité de source est donnée par la discontinuité de la dérivée normale de la fonction φ, tandis que la densité de doublet correspond à la discontinuité de la fonction φ.

Si l'on considère que φ, défini dans D^+ correspond à une solution d'un problème aux limites bien déterminé, dans le domaine D^- intérieur à C la définition du champ harmonique présente un degré d'arbitraire. En effet, si le champ dans D^- est défini par la condition de Dirichlet telle que φ^- est identifié à la valeur de φ^+ sur la frontière, la résolution du problème conduit à la connaissance de $\varphi_n^{-'}$ sur C. Dans l'expression (2.1) de $\varphi(M)$, ne subsiste à la frontière que la répartition de source.

Mais on peut aussi envisager d'éliminer cette répartition de source de la manière suivante : si le flux $F = \int_C \varphi_n^{+'} ds$ à travers la frontière est nul, le champ dans D^- peut être défini par la condition de Neumann $\varphi_n^{-'} = \varphi_n^{+'}$ et la résolution du problème donne la distribution de φ^- sur C. Dans ce cas il ne reste plus que la répartition de doublet sur C dans l'expression de $\varphi(M)$. Si le flux F n'est pas nul il est toujours loisible d'introduire la fonction $\varphi_1 = \varphi - F\,G(P_0,M)$ où $G(P_0,M)$ correspond à une source ponctuelle placée au point $P_0 \in D^-$ pour se ramener au cas précédent. Finalement $\varphi(M)$ est donné par :

$$\varphi(M) = F\,G(P_0,M) - \int_C \Delta\varphi \frac{\partial G(P,M)}{\partial n_P} ds + \int_D Q_P\, G(P,M)\, dv$$

Il est encore possible de transformer une répartition de simple couche en une répartition de double couche et vice-versa. Pour le montrer bornons-nous au cas bidimensionnel (le raisonnement est le même en tridimensionnel) d'une répartition de source et tourbillon sur une courbe $\widehat{AB}$; une intégration par parties donne, en effet, l'identité suivante :

$$\int_A^B \frac{q+i\gamma}{2\pi} \log(z-z_p)\, e^{-i\beta_p} dz_p = \frac{Q_B + i\Gamma_B}{2\pi} \log(z-z_B) - \int_A^B \frac{Q_P + i\Gamma_P}{2\pi} \frac{1}{z-z_p} dz_p$$

le premier membre représente la répartition de source et de tourbillon sur la courbe $\widehat{AB}$, d'intensités respectives q et γ ; au second membre le deuxième terme représente une répartition de doublet à axe tangentiel d'intensité Q_P et de doublet à axe normal d'intensité Γ_P telles que :

$$Q_P + i\Gamma_P = \int_A^B (q+i\gamma)\, e^{-i\beta_P} dz_P$$

et le premier terme une source et un tourbillon d'intensité Q_B et Γ_B placés en B.

Les considérations qui précèdent montrent qu'il n'y a pas unicité de la répartition de singularité dans la création d'un potentiel. L'intérêt de cette non-unicité est de permettre, dans une certaine mesure, le choix de la nature de la singularité à répartir sur les frontières de façon à réaliser au mieux le type de conditions aux limites imposées.

2.2. - Formulation de la méthode.

En se limitant au cas de champs harmoniques et lorsque l'on a choisi la nature de singularité la plus appropriée pour les conditions aux limites imposées $f(P')$ sur C, le problème revient à déterminer la densité X_P, a priori inconnue, de la singularité par l'équation intégrale :

$$\int_C X_P \, K(P,P') \, ds_P = f(P') \quad , \quad P \text{ et } P' \in C \qquad (2.2)$$

Le noyau $K(P,P')$, qui dépend des données aux limites et de la nature de la singularité n'est pas toujours régulier lorsque $P \to P'$. La méthode, dite à répartition discrétisée, consiste à diviser la frontière C en un nombre fini de petits éléments Δs (facettes ou segments) sur chacun desquels on définit X_P par sa valeur moyenne X_j considérée comme constante sur toute l'étendue de l'élément, son numéro d'ordre étant j. La condition précédente (2.2), où l'intégrale est remplacée par une somme, est satisfaite en des points de contrôle fixés au centre de chacun des éléments. L'équation intégrale est ainsi remplacée par un système d'équations linéaires définissant les X_j :

$$[A_{ij}][X_j] = [F_i]$$

où F_i est la valeur de f au point de contrôle P_i et où A_{ij} représente l'intégrale $\int_{\Delta s} K(P,P') \, ds_P$ sur l'étendue Δs_j pour un point P_i imposé. Même si $K(P,P_i)$ est singulier au voisinage de P_i le passage aux limites permet en général de définir A_{ij} en ce point.

Pour faciliter la résolution pratique de ce problème il y a évidemment intérêt à choisir la nature de la singularité, en fonction des données aux limites à traiter, de manière à rendre la diagonale principale de la matrice $[A_{ij}]$ prépondérante afin de rendre aisée l'utilisation de méthodes itératives, rapides et précises comme celle de Gauss Siedel, pour résoudre le système.

2.3. - Distributions périodiques de singularités.

Il est hors de propos de reprendre ici le calcul des A_{ij}, c'est-à-dire des effets produits par des répartitions de densité constante de singularités de nature variée en vue de leur utilisation dans les problèmes aux limites usuels de types Neumann, Dirichlet, Fourier. Un recueil de ces formules existe dans divers articles de synthèse parus à ce sujet (cf. ref.).

Dans le problème posé précédemment il s'agit de déterminer la répartition optimale de circulation $\Gamma = \varphi^+ - \varphi^-$ sur une surface-coupure d'un espace illimité, avec des conditions aux limites de Neumann pour le potentiel harmonique φ. Il est évident qu'il s'agit ici d'un potentiel de double-couche : la singularité la plus adéquate correspond donc à une distribution de doublet à axe normal.

2.3.1. Pour le cas bidimensionnel, rappelons que le potentiel produit par une répartition de doublet de densité constante $\Delta\varphi$ sur un segment $z_1 z_2$ est donné par :

$$\varphi = \mathcal{R}_e \frac{i\Delta\varphi}{2\pi} \int_{z_1}^{z_2} \frac{e^{i\theta_0}}{z - z_0} e^{-i\theta_0} dz_0$$

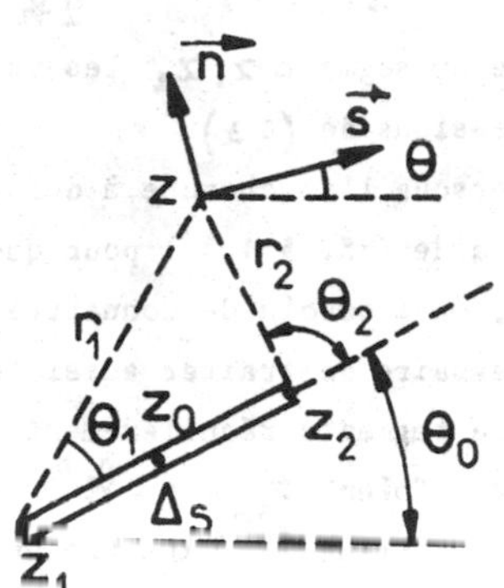

soit

$$\varphi = \mathcal{R}_e \frac{i\Delta\varphi}{2\pi} \log \frac{z - z_1}{z - z_2} = -\frac{\Delta\varphi}{2\pi}(\theta_1 - \theta_2)$$

La vitesse induite par cette répartition est

$$\varphi'_x - i\varphi'_y = \frac{i\Delta\varphi}{2\pi}\left(\frac{1}{z - z_1} - \frac{1}{z - z_2}\right).$$

Soit encore, pour les composantes tangentielle et normale rapportées à un repère local lié à z :

$$\varphi'_s - i\varphi'_n = e^{i\theta}(\varphi'_x - i\varphi'_y)$$

Bien que la fonction φ et son gradient soient singuliers aux deux extrémités z_1 et z_2 du segment, leurs valeurs restent finies lorsque z tend vers la face supérieure ou inférieure de ce segment. En désignant par $\varphi^\pm$, $\varphi_s^{\pm'}$, $\varphi_n^{\pm'}$ les valeurs correspondantes, on a :

$$\varphi^\pm = \pm \frac{\Delta\varphi}{2}, \quad \varphi_s^{\pm'} = 0, \quad \varphi_n^{\pm'} = -\frac{\Delta\varphi}{\pi}\frac{2}{\Delta s} \qquad (2.3)$$

On notera, d'après ces formules, la contribution prépondérante, au point de contrôle situé au centre du segment, que donne une répartition de doublet pour une condition de Neumann.

Pour le problème à traiter d'un sillage à géométrie périodique Σ_0 on est conduit à considérer une infinité de segments identiques, périodiquement espacés et supportant une même densité constante $\Delta\varphi$ de doublet.

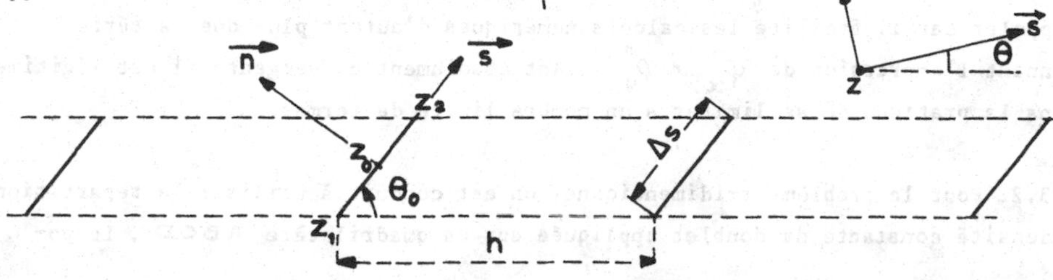

L'expression correspondante du potentiel φ en un point z est donnée par :

$$\varphi = \mathcal{R}_e \, \frac{i\Delta\varphi}{2h} \int_{z_1}^{z_2} \operatorname{cotg} \frac{\pi(z-z_0)}{h} \, dz_0$$

soit encore

$$\varphi = \mathcal{R}_e \, \frac{i\Delta\varphi}{2\pi} \log \frac{\sin \frac{\pi}{h}(z-z_1)}{\sin \frac{\pi}{h}(z-z_2)}$$

et la vitesse induite repérée suivant $\vec{s}$ et $\vec{n}$ attachés à z, par :

$$\varphi'_s - i\varphi'_n = \frac{i\Delta\varphi}{2h} e^{i\theta} \left[\operatorname{cotg} \frac{\pi}{h}(z-z_1) - \operatorname{cotg} \frac{\pi}{h}(z-z_2) \right]$$

Au centre du segment $z_1 z_2$ les valeurs $\varphi_0^{\pm}$, $\varphi_s^{\pm}$, $\varphi_n^{\pm}$ sont toujours données par les expressions de (2.3)

Lorsque l'on cherche à définir la loi du mouvement qu'il faut donner au profil d'aile (cf. § 1.1.) pour que sa circulation $\Gamma(t)$ soit effectivement optimale, on a besoin de connaître l'influence d'un sillage semi-infini. Il est donc nécessaire de traiter aussi la contribution au potentiel φ d'une <u>file semi-infinie</u> de segments régulièrement espacés porteurs d'une densité constante $\Delta\varphi$ de doublet. Soient $z_{1k} = z_1 + kh$ et $z_{2k} = z_2 + kh$ les affixes des extrémités du segment de rang k $(0 < k < \infty)$. Le potentiel résultant de cette file et la vitesse induite à l'affixe z sont donnés par :

$$\varphi = \mathcal{R}_e \, \frac{i\Delta\varphi}{2\pi} \sum_{k=0}^{k=\infty} \log \frac{z - z_{1k}}{z - z_{2k}} = \mathcal{R}_e \, \frac{i\Delta\varphi}{2\pi} \sum_{0}^{\infty} \log \frac{z - z_0 - kh + \delta}{z - z_0 - kh - \delta}$$

avec $\begin{matrix} z_{1k} \\ z_{2k} \end{matrix} = z_0 + kh \begin{matrix} -\delta \\ +\delta \end{matrix}$

$$\varphi'_x - i\varphi'_y = \frac{i\Delta\varphi}{2\pi} \sum_{k=0}^{k=\infty} \left(\frac{1}{z - z_0 - kh + \delta} - \frac{1}{z - z_0 - kh - \delta} \right)$$

Pour k suffisamment grand, on a :

$$\log \frac{z - z_0 - kh + \delta}{z - z_0 - kh - \delta} = \frac{\Delta s \, e^{i\theta_0}}{z - z_0 - kh}$$

$$\frac{1}{z - z_0 - kh - \delta} - \frac{1}{z - z_0 - kh + \delta} = \frac{\Delta s \, e^{i\theta_0}}{(z - z_0 - kh)^2}$$

c'est-à-dire que les segments lointains peuvent être remplacés par des doublets ponctuels de même axe et même intensité. Ce résultat évident est important à rappeler car il facilite les calculs numériques d'autant plus que la série donnant l'expression de $\varphi'_x - i\varphi'_y$ étant absolument convergente il est légitime dans la pratique de se limiter à un nombre limité de termes.

2.3.2. Pour le problème tridimensionnel on est conduit à utiliser la répartition à densité constante de doublet appliquée sur un quadrilatère $ABCD$. Le potentiel et la vitesse induite s'écrivent :

$$\varphi = \frac{\Delta\varphi}{4\pi}\int_{\Delta s}\frac{\partial}{\partial n_p}\left(\frac{1}{r_{PM}}\right)ds_p$$

$$\text{grad}\ \varphi = \frac{\Delta\varphi}{4\pi}\int_{\Delta s}\text{grad}\frac{\partial}{\partial n_p}\left(\frac{1}{r_{PM}}\right)ds_p$$

Mais il est bien connu que cette répartition constante de doublet produit un champ identique à celui de l'anneau de tourbillon formé par les quatre côtés du quadrilatère, la circulation correspondante étant identique à la densité $\Delta\varphi$. Pour le calcul de $\overrightarrow{\text{grad}}\,\varphi$ on a donc intérêt à appliquer la formule de Biot et Savart pour chacun des côtés tourbillons du quadrilatère ; ainsi la contribution $\vec{V}$ à $\overrightarrow{\text{grad}}\,\varphi$ donnée par le côté AB en un point du champ M s'écrira :

$$\vec{V} = \frac{\Delta\varphi}{4\pi}\ \frac{\overrightarrow{AM}\wedge\overrightarrow{BM}}{|\overrightarrow{AM}\wedge\overrightarrow{BM}|^2}\left[\overrightarrow{AB}\left(\frac{\overrightarrow{AM}}{|\overrightarrow{AM}|}-\frac{\overrightarrow{BM}}{|\overrightarrow{BM}|}\right)\right]$$

Pour le calcul du potentiel $\varphi(M)$ on peut remplacer le quadrilatère en général vrillé, par un élément plan dont la normale se déduit du produit vectoriel des deux diagonales AC et BD. En glissant un plan perpendiculaire à cette normale à mi-distance entre les deux diagonales et en prenant la projection des quatre sommets sur ce plan on obtient le quadrilatère plan $A'B'C'D'$. Cette opération est avantageuse car le potentiel $\varphi(M)$ résultant d'une densité unitaire de doublet supportée par cet élément plan est identique à la composante suivant $\vec{n}$ de la vitesse induite en M par une répartition de source de densité unitaire sur ce même élément. Or la formulation des composantes de cette vitesse a déjà été donnée par Hess et Smith [2] de sorte qu'il suffit de transposer leurs résultats et l'on obtient :

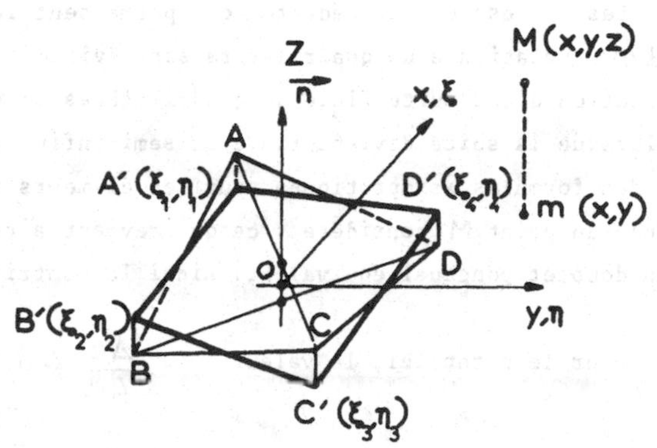

$$\varphi(M) = \frac{\Delta\varphi}{4\pi}\int_{A'B'C'D'}\frac{\partial}{\partial n}\left(\frac{1}{r_{PM}}\right)ds$$

$$= \frac{\Delta\varphi}{4\pi}\left(\text{signe de } \vec{n}\cdot\overrightarrow{OM}\right)\left[\Delta\theta - J_{12} - J_{23} - J_{34} - J_{41}\right]$$

où :

$$J_{mn} = \operatorname{arc\,tg}\left[\frac{R_{mn}|z|\left(r_m s_{mn}^{(m)} - r_n s_{mn}^{(n)}\right)}{r_m r_n R_{mn}^2 - z^2 s_{mn}^{(m)} s_{mn}^{(n)}}\right]$$

$$r_i = \sqrt{(x-\xi_i)^2 + (y-\eta_i)^2 + z^2} \quad (i = m \text{ ou } n)$$

$$s_{mn}^{(i)} = (\xi_i - x)\, C_{mn} - (\eta_i - y)\, S_{mn}$$

$$C_{mn} = \frac{\xi_n - \xi_m}{d_{mn}} \qquad S_{mn} = \frac{\eta_m - \eta_n}{d_{mn}}$$

$$d_{mn} = \sqrt{(\xi_n - \xi_m)^2 + (\eta_n - \eta_m)^2}$$

$$R_{mn} = (x - \xi_m)\, S_{mn} - (y - \eta_m)\, C_{mn}$$

$\Delta\theta = 2\pi$ si m se trouve à l'intérieur de l'élément, nul dans le cas contraire.

Les expressions précédentes qui permettent le calcul pratique de $\varphi(M)$ et $\overrightarrow{\mathrm{grad}}\,\varphi$ relatifs à un quadrilatère sont évidemment utilisables pour définir la contribution d'une suite finie de quadrilatères identiques régulièrement espacés. Mais lorsque la suite devient finie ou semi-infinie, on peut se contenter d'utiliser des formules asymptotiques pour les éléments inducteurs placés à grande distance du point M considéré ; ce qui revient à remplacer l'élément lointain par un doublet ponctuel équivalent. Ainsi la contribution d'un tel élément donnera :

pour le potentiel, la valeur $$\frac{\Delta\varphi}{4\pi}\,\Delta s\,\frac{\vec{r}_K\cdot\vec{n}}{r_K^3} \qquad (2.4)$$

pour le gradient, la valeur $$\frac{\Delta\varphi}{4\pi}\,\Delta s\left(\frac{\vec{n}}{r_K^3} - z\,\frac{\vec{r}\cdot\vec{n}}{r_K^5}\,\vec{r}_K\right) \qquad (2.5)$$

où $\vec{r}_K = \vec{r}_{P_oM} + K\vec{h}$

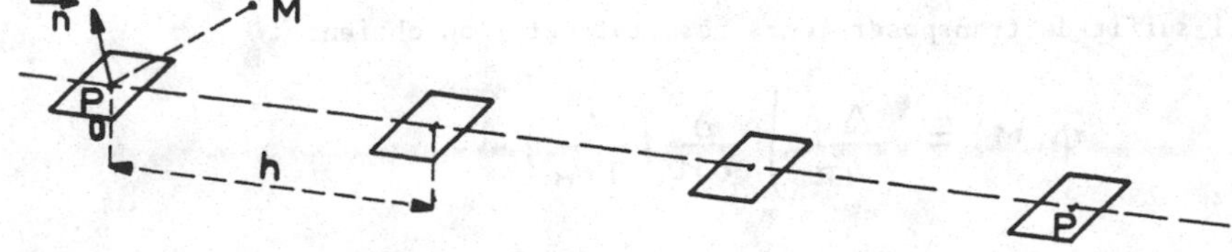

Une série dont les éléments sont formés des expressions (2.4) ou (2.5) est absolument convergente.

3. APPLICATIONS

Dans les paragraphes qui suivent on présente quelques études de systèmes portants ou propulsifs, bi et tridimensionnels, en vue d'illustrer, pour chaque cas, les particularités d'application de la méthode décrite précédemment.

3.1. Effet propulsif d'un profil en mouvement sinusoïdal.

On considère un profil, formé d'une plaque plane, dont le bord de fuite F décrit une sinusoïde ; la composante horizontale V_0 de la vitesse de déplacement est constante et dirigée suivant le sens négatif de l'axe des x. La vitesse de déplacement du bord de fuite s'écrit :

$$\vec{V}_F = -V_0 \vec{i} + V_0 \operatorname{tg}\theta \, \vec{j} \, .$$

On se propose de déterminer :

1. la loi de circulation $\Gamma(t)$ du profil en fonction du temps pour que la perte d'énergie soit minimale.
2. la loi de braquage du profil, par rapport à la direction de $\vec{V}_F$, qu'il faut réaliser à chaque instant pour que la condition optimale soit satisfaite.

3.1.1. Détermination de la loi de circulation. Le sillage Σ , réduit ici à la courbe sinusoïdale décrite par F , est supposé en équilibre au sein du fluide ; cet équilibre des pressions de part et d'autre de Σ exige alors d'après le théorème de Bernoulli et l'hypothèse des faibles perturbations que $\partial(\overset{+}{\varphi} - \overset{-}{\varphi})/\partial t$ soit nul. L'intensité $\Delta\varphi = \overset{+}{\varphi} - \overset{-}{\varphi}$ correspond donc, d'après les conditions rappelées au § 1.1., à la circulation $\Gamma(t)$ autour du profil au moment où son bord de fuite passe par le point correspondant de Σ . La détermination de la loi de circulation $\Gamma(t)$ revient donc à la recherche de la densité $\Delta\varphi$ de doublet sur Σ pour que la condition d'optimum de l'effet propulsif soit réalisée : on devra donc vérifier que sur Σ_0 , correspondant à une période, on a :

$$\varphi'_n = c V_0 \vec{n} . \vec{i}$$

Le problème aux limites est donc traduit par l'équation intégrale :

$$\mathcal{I}_m \int_{\Sigma_0} \frac{i\Delta\varphi}{2h} \; \frac{\frac{\pi}{h} e^{i\theta}}{\sin^2 \frac{\pi}{h}(z - z_0)} dz_0 = c V_0 \vec{n} . \vec{i} \qquad (3.1)$$

La solution n'est définie qu'à une constante près car le sillage Σ, constituant la frontière, partage le plan complexe z en deux parties indépendantes; mais une répartition $\Delta\varphi = C^{te}$ n'apporte aucun effet sur la dérivée normale. La résolution de (3.1) est effectuée suivant la technique de discrétisation décrite au paragraphe précédent 2.3.1. L'indétermination due à la constante additive est éliminée par la discrétisation car le système d'équations linéaires remplaçant (3.1) est bien conditionné et sa résolution donne une répartition $\Delta\varphi$ sur le sillage qui correspond sur le sillage à une constante additive nulle.

3.1.2. Détermination de la loi de braquage. Une fois déterminée la loi de circulation $\Gamma(t)$ du profil en fonction du temps, il faut pour déterminer la loi de braquage résoudre un problème de champ à tout instant t en tenant compte cette fois de la présence du profil dont la circulation est connue à l'instant considéré et dont le sillage, semi infini, est caractérisé par sa forme et la loi optimale précédente des $\Delta\varphi$.

Considérons l'instant t où le bord de fuite du profil rectiligne passe au point F de sa trajectoire sinusoïdale et soit $\alpha(t)$ l'angle que fait le profil AF avec la direction de l'axe x .

Compte-tenu du pivotement du profil autour de F , la vitesse d'un de ses points tel que M à la distance $MF=r$ est donc :

$$\vec{V}(M) = \vec{V}_F + \dot{\alpha}\, \vec{k}\wedge\vec{r}$$

avec $|\vec{V}_F| = V_0/\cos\theta$

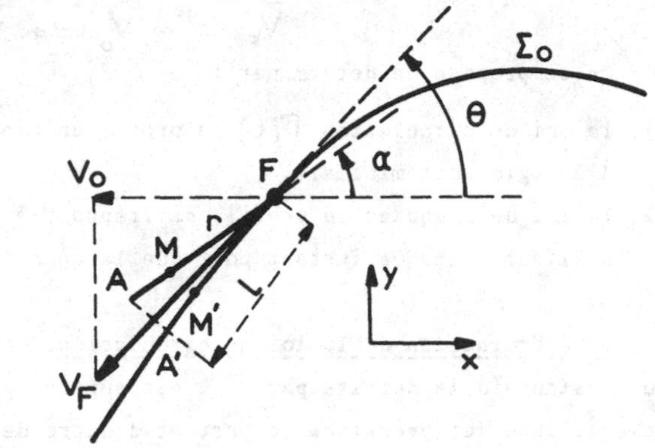

La condition de glissement (cf. 1.1.) exige donc qu'en ce point M la dérivée normale du potentiel φ , défini à cet instant, soit :

$$\varphi'_n(M) = \frac{V_0}{\cos\theta}\sin(\alpha-\theta) - \dot{\alpha} r \qquad (3.2)$$

où, avec les hypothèses admises, $\sin(\alpha-\theta)$ peut être confondu avec l'arc ; la condition de Neumann précédente peut aussi être aplatie sur la sinusoïde que décrira F , c'est-à-dire sur $FM'A'$ projection du profil sur celle-ci.

Sur le sillage semi-infini Σ , qui s'étend de F jusqu'à l'infini aval, on devra imposer la répartition optimale de circulation $\Gamma(s)$, s étant l'abscisse curviligne de Σ comptée à partir de F . Cette loi optimale est connue après la résolution du problème précédent (cf. 3.1.1.) qui donne la distribution des $\Delta\varphi(s)$ ou encore la densité $\gamma(s)$ des tourbillons libres du sillage Σ , c'est-à-dire

$$\gamma(s) = d(\Delta\varphi)/ds\ .$$

Enfin il conviendra de satisfaire la condition de Joukowsky au bord de fuite, qui exige, tout en imposant la circulation $\Gamma_F(t)$ connue du profil, de vérifier que F est un point régulier de l'écoulement où, en particulier, la dérivée normale φ'_n demeure continue.

Pour satisfaire la condition aux limites $(3,2)$ qui contient l'inconnue $\alpha(t)$ et sa dérivée $\dot{\alpha}$, il est commode de décomposer le potentiel des vitesses en trois parties, en écrivant :

$$\varphi = \varphi_1 + \frac{\alpha}{\cos\theta}\varphi_2 + \frac{\dot{\alpha} l}{V_0}\varphi_3$$

Les conditions aux limites à satisfaire pour chacune de ces fonctions sont résumées dans le tableau suivant :

Sur le profil	Sur le sillage	Circulation du profil
$\frac{\varphi'_n}{V_0} = -\frac{\theta}{\cos\theta} + \frac{\alpha}{\cos\theta} - \dot{\alpha} r$	$\frac{d}{ds}\Delta\varphi = \gamma(s)$ connu	$\Gamma_F(t)$ connu
$\frac{\varphi'_{1n}}{V_0} = -\frac{\theta}{\cos\theta}$	$\frac{d}{ds}\Delta\varphi_1 = \gamma(s)$ connu	$\Gamma_1(t)$ à déterminer
$\frac{\varphi'_{2n}}{V_0} = 1$	$\frac{d}{ds}\Delta\varphi_2 = 0$	Γ_2 à déterminer
$\frac{\varphi'_{3n}}{V_0} = -\frac{r}{l}$	$\frac{d}{ds}\Delta\varphi_3 = 0$	Γ_3 à déterminer

Compte-tenu de la condition ci-dessus de Joukowsky à satisfaire dans les trois cas ces conditions aux limites fixent sans ambiguité chacune de ces trois fonctions φ_1, φ_2, φ_3

La détermination des potentiels φ_2 et φ_3 est classique (absence du sillage des tourbillons libres) et les solutions donnent les valeurs des circulations Γ_2 et Γ_3, indépendantes du temps t.

Par contre le potentiel φ_1 dépend du temps t, en pratique on effectue sa détermination à des séquences consécutives séparées par un intervalle de temps Δt pris constant sur une période T_0. A chaque séquence la résolution numérique est obtenue en appliquant le procédé du § 2.3.1. pour une file semi-infinie de singularités ; on en déduit ainsi $\Gamma_1(t)$.

Connaissant $\Gamma_1(t)$, Γ_2 et Γ_3 il est possible de calculer la loi de braquage $\alpha(t)$ cherchée. La méthode utilisée est la suivante. Soit α_j la valeur de α pour la séquence d'ordre j, on peut écrire :

$$\alpha_{j+1} = \alpha_j + \frac{1}{2}(\dot{\alpha}_j + \dot{\alpha}_{j+1})\Delta t$$

Soit encore, en remplaçant $\dot{\alpha}_j$ par $\Delta\alpha_j/\Delta t$

$$\alpha_j - \alpha_{j+1} + \frac{1}{2}(\Delta\alpha_j + \Delta\alpha_{j+1}) = 0 \qquad (A)$$

Par ailleurs, la valeur $\Gamma_F(t)$, pour l'instant t considéré, doit être respectée, d'où une seconde équation :

$$\alpha_j \frac{\Gamma_2}{\cos\theta_j} + \Delta\alpha_j \frac{\ell}{V_0 \Delta t} \Gamma_3 = \Gamma_{Fj} - \Gamma_1 \qquad (B)$$

Pour chaque séquence on dispose ainsi de deux équations (A) et (B) et si la période est divisée en N séquences, on a $2N$ équations pour déterminer les $2N$ inconnues α_j et $\Delta\alpha_j$.

En posant $a_j = \dfrac{\Gamma_2}{\cos\theta_j}$, $b = \Gamma_3 \dfrac{\ell}{V_0 \Delta t}$, $c_j = \Gamma_{Fj} - \Gamma_1$ l'équation (B) s'écrit

$$a_j \alpha_j + b\,\Delta\alpha_j = c_j$$

et pour les N séquences on a le système :

$$\left(\begin{array}{cccc:cccc} a_1 & & & & b & & & \\ & a_2 & & & & b & & \\ & & \ddots & & & & \ddots & \\ & & & a_N & & & & b \\ \hdashline 1 & -1 & & & \frac{1}{2} & & & \\ & 1 & -1 & & & \frac{1}{2} & \frac{1}{2} & \\ & & \ddots & \ddots & & & \ddots & \ddots \\ -1 & & & 1 & \frac{1}{2} & & & \frac{1}{2} \end{array}\right) \begin{pmatrix} \alpha_1 \\ \vdots \\ \alpha_N \\ \hdashline \Delta\alpha_1 \\ \vdots \\ \Delta\alpha_N \end{pmatrix} = \begin{pmatrix} c_1 \\ \vdots \\ c_N \\ \hdashline 0 \\ \vdots \\ 0 \end{pmatrix} \begin{matrix} 1 \\ \\ N \\ N+1 \\ \\ 2N \end{matrix}$$

Soit encore

$$\begin{matrix} (1)+(2) \\ \\ \\ (N)+(1) \\ \\ \\ \\ \end{matrix} \left(\begin{array}{cccc:cccc} a_1 & a_2 & & & b & b & & \\ & & \ddots & & & b & b & \\ & & & & & & \ddots & \\ a_1 & & & a_N & b & & & b \\ \hdashline 2b & -2b & & & b & b & & \\ & 2b & -2b & & & b & b & \\ & & \ddots & \ddots & & & \ddots & \\ -2b & & & 2b & b & & & b \end{array}\right) \begin{pmatrix} \alpha_1 \\ \vdots \\ \alpha_N \\ \hdashline \Delta\alpha_1 \\ \vdots \\ \Delta\alpha_N \end{pmatrix} = \begin{pmatrix} c_1 + c_2 \\ c_2 + c_3 \\ \vdots \\ c_N + c_1 \\ \hdashline 0 \\ \vdots \\ 0 \end{pmatrix} \begin{matrix} 1 \\ \\ \\ N \\ N+1 \\ \\ 2N \end{matrix}$$

L'élimination des $\Delta\alpha$ donne :

$$\begin{matrix} (1)-(N+1) \\ (2)-(N+2) \\ \\ \\ \\ \end{matrix} \begin{pmatrix} (a_1 - 2b) & (a_2 + 2b) & & & \\ & (a_2 - 2b) & (a_3 + 2b) & & \\ & & \ddots & \ddots & \\ & & & & \\ (a_1 + 2b) & & & & (a_N - 2b) \end{pmatrix} \begin{pmatrix} \alpha_1 \\ \\ \vdots \\ \\ \alpha_N \end{pmatrix} = \begin{pmatrix} c_1 + c_2 \\ \\ \vdots \\ \\ c_N + c_1 \end{pmatrix}$$

Posons

$$p_j = -\frac{a_{j+1} + 2b}{a_j - 2b} \qquad p_N = -\frac{a_1 + 2b}{a_N - 2b}$$

$$q_j = \frac{c_i + c_{j+1}}{a_j - 2b} \qquad q_N = \frac{c_N + c_1}{a_N - 2b}$$

le système précédent devient

$$\alpha_1 = q_1 + p_1\alpha_2$$
$$\alpha_2 = q_2 + p_2\alpha_3$$
$$\text{----} \quad \text{-----------}$$
$$\alpha_N = q_N + p_N\alpha$$

d'où l'on tire finalement :

$$\alpha_1 = \frac{q_1 + p_1 q_2 + p_1 p_2 q_3 + \ldots\ldots \left(\prod_{j=1}^{N-1} p_j\right) q_N}{1 - \left(\prod_{j=1}^{N} p_j\right)}$$

Les autres valeurs de α_j se déterminent par substitution.

Un exemple de résultat est donné sur la figure ci-contre pour un profil rectiligne dont le bord de fuite décrit une sinusoïde telle que l'amplitude soit égale au déplacement h pour une période ; la corde du profil $l = 0,07\,h$. la loi de braquage $(\theta - \alpha)$ est donnée pour trois valeurs de la constante C de la condition optimale (3.1) . La valeur $C = 0$ correspond au mouvement à donner au profil pour que la circulation $\Gamma_F(t)$ soit nulle à tout instant t : dans ce cas le sillage Σ disparait ainsi d'ailleurs que l'effet propulsif.

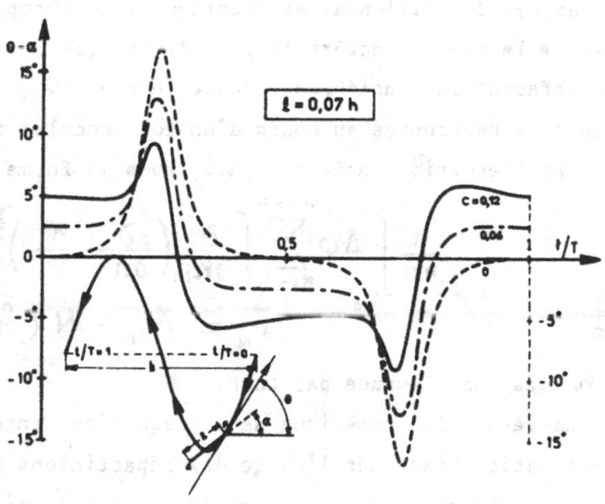

3.2. Loi de circulation optimale pour des systèmes tridimensionnels.

Des applications ont été effectuées pour des systèmes portants et propulsifs de types ailes oscillantes, ailes battantes, voilures tournantes. Il s'agit donc de déterminer la densité de doublet $\Delta\varphi$ sur la surface sillage Σ pour que la dérivée normale correspondante soit égale à $c\,V_0\,\vec{n}.\vec{\lambda}$. Dans le cas général $\Delta\varphi$ est donné par la solution de l'équation intégrale suivante :

$$\frac{1}{4\pi}\int_{\Sigma}\Delta\varphi\left[\frac{\partial}{\partial n_M}\left(\frac{\partial}{\partial n_P}\frac{1}{r_{PM}}\right)\right]d\Sigma_P = cV_0\vec{n}_M.\vec{\lambda} \qquad (3.3)$$

Pour les systèmes précédents à mouvement cyclique, le caractère périodique de la nappe permet de remplacer l'intégrale précédente par une intégrale étendue à la surface Σ_0 d'une seule période ; en introduisant $\vec{r}_N = \vec{r}_{PM} + N\vec{h}$, où $\vec{h}$ désigne le pas géométrique ou avance du système par période, on a :

$$\frac{1}{4\pi}\int_{\Sigma_0}\Delta\varphi\sum_{N=-\infty}^{N=+\infty}\left[\frac{\partial}{\partial n_M}\left(\frac{\partial}{\partial n_P}\frac{1}{r_N}\right)\right]d\Sigma_P = cV_0\vec{n}_M.\vec{\lambda}$$

En général pour les systèmes à ailes oscillantes ou à ailes battantes la symétrie des mouvements des parties droite et gauche de l'envergure entraine une symétrie de même caractère pour le sillage Σ_0, il est avantageux d'en tenir compte dans l'écriture de la condition précédente

$$\frac{1}{4\pi}\int_{\Sigma_0/2}\Delta\varphi\sum_{N=-\infty}^{N=\infty}\left[\frac{\partial}{\partial n_M}\left(\frac{\partial}{\partial n_g}\frac{1}{r_{gN}}\right)+\frac{\partial}{\partial n_M}\left(\frac{\partial}{\partial n_d}\frac{1}{r_{dN}}\right)\right]d\Sigma_P = cV_0\vec{n}.\vec{\lambda}$$

Dans le cas d'un système à voilure tournante, un rotor d'hélicoptère par exemple, formé de p pales identiques régulièrement espacées, le sillage comprend p nappes tourbillonnaires identiques. Le champ du potentiel des vitesses présente alors le même caractère de périodicité que ces nappes et le calcul des $\Delta\varphi$ peut être effectué en considérant une seule nappe Σ_0 engendrée par le bord de fuite d'une pale quelconque au cours d'un tour complet de celle-ci. Cette remarque permet d'écrire l'équation intégrale (3.3) sous la forme suivante :

$$\frac{1}{4\pi}\int_{\Sigma_0}\Delta\varphi\sum_{N=-\infty}^{N=+\infty}\left[\frac{\partial}{\partial n_M}\left(\frac{\partial}{\partial n_P}\frac{1}{r_N}\right)\right]d\Sigma_P = cV_0\vec{n}.\vec{\lambda}$$

avec :

$$\vec{r}_N = \vec{r}_{PM} - N(\vec{h}/p)$$

où $\vec{h}$ désigne l'avance par tour.

La résolution numérique de ces équations intégrales est obtenue par la méthode de colocation basée sur l'usage des répartitions discrétisées du paragraphe précédent. Elle fournit, dans chaque cas, la loi de circulation optimale qui permet d'abord de caractériser les performances globales du système par une évaluation des efforts moyens portant et propulsif et, en seconde étape, de définir les lois de déformation en envergure à donner à l'aile ou à la pale au cours d'une période pour obtenir les résultats de l'optimum.

Pour les applications pratiques il est important de rechercher des critères de qualités permettant de comparer les systèmes entre eux. Ces critères se déduisent des valeurs des efforts moyens de portance et de propulsion et de l'énergie communiquée au fluide au cours d'une période ; or, il suffit de trois coefficients pour caractériser un système en fonctionnement optimal.

Pour obtenir ces coefficients il faut résoudre deux problèmes d'optimum pour la surface-sillage Σ_o du système.

1°. Sur Σ_o on impose la condition d'optimum :

$$\varphi'_{1n} = -V_o \vec{n}.\vec{i}$$

la solution du problème fournit la loi de répartition de circulation optimale : $\Gamma_1 = \varphi_1^+ - \varphi_1^-$ et donc les deux intégrales :

$$A_{11} = \int_{\Sigma_o} \frac{\Gamma_1}{V_o L} \vec{n}.\vec{i} \frac{d\Sigma}{L^2}$$

$$A_{12} = \int_{\Sigma_o} \frac{\Gamma_1}{V_o L} \vec{n}.\vec{k} \frac{d\Sigma}{L^2}$$

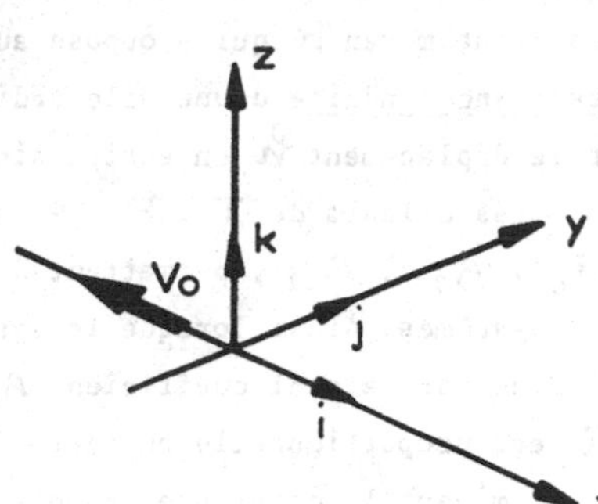

(où L est une longueur de référence, l'envergure par exemple).

2°. Sur Σ_o, on impose une autre condition d'optimum

$$\varphi'_{2n} = -V_o \vec{n}.\vec{k}$$

on en déduit une autre loi de circulation optimale, soit Γ_2 et les intégrales :

$$A_{11} = \int_{\Sigma_o} \frac{\Gamma_2}{V_o L} \vec{n}.\vec{k} \frac{d\Sigma}{L^2}$$

$$A_{21} = \int_{\Sigma_o} \frac{\Gamma_2}{V_o L} \vec{n}.\vec{i} \frac{d\Sigma}{L^2}$$

Les intégrales A_{12} et A_{21} sont égales, comme on le vérifie immédiatement en appliquant la formule de Green aux potentiels φ_1 et φ_2 et leurs dérivées normales φ'_{1n}, φ'_{2n}.

Soit maintenant à résoudre le problème d'optimum pour la direction de $\vec{\lambda} = \lambda_x \vec{i} + \lambda_z \vec{k}$, avec la condition $\varphi'_n = -cV_o \vec{n}.\vec{\lambda}$, la solution concernant la circulation Γ s'obtient par combinaison

$$\Gamma = c(\lambda_x \Gamma_1 + \lambda_z \Gamma_2)$$

L'effort propulsif moyen, ou <u>traction</u> T, est alors donné par :

$$T = \frac{\rho}{T_o} \int_{\Sigma_o} \Gamma \vec{n}.\vec{i} \, d\Sigma = \rho V_o^2 L^2 \left(\frac{L}{h}\right)\left(\lambda_x A_{11} + \lambda_z A_{12}\right)$$

où est la longueur d'une période. De même la <u>portance</u> moyenne P est donnée par

$$P = \frac{\rho}{T_o} \int_{\Sigma_o} \Gamma \vec{n}.\vec{k} \, d\Sigma = \rho V_o^2 L^2 \left(\frac{L}{h}\right)\left(\lambda_z A_{12} + \lambda_z A_{22}\right)$$

L'énergie E communiquée au fluide se calcule de même :

$$E = -\frac{\rho}{2}\int_{\Sigma_0} \Gamma \dot{\varphi}_n \, d\Sigma \qquad \text{avec pour l'optimum} \qquad \varphi'_n = -cV_0 \vec{n}.\vec{\lambda}$$

soit finalement :

$$E = \frac{\rho}{2} V_0^2 L^3 c^2 \left(\lambda_x^2 A_{11} + 2\lambda_x \lambda_z A_{12} + \lambda_z^2 A_{22}\right)$$

Il est souvent commode d'interpréter cette énergie E comme le travail d'un effort résistant moyen R qui s'oppose au mouvement du système, effort analogue à la résistance induite d'une aile ordinaire en translation uniforme. Pour la période T_0 et le déplacement h on écrira ainsi $R = E/h$

Les calculs de T, P, E ou R, où ne figurent que les trois coefficients A_{11}, A_{22}, A_{12}, permettent d'établir d'utiles comparaisons entre les qualités des systèmes. Ainsi lorsque le système est purement portant sa qualité est caractérisée par le seul coefficient A_{22} (les autres étant nuls), sa résistance induite R est proportionnelle au carré de la portance comme on le vérifie immédiatement en éliminant la constante c entre P et E (ou R), on obtient ainsi

$$R = P / \rho V_0^2 L^2 \left(2 A_{22} \frac{L}{h}\right)$$

Soit encore, en passant à des coefficients sans dimension familiers aux aérodynamiciens :

$$C_x = C_z^2 / \mathcal{R} \left(4 A_{22} \frac{L}{h}\right)$$

expression qui montre, qu'à égalité de C_z et d'allongement $\mathcal{R}$, le système sera d'autant plus avantageux que le terme entre parenthèse est grand.

Pour un système purement propulsif on pourrait de même calculer une résistance R et la comparer à la traction T par une formule analogue à la précédente, mais où apparait cette fois le seul coefficient A_{11}. Dans le cas général d'un système portant et propulsif il est plus indiqué de s'intéresser à un coefficient η_i rapport de la puissance propulsive TV_0 à la somme de la puissance propulsive et de l'énergie cinétique communiquée au fluide par unité de temps, soit E/T_0. D'après les formules précédentes ce coefficient, que l'on peut désigner par "indice de rendement", est donné par :

$$\eta_i = \frac{1}{1 + \frac{c}{2}\left(\frac{\lambda_x T + \lambda_z P}{T}\right)}$$

pour un coefficient de portance imposée, soit $f = hLP/2\rho V_0^2 L^2$, η_i peut être calculé en fonction de $\alpha = T/P$ à partir des 3 coefficients A_{11}, A_{22}, A_{12}. Les résultats montrent qu'il existe, pour chaque valeur de l'amplitude d'une aile oscillante ou battante ou de l'inclinaison d'un rotor une valeur maximale de $\eta_i(\alpha)$ pour f fixé.

Pour illustrer ces considérations nous donnons ci-dessous quelques résultats des calculs numériques :

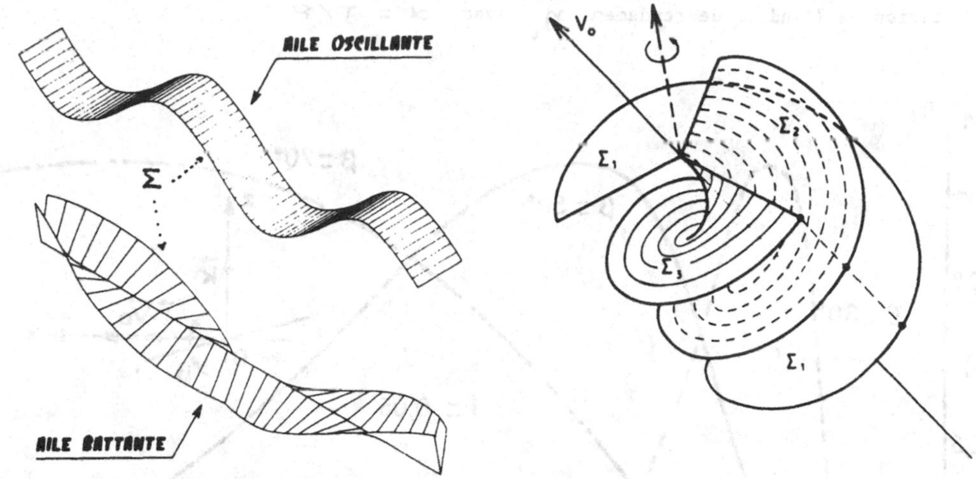

Aile oscillante. longueur de référence : envergure de l'aile L .
longueur h pour une période : $h = L$

amplitude	A_{11}	A_{22}	$A_{12} = A_{21}$
0	0	0,7854 = $\pi/4$	0
0,3	0,3070	0,6528	0
0,5	0,6114	0,5188	0
0,8	1,0816	0,3896	0

Aile battante.

0	0	0,7854	0
0,3	0,10434	0,5583	0
0,4	0,18068	0,4278	0
0,5	0,4424	0,1429	0

Dans les deux cas, l'amplitude nulle correspond à l'aile ordinaire en translation uniforme V_o , caractérisée par le seul effet portant c'est-à-dire par le coefficient A_{22} qui vaut ici $\pi/4$, puisque $L = h$.

Rotor tripale. longueur de référence : rayon d'une pale $L = R$ et $h/R = 2\pi/10$
β : angle du plan de rotation avec Ox

angle β	A_{11}	A_{22}	A_{12}
30°	0,50014	1,4491	0,84398
50°	1,1880	0,82072	0,97114
70°	1,8012	0,25521	0,63873

La figure suivante donne, pour ces trois inclinaisons β et $f = 0,05$, la variation de l'indice de rendement η_i avec $\alpha = T/P$

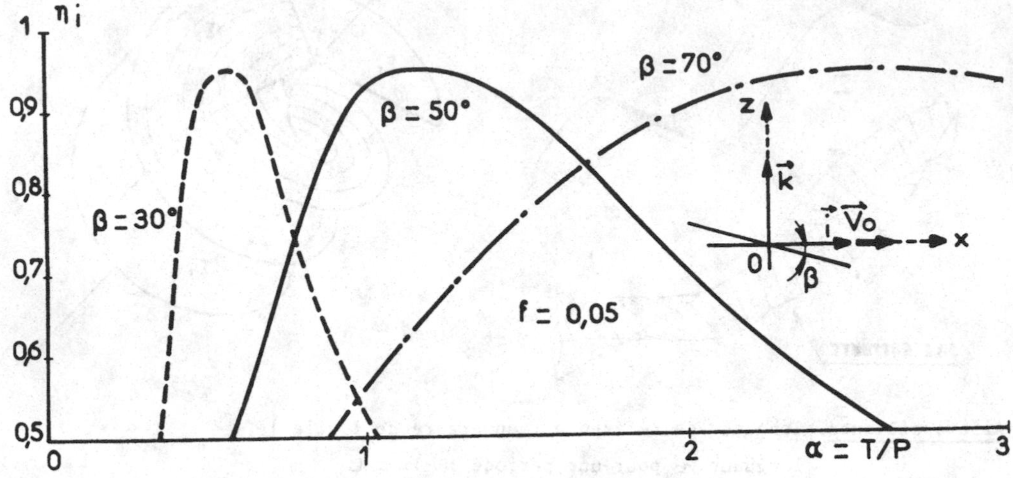

CONCLUSION

Si le choix d'un système portant et propulsif peut être effectué d'après des performances globales les mieux adaptées à un régime de fonctionnement imposé, il reste ensuite à déterminer les lois de braquage et de vrillage à donner, à chaque instant t , à l'aile ou aux pales pour satisfaire la répartition optimale de circulation $\Gamma(t)$ en envergure. Le problème est analogue à celui abordé en 3.1.2. pour le cas bidimensionnel d'un profil, mais le cas d'un système tridimensionnel exige une mise en oeuvre numérique beaucoup plus laborieuse. Son exploitation est néanmoins en cours en utilisant toujours la décomposition du potentiel φ en éléments plus simples, puis en satisfaisant les conditions par combinaisons linéaires.

Bien que basé sur des principes considérés comme classiques et élémentaires la méthode des singularités à répartitions discrétisées ne parait pas avoir eu l'audience qu'elle méritait. Il faut reconnaître que sa pratique exige souvent une très bonne connaissance des subtilités de la modélisation théorique du problème physique analysé. Par cette communication, traitant d'un exemple typique d'aéro-hydrodynamique, nous espérons avoir attiré l'attention sur l'intérêt et la souplesse de ses possibilités. Telle qu'elle a été développée au LIMSI, dans les travaux de Luu, Coulmy, Corniglion et al, la méthode peut être utilisée dans des applications très diverses et notamment pour la résolution d'équations non linéaires, de type mixte elliptique-hyperbolique pour la détermination d'écoulements compressibles autour d'obstacles. Il faut dire que les développements donnés par ces auteurs leur furent souvent suggérés par analogie avec des procédés de calcul et simulation rhéoélectriques auxquels ils étaient auparavant rompus. A ce propos on peut d'ailleurs noter que le problème général dont il a été question ici aurait pu faire l'objet d'une telle simulation : son principe est aisé à concevoir (cf. ref. 12), mais le modèle correspondant, souvent plus difficile à réaliser.

REFERENCES

Hess, J.L. et Smith, A.M.O., Journal of Ship Research, vol. 8, n° 2, septembre 1964.

Hess, J.L. et Smith, A.M.O., Progress in Aeronautical Sciences, vol. 8, Pergamon Press, 1967.

Giesing, J.P., Journal of Bassic Engineering, Trans. ASME, series D, vol. 90 n° 3, septembre 1968.

Luu, T.S., Coulmy, G. et Corniglion, J., Bull. Ass. Tech. Maritime et Aéron. (ATMA), session de 1969.

Luu, T.S., ATMA, session de 1970.

Luu, T.S., Coulmy, G. et Corniglion, J., ATMA, session de 1971.

Luu, T.S., Coulmy, G. et Sagnard, J., ATMA, session de 1971.

Luu, T.S., C.R. du Colloque du C.N.R.S., Marseille, 2-5 novembre 1971.

Luu, T.S., Coulmy, G. et Dulieu, A., ATMA, session de 1972.

Luu, T.S., Corniglion, J., ATMA, session de 1972.

Luu, T.S., Coulmy, G., Proceeding 3^{e} Conf. Numerical Methods in Fluid Mechanics, juillet 1972, Ed. Springer-Verlag.

Malavard, L., Agardograph n° 18, août 1956, Ed. AGARD-NATO, Paris, France.

SOME CONTRIBUTIONS TO NON-LINEAR SOLID MECHANICS

J.H.Argyris and P.C.Dunne

Imperial College of Science and Technology, University of London

Institut für Statik und Dynamik der Luft-und Raumfahrtkonstruktionen, University of Stuttgart

SUMMARY

The finite element method has now developed to the point where practically any linear problem can be solved with adequate accuracy. There is still room for improvement, much dead wood remains to be removed and procedures have not yet reached the degree of standarization which will eventually be possible. On the other hand the treatment of non-linear problems by the finite element method, and indeed by any method on the scale required by engineers, is still at the beginning.

Non-linear problems are very difficult to visualize. It seems that there is a built-in tendency for the human brain to think linearly. Analogies are especially helpful in this respect. A problem often becomes easier to think about when it is translated into the field to which one is accustomed.

The present report is mainly concerned with non-linear problems in structural engineering but some other types of problems are mentioned.

Part I attempts to make the theory of large strains more accessible to the engineer who has no background in tensor calculus. This is done mainly through extending the idea of natural stresses and strains to the case of large strains. The simplicity of this approach is greatest with the family of elements deriving from triangular TRIM 3 and tetrahedronal TET 4.

Part II reports on recent work at ISD on the dynamics of very large structural systems. Two types of integrating algorithms have been developed. The first which requires small time steps is applicable to both linear and non-linear systems. The second type enables linear systems to be integrated with very large time steps and is an alternative to modal analysis. The development of a similar method for non-linear systems is discussed. Although the small step algorithms are especially suitable for structural dynamics they are also applicable to other problems. The classic n-body problem is one example and another is the dynamics of an underground explosion with idealized non-linear material.

ACKNOWLEDGEMENTS

The work represented here is the work of a team. Of this team we must mention especially T. Angelopoulos who was responsible for the development and implementation on the computer of the dynamics algorithms of Part II and the shape finding technique of Part III.
A valuable contribution to the theoretical work was made by Maria Haase and a large proportion of the programming was the work of B. Bichat. The problem on elasto-plastic wave propagation was contributed by J. Doltsinis.
Others who must be thanked for their extensive and unselfish help in the preparation of the paper are G. Grimm, I. Hucklenbroich, K. Mai, H. Ries and K. Strauß.

I. LARGE STRAIN THEORY FOR FINITE ELEMENTS

1. Introduction

The theory of large strains and its application to non-linear elasticity is generally considered by practising engineers to be a subject difficult for them to follow. The idea is prevalent that a proper understanding of the subject requires facility in the tensor calculus. Particularly confusing to the non-specialist is the multiplicity of strain and stress tensors such as the Green and Almansi strains, and the Eulerian, Lagrangian and Kirchhoff stresses. Whereas in small strain theory the shear strain is the easily understood change in the angle between two originally orthogonal lines, in large strain theory it depends also on the direct strains along these lines.

In the book of O.H.Varga [1] the behaviour of isotropic material is described almost entirely in terms of the principal strains and stresses. This approach is easy for the engineer to understand. Another relatively simple way of treating the problem is through the idea of natural strains in simplex finite elements. These latter are the triangular (TRIM) and tetrahedronal (TET) family of finite elements. In the following we particularly develop this method.

The natural large strains of the TRIM 3 and TET 4 elements are constant and are the Green strains along the edges. The associated natural stresses are the component stresses parallel to the sides of the triangle or tetrahedron in its final position. For higher order simplex elements these definitions may be used in relation to the constituting small subelements.

The present work is restricted to consideration of TRIM 3, TET 4 and TRIAX 3 with and without axial symmetry. In the latter case it is necessary to make use of cartesian strains in conjunction with circumferential Fourier components.

The non-linear stiffness matrices for the TRIM 3, TET 4 and TRIAX 3 axial symmetrical case are established for an arbitrary polynomial strain energy function in terms of the natural strains. For isotropic materials the strain energy polynomials are expressed in terms of the strain invariants.

2. Two-Dimensional Strain

The strain is supposed to be a pure extension in the direction of the cartesian axes Ox , Oy (Fig.1.1) A point $P(x,y)$ moves to $P'(x',y')$. Then if

$$\lambda = r'/r \tag{1.1}$$

$$\lambda^2 = \lambda_I^2 \cos^2\theta + \lambda_{II}^2 \sin^2\theta \tag{1.2}$$

and if

$$\varepsilon = \frac{1}{2}(\lambda^2 - 1) \tag{1.3}$$

$$\varepsilon = \varepsilon_I \cos^2\theta + \varepsilon_{II} \sin^2\theta \tag{1.4}$$

Thus the strain measures λ^2 and ε transform as in the Mohr Circle. ε is the Green strain which is related to the ordinary Cauchy strain ϵ by the equations

$$\epsilon = \lambda - 1 \qquad \text{or} \qquad \varepsilon - \epsilon + \frac{1}{2}\epsilon^2 \tag{1.5}$$

The Green shear strain is obtained from ε_I and ε_{II} by the usual transformation. However, it has no longer the simple physical meaning that it has in the small strain case.

Now consider a triangle 1,2,3 which is uniformly strained and displaced to a new position 1',2',3'. The strains of the sides 1 2, 2 3, 3 1 as defined in eq. (1.3) are called the total natural strains which form the vector

$$\boldsymbol{\varepsilon}_t = \{ \varepsilon_{t\alpha} \ \ \varepsilon_{t\beta} \ \ \varepsilon_{t\gamma} \} \tag{1.6}$$

Then

$$\begin{aligned}
\varepsilon_{t\alpha} &= \varepsilon_I \cos^2\psi + \varepsilon_{II} \sin^2\psi \\
\varepsilon_{t\beta} &= \varepsilon_I \cos^2(\psi+\gamma) + \varepsilon_{II} \sin^2(\psi+\gamma) \\
\varepsilon_{t\gamma} &= \varepsilon_I \cos^2(\psi-\beta) + \varepsilon_{II} \sin^2(\psi-\beta)
\end{aligned} \tag{1.7}$$

These equations are the same as those for the small strains. It follows that the device of component strains ε_c may be used although they are no longer physically superposable.

Thus, with,

$$\boldsymbol{\varepsilon}_c = \{ \varepsilon_{c\alpha} \ \ \varepsilon_{c\beta} \ \ \varepsilon_{c\gamma} \}$$

$$\boldsymbol{\varepsilon}_t = \boldsymbol{A}\boldsymbol{\varepsilon}_c \qquad \text{or} \qquad \boldsymbol{\varepsilon}_c = \boldsymbol{A}^{-1}\boldsymbol{\varepsilon}_t \tag{1.8}$$

where,

$$\boldsymbol{A} = \begin{bmatrix} 1 & \cos^2\gamma & \cos^2\beta \\ \cos^2\gamma & 1 & \cos^2\alpha \\ \cos^2\beta & \cos^2\alpha & 1 \end{bmatrix} \tag{1.9}$$

The strain invariants are,

$$J_1 = \varepsilon_I + \varepsilon_{II} = \varepsilon_{c\alpha} + \varepsilon_{c\beta} + \varepsilon_{c\gamma} = \boldsymbol{e}_3^t \boldsymbol{\varepsilon}_c = \boldsymbol{e}_3^t \boldsymbol{A}^{-1} \boldsymbol{\varepsilon}_t \tag{1.10}$$

and

$$J_2 = \varepsilon_I \varepsilon_{II} = \frac{1}{2}\left(J_1^2 - \boldsymbol{\varepsilon}_t^t \boldsymbol{\varepsilon}_c\right) = \frac{1}{2} \boldsymbol{\varepsilon}_c^t \left[\boldsymbol{E}_3 - \boldsymbol{A}\right] \boldsymbol{\varepsilon}_c \tag{1.11}$$

where

$$\boldsymbol{e}_3 = \{1\ 1\ 1\} \quad ; \quad \boldsymbol{E}_3 = \boldsymbol{e}_3 \boldsymbol{e}_3^t = \begin{bmatrix} 1 & 1 & 1 \\ 1 & 1 & 1 \\ 1 & 1 & 1 \end{bmatrix} \tag{1.12}$$

The membrane incompressibility condition is,

$$\lambda_I \lambda_{II} = 1$$

or from (1.3)

$$(1 + 2\varepsilon_I)(1 + 2\varepsilon_{II}) = 1$$

or

$$J_1 + 2J_2 = 0 \tag{1.13}$$

For small strains this condition reduces to,

$$J_1 \rightarrow F_1 = \epsilon_I + \epsilon_{II} = \boldsymbol{e}_3^t \boldsymbol{\epsilon}_c = 0 \tag{1.14}$$

The small cartesian (Cauchy) strains ϵ are related to the small total strains ϵ_t through

$$\boldsymbol{\epsilon}_t = \boldsymbol{C}^t \boldsymbol{\epsilon} \tag{1.15}$$

where

$$\boldsymbol{\epsilon} = \left\{ \epsilon_{xx}\ \epsilon_{yy}\ \sqrt{2}\epsilon_{xy} \right\} \tag{1.15a}$$

and

$$\mathbf{C}^t = \begin{bmatrix} c_{23x} & c_{23y} & \sqrt{2}\, c_{23x}\, c_{23y} \\ c_{31x} & c_{31y} & \sqrt{2}\, c_{31x}\, c_{31y} \\ c_{12x} & c_{12y} & \sqrt{2}\, c_{12x}\, c_{12y} \end{bmatrix} \qquad (1.16)$$

where c_{23x} = cosine (23, O_x) etc.

Note that

$$\mathbf{C}^t\mathbf{C} = \mathbf{A} \qquad (1.17)$$

In large strain theory the parallel results are

$$\boldsymbol{\varepsilon}_t = \mathbf{C}^t\,\boldsymbol{\varepsilon} \qquad (1.18)$$

where

$$\boldsymbol{\varepsilon} = \{ \varepsilon_{xx} \quad \varepsilon_{yy} \quad \sqrt{2}\,\varepsilon_{xy} \} \qquad (1.18a)$$

It will be convenient in what follows to use the notation x^1, u^1 for x, u and x^2, u^2 for y, v. Also we define,

$$\mathbf{x} = \{ x^1 \quad x^2 \} \quad ; \quad \mathbf{u} = \{ u^1 \quad u^2 \} \qquad (1.19)$$

$$u^1_{,1} = \frac{\partial u^1}{\partial x^1} \qquad \text{etc.} \qquad (1.20)$$

and

$$\mathbf{D} = \begin{bmatrix} u^1_{,1} & u^2_{,1} \\ u^1_{,2} & u^2_{,2} \end{bmatrix} = \left[\frac{\partial \mathbf{u}}{\partial \mathbf{x}} \right]^t \qquad (1.21)$$

With this notation the cartesian small strain tensor may be written,

$$\boldsymbol{\epsilon} = \begin{bmatrix} \epsilon_{11} & \epsilon_{12} \\ \epsilon_{21} & \epsilon_{22} \end{bmatrix} = \frac{1}{2}\left[\mathbf{D} + \mathbf{D}^t \right] \qquad (1.22)$$

and the cartesian Green strain tensor is,

$$\mathbf{Ʒ} = \begin{bmatrix} \varepsilon_{11} & \varepsilon_{12} \\ \varepsilon_{21} & \varepsilon_{22} \end{bmatrix} = \frac{1}{2}\left[\boldsymbol{D} + \boldsymbol{D}^{t} + \boldsymbol{D}\boldsymbol{D}^{t} \right] \tag{1.23}$$

An alternative formulation of the last result is obtained by writing

$$\boldsymbol{y} = \boldsymbol{x} + \boldsymbol{u} \tag{1.24}$$

Thus y is the coordinate vector of the point x in its displaced position with respect to the same axes Ox^1, Ox^2 . Then introducing the mapping matrix

$$\boldsymbol{M} = \frac{\partial \boldsymbol{y}}{\partial \boldsymbol{x}} = \boldsymbol{I}_2 + \boldsymbol{D}^{t} \tag{1.25}$$

the expression (1.23) becomes,

$$\mathbf{Ʒ} = \frac{1}{2}\left[\boldsymbol{M}^{t}\boldsymbol{M} - \boldsymbol{I}_2 \right] \tag{1.26}$$

If n transformations $\boldsymbol{M}^i$ are applied the mapping of the final configuration with respect to the original one is

$$\boldsymbol{M}^* = \boldsymbol{M}^n \boldsymbol{M}^{n-1} \ldots \boldsymbol{M}^i \ldots\ldots \boldsymbol{M}^2 \boldsymbol{M}^1 \tag{1.27}$$

which may replace $\boldsymbol{M}$ in (1.26). Interestingly enough we may assign to each mapping a distinct physical content. For example, $\boldsymbol{M}_1$ may describe a pure plastic and $\boldsymbol{M}_2$ a pure elastic deformation. By the cosine formula the angle α' in the deformed state is given by,

$$\cos\alpha' = \frac{\lambda_\beta^2 l_\beta^2 + \lambda_\gamma^2 l_\gamma^2 - \lambda_\alpha^2 l_\alpha^2}{2\lambda_\beta l_\beta \lambda_\gamma l_\gamma}$$

$$= \frac{\varepsilon_{t\beta} l_\beta^2 + \varepsilon_{t\gamma} l_\gamma^2 - \varepsilon_{t\alpha} l_\alpha^2}{\lambda_\beta l_\beta \lambda_\gamma l_\gamma} + \frac{\cos\alpha}{\lambda_\beta \lambda_\gamma} \tag{1.28}$$

When α is $\frac{\pi}{2}$ and $l_\beta = l_\gamma$ lie along the cartesian axes,

$$\cos\alpha' = \frac{\varepsilon_{11} + \varepsilon_{22} - 2\varepsilon_{t\alpha}}{\lambda_\beta\lambda_\gamma} = \frac{2\varepsilon_{12}}{\lambda_\beta\lambda_\gamma} \tag{1.29}$$

2. Three-Dimensional Strain

In the same way as in the two-dimensional case a point P moves to P' under a uniform extension in the directions x^1, x^2, x^3. Thus $P(x^1, x^2, x^3)$ becomes $P'(\lambda_I x^1, \lambda_{II} x^2, \lambda_{III} x^3)$. Then

$$\lambda^2 = \left(\frac{OP'}{OP}\right)^2 = \frac{\lambda_I^2 (x^1)^2 + \lambda_{II}^2 (x^2)^2 + \lambda_{III}^2 (x^3)^2}{r^2}$$

$$= \lambda_I^2 c_I^2 + \lambda_{II}^2 c_{II}^2 + \lambda_{III}^2 c_{III}^2 \tag{1.30}$$

Defining as before $\varepsilon = \frac{1}{2}(\lambda^2 - 1)$

$$\varepsilon = \varepsilon_I c_I^2 + \varepsilon_{II} c_{II}^2 + \varepsilon_{III} c_{III}^2 \tag{1.31}$$

This result again shows that the principal Green strains transform by the same transformation rules as the small strains. c_I, c_{II}, c_{III} are the direction cosines of OP with the principal strain axes before deformation.

Now consider a tetrahedron 1,2,3,4 . The total strains along the edges form the vector

$$\boldsymbol{\varepsilon}_t = \{ \varepsilon_{t12} \;\; \varepsilon_{t34} \;\; \varepsilon_{t41} \;\; \varepsilon_{t23} \;\; \varepsilon_{t31} \;\; \varepsilon_{t24} \} \tag{1.32}$$

If the direction cosines of the edges with respect to the principal directions before deformation are c_{12I} etc., then,

$$\boldsymbol{\varepsilon}_t = \mathbf{C}_P^t \boldsymbol{\varepsilon}_P \tag{1.33}$$

where

$$\boldsymbol{\varepsilon}_P = \{ \varepsilon_I \;\; \varepsilon_{II} \;\; \varepsilon_{III} \} \tag{1.34}$$

and,

$$
\mathbf{C}_p^t = \begin{bmatrix} c_{12\,I}^2 & c_{12\,II}^2 & c_{12\,III}^2 \\ c_{34\,I}^2 & c_{34\,II}^2 & c_{34\,III}^2 \\ c_{41\,I}^2 & c_{41\,II}^2 & c_{41\,III}^2 \\ c_{23\,I}^2 & c_{23\,II}^2 & c_{23\,III}^2 \\ c_{31\,I}^2 & c_{31\,II}^2 & c_{31\,III}^2 \\ c_{24\,I}^2 & c_{24\,II}^2 & c_{24\,III}^2 \end{bmatrix} \tag{1.35}
$$

These equations are exactly as in the small strain case and we may again use the concept of component strains. Thus, the component strains are defined by

$$
\boldsymbol{\varepsilon}_t = \boldsymbol{A}\boldsymbol{\varepsilon}_c \tag{1.36}
$$

or

$$
\boldsymbol{\varepsilon}_c = \boldsymbol{A}^{-1}\boldsymbol{\varepsilon}_t \tag{1.37}
$$

where

$$
\boldsymbol{\varepsilon}_c = \{ \varepsilon_{c12} \;\; \varepsilon_{c34} \;\; \varepsilon_{c41} \;\; \varepsilon_{c23} \;\; \varepsilon_{c31} \;\; \varepsilon_{c24} \} \tag{1.38}
$$

and,

$$
\boldsymbol{A} = \begin{bmatrix} 1 & c_{12,34}^2 & c_{12,41}^2 & c_{12,23}^2 & c_{12,31}^2 & c_{12,24}^2 \\ & 1 & c_{34,41}^2 & c_{34,23}^2 & c_{34,31}^2 & c_{34,24}^2 \\ & & 1 & c_{41,23}^2 & c_{41,31}^2 & c_{41,24}^2 \\ & & & 1 & c_{23,31}^2 & c_{23,24}^2 \\ & \text{sym.} & & & 1 & c_{31,24}^2 \\ & & & & & 1 \end{bmatrix} \tag{1.39}
$$

All the transformations valid for small strain theory are valid also for the large strains. As before the component strains are no longer superposable. Then for the cartesian Green strains $\boldsymbol{\varepsilon}$ one has,

$$
\boldsymbol{\varepsilon}_t = \boldsymbol{C}^t\boldsymbol{\varepsilon} \tag{1.40}
$$

where

$$\boldsymbol{C}^t = \begin{bmatrix} c_{121}^2 & c_{122}^2 & c_{123}^2 & \sqrt{2}c_{121}c_{122} & \sqrt{2}c_{122}c_{123} & \sqrt{2}c_{123}c_{121} \\ c_{341}^2 & c_{342}^2 & c_{343}^2 & \sqrt{2}c_{341}c_{342} & \sqrt{2}c_{342}c_{343} & \sqrt{2}c_{343}c_{341} \\ c_{411}^2 & c_{412}^2 & c_{413}^2 & \sqrt{2}c_{411}c_{412} & \sqrt{2}c_{412}c_{413} & \sqrt{2}c_{413}c_{411} \\ c_{231}^2 & c_{232}^2 & c_{233}^2 & \sqrt{2}c_{231}c_{232} & \sqrt{2}c_{232}c_{233} & \sqrt{2}c_{233}c_{231} \\ c_{311}^2 & c_{312}^2 & c_{313}^2 & \sqrt{2}c_{311}c_{312} & \sqrt{2}c_{312}c_{313} & \sqrt{2}c_{313}c_{311} \\ c_{241}^2 & c_{242}^2 & c_{243}^2 & \sqrt{2}c_{241}c_{242} & \sqrt{2}c_{242}c_{243} & \sqrt{2}c_{243}c_{241} \end{bmatrix} \tag{1.41}$$

$$c_{121} = \text{cosine } (12, 0x^1) \quad \text{etc.}$$

and

$$\boldsymbol{\varepsilon} = \{ \varepsilon_{11} \;\; \varepsilon_{22} \;\; \varepsilon_{33} \;\; \sqrt{2}\varepsilon_{12} \;\; \sqrt{2}\varepsilon_{23} \;\; \sqrt{2}\varepsilon_{31} \} \tag{1.42}$$

If ε_p is a principal strain with direction cosines c_{p1}, c_{p2}, c_{p3} then

$$\begin{aligned} \varepsilon_p &= \sum_6 \varepsilon_{c12} (c_{121} c_{p1} + c_{122} c_{p2} + c_{123} c_{p3})^2 \\ &= c_{p1}^2 \sum_6 c_{121}^2 \varepsilon_{c12} + c_{p2}^2 \sum_6 c_{122}^2 \varepsilon_{c12} + c_{p3}^2 \sum_6 c_{123}^2 \varepsilon_{c12} \\ &+ 2c_{p1} c_{p2} \sum_6 c_{121} c_{122} \varepsilon_{c12} + 2c_{p2} c_{p3} \sum_6 c_{122} c_{123} \varepsilon_{c12} \\ &+ 2c_{p3} c_{p1} \sum_6 c_{123} c_{121} \varepsilon_{c12} \end{aligned} \tag{1.43}$$

The principal strains will correspond to the values of c_{p1}, c_{p2} and c_{p3} making ε_p stationary subject to,

$$c_{p1}^2 + c_{p2}^2 + c_{p3}^2 = 1 \tag{1.44}$$

This leads to the determinant

$$\begin{vmatrix} \left(\sum_6 c_{121}^2 \varepsilon_{c12} - \varepsilon_p \right) & \sum_6 c_{121} c_{122} \varepsilon_{c12} & \sum_6 c_{121} c_{123} \varepsilon_{c12} \\ & \left(\sum_6 c_{122}^2 \varepsilon_{c12} - \varepsilon_p \right) & \sum_6 c_{122} c_{123} \varepsilon_{c12} \\ \text{sym.} & & \left(\sum_6 c_{123}^2 \varepsilon_{c12} - \varepsilon_p \right) \end{vmatrix} = 0 \tag{1.45}$$

This must be identical with the standard cubic equation for the principal strains in terms of the strain invariants

$$J_1 = \varepsilon_I + \varepsilon_{II} + \varepsilon_{III} \; ; \quad J_2 = \varepsilon_I \varepsilon_{II} + \varepsilon_{II} \varepsilon_{III} + \varepsilon_{III} \varepsilon_I \qquad J_3 = \varepsilon_I \varepsilon_{II} \varepsilon_{III} \tag{1.46}$$

$$\varepsilon_p^3 - J_1 \varepsilon_p^2 + J_2 \varepsilon_p - J_3 = 0 \tag{1.47}$$

Thus,

$$J_1 = \sum_6 (c_{121}^2 + c_{122}^2 + c_{123}^2) \varepsilon_{c12} = \sum \varepsilon_{c12} = \boldsymbol{e}_6^t \boldsymbol{\varepsilon}_c \tag{1.48}$$

$$J_2 = \sum_{15} \sin^2 \varphi_{ij,pq} \, \varepsilon_{cij} \, \varepsilon_{cpq} \tag{1.49}$$

$$= \frac{1}{2} \left[J_1^2 - \boldsymbol{\varepsilon}_t^t \boldsymbol{\varepsilon}_c \right] = \frac{1}{2} \boldsymbol{\varepsilon}_c^t \left[\boldsymbol{E}_6 - \boldsymbol{A} \right] \boldsymbol{\varepsilon}_c \tag{1.50}$$

The third invariant J_3 is equal to the determinant of (1.45) with $\varepsilon_p = 0$ and reduces to

$$J_3 = 36 \, V^2 \sum_{16} \frac{\varepsilon_{cij} \, \varepsilon_{cpq} \, \varepsilon_{crs}}{l_{ij}^2 \, l_{pq}^2 \, l_{rs}^2} \tag{1.51}$$

where V = volume of tetrahedron (1,2,3,4) and the terms in (1.51) include all non-coplanar combinations of the edges.

The incompressibility is

$$\lambda_I \; \lambda_{II} \; \lambda_{III} = 1 \qquad \text{or} \qquad J_1 + 2 J_2 + 4 J_3 = 0 \tag{1.52}$$

For small strains this reduces to

$$J_1 \rightarrow F_1 = \epsilon_I + \epsilon_{II} + \epsilon_{III} = \boldsymbol{e}_6^t \boldsymbol{\epsilon}_c = 0 \tag{1.53}$$

3.1 Cartesian Strain Increment-Relations

We collect here some results in cartesian strains which are given for three dimensions but are immediately valid for two dimensions. The Green strain tensor following (1.26) is,

$$\boldsymbol{\varepsilon} = \frac{1}{2}\left[\boldsymbol{M}^t\boldsymbol{M} - \boldsymbol{I}_3\right] \tag{1.54}$$

Correspondingly the Almansi tensor is,

$$\boldsymbol{\varepsilon}_A = -\frac{1}{2}\left[\boldsymbol{N}^t\boldsymbol{N} - \boldsymbol{I}_3\right] \tag{1.55}$$

where

$$\boldsymbol{M} = \frac{\partial \boldsymbol{y}}{\partial \boldsymbol{x}} \quad ; \quad \boldsymbol{N} = \frac{\partial \boldsymbol{x}}{\partial \boldsymbol{y}} \tag{1.56}$$

Thus

$$\boldsymbol{N} = \boldsymbol{M}^{-1} \tag{1.57}$$

since $\boldsymbol{x}$ and $\boldsymbol{y}$ are referred to the same cartesian axes. The increments of $\boldsymbol{\varepsilon}$ and $\boldsymbol{\varepsilon}_A$ due to an increment $\delta\boldsymbol{u}$ are, from (1.54) and (1.55),

$$\delta\boldsymbol{\varepsilon} = \frac{1}{2}\left[\boldsymbol{M}^t\delta\boldsymbol{M} + \delta\boldsymbol{M}^t\boldsymbol{M}\right] \tag{1.58}$$

$$\delta\boldsymbol{\varepsilon}_A = -\frac{1}{2}\left[\boldsymbol{N}^t\delta\boldsymbol{N} + \delta\boldsymbol{N}^t\boldsymbol{N}\right] \tag{1.59}$$

For the purpose of calculating the virtual work of the stresses it is useful to have expressions for the increment of Cauchy strain $\delta\boldsymbol{\epsilon}$ based on the final configuration ($\boldsymbol{y}$ state). In the neighbourhood of a point P which becomes P' in final state, one has

$$\boldsymbol{y} - \boldsymbol{y}_{P'} = \boldsymbol{M}\left[\boldsymbol{x} - \boldsymbol{x}_P\right] \tag{1.60}$$

But

$$\boldsymbol{y} - \boldsymbol{y}_{P'} = (\boldsymbol{x} - \boldsymbol{x}_P) + (\boldsymbol{u} - \boldsymbol{u}_P)$$

Therefore,

$$\boldsymbol{u} - \boldsymbol{u}_P = \left[\boldsymbol{M} - \boldsymbol{I}_3\right]\left[\boldsymbol{x} - \boldsymbol{x}_P\right]$$

Then for an increment $\delta \boldsymbol{u}$

$$\delta [\, \boldsymbol{u} - \boldsymbol{u}_P \,] = \delta \boldsymbol{M} [\boldsymbol{x} - \boldsymbol{x}_P] \tag{1.61}$$

But

$$\boldsymbol{x} - \boldsymbol{x}_P = \boldsymbol{N} [\boldsymbol{y} - \boldsymbol{y}_{P'}]$$

So that

$$\delta [\, \boldsymbol{u} - \boldsymbol{u}_P \,] = \delta \boldsymbol{M} \boldsymbol{N} [\boldsymbol{y} - \boldsymbol{y}_{P'}] \tag{1.62}$$

Thus $\delta[\boldsymbol{u} - \boldsymbol{u}_P]$ is of the form

$$\boldsymbol{D}^t [\, \boldsymbol{y} - \boldsymbol{y}_{P'}] \qquad \text{(see eq.(1.21)}$$

and hence

$$\delta \boldsymbol{\exists} = \frac{1}{2} \left[\boldsymbol{N}^t \delta \boldsymbol{M}^t + \delta \boldsymbol{M} \boldsymbol{N} \right] \tag{1.63}$$

Now from (1.58) with (1.63)

$$\boldsymbol{M}^t \delta \boldsymbol{\exists} \boldsymbol{M} = \delta \boldsymbol{\varepsilon} \tag{1.64}$$

or

$$\boldsymbol{N}^t \delta \boldsymbol{\varepsilon} \boldsymbol{N} = \delta \boldsymbol{\exists}$$

4. Strain in Bodies of Revolution

In bodies of revolution with symmetrical loading and properties one may work in terms of triangular elements in the radial plane. For non-symmetrical loading there are two alternatives. The elements may be in the form of annular rings of triangular radial section and the circumferential displacements developed as Fourier series. Or one may use segmental or even tetrahedron elements. Although for large displacements the Fourier components will no longer be orthogonal, it is thought that the total degrees of freedom for a given precision should be less by the Fourier method, at least for fairly smoothly distributed loading.

4.1 Axi-Symmetric Strain

Since the displacement normal to the radial plane is zero the strain in that direction, which is also the principal strain ε_{II}, is given by,

$$\varepsilon_{22} = \varepsilon_{II} = \frac{u^1}{x^1} + \frac{1}{2}\left(\frac{u^1}{x^1}\right)^2 \tag{1.65}$$

In the radial plane the strains will be defined as in (1.2) and are always reducible to the principal strains ε_I , ε_{III} .

4.2 Non-Axi-Symmetric Strain

The cylindrical coordinates of a point of the body are x^1 , x^2 , x^3 so that x^2 is now an angle. To obtain in this system the strains

$$\boldsymbol{\varepsilon} = \left\{ \varepsilon_{11} \quad \varepsilon_{22} \quad \varepsilon_{33} \quad \sqrt{2}\varepsilon_{12} \quad \sqrt{2}\varepsilon_{23} \quad \sqrt{2}\varepsilon_{31} \right\} \tag{1.66}$$

we require the matrix $\boldsymbol{M}$ in terms of the cylindrical coordinates. Thus $\boldsymbol{M}$ is expressed with reference to the orthogonal triad of axes in the directions of x^1 , x^2 and x^3 at P .

$$\boldsymbol{M} = \left[\boldsymbol{I}_3 + \boldsymbol{D}^t \right] \tag{1.67}$$

where,

$$\boldsymbol{D} = \begin{bmatrix} u^1_{,1} & u^2_{,1} & u^3_{,1} \\ \frac{1}{x^1}\left(u^1_{,2} - u^2\right) & \frac{1}{x^1}\left(u^2_{,2} + u^1\right) & \frac{1}{x^1} u^3_{,2} \\ u^1_{,3} & u^2_{,3} & u^3_{,3} \end{bmatrix} \tag{1.68}$$

The corresponding Green strain tensor is then given by eq. (1.54).

We now define the Fourier components of the displacement in symmetric and anti-symmetric groups with reference to the generating triangle of each ring at $x^2 = 0$.

Thus using u for the symmetric and v for the anti-symmetric terms the nth Fourier components are

$$\begin{aligned} u^1 &\propto \cos n x^2 \quad ; \quad v^1 \propto \sin n x^2 \\ u^2 &\propto \sin n x^2 \quad ; \quad v^2 \propto \cos n x^2 \\ u^3 &\propto \cos n x^2 \quad ; \quad v^3 \propto \sin n x^2 \end{aligned} \tag{1.69}$$

Defining,

$$\boldsymbol{c}_n = \lceil \cos nx^2 \quad \sin nx^2 \quad \cos nx^2 \rfloor$$
$$\boldsymbol{s}_n = \lceil \sin nx^2 \quad -\cos nx^2 \quad \sin nx^2 \rfloor \qquad (1.70)$$

or more briefly

$$\boldsymbol{c}_n = \lceil c_n \quad s_n \quad c_n \rfloor \quad ; \quad \boldsymbol{s}_n = \lceil s_n \quad -c_n \quad s_n \rfloor \qquad (1.71)$$

then

$$\frac{d\boldsymbol{s}_n}{dx^2} = n\boldsymbol{c}_n \quad ; \quad \frac{d\boldsymbol{c}_n}{dx^2} = -n\boldsymbol{s}_n \qquad (1.72)$$

In what follows we restrict ourselves to the symmetrical component $\boldsymbol{u}$.

For the TRIAX 3 finite element presentation it is convenient to define two types of displacement vector. Thus the displacements at the ith node are

$$\boldsymbol{u}_i = \{ u_i^1 \quad u_i^2 \quad u_i^3 \} \qquad (1.73)$$

and the vector of the displacements u^j at the nodes 1, 2, 3 is,

$$\boldsymbol{u}^j = (u_1^j \quad u_2^j \quad u_3^j) \qquad (1.74)$$

Three ways of expressing the nine nodal displacements are now defined.

$$\boldsymbol{u}_I = \{ \boldsymbol{u}_1 \quad \boldsymbol{u}_2 \quad \boldsymbol{u}_3 \}$$
$$\boldsymbol{u}^I = \{ \boldsymbol{u}^1 \quad \boldsymbol{u}^2 \quad \boldsymbol{u}^3 \} \qquad (1.75)$$
$$\bar{\boldsymbol{u}}_I = \{ \boldsymbol{u}_1^t \quad \boldsymbol{u}_2^t \quad \boldsymbol{u}_3^t \}$$

The vector $\boldsymbol{u}$ within the basic triangle is interpolated linearly between the nodal values. Thus

$$\boldsymbol{u}^t = [\, \zeta^1 \quad \zeta^2 \quad \zeta^3 \,]\, \bar{\boldsymbol{u}}_I = \boldsymbol{\omega}\, \bar{\boldsymbol{u}}_I \qquad (1.76)$$

and also $u^j = \boldsymbol{\omega} \boldsymbol{u}^j$ where the ζ 's are the natural (areal) coordinates of the triangle. Alternatively

$$\boldsymbol{u} = \left[\zeta^1 \boldsymbol{I}_3 \quad \zeta^2 \boldsymbol{I}_3 \quad \zeta^3 \boldsymbol{I}_3 \right] \boldsymbol{u}_I = \boldsymbol{\omega}_e \boldsymbol{u}_I \qquad (1.77)$$

For the displacement in the nth mode we introduce the inferior index n and write,

$$\underset{n}{\boldsymbol{u}} = \boldsymbol{c}_n \boldsymbol{\omega}_e \underset{n}{\boldsymbol{u}}_I$$

or

$$\underset{n}{\boldsymbol{u}}^t = \boldsymbol{\omega} \underset{n}{\bar{\boldsymbol{u}}}_I \boldsymbol{c}_n \qquad (1.78)$$

With the above notation we find, for the Cauchy strain $\boldsymbol{\partial}_{cn}$ in the nth mode

$$\boldsymbol{\partial}_{cn} =$$

$$\begin{bmatrix} c_n \boldsymbol{\omega}_{,1} \underset{n}{\boldsymbol{u}}^1 & \frac{1}{2} s_n \left[\boldsymbol{\omega}_{,1} \underset{n}{\boldsymbol{u}}^2 + \frac{1}{x^1} \boldsymbol{\omega} \left(-n \underset{n}{\boldsymbol{u}}^1 - \underset{n}{\boldsymbol{u}}^2 \right) \right] & \frac{1}{2} c_n \left[\boldsymbol{\omega}_{,3} \underset{n}{\boldsymbol{u}}^1 + \boldsymbol{\omega}_{,1} \underset{n}{\boldsymbol{u}}^3 \right] \\ & \frac{c_n}{x^1} \boldsymbol{\omega} \left[\underset{n}{\boldsymbol{u}}^1 + n \underset{n}{\boldsymbol{u}}^2 \right] & \frac{1}{2} s_n \left[\boldsymbol{\omega}_{,3} \underset{n}{\boldsymbol{u}}^2 - \frac{n}{x^1} \boldsymbol{\omega} \underset{n}{\boldsymbol{u}}^3 \right] \\ \text{symmetric} & & c_n \boldsymbol{\omega}_{,3} \underset{n}{\boldsymbol{u}}^3 \end{bmatrix} \qquad (1.79)$$

The individual components ∂_{ij} etc., of this tensor can easily be written in the matrix form $\boldsymbol{a}_{ij} \underset{n}{\boldsymbol{u}}^I$. In the above matrix,

$$\frac{\partial \boldsymbol{\omega}}{\partial x^1} = \boldsymbol{\omega}_{,1} = -\frac{1}{2\Omega} \left[x^3_{23} \quad x^3_{13} \quad x^3_{12} \right] \qquad (1.80)$$

$$\frac{\partial \boldsymbol{\omega}}{\partial x^3} = \boldsymbol{\omega}_{,3} = -\frac{1}{2\Omega} \left[x^1_{23} \quad x^1_{13} \quad x^1_{12} \right]$$

$x_{23} = x_3 - x_2$ etc. and Ω = original area of triangle.

To evaluate the Green strain $\boldsymbol{\partial}$ we must expand the expression

$$\boldsymbol{D}\boldsymbol{D}^t$$

We do not multiply out this expression but form instead the contribution of the symmetrical and anti-symmetrical Fourier components. Thus there will be terms of the form,

$$\mathfrak{D}_{cmcn} = \frac{1}{2}\left[\boldsymbol{D}_{cm}\boldsymbol{D}^{t}_{cn} + \boldsymbol{D}_{cn}\boldsymbol{D}^{t}_{cm} \right] \; ; \; \frac{1}{2}\boldsymbol{D}_{cn}\boldsymbol{D}^{t}_{cn}$$

$$\mathfrak{D}_{smcn} = \frac{1}{2}\left[\boldsymbol{D}_{sm}\boldsymbol{D}^{t}_{cn} + \boldsymbol{D}_{cn}\boldsymbol{D}^{t}_{sm} \right] \; ; \; \frac{1}{2}\boldsymbol{D}_{sn}\boldsymbol{D}^{t}_{cn}$$

$$\mathfrak{D}_{cmsn} = \frac{1}{2}\left[\boldsymbol{D}_{cm}\boldsymbol{D}^{t}_{sn} + \boldsymbol{D}_{sn}\boldsymbol{D}^{t}_{cm} \right] \; ; \; \frac{1}{2}\boldsymbol{D}_{cn}\boldsymbol{D}^{t}_{sn} \tag{1.81}$$

$$\mathfrak{D}_{smsn} = \frac{1}{2}\left[\boldsymbol{D}_{sm}\boldsymbol{D}^{t}_{sn} + \boldsymbol{D}_{sn}\boldsymbol{D}^{t}_{sm} \right] \; ; \; \frac{1}{2}\boldsymbol{D}_{sn}\boldsymbol{D}^{t}_{sn}$$

When $m = n$ the general expressions reduce to the R.H.S. members.
Then the total large strain tensor $\boldsymbol{\mathfrak{E}}$ is

$$\boldsymbol{\mathfrak{E}} = \mathfrak{e} + \sum_{m,n}\left[\mathfrak{D}_{cmcn} + \mathfrak{D}_{smcn} + \mathfrak{D}_{cmcn} + \mathfrak{D}_{smsn}\right] \quad (3\times 3) \tag{1.82}$$

where $\mathfrak{e}$ is the total Cauchy strain given by

$$\mathfrak{e} = \sum_{n}\left(\mathfrak{e}_{cn} + \mathfrak{e}_{sn} \right) \tag{1.82a}$$

Introducing the notation for a typical $\mathfrak{D}$ matrix,

$$\mathfrak{D}_{cmcn} = \begin{bmatrix} \mathfrak{D}^{11}_{cmcn} & \mathfrak{D}^{12}_{cmcn} & \mathfrak{D}^{13}_{cmcn} \\ & \mathfrak{D}^{22}_{cmcn} & \mathfrak{D}^{23}_{cmcn} \\ \text{sym.} & & \mathfrak{D}^{33}_{cmcn} \end{bmatrix} \tag{1.83}$$

the individual entries of which are effectively contributions to the higher order strain components, and also

$$\boldsymbol{\Omega} = (x^{1})^{-2}\boldsymbol{\omega}^{t}\boldsymbol{\omega} \; , \; \boldsymbol{\Omega}_{,1} = (x^{1})^{-1}\boldsymbol{\omega}^{t}_{,1}\boldsymbol{\omega} \; , \; \boldsymbol{\Omega}_{,3} = (x^{1})^{-1}\boldsymbol{\omega}^{t}_{,3}\boldsymbol{\omega}$$

$$\boldsymbol{\Omega}_{,11} = \boldsymbol{\omega}^{t}_{,1}\boldsymbol{\omega}_{,1} \; , \; \boldsymbol{\Omega}_{,13} = \boldsymbol{\omega}^{t}_{,1}\boldsymbol{\omega}_{,3} \; , \; \boldsymbol{\Omega}_{,33} = \boldsymbol{\omega}^{t}_{,3}\boldsymbol{\omega}_{,3} \tag{1.84}$$

we find, for

$$\mathfrak{D}^{11}_{cmcn} = \underset{m}{\boldsymbol{u}}^{It} c_m c_n \left\lceil \boldsymbol{\Omega}_{,11} \quad \boldsymbol{\Omega}_{,11} \quad \boldsymbol{\Omega}_{,11} \right\rfloor \underset{n}{\boldsymbol{u}}^{I}$$

$$\mathfrak{D}^{12}_{cmcn} =$$

$$\frac{1}{2} \underset{m}{\boldsymbol{u}}^{It} \left[\begin{array}{c|c|c} -\left[nc_m s_n \boldsymbol{\Omega}_{,1} + ms_m c_n \boldsymbol{\Omega}^{t}_{,1}\right] & c_m\left[-s_n \boldsymbol{\Omega}_{,1} c_n \boldsymbol{\Omega}^{t}_{,1}\right] & \boldsymbol{0}_3 \\ c_n\left[c_m \boldsymbol{\Omega}_{,1} - s_m \boldsymbol{\Omega}^{t}_{,1}\right] & c_m c_n\left[n\boldsymbol{\Omega}_{,1} + m\boldsymbol{\Omega}^{t}_{,1}\right] & \boldsymbol{0}_3 \\ \boldsymbol{0}_3 & \boldsymbol{0}_3 & -\left[nc_m s_n \boldsymbol{\Omega}_{,1} + ms_m c_n \boldsymbol{\Omega}^{t}_{,1}\right] \end{array} \right] \underset{n}{\boldsymbol{u}}^{I}$$

$$\mathfrak{D}^{13}_{cmcn} = \frac{1}{2} \underset{m}{\boldsymbol{u}}^{It} c_m c_n \left\lceil \left[\boldsymbol{\Omega}_{,13} + \boldsymbol{\Omega}^{t}_{,13}\right] \quad \left[\boldsymbol{\Omega}_{,13} + \boldsymbol{\Omega}^{t}_{,13}\right] \quad \left[\boldsymbol{\Omega}_{,13} + \boldsymbol{\Omega}^{t}_{,13}\right] \right\rfloor \underset{n}{\boldsymbol{u}}^{I}$$

$$\mathfrak{D}^{22}_{cmcn} =$$

$$\underset{m}{\boldsymbol{u}}^{It} \left[\begin{array}{c|c|c} (mn\, s_m s_n + c_m c_n)\,\boldsymbol{\Omega} & (ms_m s_n + nc_m c_n)\,\boldsymbol{\Omega} & \boldsymbol{0}_3 \\ (ns_m s_n + mc_m c_n)\,\boldsymbol{\Omega} & (s_m s_n + mnc_m c_n)\,\boldsymbol{\Omega} & \boldsymbol{0}_3 \\ \boldsymbol{0}_3 & \boldsymbol{0}_3 & mns_m s_n \boldsymbol{\Omega} \end{array} \right] \underset{n}{\boldsymbol{u}}^{I}$$

$\mathfrak{D}^{23}_{cmcn}$ derives from $\mathfrak{D}^{12}_{cmcn}$ by substituting $\boldsymbol{\Omega}_{,3}$ in place of $\boldsymbol{\Omega}_{,1}$

$$\mathfrak{D}^{33}_{cmcn} = \underset{m}{\boldsymbol{u}}^{It} c_m c_n \left\lceil \boldsymbol{\Omega}_{,33} \quad \boldsymbol{\Omega}_{,33} \quad \boldsymbol{\Omega}_{,33} \right\rfloor \underset{n}{\boldsymbol{u}}^{I} \qquad (1.85)$$

For the case $m = n$ we have,

$$\mathfrak{D}^{11}_{cncn} = \frac{1}{2} \underset{n}{\boldsymbol{u}}^{It} c_n^2 \left[\boldsymbol{\Omega}_{,11} \quad \boldsymbol{\Omega}_{,11} \quad \boldsymbol{\Omega}_{,11} \right] \underset{n}{\boldsymbol{u}}^{I}$$

$$\mathfrak{D}^{12}_{cncn} = \frac{1}{2} \underset{n}{\boldsymbol{u}}^{It} c_n \begin{bmatrix} -n s_n \boldsymbol{\Omega}_{,1} & -s_n \boldsymbol{\Omega}_{,1} & \boldsymbol{0}_3 \\ c_n \boldsymbol{\Omega}_{,1} & n c_n \boldsymbol{\Omega}_{,1} & \boldsymbol{0}_3 \\ \boldsymbol{0}_3 & \boldsymbol{0}_3 & -n s_n \boldsymbol{\Omega}_{,1} \end{bmatrix} \underset{n}{\boldsymbol{u}}^{I}$$

$$\mathfrak{D}^{13}_{cncn} = \frac{1}{2} \underset{n}{\boldsymbol{u}}^{It} c_n^2 \left[\boldsymbol{\Omega}_{,13} \quad \boldsymbol{\Omega}_{;13} \quad \boldsymbol{\Omega}_{,13} \right] \underset{n}{\boldsymbol{u}}^{I}$$

$$\mathfrak{D}^{22}_{cncn} = \frac{1}{2} \underset{n}{\boldsymbol{u}}^{It} \begin{bmatrix} (n^2 s_n^2 + c_n^2)\boldsymbol{\Omega} & n\boldsymbol{\Omega} & \boldsymbol{0}_3 \\ n\boldsymbol{\Omega} & (s_n^2 + n^2 c_n^2)\boldsymbol{\Omega} & \boldsymbol{0}_3 \\ \boldsymbol{0}_3 & \boldsymbol{0}_3 & n^2 s_n^2 \boldsymbol{\Omega} \end{bmatrix} \underset{n}{\boldsymbol{u}}^{I}$$

$$\mathfrak{D}^{33}_{cncn} = \frac{1}{2} \underset{n}{\boldsymbol{u}}^{It} c_n^2 \left[\boldsymbol{\Omega}_{,33} \quad \boldsymbol{\Omega}_{,33} \quad \boldsymbol{\Omega}_{,33} \right] \underset{n}{\boldsymbol{u}}^{I}$$

$\mathfrak{D}^{23}_{cncn}$ derives from $\mathfrak{D}^{12}_{cncn}$ by substituting $\boldsymbol{\Omega}_{,3}$ in place $\boldsymbol{\Omega}_{,1}$

(I.86)

The terms corresponding to the anti-symmetrical components $\boldsymbol{\mathfrak{D}}_{smsn}$ are obtained from $\boldsymbol{\mathfrak{D}}_{cmcn}$ by changing c into s, s into $-c$ and $\boldsymbol{u}$ into $\boldsymbol{v}$. The terms $\boldsymbol{\mathfrak{D}}_{snsn}$ are found by the same rules from $\boldsymbol{\mathfrak{D}}_{cncn}$. The coupled terms $\boldsymbol{\mathfrak{D}}_{cmsn}$ ($\boldsymbol{\mathfrak{D}}_{smcn}$) are obtained from $\boldsymbol{\mathfrak{D}}_{cmcn}$ by changing c_n into s_n (c_m into s_m), s_n into $-c_n$ (s_m into $-c_m$) and $\boldsymbol{u}_n$ into $\boldsymbol{v}_n$

($\boldsymbol{u}_m$ into $\boldsymbol{v}_m$) For $\mathfrak{D}_{cnsn}$ and $\mathfrak{D}_{sncn}$ put $m = n$ in the corresponding general case.

It is finally necessary to express each component ε_{ij} of the Green tensor as the sum of linear and quadratic forms in the nodal vectors $\boldsymbol{u}_n^I$ and $\boldsymbol{v}_n^I$ The (1 x 9) linear transformation matrix and the (9 x 9) matrix of the quadratic form are only dependent on the initial geometry and the Fourier modes involved.

5. Virtual Work and Stress

5.1 Two-Dimensional Case - TRIM 3

If

$$\boldsymbol{\sigma}_c = \{ \sigma_{c\alpha} \quad \sigma_{c\beta} \quad \sigma_{c\gamma} \} \tag{1.87}$$

are the component stresses on the final configuration the work done during an increment of the total strains may be obtained by considering only one strain at a time. We take $\varepsilon_{t\alpha}$ Then if $\delta\epsilon_{t\alpha}$ is an increment in the Cauchy strain on the final configuration

$$\delta W = \frac{1}{2} \sigma_{c\alpha} h_\alpha t \lambda_\alpha l_\alpha \delta \epsilon_{t\alpha} \tag{1.88}$$

But $\frac{1}{2} h_\alpha \lambda_\alpha l_\alpha = \Omega_1$, the final area.

So,

$$\delta W = \Omega_1 t \sigma_{c\alpha} \delta \epsilon_{t\alpha}$$

Now

$$\delta \epsilon_{t\alpha} = \delta\lambda_\alpha / \lambda_\alpha = \delta\varepsilon_{t\alpha} / \lambda_\alpha^2$$

Therefore,

$$\delta W = \Omega_1 t \sigma_{c\alpha} \lambda_\alpha^{-2} \delta \varepsilon_{t\alpha} \tag{1.89}$$

For all strains,

$$\delta W = \Omega_1 t \boldsymbol{\sigma}_c^t \boldsymbol{\lambda}^{-2} \delta \boldsymbol{\varepsilon}_t \tag{1.90}$$

where $\boldsymbol{\lambda} = \lceil \lambda_\alpha \quad \lambda_\beta \quad \lambda_\gamma \rfloor$

In terms of the cartesian stresses and strains, since

$$\boldsymbol{\epsilon}_t = \boldsymbol{C}_0^t \boldsymbol{\epsilon} \quad \text{and} \quad \boldsymbol{\sigma} = \boldsymbol{C}_1 \boldsymbol{\sigma}_c \tag{I.91}$$

where $\boldsymbol{\sigma} = \left\{ \sigma_{11} \ \ \sigma_{22} \ \sqrt{2}\sigma_{12} \right\}$

and $\boldsymbol{C}_0$ and $\boldsymbol{C}_1$ refer to the original and final geometry,

$$\delta W = \Omega_1 t \boldsymbol{\sigma}^t \boldsymbol{C}_1^{-1,t} \boldsymbol{\lambda}^{-2} \boldsymbol{C}_0^t \delta \boldsymbol{\epsilon} \tag{I.92}$$

which may be shown to be equivalent to

$$\delta W = \Omega_1 t \boldsymbol{\sigma}^t \delta \boldsymbol{\epsilon} \tag{I.93}$$

where $\delta\boldsymbol{\epsilon}$ is the increment of cartesian Cauchy strain on the final configuration.

5.2 Three-Dimensional Case - TET4

The parallel results for the three-dimensional case may be given briefly. Thus the component stress vector on the final configuration of volume V_1 is

$$\boldsymbol{\sigma}_c = \left\{ \sigma_{c12} \ \ \sigma_{c34} \ \ \sigma_{c41} \ \ \sigma_{c23} \ \ \sigma_{c31} \ \ \sigma_{c24} \right\} \tag{I.94}$$

Then by a similar argument to that used for TRIM3,

$$\delta W = V_1 \boldsymbol{\sigma}^t \boldsymbol{\lambda}_c^{-2} \delta \boldsymbol{\epsilon}_t \tag{I.95}$$

In terms of the cartesian stresses and strains

$$\delta W = V_1 \boldsymbol{\sigma}^t \delta \boldsymbol{\epsilon} = V_1 \boldsymbol{\sigma}^t \boldsymbol{C}^{-1,t} \boldsymbol{\lambda}^{-2} \boldsymbol{C}_0 \delta \boldsymbol{\epsilon} \tag{I.96}$$

where

$$\boldsymbol{\sigma} = \left\{ \sigma_{11} \ \ \sigma_{22} \ \ \sigma_{33} \ \sqrt{2}\sigma_{12} \ \ \sqrt{2}\sigma_{23} \ \sqrt{2}\sigma_{31} \right\}$$

5.3 Bodies of Revolution

In cylindrical polar coordinates the internal virtual work equation for an increment of strain on a volume element of the final configuration is,

(I.97)

If y^1, y^2, y^3 is the triad of orthogonal directions along the cylindrical coordinates in the final position we require $\delta\boldsymbol{\mathfrak{E}}$ to be referred to these directions. But in terms of $\delta\boldsymbol{\varepsilon}$ we have $\delta\boldsymbol{\mathfrak{E}}'$ referred to the original directions x^1, x^2, x^3 so that from (1.64)

$$\delta\boldsymbol{\mathfrak{Z}}' = \boldsymbol{M}^{t,-1}\delta\boldsymbol{\mathfrak{z}}\boldsymbol{M}^{-1} \tag{1.98}$$

where $\boldsymbol{M}$ is given by eq. (1.25) with $\boldsymbol{D}$ by (1.68).
Then transforming to the axes y^1, y^2, y^3 by the rotation operation

$$\boldsymbol{J} = \begin{bmatrix} \cos(y^2 - x^2) & \sin(y^2 - x^2) & 0 \\ -\sin(y^2 - x^2) & \cos(y^2 - x^2) & 0 \\ 0 & 0 & 1 \end{bmatrix} \tag{1.99}$$

we obtain

$$\delta\boldsymbol{\mathfrak{Z}} = \boldsymbol{J}\delta\boldsymbol{\mathfrak{Z}}'\boldsymbol{J}^t \tag{1.100}$$

or finally

$$\delta\boldsymbol{\mathfrak{Z}} = \boldsymbol{J}\boldsymbol{M}^{t,-1}\delta\boldsymbol{\mathfrak{z}}\boldsymbol{M}^{-1} \tag{1.101}$$

This equation may be rewritten in the form of the vector transformation

$$\delta\boldsymbol{\mathfrak{E}} = \boldsymbol{T}\delta\boldsymbol{\varepsilon} \tag{1.102}$$

and hence,

$$\delta W = \boldsymbol{\sigma}^t\boldsymbol{T}\delta\boldsymbol{\varepsilon}\,\frac{dV_1}{dV_0}\,dV_0 \tag{1.103}$$

6. Strain Energy Functions

The choice of a strain energy function to represent the behaviour of a real material is a difficult one. This question is discussed in many books on finite elasticity [1,2,3,5,6,7]. From the computational point of view it is a great advantage if the strain energy can be represented in the form of a polynomial in the Green strains, or in the case of isotropic materials, in the strain invariants. Of course, the advantage of this approach depends on the polynomials being of relatively low degree which may not always be possible for a true representation of the material for large strains.

6.1 Strain Energy Functions for Isotropic Membranes

For isotropic material we may assume for the strain energy density $\bar{\Phi}$ based on a nominal thickness t to be of the form,

$$\bar{\Phi} = \sum_{m=2}^{n} \bar{\Phi}_m \tag{1.104}$$

where

$$\bar{\Phi}_m = \sum_{r,s} A_{rs} J_1^r \, J_2^s \tag{1.105}$$

and

$$r + 2s = m$$

J_1 and J_2 are the strain invariants defined in eqs. (1.10) and (1.11). The first two members are,

$$\begin{aligned} \bar{\Phi}_2 &= A_{20} J_1^2 + A_{01} J_2 \\ \bar{\Phi}_3 &= A_{30} J_1^3 + A_{11} J_1 \, J_2 \end{aligned} \tag{1.106}$$

For incompressible isotropic material

$$\bar{\Phi} = \sum_{m=1}^{n} A_m \, J_1^m \tag{1.107}$$

with the incompressibility condition

$$J_1 + 2J_2 = 0 \tag{1.13}$$

More general forms for $\bar{\Phi}$ are

$$\bar{\Phi} = \text{Function} \left(J_1 \, , \, J_2 \right) \tag{1.108}$$

or in the incompressible case

$$\bar{\Phi} = \text{Function} \left(J_1 \right) \quad \text{or} \quad \text{Function} \left(J_2 \right) \tag{1.109}$$

From (1.108) the principal stresses are obtained by virtual work (see also three-dimensional case below) as

$$\sigma_{I} = \frac{\lambda_{I}}{\lambda_{II}} \left[\frac{\partial \bar{\Phi}}{\partial J_1} + \varepsilon_{II} \frac{\partial \bar{\Phi}}{\partial J_2} \right] \tag{1.110}$$

and similarly for σ_{II}. In the incompressible case

$$\sigma_{I} = \sigma_h + \left(\varepsilon_{I} - \varepsilon_{II} \right) \frac{\partial \bar{\Phi}}{\partial J_1}$$
$$\sigma_{II} = \sigma_h - \left(\varepsilon_{I} - \varepsilon_{II} \right) \frac{\partial \bar{\Phi}}{\partial J_2} \tag{1.111}$$

σ_h is the total hydrostatic stress equal to $\frac{1}{2}(\sigma_1 + \sigma_{II})$. The part of this stress depending on the strain energy function is

$$\sigma_h' = \left(1 + J_1 \right) \frac{\partial \bar{\Phi}}{\partial J_1} \tag{1.112}$$

when $\bar{\Phi}$ is given in terms of J_1 or

$$\sigma_h' = J_2 \frac{\partial \bar{\Phi}}{\partial J_2} \tag{1.113}$$

when $\bar{\Phi}$ is given in terms of J_2. The remainder of σ_h is due to the compressibility constraint.

6.1.1 Some Special Cases

The simplest strain energy expression is

$$\bar{\Phi}_2 = A J_1^2 - B J_2 \tag{1.52}$$

which gives

$$\sigma_{I} = \frac{\lambda_{I}}{\lambda_{II}} \left[2 A J_1 - B \varepsilon_{II} \right] \tag{1.114}$$

The simplest incompressible case is,

$$\bar{\Phi} = \frac{1}{2} B J_1 \qquad \text{or} \qquad \bar{\Phi} = B J_2 \tag{1.115}$$

from which

$$\begin{matrix}\sigma_{I}\\ \sigma_{II}\end{matrix} = \sigma_h \pm \frac{1}{2} B\left(\varepsilon_{I} - \varepsilon_{II}\right) \tag{1.116}$$

Note that

$$\sigma_{I} - \sigma_{II} = B\left(\varepsilon_{I} - \varepsilon_{II}\right)$$

so that the shear stress and strain are in this case proportional. Membranes characterised by (1.115) are analogous to the Mooney three-dimensional material (see below).

6.2 Three-Dimensional Isotropic Materials

Equation (1.104) is still valid but

$$\bar{\Phi}_m = \sum_{m=2}^{n} A_{rst} J_1^r J_2^s J_3^t \tag{1.117}$$

and

$$r + 2s + 3t = m$$

The first two members are,

$$\bar{\Phi}_2 = A_{200} J_1^2 + A_{010} J_2$$

and

$$\bar{\Phi}_3 = A_{300} J_1^3 + A_{110} J_1 J_2 + A_{001} J_3 \tag{1.118}$$

In the incompressible case

$$\bar{\Phi} = \sum_{m=1}^{n} \bar{\Phi}_m$$

where

$$\bar{\Phi}_m = \sum_{p,q} A_{pq} J_1^p J_2^q \tag{1.119}$$

and

$$p + 2q = m$$

with which is associated the incompressibility condition

$$J_1 + 2J_2 + 4J_3 = 0 \tag{1.52}$$

We note that all the strain energy expressions proposed satisfy the condition that $\bar{\Phi} = 0$ and also it is a minimum for zero strain. A more general strain energy expression is

$$\bar{\Phi} = \text{Function}\left(J_1, J_2, J_3\right) \tag{1.120}$$

for which the principal stresses are typically

$$\sigma_{I} = \frac{\lambda_{I}}{\lambda_{II}\lambda_{III}}\left[\frac{\partial\bar{\Phi}}{\partial J_1} + (\varepsilon_{II} + \varepsilon_{III})\frac{\partial\bar{\Phi}}{\partial J_2} + \varepsilon_{II}\varepsilon_{III}\frac{\partial\bar{\Phi}}{\partial J_3}\right] \tag{I.121}$$

This equation is obtained from the virtual work due to $\delta\lambda_I$ on a unit cube.
Thus

$$\delta\bar{\Phi} = \lambda_{II}\lambda_{III}\sigma_I\,\delta\lambda_I$$

so that

$$\sigma_I = \frac{1}{\lambda_{II}\lambda_{III}}\frac{\partial\bar{\Phi}}{\partial\lambda_I} = \frac{\lambda_I}{\lambda_{II}\lambda_{III}}\frac{\partial\bar{\Phi}}{\partial\varepsilon_I} \tag{I.122}$$

from which (I.121) follows. In the incompressible case only two of the J's are independent and one may express $\bar{\Phi}$ in terms of any two of them. We take

$$\bar{\Phi} = \text{function}\,(J_1, J_2) \tag{I.123}$$

from which, with the incompressibility condition (I.52),

$$\sigma_I = \sigma_h + 2\left(\varepsilon_I - \frac{1}{3}J_1\right)\frac{\partial\bar{\Phi}}{\partial J_1} + \left[2\varepsilon_I\left(J_1 - \varepsilon_1 - \frac{1}{2}\right) + \frac{1}{3}J_1 - \frac{4}{3}J_2\right]\frac{\partial\bar{\Phi}}{\partial J_2} \tag{I.124}$$

which follows from (I.121) by introducing the mean hydrostatic stress

$$\sigma_h = \frac{1}{3}\left(\sigma_I + \sigma_{II} + \sigma_{III}\right)$$

and remembering that J_3 does not appear in $\bar{\Phi}$.

When σ_I, σ_{II} and σ_{III} are specified any two of eqs. (I.124) together with the volumetric constraint (I.52) suffice to determine the strains. However, in a practical problem the σ's are unknown. The hydrostatic part of the stress will consist of two parts. The first part is associated with the strain energy and is given by

$$\sigma_h' = \frac{1}{3}\left[(3 + J_1)\frac{\partial\bar{\Phi}}{\partial J_1} + 2(J_1 + 2J_2)\frac{\partial\bar{\Phi}}{\partial J_2}\right] \tag{I.125}$$

The second part may be considered as the hydrostatic constraint which maintains the volume constant and is denoted by σ_h''. This has the nature of a Lagrange multiplier although it is preferable to regard it as the pressure of an actual fluid which can be varied at will.

6.2.1 Some Special Cases

The simplest special case is the material characterised by $\bar{\Phi}_2$ of eq. (I.106). This gives,

$$\sigma_I = \frac{\lambda_I}{\lambda_{II}\lambda_{III}}\left[2A_{20}J_1 + A_{01}\left(\varepsilon_{II} + \varepsilon_{III}\right)\right] \tag{I.126}$$

For incompressible materials (I.126) takes the form,

$$\begin{aligned}\sigma_I &= \sigma_h + 4A_{20}J_1\left(\varepsilon_I - \tfrac{1}{3}J_1\right)\\ &\quad + A_{01}\left[\tfrac{1}{3}J_1 - \tfrac{4}{3}J_2 + 2\varepsilon_I\left(J_1 - \varepsilon_I - \tfrac{1}{2}\right)\right]\end{aligned} \tag{I.127}$$

Another example is

$$\bar{\Phi} = AJ_1 + BJ_2 \tag{I.128}$$

which is the so-called Mooney material. This does not apparently fit into the general class (I.119), but since for incompressibility $J_1 = -2(J_2 + 2J_3)$ it may be construed as a special case of the form

$$\bar{\Phi} = \bar{\Phi}_2 + \bar{\Phi}_3$$

The stress is,

$$\begin{aligned}\sigma_I &= \sigma_h + 2A\left(\varepsilon_I - \tfrac{1}{3}J_1\right)\\ &\quad + B\left[\tfrac{1}{3}J_1 - \tfrac{4}{3}J_2 + 2\varepsilon_I\left(J_1 - \varepsilon_I - \tfrac{1}{2}\right)\right]\end{aligned} \tag{I.129}$$

and

$$\sigma_h' = \frac{1}{3}\left[A\left(3 + 2J_1\right) + 2B\left(J_1 + 2J_2\right)\right] \tag{I.130}$$

Note that the equivalent form in terms of J_2 and J_3 yields $\sigma_h' = 0$ at zero strain. This may be compared with the membrane case (I.112) and (I.113).

6.3 Strain Energy Density for Anisotropic Materials

The simplicity of the isotropic case is due to the fact that the strain energy is a function only of the principal strains without reference to their directions. However it will still be possible to approximate the strain energy by a polynomial in the six strain components and advantage may be taken of any axes of symmetry.

In general the strain energy density function will vary with position. There seems little point in attempting to take account of this variation within a finite element. The assumption of uniform anisotropy within each element may be regarded as part of the discretization process. Many technical materials, although not isotropic, may be well approximated by the assumption of orthotropy. In such cases there will exist three orthogonal directions (two in membranes) for which the principal stresses and strains co-incide.

The idea developed by Varga in reference [1] of making the principal stresses and strains the basis for a discussion of large strains in isotropic materials has great conceptual simplicity. In anisotropic materials some of this simplicity is retained if the strain energy is expressed in terms of the principal strains but with coefficients depending on their directions.

As an illustration the case of an anisotropic membrane is considered.

Thus,

$$\bar{\Phi} = f_1(\varepsilon_I, \varepsilon_{II}) + f_2(\varepsilon_I, \varepsilon_{II})\cos 2\varphi + f_4(\varepsilon_I, \varepsilon_{II})\cos 4\varphi + \cdots\cdots$$

$$+ g_2(\varepsilon_I, \varepsilon_{II})\sin 2\varphi + g_4(\varepsilon_I, \varepsilon_{II})\sin 4\varphi + \cdots\cdots \tag{1.131}$$

The omission of the odd φ terms is justified by the fact that $\bar{\Phi}$ will not be altered by a change of 180° in the directions of the axes. If there is an axis of symmetry from which φ is measured the sine terms will vanish.

In the particular case of an orthotropic sheet the small strain energy density may be written

$$\bar{\Phi} = \frac{1}{2}\left[E_{11}\epsilon_{11}^2 + E_{12}(\epsilon_{11} + \epsilon_{22})^2 + E_{22}\epsilon_{22}^2 + 4G\epsilon_{12}^2 \right] \tag{1.132}$$

If the principal strains ϵ_I , ϵ_{II} are inclined to the axis Ox by angle φ , then

$$\begin{aligned} \epsilon_{11} &= \cos^2\varphi\, \epsilon_I + \sin^2\varphi\, \epsilon_{II} \\ \epsilon_{22} &= \sin^2\varphi\, \epsilon_I + \cos^2\varphi\, \epsilon_{II} \\ \epsilon_{12} &= \sin\varphi \cos\varphi\, (\epsilon_I - \epsilon_{II}) \end{aligned} \tag{1.133}$$

Substituting these values in (1.132) we find,

$$\begin{aligned} \bar{\Phi} = \frac{1}{16}\{ &(E_{11} + E_{22})(3\epsilon_I^2 + 3\epsilon_{II}^2 + 2\epsilon_I\epsilon_{II}) \\ &+ 8E_{12}(\epsilon_I + \epsilon_{II})^2 + 4G(\epsilon_I - \epsilon_{II})^2 \\ &+ 4(E_{11} - E_{22})(\epsilon_I^2 - \epsilon_{II}^2)\cos 2\varphi \\ &+ (E_{11} + E_{22} - 4G)(\epsilon_I - \epsilon_{II})^2 \cos 4\varphi \} \end{aligned} \tag{1.134}$$

Thus $\bar{\Phi}$ is of the form (1.131). The same result is obtained if (1.132) is considered valid for large strains expressed in terms of $\boldsymbol{\epsilon}$.

7. Stiffness Matrices

The stiffness matrices for the TRIM 3, TET 4 and axisymmetric TRIAX 3 elements with large strains are now derived. These elements are also the basis for developing the properties of higher order simplex elements using the natural stresses and strains.

7.1 TRIM 3

The virtual work eq. (1.90) for the case where the stress arises purely from the elastic strain of the element is

$$\delta\Phi = \Omega_1 t\, \boldsymbol{\sigma}_c^t \boldsymbol{\lambda}^{-2} \delta\boldsymbol{\epsilon}_t \tag{1.135}$$

where Φ is the total strain energy of the element.

Thus

$$\boldsymbol{\sigma}_c = \frac{1}{\Omega_1 t}\boldsymbol{\lambda}^2 \frac{\partial\Phi}{\partial\boldsymbol{\epsilon}_t^t} \tag{1.136}$$

In terms of the strain energy density

$$\boldsymbol{\sigma}_c = \frac{\Omega_0}{\Omega_1} \boldsymbol{\lambda}^2 \frac{\partial \bar{\Phi}}{\partial \boldsymbol{\varepsilon}_t^t} \tag{I.137}$$

From $\boldsymbol{\sigma}_c$ we may obtain $\boldsymbol{\sigma}_t$ and the cartesian stresses $\boldsymbol{\sigma}$ by the usual transformations. The strain energy density of an isotropic element will be supposed given in the form (I.106). J_1 and J_2 in terms of $\boldsymbol{\varepsilon}_t$ are found from eqs. (I.10) and (I.11).
Thus

$$\begin{aligned} J_1 &= \boldsymbol{e}_3^t \boldsymbol{A}^{-1} \boldsymbol{\varepsilon}_t \\ J_2 &= \frac{1}{2} \boldsymbol{\varepsilon}_t^t \boldsymbol{A}^{-1} \left[\boldsymbol{E}_3 - \boldsymbol{A} \right] \boldsymbol{A}^{-1} \boldsymbol{\varepsilon}_t \\ J_1^2 &= \boldsymbol{\varepsilon}_t^t \boldsymbol{A}^{-1} \boldsymbol{E}_3 \boldsymbol{A}^{-1} \boldsymbol{\varepsilon}_t \end{aligned} \tag{I.138}$$

In the small strain case

$$\bar{\Phi} = \frac{E}{2(1-\nu^2)} \left[J_1^2 - 2(1-\nu) J_2 \right] \tag{I.139}$$

This is of the form (I.106) with

$$A_{20} = \frac{E}{2(1-\nu^2)} \quad ; \quad A_{01} = -\frac{E}{1+\nu} \tag{I.140}$$

If the use of expression (I.139) is extended to large strains the quantity ν will lose its significance as Poisson's ratio. Then in terms of $\boldsymbol{\varepsilon}_t$ the strain energy density $\bar{\Phi}_2$ is,

$$\bar{\Phi}_2 = \frac{1}{2} \boldsymbol{\varepsilon}_t^t \bar{\boldsymbol{k}}_{N2} \boldsymbol{\varepsilon}_t \tag{I.141}$$

where

$$\bar{\boldsymbol{k}}_{N2} = \frac{E}{1+\nu} \left[\boldsymbol{A}^{-1} + \frac{\nu}{1-\nu} \boldsymbol{A}^{-1} \boldsymbol{E}_3 \boldsymbol{A}^{-1} \right] \tag{I.142}$$

is the natural stiffness matrix for large strains. The natural stiffness for the TRIM 3 element is hence

$$\boldsymbol{k}_{N2} = \Omega_0 \, t \, \bar{\boldsymbol{k}}_{N2} \qquad (1.142a)$$

A physical interpretation of the generalised forces based on the total strain energy Φ_2 of the TRIM 3,

$$\frac{\partial \Phi_2}{\partial \boldsymbol{\varepsilon}_t^t} = \boldsymbol{k}_{N2} \boldsymbol{\varepsilon}_t \qquad (1.143)$$

is as follows.

Denoting the component stress resultant force along the side l_α by P_α we have,

$$P_\alpha l_\alpha d\lambda_\alpha = \frac{\partial \Phi_2}{\partial \varepsilon_{t\alpha}} \delta\varepsilon_{t\alpha} = \frac{\partial \Phi_2}{\partial \varepsilon_{t\alpha}} \lambda_\alpha d\lambda_\alpha$$

Therefore,

$$P_\alpha = \frac{\lambda_\alpha}{l_\alpha} \frac{\partial \Phi_2}{\partial \varepsilon_{t\alpha}} = \frac{\partial \Phi_2}{\partial (\lambda_\alpha l_\alpha)} \qquad (1.144)$$

The vector of the P 's is called the natural force vector

$$\boldsymbol{P}_N = \{P_\alpha \quad P_\beta \quad P_\gamma\} = \boldsymbol{\lambda} \boldsymbol{l}^{-1} \frac{\partial \Phi}{\partial \boldsymbol{\varepsilon}_t^t} = \boldsymbol{\lambda} \boldsymbol{l}^{-1} \boldsymbol{k}_{N2} \boldsymbol{\varepsilon}_t \qquad (1.145)$$

We now see that the action of the TRIM 3 finite element is fully represented by three pairs of opposing forces P_α, P_β, P_γ acting parallel to the sides at the vertices, For the particular case of an equilateral triangle with $\nu = 1/3$ the matrix $\boldsymbol{k}_{N2}$ may be represented by three pin-jointed bars each with area $ht/2 = \sqrt{3}\, lt/4$. For application of the TRIM 3 element one must obtain the total strains $\boldsymbol{\varepsilon}_t$ in terms of the positions of the nodes expressed in the cartesian coordinates $\boldsymbol{x} = \{x^1 \quad x^2 \quad x^3\}$. Since $l_\alpha, l_\beta, l_\gamma$ are the lengths of the sides of the unstrained triangle - including however any effect of temperature considered uniform over the element - then for the side l_α ,for example, the strain is,

$$\varepsilon_{t\alpha} = \frac{1}{2}\left(\lambda_\alpha^2 - 1\right) = \frac{1}{2l_\alpha^2}\left[\left(x_{23}^1\right)^2 + \left(x_{23}^2\right)^2 + \left(x_{23}^3\right)^2 - l_\alpha^2\right]$$

$$= \frac{1}{2l_\alpha^2}\left[\mathbf{x}_{23}^t \mathbf{x}_{23} - l_\alpha^2\right] \tag{I.146}$$

where

$$x_{23}^1 = x_3^1 - x_2^1 \qquad \text{etc.}$$

and

$$\mathbf{x}_{23} = \mathbf{x}_3 - \mathbf{x}_2 = \left\{\left(x_3^1 - x_2^1\right) \quad \left(x_3^2 - x_2^2\right) \quad \left(x_3^3 - x_2^3\right)\right\} \tag{I.147}$$

When using an incremental procedure it is useful to have $\boldsymbol{\varepsilon}_t$ in the form

$$\boldsymbol{\varepsilon}_t = \boldsymbol{\varepsilon}_{t0} + \delta\boldsymbol{\varepsilon}_t \tag{I.148}$$

where $\boldsymbol{\varepsilon}_{t0}$ is the value at the beginning of the step and $\delta\boldsymbol{\varepsilon}_t$ is the increment of $\boldsymbol{\varepsilon}_t$ due to displacements $\mathbf{u} = \{u^1 \ u^2 \ u^3\}$

Thus

$$\varepsilon_{t\alpha} = \frac{1}{2l_\alpha^2}\left[\left(\mathbf{x}_{23}^t + \mathbf{u}_{23}^t\right)\left(\mathbf{x}_{23} + \mathbf{u}_{23}\right) - l_\alpha^2\right] \tag{I.149}$$

where

$$\mathbf{u}_{23} = \mathbf{u}_3 - \mathbf{u}_2 = \left\{\left(u_3^1 - u_2^1\right) \quad \left(u_3^2 - u_2^2\right) \quad \left(u_3^3 - u_2^3\right)\right\} \tag{I.150}$$

Expanding (I.149), we obtain

$$\varepsilon_{t\alpha} = \varepsilon_{t\alpha 0} + \frac{1}{l_\alpha^2}\left[\mathbf{x}_{23}^t + \frac{1}{2}\mathbf{u}_{23}^t\right]\mathbf{u}_{23} \tag{I.151}$$

The vector $\boldsymbol{\varepsilon}_t$ may be written concisely as

$$\boldsymbol{\varepsilon}_t = \{\varepsilon_{t\alpha} \;\; \varepsilon_{t\beta} \;\; \varepsilon_{t\gamma}\} = \boldsymbol{\varepsilon}_{t0} + \boldsymbol{l}^{-2}\left[\boldsymbol{x}_\Delta^t + \frac{1}{2}\boldsymbol{u}_\Delta^t\right]\begin{bmatrix}\boldsymbol{u}_{23}\\ \boldsymbol{u}_{31}\\ \boldsymbol{u}_{12}\end{bmatrix} \tag{1.152}$$

where

$$\boldsymbol{x}_\Delta = \left\lceil \boldsymbol{x}_{23} \;\; \boldsymbol{x}_{31} \;\; \boldsymbol{x}_{12} \right\rfloor \quad ; \quad \boldsymbol{u}_\Delta = \left\lceil \boldsymbol{u}_{23} \;\; \boldsymbol{u}_{31} \;\; \boldsymbol{u}_{12} \right\rfloor \tag{1.153}$$

and

$$\begin{bmatrix}\boldsymbol{u}_{23}\\ \boldsymbol{u}_{31}\\ \boldsymbol{u}_{12}\end{bmatrix} = \boldsymbol{\Delta}\,\boldsymbol{u}_I \tag{1.154}$$

where

$$\boldsymbol{\Delta} = \begin{bmatrix} \boldsymbol{O}_3 & -\boldsymbol{I}_3 & \boldsymbol{I}_3 \\ \boldsymbol{I}_3 & \boldsymbol{O}_3 & -\boldsymbol{I}_3 \\ -\boldsymbol{I}_3 & \boldsymbol{I}_3 & \boldsymbol{O}_3 \end{bmatrix} \tag{1.155}$$

and remembering that,

$$\boldsymbol{u}_I = \{\boldsymbol{u}_1 \;\; \boldsymbol{u}_2 \;\; \boldsymbol{u}_3\} = \{u_1^1 \;\; u_1^2 \;\; u_1^3 \;\; u_2^1 \;\; u_2^2 \;\; u_2^3 \;\; u_3^1 \;\; u_3^2 \;\; u_3^3\}$$

Then

$$\boldsymbol{\varepsilon}_t = \boldsymbol{\varepsilon}_{t0} + \boldsymbol{l}^{-2}\left[\boldsymbol{x}_\Delta^t + \frac{1}{2}\boldsymbol{u}_\Delta^t\right]\boldsymbol{\Delta}\,\boldsymbol{u}_I \tag{1.156}$$

Now the vector of nodal forces in the directions of the cartesian axes may be found by direct resolution, or by the virtual work on an increment in $\boldsymbol{u}_I$ as,

$$\begin{aligned}\boldsymbol{U}_I &= \{\boldsymbol{U}_1 \;\; \boldsymbol{U}_2 \;\; \boldsymbol{U}_3\} = \{U_1^1 \;\; U_1^2 \;\; U_1^3 \;\; U_2^1 \;\; U_2^2 \;\; U_2^3 \;\; U_3^1 \;\; U_3^2 \;\; U_3^3\} \\ &= \boldsymbol{\Delta}^t\left[\boldsymbol{x}_\Delta + \boldsymbol{u}_\Delta\right]\boldsymbol{\lambda}^{-1}\boldsymbol{l}^{-1}\boldsymbol{P}_N\end{aligned} \tag{1.157}$$

Finally with $\boldsymbol{P}_N$ from (1.145) and $\boldsymbol{\varepsilon}_t$ from (1.152) eq. (1.157) yields,

$$\boldsymbol{U}_I = \boldsymbol{\Delta}^t\left[\boldsymbol{x}_\Delta + \boldsymbol{u}_\Delta\right]\boldsymbol{l}^{-2}\boldsymbol{k}_{N2}\boldsymbol{\varepsilon}_{t0} + \boldsymbol{\Delta}^t\left[\boldsymbol{x}_\Delta + \boldsymbol{u}_\Delta\right]\boldsymbol{l}^{-2}\boldsymbol{k}_{N2}\boldsymbol{l}^{-2}\left[\boldsymbol{x}_\Delta^t + \frac{1}{2}\boldsymbol{u}_\Delta^t\right]\boldsymbol{\Delta}\boldsymbol{u}_I \quad (1.158)$$

Thus $\boldsymbol{U}$ turns out to be a cubic function of the nodal displacements. If u is small so that u^2 is negligible $\boldsymbol{U}$ becomes linear in $\boldsymbol{u}$ and reduces to,

$$\boldsymbol{U}_I = \boldsymbol{\Delta}^t\boldsymbol{x}_\Delta\boldsymbol{l}^{-2}\boldsymbol{k}_{N2}\boldsymbol{\varepsilon}_{t0} + \boldsymbol{\Delta}^t\boldsymbol{u}_\Delta\boldsymbol{l}^{-2}\boldsymbol{k}_{N2}\boldsymbol{\varepsilon}_{t0} + \boldsymbol{\Delta}^t\boldsymbol{x}_\Delta\boldsymbol{l}^{-2}\boldsymbol{k}_{N2}\boldsymbol{l}^{-2}\boldsymbol{x}_\Delta^t\boldsymbol{\Delta}\boldsymbol{u}_I \quad (1.159)$$

In small strain theory [4] the first term is the initial load vector $\boldsymbol{J}_I$, the second term corresponds to the contribution of the geometrical stiffness $\boldsymbol{k}_G$ and the third to that of the tangent stiffness $\boldsymbol{k}_E$ at the beginning of the step. The term $\boldsymbol{\Delta}^t\boldsymbol{u}_\Delta\,\boldsymbol{l}^{-2}\boldsymbol{k}_{N2}\boldsymbol{\varepsilon}_{t0}$ is inconvenient for direct step-by-step solution of a load increment since it is required in the form of some matrix $\boldsymbol{T}$ post-multiplied by $\boldsymbol{u}_I$. To find $\boldsymbol{T}$ we have from (1.145),

$$\boldsymbol{l}^{-2}\boldsymbol{k}_{N2}\boldsymbol{\varepsilon}_{t0} = \boldsymbol{\lambda}_0^{-1}\boldsymbol{l}^{-1}\boldsymbol{P}_{N0} \quad (1.160)$$

where the suffix 0 refers to the beginning of the step. Then,

$$\boldsymbol{u}_\Delta\boldsymbol{\lambda}_0^{-1}\boldsymbol{l}^{-1}\boldsymbol{P}_{N0} = \begin{bmatrix} (P_{\alpha 0}/\lambda_{\alpha 0}l_\alpha)\,\boldsymbol{u}_{23} \\ (P_{\beta 0}/\lambda_{\beta 0}l_\beta)\,\boldsymbol{u}_{31} \\ (P_{\gamma 0}/\lambda_{\gamma 0}l_\gamma)\,\boldsymbol{u}_{12} \end{bmatrix} = \begin{bmatrix} \boldsymbol{O}_3 & -\bar{P}_{\alpha 0}\boldsymbol{I}_3 & \bar{P}_{\alpha 0}\boldsymbol{I}_3 \\ \bar{P}_{\beta 0}\boldsymbol{I}_3 & \boldsymbol{O}_3 & -\bar{P}_{\beta 0}\boldsymbol{I}_3 \\ -\bar{P}_{\gamma 0}\boldsymbol{I}_3 & \bar{P}_{\gamma 0}\boldsymbol{I}_3 & \boldsymbol{O}_3 \end{bmatrix}\begin{bmatrix} \boldsymbol{u}_1 \\ \boldsymbol{u}_2 \\ \boldsymbol{u}_3 \end{bmatrix} \quad (1.161)$$

where

$$\bar{P}_{\alpha o} = \left(P_{\alpha o} / \lambda_{\alpha o} l_\alpha \right) \qquad \text{etc.} \tag{1.162}$$

Hence

$$\boldsymbol{\Delta}^t \mathbf{u}_\Delta \boldsymbol{l}^{-1} \boldsymbol{k}_{N2} \boldsymbol{\varepsilon}_{to} = \bar{\boldsymbol{P}}_{20} \mathbf{u}_1 \tag{1.163}$$

where

$$\bar{\boldsymbol{P}}_{20} = \begin{bmatrix} (\bar{P}_{\beta o} + \bar{P}_{\gamma o})\boldsymbol{I}_3 & -\bar{P}_{\gamma o}\boldsymbol{I}_3 & -\bar{P}_{\beta o}\boldsymbol{I}_3 \\ -\bar{P}_{\gamma o}\boldsymbol{I}_3 & (\bar{P}_{\gamma o} + \bar{P}_{\alpha o})\boldsymbol{I}_3 & -\bar{P}_{\alpha o}\boldsymbol{I}_3 \\ -\bar{P}_{\beta o}\boldsymbol{I}_3 & -\bar{P}_{\alpha o}\boldsymbol{I}_3 & (\bar{P}_{\alpha o} + \bar{P}_{\beta o})\boldsymbol{I}_3 \end{bmatrix} \tag{1.164}$$

with this notation eq. (1.159) becomes

$$\boldsymbol{U}_1 = \left[\bar{\boldsymbol{P}}_{20} \boldsymbol{x}_1 + \bar{\boldsymbol{P}}_{20} + \boldsymbol{\Delta}^t \boldsymbol{x}_\Delta \boldsymbol{l}^{-2} \boldsymbol{k}_{N2} \boldsymbol{l}^{-2} \boldsymbol{x}_\Delta^t \boldsymbol{\Delta} \right] \mathbf{u}_1 \tag{1.165}$$

which is equivalent to the form,

$$\boldsymbol{U}_1 = \boldsymbol{J}_1 + \left[\boldsymbol{k}_G + \boldsymbol{k}_E \right] \mathbf{u}_1 \tag{1.166}$$

7.1.1 Higher Order Strain Energies

The cubic strain energy for an isotropic material as derived from $\bar{\bar{\Phi}}_3$ in (1.105) may be written

$$\bar{\bar{\Phi}}_3 = \frac{1}{2} J_1 \boldsymbol{\varepsilon}_t^t \bar{\boldsymbol{k}}_{N3} \boldsymbol{\varepsilon}_t \tag{1.167}$$

where $\bar{\boldsymbol{k}}_{N3}$ is a symmetrical (3 x 3) matrix. The quartic strain energy can be written in the form

$$\bar{\Phi}_4 = \frac{1}{2} J_1^2 \boldsymbol{\varepsilon}_t^t \bar{\boldsymbol{k}}_{N4}^1 \boldsymbol{\varepsilon}_t + \frac{1}{2} \boldsymbol{\varepsilon}_t^t \boldsymbol{A}^{-1} \boldsymbol{\varepsilon}_t \boldsymbol{\varepsilon}_t^t \bar{\boldsymbol{k}}_{N4}^2 \boldsymbol{\varepsilon}_t \tag{1.168}$$

where $\bar{\boldsymbol{k}}_{N4}^1$ and $\bar{\boldsymbol{k}}_{N4}^2$ are also symmetrical. In general the energy expressions may be written as polynomials of increasing degrees in $\varepsilon_{t\alpha}$, $\varepsilon_{t\beta}$, $\varepsilon_{t\gamma}$. Thus, in general, one may express the vectorial derivative of the mth degree energy Φ_m of the TRIM 3 as

$$\frac{\partial \Phi_m}{\partial \boldsymbol{\varepsilon}_t^t} = \boldsymbol{k}_{Nm} \boldsymbol{\varepsilon}_t \tag{1.169}$$

$\boldsymbol{k}_{Nm}$ is not unique except in the case m = 2. However it may be conveniently defined as the symmetrical special secant modulus $\boldsymbol{k}_{Nsm}$ between zero strain and $\boldsymbol{\varepsilon}_t$. This is equal to

$$\boldsymbol{k}_{Nsm} = \frac{1}{m-1} \boldsymbol{k}_{NTm} \tag{1.170}$$

where $\boldsymbol{k}_{NTm}$ is the tangent modulus at $\boldsymbol{\varepsilon}_t$. Note that the elements of $\boldsymbol{k}_{NSm}$ are polynomials of degree (m - 2) in the ε_t 's. The analysis now proceeds as after eq. (1.143) and one obtains

$$\boldsymbol{U}_I = \boldsymbol{\Delta}^t \left[\boldsymbol{x}_\Delta + \boldsymbol{u}_\Delta \right] \boldsymbol{l}^{-2} \boldsymbol{k}_{NSm} \boldsymbol{\varepsilon}_t \tag{1.171}$$

This may be rewritten as,

$$\begin{aligned} \boldsymbol{U}_I = {} & \boldsymbol{\Delta}^t \boldsymbol{x}_\Delta \boldsymbol{l}^{-2} \boldsymbol{k}_{NSm0} \boldsymbol{\varepsilon}_{t0} + \boldsymbol{\Delta}^t \boldsymbol{u}_\Delta \boldsymbol{l}^{-2} \boldsymbol{k}_{NSm} \boldsymbol{\varepsilon}_t \\ & + \boldsymbol{\Delta}^t \boldsymbol{x}_\Delta \boldsymbol{l}^{-2} \left[\boldsymbol{k}_{NSm} \boldsymbol{\varepsilon}_t - \boldsymbol{k}_{NSm0} \boldsymbol{\varepsilon}_{t0} \right] \end{aligned} \tag{1.172}$$

When the increment $\boldsymbol{u}_I$ is small eq. (1.172) is linearised as,

$$U_I = \boldsymbol{\Delta}^t \boldsymbol{x}_\Delta \boldsymbol{l}^{-2} \boldsymbol{k}_{NSmo} \boldsymbol{\varepsilon}_{to} + \boldsymbol{\Delta}^t \boldsymbol{u}_\Delta \boldsymbol{l}^{-2} \boldsymbol{k}_{NSmo} \boldsymbol{\varepsilon}_{to} + \boldsymbol{\Delta}^t \boldsymbol{x}_\Delta \boldsymbol{l}^{-2} \boldsymbol{k}_{NTmo} \left[\boldsymbol{\varepsilon}_t - \boldsymbol{\varepsilon}_{to} \right]$$

which with (1.163) and (1.152) becomes

$$\boldsymbol{U}_I = \bar{\boldsymbol{P}}_{mo} \boldsymbol{x} + \left[\bar{\boldsymbol{P}}_{mo} + \boldsymbol{\Delta}^t \boldsymbol{x}_\Delta \boldsymbol{l}^{-2} \boldsymbol{k}_{NTmo} \boldsymbol{l}^{-2} \boldsymbol{x}_\Delta^t \boldsymbol{\Delta} \right] \boldsymbol{u}_I \tag{1.173}$$

The derivation of $\bar{\boldsymbol{P}}_{mo}$ was given, for m = 2, in eq. (1.163) and is repeated here for convenience.

$$\boldsymbol{\Delta}^t \boldsymbol{u}_\Delta \boldsymbol{l} \boldsymbol{k}_{NSmo} \boldsymbol{\varepsilon}_{to} = \bar{\boldsymbol{P}}_{mo} \boldsymbol{u}_I \tag{1.174}$$

where

$$\boldsymbol{P}_{mo} = \begin{bmatrix} \left(\bar{P}_{\beta o} + \bar{P}_{\gamma o}\right)\boldsymbol{I}_3 & -\bar{P}_{\gamma o}\boldsymbol{I}_3 & -\bar{P}_{\beta o}\boldsymbol{I}_3 \\ -\bar{P}_{\gamma o}\boldsymbol{I}_3 & \left(\bar{P}_{\gamma o} + \bar{P}_{\alpha o}\right)\boldsymbol{I}_3 & -\bar{P}_{\alpha o}\boldsymbol{I}_3 \\ -\bar{P}_{\beta o}\boldsymbol{I}_3 & -\bar{P}_{\alpha o}\boldsymbol{I}_3 & \left(\bar{P}_{\alpha o} + \bar{P}_{\beta o}\right)\boldsymbol{I}_3 \end{bmatrix} \tag{1.175}$$

and

$$\left(\bar{P}_{\alpha o}\right)_m = \left(P_{\alpha o}\right)_m / \lambda_{\alpha o} l_\alpha$$

Note that eqs. (1.171), (1.172) and (1.173) are valid for a material characterised by

$$\Phi = \sum_{m=2}^{k} \Phi_m \tag{1.176}$$

with

$$\bar{\boldsymbol{P}}_o = \sum_{m=2}^{k} \bar{\boldsymbol{P}}_{mo} \qquad \text{in place of} \qquad \bar{\boldsymbol{P}}_{mo} \tag{1.177}$$

and

$$\boldsymbol{k}_{NTo} = \sum_{m=2}^{k} \boldsymbol{k}_{NTmo} \qquad \text{etc.}$$

The assembly of the global equations for the complete structure proceeds as in the standard linear case.

7.1.2 Anisotropic TRIM 3

The strain energy function for an anisotropic material may also be approximated by a polynomial in the ε_t 's. Other strain energy functions may be used but they will not result in a polynomial form of the displacement functions and for this reason are computationally inconvenient. Once the strain energy function is fixed, which is of course the most difficult and highly technical question (see ref. [1,2]) the analysis proceeds exactly as before.

7.1.3 Incompressible Materials

Although no really incompressible materials exist, in the case of certain rubbers the assumption of incompressibility is justified and circumvents the computational difficulties encountered with the nearly incompressible case. For the TRIM 3 element the incompressibility condition is most conveniently considered by first supposing that each element has a constant internal pressure σ_h''. The area of one element is

$$\Omega = \Omega_0 (1 + 2\varepsilon_{I})^{1/2} (1 + 2\varepsilon_{II})^{1/2}$$

so that

$$\Omega = \Omega_0 (1 + 2J_1 + 4J_2)^{1/2} \tag{1.178}$$

If the fluid constant pressure is σ_h'' the potential of σ_h'' is

$$-\Omega \sigma_h''$$

Then the corresponding natural loads are

$$\boldsymbol{P}_{N0} = \boldsymbol{\lambda} \boldsymbol{\iota}^{-1} \frac{\partial(-\Omega \sigma_h'')}{\partial \boldsymbol{\varepsilon}_t^t} = -\sigma_h'' \boldsymbol{\lambda} \boldsymbol{\iota}^{-1} \frac{\partial}{\partial \boldsymbol{\varepsilon}_t^t} \Omega \tag{1.179}$$

$$= -\sigma_h'' \boldsymbol{\lambda} \boldsymbol{\iota}^{-1} \frac{\Omega_0^2}{\Omega} \frac{\partial}{\partial \boldsymbol{\varepsilon}_t^t} (J_1 + 2J_2)$$

Hence we find

$$\boldsymbol{P}_{N\sigma} = -\sigma_h'' \frac{\Omega_0^2}{\Omega} \boldsymbol{\lambda} \boldsymbol{\iota}^{-1} \boldsymbol{A}_0^{-1} \left[\boldsymbol{e}_3 + \left[\boldsymbol{E}_3 \boldsymbol{A}_0^{-1} - \boldsymbol{I}_3 \right] \boldsymbol{\varepsilon}_t \right] \tag{1.180}$$

The nodal loads, following eq. (I.157) are therefore,

$$\boldsymbol{U}_{I\sigma} = \boldsymbol{\Delta}^t\left[\boldsymbol{x}_\Delta + \boldsymbol{u}_\Delta\right]\boldsymbol{\lambda}^{-1}\boldsymbol{l}^{-1}\boldsymbol{P}_{N\sigma}$$

$$= -\sigma''_h \frac{\Omega_0^2}{\Omega}\boldsymbol{\Delta}^t\left[\boldsymbol{x}_\Delta + \boldsymbol{u}_\Delta\right]\boldsymbol{l}^{-2}\boldsymbol{A}_0^{-1}\left[\boldsymbol{e}_3 + \left[\boldsymbol{E}_3\boldsymbol{A}_0^{-1} - \boldsymbol{I}_3\right]\boldsymbol{\varepsilon}_t\right] \tag{I.181}$$

This expression must now be added to the R.H.S. of the equilibrium eq. (I.171). The constraint equation for incompressibility is,

$$J_1 + 2J_2 = 0 \tag{I.13}$$

or

$$\left[\boldsymbol{e}_3^t + \boldsymbol{\varepsilon}_t^t\left[\boldsymbol{A}_0^{-1}\boldsymbol{E}_3 - \boldsymbol{I}_3\right]\right]\boldsymbol{A}_0^{-1}\boldsymbol{\varepsilon}_t \tag{I.182}$$

Thus when the constraint condition is applied the σ''_h in (I.182) must be regarded as unknown quantities and in this case Ω_0^2/Ω reduces to Ω_0. The complete set of equations for the incompressible membrane element is therefore,

$$\begin{aligned}\boldsymbol{U}_I &= \boldsymbol{\Delta}^t\left[\boldsymbol{x}_\Delta + \boldsymbol{u}_\Delta\right]\boldsymbol{l}^{-2}\boldsymbol{k}_{NSm}\,\boldsymbol{\varepsilon}_t \\ &\quad - \boldsymbol{\Delta}^t\left[\boldsymbol{x}_\Delta + \boldsymbol{u}_\Delta\right]\boldsymbol{l}^{-2}\boldsymbol{A}_0^{-1}\left[\boldsymbol{e}_3 + \left[\boldsymbol{E}_3\boldsymbol{A}_0^{-1} - \boldsymbol{I}_3\right]\boldsymbol{\varepsilon}_t\right]\Omega_0\sigma''_h\end{aligned} \tag{I.183}$$

with the constraint conditions (I.182). When the increment $\boldsymbol{u}_I$ is small eq. (I.183) is linearised in the same manner as eq. (I.173) in conjunction with (I.177), and becomes

$$\begin{aligned}\boldsymbol{U}_I = &\left[\bar{\boldsymbol{P}}_0 - \sigma''_{ho}\bar{\boldsymbol{P}}_h\right]\boldsymbol{x}_I + \\ &\left[\left[\bar{\boldsymbol{P}}_0 - \sigma''_{ho}\bar{\boldsymbol{P}}_h\right] + \boldsymbol{\Delta}^t\boldsymbol{x}_\Delta\boldsymbol{l}^{-2}\boldsymbol{k}_{NTo}\boldsymbol{x}_\Delta^t\boldsymbol{\Delta}\right. \\ &\left.-\Omega_0\sigma''_{ho}\boldsymbol{\Delta}^t\boldsymbol{x}_\Delta\boldsymbol{l}^{-2}\boldsymbol{A}_0^{-1}\boldsymbol{E}_3\boldsymbol{A}_0^{-1}\boldsymbol{l}^{-2}\boldsymbol{x}_\Delta^t\boldsymbol{\Delta}\right]\boldsymbol{u}_I \\ &-\bar{\boldsymbol{P}}_h\bar{\boldsymbol{x}}_I\sigma''_{h\Delta}\end{aligned} \tag{I.184}$$

where

$$\bar{\boldsymbol{P}}_h = \begin{bmatrix} (\bar{P}_{\beta h} + \bar{P}_{\gamma h})\boldsymbol{I}_3 & -\bar{P}_{\gamma h}\boldsymbol{I}_3 & -\bar{P}_{\beta h}\boldsymbol{I}_3 \\ -\bar{P}_{\gamma h}\boldsymbol{I}_3 & (\bar{P}_{\gamma h} + \bar{P}_{\alpha h})\boldsymbol{I}_3 & -\bar{P}_{\alpha h}\boldsymbol{I}_3 \\ -\bar{P}_{\beta h}\boldsymbol{I}_3 & -\bar{P}_{\alpha h}\boldsymbol{I}_3 & (\bar{P}_{\alpha h} + \bar{P}_{\beta h})\boldsymbol{I}_3 \end{bmatrix} \tag{I.185}$$

with

$$\bar{\boldsymbol{P}}_{Nh} = \{\bar{P}_{\alpha h} \quad \bar{P}_{\beta h} \quad \bar{P}_{\gamma h}\} = \Omega_0 \boldsymbol{l}^{-2}\boldsymbol{A}_0^{-1}\left[\boldsymbol{e}_3 + [\boldsymbol{E}_3\boldsymbol{A}_0^{-1} - \boldsymbol{I}_3]\,\boldsymbol{\epsilon}_{t0}\right] \tag{I.186}$$

At the end of the step

$$\sigma''_{h1} = \sigma''_{h0} + \sigma''_{h\Delta} \tag{I.187}$$

The linearised constraint condition is,

$$\left[\boldsymbol{e}_3^t\boldsymbol{A}_0^{-1} - 2\boldsymbol{\epsilon}_{t0}^t\boldsymbol{A}_0^{-1}[\boldsymbol{A}_0^{-1}\boldsymbol{E}_3 - \boldsymbol{I}_3]\right]\boldsymbol{l}^{-2}\boldsymbol{x}_\Delta^t\boldsymbol{\Delta u}_I = 0 \tag{I.188}$$

The linearised equations may be assembled by the usual Boolean process – each $\sigma''_{h\Delta}$ will appear in three sets of equilibrium equations. It should be noted that the hydrostatic stress σ''_h will not, in general, include the total hydrostatic component of stress in the material. It is additional to the stress σ'_h obtained from eq. (I.112) or (I.113) for isotropic materials.

7.1.4 Mass Matrix

The consistent mass matrix for large strain TRIM 3 elements will be exactly as for the small strain element. Thus with $\boldsymbol{u}_I$ as the displacement vector of the element the mass matrix is,

$$\boldsymbol{m} = \boldsymbol{b}^t\bar{\boldsymbol{m}}_e\boldsymbol{b} \tag{I.189}$$

where

$$\bar{\boldsymbol{m}}_e = \lceil \bar{\boldsymbol{m}} \quad \bar{\boldsymbol{m}} \quad \bar{\boldsymbol{m}} \rfloor$$

$$\bar{\boldsymbol{m}} = \frac{1}{12} \rho_o \Omega_o t \begin{bmatrix} 2 & 1 & 1 \\ 1 & 2 & 1 \\ 1 & 1 & 2 \end{bmatrix} \tag{1.190}$$

and

$$\boldsymbol{b} = \{ (1)\ (4)\ (7)\ (2)\ (5)\ (8)\ (3)\ (6)\ (9) \} \tag{1.191}$$

where the numbers in the brackets represent the position of the Boolean instruction 'one' in the relevant rows. If the simpler lumped mass is considered adequate this is

$$\boldsymbol{m} = \frac{1}{3} \rho_o \Omega_o t\ \boldsymbol{I}_9 \tag{1.189a}$$

7.2 TET4

The TET4 element may be treated in an analogous way. It is important that the ordering of the $\boldsymbol{\varepsilon}_t$ vector should follow that of eq. (1.32) and that all other relevant matrices such as $\boldsymbol{A}$, $\boldsymbol{x}_\Delta$, $\boldsymbol{u}_\Delta$ etc., should also conform to this ordering. The volume is more simply expressed in terms of the nodal coordinates than in terms of $\boldsymbol{\varepsilon}_t$.

Thus

$$V = \frac{1}{6} \begin{vmatrix} (x_1^1 + u_1^1) & (x_1^2 + u_1^2) & (x_1^3 + u_1^3) & 1 \\ (x_2^1 + u_2^1) & (x_2^2 + u_2^2) & (x_3^3 + u_3^3) & 1 \\ (x_3^1 + u_3^1) & (x_3^2 + u_3^2) & (x_3^3 + u_3^3) & 1 \\ (x_4^1 + u_4^1) & (x_4^2 + u_4^2) & (x_4^3 + u_4^3) & 1 \end{vmatrix} \tag{1.192}$$

The potential of the hydrostatic constraint pressure is,

$$- V \sigma_h'' \tag{1.193}$$

and the corresponding nodal loads are

$$\begin{aligned} \boldsymbol{U}_{I\sigma} &= -\sigma_h'' \frac{\partial V}{\partial \boldsymbol{u}_I^t} \\ &= -\frac{1}{6} \sigma_h'' \{ V_{11}\ V_{12}\ V_{13}\ V_{21}\ V_{22}\ V_{23}\ V_{31}\ V_{32}\ V_{33}\ V_{41}\ V_{42}\ V_{43} \} \end{aligned} \tag{1.194}$$

where V_{ij} is the co-factor of the element ij of the determinant V. For small step integration of dynamic problems $\boldsymbol{U}_{I\sigma}$ is conveniently left in the above form. When linearised one may write

$$\boldsymbol{U}_{I\sigma} = \boldsymbol{U}_{I\sigma 0} - \sigma_h'' \left[\frac{\partial^2 V}{\partial \boldsymbol{u}_I \partial \boldsymbol{u}_I^t} \right]_0 \boldsymbol{u}_I \tag{1.195}$$

The elements of $\left[\frac{\partial^2 V}{\partial \boldsymbol{u} \, \partial \boldsymbol{u}_I^t} \right]_0$ are either zero or of the form $\pm x_{jk}^i$

The constraint equation may also be written

$$\delta V = \left[\frac{\partial V}{\partial \boldsymbol{u}_I} \right]_0 \boldsymbol{u}_I + \frac{1}{2} \boldsymbol{u}_I^t \left[\frac{\partial^2 V}{\partial \boldsymbol{u}_I \partial \boldsymbol{u}_I^t} \right]_0 \boldsymbol{u}_I + \ldots\ldots \tag{1.196}$$

so that the linearised form is,

$$\left[\frac{\partial V}{\partial \boldsymbol{u}_I} \right]_0 \boldsymbol{u}_I = 0 \tag{1.197}$$

7.3 <u>TRIAX3 Axisymmetric</u>

Referring to 4.1 the principal strains will be ε_{I}, $\varepsilon_{\mathrm{III}}$ in the axial plane and $\varepsilon_{\mathrm{II}}$ in the circumferential direction. For simplicity the equations will be written starting from zero initial strain.

Thus

$$\begin{aligned} \varepsilon_{\mathrm{II}} &= \frac{u^1}{x^1} + \frac{1}{2}\left(\frac{u^1}{x^1}\right)^2 \\ &= \frac{1}{x^1}\left[1 + \frac{1}{2}\frac{u^1}{x^1}\right] u_1 \end{aligned} \tag{1.198}$$

Also

$$x^1 = \boldsymbol{\omega} \boldsymbol{x}^1 \quad ; \quad u^1 = \boldsymbol{\omega} \boldsymbol{u}^1 \tag{1.199}$$

where

$$\boldsymbol{\omega} = [\ \zeta^1 \ \ \zeta^2 \ \ \zeta^3\ ] \tag{1.76a}$$

and $\boldsymbol{x}^1, \boldsymbol{u}^1$ are respectively the vectors of x_i^1 and u_i^1 at the nodes 1 2 3. The strain vector at any point is now,

$$\boldsymbol{\varepsilon} = \{\ \varepsilon_{t\alpha} \ \ \varepsilon_{t\beta} \ \ \varepsilon_{t\gamma} \ \ \varepsilon_{\text{II}}\ \} \quad (4 \times 1) \tag{1.200}$$

The strain energy density for the quadratic case may be written in the form,

$$\bar{\Phi} = AJ_1^2 + BJ_2 = A\left(J_1^P + \varepsilon_{\text{II}}\right)^2 + B\left(J_2^P + \varepsilon_{\text{II}} J_1^P\right) \tag{1.201}$$

where $J_1^P = \varepsilon_{\text{I}} + \varepsilon_{\text{II}}$, $J_2^P = \varepsilon_{\text{I}}\, \varepsilon_{\text{II}}$ are strain invariants in the axial plane which can be expressed (see Section 2) in terms of the natural strains $\varepsilon_{t\alpha}$ etc. Thus (1.201) may always be written as

$$\bar{\Phi} = \frac{1}{2} \boldsymbol{\varepsilon}^{t}\, \bar{\boldsymbol{k}}_{N2}\, \boldsymbol{\varepsilon} \tag{1.202}$$

where $\bar{\boldsymbol{k}}_{N2}$ is a symmetric square matrix independent of $\boldsymbol{\varepsilon}$. Higher order strain energy densities can be expressed as polynomials in $\varepsilon_{t\alpha}, \varepsilon_{t\beta}, \varepsilon_{t\gamma}$ and ε_{II} . $\boldsymbol{u}_I$ now takes the form

$$\boldsymbol{u}_I = \{\ u_1^1 \ \ u_1^3 \ \ u_2^1 \ \ u_2^3 \ \ u_3^1 \ \ u_3^3\ \} \tag{1.203}$$

and

$$\boldsymbol{\varepsilon} = \boldsymbol{\alpha}\, \boldsymbol{u}_I \tag{1.204}$$

where

$$\boldsymbol{\alpha} = \begin{bmatrix} \boldsymbol{l}^{-2}\left[\boldsymbol{x}_{\Delta}^{t} + \frac{1}{2}\boldsymbol{u}_{\Delta}^{t}\right]\boldsymbol{\Delta} \\ \frac{1}{\boldsymbol{\omega x}^1}\left[1 + \frac{1}{2}\,\frac{\boldsymbol{\omega u}^1}{\boldsymbol{\omega x}^1}\right]\boldsymbol{\omega b} \end{bmatrix} \tag{1.205}$$

and the Boolean matrix,

$$\boldsymbol{b} = \begin{bmatrix} 1 & 0 & 0 & 0 & 0 & 0 \\ 0 & 0 & 1 & 0 & 0 & 0 \\ 0 & 0 & 0 & 0 & 1 & 0 \end{bmatrix} \tag{1.206}$$

Then

$$\bar{\Phi} = \frac{1}{2} \boldsymbol{u}_I^t \boldsymbol{\alpha}^t \bar{\boldsymbol{k}}_{N2} \boldsymbol{\alpha} \boldsymbol{u}_I \tag{1.207}$$

To obtain the force vector $\boldsymbol{U}_I$ one must first calculate $\dfrac{\partial \Phi}{\partial \boldsymbol{u}_I^t}$

Now since $\bar{\boldsymbol{k}}_{N2}$ is symmetrical the increment of $\bar{\Phi}$ is,

$$\delta\bar{\Phi} = \delta \boldsymbol{u}_I^t \boldsymbol{\alpha}^t \bar{\boldsymbol{k}}_{N2} \boldsymbol{\alpha} \boldsymbol{u}_I + \boldsymbol{u}_I^t \delta \boldsymbol{\alpha}^t \bar{\boldsymbol{k}}_{N2} \boldsymbol{\alpha} \boldsymbol{u}_I$$

But

$$\boldsymbol{u}_I^t \delta \boldsymbol{\alpha}^t = \left[\frac{1}{2} \boldsymbol{u}_I^t \boldsymbol{\Delta}^t \delta \boldsymbol{u}_\Delta \boldsymbol{l}^{-2} \;\middle|\; \frac{1}{2} \boldsymbol{u}_I^t \frac{[\delta \boldsymbol{u}_I^t \boldsymbol{b}^t \boldsymbol{\omega}^t]\, \boldsymbol{b}^t \boldsymbol{\omega}^t}{(\boldsymbol{\omega} \boldsymbol{x}^1)^2} \right]$$

$$= \delta \boldsymbol{u}_I^t \left[\frac{1}{2} \boldsymbol{\Delta}^t \boldsymbol{u}_\Delta \boldsymbol{l}^{-2} \;\middle|\; \frac{1}{2} \frac{[\boldsymbol{u}_I^t \boldsymbol{b}^t \boldsymbol{\omega}^t]\, \boldsymbol{b}^t \boldsymbol{\omega}^t}{(\boldsymbol{\omega} \boldsymbol{x}^1)^2} \right]$$

Therefore,

$$\frac{\partial \Phi}{\partial \boldsymbol{u}_I^t} = \boldsymbol{\alpha}^t \bar{\boldsymbol{k}}_{N2} \boldsymbol{\alpha} \boldsymbol{u}_I + \left[\frac{1}{2} \boldsymbol{\Delta}^t \boldsymbol{u}_\Delta \boldsymbol{l}^{-2} \quad \frac{1}{2} \frac{\boldsymbol{\omega} \boldsymbol{u}^1}{(\boldsymbol{\omega} \boldsymbol{x}^1)^2} \boldsymbol{b}^t \boldsymbol{\omega}^t \right] \bar{\boldsymbol{k}}_{N2} \boldsymbol{\alpha} \boldsymbol{u}_I$$

$$= \bar{\boldsymbol{\alpha}}^t \bar{\boldsymbol{k}}_{N2} \boldsymbol{\alpha} \boldsymbol{u}_I \tag{1.208}$$

where

$$\bar{\boldsymbol{\alpha}} = \begin{bmatrix} \boldsymbol{l}^{-2}\left[\boldsymbol{x}_{\Delta}^{t} + \boldsymbol{u}_{\Delta}^{t}\right]\boldsymbol{\Delta} \\ \dfrac{1}{\boldsymbol{\omega x}^{1}}\left[1 + \dfrac{\boldsymbol{\omega u}^{1}}{\boldsymbol{\omega x}^{1}}\right]\boldsymbol{\omega b} \end{bmatrix} \tag{I.209}$$

Note the agreement of the first sub-matrix with the TRIM3 result (eq.(I.158)). The element force vector $\boldsymbol{U}_I$ is,

$$\boldsymbol{U}_I = 2\pi\,\Omega_0 \int \boldsymbol{\omega x}^1 \frac{\partial \bar{\Phi}}{\partial \boldsymbol{u}_I^t}\, d\zeta^1 d\zeta^2 \tag{I.210}$$

When the energy is of a higher order one may express $\bar{\Phi}$ as a polynomial in the entries of $\boldsymbol{\varepsilon}$ Adopting an argument akin to that used for TRIM3 the energy is expressed in the form,

$$\bar{\Phi} = \frac{1}{m}\boldsymbol{\varepsilon}^t \boldsymbol{k}_{NSm}\boldsymbol{\varepsilon} \tag{I.211}$$

where $\boldsymbol{k}_{NSm}$ is the special secant modulus defined in (I.170).

Then

$$\bar{\Phi} = \frac{1}{m}\boldsymbol{u}_I^t \boldsymbol{\alpha}^t \boldsymbol{k}_{NSm}\boldsymbol{\varepsilon}$$

$$\delta\bar{\Phi} = \frac{1}{m}\delta\boldsymbol{u}_I^t \bar{\boldsymbol{\alpha}}^t \boldsymbol{k}_{NSm}\boldsymbol{\varepsilon} + \frac{1}{m}\boldsymbol{u}_I^t \boldsymbol{\alpha}^t \delta(\boldsymbol{k}_{NSm}\boldsymbol{\varepsilon})$$

But

$$\delta(\boldsymbol{k}_{NSm}\boldsymbol{\varepsilon}) = \boldsymbol{k}_{NTm}\delta\boldsymbol{\varepsilon} = (m-1)\boldsymbol{k}_{NSm}\delta\boldsymbol{\varepsilon}$$

$$= (m-1)\boldsymbol{k}_{NSm}\bar{\boldsymbol{\alpha}}\,\delta\boldsymbol{u}_I$$

Therefore,

$$\delta\bar{\Phi} = \frac{1}{m}\delta \boldsymbol{u}_I^t \bar{\boldsymbol{\alpha}}^t \boldsymbol{k}_{NSm} \boldsymbol{\varepsilon} + \frac{m-1}{m} \boldsymbol{\varepsilon}^t \boldsymbol{k}_{NSm} \bar{\boldsymbol{\alpha}} \delta \boldsymbol{u}_I$$

$$= \delta \boldsymbol{u}_I^t \bar{\boldsymbol{\alpha}}^t \boldsymbol{k}_{NSm} \boldsymbol{\varepsilon}$$

Thus

$$\frac{\partial \bar{\Phi}}{\partial \boldsymbol{u}_I^t} = \bar{\boldsymbol{\alpha}}^t \boldsymbol{k}_{NSm} \boldsymbol{\alpha} \boldsymbol{u}_I \tag{1.212}$$

which is of the same form as (1.208). The equation for $\boldsymbol{U}_I$, (1.210) is valid also for the present case.

The stresses are most conveniently obtained from the principal strains and their directions.

ε_I and ε_{III} are found from $\varepsilon_{t\alpha}$, $\varepsilon_{t\beta}$, $\varepsilon_{t\gamma}$

Thus

$$\begin{aligned} \varepsilon_I &= \frac{1}{2}\left[J_1^p + \left[\left(J_1^p \right)^2 - 4 J_2^p \right]^{1/2} \right] \\ \varepsilon_{III} &= \frac{1}{2}\left[J_1^p - \left[\left(J_1^p \right)^2 - 4 J_2^p \right]^{1/2} \right] \end{aligned} \tag{1.213}$$

with

$$\psi = \frac{1}{2}\tan^{-1} \frac{\varepsilon_{c\gamma}\sin 2\beta - \varepsilon_{c\beta}\sin 2\gamma}{\varepsilon_{c\alpha} + \varepsilon_{c\beta}\cos 2\gamma + \varepsilon_{c\gamma}\cos 2\beta} \tag{1.214}$$

8. References

1 Varga, O.H., Stress-Strain Behaviour of Elastic Materials, Interscience Publishers, Wiley, New York, (1966)

2 Green, A.E. and Adkins, J.E., Large Elastic Deformations, Clarendon Press, Oxford (1960)

3 Oden, J.T. and Key, J.E., Analysis of Finite Deformations, High Speed Computing of Elastic Structures, Tome 1, University of Liège (1971). This reference contains a useful bibliography.

4 Argyris, J.H., Recent Advances in Matrix Methods of Structural Analysis, Progress in Aeronautical Sciences, Pergamon Press, (1964)

5 Prager, W., Introduction to Mechanics of Continua, Ginn and Co. Boston, (1961)

6 Murnaghan, F.D., Finite Deformation of an Elastic Solid, Wiley, New York, (1951)

7 Fung, Y.C., Foundations of Solid Mechanics, Prentice Hall, Englewood Cliffs (1965)

8 Argyris, J.H., Three-dimensional Anisotropic and Inhomogeneous Elastic Media Matrix Analysis for Small and Large Displacements, Ingenieur-Archiv, 34, 33-55 (1965)

9 Argyris, J.H., Continua and Discontinua, Opening paper to the Air Force Conference on Matrix Methods in Structural Mechanics at Wright Patterson Air Force Base, Dayton, Ohio (1965).

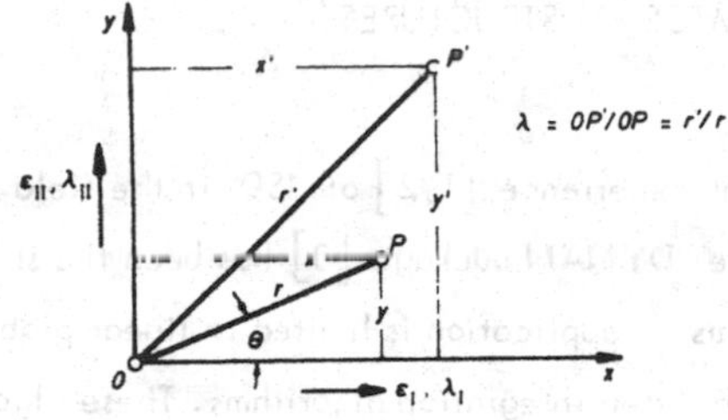

Fig . I -1 Two-Dimensional Strain

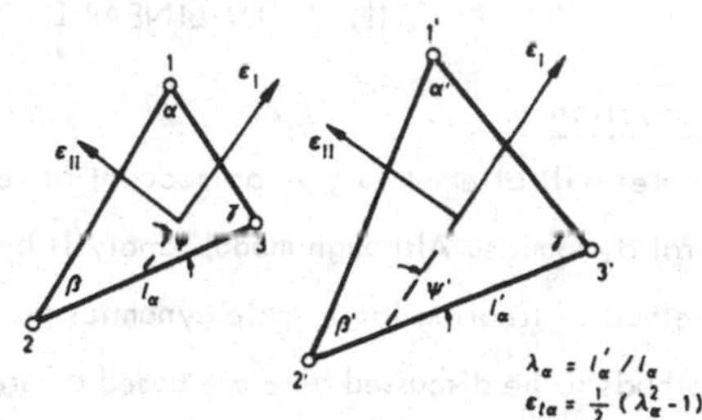

Fig . I - 2 Large Strain TRIM 3

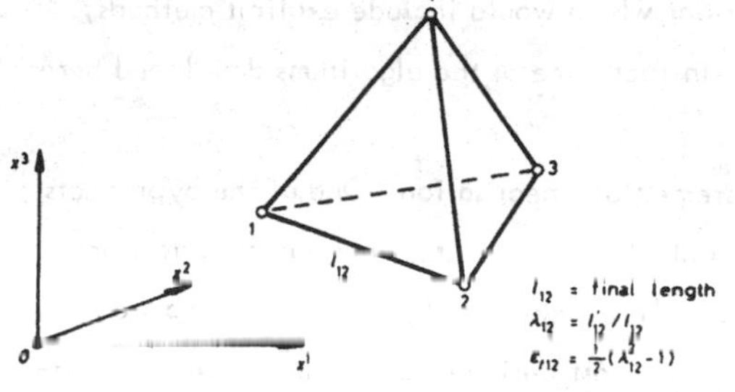

Fig . I - 3 Large Strain TET4

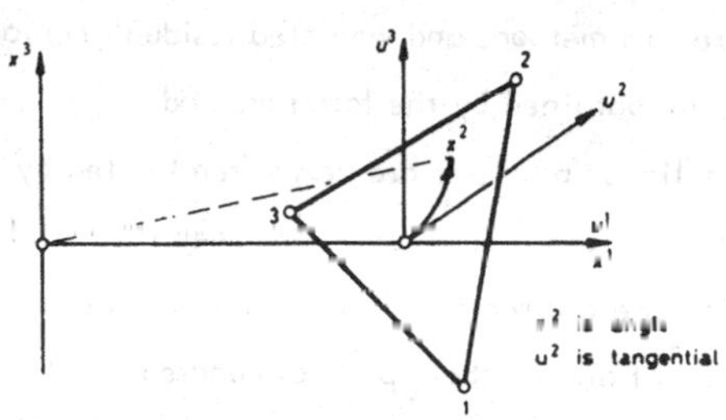

Fig . I - 4 Axisymmetric Strains Coordinate System

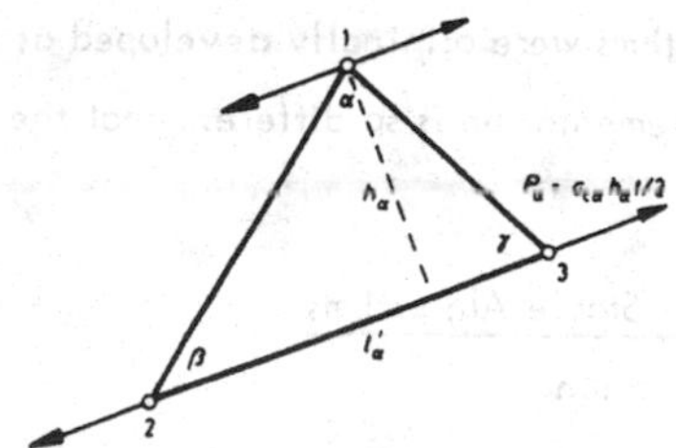

Fig . I - 5 Virtual Work of Natural Stresses σ_c

II. NON-LINEAR DYNAMICS OF STRUCTURES

1. Introduction

These notes will attempt to give an account of recent experience [1,2] at ISD in the field of structural dynamics. Although modal analysis by the DYNAN package [3] has been the standard method of treating large scale dynamics problems its application is limited to linear problems. The methods to be discussed here are based on step-by-step integration algorithms. These algorithms are all single step and work in terms of the inertia force vector and its time derivatives at the beginning and end of a step. Thus they are implicit methods and in general each step is solved iteratively. No excuse is made for concentrating on this type of algorithm. Our initial experience in applying these algorithms encouraged us to limit our efforts to improving and extending them, rather than making an attack on a broader front which would include explicit methods, extremum methods and weighted residual methods. In fact some of the algorithms developed here may be obtained by the latter method.

Non-linear problems are very often treated by incremental linearisation. One of the byproducts of the present investigation has been the development of large time step integrating algorithms which are a powerful alternative to modal analysis of linear systems. By large time step we mean a step of any number, perhaps hundreds, of times the least period of a dynamic system. Extension of large time step methods to non-linear systems is difficult for technical rather than theoretical reasons. Broadly speaking one may say that to attempt large step solutions of non-linear systems is to swim against the tide. The solution of a large time step is similar to the solution of a non-linear static problem by direct iteration - that is, not incrementally. Nevertheless if really large time steps can be achieved the effort may be worthwhile.

Although the large step algorithms were originally developed as modifications of the small step algorithms their practical implementation is so different that the two types of algorithm will be considered separately.

2. Small Step or Conditionally Stable Algorithms

Starting from the equation of motion

$$\ddot{\boldsymbol{r}} = \boldsymbol{M}^{-1}\boldsymbol{R}(\boldsymbol{r}, \dot{\boldsymbol{r}}, t) \qquad \text{(II.1)}$$

where $\boldsymbol{r}$ = displacement vector

$\boldsymbol{R}$ = inertia force vector

$\boldsymbol{M}$ = mass matrix

we represent $\boldsymbol{R}$ in terms of the values of $\boldsymbol{R}$, $\dot{\boldsymbol{R}}$, $\ddot{\boldsymbol{R}}$ etc. at the beginning and end of an interval of time $\tau = t_1 - t_0$. Thus $\boldsymbol{R}$ is represented by Hermitian interpolation polynomials of order 2,4,6 --- 2 n corresponding to polynomials which are linear, cubic, quintic --- (2 n - 1) tic.

The first member of the family n = 1, is the well-known linear acceleration algorithm. The second, n = 2, is the algorithm first used in references [4], [5], where the term "finite element in time" was coined by analogy with the cubic beam displacement function of standard finite element theory.

Integrating eq. (1) twice one obtains

$$\dot{\boldsymbol{r}}_1 = \dot{\boldsymbol{r}}_0 + \boldsymbol{M}^{-1}\int_{t_0}^{t_1}\left[\varphi_1\boldsymbol{R}_0 + \varphi_2\boldsymbol{R}_1 + \varphi_3\dot{\boldsymbol{R}}_0 + \varphi_4\dot{\boldsymbol{R}}_1 + \cdots\right]dt \qquad (II.2)$$

$$\boldsymbol{r}_1 = \boldsymbol{r}_0 + \tau\dot{\boldsymbol{r}} + \boldsymbol{M}^{-1}\int_{t_0}^{t}\int_{t_0}^{t}\left[\varphi_1\boldsymbol{R}_0 + \varphi_2\boldsymbol{R}_1 + \varphi_3\dot{\boldsymbol{R}}_0 + \varphi_4\dot{\boldsymbol{R}}_1 + \cdots\right]dt \qquad (II.3)$$

where the φ are the Hermitian interpolation polynomials. The first four algorithms are set out in Table .

If $\boldsymbol{R}$ were a polynomial in t of degree (2 n - 1) the nth algorithm would integrate both $\ddot{\boldsymbol{r}}, \dot{\boldsymbol{r}}, \boldsymbol{r}$ exactly. Since $\boldsymbol{R}$ may include a forcing function $\boldsymbol{f}(t)$ it is clear that should be represented by a (2 n - 1)tic or less in t. Impulse loads should be applied at the beginning of a time interval and require that velocity discontinuities are included in the program. However real impulse loads are not meaningful in the context of finite step integration and in practice all loads should be applied over at least one integration step. This avoids special consideration of impulses.

2.1 Stability of the Algorithms

When the algorithms are applied to a simple oscillator

$$\ddot{r} + \omega^2 r = 0 \qquad (II.4)$$

one has

$$\ddot{r} = R = -\omega^2 r$$

so that

$$\dot{R} = -\omega^2\dot{r}\,, \qquad \ddot{R} = -\omega^2\ddot{r} = \omega^4 r$$

$$\dddot{R} = \omega^4\dot{r} \qquad \text{etc.}$$

Thus all derivatives of R are expressible in terms of r or $\dot{r}$ and the algorithms lead to

$$\begin{bmatrix} r_1 \\ \dot{r}_1 \end{bmatrix} = \boldsymbol{A}\begin{bmatrix} r_0 \\ \dot{r}_0 \end{bmatrix} \approx \begin{bmatrix} \boldsymbol{A}_0 + \boldsymbol{A}_e \end{bmatrix}\begin{bmatrix} r_0 \\ \dot{r}_0 \end{bmatrix} \qquad (II.5)$$

The matrix $\boldsymbol{A}_0$ is the harmonic operator

$$\boldsymbol{A}_0 = \begin{bmatrix} \cos \omega\tau & \omega^{-1}\sin \omega\tau \\ -\omega \sin \omega\tau & \cos \omega\tau \end{bmatrix} \tag{II.6}$$

and $\boldsymbol{A}_e$ is composed of the first terms of the error matrix. The error matrix for the first and second algorithms are

$$\boldsymbol{A}_e = \frac{1}{12}\,\omega^4\tau^3 \begin{bmatrix} \frac{1}{2}\tau & \frac{7}{30}\tau^2 \\ 1 & \frac{1}{2}\tau \end{bmatrix} \tag{II.7}$$

and

$$\boldsymbol{A}_e = \frac{1}{720}\,\omega^6\tau^5 \begin{bmatrix} \frac{1}{2}\tau & \frac{17}{70}\tau^2 \\ 1 & \frac{1}{2}\tau \end{bmatrix} \tag{II.8}$$

For the nth algorithm $\boldsymbol{A}_e$ is of order τ^{2n+1}. The error matrix gives a good idea of the accuracy of the algorithms applied to linear systems with small time steps. It may be shown that the eigenvalues of the matrix $\boldsymbol{A}$ have modulus equal to unity for integration step τ less than about half the period $T_0 = 2\pi/\omega$. For example, $n = 1$, $\tau = 0.551\ T_0$; for $n = 2$, $\tau = 0.503\ T_0$. For greater values of τ the algorithms become divergent and are for this reason called conditionally stable. Quite independently of the time step required for sufficient accuracy of the response in the main modes of a multi-degree of freedom system, the maximum integration step is determined by the highest frequency mode of the system.

2.2 Implementation of the Algorithms

Because of the limitation on the integration step discussed in the previous section these algorithms are most suited to a direct Jacobi type iterative solution of each time step. The time step for convergence of the algorithms with Jacobi iteration when applied to a linear oscillator is of the same order as that required for stability of the algorithm. Thus the allowable maximum integration step is again conditioned by the highest natural frequency of a linear system, or in the case of non-linear systems by the highest pseudo frequency corresponding to the current tangent stiffness. For the simple oscillator of eq. (II.4) one may obtain by inspection from Table 1 the equation

$$\begin{bmatrix} \dot r_1 \\ r_1 \end{bmatrix} = \begin{bmatrix} a & b \\ c & d \end{bmatrix} \begin{bmatrix} \dot r_1 \\ r_1 \end{bmatrix} + \text{terms not involving } \dot r_1 + r_1 \tag{II.9}$$

Convergence of the Jacobi iteration requires that the eigenvalues λ of the matrix have modulus less than 1. The second algorithm, for example, gives,

$a = -\frac{1}{12}\omega^2\tau^2$, $b = \frac{1}{2}\omega^2\tau$, $c = -\frac{1}{30}\omega^2\tau^3$, $d = \frac{3}{20}\omega^2\tau^2$

and $|\lambda| = \omega^2\tau^2/4\sqrt{15}$. Then $\tau/T_0 < 0.63$ and for rapid convergence one requires τ/T_0 less than half this - say $\tau/T_0 < 0.3$. The criteria for the higher algorithms come out almost the same.

A number of variations of the actual implementation of the method are discussed in the references quoted. Experience has shown that the most economical and accurate procedure in non-linear systems is to carry out the iteration without incremental linearization. This avoids the necessity to store the global tangent stiffness matrix - only the element topology, geometry and material properties have to be stored.

In most problems the inertia force $\boldsymbol{R}$ is of the form,

$$\boldsymbol{R} = -\boldsymbol{R}_S - \boldsymbol{C}\dot{\boldsymbol{r}} + \boldsymbol{f}(t) \tag{II.10}$$

where $\boldsymbol{R}_S$ = internal elastic force vector

$\boldsymbol{C}$ = damping matrix, generally assumed constant

$\boldsymbol{f}(t)$ = applied loading.

In linear systems $\boldsymbol{R}_S = \boldsymbol{K}\boldsymbol{r}$ where $\boldsymbol{K}$ is the stiffness matrix. In non-linear problems $\boldsymbol{R}_S$ may be considered as $\boldsymbol{K}_s\boldsymbol{r}$ where $\boldsymbol{K}_s$ is the secant stiffness matrix which is a function of $\boldsymbol{r}$. Now eq. (II.10) may be written without using the global matrices $\boldsymbol{C}$ and $\boldsymbol{K}$ or $\boldsymbol{K}_s$. The contribution of each element g to the internal elastic and damping forces may be calculated from,

$$\boldsymbol{R}_g = -\boldsymbol{k}_{gs}\boldsymbol{\rho}_g - \boldsymbol{c}_g\dot{\boldsymbol{\rho}}_g = -\boldsymbol{P}_g - \boldsymbol{c}_g\dot{\boldsymbol{\rho}}_g \tag{II.11}$$

where $\boldsymbol{\rho}_g$ and $\boldsymbol{P}_g$ are the element nodal displacements and forces and $\boldsymbol{k}_{gs}$ is the secant modulus of the element g. The time derivatives of $\boldsymbol{R}$ and therefore of $\boldsymbol{R}_g$ are required for application of all but the first (linear) algorithm.

Thus

$$\dot{\boldsymbol{R}}_g = -\dot{\boldsymbol{P}}_g - \boldsymbol{c}_g \ddot{\boldsymbol{\varrho}}_g = -\left(\boldsymbol{k}_{gs}\boldsymbol{\varrho}_g\right)^{\cdot} - \boldsymbol{c}_g \ddot{\boldsymbol{\varrho}}_g$$
$$= -\boldsymbol{k}_{gt}\dot{\boldsymbol{\varrho}}_g - \boldsymbol{c}_g \ddot{\boldsymbol{\varrho}}_g \qquad (II.12)$$

where $\boldsymbol{k}_{gt}$ is the tangent stiffness matrix of the element. For the large displacement small strain case $\boldsymbol{k}_{gt}$ is equivalent to the sum of the elastic and geometric stiffness $\boldsymbol{k}_{Eg} + \boldsymbol{k}_{Gg}$ (Ch.III)
For $\ddot{\boldsymbol{R}}_g$ one has,

$$\ddot{\boldsymbol{R}}_g = -\ddot{\boldsymbol{P}}_g - \boldsymbol{c}_g \ddot{\boldsymbol{\varrho}}_g = -\boldsymbol{k}_{gt}\ddot{\boldsymbol{\varrho}}_g - \dot{\boldsymbol{k}}_{gt}\dot{\boldsymbol{\varrho}}_g - \boldsymbol{c}_g \dddot{\boldsymbol{\varrho}}_g \qquad (II.13)$$

Note that $\dot{\boldsymbol{k}}_{gt}$ is best left in this form.
Continuing in this way the higher derivatives may be derived. Assembling the $\boldsymbol{R}_g$ etc. by pre-multiplication by the Boolean location matrices $\boldsymbol{a}_g^t$, and noting that,

$$\boldsymbol{\varrho}_g = \boldsymbol{a}_g \boldsymbol{r}$$

we obtain by summation over

$$\boldsymbol{R} = \sum_g \boldsymbol{a}_g^t \boldsymbol{R}_g + \boldsymbol{f}(t) \qquad (II.14)$$
$$= -\sum_g \boldsymbol{a}_g^t \boldsymbol{P}_g - \sum_g \boldsymbol{a}_g^t \boldsymbol{c}_g \dot{\boldsymbol{\varrho}}_g + \boldsymbol{f}(t)$$

$$\dot{\boldsymbol{R}} = \sum_g \boldsymbol{a}_g^t \dot{\boldsymbol{R}}_g + \dot{\boldsymbol{f}}(t) \qquad (II.15)$$
$$= -\sum_g \boldsymbol{a}_g^t \dot{\boldsymbol{P}}_g - \sum_g \boldsymbol{a}_g^t \boldsymbol{c}_g \ddot{\boldsymbol{\varrho}}_g + \dot{\boldsymbol{f}}(t)$$

$$\ddot{\boldsymbol{R}} = \sum_g \boldsymbol{a}_g^t \ddot{\boldsymbol{R}}_g + \ddot{\boldsymbol{f}}(t) \qquad (II.16)$$
$$= -\sum_g \boldsymbol{a}_g^t \ddot{\boldsymbol{P}}_g - \sum_g \boldsymbol{a}_g^t \boldsymbol{c}_g \dddot{\boldsymbol{\varrho}}_g + \ddot{\boldsymbol{f}}(t)$$

Equations(II.14) to (II.16) are equivalent to the global expressions.

$$\begin{aligned} \boldsymbol{R} &= -\boldsymbol{K}_s \boldsymbol{r} - \boldsymbol{C}\dot{\boldsymbol{r}} + \boldsymbol{f}(t) \\ \dot{\boldsymbol{R}} &= -\boldsymbol{K}_t \dot{\boldsymbol{r}} - \boldsymbol{C}\ddot{\boldsymbol{r}} + \dot{\boldsymbol{f}}(t) \\ \ddot{\boldsymbol{R}} &= -\boldsymbol{K}_t \ddot{\boldsymbol{r}} - \dot{\boldsymbol{K}}_t \dot{\boldsymbol{r}} - \boldsymbol{C}\dddot{\boldsymbol{r}} + \ddot{\boldsymbol{f}}(t) \end{aligned} \qquad (II.17)$$

The global equilibrium equation is

$$\boldsymbol{R} = \boldsymbol{M}\ddot{\boldsymbol{r}} \qquad (II.18)$$

and this equation must be used to substitute for the derivatives of $\boldsymbol{r}$ higher than $\dot{\boldsymbol{r}}$ in the above expressions for $\dot{\boldsymbol{R}}$, $\ddot{\boldsymbol{R}}$ etc. The element wise programming of this procedure is therefore greatly simplified when $\boldsymbol{M}$ is a diagonal lumped mass matrix. It will in general be easier to carry a greater number of lumped mass freedoms than to use a smaller consistent mass matrix.

A previously developed procedure for solving non-linear problems was the so-called $\boldsymbol{K}^*$ method discussed in ref. [1]. This method uses an effective global tangent stiffness which is the mean of the tangent stiffness at the beginning and of a time step. Accumulation of the increments of the internal elastic loading $\boldsymbol{R}_S$ is used although it is also possible to incorporate a periodic check of $\boldsymbol{R}_S$ calculated directly from the current displacements. This procedure may be the most economical for problems with less than about 600 degrees of freedom. Each step is again solved by Jacobi iteration. There are several other variations possible in the detailed implementation of the small step algorithm. In Fig. II.1 are shown three possible flow charts two of which refer to non-linear and one to linear problems. For very large linear systems the non-linear algorithm without linearization (Fig. II.2) may often prove the most accurate and economical. Some examples of applications of the algorithms are shown in Figs. II- 3-17.

2.3 Non-Structural Applications of the Small Step Algorithms

Although the algorithms are especially suited to multi-degree of freedom structural systems their high accuracy and ease of programming should be useful in other applications. For example, the classical n-body problem is rather like the problem of masses connected by non-linear elastic cords. The accuracy achievable in this type of problem is demonstrated in Figs. II -13 - 22.

Another problem is that of elastic or elasto-plastic wave propagation. Figures II- 23 - 33 show some examples of applications in this field.

Problems depending on systems of first order differential equations may be solved by use of the first lines only of the algorithms in Table I, with $\dot{\boldsymbol{r}}$ replaced by $\boldsymbol{r}$, $\boldsymbol{R}$ by $\dot{\boldsymbol{r}}$ and so on.

3. Large Step or Unconditionally Stable Algorithms

Our interest in large step algorithms was stimulated by a paper by Goudreau and Taylor [6]. They showed that the Newmark average acceleration algorithm, which may be considered as a modification of the linear acceleration method, was superior to other existing algorithms. The linear acceleration method is the case n = 1 of the previous section. We therefore attempted to modify the higher members of the family in order that they should have unconditional stability. It was noticed that the Newmark algorithm when applied to a simple oscillator of circular frequency always gave the following relation between the vectors $\{r_1 \quad \dot{r}_1\}$ and $\{r_0 \quad \dot{r}_0\}$.

$$\begin{bmatrix} r_1 \\ \dot{r}_1 \end{bmatrix} = \begin{bmatrix} \cos\varphi & \omega^{-1}\sin\varphi \\ -\omega\sin\varphi & \cos\varphi \end{bmatrix} \begin{bmatrix} r_0 \\ \dot{r}_0 \end{bmatrix} \tag{II.19}$$

where

$$\varphi = 2\tan^{-1}\frac{\frac{1}{2}\omega\tau}{1-\frac{1}{12}(\omega\tau)^2} \tag{II.20}$$

For small time steps $\varphi \simeq \omega\tau$ but when τ is large the effective period of the oscillation is increased. The total energy, however, remains unaltered. It was found possible to modify the coefficients of the second lines in the algorithms of Table I so that all of them reproduce eq.(II.19) when applied to a simple oscillator. Afterwards it was realised that the synthesis of the algorithms could be described very easily as follows. Calculate $\boldsymbol{r}_1$ by the same Hermitian quadrature as is used to calculate $\dot{\boldsymbol{r}}_1$. For example, we give in detail the second member, viz.

$$\dot{\boldsymbol{r}}_1 = \dot{\boldsymbol{r}}_0 + \frac{1}{2}\tau\boldsymbol{M}^{-1}\left[\boldsymbol{R}_0 + \boldsymbol{R}_1\right] + \frac{1}{12}\tau^2\boldsymbol{M}^{-1}\left[\dot{\boldsymbol{R}}_0 - \dot{\boldsymbol{R}}_1\right] \tag{II.21}$$

$$\boldsymbol{r}_1 = \boldsymbol{r}_0 + \frac{1}{2}\tau\left[\dot{\boldsymbol{r}}_0 + \dot{\boldsymbol{r}}_1\right] + \frac{1}{12}\tau^2\boldsymbol{M}^{-1}\left[\boldsymbol{R}_0 - \boldsymbol{R}_1\right] \tag{II.22}$$

Substituting for $\dot{\boldsymbol{r}}_1$ from (II.21) in (II.22) one has

$$\boldsymbol{r}_1 = \boldsymbol{r}_0 + \tau\dot{\boldsymbol{r}}_0 + \frac{1}{6}\tau^2\boldsymbol{M}^{-1}\left[2\boldsymbol{R}_0 + \boldsymbol{R}_1\right] + \frac{1}{24}\tau^3\boldsymbol{M}^{-1}\left[\dot{\boldsymbol{R}}_0 - \dot{\boldsymbol{R}}_1\right] \tag{II.23}$$

The complete algorithms are set out in Table II. Note that for some purposes it may be more convenient to use the second algorithm in the form of (II.22) rather than (II.23). In Table III a summary of some important properties of the algorithms is given. Fig II- 34 shows curves of the period elongations together with that for the method of Wilson.

Naturally there is some reduction in the small time step accuracy compared with the conditionally stable algorithms. The error matrix for the second member, n = 2, is

$$\boldsymbol{A}_e = \frac{1}{720}\,\omega^6\tau^5\begin{bmatrix}\tau & -\omega^{-2}\\ 1 & \tau\end{bmatrix} \qquad (II.24)$$

which is of no greater order then the $\boldsymbol{A}_e$ of eq. (II.8). It was noted that the conditionally stable algorithms integrate exactly forcing functions up to the power (2 n - 1) in the time. The present algorithms will integrate the velocity exactly but will give the displacement correctly only up to the (2n - 2)th power of t.

Compared with previously developed algorithms, known to the authors at least, the algorithms for n = 2, 3 and 4 are remarkably accurate.

3.1 Implementation of the Algorithms

The implementation of the large step algorithms is entirely different from that for the small step algorithms. The large time step precludes the use of the Jacobi iterative solution and it is necessary always to form the global matrices and to solve each step by a direct method such as elimination or matrix inversion. The algorithms are therefore ideal for linear systems. It may be shown that the algorithms retain their unconditional stability for multi-degree linear systems with or without damping $\boldsymbol{C}$. The damping need not be proportional to the stiffness or mass matrix but it supposed positive.

When $\boldsymbol{R}$ is as in eq. (II.10) all algorithms lead to an equation of the form

$$\boldsymbol{D}_1\begin{bmatrix}\boldsymbol{r}_1\\ \dot{\boldsymbol{r}}_1\end{bmatrix} = \boldsymbol{D}_0\begin{bmatrix}\boldsymbol{r}_0\\ \dot{\boldsymbol{r}}_0\end{bmatrix} + \boldsymbol{F} \qquad (II.25)$$

where $\boldsymbol{D}_1$, $\boldsymbol{D}_0$ are square matrices of order(2 n x 2 n) and $\boldsymbol{F}$ is a vector of the load terms. $\boldsymbol{D}_1$, $\boldsymbol{D}_0$ and $\boldsymbol{F}$ are given in Figs. II-35,36 for the first three algorithms. Some examples of applications to linear systems appear in Figs II-37 - 42.

3.2 Algorithmic Damping

Many authors have considered algorithmic damping to be a desirable property of algorithms designed for multi-degree of freedom systems. By algorithmic damping we mean the eventual disappearance of the harmonic components of the higher frequencies of the system. This is considered desirable for two reasons. Firstly, because higher modes are often inaccurately represented by the inevitable discretisation of the system. Secondly because the period elongations of the higher frequencies become so large that, although the maximum amplitudes of the high frequencies are present, their occurrence in time is completely different from the exact solution. However, we have not introduced algorithmic damping into the present algorithms. The reason is that the application of the algorithms only becomes meaningful in relation to the loading function. From the pseudo-indicial admittance curves of Fig. II- 43 , one sees that for large integration steps compared with the period of the oscillator the high frequency modes will not be excited appreciably if the changes in the loading function occur over at least one integration step. Real step functions or impulses will excite the higher modes and should not be present in the load function. Such loadings obviously require very small time step if their response is to be accurately represented.

If for some reason algorithmic damping is desired it can be introduced by weighting the terms $\dot{\boldsymbol{r}}_1$, $\boldsymbol{R}_1$, $\dot{\boldsymbol{R}}_1$,etc. more than $\boldsymbol{r}_0$, $\boldsymbol{R}_0$, $\dot{\boldsymbol{R}}_0$ in the algorithms of Table II or eqs. (II.21) and (II.22). The effect of this can be shown by considering a general algorithm of the form (single degree system)

$$\dot{r}_1 = \dot{r}_0 + A\left[\lambda\ddot{r}_0 + (2-\lambda)\ddot{r}_1\right] + B\left[\lambda\dddot{r}_0 - (2-\lambda)\dddot{r}_1\right] + C\left[\lambda r_0^{\mathrm{IV}} + (2-\lambda)r_1^{\mathrm{IV}}\right] + \dots\dots \tag{II.26}$$

$$r_1 = r_0 + A\left[\lambda\dot{r}_0 + (2-\lambda)\dot{r}_1\right] + B\left[\lambda\ddot{r}_0 - (2-\lambda)\ddot{r}_1\right] + C\left[\lambda\dddot{r}_0 + (2-\lambda)\dddot{r}_1\right] + \dots\dots \tag{II.27}$$

where $A,B,C,$ etc. are dependent on the time step τ . Applying this to the simple oscillator

$$\ddot{r} = -\omega^2 r \tag{II.28}$$

we obtain

$$\begin{aligned} \left[1+(2-\lambda)X\right]\dot{r}_1 - (1+\lambda X)\dot{r}_0 &= -\omega^2 Y\left[\lambda r_0 + (2-\lambda)r_1\right] \\ (2-\lambda)Y\dot{r}_1 + \lambda Y\dot{r}_0 &= \left[1+(2-\lambda)X\right]r_1 - (1+\lambda X)r_0 \end{aligned} \tag{II.29}$$

where

$$\begin{aligned} X &= \quad -\omega^2 B + \omega^4 D + \dots\dots \\ Y &= A - \omega^2 C + \omega^4 E + \dots\dots \end{aligned} \tag{II.30}$$

Solving for $\dot{r}_1$ and r_1 in terms of $\dot{r}_0$ and r_0 and writing the total energy

$$\Phi = \frac{1}{2}\left(\dot{r}^2 + \omega^2 r^2\right) \tag{II.31}$$

one obtains

$$\Phi_1 = \Phi_0 \frac{\left[1 + \lambda X\right]^2 + \omega^2\lambda^2 Y^2}{\left[1 + (2-\lambda)X\right]^2 + \omega^2 Y^2 (2-\lambda)^2} \tag{II.32}$$

Thus, when $\lambda = 1$ as in the algorithms of Table II we have $\Phi_1 = \Phi_0$. It may be shown that when the coefficients $A, B, C,$ etc. have the values of Table II (or values of the same order of magnitude)

$$\Phi_1 \gtreqless \Phi_0 \tag{II.33}$$

according as $\lambda \gtreqless 1$,

It follows that our family of algorithms may be modified for algorithmic damping by simply taking λ a little less then unity. This will reduce a little the accuracy of the low modes and that of the free mass response to a forcing function. It may be noted finally that if we modify only the coefficients in the last term of each line of the algorithms the algorithm becomes convergent for large τ but there will be range of τ for which the algorithms become divergent. This may not preclude the use of such algorithms because in the range of theoretical divergence for a lower mode the truncation error will be in any case very small.

3.3 Application to Non-Linear Systems

The unconditional stability of the algorithms is defined only in relation to linear systems. It must not be expected, therefore, that these algorithms will perform better than the conditionally stable ones when applied to non-linear systems. In fact their small time step truncation error will be greater. An idea of their behaviour with non-linear conservative systems may be seen by applying the first member to a non-linear oscillator (for a unit mass)

$$\ddot{r} = -R_S(r) \tag{II.34}$$

Thus

$$\begin{aligned} r_1 &= r_0 + \frac{1}{2}\tau\left(\dot{r}_0 + \dot{r}_1\right) \\ \dot{r}_1 &= \dot{r}_0 + \frac{1}{2}\tau\left(R_{S0} + R_{S1}\right) \end{aligned} \tag{II.35}$$

and eliminating τ one has,

$$\frac{1}{2}(\dot{r}_1^2 - \dot{r}_0^2) = -\frac{1}{2}(r_1 - r_0)(R_{S0} + R_{S1}) \qquad (II.36)$$

Thus the change in kinetic energy does not equal the change in potential energy - see Fig.II-44. Although an individual time step will never become divergent it is possible by changing the integration step periodically to arrange for arbitrary in-put of energy to the system. The higher algorithms lead to similar but more complex energy balance conditions. The general conclusion must be that the present large step algorithms must not be applied to non-linear problems.

4. Large Step Algorithms for Non-Linear Problems

There are many structural problems in which the non-linearity is elastic and in which the force displacement relation is well approximated by a polynomial. The non-linear problem of Fig.II-3 is approximately cubic for reasonably large deflections and materials with a polynomial strain energy function of the large strains (Green strains) lead to polynomial load deflection relations.

4.1 Single Degree of Freedom System

The equation of motion of a non-linear undamped system may be written

$$\ddot{r} = -R_S + f(t) \qquad (II.37)$$

If the displacement is given in terms of the velocity as in the linear algorithm

$$r_1 = r_0 + \frac{1}{2}\tau(\dot{r}_0 + \dot{r}_1) \qquad (II.38)$$

Now suppose that exact energy balance is maintained. Then

$$\frac{1}{2}(\dot{r}_1^2 - \dot{r}_0^2) = -R_{Sav}(r_1 - r_0) + f_{av}(r_1 - r_0) \qquad (II.39)$$

where R_{Sav} and f_{av} are the average values of R_S considering them as functions of r. Since from (II.38)

$$\frac{1}{2}(\dot{r}_0 + \dot{r}_1) = \frac{1}{\tau}(r_1 - r_0)$$

one has, dividing the two sides of (II.39) by $\frac{1}{2}(\dot{r}_0 + \dot{r}_1)$ and $\frac{1}{\tau}(r_0 - r_1)$ respectively,

$$\dot{r}_1 = \dot{r}_0 - \tau R_{Sav} + \tau f_{av} \tag{II.40}$$

Equations (II.38) and (II.40) constitute the algorithm, but in order to apply it a meaning has to be given to R_{Sav} and f_{av}.

$$\begin{aligned} R_{Sav}(r_1 - r_0) &= \int_{r_0}^{r_1} R_S \, dr \\ &= \int_{r_0}^{r_1} \left[R_{S0} + \int_{r_0}^{r} R_S' \, dr \right] dr = R_{S0}(r_1 - r_0) + \int_{r_0}^{r_1}\int_{r_0}^{r} R_S' \, dr \, dr \end{aligned} \tag{II.41}$$

where

$$R_S' = \frac{dR_S}{dr} = K_t \tag{II.42}$$

is the tangent modulus.

The double integral in (II.41) may be evaluated to various degrees of precision by Hermitian quadrature. Thus, if R_S is a quadratic function of r,

$$R_{Sav} = R_{S0} + \left(\frac{1}{3}K_0 + \frac{1}{6}K_1\right)(r_1 - r_0) \tag{II.43}$$

If R_S is up to quartic in r,

$$\begin{aligned} R_{Sav} = R_{S0} &+ \left(\frac{7}{20}K_0 + \frac{3}{20}K_1\right)(r_1 - r_0) \\ &+ \left(\frac{1}{20}K_0' - \frac{1}{30}K_1'\right)(r_1 - r_0)^2 \end{aligned} \tag{II.44}$$

Note that the coefficients in (II.43) and (II.44) are as in the second lines of the conditional algorithms of Table I, and higher order approximations may be obtained immediately from this Table. For f_{av} we may use the approximations

$$f_{av} = \frac{1}{2}(f_0 + f_1) \tag{II.45}$$

or

$$f_{av} = \frac{1}{2}(f_0 + f_1) + \frac{1}{12}\tau(\dot{f}_0 - \dot{f}_1) \qquad (II.46)$$

which amounts to replacing the average f's over the displacement by those over the time.

In conjunction with (II.43) and (II.45) the equation (II.40) becomes,

$$\dot{r}_1 = \dot{r}_0 - \tau\left[R_{S0} + \left(\frac{1}{3}K_0 + \frac{1}{6}K_1\right)(r_1 - r_0)\right] + \frac{1}{2}\tau(f_0 + f_1) \qquad (II.47)$$

If we substitute for $\dot{r}_1$ from (II.47) in (II.38)

$$r_1 = r_0 + \tau\dot{r}_0 - \frac{1}{2}\tau^2\left[R_{S0} + \left(\frac{1}{3}K_0 + \frac{1}{6}K_1\right)(r_1 - r_0)\right] + \frac{1}{4}\tau^2(f_0 + f_1) \qquad (II.48)$$

Equations (II.47) and (II.48) may be extended to multi-degree of freedom systems but a more accurate algorithm will now be considered which represents an extension of the second algorithm of Table II to non-linear systems.

We consider a free single degree of freedom system and assume that the equation for the displacement is obtained as before by Hermitian quadrature

$$r_1 = r_0 + \frac{1}{2}\tau(\dot{r}_0 + \dot{r}_1) + \frac{1}{12}\tau^2(\ddot{r}_0 - \ddot{r}_1) \qquad (II.49)$$

with

$$\ddot{r} = -R_S(r) \qquad (II.50)$$

For energy balance we have

$$\frac{1}{2}(\dot{r}_1^2 - \dot{r}_0^2) = -R_{Sav}(r_1 - r_0) \qquad (II.51)$$

Equation (II.49) may be written, with (II.50)

$$r_1 - r_0 = \frac{1}{2}\tau(\dot{r}_0 + \dot{r}_1) + \frac{1}{12}\tau^2 K_c(r_1 - r_0) \qquad (II.52)$$

where K_c is the chord stiffness modulus between r_0 and r_1. From (II.51)

$$\frac{\dot{r}_1 - \dot{r}_0}{r_1 - r_0} = -2\,\frac{R_{Sav}}{(\dot{r}_1 + \dot{r}_0)} \tag{II.53}$$

Multiplying each term of (II.52) by one side of (II.53)

$$\dot{r}_1 = \dot{r}_0 - \tau R_{Sav} - \frac{1}{12}\tau^2 K_c \tag{II.54}$$

Substituting for $\dot{r}_1$ in (II.52) one has,

$$r_1 = r_0 + \tau\dot{r}_0 - \frac{1}{2}\tau^2\left[R_{Sav} + \frac{1}{6}(R_{S0} - R_{S1})\right] - \frac{1}{24}\tau^3 K_c(\dot{r}_0 - \dot{r}_1) \tag{II.55}$$

Now R_{Sav} and K_c must be expressed with consistent accuracy. Thus if we wish the energy balance equation to remain accurate for up to a quartic load displacment law R_{Sav} will be expressed by eq. (II.44) and

$$K_c = \frac{1}{2}(K_0 + K_1) + \frac{1}{12}(K_0' - K_1')(r_1 - r_0) \tag{II.56}$$

where $K' = \dfrac{dK}{dr}$

If the loading terms are included as in the linear case the complete algorithm is

$$\dot{r}_1 = \dot{r}_0 - \tau\left[R_{S0} + \frac{1}{2}\bar{K}(r_1 - r_0)\right] - \frac{1}{12}\tau^2 K_c(\dot{r}_0 - \dot{r}_1) + \frac{1}{2}\tau(f_0 + f_1) + \frac{1}{12}\tau^2(\dot{f}_0 - \dot{f}_1) \tag{II.57}$$

$$r_1 = r_0 + \frac{1}{2}\tau(\dot{r}_0 + \dot{r}_1) + \frac{1}{12}\tau^2 K_c(r_1 - r_0) + \frac{1}{12}\tau^2(f_0 - f_1) \tag{II.58}$$

where K_c appears in (II.56) and

$$\bar{K} = \frac{7}{10}K_0 + \frac{3}{10}K_1 + \left(\frac{1}{10}K_0' - \frac{1}{15}K_1'\right)(r_1 - r_0) \tag{II.59}$$

An alternative, but equivalent, form for r_1 may be obtained by substituting for $\dot{r}_1$ in (II.58) in (II.57). When the system is linear K_c and $\bar{K}$ are both equal to the stiffness K and the algorithm reduces to the standard unconditionally stable algorithm with $n = 2$.

A free oscillator with a conservative load displacement relation up to quartic will give a bounded response when integrated by the above algorithm. As in the linear case the period will be alongated. When the integration time step is very large eq. (II.58) shows that r_1 will tend to follow the static deflection provided r_0 already corresponds to f_0. However, it cannot be concluded from eq. (II.57) that $\dot{r}_1$ also tends to follow the rate of change of the static deflection as it does in the linear case. Ideally if this condition could be satisfied one would be confident of the behaviour of the algorithm for really large steps. Nevertheless the algorithm should behave well for the free system and also for the extreme case of a free mass. To extend the use of the non-linear algorithm to multi-degree of freedom systems it is necessary to define what is meant by $\bar{K}$ and K_c in this case.

4.1 Multi-Degree of Freedom Conservative Systems

If the vector

$$\boldsymbol{R}_S = \boldsymbol{R}_S(\boldsymbol{r}) \tag{II.60}$$

is written in the form

$$\boldsymbol{R}_S = \boldsymbol{R}_{S0} + \boldsymbol{K}_c[\boldsymbol{r}_1 - \boldsymbol{r}_0] \tag{II.61}$$

where $\boldsymbol{K}_c$ is a square matrix there are in general many ways of writing $\boldsymbol{K}_c$. However we require $\boldsymbol{K}_c$ to be expressed in terms of the states $\boldsymbol{r}_0$ and $\boldsymbol{r}_1$. Now

$$\boldsymbol{R}_S = \boldsymbol{R}_{S0} + \int_{\boldsymbol{r}_0}^{\boldsymbol{r}} \boldsymbol{K}_t \, d\boldsymbol{r} \tag{II.62}$$

which is independent of the path of integration. $\boldsymbol{K}_t$ is the tangent stiffness matrix. The integral in (II.62) may be written with various degrees of approximation and by analogy with the single degree of freedom eq. (II.56) we take

$$\boldsymbol{K}_c = \frac{1}{2}[\boldsymbol{K}_0 + \boldsymbol{K}_1] + \frac{1}{12}\sum_{m=1}^{n}(r_1^m - r_0^m)[\boldsymbol{K}^0_{,m} - \boldsymbol{K}^1_{,m}] \tag{II.63}$$

where

$$\boldsymbol{K}^0_{,m} = \left[\frac{\partial}{\partial r_m} \boldsymbol{K}_t \right]_{\boldsymbol{r}=\boldsymbol{r}_0} \tag{II.64}$$

and r^m is the mth element of the vector $\boldsymbol{r}$. Similarly $\boldsymbol{R}_{Sav}$ may be defined by the relation,

$$\begin{aligned}
[\boldsymbol{r}_1 - \boldsymbol{r}_0]^t \boldsymbol{R}_{Sav} &= \int_{\boldsymbol{r}}^{\boldsymbol{r}} \boldsymbol{R}_S^t \, d\boldsymbol{r} \\
&= [\boldsymbol{r}_1 - \boldsymbol{r}_0]^t \boldsymbol{R}_{S0} + \int_{\boldsymbol{r}_0}^{\boldsymbol{r}_1}\int_{\boldsymbol{r}_0}^{\boldsymbol{r}} d\boldsymbol{r}^t \boldsymbol{K} \, d\boldsymbol{r} \\
&= [\boldsymbol{r}_1 - \boldsymbol{r}_0]^t \boldsymbol{R}_{S0} + \frac{1}{2} [\boldsymbol{r}_1 - \boldsymbol{r}_0]^t \bar{\boldsymbol{K}} [\boldsymbol{r}_1 - \boldsymbol{r}_0]
\end{aligned}$$

Thus

$$\boldsymbol{R}_{Sav} = \boldsymbol{R}_{S0} + \frac{1}{2} \bar{\boldsymbol{K}} [\boldsymbol{r}_1 - \boldsymbol{r}_0]$$

where

$$\begin{aligned}
\bar{\boldsymbol{K}} = \frac{7}{10} \boldsymbol{K}_0 + \frac{3}{10} \boldsymbol{K}_1 &+ \frac{1}{10} \sum_{m=1}^{n} (r_1^m - r_0^m) \boldsymbol{K}^0_{,m} \\
&- \frac{1}{15} \sum_{m=1}^{n} (r_1^m - r_0^m) \boldsymbol{K}^1_{,m}
\end{aligned} \tag{II.65}$$

The complete algorithm is as follows

$$\begin{aligned}
\dot{\boldsymbol{r}}_1 = \dot{\boldsymbol{r}}_0 - \tau \boldsymbol{M}^{-1} \left[\boldsymbol{R}_{S0} + \frac{1}{2} \bar{\boldsymbol{K}} [\boldsymbol{r}_1 - \boldsymbol{r}_0] \right] &- \frac{1}{12} \tau^2 \boldsymbol{M}^{-1} \boldsymbol{K}_c [\dot{\boldsymbol{r}}_0 - \dot{\boldsymbol{r}}_1] \\
+ \frac{1}{2} \tau \boldsymbol{M}^{-1} [\boldsymbol{f}_0 + \boldsymbol{f}_1] &+ \frac{1}{12} \tau^2 \boldsymbol{M}^{-1} [\dot{\boldsymbol{f}}_0 - \dot{\boldsymbol{f}}_1]
\end{aligned} \tag{II.66}$$

$$\begin{aligned}
\boldsymbol{r}_1 = \boldsymbol{r}_0 + \frac{1}{2} \tau \boldsymbol{M}^{-1} [\dot{\boldsymbol{r}}_0 + \dot{\boldsymbol{r}}_1] &+ \frac{1}{12} \tau^2 \boldsymbol{M}^{-1} \boldsymbol{K}_c [\boldsymbol{r}_1 - \boldsymbol{r}_0] \\
&+ \frac{1}{12} \tau^2 \boldsymbol{M}^{-1} [\boldsymbol{f}_0 - \boldsymbol{f}_1]
\end{aligned} \tag{II.67}$$

This algorithm will maintain exact energy balance for a free system in which the load displacement relation is up to quartic in $\boldsymbol{r}$ - or when the elastic energy is up to a quintic in $\boldsymbol{r}$ Higher order algorithms may be obtained but will involve higher derivatives of the $\boldsymbol{K}_t$ matrix.

4.2 Implementation of Algorithm

The algorithm of eqs. (II.66) and (II.67) will be competitive with the small step algorithms of Section 2 only if it is possible to use it with really large steps. Since $\boldsymbol{K}_c$ and $\bar{\boldsymbol{K}}$ depend on $\boldsymbol{r}_1$, the solution of each time step is iterative in the sense that $\boldsymbol{K}_c$ and $\bar{\boldsymbol{K}}$ must be recalculated several times. However, for given $\boldsymbol{K}_c$ and $\bar{\boldsymbol{K}}$ the vector $\{\boldsymbol{r}_1 \ \dot{\boldsymbol{r}}_1\}$ has to be obtained by a direct method. Thus the method is similar to the large step linear case except that the matrices $\boldsymbol{D}_1$ and $\boldsymbol{D}_0$ are no longer independent of r_0 and r_1.
As mentioned in the introduction the solution of a large time step is similar to the solving of a static problem without using an incremental method. If it is necessary to solve incrementally the whole object of the exercise would be defeated. It appears from the examples calculated by the method that convergence is obtained with no special precautions provided the time step does not exceed about one quarter of the period corresponding to the maximum amplitude. This time step is not large by the standard set by the linear algorithm. It would mean that the presence of a high frequency and unimportant non-linear "mode" would preclude the use of a large time step. Because the large step algorithm already requires sophisticated programming any further complications to ensure convergence would be uneconomic. From eq. (II.67) it may be seen that when is large and the initial conditions are $r_1 = \dot{r}_0 = f_0 = 0$ then

$$r_1 = K_c^{-1} f_1 \tag{II.68}$$

But $K_c = r_1^2$ in this case. Thus the algorithm will diverge. However, the simple device of taking the average of successive iterates will ensure convergence. In general, averaging will increase convergence when the static load deflection curve is concave upwards for positive loads. In other cases it will slow but not destroy convergence. In a multi-degree freedom system there may be opposing criteria for the various "modes".
The method has been tried out on the plane net problem which was solved previously by the small step algorithm. The results for a time step of $\tau = 0.01$ sec are given in Fig. II - 45 where for comparison the accurate curve for $\tau = 0.0005$ sec by the conditional small step method is shown. Above $\tau = 0.01$ the method does not converge. This is about five times the limiting time step for the conditional algorithm.
Other examples are shown in Figs. II- 46 - 48.

5. References

1 Argyris, J.H., Dunne, P.C. and Angelopoulos, T., Non-linear Oscillations Using the Finite Element Technique, Computer Methods in Applied Mechanics and Engineering, 2, 203-250 (1973)

2 Argyris, J.H., Dunne, P.C. and Angelopoulos, T., Dynamic Response by Large Step Integration, Earthquake Engineering and Structural Dynamics, 2, 185-203 (1973)

3 Braun, K.A., Brönlund, O.E., Bühlmeier, J., Dietrich, G., Frik, G., Johnsen, T.L., Kiesbauer, H.T., Malejannakis, G.A., Straub, K. and Vallianos, G., DYNAN Lecture Notes with Computational Examples, ISD Report No.109, University of Stuttgart (1971)

4 Argyris, J.H., The Impact of the Digital Computer on Engineering Sciences, Twelfth Lanchester Memorial Lecture, The Aeronautical Journal of the Roy.Aeron.Soc., 74, Nos.709,710 (1970)

5 Argyris, J.H. and Chan, A.S.L., Application of Finite Elements in Space and Time, Ingenieur Archiv, 41, 235-257 (1972)

6 Goudreau, G.L. and Taylor, R.L., Evaluation of Numerical Integration Methods in Elastodynamics, Computer Methods in Applied Mechanics and Engineering, 2, [illegible] ([illegible])

7 Haase, M., Note on Stability of Large Step algorithms Applied to Multidegree Freedom Arbitrarily Damped Systems, ISD Internal Report, University of Stuttgart (1973)

8 Newmark, N.M., A Method of Computation for Structural Dynamics, Proceedings ASCE 85, EM 3 (1959)

9 Wilson, E.L., Farhoomand, I. and Bathe, K.J., Non-linear Dynamic Analysis of Complex Structures, Earthquake Engineering and Structural Dynamics, 1, 241-252 (1973)

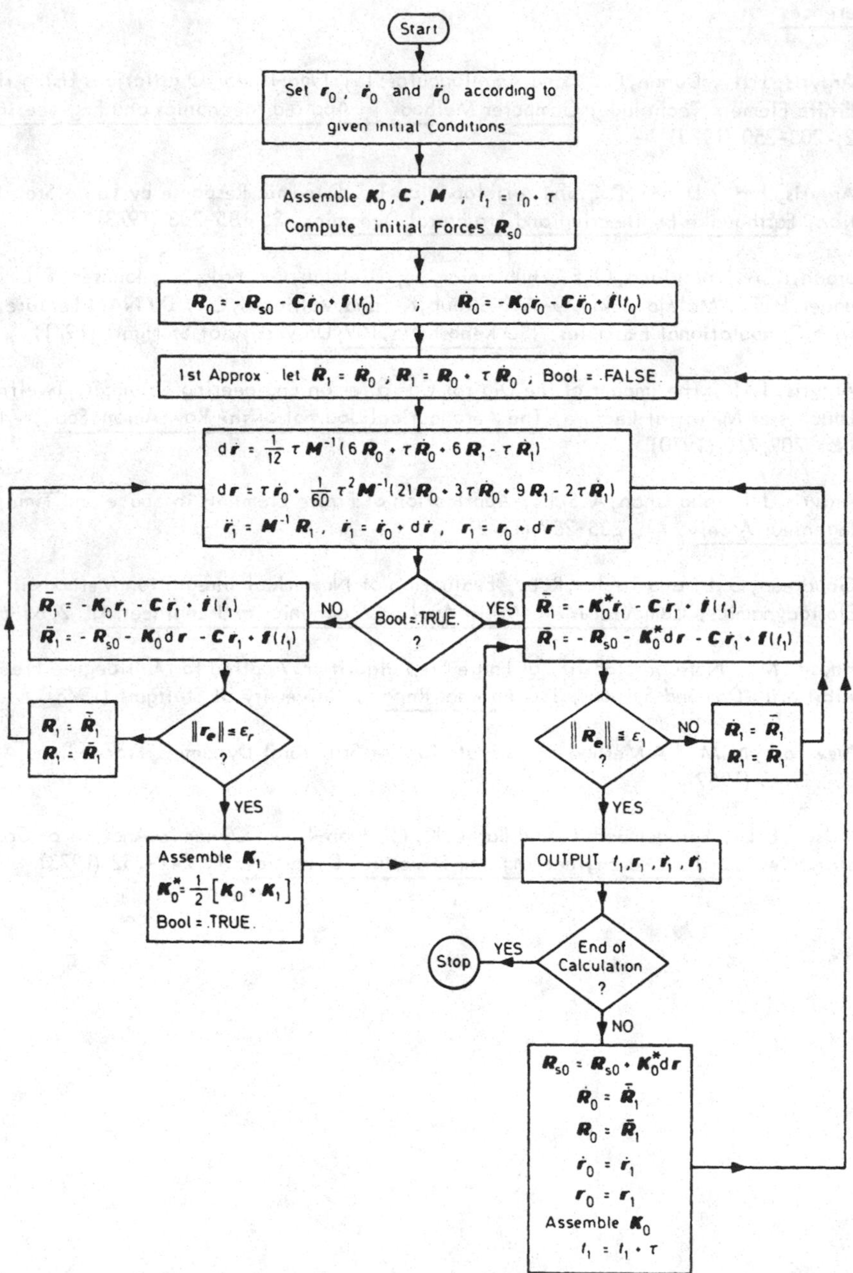

Fig. II-1a Flow Chart for Non-linear Oscillations Using Modified Stiffness Matrix with Accumulation

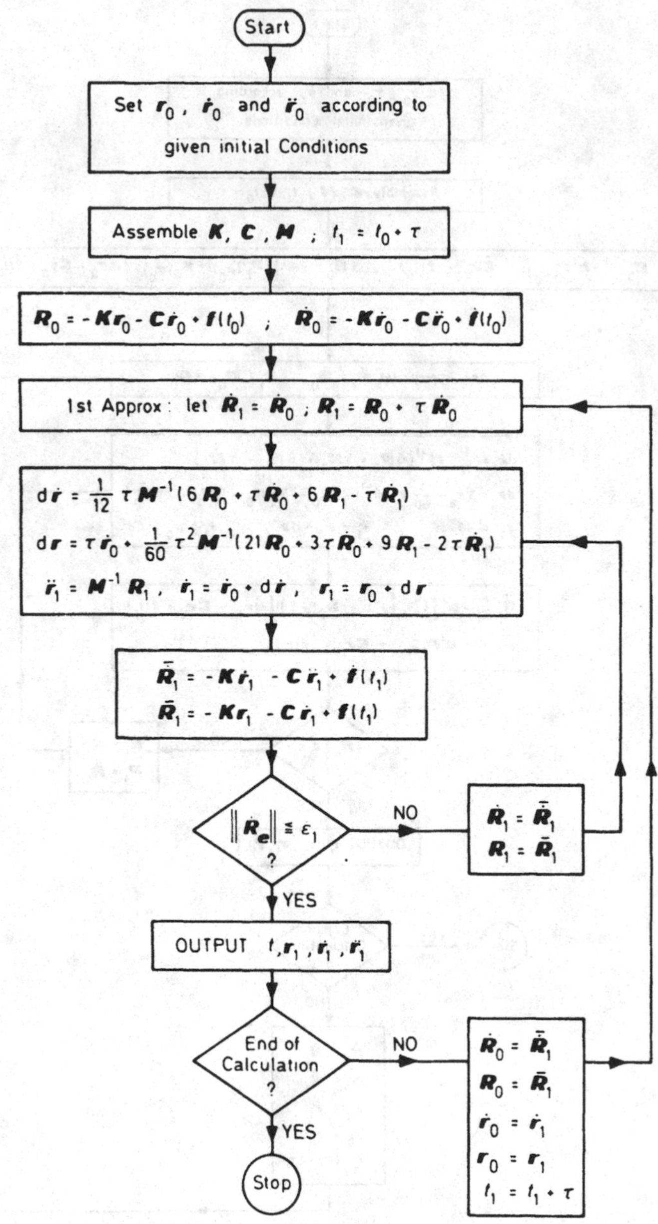

Fig. II-1b Flow Chart for Linear Oscillations

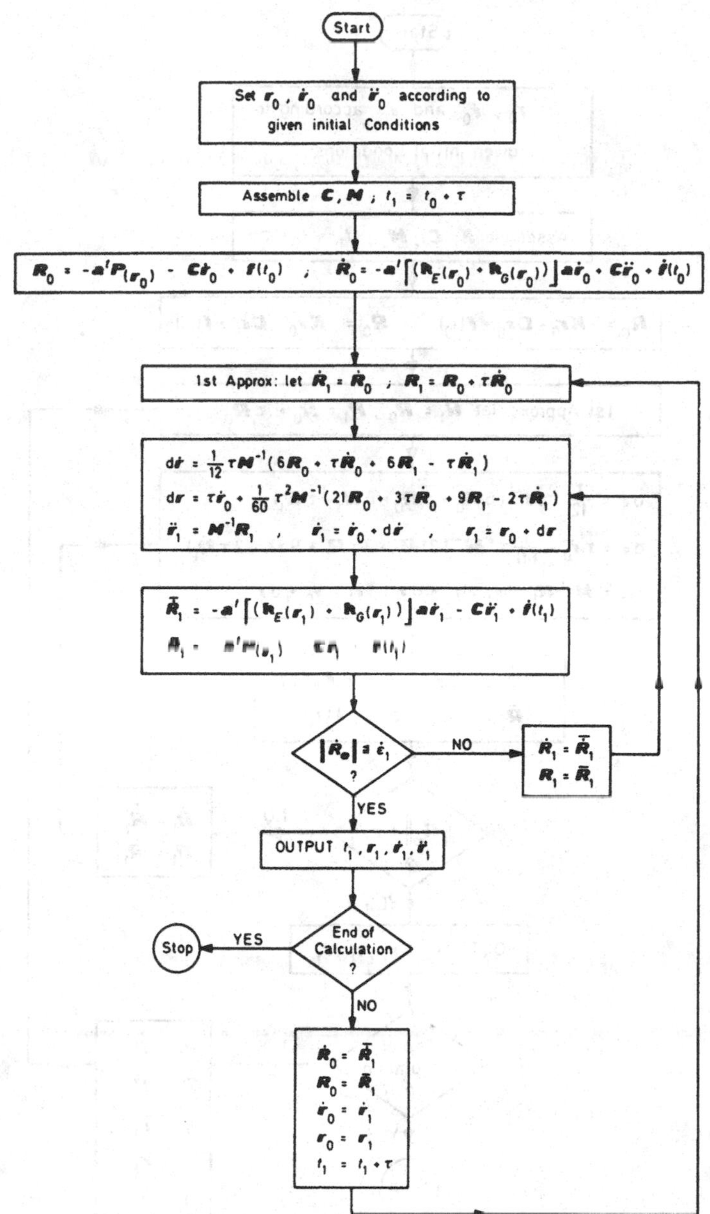

Fig. II – 2 Flow Chart for Non-Linear Oscillations Using Total Displacements

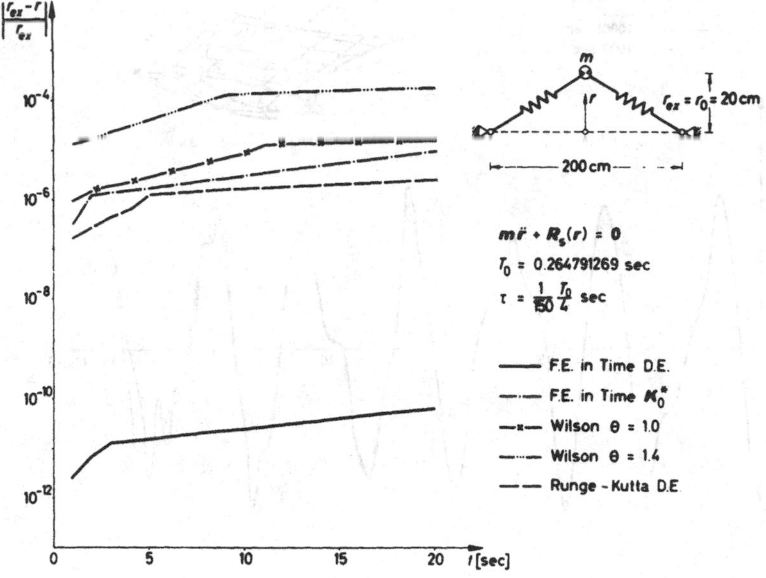

Fig. II - 3 Graph Showing Relative Error in the Displacement During 20 Seconds of Free Oscillation

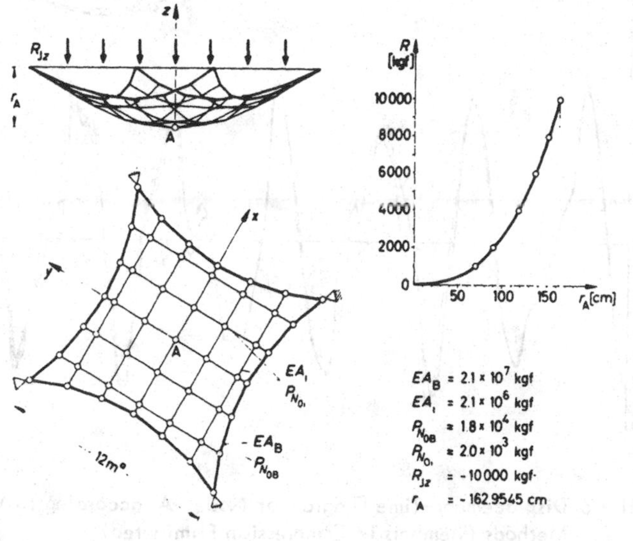

Fig. II - 4 Plane Prestressed Network Loaded Vertically

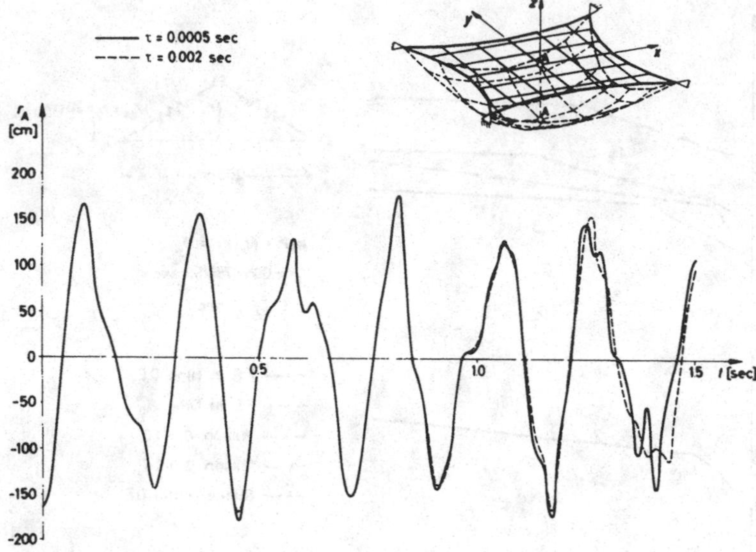

Fig. II – 5 Free Oscillations of Plane Net. Modified Stiffness Matrix with Accumulation (Members in Compression included)

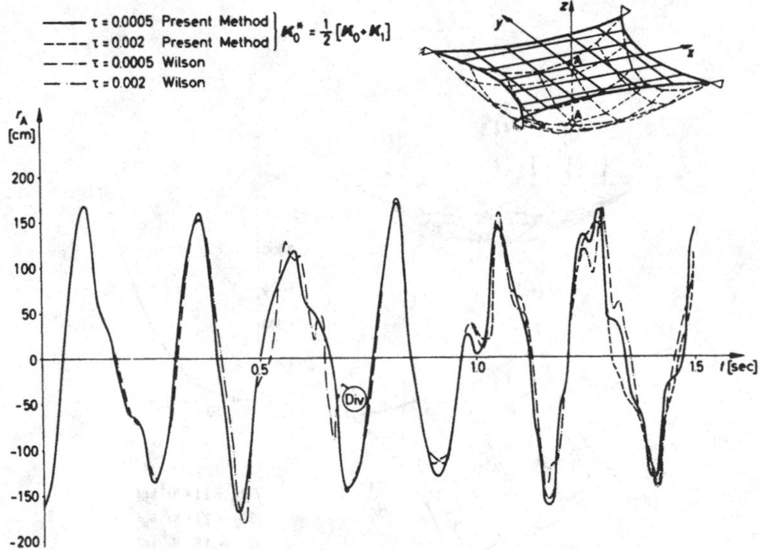

Fig. II – 6 Displacement-Time Diagram of Node A according to Various Methods (Members in Compression Eliminated)

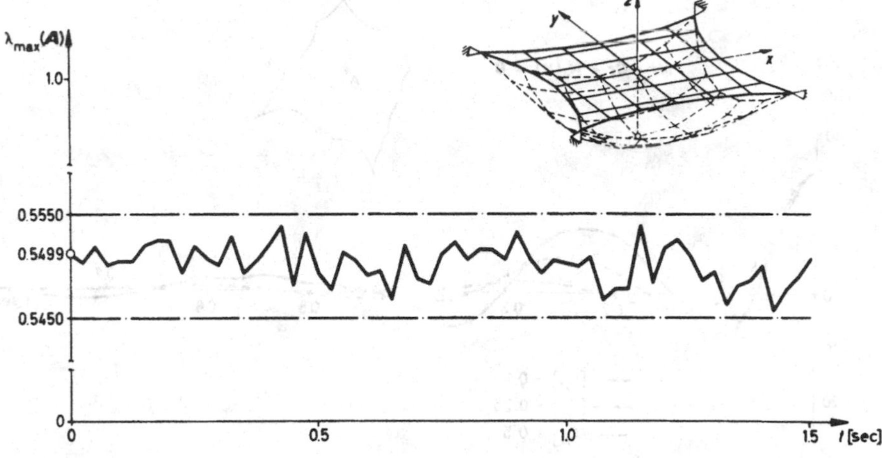

Fig. II - 7 Calculated Maximum Eigenvalue of the Iteration Matrix with Respect to Time

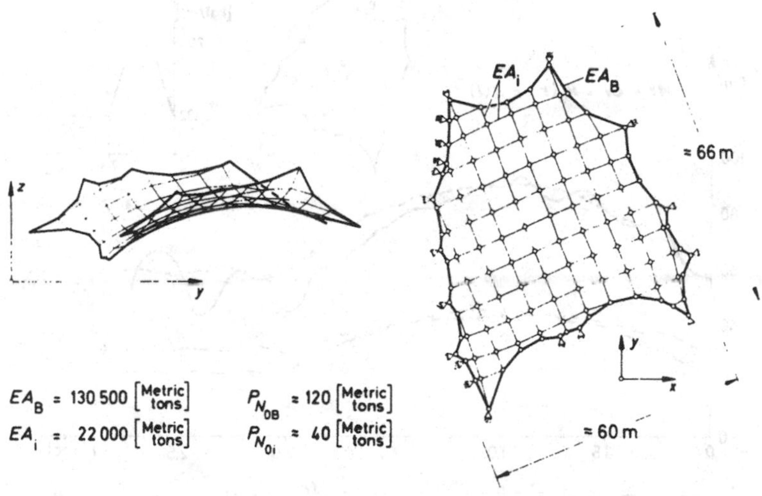

Fig. II - 8 Three-Dimensional Prestressed Network (Eastern Grandstand of the Olympic Stadium in Munich, 288 Unknowns)

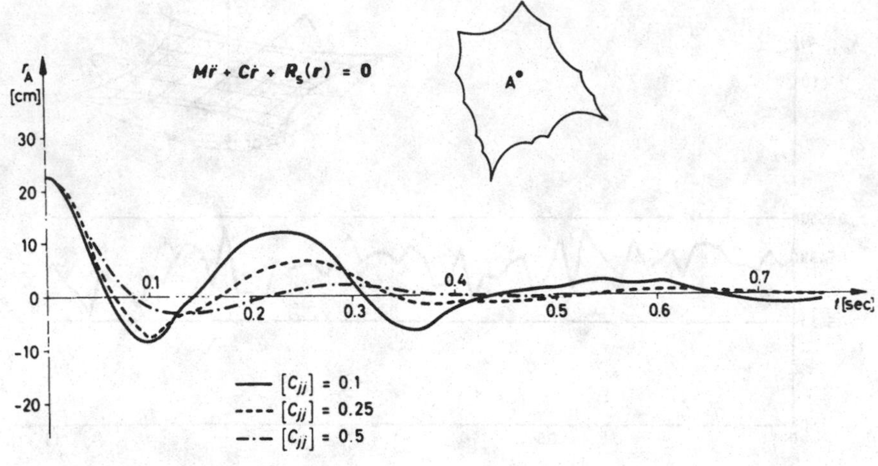

Fig. II - 9 Damped Oscillation of the Node A

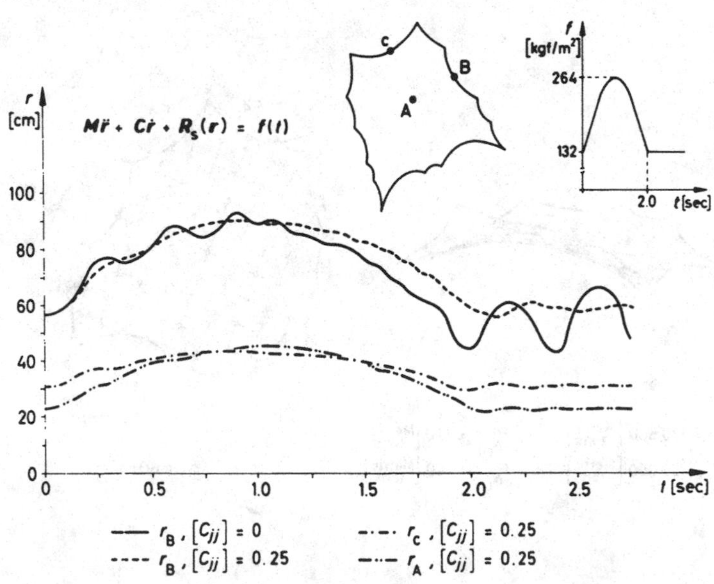

Fig. II - 10 Transient plus Constant Wind Loading on Net with Influence of Damping

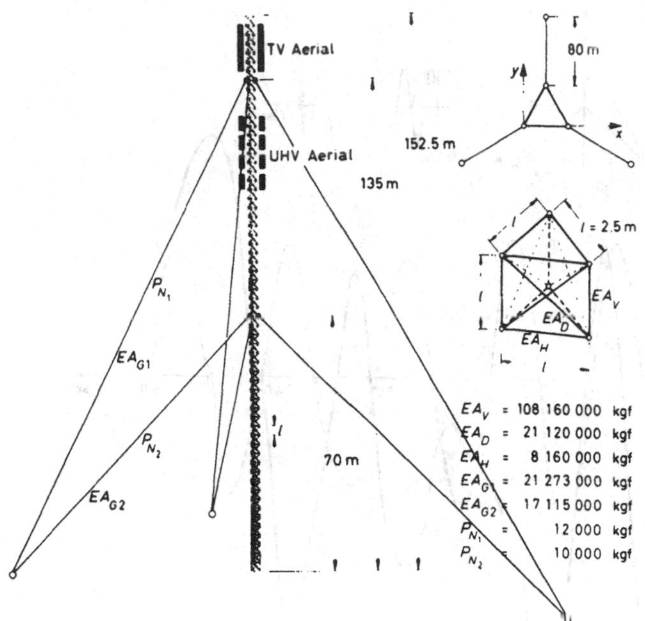

Fig. II - 11 Transmitter Tower (549 - Unknowns)

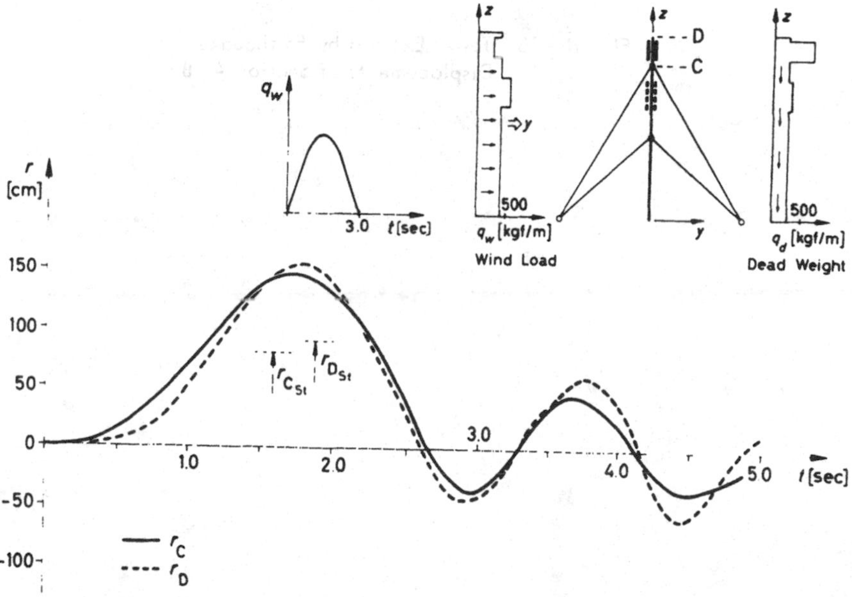

Fig. II - 12 Transient Wind Loading, Displacement of Sections C, D

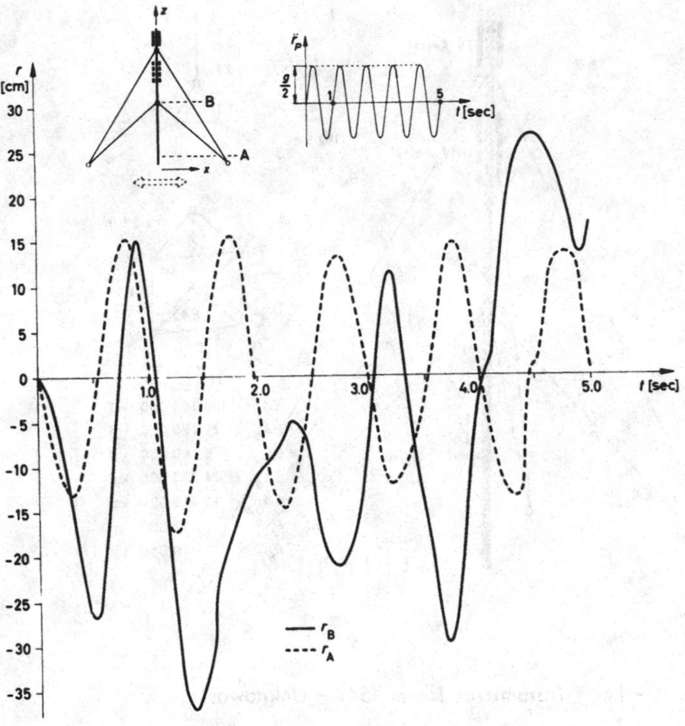

Fig. II - 13 Tower Excited by Earthquake
Displacements of Section A, B

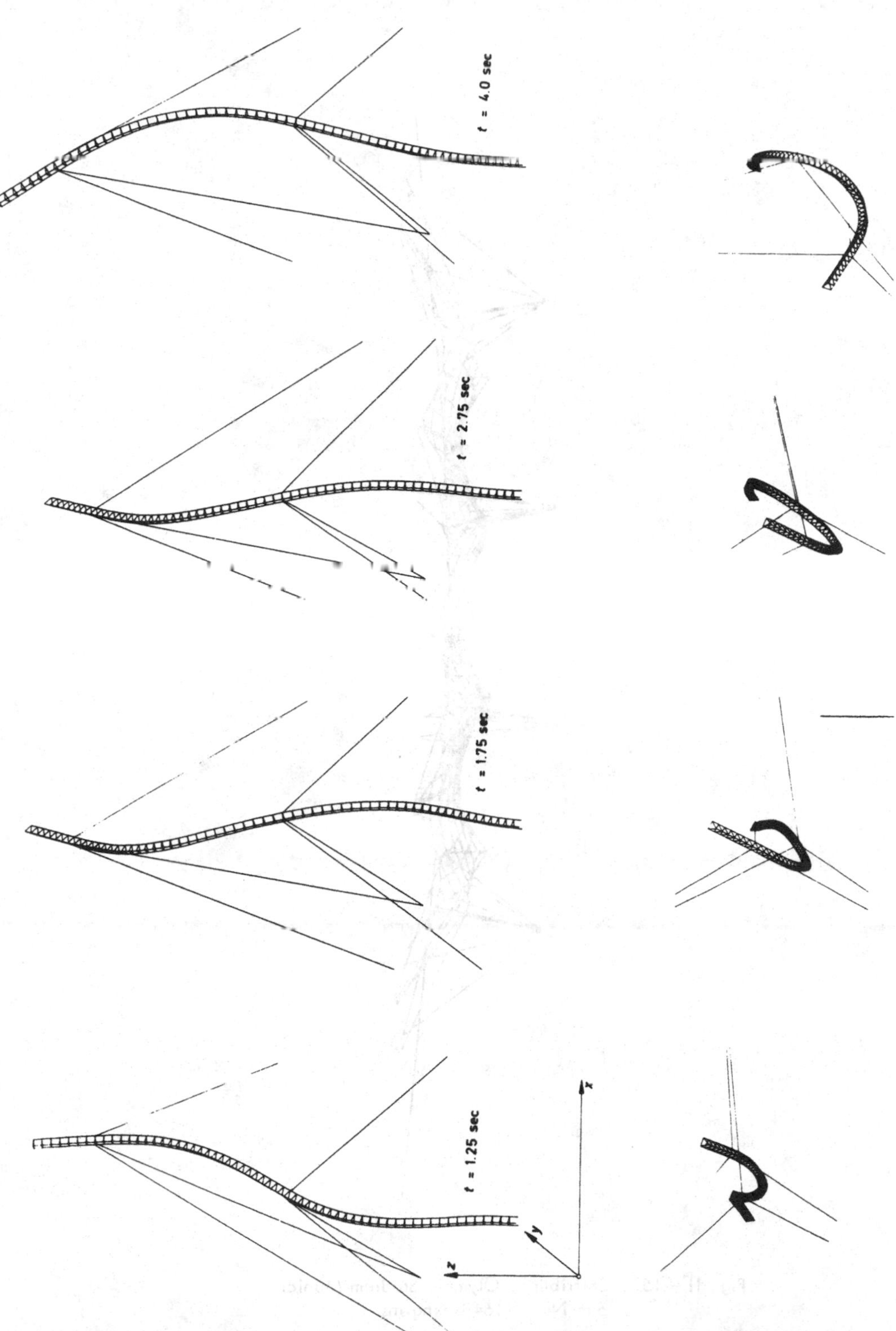

Fig. II - 14 Deformation of the Tower at Various Times During the Earthquake

Fig. II - 15 Osttribüne, Olympic Stadium Munich
6 m Net 1164 Unknowns

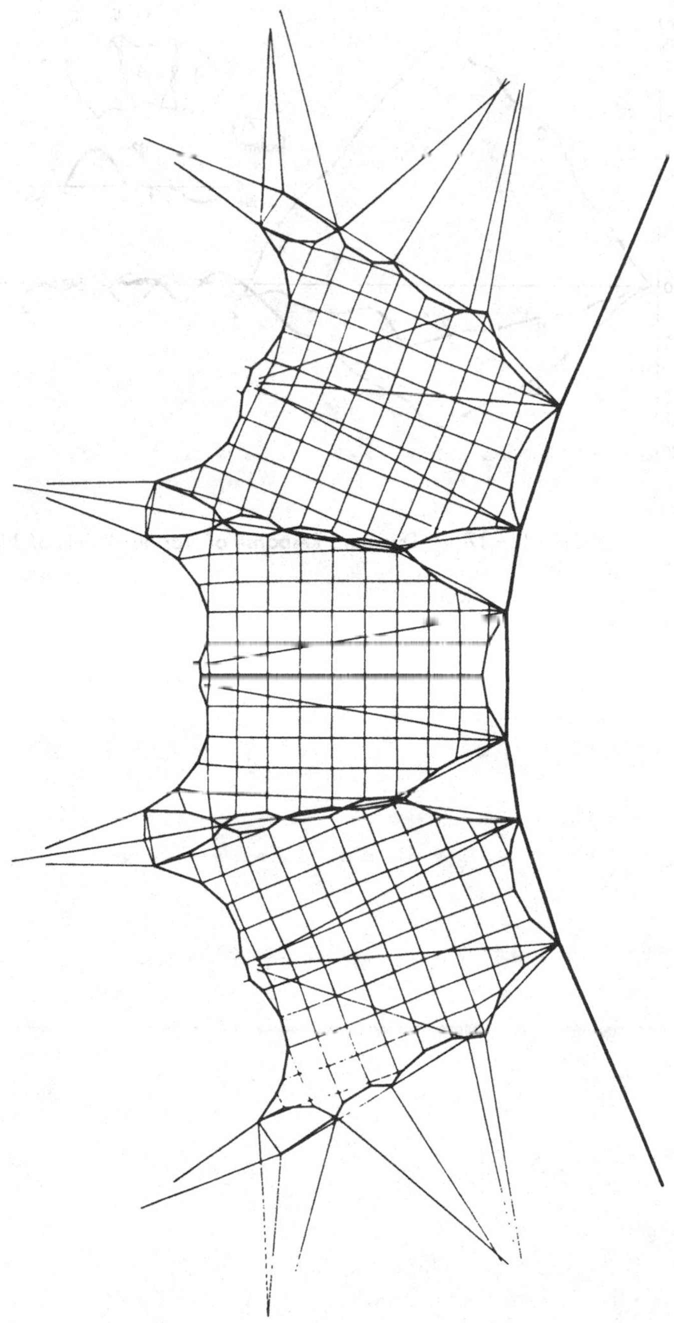

Fig. II - 16 Osttribüne, Olympic Stadium Munich
6 m Net 1164 Unknowns

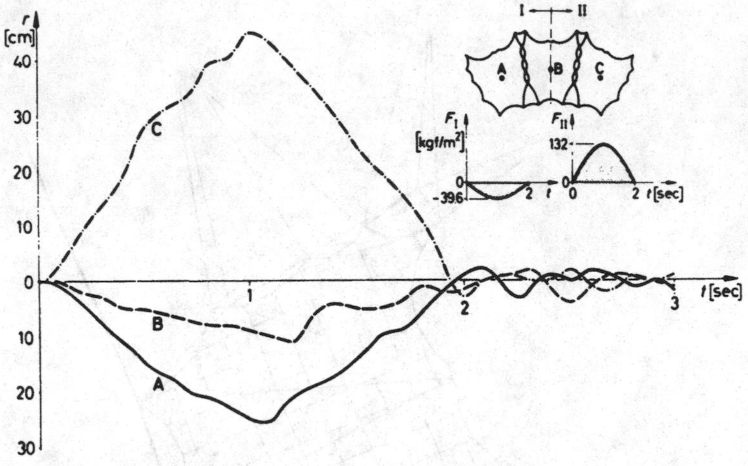

Fig. II - 17 Dynamic Response of Various Points of Net

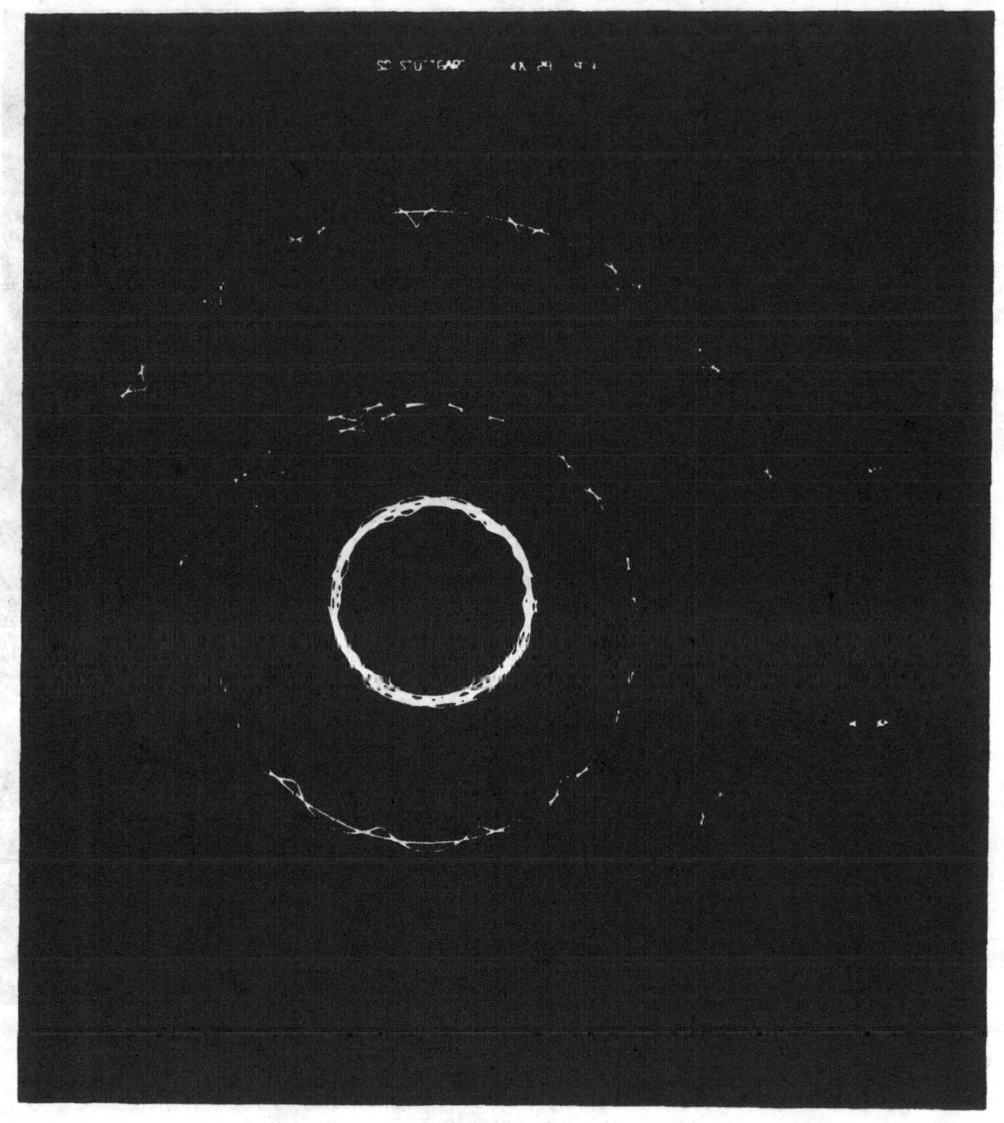

Fig. II-18 Three Planets and Moons - Small Step Algorithm - Hermitian Fifth Degree

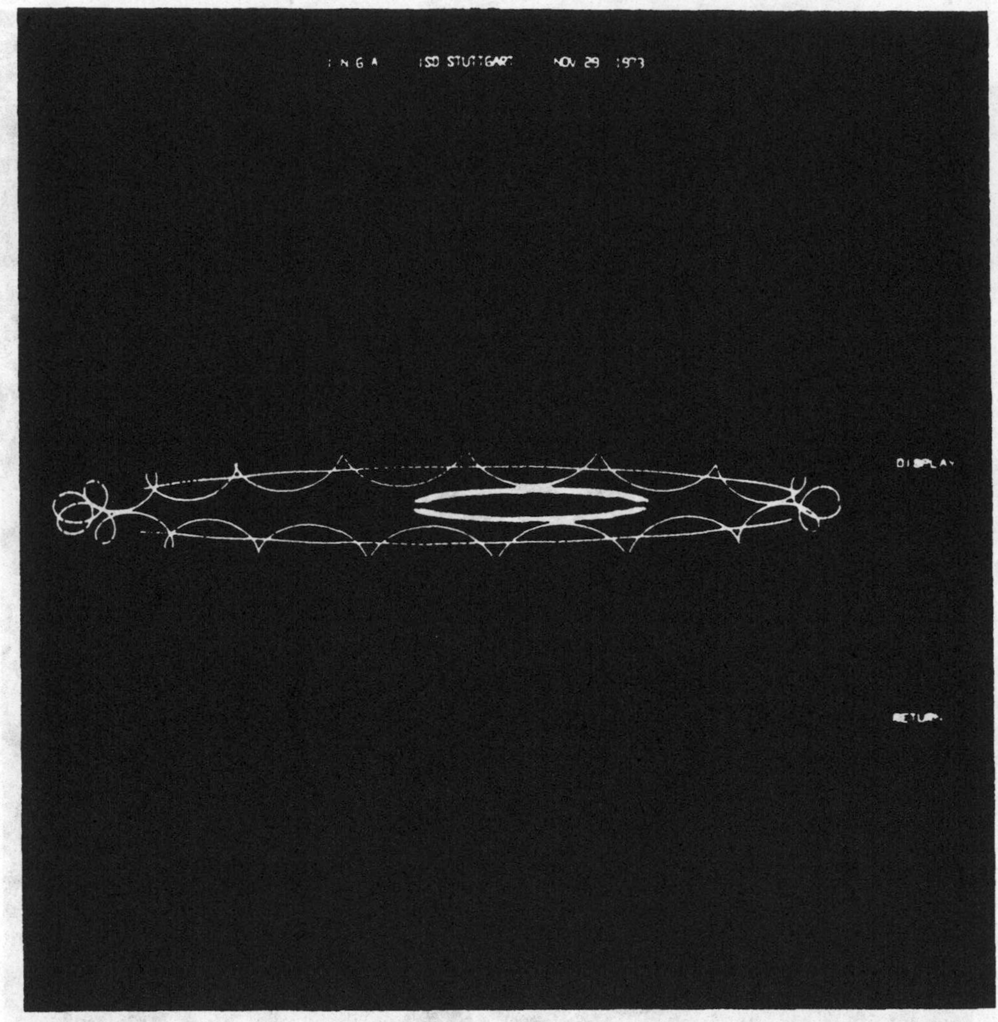

Fig. II - 19 Earth - Moon - Mercury Problem - Small Step Algorithm
Hermitian Fifth Degree

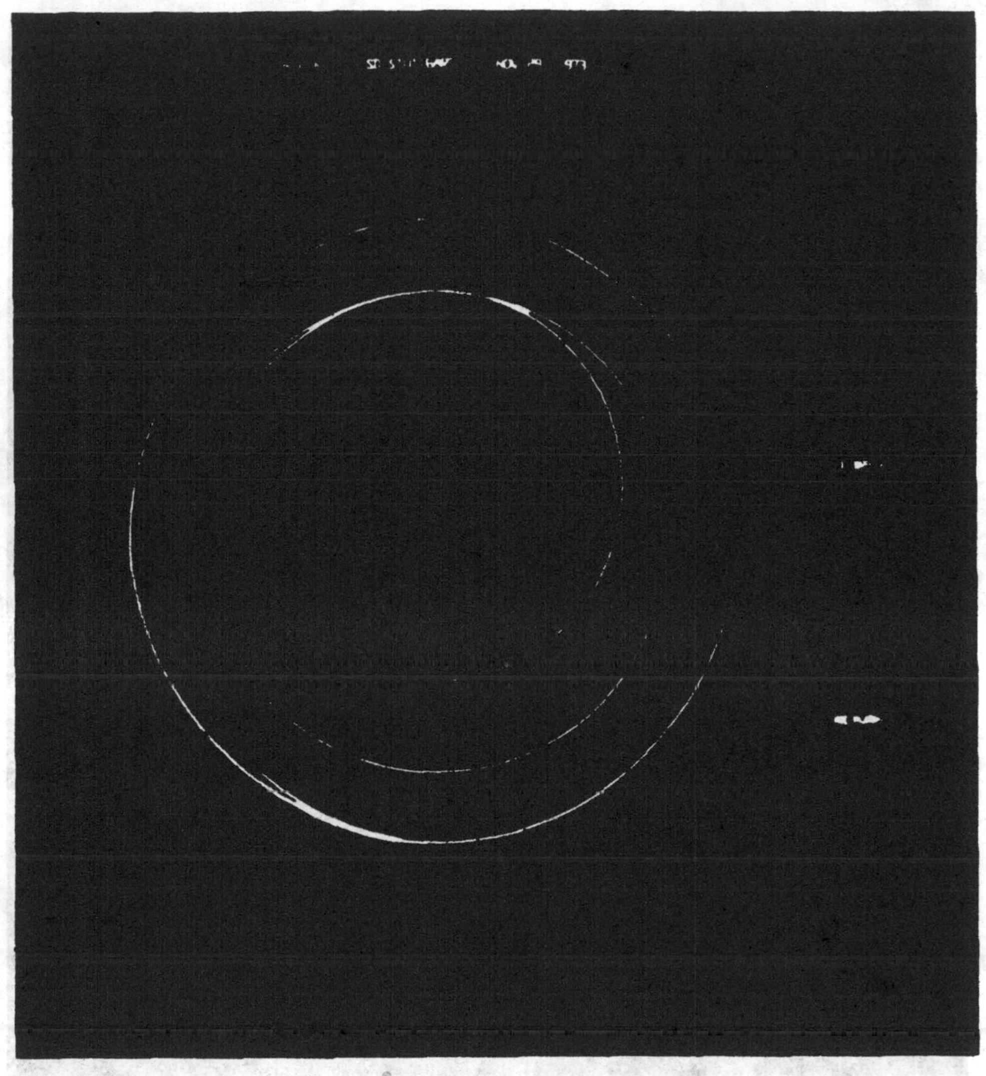

Fig. II - 20   Rendez-vous - Hohmann's Transfer
Small Step Algorithm - Hermitian Fifth Degree

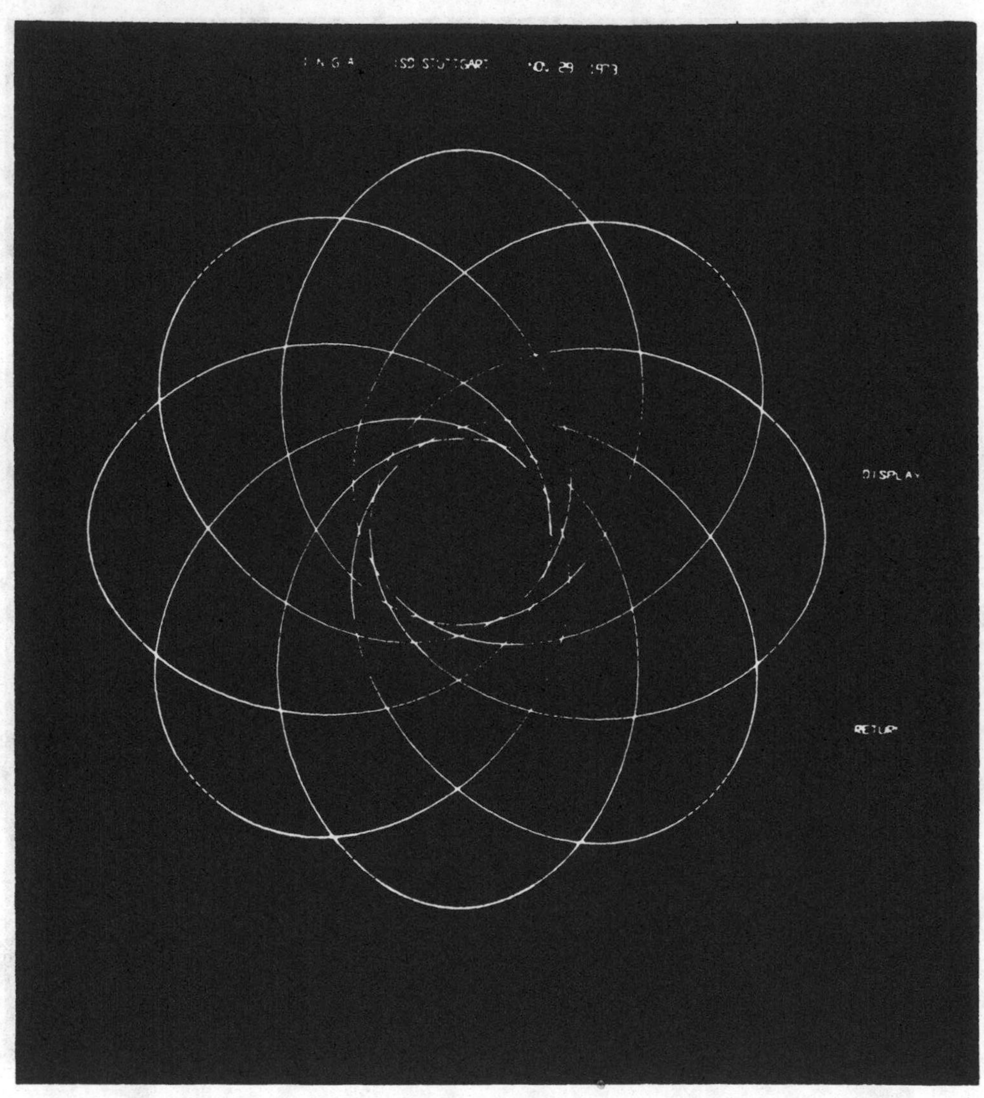

Fig. II - 21 Eight - Body Problem - Small Step Algorithm - Hermitian Fifth Degree

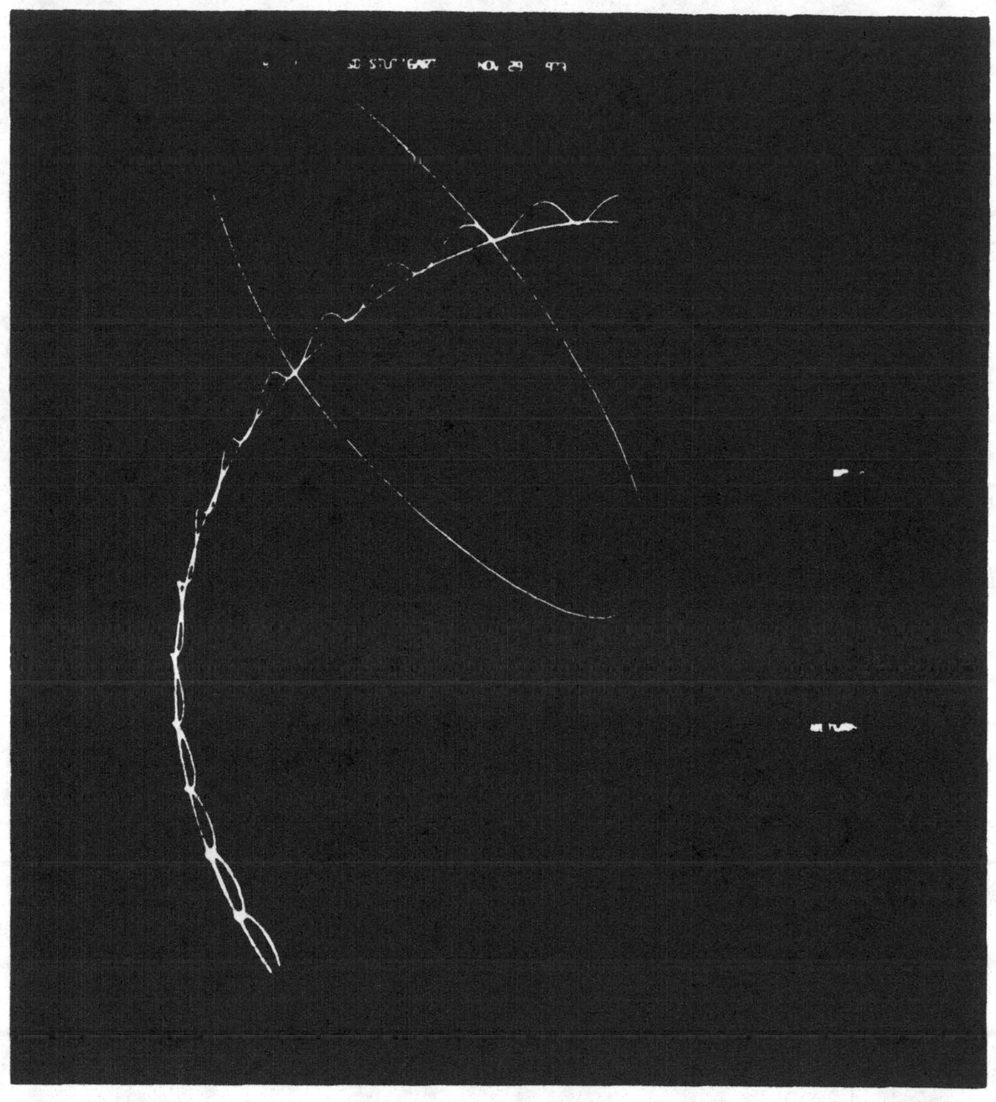

Fig. II - 22 Comet Passing Earth and Sun - Small Step Algorithm - Hermitian Fifth Degree

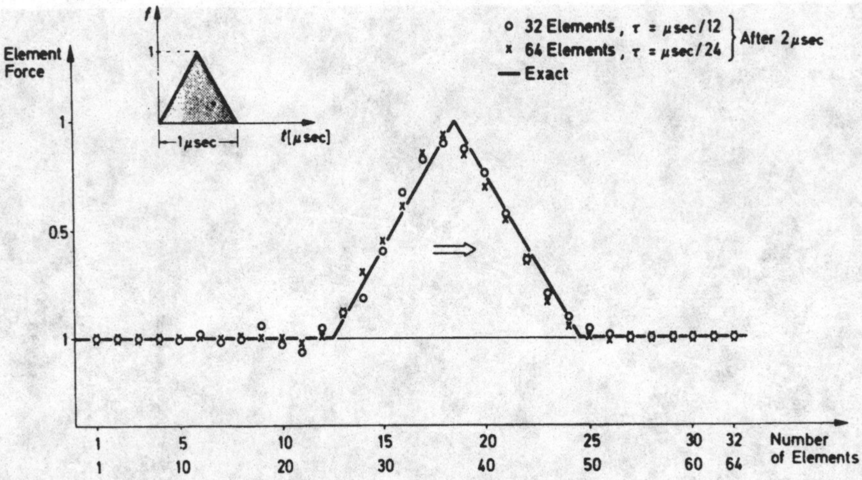

Fig. II - 23 Triangular Pulse Through Elastic Slab

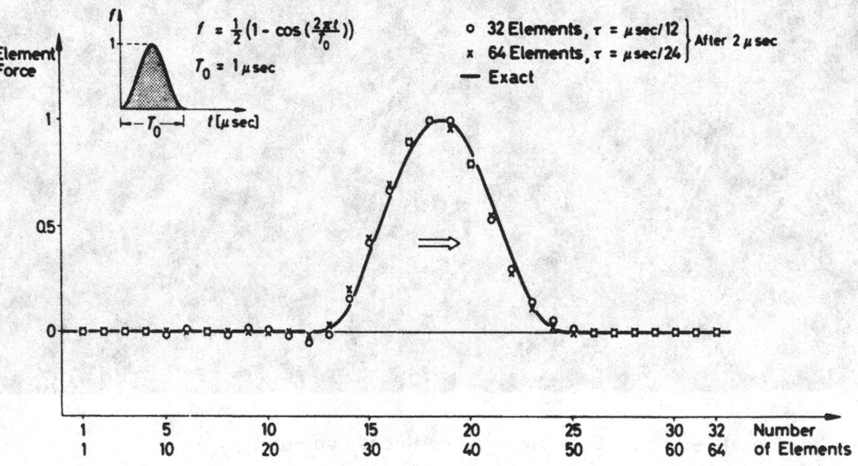

Fig. II - 24 Cosine Pulse through Elastic Slab

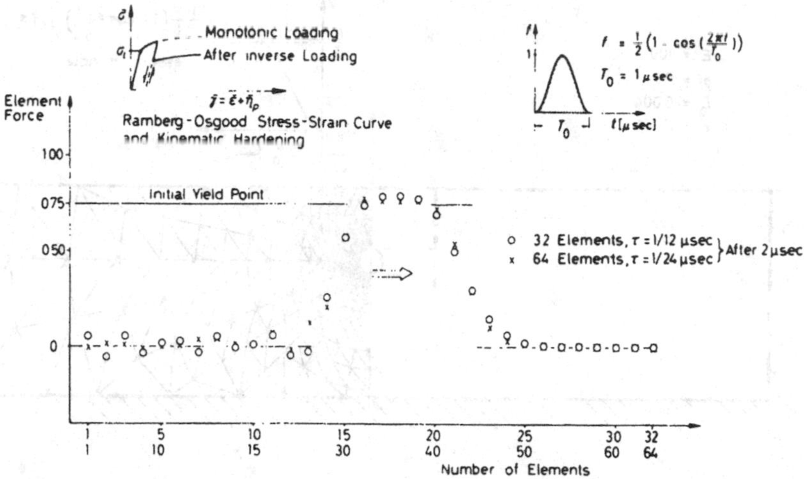

Fig. II.25 Propagation of Cosine Pulse in Elastoplastic Free-Free Slab
Comparison for Different Idealisations in Time and Space

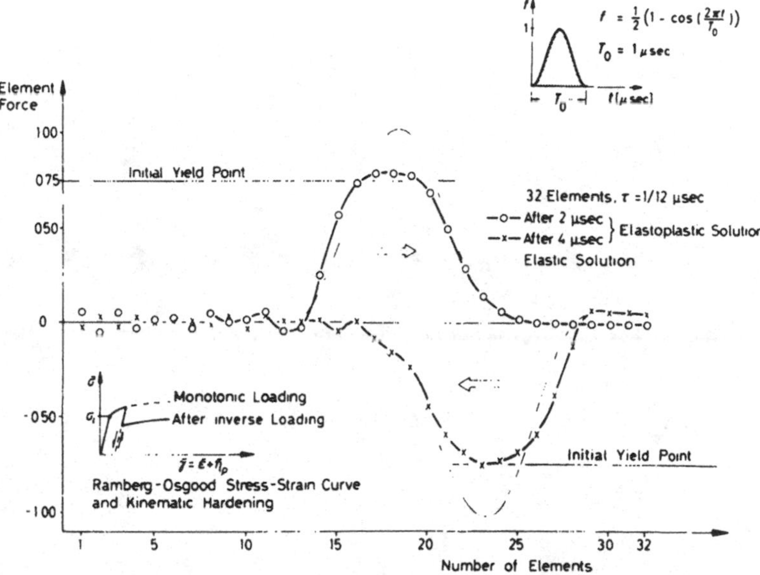

Fig. II.26 Propagation of Cosine Pulse in Elastoplastic Free-Free Slab

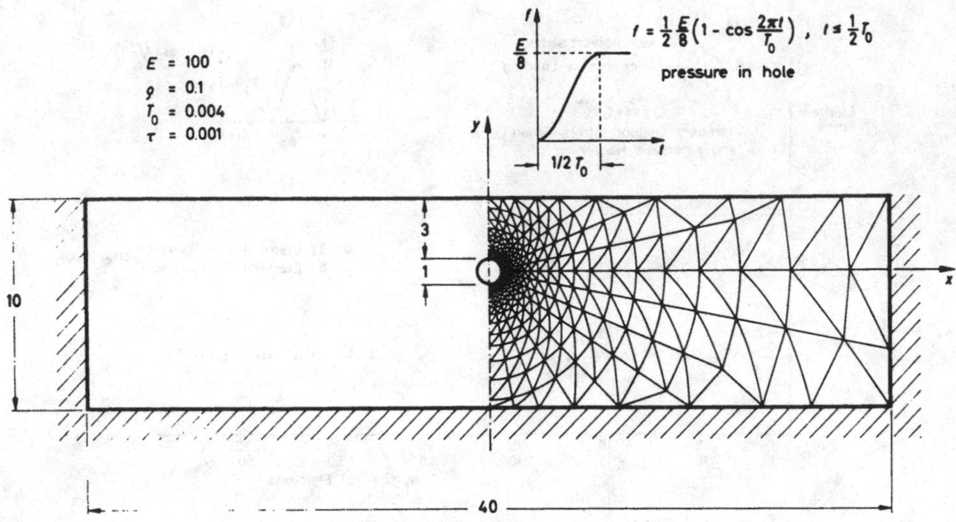

Fig. II-27 Underground Explosion with Large Strain
Simplified Material with Quadratic Green Strain Energy

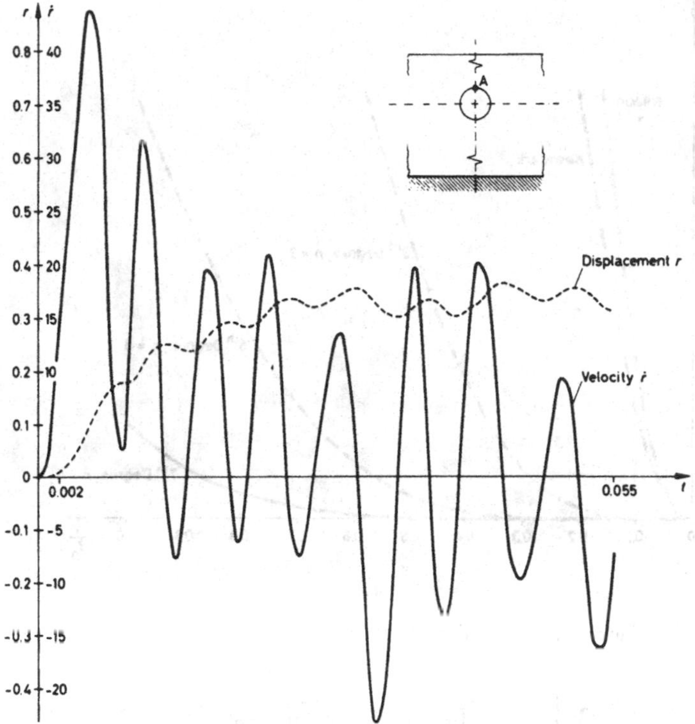

Fig. II-28 Displacement and Velocity of Point A up to 55 Time Steps τ

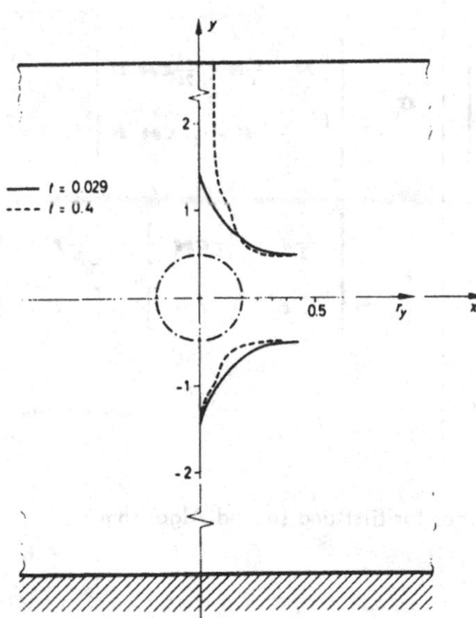

Fig. II-29 Underground Explosion with Green Strain Energy
Displacement of Points along Axis of Symmetry at $t = 0.029$ and 0.4

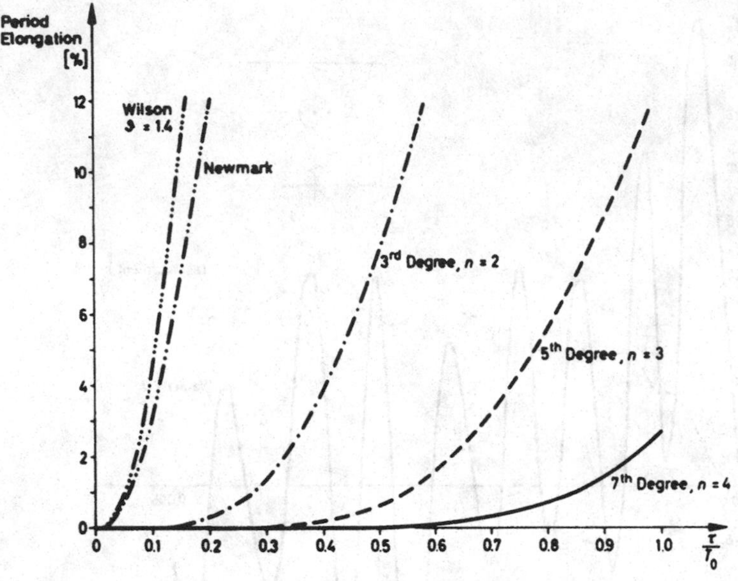

Fig. II - 34 Percentage Period Elongation

$$\boldsymbol{D}_1 = \begin{bmatrix} \left[\boldsymbol{M} + \frac{\tau^2}{4}\boldsymbol{K}\right] & \frac{\tau^2}{4}\boldsymbol{C} \\ \frac{\tau}{2}\boldsymbol{K} & \left[\boldsymbol{M} + \frac{\tau}{2}\boldsymbol{C}\right] \end{bmatrix}$$

$$\boldsymbol{D}_0 = \begin{bmatrix} \left[\boldsymbol{M} - \frac{\tau^2}{4}\boldsymbol{K}\right] & \left[\tau\boldsymbol{M} - \frac{\tau^2}{4}\boldsymbol{C}\right] \\ -\frac{\tau}{2}\boldsymbol{K} & \left[\boldsymbol{M} - \frac{\tau}{2}\boldsymbol{C}\right] \end{bmatrix}$$

$$\boldsymbol{F} = \begin{bmatrix} \frac{\tau^2}{4}\left[\boldsymbol{f}_0 + \boldsymbol{f}_1\right] \\ \frac{\tau}{2}\left[\boldsymbol{f}_0 + \boldsymbol{f}_1\right] \end{bmatrix}$$

$n = 1$, 2nd Order Hermitian Polynomial of 1st Degree (Newmark Algorithm)

$$\boldsymbol{D}_1 = \begin{bmatrix} \left[\boldsymbol{M} + \frac{\tau^2}{6}\boldsymbol{K} + \frac{\tau^3}{24}\boldsymbol{C}\boldsymbol{M}^{-1}\boldsymbol{K}\right] & \left[\frac{\tau^2}{6}\boldsymbol{C} - \frac{\tau^3}{24}\left(\boldsymbol{K} - \boldsymbol{C}\boldsymbol{M}^{-1}\boldsymbol{C}\right) \right. \\ \left[\frac{\tau}{2}\boldsymbol{K} + \frac{\tau^2}{12}\boldsymbol{C}\boldsymbol{M}^{-1}\boldsymbol{K}\right] & \left[\boldsymbol{M} + \frac{\tau}{2}\boldsymbol{C} - \frac{\tau^2}{12}\left(\boldsymbol{K} - \boldsymbol{C}\boldsymbol{M}^{-1}\boldsymbol{C}\right) \right. \end{bmatrix}$$

$$\boldsymbol{D}_0 = \begin{bmatrix} \left[\boldsymbol{M} - \frac{\tau^2}{3}\boldsymbol{K} + \frac{\tau^3}{24}\boldsymbol{C}\boldsymbol{M}^{-1}\boldsymbol{K}\right] & \left[\tau\boldsymbol{M} - \frac{\tau^2}{3}\boldsymbol{C} - \frac{\tau^3}{24}\left(\boldsymbol{K} - \boldsymbol{C}\boldsymbol{M}^{-1}\boldsymbol{C}\right) \right. \\ \left[-\frac{\tau}{2}\boldsymbol{K} + \frac{\tau^2}{12}\boldsymbol{C}\boldsymbol{M}^{-1}\boldsymbol{K}\right] & \left[\boldsymbol{M} - \frac{\tau}{2}\boldsymbol{C} - \frac{\tau^2}{12}\left(\boldsymbol{K} - \boldsymbol{C}\boldsymbol{M}^{-1}\boldsymbol{C}\right) \right. \end{bmatrix}$$

$$\boldsymbol{F} = \begin{bmatrix} \left[\frac{\tau^2}{3}\boldsymbol{I} - \frac{\tau^3}{24}\boldsymbol{C}\boldsymbol{M}^{-1}\right] & \left[\frac{\tau^2}{6}\boldsymbol{I} + \frac{\tau^3}{24}\boldsymbol{C}\boldsymbol{M}^{-1}\right] \\ \left[\frac{\tau}{2}\boldsymbol{I} - \frac{\tau^2}{12}\boldsymbol{C}\boldsymbol{M}^{-1}\right] & \left[\frac{\tau}{2}\boldsymbol{I} + \frac{\tau^2}{12}\boldsymbol{C}\boldsymbol{M}^{-1}\right] \end{bmatrix} \begin{bmatrix} \boldsymbol{f}_0 \\ \boldsymbol{f}_1 \end{bmatrix} + \begin{bmatrix} \frac{\tau^3}{24}\left(\dot{\boldsymbol{f}}_0 - \dot{\boldsymbol{f}}_1 \right. \\ \frac{\tau^2}{12}\left(\dot{\boldsymbol{f}}_0 - \dot{\boldsymbol{f}}_1 \right. \end{bmatrix}$$

$n = 2$, 4th Order Hermitian Polynomial of 3rd Degree

Fig. II - 35 Matrices for first and second Algorithm

$$D_1 = \begin{bmatrix} \left[M + \frac{3}{20}\tau^2 K + \frac{\tau^3}{24} CM^{-1}K - \frac{\tau^4}{240}\left(KM^{-1} - (CM^{-1})^2\right)K \right] & \left[\frac{3}{20}\tau^2 C - \frac{\tau^3}{24}\left(K - CM^{-1}C\right) - \frac{\tau^4}{240} KM^{-1}C \right] \\ \left[\frac{\tau}{2} K + \frac{\tau^2}{10} CM^{-1}K - \frac{\tau^3}{120}\left(KM^{-1} - (CM^{-1})^2\right)K \right] & \left[M + \frac{\tau}{2} C - \frac{\tau^2}{10}\left(K - CM^{-1}C\right) - \frac{\tau^3}{120}\left(CM^{-1}K + (KM^{-1} - (CM^{-1})^2)C\right) \right] \end{bmatrix}$$

$$D_2 = \begin{bmatrix} \left[M - \frac{7}{20}\tau^2 K + \frac{7}{120}\tau^3 CM^{-1}K + \frac{\tau^4}{240}\left(KM^{-1} - (CM^{-1})^2\right)K \right] & \left[\tau M - \frac{7}{20}\tau^2 C - \frac{7}{120}\tau^3\left(K - CM^{-1}C\right) + \frac{\tau^4}{240} KM^{-1}C \right] \\ \left[-\frac{\tau}{2} K + \frac{\tau^2}{10} CM^{-1}K + \frac{\tau^3}{120}\left(KM^{-1} - (CM^{-1})^2\right)K \right] & \left[M - \frac{\tau}{2} C - \frac{\tau^2}{10}\left(K - CM^{-1}C\right) + \frac{\tau^3}{120}\left(CM^{-1}K + (KM^{-1} - (CM^{-1})^2)C\right) \right] \end{bmatrix}$$

$$F = \begin{bmatrix} \left[\frac{7}{20}\tau^2 I - \frac{7}{120}\tau^3 CM^{-1} - \frac{\tau^4}{240}\left(KM^{-1} - (CM^{-1})^2\right) \right] & \left[\frac{3}{20}\tau^2 I + \frac{\tau^3}{24} CM^{-1} - \frac{\tau^4}{240}\left(KM^{-1} - (CM^{-1})^2\right) \right] \\ \left[\frac{\tau}{2} I - \frac{\tau^2}{10} CM^{-1} - \frac{\tau^3}{120}\left(KM^{-1} - (CM^{-1})^2\right) \right] & \left[\frac{\tau}{2} I + \frac{\tau^2}{10} CM^{-1} - \frac{\tau^3}{120}\left(KM^{-1} - (CM^{-1})^2\right) \right] \end{bmatrix} \begin{bmatrix} f_2 \\ f_1 \end{bmatrix} + \begin{bmatrix} \left[\frac{7}{120}\tau^3 I - \frac{\tau^4}{240} CM^{-1} \right] & \left[-\frac{\tau^3}{24} I - \frac{\tau^4}{240} CM^{-1} \right] \\ \left[\frac{\tau^2}{10} I - \frac{\tau^3}{120} CM^{-1} \right] & \left[-\frac{\tau^2}{10} I - \frac{\tau^3}{120} CM^{-1} \right] \end{bmatrix} \begin{bmatrix} f_2 \\ f_1 \end{bmatrix} + \begin{bmatrix} \frac{\tau^4}{240}\left(f_2 + f_1\right) \\ \frac{\tau^3}{120}\left(f_2 + f_1\right) \end{bmatrix}$$

Fig. II - 36 Matrices for Third Algorithm of Family

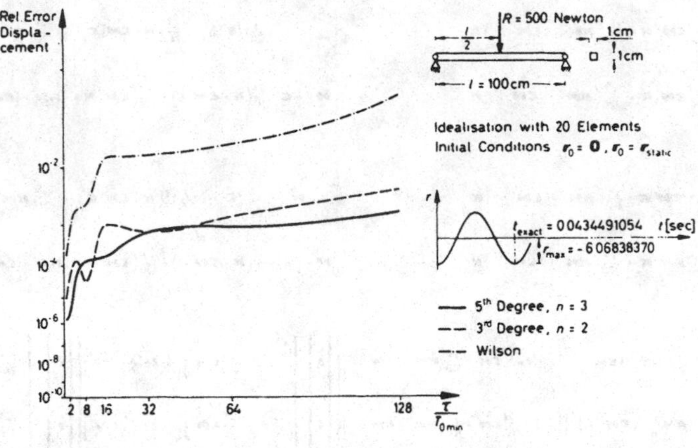

Fig. II - 37 Free Oscillation of Beam

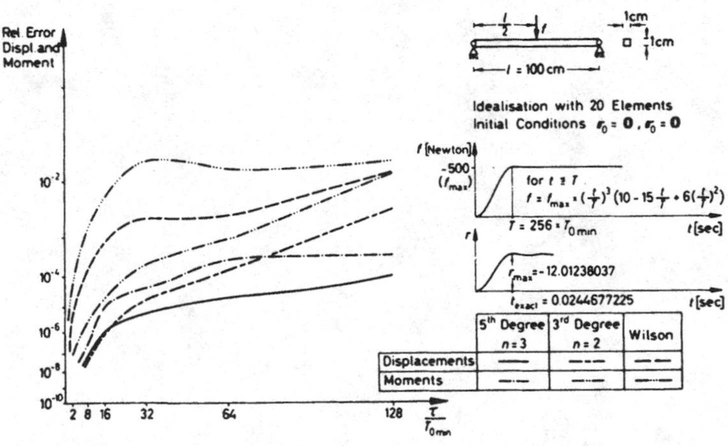

Fig. II - 38 Forced Oscillation of Beam

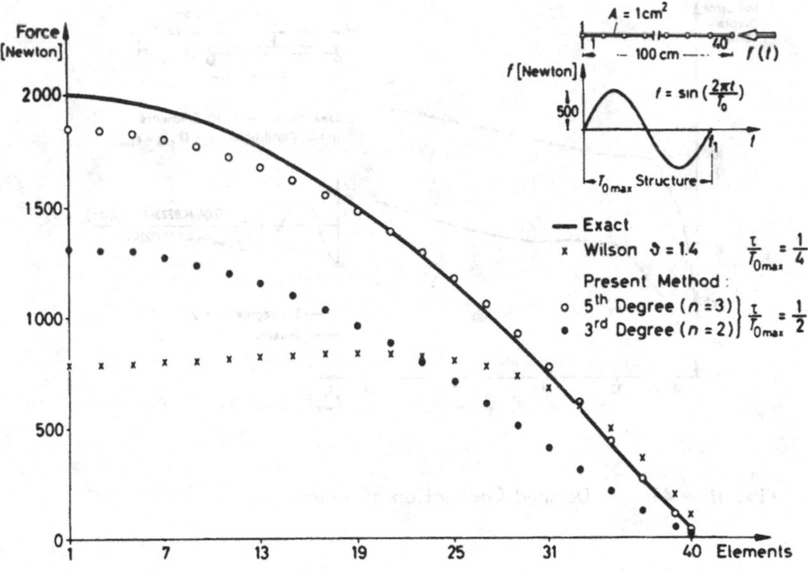

Fig. II - 39 Force Along Length of Bar at $t_1 = T_{0\ max}$

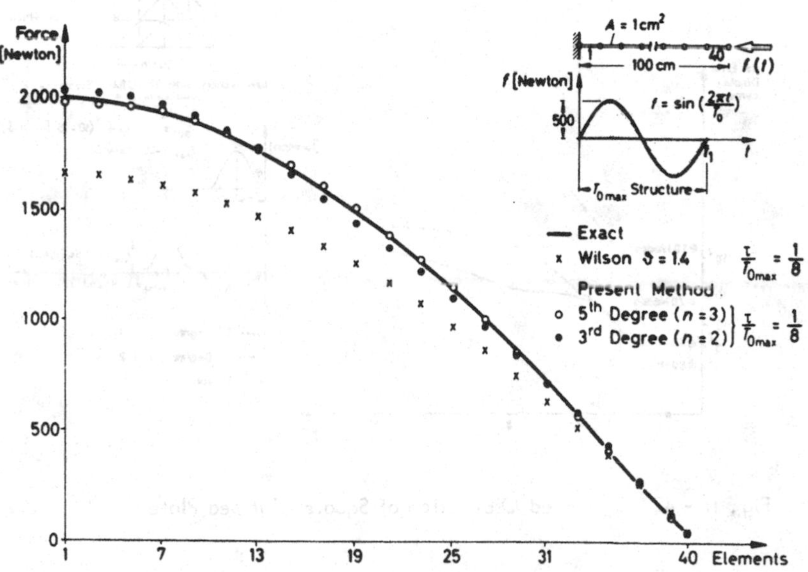

Fig. II - 40 Force Along Length of Bar at $t_1 = T_{0\ max}$

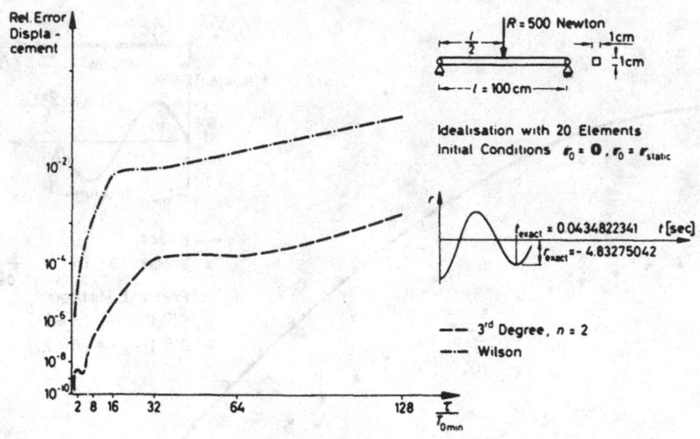

Fig. II - 41 Damped Oscillation of Beam

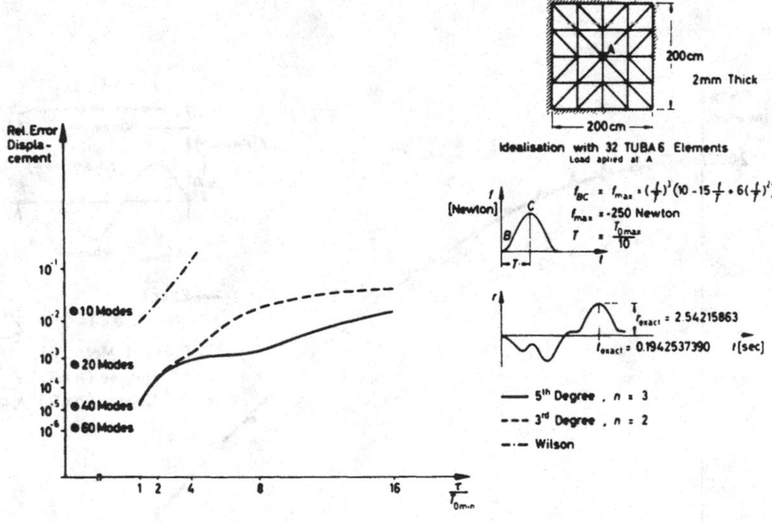

Fig. II - 42 Forced Oscillation of Square Clamped Plate

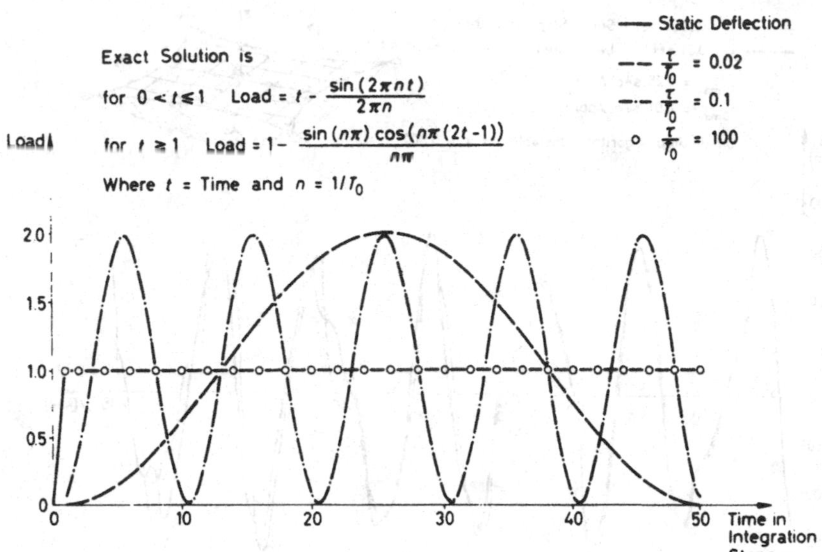

Fig. II 43 Pseudo Indicial Admittance for Unconditionally Stable Algorithm n = 2

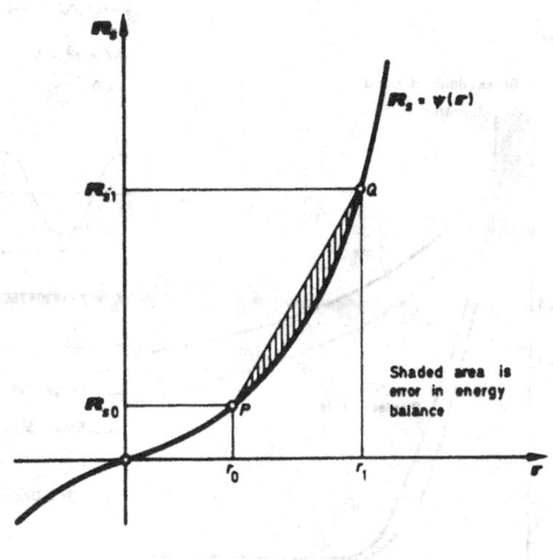

Fig. II - 44 Newmark Algorithm Applied to Non-Linear Oscillator

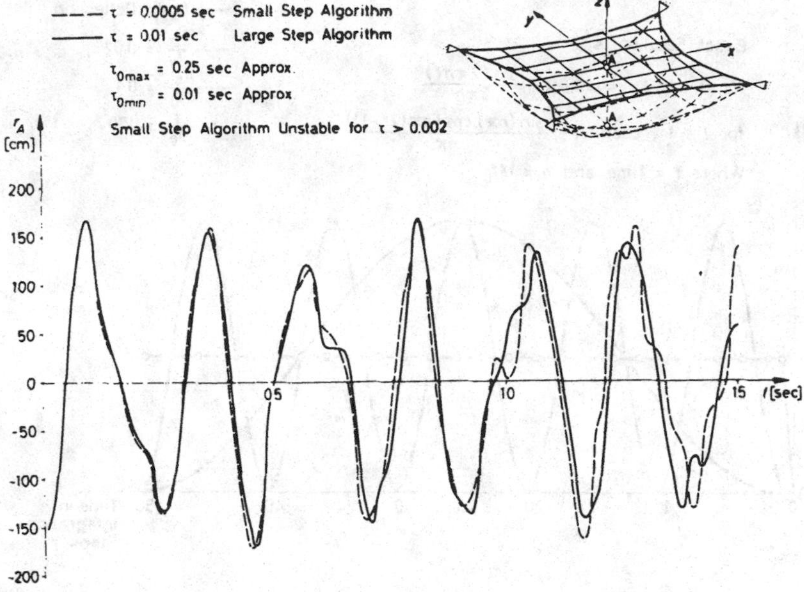

Fig. II-45 Free Oscillations of Plane Net - Small Step and Large Step Algorithms

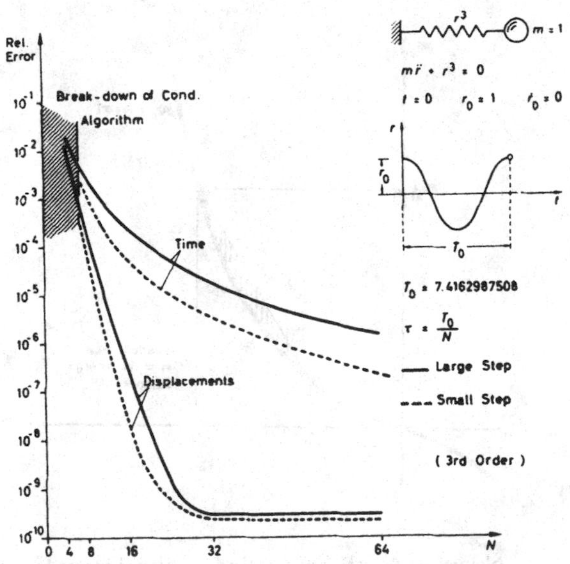

Fig. II-46 Simple Cubic Oscillator
Free Vibration, Non-linear Large and Small Step Algorithms
Error in Maximum Displacement and Time after One Period

		Coefficients of $M^{-1}x$							
n		R_0	R_1	$\dot{R}_0$	$\dot{R}_1$	$\ddot{R}_0$	$\ddot{R}_1$	$\dddot{R}_0$	$\dddot{R}_1$
1	$\dot{r}_1 = \dot{r}_0 +$	$\frac{1}{2}\tau$	$\frac{1}{2}\tau$						
	$r_1 = r_0 + \tau\dot{r}_0 +$	$\frac{1}{3}\tau^2$	$\frac{1}{6}\tau^2$						
2	$\dot{r}_1 = \dot{r}_0 +$	$\frac{1}{2}\tau$	$\frac{1}{2}\tau$	$\frac{1}{12}\tau^2$	$-\frac{1}{12}\tau^2$				
	$r_1 = r_0 + \tau\dot{r}_0 +$	$\frac{7}{20}\tau^2$	$\frac{3}{20}\tau^2$	$\frac{1}{20}\tau^3$	$-\frac{1}{30}\tau^3$				
3	$\dot{r}_1 = \dot{r}_0 +$	$\frac{1}{2}\tau$	$\frac{1}{2}\tau$	$\frac{1}{10}\tau^2$	$-\frac{1}{10}\tau^2$	$\frac{1}{120}\tau^3$	$\frac{1}{120}\tau^3$		
	$r_1 = r_0 + \tau\dot{r}_0 +$	$\frac{5}{14}\tau^2$	$\frac{1}{7}\tau^2$	$\frac{13}{210}\tau^3$	$-\frac{4}{105}\tau^3$	$\frac{1}{210}\tau^4$	$\frac{1}{280}\tau^4$		
4	$\dot{r}_1 = \dot{r}_0 +$	$\frac{1}{2}\tau$	$\frac{1}{2}\tau$	$\frac{3}{28}\tau^2$	$-\frac{3}{28}\tau^2$	$\frac{1}{84}\tau^3$	$\frac{1}{84}\tau^3$	$\frac{1}{1680}\tau^4$	$-\frac{1}{1680}\tau^4$
	$r_1 = r_0 + \tau\dot{r}_0 +$	$\frac{13}{36}\tau^2$	$\frac{5}{36}\tau^2$	$\frac{17}{252}\tau^3$	$-\frac{5}{126}\tau^3$	$\frac{1}{144}\tau^4$	$\frac{5}{1008}\tau^4$	$\frac{1}{3024}\tau^5$	$-\frac{1}{3780}\tau^5$

Table II - I - Family of Conditionally Stable Algorithms

n		Coefficients of $M^{-1}x$							
		R_0	R_1	$\dot{R}_0$	$\dot{R}_1$	$\ddot{R}_0$	$\ddot{R}_1$	$\dddot{R}_0$	$\dddot{R}_1$
1	$\dot{r}_1 = \dot{r}_0 +$	$\frac{1}{2}\tau$	$\frac{1}{2}\tau$						
	$r_1 = r_0 + \tau\dot{r}_0 +$	$\frac{1}{4}\tau^2$	$\frac{1}{4}\tau^2$						
2	$\dot{r}_1 = \dot{r}_0 +$	$\frac{1}{2}\tau$	$\frac{1}{2}\tau$	$\frac{1}{12}\tau^2$	$-\frac{1}{12}\tau^2$				
	$r_1 = r_0 + \tau\dot{r}_0 +$	$\frac{1}{3}\tau^2$	$\frac{1}{6}\tau^2$	$\frac{1}{24}\tau^3$	$-\frac{1}{24}\tau^3$				
3	$\dot{r}_1 = \dot{r}_0 +$	$\frac{1}{2}\tau$	$\frac{1}{2}\tau$	$\frac{1}{10}\tau^2$	$-\frac{1}{10}\tau^2$	$\frac{1}{120}\tau^3$	$\frac{1}{120}\tau^3$		
	$r_1 = r_0 + \tau\dot{r}_0 +$	$\frac{7}{20}\tau^2$	$\frac{3}{20}\tau^2$	$\frac{7}{120}\tau^3$	$-\frac{1}{24}\tau^3$	$\frac{1}{240}\tau^4$	$\frac{1}{240}\tau^4$		
4	$\dot{r}_1 = \dot{r}_0 +$	$\frac{1}{2}\tau$	$\frac{1}{2}\tau$	$\frac{3}{28}\tau^2$	$-\frac{3}{28}\tau^2$	$\frac{1}{84}\tau^3$	$\frac{1}{84}\tau^3$	$\frac{1}{1680}\tau^4$	$-\frac{1}{1680}\tau^4$
	$r_1 = r_0 + \tau\dot{r}_0 +$	$\frac{5}{14}\tau^2$	$\frac{1}{7}\tau^2$	$\frac{11}{168}\tau^3$	$-\frac{1}{24}\tau^3$	$\frac{11}{1680}\tau^4$	$\frac{3}{560}\tau^4$	$\frac{1}{3600}\tau^5$	$-\frac{1}{3600}\tau^5$

Table II – II Unconditionally Stable Algorithm $n = 1$ to 4

Order n	$\tan \phi/2$	Period elongation	Period elongation for small $\omega\tau$	ϕ for $\tau \to \infty$
1 (Newmark)	$\frac{1}{2}\omega\tau$	$\omega\tau/\phi$	$1 + \frac{\omega^2\tau^2}{12}$	π
2 (Ref 1)	$\frac{1}{2}\omega\tau \Big/ \left(1 - \frac{1}{12}\omega^2\tau^2\right)$	"	$1 + \frac{\omega^4\tau^4}{720}$	2π
3	$\frac{1}{2}\omega\tau\left(1 - \frac{\omega^2\tau^2}{60}\right) \Big/ \left(1 - \frac{\omega^2\tau^2}{10}\right)$	"	$1 + \frac{\omega^6\tau^6}{100800}$	3π
4	$\frac{1}{2}\omega\tau\left(1 - \frac{\omega^2\tau^2}{42}\right) \Big/ \left(1 - \frac{3\omega^2\tau^2}{28} + \frac{\omega^4\tau^4}{1680}\right)$	"	$1 + O(\omega^8\tau^8)$	4π

Table II - III Summary of Properties of Matrix A

ONE-SIDED APPROXIMATION AND PLATE BENDING

Gilbert Strang
Massachusetts Institute of Technology

We discuss a problem which arose in the theory of one-sided approximation, but has at the same time a natural physical interpretation. Consider a triangular plate, supported at its vertices but with all edges free, subject to a point load acting at a distance Δ from a vertex. The problem is to compute the deflection for small Δ. We shall describe how this computation promised to be useful in estimating the distance from a nonnegative function u to the set of nonnegative linear functions $v \leq u$. The latter estimate leads to an error bound for finite element approximation of continuous quadratic programming problems, including the obstacle problem and the deformation of elastic-perfectly plastic materials.

This paper was prepared for the International Symposium on Computing Methods in Applied Sciences and Engineering at IRIA, Rocquencourt, France, in December, 1973. It will be published in the Proceedings of the Symposium. I am grateful for the support of the National Science Foundation (GP 22928).

INTRODUCTION

This paper represents one step, and unfortunately only a small one, toward an understanding of the rate of convergence of Ritz methods for variational inequalities. It applies most directly to a subclass of variational inequalities, which we might describe as continuous quadratic programming problems--the problem is to minimize a quadratic functional of the usual "potential energy" type, but with the class of admissible trial functions subject to inequality constraints as well as equations. The central problems of plasticity theory fall naturally into this framework.

The Ritz method chooses a family of trial functions $\Sigma\, q_j\, \varphi_j$, depending only on a finite number of free parameters q_j, and minimizes the potential energy under the given constraints. This produces an ordinary (discrete) quadratic programming problem. Our goal is not to solve this latter problem--a number of good algorithms already exist, and this source of quadratic programming problems ought to inspire new ones--but rather to estimate the distance between the true solution u and its Ritz approximation u_h.

First, we recall how such estimates are established in the classical case, when there are no inequality constraints and the problem is linear. There are three steps to an error estimate:

1) To establish some smoothness, or regularity, for the true solution u. Without this step we can still prove convergence (this has already been done for many variational inequalities), but normally we cannot establish anything about its rate.

2) To show that if such a smooth function u can be well approximated by the given family of trial functions, then the particular trial function u_h chosen by the Ritz method will be close to u.

In the classical case, this step is made simple by the fundamental theorem of the Ritz method: u_h is the projection of u, in the inner product natural to the problem, onto the trial subspace. In nonlinear problems, u_h will no longer be the closest trial function to u; we have somehow to find an a priori estimate for $u - u_h$, given only the approximation properties of the trial subspace.

3) To study the approximation properties of the trial subspace, and extract the information required in Step 2. At this stage the given variational problem and the Ritz method are no longer involved; we are assured that the unknown function u possesses a certain number of derivatives, and asked to approximate it. For the finite element method, with piecewise polynomial trial functions, this approximation problem is discussed in [4].

When the problem is governed by a variational inequality, rather than an equation, each of these three steps becomes more difficult. Nevertheless, some results are known. Brézis, Stampacchia, Lewy, and others have established a limited regularity of u--limited not by the smoothness of the data, as in linear problems, but rather by the appearance of an internal "free boundary" across which an active inequality constraint becomes inactive. Step 2 has been studied by Falk, and by Mosco and the author. The two approaches have led to different approximation problems in Step 3, and I believe that Falk's analysis may prove to be simpler. But in this paper we adopt the approach described in [3], and prove the approximation theorem which it requires. Taken together with [3], this paper establishes an h^2 estimate for the strain energy in the error $u - u_h$, when piecewise linear finite elements are applied to variational inequalities like the St. Venant torsion problem.

PIECEWISE LINEAR APPROXIMATION FROM BELOW

We shall describe two attempts at proving a theorem on one-sided approximation. The first attempt ended in a problem of independent interest in the theory of plate bending--to find the deflection of a plate under certain loads. (The applications which originally motivated the theorem were _not_ to plate bending; it is only that the approximation theorem which was finally wanted could be restated in terms of plates.) Unfortunately, the deflection was too great to prove the one-sided approximation theorem. But a modification of this unsuccessful argument, described at the end of this note, does yield a proof.

The theorem in question can be stated in the following way:

THEOREM 1: _Suppose_ $u(x,y)$ _is a nonnegative function on the plane, and let_ T _be the triangle with vertices_ $P_1 = (0,0)$, $P_2 = (1,0)$, $P_3 = (0,1)$. _Then for some absolute constant_ c, _there exists a linear function_ $v(x,y)$ _such that_

(1) $$0 \leq v \leq u \quad \text{on } T$$

(2) $$u(P_i) - v(P_i) \leq c|u|_{2,T}, \quad i = 1,2,3.$$

The last quantity is the standard $\mathcal{H}^2$ seminorm, which must be finite or the result is vacuous:

$$|u|^2_{2,T} = \iint_T (u^2_{xx} + 2u^2_{xy} + u^2_{yy})\, dx\, dy.$$

This is not the only norm of interest. One could prove the result more simply, and admit more independent variables, by using appropriate L_p rather than L_2 norms of the second derivatives. In fact, this weaker result would be sufficient for the applications we have made, in a joint paper [3] with Mosco, to error estimates in quadratic programming. But the $\mathcal{H}^2$ norm is the optimal one for those applications, so we shall stay with it here.

First, we describe the consequences of Theorem 1 for piecewise linear approximations. Suppose the plane is covered by triangles like T. Within each triangle T_j there is a linear function v_j satisfying (1) and (2). Let w be the continuous piecewise linear function whose value at every vertex P_i is the smallest value $v_j(P_i)$, chosen from the triangles surrounding that vertex. Then w must satisfy

(3) $$0 \leq w \leq u \quad \text{over the whole plane}$$

(4) $$u(P_i) - w(P_i) \leq c|u|_{2,i}.$$

The seminorm is also computed over the triangles surrounding P_i.

Estimates of $u - w$ in other norms are almost immediate. If u_I is the interpolate of u--the continuous piecewise linear function determined by $u_I(P_i) = u(P_i)$--then it is a central result of approximation theory [4] that within each triangle

(5) $$\max_{T_j}|u-u_I| \leq C|u|_{2,T_j};$$

(6) $$|u-u_I|_{0,T_j} \leq C|u|_{2,T_j};$$

(7) $$|u-u_I|_{1,T_j} \leq C|u|_{2,T_j}.$$

The left sides of (6) and (7) are L_2 norms of $u - w$ and of its first derivatives, respectively. From (4), we already know the size of $u_I - w$ at the vertices. But this is a linear function within each triangle, and therefore the estimates (5-7) apply also to $u_I - w$--except that the $|u|_2$ norms are taken over the union Ω_j

of all neighbors of T_j. By the triangle inequality, the same estimates hold for $u - w$. In fact, they remain valid for any triangulation of the plane, with a constant c depending only on the smallest angle and the largest side--a simple affine transformation maps each triangle into the original triangle T.

Finally, we rescale the independent variables so that the longest side is h, and look to see how this scaling affects each seminorm:

THEOREM 2. <u>Given</u> $u \geq 0$ <u>on the plane, there exists a continuous piecewise linear function</u> w_h <u>such that</u>

(8) $$0 \leq w_h \leq u;$$

(9) $$\max_{T_j} u - w_h \leq C\, h^{3/2} |u|_{2,\Omega_j};$$

(10) $$|u-w_h|_{0,T_j} \leq C\, h^2 |u|_{2,\Omega_j}, \qquad |u-w_h|_0 \leq C\, h^2 |u|_2;$$

(11) $$|u-w_h|_{1,T_j} \leq C\, h |u|_{2,\Omega_j}, \qquad |u-w_h|_1 \leq C\, h |u|_2.$$

The second inequalities in (10-11) come from the first, by squaring and summing over all triangles; the constant C depends only on the smallest angle. The underlying domain can be altered from the whole plane to a polygon.

The theorem leads to error bounds for the finite element approximation of variational inequalities. We describe in [3] a first application of this kind, to the <u>obstacle problem</u> of minimizing $\iint |\text{grad } v|^2$ under the constraint $v \geq \psi$. (An additional constraint $v \leq \chi$ could be handled by the same approach, at least if the two obstacles are separated: $\psi < \chi$.) The argument can be extended to St. Venant's torsion problem for an elastic-plastic cylinder--where there is an unknown boundary between elliptic and hyperbolic regions (and, if the cylinder is hollow, a lower as well as an upper obstacle). This free boundary appears automatically in the discrete approximation, which need not distinguish during the computation between the elliptic and hyperbolic domains: it simply minimizes over those piecewise linear functions which satisfy the stress constraints. For an exposition of these methods, we refer to Glowinski-Lions-Trémolières [1].

AN UNSUCCESSFUL PROOF OF THEOREM 1

Suppose we choose any linear function v which satisfies $0 \leq v \leq u$ in the triangle T, and which is tangent to u at a point ξ in T. (Everything now takes place in T, and we drop this subscript from the norms.) Since there are functions u in $\mathcal{H}^2$ (i.e., functions with $|u|_2 < \infty$) which are not pointwise differentiable, we must be more precise about the word "tangent": we mean that $v(\xi) = u(\xi)$, and that none of the nodal values $v(P_i)$ can be increased without violating the constraint $v \leq u$ in T. We hoped to prove that the difference $g = u - v$ satisfies the estimate (2) of the theorem, by the argument which follows.

Since $|g|_2 = |u|_2$, our problem is to show that <u>if</u> $g \geq 0$ is <u>tangent to zero at</u> ξ, <u>then</u> $g(P_i) \leq c|g|_2$. The best grasp we have on the function class $\mathcal{H}^2$, in fact almost the only one, is by way of the interpolates g_I. We know that $g - g_I$ vanishes at the vertices; suppose we can evaluate the quantity

$$(12) \qquad d(\xi) = \max\{f(\xi) \mid f(P_i) = 0, \ |f|_2 = 1\}.$$

Then we will have

$$g_I(\xi) = (g_I - g)(\xi) \leq d(\xi)\ |g_I - g|_2 = d(\xi)|g|_2 .$$

Since g_I is nonnegative and linear, <u>it cannot get very large at the vertices and remain small at the point</u> ξ. More precisely, suppose it were true that $d(\xi)$ could be bounded by the distance from ξ to the nearest vertex:

$$(13) \qquad d(\xi) \leq C\,\Delta, \qquad \Delta = \min|\xi - P_i| .$$

Then, from $g_I(\xi) \leq C \Delta |g|_2$ and $g_I \geq 0$, it would follow that the slope of g_I could not exceed $C|g|_2$--in the extreme case $g_I = 0$ at the vertex nearest to ξ and climbs as fast as possible. (A limiting argument would be required if $\Delta = 0$.) Therefore, g_I cannot exceed $\sqrt{2}\, C|g|_2$ at any vertex, which (since $g = g_I$ at the vertices) is what we want to prove.

So the problem is to test the bound (13) on $d(\xi)$. Fortunately, $d(\xi)$ has a natural interpretation in engineering terms; it is the square of the deflection (at ξ) of a triangular plate which is supported at the vertices P_i and acted on by a unit load at the point ξ. To verify this equivalence, renormalize (12) to

$$(14) \qquad 1/d^2 = \min\{|f|_2^2 \mid f(P_i) = 0,\ f(\xi) = 1\}.$$

Introducing Lagrange multipliers and the Dirac functions $\delta_i = \delta(x-P_i)$, $\delta_\xi = \delta(x-\xi)$, the problem is to minimize

$$(15) \qquad \iint_T (f_{xx}^2 + 2f_{xy}^2 + f_{yy}^2 - 2\Sigma\lambda_i\, \delta_i f - 2\lambda_\xi \delta_\xi f)\, dx\, dy.$$

The Euler equation for the minimizing F is the biharmonic:

$$(16) \qquad \Delta^2 F = \sum_1^3 \lambda_i \delta_i + \lambda_\xi \delta_\xi .$$

This corresponds to the normal deflection of a plate with supports at the vertices and free edges (and Poisson ratio equal to 1, but that could easily be changed) under a point load at ξ of amplitude λ_ξ. The four multipliers λ are chosen, as usual, to satisfy the four constraints in (14). Multiplying (16) by F and integrating over T (by parts, on the left side), we find $|F|_2^2 = \lambda_\xi\, F(\xi) = \lambda_\xi$, so that the Lagrange multiplier λ_ξ

coincides with $1/d^2$. Since a load $1/d^2$ produced a unit deflection $F(\xi) = 1$, a unit load would produce a deflection $F(\xi) = d^2$.

There is still another equivalent statement of the problem: to find the fundamental frequency $1/d^2$ of a free triangular plate, supported at the vertices and carrying a concentrated mass at ξ.

The difficulty is now to solve the boundary value problem (16). The lists of exact solutions to biharmonic equations yielded nothing for triangular plates with free edges--not surprisingly, since the solution must be very complicated. But we want only a good estimate for λ_ξ (and thus for d), not necessarily its exact value. <u>Here some familiar and comparatively deep results from function theory can actually play a useful role</u>. In fact, this is our main justification for pursuing the problem; we want to show how an engineer's guess for the deflection (he would surely have got the estimate right) can be rigorously confirmed in spite of difficulties with the geometry.

Our first step is to compare the minimum in (14) with

$$b(\xi) = \min\{ \iint_{-\infty}^{\infty} f_{xx}^2 + 2 f_{xy}^2 + f_{yy}^2 + f^2 \mid f(P_i) = 0,\ f(\xi) = 1\}.$$

Certainly, the minimum has been increased by including the f^2 term and integrating over the whole plane instead of the triangle T. On the other hand, we claim that the new minimum b is bounded by a constant times the old one. This is true of the inclusion of f^2, because according to (6)

$$\iint_T f^2 = |f|_{0,T}^2 = |f-f_I|_{0,T}^2 \le C|f|_{2,T}^2.$$

The change from T to the whole plane P is made legitimate by Calderon's extension theorem: there is an extension of f such that $||f||_{2,P} \le C'||f||_{2,T}$. Therefore, $b(\xi)$ is no larger than $(1+C)(C'/d)^2$.

The boundary value problem associated with b is very much simpler than (16): the boundary disappears, and the extremal function now satisfies, for $-\infty < x,y < \infty$,

$$\Delta^2 F + F = \sum_1^3 \lambda_i \delta_i + \lambda_\xi \delta_\xi . \tag{17}$$

By superposition, F must be the sum of the responses to four point loads, acting at the vertices P_i and at ξ. More precisely, let G be the fundamental solution, or Green's function, over the whole plane:

$$\Delta^2 G + G = \delta(x,y). \tag{18}$$

Then F is a combination of translates of G:

$$F = \lambda_1 G(x,y) + \lambda_2 G(x-1,y) + \lambda_3 G(x,y-1) + \lambda_\xi G(x-\xi_1, y-\xi_2).$$

The weights λ are chosen so that $F(P_i) = 0$, $F(\xi) = 1$. This yields a set of four simultaneous equations, and by Cramer's rule (denoting ξ by P_4 for convenience)

$$\lambda_\xi = \frac{\det M'}{\det M}, \quad M_{ij} = G(P_i - P_j), \qquad i,j = 1,\ldots,4. \tag{19}$$

M' is the submatrix of order 3, formed by deleting the last row and column. Therefore, it is independent of ξ, and the numerator in (19) is a fixed constant. We want to estimate the denominator when Δ is small, say when $P_4 = \xi$ is close to P_3.

The matrix M is positive definite by <u>Bochner's theorem</u>, because the Fourier transform of G is everywhere positive: $\hat{G} = ((\theta_1^2 + \theta_2^2)^2 + 1)^{-1}$. Surprisingly, the determinant of a positive definite matrix is bounded [2] by

$$\text{(20)} \qquad \det M \leq M_{11} M_{22} \det \begin{pmatrix} M_{33} & M_{34} \\ M_{43} & M_{44} \end{pmatrix} .$$

The factors $M_{11} = M_{22} = G(0,0)$ are independent of ξ, and the remaining factor is $G^2(0,0) - G(P_3-\xi)\, G(\xi-P_3)$. Obviously, G in (18) depends only on the radial distance from the origin, and for small r it is known that

$$G(r) - G(0) \sim c\, r^2 \log r^{-1}.$$

Therefore the 2 x 2 determinant in (20) behaves like $c\, G^2(0)\, \Delta^2 \log \Delta^{-1}$, and this provides an upper bound for $\det M$, and therefore a lower bound for λ_ξ. It is not difficult to find a similar upper bound for λ_ξ. Therefore it must be that <u>the deflection of the plate includes a logarithmic term,</u> and

$$\text{(21)} \qquad d = (\lambda_\xi)^{-\frac{1}{2}} \sim \Delta(\log \Delta^{-1})^{\frac{1}{2}}.$$

The unlucky estimate (13) is not correct, and our proof fails.

A MORE SUCCESSFUL PROOF

Since the argument came to grief only for small Δ, we look for a modification which will avoid this possibility. The idea we shall sketch is unnecessarily crude, but it seems to work. It does use the facts already proved, that if $g \geq 0$ in T and $g(\xi) = 0$, then $g(P_i) \leq C(\xi)|g|_2$--as ξ approaches a vertex, the coefficient C at that vertex actually goes to zero (because d does), but we could not establish that the coefficients at the other vertices remain bounded.

We shall denote by K the specific constant which occurs in (5):

$$\max_T |u-u_I| \leq K|u|_{2,T}. \tag{22}$$

Two cases of Theorem 1 are particularly easy. If u exceeds $K|u|_2$ at all three vertices of T, we may choose the approximation $v = u_I - K|u|_2$; then $v \leq u$, and $u - v = K|u|_2$ at the vertices. If at all three vertices u is less than $K|u|_2$, then we take $v = 0$ and again inequality (2) in the theorem holds.

Suppose that $u(P_1)$ and $u(P_2)$, say, are less than $K|u|_2$, but $u(P_3) = u(0,1)$ is not. Then we construct $v = cy$, choosing the largest c for which $v \leq u$ in T. At the vertices P_1 and P_2, $v = 0$ and $g = u - v$ is still less than $K|u|_2$; and at some point ξ, because c was maximal, $g(\xi) = 0$. We introduce the following device: think of the larger triangle whose vertices are at $(0,-1)$, $(2,-1)$, and $P_3 = (0,1)$. On this triangle we still have $g \geq 0$, because $u \geq 0$ and $v \leq 0$ in the new part below the x-axis. The point ξ is certainly not near either of the two new vertices, and even if it is near the old P_3, it would still follow that $g(P_3) \leq C|g|_2$. So this case is settled.

Suppose finally that u is near zero at only one of the vertices, for example the origin: $u(P_1) \leq K|u|_2$. Then we replace the origin by a vertex at $Q = (-1,-1)$, and consider the larger triangle $T' = Q\, P_2\, P_3$. If we still choose $v = cy$, with the largest c for which $v \leq u$ in T', a coincidence point ξ will again be on or above the x-axis, and not near Q. Nor will the point ξ be near to P_2, because by hypothesis $g(P_2) = u(P_2)$ exceeds $K|u|_2$. Therefore, we can conclude that g is small at P_3: $g(P_3) \leq C|u|_2$ for some absolute constant C. If it happened that $g(P_2) \leq g(P_3)$ then this choice of v would establish the theorem; but it is more likely that $g(P_2) > g(P_3)$, and we must look for another v.

If we carry out the same argument for v of the form cx, the roles of P_2 and P_3 are reversed: either it happens that $g(P_3) \leq g(P_2) \leq C|u|_2$, or else $g(P_3) > g(P_2)$ and this v is also not satisfactory.

Our last idea is this: consider the family

$$v_\theta = c_\theta(x \cos \theta + y \sin \theta), \quad 0 \leq \theta \leq \pi/2.$$

For each θ, c_θ is chosen to be maximal under the constraint $v \leq u$ in T', so there is a coincidence point ξ_θ (not near to Q!). The values $g_\theta(P_i) = u(P_i) - v_\theta(P_i)$ depend continuously on θ. Therefore (unless the proof was settled by one of the previous cases) there is a value $\theta = \alpha$ for which $g_\alpha(P_2) = g_\alpha(P_3)$. The corresponding v_α is the one-sided approximation we want in Theorem 1. It is zero at the origin, where by assumption $u(P_1) \leq K|u|_2$. Evidently, the point ξ_α cannot be close to both vertices P_2 and P_3, so that $g_\alpha \leq C|u|_2$ at one vertex or the other--and therefore at both.

This proof appears to extend to three dimensional problems. Whether the theorem holds in all dimensions, and whether a higher order of one-sided approximation is assured for piecewise polynomials of higher degree, is at this moment unknown.

REFERENCES

1. R. Glowinski, J. L. Lions, and R. Trémolières, Résolution Numérique des Inéquations de la Mécanique et de la Physique, Dunod, Paris, 1974.

2. L. Mirsky, An Introduction to Linear Algebra, Oxford University Press, 1955.

3. U. Mosco and G. Strang, One-sided approximation and variational inequalities, Bull. Amer. Math. Soc., to appear.

4. G. Strang and G. Fix, An Analysis of the Finite Element Method, Prentice-Hall, New York, 1973.

QUELQUES METHODES D'ELEMENTS FINIS POUR LE PROBLEME D'UNE PLAQUE ENCASTREE

P.G. CIARLET
Analyse Numérique, Tour 55
Université de Paris VI
11, Quai Saint-Bernard, 75230 PARIS CEDEX 05

Communication présentée au Colloque International sur les Méthodes de Calcul Scientifique et Technique, I.R.I.A., Le Chesnay, 17-21 Décembre 1973.

O. INTRODUCTION

L'objet de cet article est de présenter diverses méthodes d'éléments finis, effectivement utilisées par les Ingénieurs, pour résoudre numériquement le problème d'une plaque encastrée.

Nous n'avons pas considéré toutes les méthodes : C'est ainsi que nous ne disons rien des méthodes "hybrides" ou "mixtes" (cf. Oden [31] , Pian [32]), qui sont associées à d'autres formulations variationnelles que celle que nous donnons ici. Nous renvoyons le lecteur intéressé par l'analyse numérique de ces méthodes à Brezzi [10] , Oden [31] et aux travaux de Johnson [23,24] . De même, nous renvoyons à Glowinski [21] et à un article à paraître de Ciarlet & Raviart [16] pour des méthodes "par décomposition" qui, tout en étant des méthodes non conformes, correspondent à une façon de poser le problème discret différente de celle décrite dans cet article.

Le plan de l'article est le suivant : Au §1, on rappelle la formulation variationnelle du problème d'une plaque encastrée. On donne ensuite au §2 des exemples variés d'éléments finis <u>conformes</u> utilisés pour approcher la solution de ce problème. Enfin, nous examinons au §3 diverses méthodes d'éléments finis <u>non conformes</u> pour lesquelles un essai de <u>justification a priori du "patch test" de B.</u> Irons a été fait, suivant les travaux récents de M. Crouzeix, P. Lasaux, P. Lesaint, P.-A. Raviart, G. Strang, et par l'intermédiaire d'un "lemme de Bramble-Hilbert sur les formes bilinéaires", introduit en [12] . On indique aussi une méthode de pénalisation, introduite par Babuška & Zlámal [4] .

Chaque fois qu'elle apparaît dans une inégalité, la lettre C désigne une constante indépendante des diverses fonctions intervenant dans l'inégalité en question, ainsi que du sous-espace V_h considéré.

1. LE PROBLEME CONTINU

Dans tout ce qui suit, on désigne par Ω un ouvert borné du plan. Etant donné un entier m, les expressions

$$|v|_{m,\Omega} = \Big(\sum_{|\alpha|=m} \int_\Omega |\partial^\alpha v|^2 dxdy \Big)^{1/2} , \quad \| v \|_{m,\Omega} = \Big(\sum_{\ell=0}^{m} |v|^2_{\ell,\Omega} \Big)^{1/2}$$

représentent les semi-normes et normes usuelles de Sobolev; on rappelle que sur l'espace de Sobolev $H^m_0(\Omega)$, la semi-norme $|v|_{m,\Omega}$ est une norme équivalente à la norme $\| v \|_{m,\Omega}$.

Considérons le problème de l'équilibre d'une plaque, tel qu'il est décrit dans le livre de Landau et Lifchitz [26] , par exemple. En l'absence de forces, la plaque est représentée par l'ensemble $\bar{\Omega}$ du plan, supposé horizontal. On note respectivement e, E, et μ, l'épaisseur, le module d'Young, et le coefficient de Poisson de la plaque. La fonction inconnue u, qui représente la cote de la plaque par rapport au plan horizontal lorsqu'une force verticale de densité F est appliquée à la plaque, rend minimale l'énergie de la plaque qui, pour une cote donnée v, est donnée par l'expression

$$(1.1)\qquad E(v) = \frac{Ee^3}{24(1-\mu^2)} \int_\Omega \left\{(\Delta v)^2 + 2(1-\mu)\left(\frac{\partial^2 v}{\partial x \partial y} - \frac{\partial^2 v}{\partial x^2}\frac{\partial^2 v}{\partial y^2}\right)\right\} dxdy - \int_\Omega Fv \, dxdy.$$

Si l'on pose $f = \frac{12(1-\mu^2)}{Ee^3} F$, l'énergie de la plaque s'écrit (à un facteur multiplicatif constant près)

$$(1.2)\qquad J(v) = \frac{1}{2}\, a(v,v) - (f,v)$$

où $(.,.)$ est le produit scalaire de l'espace $L^2(\Omega)$, en supposant par conséquent l'appartenance de f à $L^2(\Omega)$, et où la forme bilinéaire $a(.,.)$ est donnée par

$$(1.3)\qquad a(u,v) = \int_\Omega \left\{\Delta u\, \Delta v + (1-\mu)\left(2\frac{\partial^2 u}{\partial x \partial y}\frac{\partial^2 v}{\partial x \partial y} - \frac{\partial^2 u}{\partial x^2}\frac{\partial^2 v}{\partial y^2} - \frac{\partial^2 u}{\partial y^2}\frac{\partial^2 v}{\partial x^2}\right)\right\} dxdy$$

$$= \int_\Omega \left\{\mu\, \Delta u\, \Delta v + (1-\mu)\left(\frac{\partial^2 u}{\partial x^2}\frac{\partial^2 v}{\partial x^2} + \frac{\partial^2 u}{\partial y^2}\frac{\partial^2 v}{\partial y^2} + 2\frac{\partial^2 u}{\partial x \partial y}\frac{\partial^2 v}{\partial x \partial y}\right)\right\} dxdy.$$

La forme bilinéaire ci-dessus est continue sur l'espace $H^2(\Omega) \times H^2(\Omega)$ et, de plus, elle est $H_0^2(\Omega)$-elliptique; pour le voir, on remarque que

$$(1.4)\qquad a(v,v) = \mu|\Delta v|^2_{0,\Omega} + (1-\mu)|v|^2_{2,\Omega}$$

et on utilise le fait que, physiquement le coefficient de Poisson μ vérifie les inégalités $0 < \mu < \frac{1}{2}$. Dans ces conditions, il existe une et une seule fonction u dans l'espace $V = H_0^2(\Omega)$ telle que

$$(1.5)\qquad J(u) = \min_{v \in V} J(v),$$

ou, de façon équivalente, qui vérifie les équations

$$(1.6)\qquad a(u,v) = (f,v) \text{ pour tout } v \in V.$$

Pour interpréter - au moins formellement - le problème variationnel (1.6), on utilise les formules de Green suivantes :

$$(1.7)\qquad \int_\Omega \Delta u\, \Delta v\, dxdy = \int_\Omega \Delta^2 u\, v\, dxdy - \oint_{\partial\Omega} \frac{\partial \Delta u}{\partial n} v\, d\gamma + \oint_{\partial\Omega} \Delta u \frac{\partial v}{\partial n} d\gamma,$$

$$(1.8)\qquad \int_\Omega \left\{2\frac{\partial^2 u}{\partial x \partial y}\frac{\partial^2 v}{\partial x \partial y} - \frac{\partial^2 u}{\partial x^2}\frac{\partial^2 v}{\partial y^2} - \frac{\partial^2 u}{\partial y^2}\frac{\partial^2 v}{\partial x^2}\right\} dxdy =$$

$$= \oint_{\partial\Omega} \left\{-\frac{\partial^2 u}{\partial t^2}\frac{\partial v}{\partial n} + \frac{\partial^2 u}{\partial n \partial t}\frac{\partial v}{\partial t}\right\} d\gamma,$$

où $\frac{\partial}{\partial n}$ et $\frac{\partial}{\partial t}$ représentent respectivement les dérivées normales et tangentielles le long de la frontière $\partial\Omega$ de l'ouvert Ω. Dans ces conditions, si la solution u du problème variationnel (1.6) est suffisamment régulière, elle est aussi la solution du problème

(1.9) $$\Delta^2 u = f \text{ dans } \Omega,$$

(1.10) $$u = \frac{\partial u}{\partial n} = 0 \text{ sur } \partial\Omega,$$

qui est effectivement le modèle "classique" le plus simple pour une plaque encastrée, l'encastrement étant pris en compte par les conditions aux limites (1.10).

L'application de la seconde formule de Green (1.8) montre que la contribution du terme $\int_\Omega (1-\mu)\left(2\frac{\partial^2 u}{\partial x\partial y}\frac{\partial^2 v}{\partial x\partial y} - \frac{\partial^2 u}{\partial x^2}\frac{\partial^2 v}{\partial y^2} - \frac{\partial^2 u}{\partial y^2}\frac{\partial^2 v}{\partial x^2}\right)dxdy$ est nulle. En d'autres termes, on pourrait se contenter de la forme bilinéaire $a'(u,v) = \int_\Omega \Delta u\ \Delta v\ dxdy$, et c'est d'ailleurs ce choix qui est fréquemment fait, puisqu'il conduit à la formulation variationnelle la plus simple qu'on puisse attacher au problème (1.9)-(1.10). La forme bilinéaire a' est encore V-elliptique car la semi-norme $|\Delta v|_{0,\Omega}$ est une norme sur l'espace $V = H_0^2(\Omega)$, équivalente à la norme $\|v\|_{2,\Omega}$. En fait, la possibilité de remplacer la forme bilinéaire a par la forme bilinéaire a' tient à ce que l'on se place dans l'espace $H_0^2(\Omega)$, et non dans un espace strictement plus grand, comme l'espace $H^2(\Omega)$; autrement dit, cette possibilité serait supprimée si l'on choisissait des conditions aux limites autres que celles d'une plaque encastrée.

On voit aussi que la forme bilinéaire a' correspond à la valeur $\mu = 1$ dans l'expression (1.3) et qu'en fait, toute valeur μ de l'intervalle $[0,1]$ conduira également au même problème (1.9)-(1.10), la V-ellipticité étant toujours assurée; cf (1.4). De la même façon, toute l'analyse faite au §2 pour les méthodes conformes s'applique sans changement à toute valeur μ de l'intervalle $[0,1]$. Cependant, pour certaines des méthodes non conformes du §3, certains résultats ne sont plus valables si μ est égal à 1, alors qu'ils restent vrais pour les valeurs physiquement admissibles de μ, i.e., dans l'intervalle $]0,\frac{1}{2}[$.

En ce qui concerne la régularité de la solution u du problème (1.5), on peut montrer (voir Kondrat'ev [25]) que celle-ci appartient à l'espace $H^3(\Omega) \cap H_0^2(\Omega)$ dès que l'ensemble $\bar\Omega$ est un polygone convexe, ce qui est effectivement souvent le cas des plaques. A cet égard, il est intéressant de remarquer que (sauf pour l'élément de Morley; cf §3), l'hypothèse "$u \in H^3(\Omega)$" est aussi l'hypothèse minimale qu'on utilise pour obtenir la convergence des méthodes d'éléments finis, aussi bien conformes que non conformes.

2. METHODES CONFORMES

On suppose comme au §1 que $f \in L^2(\Omega)$. On notera $\|\cdot\|$ l'expression $|\cdot|_{2,\Omega}$, qui est une norme sur l'espace $V = H_0^2(\Omega)$. Il existe alors des constantes M et $\alpha > 0$ telles que

(2.1) $$|a(u,v)| \leq M\|u\|\,\|v\| \text{ pour tout } u,v \in V,$$

(2.2) $$\alpha\|v\|^2 \leq a(v,v) \text{ pour tout } v \in V.$$

Etant donné un sous-espace de dimension finie V_h de V, le <u>problème discret</u> consiste à trouver une fonction $u_h \in V_h$ telle que

(2.3) $$a(u_h,v_h) = (f,v_h) \text{ pour } v_h \in V_h,$$

et ce problème a une solution et une seule, d'après (2.2). Utilisant les inégalités

$$\begin{aligned} \alpha \|u-u_h\|^2 &\leq a(u-u_h,\, u-u_h) \\ &= a(u-u_h,\, u-v_h) \leq M \|u-u_h\| \, \|u-v_h\| \end{aligned}$$

vérifiées pour toute fonction $v_h \in V_h$, on en déduit l'inégalité

(2.4) $$\|u-u_h\| \leq C \inf_{v_h \in V_h} \|u-v_h\|,$$

où la constante $C = M/\alpha$ est indépendante du sous-espace V_h, de sorte que le problème de l'évaluation de l'<u>erreur</u> $\|u-u_h\|$ est ramené à un problème de théorie de l'approximation - l'évaluation de la quantité $\inf_{v_h \in V_h} \|u-v_h\|$.

Pour obtenir l'inégalité (2.4), on a utilisé de façon essentielle l'inclusion $V_h \subset V$. On dit alors que la méthode d'approximation est <u>interne</u> et que, dans le cas où l'espace V_h correspond à une méthode d'éléments finis (cf. les exemples décrits plus loin), la méthode, et les éléments finis, sont <u>conformes</u>, ou encore <u>compatibles</u>.

Pour construire un tel espace V_h, on se donne :

(a) Une <u>triangulation</u> $\mathcal{C}_h$ de l'ensemble $\bar{\Omega}$ en <u>éléments finis</u>, i.e., $\bar{\Omega} = \bigcup_{K \in \mathcal{C}_h} K$, où les éléments K sont des <u>triangles</u>, ou des <u>quadrilatères</u>, d'intérieurs deux à deux disjoints, et tels que tout côté d'un élément soit ou bien un côté d'un autre élément, ou bien une partie de $\partial\Omega$; on pose

$$h = \max_{K \in \mathcal{C}_h} h_K, \text{ avec } h_K = \operatorname{diam}(K) \text{ pour tout } K \in \mathcal{C}_h,$$

(b) Un <u>espace</u> P, de dimension finie, de fonctions réelles tel que si v_h est une fonction quelconque de l'espace V_h, alors

$$\operatorname{restr.} v_h\Big|_K \in P \text{ pour tout } K \in \mathcal{C}_h,$$

(c) Un ensemble de <u>degrés de liberté</u> attachés à un élément fini "courant" K qui, d'une part, définissent une base de l'espace P et qui, d'autre part, sont choisis de telle façon que l'inclusion $V_h \subset H^2(\Omega)$ ait lieu; comme les fonctions de l'espace P sont le plus souvent très régulières dans la pratique, l'inclusion précédente sera une conséquence de l'inclusion $V_h \subset C^1(\bar{\Omega})$, ce que l'on pourra vérifier dans chacun des exemples donnés ci-après. On vérifiera aussi sur ces mêmes exemples que les conditions aux limites (1.10) peuvent être satisfaites exactement dans les sous-espaces V_h correspondants.

Si u est une fonction suffisamment régulière définie sur $\bar{\Omega}$ (resp. sur un élément fini K), on notera $\Pi_h u$ (resp. $\Pi_K u$) la fonction de V_h (resp. de P) qui <u>interpole</u>

la fonction u sur $\bar{\Omega}$ (resp. sur K), i.e., dont les degrés de liberté sur $\bar{\Omega}$ (resp. sur K) sont identiques à ceux de la fonction u. De la sorte on voit que restr. $\Pi_h u\big|_K = \Pi_K u$ pour tout $K \in \mathcal{C}_h$. On va alors majorer la quantité $\inf_{v_h \in V_h} \| u-v_h \|$ de l'inégalité (2.4) par $\| u-\Pi_h u \|$, et comme

$$|u-\Pi_h u|_{2,\Omega} = \left(\sum_{K \in \mathcal{C}_h} |u-\Pi_K u|_{2,\Omega}^2 \right)^{1/2}, \tag{2.5}$$

le problème d'évaluation de l'erreur se trouve ramené à un problème de <u>théorie de l'interpolation</u> "locale", i.e., sur un élément fini "courant" K. Ce problème a été étudié par de nombreux auteurs ces dernières années; voir notamment Babuška & Aziz [3], Bramble & Hilbert [8], Ciarlet [11], Ciarlet & Raviart [14,15], Raviart [33], Strang [35], Strang & Fix [37], Zlámal [40].

Le résultat fondamental est le suivant: on considère une "famille" d'éléments finis pour laquelle le paramètre h tend vers zéro, et qui ne deviennent pas "plats" à la limite (pour une définition précise de cette notion, voir Ciarlet & Raviart [14]). L'hypothèse <u>fondamentale</u> est l'inclusion

$$P_k \subset P, \tag{2.6}$$

où P_k désigne l'espace vectoriel des polynômes (ici : de deux variables) de degré $\leq k$. Alors pour tout entier $m \leq k+1$ tel que $P \subset H^m(K)$, on a

$$|u-\Pi_K u|_{m,K} \leq C\, h_K^{k+1-m} |u|_{k+1,K} \tag{2.7}$$

où la constance C est indépendante de la fonction u et de h_K.

Par application de (2.4), (2.5) et (2.7) avec m = 2, nous obtenons

$$\| u-u_h \| \leq C\, h^{k-1} |u|_{k+1,\Omega}, \tag{2.8}$$

en supposant que l'inclusion (2.6) a lieu. En conséquence, <u>on obtient une convergence d'ordre</u> O(h) <u>dès que la solution</u> u <u>appartient à l'espace</u> $H^3(\Omega)$ <u>et dès que l'inclusion "minimale"</u>

$$P_2 \subset P \tag{2.9}$$

<u>est satisfaite</u>.

Utilisant les techniques de dualité, développées par Aubin [2] et Nitsche [30], on peut montrer que si l'inclusion (2.6) est vérifiée avec un entier $k \geq 3$, on a

$$\frac{\| u-u_h \|_{0,\Omega}}{\| u-u_h \|_{2,\Omega}} = O(h^2),$$

mais ce résultat est établi en supposant que la frontière de Ω est suffisamment régulière pour que la solution u soit dans l'espace $H^4(\Omega)$ pour tout second membre $f \in L^2(\Omega)$ et qu'il existe une inégalité du type $\| u \|_{4,\Omega} \leq C \| f \|_{0,\Omega}$ pour tout $f \in L^2(\Omega)$; voir Nečas [29, Théorème 2.2, page 216].

Examinons maintenant un certain nombre d'exemples. Dans les figures, on utilise les notations suivantes pour les degrés de liberté :

- u.
- ⊙ $\partial^\alpha u \quad |\alpha| = 0,1.$
- ◎ $\partial^\alpha u \quad |\alpha| = 0,1,2.$
- ┼ dérivée normale au milieu du côté.
- ✕ $\dfrac{\partial^2 u}{\partial x \partial y}$.

Exemple 1 (cf. Figure 1). Cet élément, que nous appellerons "élément à 21 degrés de liberté", est apparu en 1968, simultanément dans au moins six publications; voir

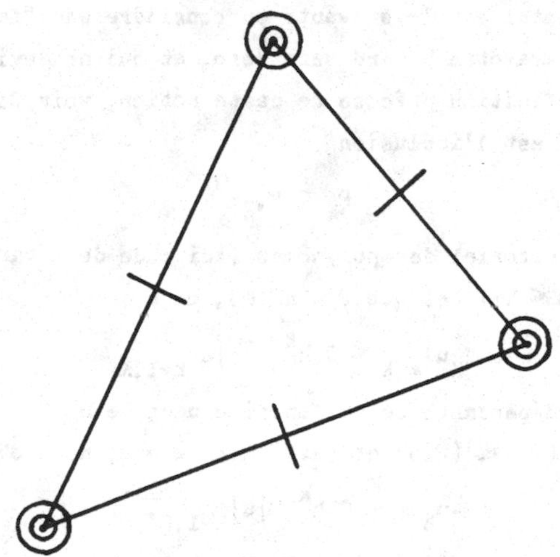

Figure 1

à ce sujet Zienkiewicz [38, page 209], et Zlámal [40] où la théorie de l'interpolation pour cet élément a été faite pour la première fois. L'espace P étant ici l'espace P_5, de dimension 21, on obtient donc

$$\| u-u_h \| \leq C\, h^4 |u|_{6,\Omega} ,$$

en supposant que $u \in H^6(\Omega)$.

A partir de cet élément, on peut construire un "élément à 18 degrés de liberté" (cf. Figure 2), qui est également apparu en 1968 (voir à ce sujet Zienkiewicz [38, page 209]). L'espace P, de dimension 18, est formé par les polynômes de degré 5 pour lesquels la dérivée normale le long de chaque côté du triangle est un polynôme (d'une variable) de degré 3. Dans ce cas, on a donc les inclusions $P_4 \subset P \subset P_5$, de sorte que, si $u \in H^5(\Omega)$,

$$\| u-u_h \| \leq C\, h^3 |u|_{5,\Omega} .$$

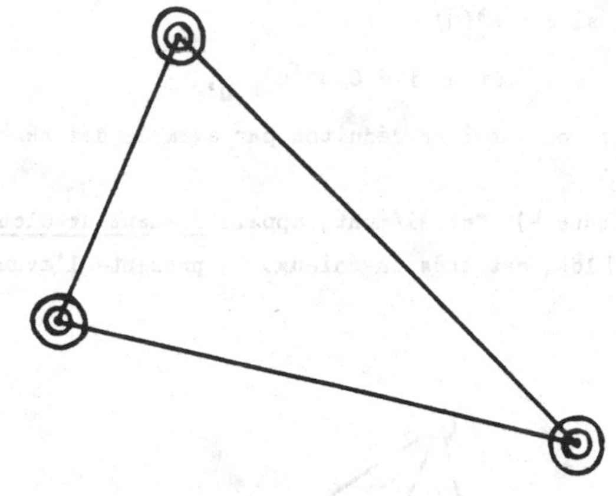

Figure 2

La théorie de l'interpolation pour cet élément a été faite par Bramble & Zlámal [9] ■

Exemple 2 (cf. Figure 3). Cet élément a été introduit par Bogner, Fox &

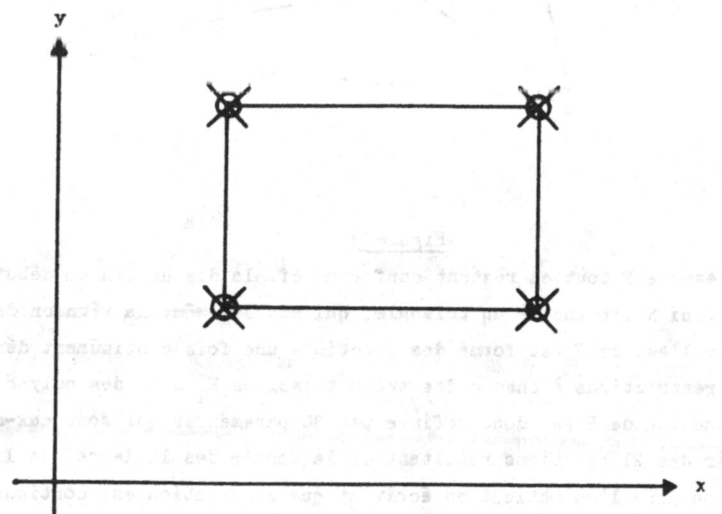

Figure 3

Schmit [7] ; il ne s'applique qu'à des plaques dont les côtés sont parallèles aux axes de coordonnées. L'espace P, de dimension 16, est formé des polynômes du type

$$p(x,y) = \sum_{0 \leq i,j \leq 3} \alpha_{ij} x^i y^j ,$$

c'est-à-dire qui sont de degré 3 par rapport à chacune des variables. De l'inclusion

$P_3 \subset P$, on déduit que, si $u \in H^4(\Omega)$,

$$\|u-u_h\| \leq C\, h^2 |u|_{4,\Omega},$$

les majorations locales pouvant être déduites par exemple des résultats de Ciarlet & Raviart [14]. ∎

Exemple 3 (cf. Figure 4). Cet élément, appelé élément de Clough et Tocher, du nom de ses inventeurs [18], est très ingénieux. Il présente l'avantage de réduire la

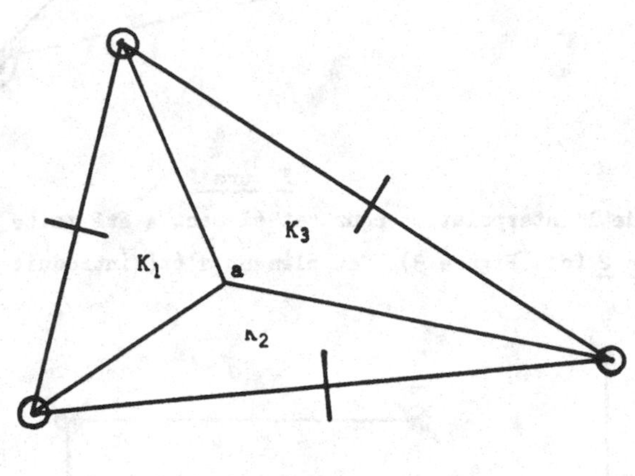

Figure 4

dimension de l'espace P tout en restant conforme ; cf. la discussion au début du §3.

L'élément fini K est encore un triangle, qui est lui-même la réunion de trois triangles K_i, et l'espace P est formé des fonctions une fois continûment dérivables sur K dont les restrictions à chacun des trois triangles K_i sont des polynômes de degré 3. Une fonction de P est donc définie par 30 paramètres qui sont eux-mêmes obtenus à partir des 21 équations résultant de la donnée des 12 degrés de liberté et des 9 équations que l'on obtient en écrivant que la fonction est continue sur K, ainsi que ses dérivées partielles premières. On montre (cf. Ciarlet [13]) que la matrice du système linéaire correspondant est régulière, quelle que soit la position du point a à l'intérieur de l'élément, et que, moyennant quelques précautions, la théorie de l'interpolation résulte encore de l'inclusion $P_3 \subset P$. On obtient ainsi, si $u \in H^4(\Omega)$,

$$\|u-u_h\| \leq C\, h^2 |u|_{4,\Omega}.$$

L'ordre asymptotique de convergence est donc identique à celui de l'élément de l'Exemple 2, avec l'avantage de pouvoir maintenant considérer des domaines polygonaux quelconques.

De même qu'on passe de l'élément à 21 degrés de liberté à l'élément à 18 degrés de liberté (cf. Exemple 1), de même peut-on réduire de 3 le nombre de degrés de liberté de l'élément de Clough et Tocher (ici encore, les dérivées normales aux milieux des côtés) en assujetissant la dérivée normale le long de chaque côté du triangle à être une fonction linéaire (d'une variable), ce qui conduit à un espace P de dimension 9 vérifiant l'inclusion $P_2 \subset P$, et donc à une erreur en $O(h)$ si $u \in H^3(\Omega)$. ∎

<u>Exemple 4</u> (cf. Figure 5). L'élément K, que nous appellerons <u>élément de Fraeijs de Veubeke et Sander</u> [20,34], est ici un quadrilatère convexe, et sa conception

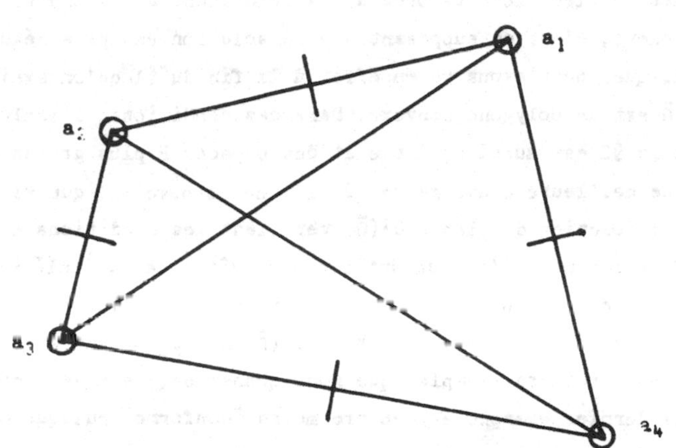

<u>Figure 5</u>

relève de la même idée que celle de l'élément de Clough et Tocher. Suivant les notations de la Figure 5 on note K_1 le triangle de sommets $a_1 a_2$ et a_4 et K_2 le triangle de sommets $a_1 a_2$ et a_3. On pose

$$R_1 = \{p \in C^1(K);\ p = 0 \text{ sur } \complement K_1,\ p \in P_3 \text{ sur } K_1\},$$
$$R_2 = \{p \in C^1(K);\ p = 0 \text{ sur } \complement K_2,\ p \in P_3 \text{ sur } K_2\},$$

les complémentaires étant pris par rapport à l'élément K. Alors l'espace P, de dimension 16, est la somme directe de P_3 et des deux espaces R_1 et R_2. Ciavaldini & Nédélec [17] ont récemment fait l'analyse de cet élément : compte-tenu de l'inclusion $P_3 \subset P$, on obtient encore, si $u \in H^4(\Omega)$,

$$\|u-u_h\| \leq C\, h^2 |u|_{4,\Omega}. \qquad ∎$$

D'autres éléments finis conformes sont également employés: par exemple, on peut "ajouter" à des espaces de polynômes des fonctions "singulières" judicieusement choisies. Ces fonctions sont singulières en ce sens que certaines de leurs dérivées, secondes par exemple, sont non bornées. Pour pouvoir appliquer les majorations du type (2.7) avec m = 2, il faudra donc d'abord s'assurer que l'inclusion $P \subset H^2(K)$ est satisfaite. On trouvera des exemples de tels éléments page 199 du livre de Zienkiewicz [38], ainsi que dans Birkhoff & Mansfield [6] où se trouve de surcroit faite une théorie de l'interpolation "locale".

3. METHODES NON CONFORMES

Les éléments conformes décrits dans le §2 sont difficiles à mettre en oeuvre car la dimension de l'espace P est relativement élevée et la structure de l'espace P est parfois compliquée (cf. Exemples 3 et 4). Naturellement, ces difficultés résultent de la nécessité d'avoir des dérivées partielles premières continues lorsqu'on passe d'un élément à un élément adjacent.

Par ailleurs, si les éléments précédents conduisent à des ordres asymptotiques de convergence élevé, c'est en supposant que la solution est plus régulière qu'elle ne l'est en pratique. Nous avons vu en effet à la fin du §1 qu'on avait seulement "$u \in H^3(\Omega)$" si $\bar{\Omega}$ est un polygone convexe. Dans ces conditions, l'inclusion minimale $P_2 \subset P$ signalée au §2 est aussi optimale et des espaces P plus grands que P_2 ne conduiront pas à une meilleure convergence. Or il se trouve que si $P = P_2$ (le cas idéal !) la seule fonction de classe $C^1(\bar{\Omega})$ vérifiant les conditions aux limites (1.10) est la fonction nulle (cf. un article à paraître de A. Ženíšek).

Les considérations qui précèdent conduisent donc naturellement à la conception de méthodes pour lesquelles l'inclusion $V_h \subset C^1(\bar{\Omega})$ <u>n'est pas</u> satisfaite : effectivement, dans les deux premiers exemples que nous donnerons, on a seulement l'inclusion $V_h \subset C^0(\bar{\Omega})$ et le dernier exemple est encore moins "conforme" puisque cette dernière inclusion n'est même pas satisfaite.

D'une façon générale, on dit que les éléments finis sont <u>non conformes</u>, ou <u>incompatibles</u>, dès que l'inclusion $V_h \subset V = H_0^2(\Omega)$ n'est pas vérifiée. On supposera que l'inclusion $V_h \subset L^2(\Omega)$ a lieu, ce qui permet d'écrire les membres de droites des relations (3.1) ci-dessous.

Puisque les fonctions de V_h sont localement régulières, la façon la plus naturelle de définir le problème discret associé à un sous-espace V_h d'éléments finis non conformes consiste à chercher une fonction $u_h \in V_h$ qui vérifie

(3.1) $$a_h(u_h,v_h) = (f,v_h) \text{ pour tout } v_h \in V_h,$$

où, par définition,

(3.2) $$a_h(u_h,v_h) = \sum_{K\in\mathcal{T}_h} \int_K \{\ldots\} dxdy,$$

l'expression $\{\ldots\}$ étant la même que celle qui intervient dans la forme bilinéaire $a(.,.)$ donnée en (1.3).

De la même façon, il nous faut définir une norme sur l'espace V_h; là encore, il est naturel de poser

(3.3) $$\| v_h \|_h = \Big(\sum_{K\in\mathcal{T}_h} |v_h|_{2,K}^2\Big)^{1/2},$$

mais encore faut-il vérifier qu'il s'agit effectivement d'une norme, la positivité n'étant pas automatique; on démontre que c'est effectivement une norme pour les trois exemples que nous décrivons plus loin; cf. Lascaux & Lesaint [27].

Des expressions (3.2) et (3.3), on déduit que

(3.4) $$\alpha \| v_h \|_h^2 \leq a_h(v_h,v_h) \text{ pour tout } v_h \in V_h,$$

où la constante $\alpha = (1-\mu)$ est indépendante du sous-espace V_h, et c'est d'ailleurs cette "uniformité" de la V_h-ellipticité qui permet d'obtenir la majoration fondamentale (3.6) de l'erreur. Signalons que si l'on avait choisi la valeur $\mu = 1$ dans la forme bilinéaire $a(.,.)$, valeur physiquement irréaliste mais admissible pour les méthodes conformes, la V_h-ellipticité ne serait plus nécessairement uniforme pour les exemples que nous considérons plus loin.

Dans ce qui suit, nous considérons que la forme bilinéaire $a_h(.,.)$ et la norme $\|.\|_h$ que nous venons de définir sur l'espace V_h sont également définies sur l'espace V où elles sont respectivement égales à la forme $a(.,.)$ et à la norme $\|.\|$.

Une simple application de l'inégalité de Cauchy-Schwarz montre pour commencer qu'il existe une constante M indépendante de l'espace V_h telle que

(3.5) $$|a_h(u_h,v_h)| \leq M \|u_h\|_h \|v_h\|_h \text{ pour tout } u_h, v_h \subset V_h.$$

Soit ensuite $v_h = u_h - w_h$ un élément quelconque du sous-espace V_h. Utilisant les relations (1.6), (3.1), (3.4) et (3.5), on obtient

$$\begin{aligned} \alpha \|w_h\|_h^2 &\leq a_h(w_h,w_h) \\ &= a_h(u-v_h,u_h-v_h) + (f,w_h) - a_h(u,w_h) \\ &\leq M \|u-v_h\|_h \|w_h\|_h + |(f,w_h)-a_h(u,w_h)|, \end{aligned}$$

de sorte que

$$\|w_h\|_h \leq \frac{M}{\alpha} \|u-v_h\|_h + \frac{|(f,w_h)-a_h(u,w_h)|}{\|w_h\|_h}.$$

Cette dernière inégalité, jointe à l'inégalité triangulaire $\|u-u_h\|_h \leq \|u-v_h\|_h + \|w_h\|_h$, conduit à l'inégalité

(3.6) $$\|u-u_h\|_h \leq C \left(\inf_{v_h \in V_h} \|u-v_h\|_h + \sup_{w_h \in V_h} \frac{|(f,w_h)-a_h(u,w_h)|}{\|w_h\|_h} \right),$$

où la constante $C = \max\{1 + \frac{M}{\alpha}, \frac{1}{\alpha}\}$ est indépendante du sous-espace V_h. Cette inégalité, fondamentale pour l'étude des méthodes non conformes, est due à Strang [36,37]. On remarque que l'inégalité (3.6) généralise l'inégalité (2.4), puisque l'expression

(3.7) $$E_h(u,w_h) = (f,w_h) - a_h(u,w_h)$$

est nulle pour tout $w_h \in V_h$, dès lors que l'inclusion $V_h \subset V$ a lieu.

Compte tenu de l'expression (3.1) de la forme bilinéaire $a_h(.,.)$, on obtient en utilisant les formules de Green (1.7) et (1.8) sur chaque élément K ($\frac{\partial}{\partial n_K}$ et $\frac{\partial}{\partial t_K}$

désignant respectivement les dérivées normales et tangentielles le long de la frontière ∂K de l'élément K):

$$(3.8)\qquad E_h(u,w_h) = E_h^0(u,w_h) + E_h^1(u,w_h),$$

avec

$$(3.9)\qquad E_h^0(u,w_h) = \sum_{K\in\mathcal{E}_h} \oint_{\partial K} \left\{\frac{\partial \Delta u}{\partial n_K} w_h + (1-\mu)\frac{\partial^2 u}{\partial n_K \partial t_K}\frac{\partial w_h}{\partial t_K}\right\} d\gamma,$$

$$(3.10)\qquad E_h^1(u,w_h) = \sum_{K\in\mathcal{E}_h} \oint_{\partial K} \left(-\Delta u + (1-\mu)\frac{\partial^2 u}{\partial t_K^2}\right)\frac{\partial w_h}{\partial n_K} d\gamma,$$

les formes bilinéaires $E_h^0(u,w_h)$ et $E_h^1(u,w_h)$ étant respectivement définies sur les espaces $H^4(\Omega) \times V_h$ et $H^3(\Omega) \times V_h$. Observons que si le sous-espace V_h vérifie l'inclusion $V_h \subset C^0(\bar\Omega)$, ce qui est le cas du rectangle d'Adini et du triangle de Zienkiewicz, le terme $E_h^0(u,w_h)$ est nul et l'hypothèse "$u \in H^3(\Omega)$" est suffisante.

Considérons le terme $\inf_{v_h\in V_h} \|u-v_h\|_h$, qui intervient dans l'inégalité (3.6). En supposant l'inclusion "minimale" $P_2 \subset P$ vérifiée, et l'appartenance de la solution u à l'espace $H^3(\Omega)$, on obtient, compte tenu de l'expression (3.3) de la norme $\|\cdot\|_h$,

$$(3.11)\qquad \inf_{v_h\in V_h} \|u-v_h\|_h \leq C\, h|u|_{3,\Omega}.$$

Dans ces conditions, au vu de la majoration fondamentale (3.6), l'idée naturelle est de démontrer une inégalité du type

$$(3.12)\qquad |E_h(u,w_h)| \leq C\, h|u|_{3,\Omega} \|w_h\|_h \text{ pour tout } u \in H^3(\Omega),\ w_h \in V_h.$$

Or on a vu en (3.8), (3.9) et (3.10) que l'expression $E_h(u,w_h)$ est elle-même une somme du type

$$(3.13)\qquad E_h(u,w_h) = \sum_{K\in\mathcal{E}_h} E_{h,K}(u,w_h),$$

chaque expression $E_{h,K}(u,w_h)$ étant associée au seul élément K; une telle décomposition n'est d'ailleurs pas unique et c'est précisément du choix d'une décomposition judicieuse que résulteront les majorations désirées; cf. l'expression (3.15).

L'objectif est alors d'obtenir des majorations du type

$$(3.14)\qquad |E_{h,K}(u,w_h)| \leq C\, h|u|_{3,K}\, |w_h|_{2,K} \text{ pour tout } u \in H^3(\Omega),\ w_h \in V_h$$

la majoration (3.12) en découlant immédiatement.

Nous allons préciser sur un exemple la démarche qui conduit à une majoration du type (3.14). On considère le terme $E_h^1(u,w_h)$ correspondant au triangle de Morley (cf. Exemple 7). Etant donné un triangle K et une fonction g définie sur la frontière du triangle, appelons $\Pi_K g$ la fonction qui, sur chacun des trois côtés $\partial_i K$, $1 \leq i \leq 3$, du triangle K, est constante et égale à la valeur moyenne $\frac{1}{h_i}\int_{\partial_i K} g\, d\gamma$ de la fonction g sur ce côté, h_i étant la longueur du côté $\partial_i K$. On peut alors transformer l'expression $E_h^1(u,w_h)$ de (3.10) en remarquant, suivant Lascaux et Lesaint [27], que l'on a aussi

(3.15) $$E_h^1(u,w_h) = \sum_{K\in\mathcal{C}_h} \oint_{\partial K} \Big(-\Delta u+(1-\mu)\frac{\partial^2 u}{\partial t_K^2}\Big)\Big(\frac{\partial w_h}{\partial n_K} - \Pi_K \frac{\partial w_h}{\partial n_K}\Big)d\gamma.$$

En effet, sur un côté $\partial_i K$ de milieu a_i, la fonction $\Pi_K \frac{\partial w_h}{\partial n_K}$ vaut $\frac{\partial w_h}{\partial n_K}(a_i)$ puisque, le long de ce côté, la fonction $\frac{\partial w_h}{\partial n_K}$ est un polynôme (d'une variable) de degré 1. La contribution des deux intégrales curvilignes associés aux deux éléments adjacents à ce côté est donc nulle si $\partial_i K$ est un côté "intérieur" à Ω, et si $\partial_i K$ est une partie de $\partial\Omega$, alors $\frac{\partial w_h}{\partial n_K}(a_i) = 0$, compte tenu de la deuxième condition aux limites, de sorte que l'intégrale correspondante $\int_{\partial_i K}(\ldots)d\gamma$ est encore nulle.

On est donc amené à évaluer des expressions du type

(3.16) $$A_{h,i,K}(u,w_h) = \int_{\partial_i K} \Big(-\Delta u+(1-\mu)\frac{\partial^2 u}{\partial t_K^2}\Big)\Big(\frac{\partial w_h}{\partial n_K} - \Pi_K \frac{\partial w_h}{\partial n_K}\Big)d\gamma.$$

On constate alors que

(3.17) $$A_{h,i,K}(u,w_h) = 0 \text{ pour tout } u \in H^3(\Omega),\ w_h \in P_1,$$

(3.18) $$A_{h,i,K}(u,w_h) = 0 \text{ pour tout } u \in P_2,\ w_h \in V_h.$$

En effet, si $w_h \in P_1$, la fonction $\frac{\partial w_h}{\partial n_K}$ est constante le long d'un côté $\partial_i K$ du triangle K et la relation (3.17) provient de l'invariance des fonctions constantes par l'application Π_K. La vérification de la relation (3.18) résulte de ce que $\int_{\partial_i K}(\phi-\Pi_K\phi)d\gamma = 0$ si $\phi \in P_1$, d'après la définition de l'application Π_K, ce qui est bien le cas pour la fonction $\phi = \frac{\partial w_h}{\partial n_K}$, puisque $w_h \in P_2$.

On démontre (cf. Ciarlet [12]) le lemme suivant, qui est la généralisation au cas des formes bilinéaires du Lemme de Bramble-Hilbert [8], établi pour des formes linéaires.

Lemme. Soit Ω un ouvert de R^n de frontière suffisamment régulière, soit k et ℓ deux entiers, et soit V un espace de fonctions vérifiant les inclusions $P_\ell \subset V \subset H^{\ell+1}(\Omega)$. L'espace V étant normé par $\|\cdot\|_{\ell+1,\Omega}$, soit $A : H^{k+1}(\Omega) \times V \to R$ une forme bilinéaire continue, de norme $\|A\|$, et telle que

(3.19) $$A(u,w) = 0 \text{ pour tout } u \in H^{k+1}(\Omega),\ w \in P_\ell,$$

(3.20) $$A(u,w) = 0 \text{ pour tout } u \in P_k,\ w \in V.$$

Alors il existe une constante C, qui ne dépend que de l'ouvert Ω, telle que

(3.21) $$|A(u,w)| \leq C\,\|A\|\ |u|_{k+1,\Omega}\ |w|_{\ell+1,\Omega}, \text{ pour tout } u \in H^{k+1}(\Omega),\ w \in V.$$

Une fois ce lemme établi, on l'applique aux expressions $A_{h,i,K}$ de (3.16): on passe comme à l'accoutumée de l'élément "courant" K à un élément "de référence" $\hat{K}$ sur lequel est appliqué le lemme, ce qui conduit à une majoration du type

(3.22) $|A_{h,i,K}(u,w_h)| \leq C\, h\, |u|_{3,K}\, |w_h|_{2,K}$ pour tout $u \in H^3(\Omega)$, $w_h \in V_h$,

le facteur h provenant des changements de variables dans les intégrales lorsqu'on passe de K à $\hat{K}$, puis de $\hat{K}$ à K. La difficulté résultant de ce que l'on considère une intégrale sur un côté plutôt que sur tout le triangle se traite comme dans Crouzeix & Raviart [19, Lemme 3].

Les autres termes intervenant dans l'expression $E_h(u,w_h)$ se traitent de façon analogue, avec éventuellement des modifications "techniques", et cela aussi bien pour le triangle de Morley que pour le triangle de Zienkiewicz ou le rectangle d'Adini (cf. les exemples).

Si nous faisons la somme de toutes les relations (3.18) sur tous les éléments finis K, nous en déduisons que

(3.23) $$E_h(u,w_h) = 0 \text{ pour tout } u \in P_2,\ w_h \in V_h,$$

or cette dernière relation n'est autre que le célèbre "patch test" des Ingénieurs, trouvé empiriquement par Irons [22] comme une condition nécessaire de "convergence" des méthodes d'éléments finis non conformes. Nous nous sommes efforcés ici précisément de faire apparaître cette nécessité en considérant le patch test comme l'une des deux invariances polynomiales nécessaires pour obtenir une majoration du type (3.14), une fois connu le lemme énoncé plus haut.

Examinons maintenant quelques exemples. Pour chacun des sous-espaces V_h correspondant aux trois exemples qui suivent, les conditions aux limites (1.10) sont prises en compte de la façon la plus simple: tous les degrés de liberté sont nuls lorsqu'ils correspondent à des noeuds situés sur la frontière. On constatera par ailleurs dans le cas du triangle de Zienkiewicz que le patch test se traduit par une restriction sur la géométrie des éléments.

Exemple 5 (cf. Figure 6). Cet élément, que l'on appelle "triangle de Zienkiewicz"

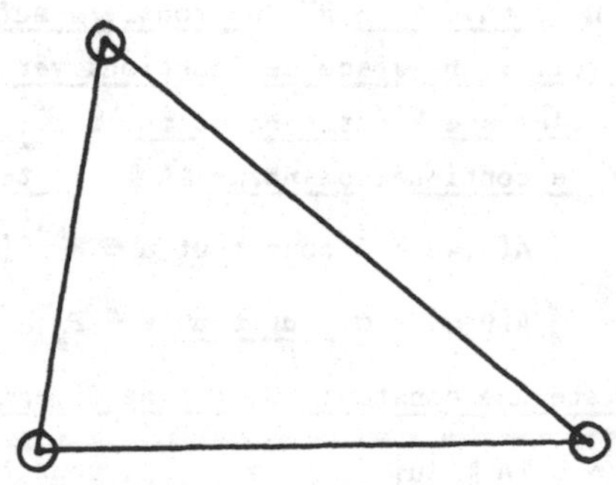

Figure 6

a été introduit dans Bazeley, Cheung, Irons & Zienkiewicz [5]. L'espace P est ici formé des polynômes $p \in P_3$ pour lesquels

$$(3.24) \qquad 6p(a) - 2\sum_{i=1}^{3} p(a_i) + \sum_{i=1}^{3} \langle Dp(a),(a_i-a)\rangle = 0,$$

où les points a_i, $1 \leq i \leq 3$, et a sont respectivement les sommets et le barycentre du triangle. L'espace P vérifie les inclusions $P_2 \subset P \subset P_3$, et sa dimension est 9. Lascaux et Lesaint [27] ont montré que le patch test est vérifié si et seulement si tous les côtés de tous les triangles d'une triangulation donnée sont parallèles à seulement trois direction, et qu'alors si $u \in H^3(\Omega)$,

$$\| u-u_h \|_h \leq C\, h\, |u|_{3,\Omega},$$

ce qui est la solution du "problème de l'Union Jack" (cf. Zienkiewicz [38, pp. 188-189]). Par ailleurs, le fait que la valeur au centre de gravité ne soit plus un degré de liberté (cf. la relation (3.24)), condition également trouvée par les Ingénieurs comme une condition empirique de convergence, voit ici sa justification dans le fait que la fonction de base correspondant au barycentre "ne passe pas" le patch test. ∎

Exemple 6 (cf. Figure 7). Cet élément, que l'on appelle "rectangle d'Adini",

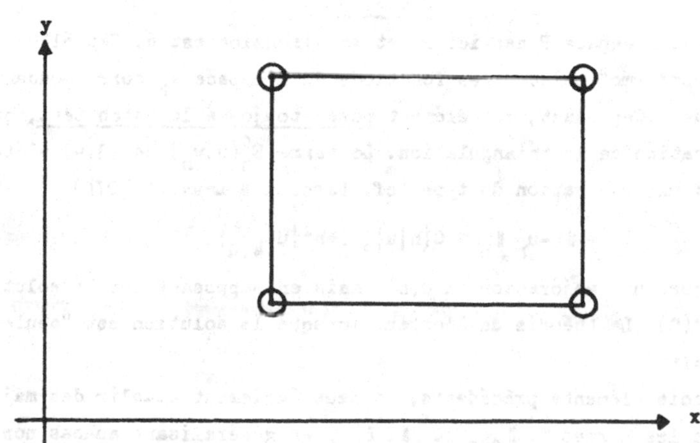

Figure 7

a été introduit dans Adini & Clough [1]. L'espace P consiste en tous les polynômes du type

$$p(x,y) = \alpha_{13}xy^3 + \alpha_{31}x^3y + \sum_{0\leq i+j\leq 3} \alpha_{ij}x^iy^j,$$

et sa dimension est 12. Lascaux et Lesaint [27] ont montré que, si $u \in H^3(\Omega)$,

$$\| u-u_h \|_h \leq C\, h\, |u|_{3,\Omega},$$

le patch test étant ici toujours vérifié. L'absence de condition géométrique n'est qu'apparente puisque l'on ne peut considérer que des domaines à côtés parallèles aux axes. ∎

Exemple 7 (cf. Figure 8). Cet élément est connu sous le nom de triangle de Morley

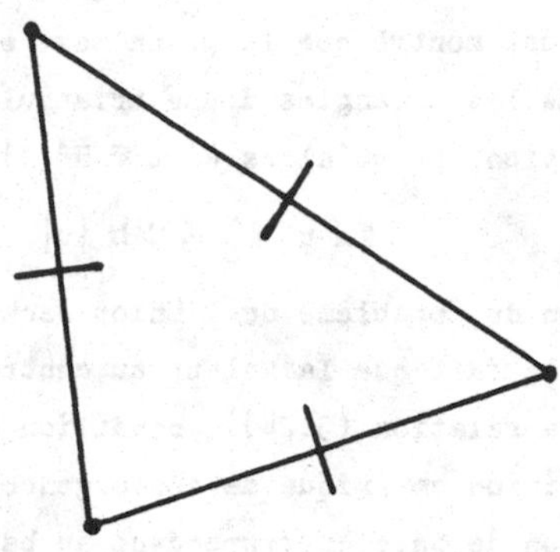

Figure 8

(cf. Morley [28]). L'espace P est ici P_2 et sa dimension est 6. Cet élément est "hautement non conforme" puisque les fonctions de l'espace V_h correspondant ne sont même pas continues. Cependant, cet élément passe toujours le patch test, quelle que soit la configuration de la triangulation. Le terme $E_h^0(u,w_h)$ de (3.9) n'étant pas nul, on arrive a une majoration du type (cf. Lascaux & Lesaint [27])

$$\|u-u_h\|_h \leq C\left(h|u|_{3,\Omega}+h^2|u|_{4,\Omega}\right),$$

c'est-à-dire encore une majoration en O(h), mais en supposant que la solution u est dans l'espace $H^4(\Omega)$. La théorie de l'erreur lorsque la solution est "seulement" dans $H^3(\Omega)$ reste à faire. ∎

Pour les trois éléments précédents, on peut également établir des majorations de l'erreur dans les normes $\|.\|_{0,\Omega}$ ou $\|.\|_{1,\Omega}$ en généralisant au cas non conforme les techniques de dualité d'Aubin-Nitsche déjà signalées au §2; à cet égard nous renvoyons à Lascaux et Lesaint [27].

Terminons par quelques considérations sur une autre façon de mettre en oeuvre des éléments non conformes. Pour fixer les idées, supposons que l'on ait l'inclusion $V_h \subset C^0(\bar{\Omega})$, mais non l'inclusion $V_h \subset C^1(\bar{\Omega})$. Les fonctions de l'espace V_h étant localement "régulières", la conformité de la méthode serait assurée si le long de tout côté "intérieur", adjacent à deux éléments K et K', on avait

$$(3.25) \qquad \frac{\partial v_h}{\partial n_K} + \frac{\partial v_h}{\partial n_{K'}} = 0 \text{ pour tout } v_h \in V_h,$$

et si l'on avait aussi sur $\partial\Omega$

(3.26) $$\frac{\partial v_h}{\partial n} = 0 \text{ pour tout } v_h \in V_h .$$

Si les relations (3.25) et (3.26) ne peuvent être satisfaites, du moins peut-on les considérer comme des contraintes et les pénaliser, suivant en cela une technique couramment utilisée en pratique; cf. par exemple Zienkiewicz [39].

Avec la définition (3.2) pour la forme bilinéaire $a_h(.,.)$, le problème discret consiste donc à chercher le minimum de la fonctionnelle

(3.27) $$J_h(v_h) = \frac{1}{2} a_h(v_h,v_h) - (f,v_h),$$

les fonctions v_h étant assujetties aux contraintes (3.25) et (3.26), que nous écrirons sous la forme $\phi(v_h) = 0$ avec

(3.28) $$\phi(v_h) = \sum_{\substack{K,K'\in\mathcal{C}_h \\ K\neq K'}} \int_{K\cap K'} \left(\frac{\partial v_h}{\partial n_K} + \frac{\partial v_h}{\partial n_{K'}}\right)^2 d\gamma + \int_\Gamma \left(\frac{\partial v_h}{\partial n}\right)^2 d\gamma .$$

La méthode de pénalisation consiste alors à chercher le minimum de la fonctionnelle

(3.29) $$J_h^*(v_h) = J_h(v_h) + \frac{1}{\varepsilon(h)} \phi(v_h)$$

lorsque v_h décrit le sous-espace V_h, ou $\varepsilon(h)$ est une fonction de h convenablement choisie qui tend vers zéro lorsque h tend vers zéro. Généralement, la fonction ε est de la forme $\varepsilon(h) = C\, h^\sigma$, où la constante $\sigma > 0$ est choisie de façon à obtenir le meilleur ordre de convergence.

Exemple 8 (cf. Figure 9). Le point a est le barycentre du triangle, et l'espace P est l'espace P_3 , dont la dimension est 10. Cet élément a été considéré par

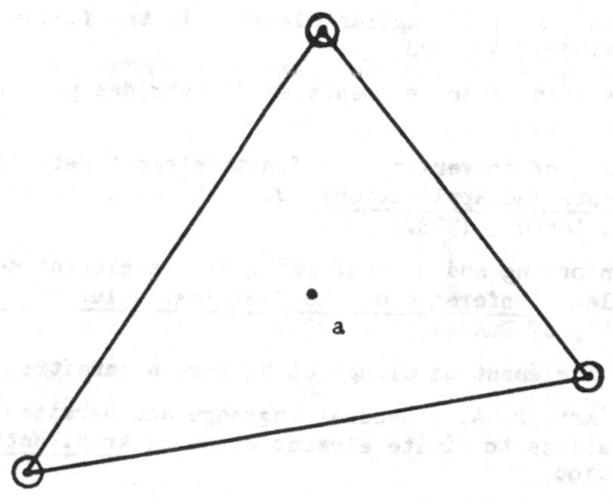

Figure 9

Babuška & Zlámal [4]. Avec le choix $\mu = 0$ dans la forme bilinéaire, ils ont montré que

(3.30) $$\|u-u_h\|_h < C\, h^{1/2} \|u\|_{3,\Omega}$$

pour le choix optimal $\varepsilon(h) = C\, h^2$.

Du fait de la pénalisation, il n'y a plus de patch test à passer, ce qui permet de conserver la valeur au barycentre comme degré de liberté, à l'inverse de ce qui se passait pour le triangle de Zienkiewicz (cf. Exemple 5).

REFERENCES

[1] Adini, A.; Clough, R.W. : Analysis of plate bending by the finite element method, NSF Report G. 7337, 1961.

[2] Aubin, J.P. : Behavior of the error of the approximate solutions of boundary value problems for linear elliptic operators by Galerkin's and finite difference methods, Ann. Scuola Norm. Sup. Pisa 21 (1967), 599-637.

[3] Babuška, I.; Aziz, A.K. : Survey Lectures on the Mathematical Foundations of the Finite Element Method, The Mathematical Foundations of the Finite Element Method with Applications to Partial Differential Equations (A.K. Aziz, Editor), pp. 3-359, Academic Press, New York, 1972.

[4] Babuška, I.; Zlámal, M.: Nonconforming elements in the finite element method Technical Note BN-729, University of Maryland, College Park, 1972.

[5] Bazeley, G.P.; Cheung, Y.K.; Irons, B.M.; Zienkiewicz, O.C. : Triangular elements in bending-conforming and nonconforming solutions, Conference on Matrix Methods in Structural Mechanics, Wright Patterson A.F.B., Ohio, 1965.

[6] Birkhoff, G.; Mansfield, L. : Compatible triangular finite elements, J. Math. Anal. Appl., à paraître.

[7] Bogner, F.K.; Fox, R.L.; Schmit, L.A. : The generation of interelement compatible stiffness and mass matrices by the use of interpolation formulas, Conference on Matrix Methods in Structural Mechanics, Wright Patterson A.F.B., Ohio 1965

[8] Bramble, J.H.; Hilbert, S.H. : Bounds for a class of linear functionals with applications to Hermite interpolation, Numer. Math. 16 (1971), 362-369.

[9] Bramble, J.H.; Zlámal, M. : Triangular Elements in the finite element method, Math. Comp. 24 (1970), 809-820.

[10] Brezzi, F. : Sur la méthode des éléments finis hybrides pour le problème biharmonique, à paraître.

[11] Ciarlet, P.G.; Orders of convergence in finite element methods, The Mathematics of Finite Elements and Applications (J.R. Whiteman, Editor), pp. 113-129, Academic Press, London, 1973.

[12] Ciarlet, P.G. : Conforming and nonconforming finite element methods for solving the plate problem, Conference on the Numerical Solution of Differential Equations, University of Dundee, July 03-06, 1973.

[13] Ciarlet, P.G.; Sur l'élément de Clough et Tocher, à paraître.

[14] Ciarlet, P.G.; Raviart, P.-A. : General Lagrange and Hermite interpolation in R^n with applications to finite element methods, Arch. Rational Mech. Anal. 46 (1972), 177-199.

[15] Ciarlet, P.G.; Raviart, P.-A. : Interpolation theory over curved elements, with applications to finite element methods, Computer Meth. in Appl. Mech. and Engnrg 1 (1972), 217-249.

[16] Ciarlet, P.G.; Raviart, P.-A. : A nonconforming method for the plate problem, à paraître.

[17] Ciavaldini, J.F.; Nédélec, J.C. : à paraître.

[18] Clough, R.W.; Tocher, J.L. : Finite element stiffness matrices for analysis of plate in bending, Conference on Matrix Methods in Structural Mechanics, Wright Patterson A.F.B., Ohio, 1965.

[19] Crouzeix, M.; Raviart, P.-A. : Conforming and nonconforming finite element methods for solving the stationary Stokes equations, I, à paraître.

[20] Fraeijs de Veubeke, B. : Bending and stretching of plates, Conference on Matrix Methods in Structural Mechanics, Wright Patterson A.F.B., Ohio, 1965.

[21] Glowinski, R. : Approximations externes, par éléments finis de Lagrange d'ordre un et deux, du problème de Dirichlet pour l'opérateur biharmonique. Méthode itérative de résolution des problèmes approchés, Conference on Numerical Analysis, Royal Irish Academy, 1972.

[22] Irons, B.M.; Razzaque, A. : Experience with the patch test for convergence of finite elements, The Mathematical Foundations of the Finite Element Method with Applications to Partial Differential Equations (A.K. Aziz, Editor), pp. 557-587, Academic Press, New York, 1972.

[23] Johnson, C. : On the convergence of some mixed finite element methods in plate bending problems, à paraître.

[24] Johnson, C. : Convergence of another mixed finite-element method for plate bending problems, Report No. 27, Department of Mathematics, Chalmers Institute of Technology and the University of Göteborg, 1972.

[25] Kondrat'ev, V.A. : Boundary value problems for elliptic equations in domains with conical or angular points, Trudy Mosk. Mat. Obšč. 16 (1967), 209-292.

[26] Landau, L.; Lifchitz, E. : Théorie de l'Elasticité, Mir, Moscou, 1967.

[27] Lascaux, P.; Lesaint, P. : Convergence de certains éléments finis non conformes pour le problème de la flexion des plaques minces, à paraître.

[28] Morley, L.S.D. : The triangular equilibrium element in the solution of plate bending problems, Aero. Quart. 19 (1968), 149-169.

[29] Nečas, J. : Les Méthodes Directes en Théorie des Equations Elliptiques, Masson, Paris, 1967.

[30] Nitsche, J. : Ein Kriterium für die quasi-optimalität des Ritzchen Verfahrens, Numer. Math. 11 (1968), 346-348.

[31] Oden, J.T., Some contributions to the mathematical theory of mixed finite element approximations, Tokyo Seminar on Finite Elements, 1973.

[32] Pian, T.H.H. : Finite element formulation by variational principles with relaxed continuity requirements, The Mathematical Foundations of the Finite Element Method with Applications to Partial Differential Equations (A.K. Aziz,Editor), pp. 671-687, Academic Press, New York, 1972.

[33] Raviart, P.-A. : Méthode des Eléments Finis, Université de Paris VI, Paris,1972.

[34] Sander, C. : Bornes supérieures et inférieures dans l'analyse matricielle des plaques en flexion-torsion, Bull. Soc. Roy. Sci. Liège 33 (1964), 456-494.

[35] Strang, G. : Approximation in the finite element method, Numer. Math. 19 (1972), 81-98.

[36] Strang, G. : Variational Crimes in the finite element method, The Mathematical Foundations of the Finite Element Method with Applications to Partial Differential Equations (A.K. Aziz, Editor), pp. 689-710, Academic Press, New York, 1972.

[37] Strang, G.; Fix, G. : An Analysis of the Finite Element Method, Prentice-Hall, Englewood Cliffs, 1973.

[38] Zienkiewicz, O.C. : The Finite Element Method in Engineering Science, McGraw-Hill, London, 1971.

[39] Zienkiewicz, O.C. : Constrained variational principles and penalty function methods in finite element analysis, Conference on the Numerical Solution of Differential Equations, University of Dundee, July 03-06, 1973.

[40] Zlámal, M. : On the finite element method, Numer. Math. 12 (1968), 394-409.

UN NOUVEL ÉLÉMENT DE COQUES GÉNÉRALES - "SEMILOOF"

Bruce M. Irons, Reader, University of Wales, Swansea.

Summary

The general purpose thin shell element described here is essentially a nonconforming quadratic Ahmad element, with minimum-order integration, and with nodal parameters which accept multiple junctions. A historical introduction clarifies the development and leads smoothly into the formulation, and the discussion of patch-test convergence. The geometry and the shell theory are new and are consistent with rigid body responses of a general patch. Implementation will be via a foolproof shape function routine.

Introduction et Motivation

"Semiloof" est probablement la dernière phase de la recherche de l'auteur pour un élément de coques,[5] une recherche motivée par un mécontentement profond envers presque tous les éléments de coques familiers. La liste suivante des conditions requises abrège cette méfiance:

(i) Il faut un élément de raideur direct, car beaucoup de millions de dollars sont déjà perdus sur les programmes d'ordinateur qui admettent tels éléments seulement.

(ii) L'élément doit être utilisable ("mixable" en anglais) - au sens exact de l'épreuve de rapiéçage[9] ("patch test" en anglais) - avec les éléments voisins triangulaires ou quadrilatéraux,† avec les membranes isoparamètriques, et avec un certain élément convenable de poutre.*

(iii) Les éléments de toutes formes ne violent jamais les mouvements rigides, ainsi que tous les assemblages de tels éléments.

† Semiloof est le premier quadrilatère de la famille Ahmad qui a satisfait numériquement aux épreuves (ii) et (iii). Les rapiéçages d'éléments triangulaires et quadrilatéraux imbriqués ont réussi aux essais d'ordinateur.

* Un élément de poutre tres spécial réalisé récemment par F. Albuquerque,[2] de Lourenço Marques.

(iv) La plupart des coques technologiques ont des angles vifs et des embranchements multiples. Donc, un élément doit modeler ceux-ci, sans exceptions pathologiques, et sans complications telles que transformations locales etc.

(v) Quelque soit le modèle choisi, on doit le traduire par l'intermédiaire d'une routine de fonctions de forme ("shape function routine" en anglais), une "boite noire" ("black box" en anglais) de laquelle l'utilisateur ne doit pas se soucier et dans laquelle se trouvent toutes les complications telles que transformations et conventions de signe. De cette façon le chercheur peut garantir fermement que l'utilisateur pourra incorporer facilement l'élément dans son programme, et que toutes les caractéristiques matricielles exotiques de l'élément, dont on aura besoin plus tard - inévitablement à court délai - pourront être ajoutées sans peine.

Note: Si les éléments iso-P sont toujours en vogue, c'est en grande partie que la routine des fonctions de forme est créée, vérifiée et bien documentée, et que tout le monde peut lui donner des tâches multiples. Nous envisageons maintenant une routine plus compliquée, mais conservant ces avantages.

(vi) La routine des fonctions de forme doit rester abordable au programmeur de maintenance grâce à une code lucide, une documentation complète, et des ordres d'impression intermédiairs facultatifs.

(vii) Toute routine doit être convenable et indéréglable. Par exemple le procédé se change souvent à la première rencontre avec un nouvel élément: il faut que l'utilisateur ne doive jamais l'en avertir.

(viii) Encore c'est un bienfait de fournir à l'utilisateur des diagnostics abondants. L'endroit naturel pour bien d'entre eux est la routine des fonctions de forme.

(ix) Il faut que l'élément ne montre aucun caprice en fonctionnement. Par exemple il doit éviter tous les pièges tels que rang défectueux.

(x) Une précision extrême n'est jamais requise, mais un maillage grossier doit donner des résultats acceptables. Selon le consensus general, les contraintes qui varient linéairement satisfont le mieux les besoins technologiques.

Disposition des Noeuds Semiloof

Il est difficile de critiquer la disposition de la fig.1 du point de vue de l'utilisateur - elle a semblé la plus attirante parmi celles examinées à la ref. 9. Aux coins et à mi-côtés nous avons u, v, w, les flèches en directions globales. Ceci suffirera pour une membrane, mais ne peut pas empêcher le pivotement pour une coque avec flexion. Afin d'assurer une conformité approximative pour les pentes, nous introduisons les rotations aux points de Gauss le long de chaque côté. Les 32 degrés de liberté devraient suffire à déterminer les champs de contraintes linéaires, à la fois pour les actions de flexion et de membrane. Pour la logique du programme nous groupons les 5 variables le long d'un côté comme si elles agissaient en son milieu. La convention de signe - à laquelle l'utilisateur s'interesse rarement - dépend des numéros de noeuds des coins voisins, disons N_1, N_2. Ceux-ci ne sont jamais égaux, car il se rapportent à des cordonnées nodales. Disons $N_2 > N_1$. Le sens des rotations aux points c et d est fixé par la règle de la main droite pour le segment orienté $N_1 \rightarrow N_2$, c précédant d.

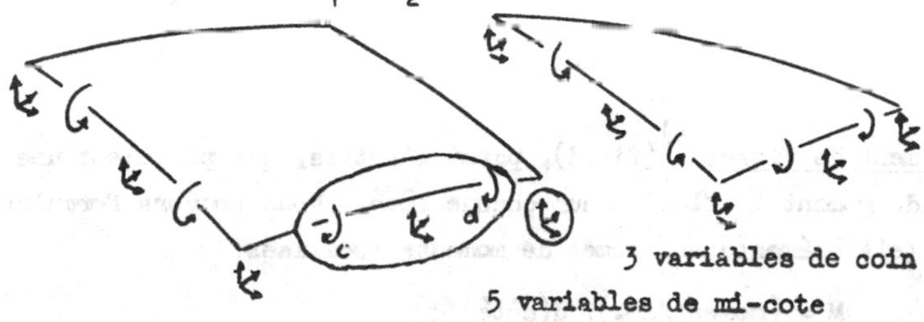

Fig.1

Précurseurs de Semiloof

1. On peut résoudre une problème 2D avec noeuds de Loof ("Loof nodes" en anglais) situés aux deux points de Gauss sur chaque côté d'un élément, comme indiqué à la fig.2. Il faut ajouter un 9me noeud au centre de l'élément: la recherche des fonctions de forme est donnée a la ref. 7. A cause des noeuds manquants aux coins, on ne peut même pas assurer $C^{(0)}$ entre les elements.

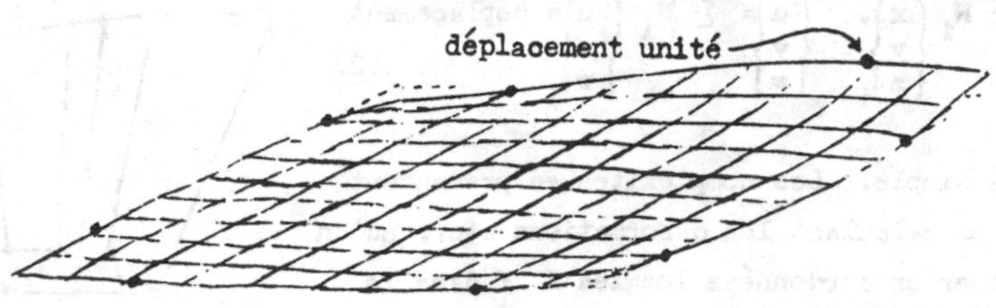

Fig.2

Pourtant, le discontinuité tend vers $P_2(\xi)$, la polynôme de Legendre qui s'annule aux deux points de Gauss (ici ξ arpente le cote, $-1 \leq \xi \leq 1$) dont l'intégrale et premier moment sont nuls. Nous examinons l'épreuve de rapiéçage, les contraintes étant maintenues constantes. Toute perturbation de cet état uniforme provoquera des discontinuités de déplacement entre les éléments. Si les sauts varient comme $P_2(\xi)$ le travail résultant est nul. Par conséquent, pourvu que le rang suffise, l'épreuve de rapiéçage est satisfaite.

Note. Nous faisons honneur a Loof. A la ref. 11 il mentionna des points de Lobatto mais il parla de son dessein d'essayer les points de Gauss quand l'occasion se présenterait.

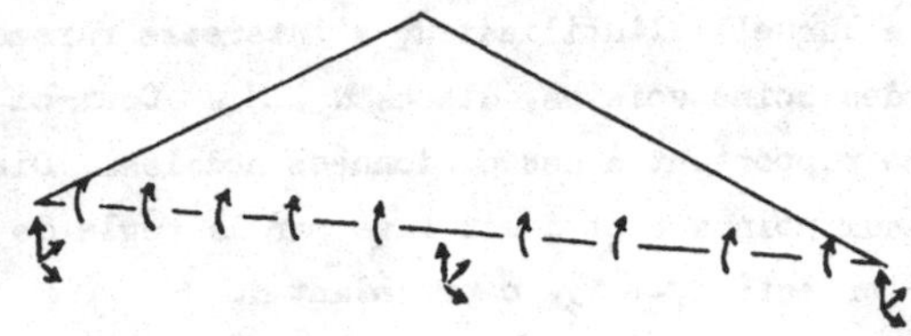

Fig.3

2. L'élément de Visser[15] (fig.3), parmi d'autres, qui postulent une variation linéaire de moment de flexion sur chaque côté. Nous pouvons formuler sans peine de tels éléments en termes de moments localisés:

$$M = (\text{moment/cm.}).\ d(\text{côté})/d \qquad (1)$$

aux deux points de Gauss, en sorte que tout travail est l'addition de M fois la rotation aux deux noeuds de Loof. Ensuite une inversion partielle[3] ("part-inversion" en anglais) donnerait précisément la version équivalente en raideur directe avec rotations de Loof.

3. La membrane isoparamètrique de fig.4 adapte les fonctions de forme $N_i(\xi,\eta)$ qui établissent une correspondence $(\xi,\eta)\rightarrow(x,y,z)$ en 3 dimensions.

$$\begin{Bmatrix} x \\ y \\ z \end{Bmatrix} = \sum N_i \begin{Bmatrix} x \\ y \\ z \end{Bmatrix}_i , \quad \begin{Bmatrix} u \\ v \\ w \end{Bmatrix} = \sum N_i \begin{Bmatrix} u \\ v \\ w \end{Bmatrix}_i = \text{déplacement} \qquad (2)$$

C'est très simple. Les complexités se présentent seulement en calculant les déformations etc., qu'on doit exprimer en cordonnées locales X, Y dans le plan tangentiel de la membrane. Nous avons

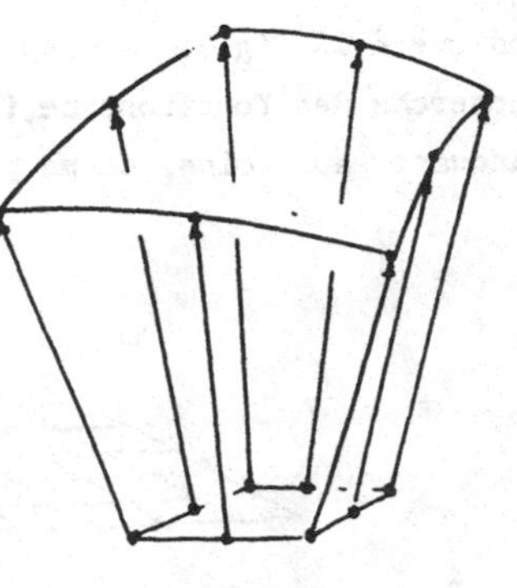

Fig.4

$$\begin{Bmatrix} \partial N_i/\partial \xi \\ \partial N_i/\partial \eta \end{Bmatrix} = \begin{bmatrix} \vec{\xi}\cdot\hat{X} & \vec{\xi}\cdot\hat{Y} \\ \vec{\eta}\cdot\hat{X} & \vec{\eta}\cdot\hat{Y} \end{bmatrix} \begin{Bmatrix} \partial N_i/\partial X \\ \partial N_i/\partial Y \end{Bmatrix} \qquad (3)$$

ou par exemple $\hat{X}$ est le vecteur unité en direction X, $\vec{\xi}$ est le vecteur base covariant ∂(position)/$\partial\xi$, et $\vec{\xi}\cdot\hat{X}$ est le produit scalaire. Nous calculons ainsi $\partial N_i/\partial X$, $\partial N_i/\partial Y$ au point donné ξ, η. Les déformations et autres quantités de ce genre suivent facilement. Par exemple, la contribution à $\partial W/\partial X$ à cause d'un déplacement $\vec{d}_i$ au noeud i est

$$\vec{d}_i \cdot \hat{Z}\, \partial N_i/\partial X \qquad (4)$$

4. La coque feuilletée d'Ahmad ("membrane-stack" en anglais) pour les coques semi-épaisses, originairement conçue quand les raisonnements vectoriels étaient manifestement absents dans les manuels d'éléments finis, était réalisée comme étude introductive.(1) Son utilisation générale était inattendu.

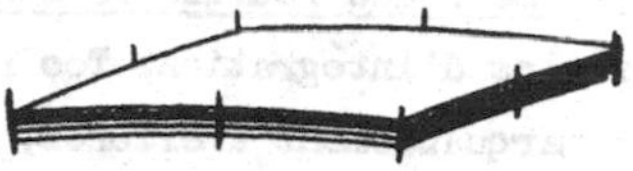

Fig.5

Nous discutons seulement le quadrilatère à 8 noeuds et 40 degrés de liberté. Chacune des 8 lignes rigides de la fig.5 se soumet aux flèches u,v,w à la mi-surface du feuillet, et lie les membranes. Chaque feuille correspond à l'intervalle (ξ, $\xi+d\xi$), comme indiqué à la fig.5. Géométriquement nous avons une brique iso-P 20-noeuds, mais x,y,z varient linéairement avec ξ, en sorte que chaque membrane peut avoir une épaisseur nonuniforme.

Élastiquement nous n'avons pas encore une coque réaliste. Les membranes ressemblent à un livre dont les pages glissent sans contrainte. Nous nous proposons de les coller afin de leur donner une raideur de flexion. Il y a deux techniques:

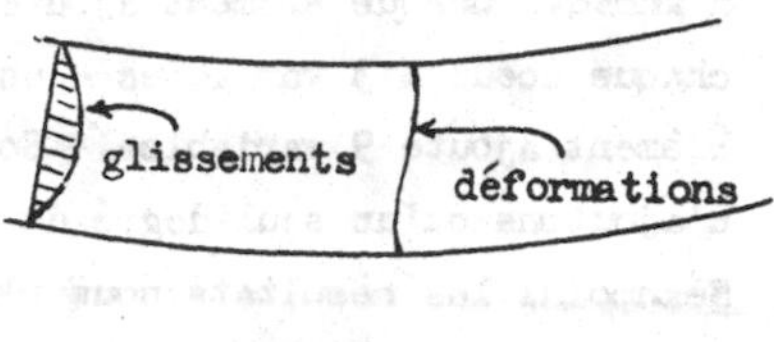

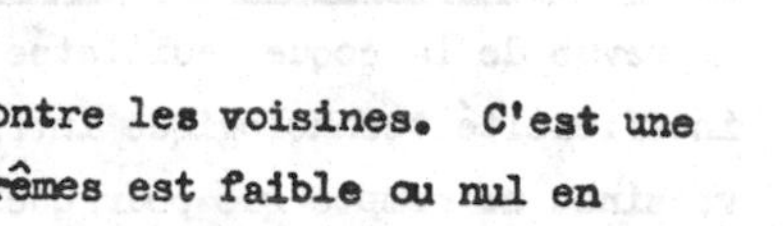

Fig.6

(i) Ahmad ajouta l'énergie de déformation de glissement à mesure que chaque membrane glisse contre les voisines. C'est une image grossière: le glissement aux membranes extrêmes est faible ou nul en réalité, hors du cas rare où des charges tangentielles sensibles s'appliquent à la surface. Toujours nous présumons que le glissement varie comme $(1 - \xi^2)$, et il suit que les normales courbent comme indiqué à la fig.6. Ahmad effectivement divise γ_{XZ} et γ_{YX} par $\sqrt{1,2}$ afin de rectifier le modèle dont les normales sont rigides. Notons que γ_{XY}, une déformation dans la membrane, n'est pas modifiée.

(ii) Alternativement, pour une coque mince nous voulons annuler γ_{XZ} et γ_{YZ}. En cas de certains éléments délinquants mais compétitifs ("delinquent elements" en anglais, avec des "discrete Kirchhoff assumptions") nous annulons γ_{XZ} et γ_{YZ} aux points isolés, choisis avec soin. Les contraintes nous permettent d'éliminer des variables nodales convenables avant d'assembler les éléments.

Note. Les deux techniques ne s'excluent pas. Par exemple, en principe on peut annuler toutes variations de glissement, afin de rendre celui-ci constant. Autrement, on peut le contraindre à varier linéairement avec ξ et η, etc.[1]

5. Le coque feuilletée d'Ahmad avec intégration 2x2. Par suite d'un examen des règles d'intégration, Too remarqua que Gauss 2x2 donne des résultats remarquablement améliorés, pouvu qu'il présente seulement les contraintes aux mêmes points 2x2. Cette observation[12,14] est toujours inexpliquée, cependant elle a inspiré au moins deux innovations importantes.

Discutons pourquoi les résultats sages nous étonnent spécialement, surtout lorsque la plaque ou la coque est mince. En tel cas l'énergie de déformation de glissement applique de fait 8 contraintes rigides, car on sait que les 2 glissements aux points de Gauss 2x2 sont reliés linéairement et indépendamment aux variables nodales. Donc examinons un maillage raffiné comme indiqué à la fig.7 pour une plaque d'Ahmad. Chaque element ajoute 3 noeuds, et chaque noeud a 3 variables - une flèche et deux pentes - de sorte que chaque élément ajoute 9 variables. Soustrayons les 8 contraintes. Alors nous n'ajoutons qu'un seul degré de liberté par élément de plaque supplémentaire. Néanmoins les résultats nous plaisent.

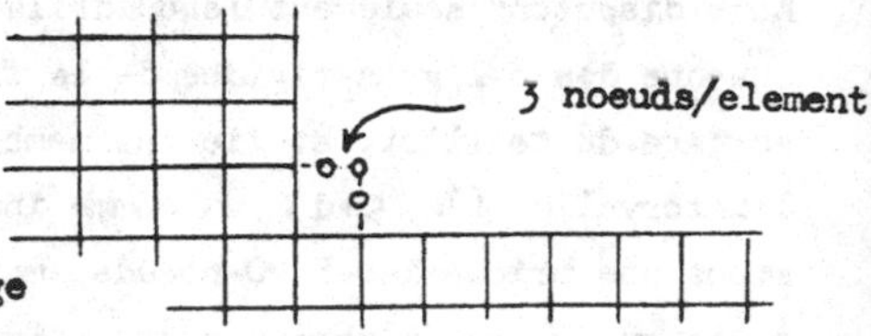

3 noeuds/element

Fig.7

6. Le premier élément délinquant iso-P se suggéra d'une part par la sagesse imprévue de la coque feuilletée avec intégration 2x2, et d'autre part par son inefficacité technologique intrinsique. Car le glissement entre les membranes voisines ne compte que pour quelques pour cent de l'énergie de déformation totale. En réalité, il importe peu qu'on l'inclue ou pas. Pourtant la coque feuilletée fournit une variation de glissement quadratique en ξ, η, mais linéaire en déformation de flexion.

Jusq'ici nous avons trop de degrés de liberté; mais quels 8 devons-nous omettre? La fig.8 nous donne un indice. Imaginons que AB soit une poutre aux flexions linéaires. On pourra la déterminer entièrement avec la flèche et la pente aux deux bouts, sans les deux variables. Nous nous demanderons si on peut aussi ôter les variables semblables en cas de plaque ou de coque.

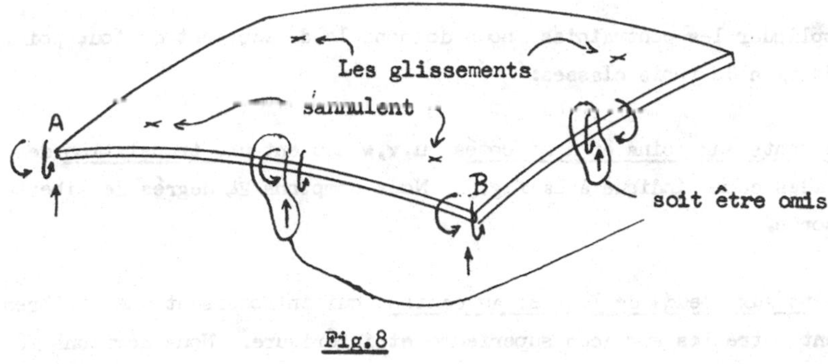

Fig.8

Note. Par conséquent, pour un grand problème chaque nouvel élément ajoute 5 variables au lieu d'une. Si nous avons en trouvé 4 en sus c'est que la flèche et la pente à mi-côté ne doivent plus se conformer entre les éléments. Les nouveaux degrés de liberté améliorent les résultats, un petit peu.

Razzaque fut le premier à coder les éléments délinquants iso P, et rapporte que la précision fut parmi les meilleures publiées pour les éléments de forme générale. Il se peut que la plaque délinquante soit l'aboutissement de la formulation iso-P.(13, 4)

Mais la coque délinquante fait défaut en pratique. Deux variables, une flèche et une pente, disparaissent de chaque mi-côté. On doit choisir avec soin leurs directions, et par conséquent on doit choisir aussi les 3 variables restantes. Razzaque a déterminé ces directions indépendamment dans chaque élément, sans se soucier des légères inconsistances.

On soupçonne qu'il a réussi à cause de la simplicité géométrique de ses problèmes. Sans doute il n'aurait pas obtenu de résultats utilisables pour des coques à angles vifs et à embranchements multiples.

Note. Les éléments délinquants sont justement dénommés. Dirigés par l'intuition physique plus que par toute théorie de coques admise, nous avons trouvé un élément compétitif. Bien qu'il ne satisfasse à l'épreuve de rapiéçage que pour un maillage de parallélogrammes (éventuellement inégaux), les éléments difformes réussissent presque. D'ailleurs, quand nous commettons ce délit particulier (et il est difficile de préciser en termes généraux ce que cela signifie quand la glissement s'annule aux points choisis), quel statut conserve-t-elle, l'épreuve de rapiéçage?

Déplacements de Semiloof Libres de Contraintes

Avant d'appliquer les contraintes, nous donnons le déplacement de tout point comme l'addition de trois classes:

1. Déplacements aux coins et à mi-côtés u,v,w causent une translation des 8 lignes rigides comme indiqué à la fig.5. Nous comptons 24 degrés de liberté de cette sorte.

2. Rotations aux noeuds de loof et au centre, qui introduisent une différence de déplacement entre les surfaces supérieure et inférieure. Nous comptons 18 degrés de liberté de plus.

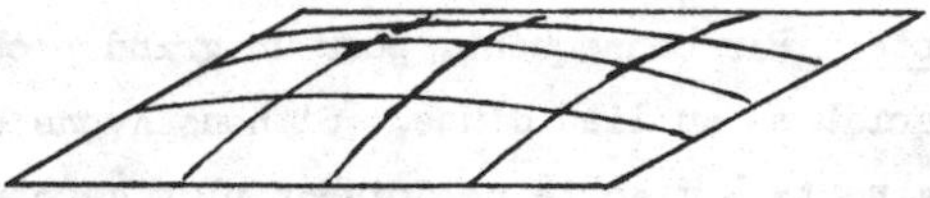

3. Une seule fonction bulle, $(1-\xi^2)(1-\eta^2)$ qui donne un déplacement dans la direction perpendiculaire a l'élément au centre ($\xi = \eta = 0$), et qui s'annule aux frontières. (fig.9) Ce supplément permit de satisfaire à l'épreuve de rapiéçage. Nous devons fournir tout état de flexion constante dans un élément, en général quadrilatéral et plat, disons

Fig.9

$$\begin{Bmatrix} x \\ y \end{Bmatrix} = \sum N_i \begin{Bmatrix} x \\ y \end{Bmatrix}_i, \quad z = 0, \quad \text{et } w = \sum N_i w_i \tag{5}$$

ou $N_i(\xi, \eta)$ sont les fonctions de forme de coins et de mi-côtés. Mais le quadrilatère n'exige pas toute la base, et par exemple

$$x = A + B\xi + C\eta + D\xi\eta$$

Si nous ajoutons le 43me degré de liberté, la fonction bulle, c'est que $w = x^2$ renferme le terme $\xi^2\eta^2$. A la ref.9 nous avons manqué cette condition requise.

Semiloof et les Contraintes de Glissement

Nous poursuivons en réduisant les 43 degrés de liberté aux 32 de la fig.1. Les 11 contraintes qui ont réussi (à la suite de plusieurs qui échouèrent) se groupent naturellement en trois classes:

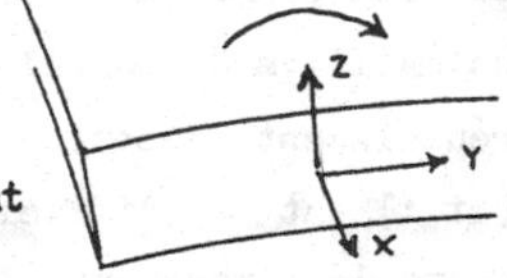

1. Les 8 pentes indésirées aux noeuds de Loof. La rotation de la normale comme indiqué à la fig.10 engendre un glissement γ_{YZ}. Donc il est naturel de contraindre la pente avec la condition $\gamma_{YZ} = 0$.

Z
Y
X

Fig.10

<u>Note.</u> Les 8 glissements aux noeuds de Loof sont reliés à peu près via la matrice identité aux 8 rotations éliminées. En outre, l'alternative la plus directe, les conditions $\gamma_{XZ} = \gamma_{YZ} = 0$ aux points de Gauss 2x2 ne sont même pas indépendantes.

<u>L'épreuve de rapiéçage.</u> Considérons encore l'influence de l'épreuve sur la feuille au niveau ζ à $\zeta + d\zeta$. Perturbons les noeuds "intérieurs" (c-a-d cernés complètement d'éléments - se reporter à la ref. 9, p.559, 583) et demandons-nous si le travail virtuel s'annule dans un champ de contraintes planes uniformes. Aux noeuds de Loof A et B à la vue en plan du rapiécage, la fig.11, les flèches normales a RS sont continues entre les éléments voisins à cause des pentes nodales communes. Si les flèches dans la direction de AB sont également continues, c'est que w_R, w_S et w_M, les flèches aux coins et à mi-côté, sont communes, et que le glissement γ_{YZ} s'annule à cause des 8 contraintes imposées. Par conséquent nous devons satisfaire l'épreuve de rapiéçage quelques soient les 3 dernières contraintes qu'il nous plaise d'imposer.

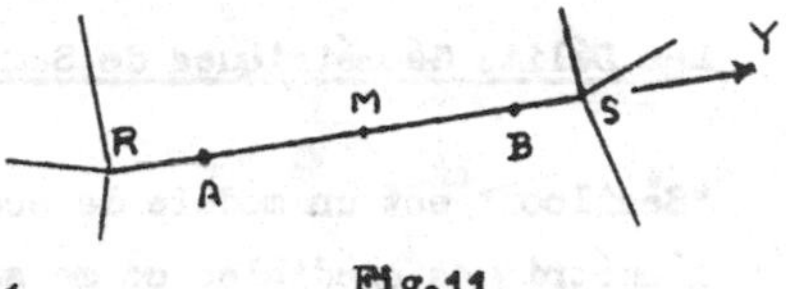

<u>Fig.11</u>

2. <u>Les 2 pentes au centre.</u> <u>Observation préliminaire.</u> Une plaque, en plan XY, a les glissements latéraux γ_{XZ}, γ_{YZ}. Or, pour Z fixe, et X,Y tournant, la quantité bidimensionnelle

$$\vec{\gamma} = \hat{X}\,\gamma_{XZ} + \hat{Y}\,\gamma_{YZ} \qquad (6)$$

se transforme comme un vecteur.

<u>Les 2 contraintes.</u> Nous réservons les vecteurs unités au centre, $\hat{X}_9$ et $\hat{Y}_9$, et nous fixons

$$\int \hat{X}_9 \cdot \vec{\gamma}\ d(\text{superficie}) = \int \hat{Y}_9 \cdot \vec{\gamma}\ d(\text{superficie}) = 0 \qquad (7)$$

employant les points de Gauss 2x2.

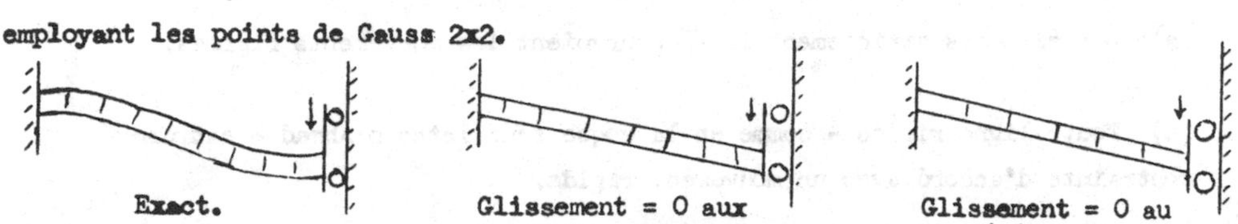

Exact. | Glissement = 0 aux 2 points de Gauss. Exact. | Glissement = 0 au mi-côté. Trop souple.

<u>Fig.12</u>

<u>Note.</u> Préalablement une version plus simple a échoué, malgré sa réussite à l'épreuve de rapiéçage. Elle se déformait trop souplement dans les champs de contraintes nonuniformes. Au lieu des deux intégrales de (7), nous avons contraint les deux glissements au centre. D'une manière semblable l'élément quadratique de poutre indiqué à la fig.12 est trop souple avec une seule contrainte.

3. <u>La fonction bulle</u> est évidemment riche d'une certaine combinaison de glissements:

$$\int \nabla \cdot \vec{\gamma}\ d(\text{superficie})$$

$$= \int \frac{\partial \gamma_{xz}}{\partial x} + \frac{\partial \gamma_{yz}}{\partial y}\ d(\text{superficie}) = 0 \qquad (8)$$

est une contrainte crédible. Nous préférons transformer l'intégrale à

$$\int_{\text{frontiere}} (\text{glissement normal})\ d(\text{arc}) = 0 \qquad (9)$$

et celle-ci est la forme employée.

<u>Les Délits Géométriques de Semiloof</u>

"Semiloof" est un modèle de coque mince, et nous faisons les suppositions géométriques crédibles comme suit.

(i) Pour commencer, nous rendons approximativement normales à la surface moyenne du feuillet les lignes nodales rigides de la fig.5. Par conséquent, les éléments ne s'imbriquent en général pas aux embranchements.

(ii) La coque est si mince que l'élément de surface d(superficie) pour toute membrane peut être confondu avec sa valeur sur la mi-surface.

(iii) Les membranes sont presque parallèles.

L'épreuve de rapiéçage a déjà admis tous les quadrilatères plates. Un autre principe domine dès maintenant: désormais nous exigerons qu'un rapiéçage d'elements <u>de toutes formes</u> ne viole jamais les mouvements rigides. A la ref.1 nous avons fait les hypothèses sans assez de soins. Notons:

(a) Les éléments strictement iso-P pourvoient les mouvements rigides.

(b) Toute ligne rigide - comme en la coque feuilletée d'Ahmad - est une contrainte d'accord avec un mouvement rigide.

(c) Un couple d'éléments fournirait un mouvement rigide <u>seulement si</u> les variables nodales qui les lient ensemble (en particulier les pentes) se définissent exactement pour tout mouvement rigide donné.

Il faut que toute ligne rigide ξ, η = constante soit normale, à chaque noeud de Loof, à la tangente frontière. Autrement un mouvement de rotation $\vec{\Omega}$, normal à la surface moyenne, comme indiqué à la fig.13, provoquerait une "rotation"

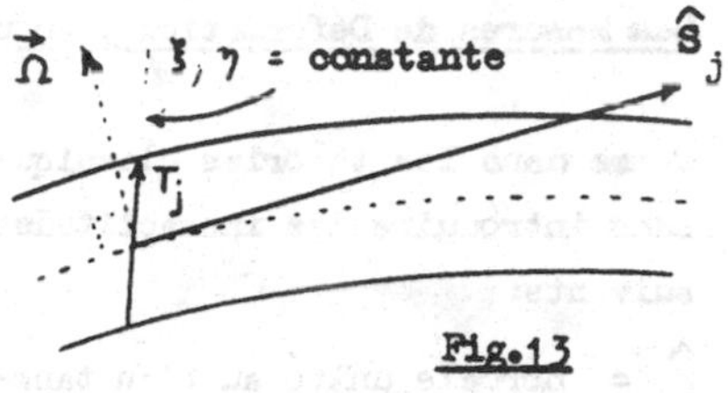

Fig.13

fausse autour de $\hat{S}_j$. Si nous devons compenser les épaisseurs donnés, c'est que cette condition n'est pas assurée automatiquement. Quand nous rencontrons un nouvel élément, nous devons remplir plusieurs tâches:

Stade 1. Nous interpolons les épaisseurs T_i, $i = 1$ a 8, données aux coins et à mi-côtés, afin d'engendrer les T_j, $j = 1$ à 9, aux noeuds de Loof et au centre. Nous élevons $\vec{T}_j$ (la première approximation) perpendiculaire à la mi-surface.

Stade 2. Afin d'assurer que les $\vec{T}_j$, $j = 1$ a 9, déterminent une base géométrique dans l'espace de fonctions de coins et de mi-côtés, $N_i(\xi, \eta)$, $i = 1$ à 8, il faut imposer une condition aux épaisseurs $\vec{T}_j$, c'est à dire $\Sigma(-1)^j\vec{T}_j^* = 0$, $j = 1$ à 8, ou $\vec{T}_j^*$ est la valeur définitive: disons

$$\vec{T}_j^* = \vec{T}_j - (-1)^j (\vec{p} - \vec{p}.\hat{S}_j \hat{S}_j) \tag{9}$$

Si la composante $\vec{T}_j.\hat{S}_j$ s'annule, $\vec{T}_j^*.\hat{S}_j = 0$ aussi. Pour calculer $\vec{p}$ nous multiplions par $(-1)^j$ et l'additionnons:

$$\sum_1^8 (-1)^j\vec{T}_j^* = \sum_1^8 (-1)^j\vec{T}_j - \sum_1^8 (\vec{p} - \vec{p}.\hat{S}_j \hat{S}_j) = 0 \tag{10}$$

Traduisons en forme matricielle:

$$\left[8\,I - \sum_1^8 \hat{S}_j \hat{S}_j^T\right]\vec{p} = \sum_1^8 (-1)^j \vec{T}_j \tag{11}$$

Beaucoup de techniques sont possibles: celle-ci est indéréglable, car la matrice 3x3 est définie positive. Notons que les ajustements forcés sont de même ordre de grandeur que les variations d'épaisseur normale T dans un élément iso-P dont les T_i sont constants aux coins et mi-côtés.

Puis nous construisons et conservons les déplacements relatifs $\vec{r}_j = \vec{T}_j \times \hat{S}_j$, qui engendrent la pente unité commune avec les éléments voisins: aussi $\vec{s}_j = \hat{S}_j T_j$, qui donnerait une pente approximativement unitaire le long du côté, une variable destinée pour l'élimination.

Stade 3. Nous construisons et réduisons la matrice des contraintes.

Stade 4. Nous nous servons de cette matrice-ci pour créer les fonctions de forme a l'endroit donné ξ, η. Sauf dans le cas d'un nouvel élément, nous sautons directement au 4me stade.

Les Mesures de Déformation pour une Coque Feuilletée Mince

Comme dans les théories classiques de coques, notre but est simplifier le calcul sans introduire des inexactitudes excessives. Nous employons les symboles suivants:

$\hat{Z}$ = normale unité au plan tangent à la surface moyenne.

$\hat{X}$ = normale dirigée vers l'extérieur dans le plan tangent à l'élément à la frontière.

$\vec{d}$ = déplacement à la surface moyenne.

$\vec{\Delta}$ = déplacement relatif entre les surfaces supérieure et inférieure, tel que $\vec{r}_j$ ou $\vec{s}_j$, au meme point ξ, η.

N_i, L_j = 8 fonctions de forme de coins et de mi-côtés, et 9 fonctions de Loof.

Ainsi $\vec{d} = \sum N_i \vec{d}_i$ et $\vec{\Delta} = \sum L_j \vec{\Delta}_j$, $i = 1$ à 8 et $j = 1$ à 9.

$\vec{T}$ = vecteur d'épaisseur

$= \sum L_j \vec{T}_j^{*} = R\hat{X} + S\hat{Y} + T\hat{Z}$ disons.

Par conséquent T est la composante normale, et R, S introduisent une pente initiale. T n'égale pas $\sum L_j T_j$. Nous inférons:

$$\begin{Bmatrix} \partial/\partial\xi \\ \partial/\partial\eta \\ \partial/\partial\zeta \end{Bmatrix} = \begin{bmatrix} a & b & 0 \\ c & d & 0 \\ \tfrac{1}{2}R & \tfrac{1}{2}S & \tfrac{1}{2}T \end{bmatrix} \begin{Bmatrix} \partial/\partial X \\ \partial/\partial Y \\ \partial/\partial Z \end{Bmatrix} \tag{12}$$

car X et Y se trouvent dans le plan ξ-η, et car le changement de position quand ζ varie de -1 a 1, tenant ξ et η constants, est $\vec{T}$. Or,

$$\partial/\partial Z = (2\,\partial/\partial\zeta - R\,\partial/\partial X - S\,\partial/\partial Y)/T \tag{13}$$

Par exemple,

$$U_Z = (\vec{\Delta}.\hat{X} - R\,U_X - S\,U_Y)/T \tag{14}$$

Les deux glissements, $\gamma_{XZ} = U_Z + W_X$ et $\gamma_{YZ} = V_Z + W_Y$ exigent les termes de correction entraînant R et S, à cause de la pente initiale de $\vec{T}$.

Les dérivées qui déterminent les déformations de membrane et le mouvement de rotation sont simples. Par exemple,

$$\varepsilon_x = U_X = \sum \vec{d}_i.\hat{X}\,\partial N_i/\partial X \tag{15}$$

Mais au lieu de <u>courbures</u> nous utilisons directement U_{XZ}, U_{YZ}, V_{XZ} et V_{YZ}:

$$-U_{XZ} \text{ au lieu de } W_{XX}$$
$$-U_{YZ} - V_{XZ} \text{ au lieu de } 2\,W_{XY}$$
$$-V_{YZ} \text{ au lieu de } W_{YY} \qquad (16)$$

Afin d'éviter la complication de (13), nous remplaçons UXZ par:

$$U_{XZ} = \vec{\Delta}_X . \hat{X}/T = \Sigma\, \vec{\Delta}_i . \hat{X}(\partial L_i/\partial X)/T \qquad (17)$$

Car en pratique nous multiplierons U_{XZ} par T, afin de calculer l'écart de déformation entre les surfaces supérieure et inférieure. De cette façon nous comparons la déformation en A, dans la fig.14, avec celle en B, pas orthogonalement au-dessus de A. Tous les deux s'annulent si le mouvement est rigide.

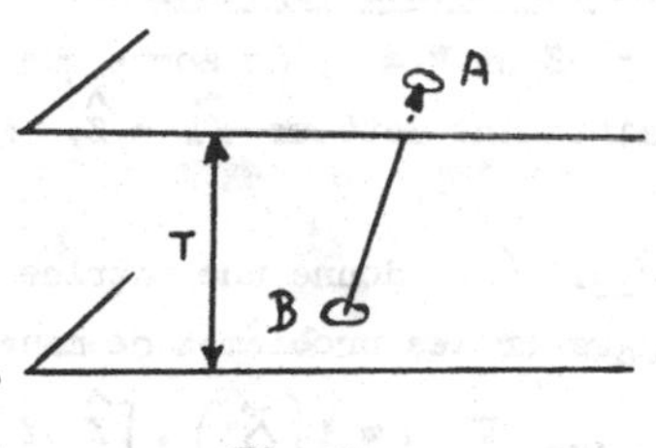

Fig.14

Il y a encore deux <u>termes supplémentaires de flexion</u>, facilement ignorés, causés par $\vec{d}$.

(a) Si $\partial N_i/\partial \xi$ et $\partial N_i/\partial \eta$ sont les mêmes aux surfaces supérieure et inférieure, c'est que N_i est une function de ξ, η seulement, mais un point X devient X + R, Y devient Y + S. Or,

$$\begin{Bmatrix} dX \\ dY \end{Bmatrix} \text{ devient } \begin{Bmatrix} dX \\ dY \end{Bmatrix} = \begin{bmatrix} 1+R_X & R_Y \\ S_X & 1+S_Y \end{bmatrix} \begin{Bmatrix} dX \\ dY \end{Bmatrix} \qquad (18)$$

$$d\varphi = [\varphi_x \quad \varphi_y] \begin{Bmatrix} dX \\ dY \end{Bmatrix} = [\varphi_X \quad \varphi_Y]^* \begin{bmatrix} 1+R_X & R_Y \\ S_X & 1+S_Y \end{bmatrix} \begin{Bmatrix} dX \\ dY \end{Bmatrix} \qquad (19)$$

$$\begin{Bmatrix} \varphi_x \\ \varphi_y \end{Bmatrix}^* = \begin{bmatrix} 1-R_X & -S_X \\ -R_Y & 1-S_Y \end{bmatrix} \begin{Bmatrix} \varphi_X \\ \varphi_Y \end{Bmatrix} \qquad (20)$$

Par exemple, U_{XZ} acquiert le terme $-(R_X U_X + S_X U_Y)/T$.

(b) Si X,Y sont dans la surface inférieure, la direction normale à la surface supérieure devient $(-T_X, -T_Y, 1)$. A cause d'une flèche W nous avons les composantes $\delta U = T_X W$, $\delta V = T_Y W$ dans la surface supérieure. Par exemple, U_{YZ} acquiert le terme $T_X W_Y/T$.

Résumons sommairement:

$$\begin{Bmatrix} \gamma_{XZ} \\ \gamma_{YZ} \end{Bmatrix} = \begin{Bmatrix} W_X \\ W_Y \end{Bmatrix} + \frac{1}{T}\vec{\Delta}\cdot\begin{Bmatrix} \hat{X} \\ \hat{Y} \end{Bmatrix} - \frac{1}{T}\begin{bmatrix} U_X & U_Y \\ V_X & V_Y \end{bmatrix}\begin{Bmatrix} R \\ S \end{Bmatrix} \qquad (21)$$

$$\begin{bmatrix} U_{XZ} & V_{XZ} \\ U_{YZ} & V_{YZ} \end{bmatrix} = \frac{1}{T}\begin{Bmatrix} \vec{\Delta}_X \\ \vec{\Delta}_Y \end{Bmatrix}\cdot\begin{bmatrix} \hat{X} & \hat{Y} \end{bmatrix} - \frac{1}{T}\begin{bmatrix} R_X & S_X \\ R_Y & S_Y \end{bmatrix}\begin{bmatrix} U_X & V_X \\ U_Y & V_Y \end{bmatrix} + \frac{1}{T}\begin{Bmatrix} W_X \\ W_Y \end{Bmatrix}\begin{bmatrix} T_X & T_Y \end{bmatrix} \qquad (22)$$

(Voir (23) aussi, la version préférée.) Démontrons que les formules obéissent aux mouvements rigides. Mettons $\vec{\Omega} = \hat{X}$; sur la surface inférieure $U = 0$, $V = -Z$ et $W = Y$, de sorte que $\vec{\Delta} = -T\hat{Y} + S\hat{Z}$. Les déformations s'annulent. Maintenant mettons $\vec{\Omega} = \hat{Z}$; etc.

Note. (22) donne une matrice antisymétrique au lieu de nulle, qui peut aggraver les problèmes de mauvais conditionnement. Nous préférons modifier (22):

$$\begin{bmatrix} U_{XZ} & V_{XZ} \\ U_{YZ} & V_{YZ} \end{bmatrix} = \frac{1}{T}\begin{Bmatrix} \vec{\Delta}_X \\ \vec{\Delta}_Y \end{Bmatrix}\cdot\begin{bmatrix} \hat{X} & \hat{Y} \end{bmatrix} - \frac{1}{T}\begin{bmatrix} R_X & S_X \\ R_Y & S_Y \end{bmatrix}\begin{bmatrix} U_X & V_X \\ U_Y & V_Y \end{bmatrix} + \frac{1}{T}\begin{Bmatrix} T_X \\ T_Y \end{Bmatrix}\begin{bmatrix} W_X & W_Y \end{bmatrix} \qquad (23)$$

Semiloof En Pratique

Cette explication courte est développée à la ref.5 qui comprend une version ancienne et défectueuse du programme. L'ensemble actuel des fonctions de forme est aussi disponible sans contrainte. Il comprend 450 instructions FORTRAN et il faut 1600 mémoires (nombre réels) pour les tableaux. Avec la documentation et les 11 essais diagnostiques, il devrait être facile à incorporer. On peut améliorer la vitesse, pourtant, car le programme a changé continuellement pendant les 14 mois de mise au point, la vitesse étant négligée au profit de la clarté et la facilité de modification.

Le rang et les mécanismes parasites. Idéalement la matrice de raideur pour un élément quadrilatéral a le rang de 26 = 32 (le nombre des variables) - 6(le nombre des mouvements rigides disponibles); pour un élément triangulaire, 18 = 24 - 6. Mais chaque point d'intégration peut contribuer au maximum 6 (le rang de la matrice d'élasticité), donnant 24 pour le quadrilatère à intégration 2x2, et 18 pour le triangle intégré par la règle de mi-côtés.

Par conséquent le quadrilatère a aux moins deux mécanismes parasites, comme ceux indiqués à la fig.15 pour un élément carré. (L'expérience n'a pas encore montré d'autre mécanisme ni pour le triangle ni pour le quadrilatère.) Il est bien possible qu'un tel

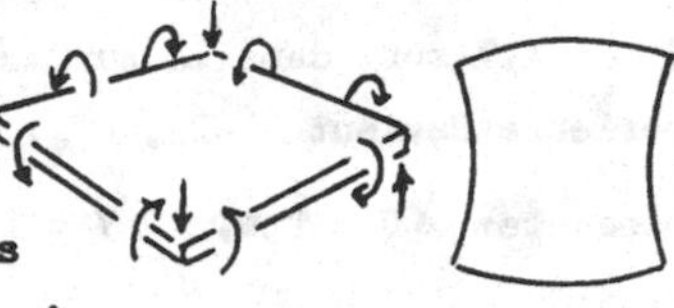

Fig.15

mécanisme puisse se transmettre à travers les éléments voisins et de là contamine toute la solution. Nous pouvons:

(a) savoir ce qu'il faut faire à propos du problème et l'éviter ordinairement.

(b) employer toujours les triangles. Quoique ceçi entraîne davantage de variables, les inexactitudes sont néanmoins cinq fois plus grandes que lorsqu'on utilise les quadrilatères.

(c) employer une règle d'intégration à 5 points:

$$\int_{-1}^{1}\int_{-1}^{1} \varphi(\xi,\eta)\, d\xi\, d\eta = a\varphi(0,0) + \sum_{1}^{4} b\varphi(\pm B, \pm B) \qquad (24)$$

ou $b = 1 - \frac{1}{4}a$ et $B = (3b)^{-\frac{1}{2}}$, disons a = .01, b = .9975, et B = .5780733131 au lieu de .577350269.

<u>La performance de l'élément</u>

1. Les éléments de coques iso-P à 8 noeuds avec intégration 2x2 et avec les mesures de déformation qui ne violent jamais les mouvements rigides, ont donné les résultats excellents pour les coques régulières. Surtout la performance avec un maillage grossier est remarquable.

2. Puisque la convergence est assurée, l'auteur s'est concentré a l'étude des maillages grossiers. La plaque circulaire chargée uniformément, comme indiqué à la fig.16 ($\nu = 0,3$) a donné des écarts de contrainte de ± 3% maximum. La plaque carrée de la fig.17 a donné une flèche centrale +0.13%.

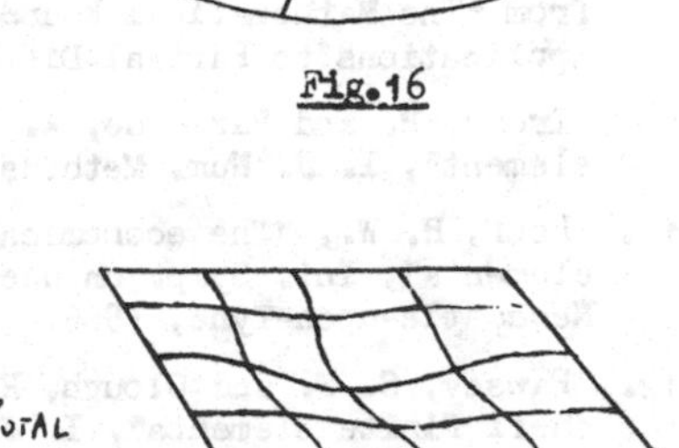

Fig.16

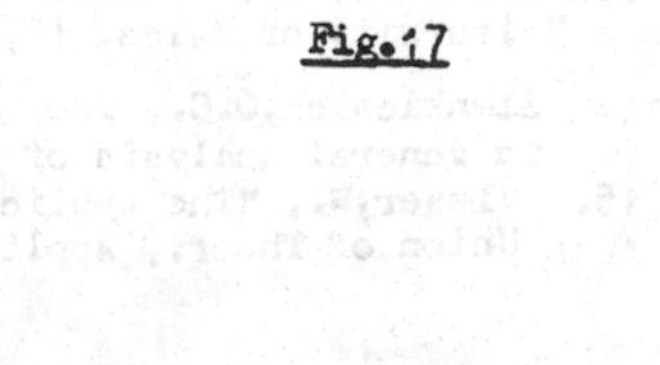

Fig.17

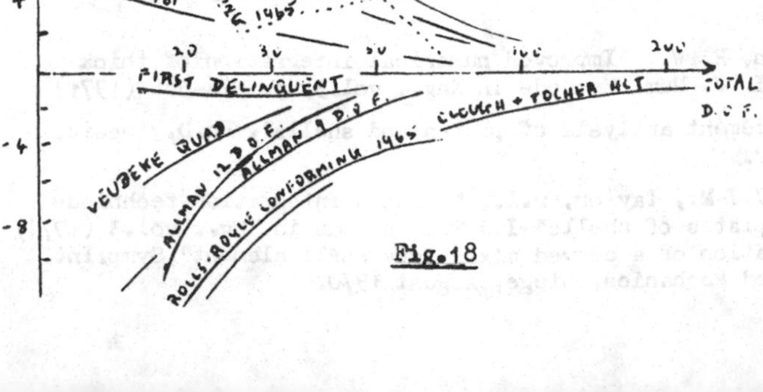

Fig.18

3. La reponse de la plaque carrée a une charge ponctuelle est moins satisfaisante comme indiquée à la fig.18, et bien pire que la ref. Nous l'admettons car:

(a) Les coins peuvent pivoter: voir la fig.19. Probablement l'élément de Visser commettrait cette faute.

(b) Ordinairement une charge ponctuelle est reprise par une poutre.

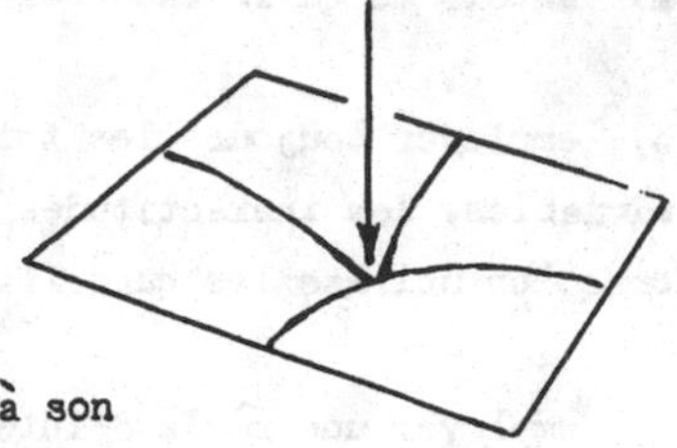

Fig.19

Reconnaissance. L'auteur veut exprimer sa gratitude à son collègue M. Ivan Cormeau de Bruxelles pour l'aide patiente à propos de la grammaire et du choix de mots.

References

1. Ahmad, S., "Curved finite elements in the analysis of solid, shell and plate structures" Ph.D. thesis, University of Wales 1969.

2. Albuquerque, F., "A beam element for use with the Semiloof shell element", M.Sc. thesis, University of Wales 1973.

3. Asplund, S.O., "Structural Mechanics: Classical and Matrix methods" Prentice-Hall, Englewood Cliffs, N.J., 1966.

4. Baldwin, J.T., Razzaque, A, and Irons, B., "Shape function subroutine for an isoparametric thin plate element", Int. J. Num. Meth., to be published.

5. Irons, B., Lecture notes, International Research Seminar on the Theory and Application fo Finite Elements (A NATO Advanced Study Institute), July-August 1973, Calcary University, Canada.

6. Irons, B., "Engineering Applications of Numerical Integration in Stiffness Methods", JAIAA vol.4 (1966) p.2035-2037.

7. Irons, B., Comment on "A Higher Order Conforming Recangular Plate Element" by S. Gopalacharyulu, I. J. Num. Methods in Eng., vol.6 no.2, p. 305-309.

8. Irons, B. and Razzaque, A., "Shape function formulations for elements other than displacement models", Conference on Variational Methods in Engineering, Southampton University, September 1972.

9. Irons, B. and Razzaque, A., "Experience with the Patch Test", p.557-587, from "The Mathematical Foundations of the Finite Element Method with Applications to Partial Differential Equations" Academic Press 1972.

10. Irons, B. and Razzaque, A., "A further modification to Ahmad's shell element", I. J. Num. Methods in Eng., Vol.5, no.4 (1973) p.588-589.

11. Loof, H. W., "The economical computation of stiffness of large structural elements", Int. Symp. on use of Comp. in Struct. Eng., University of Newcastle-upon-Tyne, 1966.

12. Pawsey, S. F. and Clough, R. W., "Improved numerical integration of thick shell finite elements", I. J. Num. Methods in Eng., vol.3, p. 576-586 (1971)

13. Razzaque, A., "Finite element analysis of plates and shells", Ph.D. thesis, University of Wales, 1972.

14. Zienkiewicz, O.C., Too, J.J-M., Taylor, r.l., "Reduced Integration technique in general analysis of plates of shells" I.J.Num.Methods in Eng., vol.3 (1971)

15. Visser, W., "The Application of a curved mixed-type shell element", Symp.Int. Union of Theor., Applied Mechanics, Liege, August 1970.

NUMERICAL SOLUTION OF THE STATIONARY NAVIER-STOKES EQUATIONS BY FINITE ELEMENT METHODS

P. JAMET (*) and P.A. RAVIART (**)

1. INTRODUCTION

Let Ω be a bounded domain of $\mathbb{R}^N$ (N=2 or 3) with boundary Γ. We consider the stationary Navier-Stokes problem for an incompressible viscous fluid confined in Ω. Find functions $\vec{u}=(u_1,\ldots,u_N)$ and p defined over Ω such that

$$(1.1)\begin{cases} -\nu\Delta\vec{u}+\sum_{i=1}^{N} u_i \dfrac{\partial\vec{u}}{\partial x_i} + \overrightarrow{\text{grad}}\, p = \vec{f} \quad \text{in } \Omega, \\ \text{div}\,\vec{u} = 0 \quad \text{in } \Omega, \\ \vec{u} = 0 \quad \text{on } \Gamma, \end{cases}$$

where $\vec{u}$ is the fluid velocity, p is the pressure, $\vec{f}$ are the body forces and $\nu>0$ is the viscosity coefficient (the density of the fluid has been set equal to 1).

In a previous paper [4], Crouzeix and the second author have developped a general theory for the finite element approximation of the Stokes problem and have constructed conforming and nonconforming triangular elements (N=2) or tetraedral elements (N=3) well suited for the numerical treatment of the constraint div $\vec{u}$=0. In the present paper, we shall extend the analysis of [4] to the finite element approximation of the nonlinear problem (1.1).

On the other hand, it has been found worthwile to use numerical quadrature for evaluating the various integrals which appear in the finite element method and particularly those associated with the nonlinear term $\sum_{i=1}^{N} u_i \frac{\partial\vec{u}}{\partial x_i}$. Thus, we shall analyze in this paper the effect of numerical quadrature.

(*) Service de Mathématiques Appliquées, Centre d'Etudes de Limeil, B.P. 27, 94190 VILLENEUVE-ST-GEORGES, FRANCE.

(**) Analyse Numérique, T.55, Université de Paris VI, 4 Place Jussieu, 75230 PARIS CEDEX 05, FRANCE.

An outline of the paper is as follows. In §2, we shall recall some standard results on the continuous problem (1.1). We shall give in §3 a general formulation of conforming finite element approximations of the Navier-Stokes problem (L;1). Section 4 will be devoted to the derivation of general error bounds for the velocity and for the pressure. We shall introduce in §5 the numerical integration method and we shall analyze in §6 the effect of numerical quadrature on error estimates. Finally, we shall briefly discuss in §7 an example of a nonconforming method.

For the sake of brevity, we have only considered a general theory for <u>conforming</u> finite element methods but, using the ideas of [4], we could have also developped a general approach including <u>nonconforming</u> methods. Similarly, we have confined ourselves to <u>polyhedral</u> domains Ω and to the use of straight elements. The case of general curved domains can be handled by using isoparametric finite elements as analyzed in Ciarlet & Raviart [2], [3] (see also Scott [11] and Zlamal [14]).

Let us mention that some of our results are related to those of Fortin [5] who first gave a mathematical analysis of the finite element approximation of the Navier-Stokes equations. For related work by the Engineers, we refer to Taylor & Hood [13] and the references therein.

2. <u>NOTATIONS AND PRELIMINARIES</u>

We shall consider real-valued functions defined on Ω. Let us denote by

$$(2.1)\qquad (u,v) = \int_\Omega u(x)v(x)dx$$

the scalar product in $L^2(\Omega)$ and by

$$(2.2)\qquad \|v\|_{0,\Omega} = (v,v)^{1/2}$$

the corresponding norm. The quotient space $L^2(\Omega)/\mathbb{R}$ is provided with the quotient norm

$$(2.3)\qquad \|v\|_{L^2(\Omega)/\mathbb{R}} = \inf_{c\in\mathbb{R}} \|v+c\|_{0,\Omega}$$

where, for simplicity, we also denote by v any function in the class $v\in L^2(\Omega)/\mathbb{R}$.

For any integer $m\geq 0$, we consider the usual Sobolev space

$$(2.4)\qquad H^m(\Omega) = \{v \mid v\in L^2(\Omega)\ ,\ \partial^\alpha v\in L^2(\Omega)\ ,\ |\alpha|\leq m\ \}$$

In (2.4), α is a multiindex : $\alpha=(\alpha_1,\dots,\alpha_N)$, $\alpha_i\geq 0$, $|\alpha|=\alpha_1+\dots+\alpha_N$ and $\partial^\alpha=(\frac{\partial}{\partial x_1})^{\alpha_1}\dots(\frac{\partial}{\partial x_N})^{\alpha_N}$. We provide $H^m(\Omega)$ with the norm and seminorm

$$(2.5)\qquad \|v\|_{m,\Omega} = (\sum_{|\alpha|\leq m} \|\partial^\alpha v\|^2_{0,\Omega})^{1/2}$$

$$(2.6)\qquad |v|_{m,\Omega} = \sum_{|\alpha|=m} \|\partial^\alpha v\|^2_{0,\Omega})^{1/2}$$

Let $(L^2(\Omega))^N$ (resp. $(H^m(\Omega))^N$) be the space of vector-valued functions $\vec{v}=(v_1,\ldots,v_N)$ with components v_i in $L^2(\Omega)$ (resp. in $H^m(\Omega)$). The scalar product in $(L^2(\Omega))^N$ is given by

$$(2.7)\qquad (\vec{u},\vec{v}) = \int_\Omega \vec{u}(x).\vec{v}(x)\,dx = \sum_{i=1}^{N} (u_i,v_i)$$

We shall use the following notations :

$$(2.8)\qquad \|\vec{v}\|_{m,\Omega} = \Big(\sum_{i=1}^{N} \|v_i\|^2_{m,\Omega}\Big)^{1/2}$$

$$(2.9)\qquad |\vec{v}|_{m,\Omega} = \Big(\sum_{i=1}^{N} |v_i|^2_{m,\Omega}\Big)^{1/2}$$

Let us introduce the spaces

$$(2.10)\qquad X = (H^1_0(\Omega))^N = \{\vec{v}\,|\,\vec{v}\in(H^1(\Omega))^N,\ \vec{v}|_\Gamma=\vec{0}\}$$

$$(2.11)\qquad V = \{\vec{v}\,|\,\vec{v}\in X\ ,\ \operatorname{div}\vec{v}=0\}$$

Note that

$$(2.12)\qquad \|\vec{v}\| = |\vec{v}|_{1,\Omega}$$

is a norm over the spaces X and V which is equivalent to the norm $\|\vec{v}\|_{1,\Omega}$. We extend the scalar product in $(L^2(\Omega))^N$ to represent the duality between V and its dual space V'. We provide V' with the dual norm

$$(2.13)\qquad \|\vec{f}\|^* = \sup_{\vec{v}\in V} \frac{|(\vec{f},\vec{v})|}{\|\vec{v}\|}\ ,\quad \vec{f}\in V'$$

Let us define :

$$(2.14)\qquad a(\vec{u},\vec{v}) = \sum_{i=1}^{N}\int_\Omega \frac{\partial\vec{u}}{\partial x_i}\cdot\frac{\partial\vec{v}}{\partial x_i}\,dx\ ,\quad \vec{u},\vec{v}\in(H^1(\Omega))^N$$

$$(2.15)\qquad b_1(\vec{u},\vec{v},\vec{w}) = \sum_{i=1}^{N}\int_\Omega u_i\,\frac{\partial\vec{v}}{\partial x_i}\cdot\vec{w}\,dx$$

$$(2.16)\qquad b(\vec{u},\vec{v},\vec{w}) = \frac{1}{2}\,(b_1(\vec{u},\vec{v},\vec{w}) - b_1(\vec{u},\vec{w},\vec{v}))$$

By the Sobolev's imbedding theorem, we have $X\subset(L^4(\Omega))^N$ $(N\leq 3)$ so that the trilinear form $b(\vec{u},\vec{v},\vec{w})$ is defined and continuous on XxXxX. Moreover, we have :

$$(2.17)\qquad b(\vec{u},\vec{v},\vec{w}) = b_1(\vec{u},\vec{v},\vec{w})\ \text{for all}\ \vec{u}\in V\ \text{and all}\ \vec{v},\vec{w}\in X$$

$$(2.18)\qquad b(\vec{u},\vec{v},\vec{v}) = 0\ \text{for all}\ \vec{u},\vec{v}\in X.$$

Then, two weak formulations of problem (1.1) are as follows :

(i) <u>Given a function</u> $\vec{f}\in V'$, <u>find functions</u> $\vec{u}\in V$ <u>and</u> $p\in L^2(\Omega)/\mathbb{R}$ <u>such that</u>

$$(2.19)\qquad \nu a(\vec{u},\vec{v})+b(\vec{u},\vec{u},\vec{v})-(p,\operatorname{div}\vec{v}) = (\vec{f},\vec{v})\ \underline{\text{for all}}\ \vec{v}\in X.$$

(ii) Given a function $\vec{f} \in V'$, find a function $\vec{u} \in V$ such that

(2.20) $\nu\, a(\vec{u},\vec{v}) + b(\vec{u},\vec{u},\vec{v}) = (f,v)$ for all $\vec{v} \in V$.

In fact, these two formulations are equivalent and we have the following result (cf. Ladyzhenskaya [9], Lions [10]).

Theorem 1 : Define

(2.21) $$\beta = \sup_{\vec{u},\vec{v},\vec{w} \in V} \frac{|b(\vec{u},\vec{v},\vec{w})|}{\|\vec{u}\|\,\|\vec{v}\|\,\|\vec{w}\|}$$

and assume that the function $\vec{f}$ satisfies

(2.22) $$\frac{\beta}{\nu^2} \|\vec{f}\|^* \leq 1-\delta$$

for some constant $0<\delta<1$. Then, there exists a unique pair of functions $(\vec{u},p) \in V \times L^2(\Omega)/\mathbb{R}$ solution of equation (2.19). Moreover, the function $\vec{u} \in V$ can be characterized as the unique solution of equation (2.20).

We shall need the following estimate for $\vec{u}$:

(2.23) $$\|\vec{u}\| < \frac{1}{\nu} \|\vec{f}\|^*$$

which follows at once from (2.18) and (2.20) with $\vec{v}=\vec{u}$. By combining (2.22) and (2.23), we obtain :

(2.24) $$\|\vec{u}\| < \frac{\nu}{\beta}$$

Note that the existence result remains valid without any restriction on the function $\vec{f}$. But we shall always assume in this paper that condition (2.22) holds in order to ensure the uniqueness of the solution $(\vec{u},p)$. We shall also assume that $\vec{f}$ belongs at least to the space $(L^2(\Omega))^N$ and that the solution $(\vec{u},p)$ is as smooth as we need for deriving the error estimates.

3. A CONFORMING FINITE ELEMENT METHOD

For the sake of simplicity, we shall assume in all the sequel that Ω is a polyhedral domain of $\mathbb{R}^N$;

Let us recall some definitions and notations given in [4]. Let $h>0$ be a parameter ; we construct a triangulation $\mathcal{T}_h$ of the set $\bar{\Omega}$ with nondegenerate N-simplices K (triangles if N=2, tetrahedrons if N=3) with diameters $\leq h$. For any $K \in \mathcal{T}_h$, we let :

(3.1) $$\begin{cases} h(K) = \text{diameter of } K, \\ \rho(K) = \text{diameter of the inscribed sphere of } K \\ \sigma(K) = h(K)/\rho(K) \end{cases}$$

We shall assume in the following that there exists a constant $\sigma>0$ independent of h such that

(3.2) $\sigma(K) \leq \sigma$ for all $K \in \mathcal{T}_h$.

Let k and k' be fixed integers such that $1 \leq k \leq k'$. With any $K \in \mathcal{T}_h$, we associate a finite-dimensional space of polynomials P_K such that

(3.3) $\quad P_k \subset P_K \subset P_{k'}$,

where, for any integer $m \geq 0$, P_m denotes the space of all polynomials of degree $\leq m$ in the N variables $x_1, \ldots, x_N$.

Let us consider the finite-dimensional spaces :

(3.4) $\quad W_h = \{v_h \mid v_h \in C^0(\bar{\Omega}), v_h|_K \in P_K \text{ for all } K \in \mathcal{C}_h\} \subset H^1(\Omega)$;

(3.5) $\quad X_h = \{\vec{v}_h \mid \vec{v}_h \in (W_h)^N, \vec{v}_h|_\Gamma = \vec{0}\} \subset X$ (1)

Then, we may introduce the space

(3.6) $\quad V_h = \{\vec{v}_h \mid \vec{v}_h \in X_h, \int_K q \operatorname{div} \vec{v}_h \, dx = 0 \text{ for all } q \in P_{k-1} \text{ and all } K \in \mathcal{C}_h\}$

which approximates the space V. Notice however that, in general, V_h is not a subspace of V.

Remark 1 : At first glance, it would seem more natural to set :

$$V_h = \{\vec{v}_h \mid \vec{v}_h \in X_h, \operatorname{div} \vec{v}_h = 0\}$$

Unfortunately, as simple examples show, this definition may lead to the rather undesirable situation $V_h = \{\vec{0}\}$. Thus, in order to get a non trivial subspace V_h of X_h, we have to weaken this condition $\operatorname{div} \vec{v}_h = 0$ as has been done in definition (3.6).

Example 1 : Just for simplicity, we shall restrict ourselves to the case N=2. Let K be a triangle of the triangulation $\mathcal{C}_h$ with vertices $a_{i,K}$, $1 \leq i \leq 3$. Denote by $a_{ij,K}$ the midpoint of the side $[a_{i,K}, a_{j,K}]$, $1 \leq i < j \leq 3$, and by $a_{123,K}$ the centroid of the triangle K.

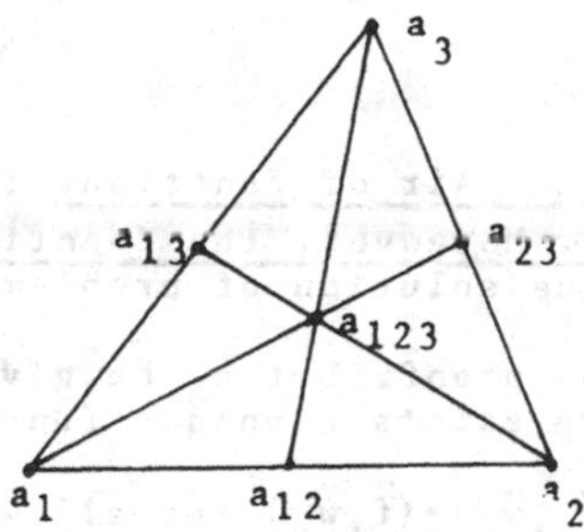

Fig. 1

Let us denote by P_K the space of polynomials spanned by

$$\lambda_1^2, \lambda_2^2, \lambda_3^2, \lambda_1\lambda_2, \lambda_2\lambda_3, \lambda_3\lambda_1, \lambda_1\lambda_2\lambda_3$$

where the λ_i's are the barycentric coordinates with respect to the vertices of the triangle K. Then, we get (3.3) with k=2, k'=3.

(1) This space X_h is denoted by $(W_{o,h})^N$ in [4].

Moreover, a function $v_h \in W_h$ is uniquely determined by its values $v_h(a_{i,K})$, $1 \leq i \leq 3$, $v_h(a_{ij,K})$, $1 \leq i < j \leq 3$, and $v_h(a_{123,K})$, $K \in \mathcal{T}_h$. For other examples of conforming finite elements (in dimension N=2 or 3) and related spaces W_h, we refer to [4, §4].

Going back to the general case, we introduce the space Φ_h of all functions φ_h defined on Ω such that $\varphi_h|_K \in P_{k-1}$ for all $K \in \mathcal{T}_h$. (Note that these functions are generally discontinuous). Thus, we may write :

(3.7) $\quad V_h = \{\vec{v}_h \mid \vec{v}_h \in X_h\ ,\ (\varphi_h, \operatorname{div} \vec{v}_h) = 0 \text{ for all } \varphi_h \in \Phi_h\}.$

Consider now the discrete analogues of problems (2.19) and (2.20):

(i) <u>Find functions $\vec{u}_h \in V_h$ and $p_h \in \Phi_h/\mathbb{R}$ such that</u>

(3.8) $\quad \nu\, a(\vec{u}_h,\vec{v}_h)+b(\vec{u}_h,\vec{u}_h,\vec{v}_h)-(p_h,\operatorname{div}\vec{v}_h)=(\vec{f},\vec{v}_h)$ <u>for all</u> $\vec{v}_h \in X_h$;

(ii) <u>Find a function $\vec{u}_h \in V_h$ such that</u>

(3.9) $\quad \nu\, a(\vec{u}_h,\vec{v}_h)+b(\vec{u}_h,\vec{u}_h,\vec{v}_h)=(\vec{f},\vec{v}_h)$ for all $\vec{v}_h \in V_h$.

Before establishing an existence and uniqueness theorem, we need the following definitions :

(3.10) $$\beta_h = \sup_{\vec{u}_h,\vec{v}_h,\vec{w}_h \in V_h} \frac{|b(\vec{u}_h,\vec{v}_h,\vec{w}_h)|}{\|\vec{u}_h\|\,\|\vec{v}_h\|\,\|\vec{w}_h\|}$$

(3.11) $$\|\vec{f}\|_h^* = \sup_{\vec{v}_h \in V_h} \frac{|(\vec{f},\vec{v}_h)|}{\|\vec{v}_h\|}$$

<u>Theorem 2</u> : <u>Assume that the function f satisfies</u>

(3.12) $$\frac{\beta_h}{\nu^2}\,\|f\|_h^* < 1.$$

<u>Then, there exists a unique pair of functions</u> $(\vec{u}_h,p_h) \in V_h \times \Phi_h/\mathbb{R}$ <u>solution of problem (3.8). Moreover, the function</u> $\vec{u}_h \in V_h$ <u>can be</u> characterized as the unique solution of problem (3.9).

<u>Proof</u> : We only sketch the proof. Let $\vec{u}_h$ be given in V_h ; by the Lax-Milgram theorem, there exists a unique function $\vec{v}_h \in V_h$ such that

$$\nu\, a(\vec{v}_h,\vec{w}_h)+b(\vec{u}_h,\vec{v}_h,\vec{w}_h)=(\vec{f},\vec{w}_h) \text{ for all } \vec{w}_h \in V_h.$$

We have thus defined a mapping $T : \vec{u}_h \in V_h \rightarrow \vec{v}_h = T(\vec{u}_h) \in V_h$. Using (2.18), it is easy to check that, under the assumption (3.12), T is a strict contraction mapping with respect to the norm (2.12). Hence, problem (3.9) has a unique solution $\vec{u}_h \in V_h$.

Then, consider the linear functional defined on X_h :

$$\vec{v}_h \rightarrow \nu\, a(\vec{u}_h,\vec{v}_h)+b(\vec{u}_h,\vec{u}_h,\vec{v}_h)-(\vec{f},\vec{v}_h)$$

which vanishes on V_h. By applying [4, Lemma 7], there exists a unique function $p_h \in \Phi_h/\mathbb{R}$ such that

$$\nu\, a(\vec{u}_h,\vec{v}_h)+b(\vec{u}_h,\vec{u}_h,\vec{v}_h)-(\vec{f},\vec{v}_h)=(p_h,\operatorname{div}\vec{v}_h) \text{ for all } \vec{v}_h \in X_h.$$

Thus, $(\vec{u}_h,p_h)$ is a solution of problem (3.8). Conversely, let $(\vec{u}_h,p_h)\in V_h \times \Phi_h/\mathbb{R}$ be a solution of (3.8). Then, u_h is the solution of problem (3.9).

By taking $\vec{v}_h=\vec{u}_h$ in (3.9) and using condition (3.12), we get the estimate :

$$(3.13)\quad \|\vec{u}_h\| \leq \frac{1}{\nu}\|\vec{f}\|_h^* < \frac{\nu}{\beta_h}$$

Here again, one can easily show that the existence result remains valid without the restriction (3.12) on the function $\vec{f}$.

4. ERROR ESTIMATES

Note : In all the sequel, we shall denote by C or c_i various constants which do not depend on the parameter h.

4.1. An estimate for $\vec{u}_h-\vec{u}$ in X

In order to derive bounds for the error $\vec{u}_h-\vec{u}$, we shall need a hypothesis concerning the approximation of an arbitrary smooth function of V by functions of V_h and which is essentially hypothesis H.1 of [4].

Hypothesis H.1 : There exists an operator $r_h \in \mathcal{L}((H^1(\Omega)\cap C^o(\bar{\Omega}))^N; (W_h)^N)\cap\mathcal{L}((H_o^1(\Omega)\cap C^o(\bar{\Omega}))^N;X_h)$ such that :

(i) (4.1) $(\operatorname{div}(r_h\vec{v}-\vec{v}),\varphi_h) = 0$ for all $\varphi_h\in\Phi_h$ and all $\vec{v}\in(H^1(\Omega)\cap C^o(\Omega))^N$;

(ii) (4.2) $\|r_h\vec{v}-\vec{v}\| \leq Ch^m|\vec{v}|_{m+1,\Omega}$ for all $\vec{v}\in(H^{m+1}(\Omega))^N$, $1\leq m\leq k$.

Note that condition (4.1) can be equivalently stated in the form

$$(4.3)\quad \int_K q\,\operatorname{div}(r_h\vec{v}-\vec{v})dx=0 \text{ for all } q\in P_{k-1},\text{ all } K\in\mathcal{C}_h \text{ and all } \vec{v}\in(H^1(\Omega)\cap C^o(\bar{\Omega}))^N.$$

Now, assuming that Hypothesis H.1 holds, we have by (4.1) $r_h\in\mathcal{L}(V\cap(C^o(\bar{\Omega}))^N;V_h)$ and by (4.2)

$$(4.4)\quad \inf_{\vec{v}_h\in V_h}\|\vec{v}_h-\vec{v}\| \leq Ch^m|\vec{v}|_{m+1,\Omega} \text{ for all } \vec{v}\in V\cap(H^{m+1}(\Omega))^N,\ 1\leq m\leq k.$$

As it has been shown in [4, §4], Hypothesis H.1 holds with k=2 in the case of example 1.

First, we consider the convergence of β_h and $\|f\|_h^*$ as h tends to zero.

Lemma 1 : Assume that Hypothesis H.1 holds. Then, we have :

$$(4.5)\quad \lim_{h\to 0}\beta_h=\beta\ ,$$

(4.6) $\lim_{h\to 0} |\vec{f}|_h^* = \|\vec{f}\|^*$

Proof : We shall only prove (4.5) since (4.6) can be obtained in a similar way. For each value of the parameter h, let $\vec{u}_h, \vec{v}_h, \vec{w}_h$ be functions in V_h such that :

$$\begin{cases} \|\vec{u}_h\| = \|\vec{v}_h\| = \|\vec{w}_h\| = 1 , \\ |b(\vec{u}_h, \vec{v}_h, \vec{w}_h)| = \beta_h \end{cases}$$

Since β_h is bounded as h tends to zero, we can find a subsequence $\{h_n\}_{n\geq 1}$ such that :

$$\begin{cases} \vec{u}_{h_n} \to \vec{u}_* , \ \vec{v}_{h_n} \to \vec{v}_* , \ \vec{w}_{h_n} \to \vec{w}_* \ \underline{\text{weakly}} \text{ in } X, \\ \beta_{h_n} \to \beta_* . \end{cases}$$

Let us show that $\vec{u}_*$, $\vec{v}_*$, $\vec{w}_* \in V$. Denote by ρ_h the orthogonal projection operator in $L^2(\Omega)$ upon Φ_h. Then, one can prove (cf. [2]) :

(4.7) $|\varphi - \rho_h \varphi|_{0,\Omega} \leq c_1 h^m |\varphi|_{m,\Omega}$ for all $\varphi \in H^m(\Omega)$, $0 \leq m \leq k$.

Since $H^k(\Omega)$ is dense in $L^2(\Omega)$, we get :

$$\lim_{h\to 0} \rho_h \varphi = \varphi \text{ in } L^2(\Omega) \text{ for all } \varphi \in L^2(\Omega).$$

Therefore

$$(\text{div } \vec{u}_*, \varphi) = \lim_{n\to\infty} (\text{div } \vec{u}_{h_n}, \rho_{h_n} \varphi) = 0 \text{ for all } \varphi \in L^2(\Omega)$$

which implies div $\vec{u}_* = 0$ and similarly div $\vec{v}_* =$ div $\vec{w}_* = 0$.

Now, since the imbedding of X into $(L^4(\Omega))^N$ is compact for $N \leq 3$, we may assume that :

$$\vec{u}_{h_n} \to \vec{u}_* , \ \vec{v}_{h_n} \to \vec{v}_* , \ \vec{w}_{h_n} \to \vec{w}_* \quad \text{strongly in } (L^4(\Omega))^N.$$

Thus, we obtain :

$$\beta_* = \lim_{n\to\infty} \beta_{h_n} = \lim_{n\to\infty} |b(\vec{u}_{h_n}, \vec{v}_{h_n}, \vec{w}_{h_n})| = |b(\vec{u}_*, \vec{v}_*, \vec{w}_*)|$$

and therefore

(4.8) $\beta_* \leq \beta$

since $\vec{u}_*, \vec{v}_*, \vec{w}_* \in V$ with $\|\vec{u}_*\|, \|\vec{v}_*\|, \|\vec{w}_*\| \leq 1$ (by the lower-semi-continuity of the norm in the weak topology).

Let us prove the reverse inequality. Let $\vec{u}$, $\vec{v}$, $\vec{w}$ be arbitrary functions in $\mathcal{V} = V \cap (H^2(\Omega))^N$. By Hypothesis H.1, we have :

$$r_h\vec{u} \to \vec{u} , \ r_h\vec{v} \to \vec{v} , \ r_h\vec{w} \to \vec{w} \text{ in } X$$

as h tends to zero so that

$$\frac{|b(r_h\vec{u},r_h\vec{v},r_h\vec{w})|}{\|r_h\vec{u}\|\,\|r_h\vec{v}\|\,\|r_h\vec{w}\|} \longrightarrow \frac{|b(\vec{u},\vec{v},\vec{w})|}{\|\vec{u}\|\,\|\vec{v}\|\,\|\vec{w}\|}$$

Hence :

$$\beta_* \geq \frac{|b(\vec{u},\vec{v},\vec{w})|}{\|\vec{u}\|\,\|\vec{v}\|\,\|\vec{w}\|} \quad \text{for all } \vec{u},\vec{v},\vec{w}\in\mathcal{V}.$$

But, since $\mathcal{V}$ is dense in V, we may write :

$$\beta = \sup_{\vec{u},\vec{v},\vec{w}\in\mathcal{V}} \frac{|b(\vec{u},\vec{v},\vec{w})|}{\|\vec{u}\|\,\|\vec{v}\|\,\|\vec{w}\|}$$

and we conclude that $\beta_* \geq \beta$. Comparing with (4.8), we get $\beta_* = \beta$. Also, it follows that the whole sequence $\{\beta_h\}$ converges to β as h tends to zero.

As a consequence of Lemma 1, condition (2.22) implies condition (3.12) for h small enough so that Theorem 2 can be applied.

Theorem 3 : Assume that Hypothesis H.1 holds and that the function $\vec{f}$ satisfies condition (2.22). Assume, in addition, that the solution $(\vec{u},p)$ of problem (2.19) verifies the smoothness properties :

(4.9) $\quad \vec{u}\in V\cap(H^{k+1}(\Omega))^N, \quad p\in H^k(\Omega).$

Then, for h small enough, problem (3.9) has a unique solution $\vec{u}_h\in V_h$ and we have the estimate

(4.10) $\quad \|\vec{u}_h-\vec{u}\| \leq Ch^k(|\vec{u}|_{k+1,\Omega} + |p|_{k,\Omega})$

where the constant C is independent of h, $\vec{u}$ and p.

Proof : By Lemma 1, we may choose h small enough so that

(4.11) $\quad \dfrac{\beta_h}{\nu^2}\|\vec{f}\|_h^* \leq 1-\dfrac{\delta}{2}$

Then, existence and uniqueness of the solution $\vec{u}_h\in V_h$ follow from Theorem 2. Now, let $\vec{v}_h$ be an arbitrary function of V_h and $\vec{w}_h=\vec{u}_h-\vec{v}_h$. We consider the expression :

(4.12) $\quad D = \nu\, a(\vec{w}_h,\vec{w}_h)+b(\vec{u}_h,\vec{u}_h,\vec{w}_h)-b(\vec{v}_h,\vec{v}_h,\vec{w}_h)$

Using (2.18), we may write :

$$D = \nu\, a(\vec{w}_h,\vec{w}_h)+b(\vec{w}_h,\vec{u}_h,\vec{w}_h)-b(\vec{u}_h,\vec{w}_h,\vec{w}_h) =$$
$$= \nu\,\|\vec{w}_h\|^2 + b(\vec{w}_h,\vec{u}_h,\vec{w}_h).$$

Thus, using (3.11) and (3.13), we get :

$$D \geq \nu\,\|\vec{w}_h\|^2-\beta_h\|\vec{u}_h\|\,\|\vec{w}_h\|^2 \geq \Big(\nu-\frac{\beta_h}{\nu}\|\vec{f}\|_h^*\Big)\|\vec{w}_h\|^2$$

and therefore by (4.11)

(4.13) $$D \geq \frac{\nu\delta}{2}\|\vec{w}_h\|^2$$

On the other hand, using (3.9) and (2.19), we have

(4.14) $$\begin{cases} D = (\vec{f},\vec{w}_h) - \nu a(\vec{v}_h,\vec{w}_h) - b(\vec{v}_h,\vec{v}_h,\vec{w}_h) = \\ \quad = \nu\, a(\vec{u}-\vec{v}_h,\vec{w}_h) + b(\vec{u},\vec{u},\vec{w}_h) - b(\vec{v}_h,\vec{v}_h,\vec{w}_h) - (p,\operatorname{div}\vec{w}_h). \end{cases}$$

But, we may write

$$b(\vec{u},\vec{u},\vec{w}_h) - b(\vec{v}_h,\vec{v}_h,\vec{w}_h) = b(\vec{u}-\vec{v}_h,\vec{u},\vec{w}_h) + b(\vec{v}_h,\vec{u}-\vec{v}_h,\vec{w}_h) \leq$$
$$\leq c_1(\|\vec{u}\|+\|\vec{v}_h\|)\|\vec{u}-\vec{v}_h\|\,\|\vec{w}_h\|$$

Next, since $\vec{w}_h \in V_h$, we have :

$$(p,\operatorname{div}\vec{w}_h) = (p-\rho_h p,\operatorname{div}\vec{w}_h)$$

and therefore

$$|(p,\operatorname{div}\vec{w}_h)| \leq c_2|p-\rho_h p|_{0,\Omega}\|\vec{w}_h\|$$

Thus, we obtain

(4.15) $$D \leq \{(\nu + c_1(\|\vec{u}\|+\|\vec{v}_h\|))\|\vec{u}-\vec{v}_h\| + c_2|p-\rho_h p|_{0,\Omega}\}\|\vec{w}_h\|$$

Now, comparing (4.13) and (4.15), we get :

$$\|\vec{w}_h\| \leq \frac{2}{\nu\delta}\{(\nu + c_1(\|\vec{u}\|+\|\vec{v}_h\|))\|\vec{u}-\vec{v}_h\| + c_2\|p-\rho_h p\|_{0,\Omega}\}$$

so that

$$\|\vec{u}_h-\vec{u}\| \leq \|\vec{w}_h\| + \|\vec{u}-\vec{v}_h\| \leq$$
$$\leq c_3\{(1+\|\vec{u}\|+\|\vec{v}_h\|)\|\vec{u}-\vec{v}_h\| + \|p-\rho_h p\|_{0,\Omega}\}$$

Choosing $\vec{v}_h$ to be the orthogonal projection in X of $\vec{u}$ upon V_h and using (2.24), we obtain :

(4.16) $$\|\vec{u}_h-\vec{u}\| \leq c_4\{\inf_{\vec{v}_h\in V_h}\|\vec{u}-\vec{v}_h\| + \inf_{\varphi_h\in\Phi_h}|p-\varphi_h|_{0,\Omega}\}$$

Then, the desired inequality (4.10) follows at once from (4.4), (4.7) and (4.16).

Remark 2 : If we assume only $\vec{u}\in V\cap(H^{m+1}(\Omega))^N$, $p\in H^m(\Omega)$ for some integer m with $1\leq m\leq k$, we get the weaker estimate

(4.17) $$\|\vec{u}_h-\vec{u}\| \leq Ch^m(|\vec{u}|_{m+1,\Omega}+|p|_{m,\Omega}).$$

Moreover, if we do not assume any regularity property on the functions $\vec{u}$ and p, it follows from (4.16) by a density argument that :

(4.18) $$\lim_{h\to 0}\vec{u}_h = \vec{u} \quad \text{in } X .$$

4.2. An estimate for $\vec{u}_h-\vec{u}$ in $(L^2(\Omega))^N$

In order to derive a L^2-estimate for the error u_h-u, we shall use the classical Aubin-Nitsche's duality argument. We write :

$$(4.19)\qquad \|\vec{u}_h-\vec{u}\|_{0,\Omega} = \sup_{\vec{g}\in(L^2(\Omega))^N} \frac{|(\vec{u}_h-\vec{u},\vec{g})|}{\|\vec{g}\|_{0,\Omega}}$$

Let us consider the following linear problem : <u>given a function</u> $\vec{g}\in(L^2(\Omega))^N$, <u>find functions</u> $\vec{\varphi}\in V$ <u>and</u> $\chi\in L^2(\Omega)/\mathbb{R}$ <u>such that</u>

$$(4.20)\qquad \nu\, a(\vec{v},\vec{\varphi})+b(\vec{u},\vec{v},\vec{\varphi})+b(\vec{v},\vec{u},\vec{\varphi})-(\chi,\mathrm{div}\,\vec{v})=(\vec{v},\vec{g}) \quad \text{for all } \vec{v}\in X$$

<u>Lemma 2</u> : <u>Problem (4.20) has a unique solution</u> $(\vec{\varphi},\chi)\in V\times L^2(\Omega)/\mathbb{R}$

<u>Proof</u> : Problem (4.20) is equivalent to the following one : find a function $\vec{\varphi}\in V$ such that

$$(4.21)\qquad \nu\, a(\vec{v},\vec{\varphi})+b(\vec{u},\vec{v},\vec{\varphi})+b(\vec{v},\vec{u},\vec{\varphi})=(\vec{v},\vec{g}) \quad \text{for all } \vec{v}\in V.$$

Since

$$\nu\, a(\vec{v},\vec{v})+b(\vec{u},\vec{v},\vec{v})+b(\vec{v},\vec{u},\vec{v})=\nu\, a(\vec{v},\vec{v})+b(\vec{v},\vec{u},\vec{v}) \geq$$

$$\geq (\nu-\beta\|\vec{u}\|)\|\vec{v}\|^2 \geq \nu\delta\|\vec{v}\|^2 \quad \text{for all } \vec{v}\in V,$$

existence and uniqueness of the solution $\vec{\varphi}\in V$ follow from the Lax-Milgram theorem.

We shall also need the following regularity property for the solution $(\vec{\varphi},\chi)$ of problem (4.20) : there exists a constant $\Lambda>0$ which does not depend on $\vec{g}$ such that :

$$(4.22)\qquad \|\vec{\varphi}\|_{2,\Omega}+|\chi|_{1,\Omega} \leq \Lambda\|\vec{g}\|_{0,\Omega}$$

In fact, by using techniques of Kondratiev [8] and Grisvard [7], one can prove that this property (4.22) holds provided the polyhedral domain Ω is <u>convex</u> and the solution $\vec{u}$ is smooth enough (for example $\vec{u}\in(C^1(\bar{\Omega}))^N$).

<u>Theorem 4</u> : <u>Assume that Hypothesis H.1, (2.22), (4.9) and (4.22) hold. Then, for h small enough, we have the estimate</u>

$$(4.23)\qquad \|\vec{u}_h-\vec{u}\|_{0,\Omega} \leq C h^{k+1}$$

<u>for some constant $C=C(\vec{u},p)$ which is independent of h.</u>

<u>Proof</u> : Taking $\vec{v}=\vec{u}_h-\vec{u}$ in (4.20), we get :

$$(4.24)\quad (\vec{u}_h-\vec{u},\vec{g})=\nu\, a(\vec{u}_h-\vec{u},\vec{\varphi})+b(\vec{u},\vec{u}_h-\vec{u},\vec{\varphi})+b(\vec{u}_h-\vec{u},\vec{u},\vec{\varphi})-(\chi,\mathrm{div}(\vec{u}_h-\vec{u}))$$

On the other hand, using (2.19) and (3.9), we may write :

$$(4.25)\qquad \nu\, a(\vec{u}_h-\vec{u},\vec{\varphi}_h)+b(\vec{u}_h,\vec{u}_h,\vec{\varphi}_h)-b(\vec{u},\vec{u},\vec{\varphi}_h)+(p,\mathrm{div}\,\vec{\varphi}_h)=0$$

for all $\vec{\varphi}_h\in V_h$. Now, combining (4.24) and (4.25) and noticing that $\mathrm{div}\,\vec{\varphi}=0$, we obtain :

$$(\vec{u}_h-\vec{u},\vec{g}) = \nu\, a(\vec{u}_h-\vec{u},\vec{\varphi}-\vec{\varphi}_h)+b(\vec{u}_h-\vec{u},\vec{u}_h,\vec{\varphi}-\vec{\varphi}_h)+ + b(\vec{u},\vec{u}_h-\vec{u},\vec{\varphi}-\vec{\varphi}_h)-b(\vec{u}_h-\vec{u},\vec{u}_h-\vec{u},\vec{\varphi}) - - (\chi,\mathrm{div}(\vec{u}_h-\vec{u}))-(p,\mathrm{div}(\vec{\varphi}-\vec{\varphi}_h))$$

Thus, we get for all $\vec{\varphi}_h \in V_h$

$$|(\vec{u}_h-\vec{u},\vec{g})| \leqslant \{\nu + c_1(\|\vec{u}\|+\|\vec{u}_h\|)\}\|\vec{u}_h-\vec{u}\|\,\|\vec{\varphi}-\vec{\varphi}_h\| + + c_1\|\vec{u}_h-\vec{u}\|^2\|\vec{\varphi}\|+|(\chi,\mathrm{div}(\vec{u}_h-\vec{u}))|+|(p,\mathrm{div}(\vec{\varphi}-\vec{\varphi}_h))| \tag{4.26}$$

Next, we have by (4.7) :

$$|(\chi,\mathrm{div}(\vec{u}_h-\vec{u}))| = |(\chi-\rho_h\chi,\mathrm{div}(\vec{u}_h-\vec{u}))| \leqslant c_2 h\|\vec{u}_h-\vec{u}\|\,|\chi|_{1,\Omega} \tag{4.27}$$

$$|(p,\mathrm{div}(\vec{\varphi}-\vec{\varphi}_h))| = |(p-\rho_h p,\mathrm{div}(\vec{\varphi}-\vec{\varphi}_h))| \leqslant c_3 h^k\|\vec{\varphi}-\vec{\varphi}_h\|\,|p|_{k,\Omega} \tag{4.28}$$

Now, we choose $\vec{\varphi}_h = r_h\vec{\varphi}$ so that we get by Hypothesis H.1 :

$$\|\vec{\varphi}-\vec{\varphi}_h\| \leqslant c_4 h|\vec{\varphi}|_{2,\Omega} \tag{4.29}$$

By combining (4.26),..., (4.29) and by applying Theorem 3 and inequality (4.17), we obtain for h small enough :

$$|(\vec{u}_h-\vec{u},\vec{g})| \leqslant c_5 h^{k+1}(|\vec{u}|_{k+1,\Omega}+|p|_{k,\Omega})(1+|\vec{u}|_{2,\Omega}+|p|_{1,\Omega}) (\|\vec{\varphi}\|_{2,\Omega}+|\chi|_{1,\Omega}) \tag{4.30}$$

Using (4.19), (4.22) and (4.30), we get the estimate (4.23) with

$$C = c_5\Lambda(|\vec{u}|_{k+1,\Omega}+|p|_{k,\Omega})(1+|\vec{u}|_{2,\Omega}+|p|_{1,\Omega})$$

4.3. An estimate for p_h-p in $L^2(\Omega)/\mathbb{R}$

In this section, we shall need a new hypothesis that we call "H.3" as in [4].

Hypothesis H.3 : Given any function $\varphi_h \in \Phi_h$ such that $\int_\Omega \varphi_h dx = 0$, there exists a function $\vec{v}_h \in X_h$ such that :

(i) (4.31) $\quad (\mathrm{div}\,\vec{v}_h-\varphi_h,\psi_h)=0$ for all $\psi_h \in \Phi_h$,

(ii) (4.32) $\quad \|\vec{v}_h\| \leqslant C\|\varphi_h\|_{0,\Omega}$

As it has been shown in [4 , §6], Hypothesis H.3 holds provided the polyhedral domain is convex and the triangulation $\mathcal{C}_h$ satisfies the uniformity condition

$$\rho(K) \geqslant Ch \quad \text{for all } K \in \mathcal{C}_h \ (2) \tag{4.33}$$

(2) This condition (4.33) is easily seen to be equivalent to the inverse assumption : $|v_h|_{1,\Omega} \leqslant Ch^{-1}\|v_h\|_{0,\Omega}$ for all $v_h \in W_h$.

Theorem 5 : With the same assumptions as in Theorem 3, we assume in addition, that hypothesis H.3 holds. Then :

$$(4.34)\qquad \|p_h - p\|_{L^2(\Omega)/\mathbb{R}} \leq Ch^k(|\vec{u}|_{k+1,\Omega} + |p|_{k,\Omega})$$

where the constant C is independent of h, $\vec{u}$ and p.

Proof : The proof is similar to that of [4 , Theorem 6] and will be only sketched. We choose p and p_h such that

$$\int_\Omega p\,dx = \int_\Omega p_h\,dx = 0$$

From (2.19) and (3.8), we get for all $\vec{v}_h \in X_h$:

$$(p_h - \rho_h p, \operatorname{div} \vec{v}_h) = (p - \rho_h p, \operatorname{div} \vec{v}_h) + \nu\, a(\vec{u}_h - \vec{u}, \vec{v}_h) + b(\vec{u}_h - \vec{u}, \vec{u}_h, \vec{v}_h) + b(\vec{u}, \vec{u}_h - \vec{u}, \vec{v}_h)$$

Now $\int_\Omega (p_h - \rho_h p)dx = 0$. Hence, by Hypothesis H.3, we may choose $\vec{v}_h \in X_h$ so that :

$$(\operatorname{div} \vec{v}_h, \psi_h) = (p_h - \rho_h p, \psi_h) \quad \text{for all } \psi_h \in \Phi_h,$$

$$\|\vec{v}_h\| \leq c_1 \|p_h - \rho_h p\|_{0,\Omega}.$$

Therefore

$$\|p_h - \rho_h p\|_{0,\Omega} \leq \|p - \rho_h p\|_{0,\Omega} + \nu\, c_1 \|\vec{u}_h - \vec{u}\| + c_2(\|\vec{u}_h\| + \|\vec{u}\|)\|\vec{u}_h - \vec{u}\|$$

and the desired estimate (4.34) follows at once.

5. THE EFFECT OF NUMERICAL INTEGRATION : GENERALITIES

The practical application of the finite element method (3.8) requires the computation of various multiple integrals. Although most of these integrals involve only polynomials and can be computed exactly, it is easier and faster to use numerical integration techniques ; we shall show that it can be performed with no loss in the order of accuracy of the method. Note that these numerical integration techniques are essential when using curved isoparametric finite element methods.

Let us describe the numerical quadrature method that we shall use. We proceed as in Ciarlet & Raviart [3]. Let $\hat{K}$ be a fixed non-degenerate N-simplex of $\mathbb{R}^N$. We choose a certain quadrature formula over the reference set $\hat{K}$:

$$(5.1)\qquad \hat{I}(\hat{\varphi}) = \int_{\hat{K}} \hat{\varphi}(\hat{x})d\hat{x} \ \text{ is approximated by } \ \hat{I}_a(\hat{\varphi}) = \sum_{\ell=1}^{L} \hat{\omega}\, \hat{\varphi}(\hat{b}_\ell)$$

for some specified points $\hat{b}_\ell \in \hat{K}$ and weights $\hat{\omega}_\ell$ which will be assumed to be positive. For each $K \in \mathcal{C}_h$, let $F_K : \hat{x} \to F_K(\hat{x}) = B_K\hat{x} + b_K$, $B_K \in \mathcal{L}(\mathbb{R}^N)$, $b_K \in \mathbb{R}^N$, be an affine invertible mapping which maps $\hat{K}$ onto K. We may assume that the Jacobian determinant $J_K = \det(B_K)$ of the mapping F_K is positive. Then, there corresponds to (5.1) the quadrature formula over K :

$$(5.2)\qquad I_K(\varphi) = \int_K \varphi(x)dx \ \text{ is approximated by } \ I_{K,a}(\varphi) = \sum_{\ell=1}^{L} \omega_{\ell,K}\, \varphi(b_{\ell,K})$$

where

(5.3) $\omega_{\ell,K} = \hat{\omega}_\ell J_K$, $b_{\ell,K} = F_K(\hat{b}_\ell)$, $1\leq\ell\leq L$.

Then, any integral over the polyhedral domain Ω

(5.4) $I(\varphi) = \int_\Omega \varphi(x)dx$

is approximated by

(5.5) $I_a(\varphi) = \sum_{K\in\mathcal{C}_h} I_{K,a}(\varphi)$.

In all the sequel, we shall assume that the <u>function $\vec{f}$ belongs to the space</u> $(C^o(\bar{\Omega}))^N$. Let $a_h(\vec{u}_h,\vec{v}_h)$, $b_h(\vec{u}_h,\vec{v}_h,\vec{w}_h)$ and $(\vec{f},\vec{v}_h)_h$ be the approximations of $a(\vec{u}_h,\vec{v}_h)$, $b(\vec{u}_h,\vec{v}_h,\vec{w}_h)$ and $(\vec{f},\vec{v}_h)$ resulting from numerical integration:

$$a_h(\vec{u}_h,\vec{v}_h) = I_a(\sum_{i=1}^N \frac{\partial\vec{u}_h}{\partial x_i} \cdot \frac{\partial\vec{v}_h}{\partial x_i}),\ldots\ldots$$

Note that the analogue of property (2.18) holds :

(5.6) $b_h(\vec{u}_h,\vec{v}_h,\vec{v}_h) = 0$ for all $\vec{u}_h,\vec{v}_h \in X_h$.

Now, we replace the discrete problems (3.8) and (3.9) by the following ones :

(i) <u>Find functions $\tilde{\vec{u}}_h\in V_h$ and $\tilde{p}_h \in \Phi_h/\mathbb{R}$ such that</u>

(5.7) $\nu\, a_h(\tilde{\vec{u}}_h,\vec{v}_h)+b_h(\tilde{\vec{u}}_h,\tilde{\vec{u}}_h,\vec{v}_h)-(\tilde{p}_h,\operatorname{div}\vec{v}_h) = (\vec{f},\vec{v}_h)_h$ <u>for all</u> $\vec{v}_h\in X_h$

(ii) <u>Find a function $\tilde{\vec{u}}_h \in V_h$ such that</u>

(5.8) $\nu\, a_h(\tilde{\vec{u}}_h,\vec{v}_h)+b_h(\tilde{\vec{u}}_h,\tilde{\vec{u}}_h,\vec{v}_h)=(f,v_h)$ for all $\vec{v}_h\in V_h$.

<u>Remark 3</u> : We shall ignore the possibility of using numerical integration in the definition of the space V_h :

$$V_h = \{\vec{v}_h | \vec{v}_h \in X_h \text{ , } I_a(\varphi_h \operatorname{div}\vec{v}_h) = 0 \text{ for all } \varphi_h \in \Phi_h\}$$

and in the computation of $(p_h,\operatorname{div}\vec{v}_h)$. The interest of this possibility is limited because we shall prove in §6 that the error $\|\tilde{\vec{u}}_h - u\|$ is optimal when the quadrature formula (5.1) is exact for all polynomials of degree $\leq k+k'-2$, which corresponds to an exact computation of $(\varphi_h,\operatorname{div}\vec{v}_h)$.

For studying problems (5.7) and (5.8), we shall need :

<u>Hypothesis H.4</u> : <u>The quadrature formula (5.1) satisfies the following properties</u> :

(i) <u>The weights $\hat{\omega}_\ell$ are positive and the set</u> $\{\hat{b}_\ell\}_{\ell=1}^L$ <u>contains a</u> $P_{k'-1}$-<u>unisolvent subset, i.e.</u>

(5.9) $p\in P_{k'-1}$, $p(\hat{b}_\ell)=0$, $1\leq\ell\leq L \implies p=0$;

(ii) <u>There exists an integer s $\geq$ k'-1 such that the quadrature formula (5.1) is exact for all polynomials of degree $\leq$ s.</u>

By Hypothesis H.4 (i) and [3 , Theorem 3] for instance, there exists a constant $\alpha>0$ independent of h such that

(5.10) $\quad a_h(\vec{v}_h,\vec{v}_h) \geq \alpha\|\vec{v}_h\|^2$ for all $\vec{v}_h \in X_h$.

As a first consequence of (5.10)

(5.11) $\quad \|\vec{v}_h\|_h = a_h(\vec{v}_h,\vec{v}_h)^{1/2}$

is a norm over X_h.

Let us now introduce the following quantities :

(5.12) $$\tilde{\beta}_h = \sup_{\vec{u}_h,\vec{v}_h,\vec{w}_h \in V_h} \frac{|b_h(\vec{u}_h,\vec{v}_h,\vec{w}_h)|}{\|\vec{u}_h\|_h\|\vec{v}_h\|_h\|\vec{w}_h\|_h}$$

(5.13) $$|\tilde{\vec{f}}|_h^* = \sup_{\vec{v}_h \in V_h} \frac{|(\vec{f},\vec{v}_h)_h|}{\|\vec{v}_h\|_h}$$

Then, we have the analogue of Theorem 2.

<u>Theorem 6 : Assume that Hypothesis H.4 (i) holds and that the function $\vec{f}$ satisfies</u>

(5.14) $$\frac{\tilde{\beta}_h}{\nu^2}\|\tilde{\vec{f}}\|_h^* < 1$$

<u>Then, there exists a unique pair of functions</u> $(\tilde{\vec{u}}_h,\tilde{p}_h) \in V_h \times \Phi_h/\mathbb{R}$ <u>solution of problem (5.7). Moreover, the function</u> $\tilde{\vec{u}}_h \in V_h$ <u>can be characterized as the unique solution of problem (5.8)</u>

<u>Proof</u> : The proof follows the same line as that of Theorem 2. ▨

By taking $\vec{v}_h=\tilde{\vec{u}}_h$ in (5.8), we get the inequality

(5.15) $$\|\tilde{\vec{u}}_h\|_h \leq \frac{1}{\nu}\|\tilde{\vec{f}}\|_h^* .$$

Before establishing the convergence of $\tilde{\beta}_h$ and $\|\tilde{\vec{f}}\|_h^*$ as h tends to zero and before deriving error estimates, we need introduce some notations. We set :

(5.16) $\quad \hat{E}(\hat{\varphi})=\hat{I}(\hat{\varphi})-\hat{I}_a(\hat{\varphi}),\ E_K(\varphi)=I_K(\varphi)-I_{K,a}(\varphi),\ E(\varphi)=I(\varphi)-I_a(\varphi).$

Given a fixed $K\in\mathcal{T}_h$, the mapping F_K determines one-to-one correspondences between the points $\hat{x}$ of $\hat{K}$ and the points x of K by

$$x=F_K(\hat{x}) \quad\text{and}\quad \hat{x}=F_K^{-1}(x) ,$$

and between the functions $\hat{\varphi} : \hat{K} \to \mathbb{R}$ and $\varphi : K \to \mathbb{R}$ by

$$\varphi=\hat{\varphi}\circ F_K^{-1} \quad\text{and}\quad \hat{\varphi}=\varphi\circ F_K.$$

We shall make constant use of the above correspondences. Note that

(5.17) $\quad I_K(\varphi)=J_K.\hat{I}(\hat{\varphi})\ ,\ I_{K,a}(\varphi)=J_K.\hat{I}_a(\hat{\varphi})\ ,\ E_K(\varphi)=J_K.\hat{E}(\hat{\varphi}).$

Let us introduce now the Sobolev spaces $W^{m,q}(\Omega)$ for any integer $m\geq 0$ and any $q\geq 1$:

(5.18) $W^{m,q}(\Omega) = \{v \mid v\in L^q(\Omega)\ ,\partial^\alpha\ v\in L^q(\Omega)\ ,\ |\alpha|\leq m\}$

We provide $W^{m,q}(\Omega)$ with the norm and seminorm

(5.19) $\|v\|_{m,q,\Omega} = \Big(\sum_{|\alpha|\leq m} \|\partial^\alpha v\|^q_{L^q(\Omega)}\Big)^{1/q}$,

(5.20) $|v|_{m,q,\Omega} = \Big(\sum_{|\alpha|= m} \|\partial^\alpha v\|^q_{L^q(\Omega)}\Big)^{1/q}$.

Note that :

$$W^{m,2}(\Omega) = H^m(\Omega)\ ,\ \|v\|_{m,2,\Omega} = \|v\|_{m,\Omega}\ ,\ |v|_{m,2,\Omega} = |v|_{m,\Omega}\ .$$

Then, we need a slightly refined version of Hypothesis H.1.

<u>Hypothesis $\widetilde{\text{H.1}}$</u> : <u>There exists an operator</u> $r_h\in \mathcal{L}((H^1(\Omega)\cap C^o(\bar\Omega))^N\ ;\ (W_h)^N)\cap \mathcal{L}((H^1_o(\Omega)\cap C^o(\bar\Omega))^N\ ;\ X_h)$ <u>such that</u>

(i) <u>(4.1) holds</u>

(ii) (5.21) $\Big(\sum_{K\in\mathcal{C}_h} |r_h\vec v-\vec v|^q_{s,q,K}\Big)^{1/q} \leq Ch^{m+1-s}|\vec v|_{m+1,q,\Omega}$, $0\leq s\leq m+1$

<u>for all</u> $\vec v\in(W^{m+1,q}(\Omega))^N$ <u>and all m with</u> $0\leq m\leq k$ <u>and</u> $m+1-\frac{N}{q}>0$ (3)

In practice, Hypothesis $\widetilde{\text{H.1}}$ holds as soon as Hypothesis H.1 does.

Now, we want to study the convergence of β_h and $\|f\|^*_h$ as h tends to zero. To this purpose, we need some technical lemmas.

<u>Lemma 3 : Assume that Hypothesis H.4 (ii) holds for some integer $s=r+k'-1$ with $r\geq 0$. Then, there exists a constant C>0 independent of h and K such that</u>

(5.22) $\Big|E_K\Big(\frac{\partial v_i}{\partial x_j}\frac{\partial w_i}{\partial x_j}\Big)\Big| \leq Ch^{r+1}\Big|\frac{\partial v_i}{\partial x_j}\Big|_{r+1,K}\Big\|\frac{\partial w_i}{\partial x_j}\Big\|_{0,K}$

<u>for all</u> $K\in\mathcal{C}_h$ <u>and all</u> $v_i,w_i\in W_h$.

<u>Proof</u> : This result is similar to [3 , Theorem 6] but it will be established in a slightly different way. Since Hypothesis H.4 (ii) holds with $s=r+k'-1$, we may write :

$$\hat E\Big(\widehat{\frac{\partial v_i}{\partial x_j}}\ \widehat{\frac{\partial w_i}{\partial x_j}}\Big) = \hat E\Big(\Big(\widehat{\frac{\partial v_i}{\partial x_j}}-\hat\pi_r\widehat{\frac{\partial v_i}{\partial x_j}}\Big)\widehat{\frac{\partial w_i}{\partial x_j}}\Big)\ ,$$

where, for any integer $m\geq 0$, $\hat\pi_m$ denotes the orthogonal projection operator in $L^2(\hat K)$ upon P_m. Since $\widehat{\frac{\partial v_i}{\partial x_j}}-\hat\pi_r\widehat{\frac{\partial v_i}{\partial x_j}}$ and $\widehat{\frac{\partial w_i}{\partial x_j}}$ belong to

(3) so that $W^{m+1,q}(\Omega)\subset C^o(\bar\Omega)$ by the Sobolev's imbedding theorem.

the finite-dimensional space $P_{k'-1}$, there exists a constant $c_1=c_1(\hat{K},k',r)$ such that

$$|\hat{E}((\widehat{\frac{\partial v_i}{\partial x_j}} - \hat{\pi}_r \widehat{\frac{\partial v_i}{\partial x_j}})| \leq c_1 \left\| \widehat{\frac{\partial v_i}{\partial x_j}} - \hat{\pi}_r \widehat{\frac{\partial v_i}{\partial x_j}} \right\|_{0,\hat{K}} \left\| \widehat{\frac{\partial w_i}{\partial x_j}} \right\|_{0,\hat{K}}$$

By the Bramble-Hilbert lemma [1] in the form given in [2 ,Lemma 7], we get :

$$\left\| \widehat{\frac{\partial v_i}{\partial x_j}} - \hat{\pi}_r \widehat{\frac{\partial v_i}{\partial x_j}} \right\|_{0,\hat{K}} \leq c_2 \left| \widehat{\frac{\partial v_i}{\partial x_j}} \right|_{r+1,\hat{K}}$$

and therefore

$$|\hat{E}(\widehat{\frac{\partial v_i}{\partial x_j}} \widehat{\frac{\partial w_i}{\partial x_j}})| \leq c_3 \left| \widehat{\frac{\partial v_i}{\partial x_j}} \right|_{r+1,\hat{K}} \left\| \widehat{\frac{\partial w_i}{\partial x_j}} \right\|_{0,\hat{K}}$$

Since (cf. [2 , formula (4.15)])

$$(5.23) \quad |\hat{\varphi}|_{\ell,q,\hat{K}} \leq J_K^{-1/q} \|B_K\|^{\ell} |\varphi|_{\ell,q,K} \leq c_4 J_K^{-1/q} h^{\ell} |\varphi|_{\ell,q,K}$$

for all $\varphi \in W^{\ell,q}(K), \ell \geq 0$,

we obtain

$$|E_K(\frac{\partial v_i}{\partial x_j} \frac{\partial w_i}{\partial x_j}) = J_K |\hat{E}(\widehat{\frac{\partial v_i}{\partial x_j}} \widehat{\frac{\partial w_i}{\partial x_j}})| \leq c_5 h^{r+1} \left| \frac{\partial v_i}{\partial x_j} \right|_{r+1,K} \left\| \frac{\partial w_i}{\partial x_j} \right\|_{0,K} \quad ▨$$

Since $a(\vec{v}_h,\vec{w}_h)-a_h(\vec{v}_h,\vec{w}_h) = \sum_{i,j=1}^{N} \sum_{K\in\mathcal{C}_h} E_K(\frac{\partial v_i}{\partial x_j} \frac{\partial w_i}{\partial x_j})$, where v_i, w_i, $1\leq i\leq N$, denote the components of $\vec{v}_h$, $\vec{w}_h \in (W_h)^N$, we get by Lemma 3

$$(5.24) \quad |a(\vec{v}_h,\vec{w}_h)-a_h(\vec{v}_h,\vec{w}_h)| \leq Ch^{r+1} (\sum_{K\in\mathcal{C}_h} |\vec{v}_h|^2_{r+2,K})^{1/2} \|\vec{w}_h\|.$$

<u>Lemma 4 : Assume that Hypothesis $\tilde{H}.1$ (ii) and H.4 (ii) hold. Then, for any sequence $\{\vec{v}_h\}$ of functions $\vec{v}_h \in X_h$ such that $\vec{v}_h \to \vec{v}$ weakly</u> in X as $h \to 0$, we have :

$$(5.25) \quad \|\vec{v}\| \leq \liminf_{h\to 0} \|\vec{v}_h\|_h$$

<u>Proof</u> : Define $\lambda = \liminf_{h\to 0} \|\vec{v}_h\|_h$. First, we extract a subsequence yet denoted by $\{\vec{v}_h\}$ such that

$$\lim_{h\to 0} \|\vec{v}_h\|_h = \lambda.$$

Now, since $\mathcal{X} = X\cap(H^2(\Omega))^N$ is dense in X, we can find a sequence $\{\vec{v}_n\}_{n\geq 1}$ of functions of $\mathcal{X}$ such that

$$\lim_{n\to\infty} \vec{v}_n = \vec{v} \quad \text{strongly in X.}$$

Then, consider the expression :

(5.26) $a_h(\vec{v}_h - r_h\vec{v}_n, \vec{v}_h - r_h\vec{v}_n) = a_h(\vec{v}_h,\vec{v}_h) - 2a_h(r_h\vec{v}_n,\vec{v}_h) + a_h(r_h\vec{v}_n, r_h\vec{v}_n)$.

By using (5.24) with r=0 and Hypothesis $\tilde{H}.1$ (ii), we get :

$$|a(r_h\vec{v}_n,\vec{v}_h) - a_h(r_h\vec{v}_n,\vec{v}_h)| \leq c_1 h\Big(\sum_{K\in\mathcal{C}_h} |r_h\vec{v}_n|^2_{2,K}\Big)^{1/2} \|\vec{v}_h\| \leq$$

$$\leq c_2 h |\vec{v}_n|_{2,\Omega} \|\vec{v}_h\|$$

and therefore

$$\lim_{h\to 0} a_h(r_h\vec{v}_n,\vec{v}_h) = \lim_{h\to 0} a(r_h\vec{v}_n,\vec{v}_h) = a(\vec{v}_n,\vec{v}).$$

Similarly, we obtain

$$\lim_{h\to 0} a_h(r_h\vec{v}_n, r_h\vec{v}_n) = \lim_{h\to 0} a(r_h\vec{v}_n, r_h\vec{v}_n) = a(\vec{v}_n,\vec{v}_n).$$

Hence

$$\lim_{h\to 0} a_h(\vec{v}_h - r_h\vec{v}_n, \vec{v}_h - r_h\vec{v}_n) = \lambda^2 - 2a(\vec{v}_n,\vec{v}) + a(\vec{v}_n,\vec{v}_n)$$

and

$$\lim_{n\to\infty}\lim_{h\to 0} a_h(\vec{v}_h - r_h\vec{v}_n, \vec{v}_h - r_h\vec{v}_n) = \lambda^2 - a(\vec{v},\vec{v}).$$

Since the expression (5.26) is ≥ 0, the conclusion follows at once.

<u>Lemma 5</u> : <u>Assume that Hypothesis H.4 (ii) holds and that the triangulation $\mathcal{C}_h$ verifies the uniformity condition (4.33)</u>. <u>Then, we have</u> :

(5.27) $|b(\vec{u}_h,\vec{v}_h,\vec{w}_h) - b_h(\vec{u}_h,\vec{v}_h,\vec{w}_h)| \leq C h^{1-\frac{N}{4}} \|\vec{u}_h\| \, \|\vec{v}_h\| \, \|\vec{w}_h\|$

<u>for all</u> $\vec{u}_h,\vec{v}_h,\vec{w}_h \in X_h$.

<u>Proof</u> : First we note that condition (4.33) implies

(5.28) $\|v_h\|_{L^\infty(\Omega)} \leq c_1 h^{-N/q} \|v_h\|_{L^q(\Omega)}$ for all $v_h \in W_h$ and all $q \geq 1$.

Let us prove this classical inequality for the reader's convenience. Let $v_h \in W_h$ and let $K \in \mathcal{C}_h$; since $\hat{v}_h \in P_{k'}$, there exists a constant $c_2 = c_2(\hat{K}, k')$ such that

$$\|\hat{v}_h\|_{L^\infty(\hat{K})} \leq c_2 \|\hat{v}_h\|_{L^q(\hat{K})}$$

and therefore

$$\|v_h\|_{L^\infty(K)} \leq c_2 J_K^{-1/q} \|v_h\|_{L^q(K)}$$

But

$$J_K^{-1} = \det(B_K^{-1}) \leq \|B_K^{-1}\|^N,$$

where $\|.\|$ denotes the spectral matrix-norm. Thus, using [2 , Lemma 2] and (4.33), we get

$$J_K^{-1} \leq \left(\frac{h(\hat{K})}{\rho(K)}\right)^N \leq c_3 h^{-N}$$

so that

$$\|v_h\|_{L^\infty(K)} \leq c_2 c_3^{1/q} h^{-N/q} \|v_h\|_{L^q(K)}$$

Hence :

$$\|v_h\|_{L^\infty(\Omega)} = \sup_{K\in\mathcal{C}_h} \|v_h\|_{L^\infty(K)} \leq c_2 c_3^{1/q} h^{-N/q} \|v_h\|_{L^q(\Omega)}$$

Next, we have :

$$(5.29) \quad b(\vec{u}_h,\vec{v}_h,\vec{w}_h)-b_h(\vec{u}_h,\vec{v}_h,\vec{w}_h)=\frac{1}{2}\sum_{i,j=1}^{N}\{E(u_i\frac{\partial v_j}{\partial x_i}w_j)-E(u_i\frac{\partial w_j}{\partial x_i}v_j)\}.$$

where u_i, v_i, w_i, $1\leq i\leq N$, denote the components of $\vec{u}_h, \vec{v}_h, \vec{w}_h \in X_h$. For example, consider the term

$$E_K(u_i \frac{\partial v_j}{\partial x_i} w_j) = J_K \hat{E}(\hat{u}_i \widehat{\frac{\partial v_j}{\partial x_i}} \hat{w}_j) .$$

Now, $\frac{\partial v_j}{\partial x_i} \in P_{k'-1}$ and, by Hypothesis H.4 (ii), we have

$$\hat{E}(\hat{u}_i \widehat{\frac{\partial v_j}{\partial x_i}} \hat{w}_j) = \hat{E}((\hat{u}_i\hat{w}_j-\hat{\pi}_o(\hat{u}_i\hat{w}_j))\widehat{\frac{\partial v_j}{\partial x_i}}) ,$$

where, again $\hat{\pi}_o$ denotes the orthogonal projection operator in $L^2(\hat{K})$ upon P_o.

Since $\hat{u}_i.\hat{w}_j-\hat{\pi}_o(\hat{u}_i.\hat{w}_j)$ and $\widehat{\frac{\partial v_j}{\partial x_i}}$ belong to the finite-dimensional spaces $P_{2k'}$ and $P_{k'-1}$ respectively, there exists a constant $c_4=c_4(\hat{K},k')$ such that

$$|\hat{E}((\hat{u}_i\hat{w}_j-\hat{\pi}_o(\hat{u}_i\hat{w}_j))\widehat{\frac{\partial v_j}{\partial x_i}})| \leq c_4 |\hat{u}_i\hat{w}_j-\hat{\pi}_o(\hat{u}_i\hat{w}_j)|_{0,\hat{K}}\cdot\left\|\widehat{\frac{\partial v_j}{\partial x_i}}\right\|_{0,\hat{K}}$$

Thus, by the Bramble-Hilbert lemma, we get for some constant $c_5=c_5(\hat{K},k')$:

$$|\hat{E}(\hat{u}_i \widehat{\frac{\partial v_j}{\partial x_i}} \hat{w}_j)| \leq c_5|\hat{u}_i\hat{w}_j|_{1,\hat{K}}\left\|\widehat{\frac{\partial v_j}{\partial x_i}}\right\|_{0,\hat{K}}$$

and by using (5.23)

$$|E_K(u_i \frac{\partial v_j}{\partial x_i} w_j)| \leq c_6 h|u_i w_j|_{1,K}\left\|\frac{\partial v_j}{\partial x_i}\right\|_{0,K} \quad \text{for all } K\in\mathcal{C}_h.$$

Hence

$$|E(u_i \frac{\partial v_j}{\partial x_i} w_j)| \leq c_6 h|u_i w_j|_{1,\Omega}\left\|\frac{\partial v_j}{\partial x_i}\right\|_{0,\Omega} \leq$$

$$\leq c_6 h(|u_i|_{L^\infty(\Omega)}|w_j|_{1,\Omega}+|u_i|_{1,\Omega}|w_j|_{L^\infty(\Omega)})\left\|\frac{\partial v_j}{\partial x_i}\right\|_{0,\Omega}$$

Now, applying (5.28) and the Sobolev's imbedding theorem, we obtain

$$|E(u_i \frac{\partial v_j}{\partial x_i} w_j)| \leq c_7 h^{1-N/4} (\|u_i\|_{L^4(\Omega)} |w_j|_{1,\Omega} + |u_i|_{1,\Omega} |w_j|_{L^4(\Omega)}) \left\|\frac{\partial v_j}{\partial x_i}\right\|_{0,\Omega} \leq$$

$$\leq c_8 h^{1-N/4} \|\vec{u}_h\| \, \|\vec{v}_h\| \, \|\vec{w}_h\|$$

Clearly, a similar estimate is valid for each term in the right-hand side of (5.29) so that inequality (5.27) is proved.

We are now able to prove

<u>Lemma 6</u> : <u>Assume that Hypotheses $\widetilde{H.1}$ and H.4 hold. Assume, in addition, that the triangulation</u> $\mathcal{T}_h$ <u>verifies condition (4.33). Then, we have</u> :

(5.30) $\lim_{h\to 0} \tilde{\beta}_h = \beta$,

(5.31) $\lim_{h\to 0} \|\tilde{\vec{f}}\|_h^* = \|\vec{f}\|^*$

<u>Proof</u> : We shall only prove (5.30). First, by Lemma 5, we get for all $\vec{u}_h, \vec{v}_h, \vec{w}_h \in X_h$:

$$|b_h(\vec{u}_h, \vec{v}_h, \vec{w}_h)| \leq |b(\vec{u}_h, \vec{v}_h, \vec{w}_h)| + c_1 h^{1-N/4} \|\vec{u}_h\| \, \|\vec{v}_h\| \, \|\vec{w}_h\| \leq$$

$$\leq c_2 (1+h^{1-N/4}) \|\vec{u}_h\| \, \|\vec{v}_h\| \, \|\vec{w}_h\| \, .$$

Using (5.10), (5.11), we obtain ($N\leq 3$)

$$\tilde{\beta}_h \leq c_2 \, \alpha^{-3/2} \, (1+h^{1-N/4}) \leq c_3 \, .$$

Next, we proceed as in the proof of Lemma 1 : for each value of the parameter h, let $\vec{u}_h$, $\vec{v}_h$, $\vec{w}_h$ be functions in V_h such that

$$\begin{cases} \|\vec{u}_h\|_h = \|\vec{v}_h\|_h = \|\vec{w}_h\|_h = 1 \, , \\ |b_h(\vec{u}_h, \vec{v}_h, \vec{w}_h)| = \tilde{\beta}_h \, . \end{cases}$$

Then, we can find a subsequence $\{h_n\}_{n\geq 1}$ such that

$$\begin{cases} \vec{u}_{h_n} \to \vec{u}_* \, , \ \vec{v}_{h_n} \to \vec{v}_* \, , \ \vec{w}_{h_n} \to \vec{w}_* \quad \text{weakly in } X \text{ and strongly} \\ \text{in } (L^4(\Omega))^N, \\ \tilde{\beta}_{h_n} \to \beta_* \, , \end{cases}$$

as $n\to\infty$. Like in the proof of Lemma 1, we have : $\vec{u}_*, \vec{v}_*, \vec{w}_* \in V$. Morevoer, by Lemma 4, we have

$$\|\vec{u}_*\| \leq 1 \, , \ \|\vec{v}_*\| \leq 1 \, , \ \|\vec{w}_*\| \leq 1.$$

On the other hand, by Lemma 5, we get :

$$\lim_{n\to\infty} b_{h_n}(\vec u_{h_n},\vec v_{h_n},\vec w_{h_n}) = \lim_{n\to\infty} b(\vec u_{h_n},\vec v_{h_n},\vec w_{h_n})$$

and therefore

$$\beta_* = \lim_{n\to\infty} |b_{h_n}(\vec u_{h_n},\vec v_{h_n},\vec w_{h_n})| = |b(\vec u_*,\vec v_*,\vec w_*)| \leqslant \frac{|b(\vec u_*,\vec v_*,\vec w_*)|}{\|\vec u_*\|\,\|\vec v_*\|\,\|\vec w_*\|}$$

which implies $\beta_* \leqslant \beta$.

Now, using Hypothesis $\widetilde{\text{H.1}}$, formula (5.24) and Lemma 5, we have

$$\lim_{h\to 0} \frac{|b_h(r_h\vec u, r_h\vec v, r_h\vec w)|}{\|r_h\vec u\|_h\,\|r_h\vec v\|_h\,\|r_h\vec w\|_h} = \frac{|b(\vec u,\vec v,\vec w)|}{\|\vec u\|\,\|\vec v\|\,\|\vec w\|}$$

for all $\vec u,\vec v,\vec w \in V \cap (H^2(\Omega))^N$. Hence, $\beta_* \geqslant \beta$ so that $\beta_* = \beta$.

Furthermore, it follows that the whole sequence $\{\tilde\beta_h\}$ converges to β as h tends to zero.

6. THE EFFECT OF NUMERICAL INTEGRATION : ERROR ESTIMATES

6.1. Error estimate in X

In order to derive an estimate for the error $\tilde{\vec u}_h-\vec u$ in X, we proceed as in § 4.1. We assume the hypotheses of Lemma 6. Thus, we may choose h small enough so that

$$(6.1)\qquad \frac{\tilde\beta_h}{\nu^2}\,\|\tilde{\vec f}\|_h^* \leqslant 1 - \frac{\delta}{2}$$

Then, existence and uniqueness of the solution $\tilde{\vec u}_h$ of (5.8) follow from Theorem 6. Now, let $\vec v_h$ be an arbitrary function of V_h and $\vec w_h=\tilde{\vec u}_h-\vec v_h$. We consider the expression :

$$(6.2)\qquad D_h = \nu\, a_h(\vec w_h,\vec w_h) + b_h(\tilde{\vec u}_h,\tilde{\vec u}_h,\vec w_h) - b_h(\vec v_h,\vec v_h,\vec w_h)$$

Using (5.6), (5.12) and (5.15), we may write :

$$D_h = \nu\, a_h(\vec w_h,\vec w_h) + b_h(\vec w_h,\tilde{\vec u}_h,\vec w_h) \geqslant \nu\,(1-\frac{\tilde\beta_h}{\nu^2}|\tilde{\vec f}|_h^*)\,\|\vec w_h\|_h^2$$

and we get by (5.10) and (6.1)

$$(6.3)\qquad D_h \geqslant \frac{\nu\alpha\delta}{2}\,\|\vec w_h\|^2$$

On the other hand, using (5.7) and (2.19), we have :

$$\begin{aligned} D_h &= (\vec f,\vec w_h)_h - \nu\, a_h(\vec v_h,\vec w_h) - b_h(\vec v_h,\vec v_h,\vec w_h) = \\ &= \nu\, a(\vec u-\vec v_h,\vec w_h) + b(\vec u,\vec u,\vec w_h) - b(\vec v_h,\vec v_h,\vec w_h) - (p,\operatorname{div}\vec w_h) + \\ &+ \nu\,\{a(\vec v_h,\vec w_h) - a_h(\vec v_h,\vec w_h) + b(\vec v_h,\vec v_h,\vec w_h) - b_h(\vec v_h,\vec v_h,\vec w_h)\} - \\ &- \{(\vec f,\vec w_h) - (\vec f,\vec w_h)_h\} \end{aligned}$$

(Compare with (4.14)). Hence, we obtain :

$$(6.4)\quad \begin{cases} D_h \leq \{(\nu + c_1(\|\vec{u}\| + \|\vec{v}_h\|))\|\vec{u}-\vec{v}_h\| + c_2|p-\rho_h p|_{0,\Omega}\}\|\vec{w}_h\| + \\ + \quad \nu|a(\vec{v}_h,\vec{w}_h)-a_h(\vec{v}_h,\vec{w}_h)| + |b(\vec{v}_h,\vec{v}_h,\vec{w}_h)-b_h(\vec{v}_h,\vec{v}_h,\vec{w}_h)| + \\ + \quad |(\vec{f},\vec{w}_h)-(\vec{f},\vec{w}_h)_h| \end{cases}$$

Comparing (6.3) and (6.4), we get for all $\vec{v}_h \in V_h$:

$$(6.5)\qquad \|\tilde{\vec{u}}_h-\vec{u}\| \leq c_3(A_1+A_2+A_3+A_4)$$

where

$$(6.6)\quad A_1 = (1+\|\vec{u}\|+\|\vec{v}_h\|)\|\vec{u}-\vec{v}_h\| + \|p-\rho_h p\|_{0,\Omega}$$

$$(6.7)\quad A_2 = \sup_{\vec{w}_h \in V_h} \frac{|a(\vec{v}_h,\vec{w}_h)-a_h(\vec{v}_h,\vec{w}_h)|}{\|\vec{w}_h\|}$$

$$(6.8)\quad A_3 = \sup_{\vec{w}_h \in V_h} \frac{|b(\vec{v}_h,\vec{v}_h,\vec{w}_h)-b_h(\vec{v}_h,\vec{v}_h,\vec{w}_h)|}{\|\vec{w}_h\|}$$

$$(6.9)\quad A_4 = \sup_{\vec{w}_h \in V_h} \frac{|(\vec{f},\vec{w}_h)-(\vec{f},\vec{w}_h)_h|}{\|\vec{w}_h\|}$$

We choose $\vec{v}_h = r_h\vec{u}$. Then, we must estimate each of the terms A_i. Note that A_1 is the same as in § 4.1 and it will be evaluated in a similar way. The three terms A_1, A_2 and A_3 come from numerical quadrature. The term A_2 has been evaluated in (5.24). Thus, it remains to evaluate the terms A_3 and A_4.

First,
$$b(\vec{v}_h,\vec{v}_h,\vec{w}_h)-b_h(\vec{v}_h,\vec{v}_h,\vec{w}_h) = \frac{1}{2}\sum_{i,j=1}^{N}\sum_{K\in\mathcal{C}_h} E_K\Big(v_i\frac{\partial v_j}{\partial x_i}w_j - v_i v_j\frac{\partial w_j}{\partial x_i}\Big)$$

Hence, for estimating A_3, we need the following lemma.

<u>Lemma 7</u> : <u>Assume that Hypothesis H.4 (ii) holds for some integer $s=r+k'-1$ with $r\geq 0$. Then, there exists a constant $C>0$ independent of h and K such that</u> :

$$(6.10)\quad \Big|E_K\Big(v_i v_j \frac{\partial w_j}{\partial x_i}\Big)\Big| \leq Ch^{r+1}\|v_i\|_{r+1,4,K}\,\|v_j\|_{r+1,4,K}\,\Big\|\frac{\partial w_j}{\partial x_i}\Big\|_{0,K}$$

$$(6.11)\quad \begin{cases} \Big|E_K\Big(v_i\frac{\partial v_j}{\partial x_i}w_j\Big)\Big| \leq Ch^{r+1}\Big\{\|v_i\|_{r,4,K}\Big\|\frac{\partial v_j}{\partial x_i}\Big\|_{r,4,K}\|w_j\|_{1,K} + \\ \qquad + \|v_i\|_{r+1,4,K}\Big\|\frac{\partial v_j}{\partial x_i}\Big\|_{r+1,K}\|w_j\|_{0,4,K}\Big\} \end{cases}$$

for all $K\in\mathcal{C}_h$ and all $v_i, v_j, w_j \in W_h$.

<u>Proof</u> : First, let us consider the term $E_K\Big(v_i v_j\frac{\partial w_j}{\partial x_i}\Big)$. As a

consequence of Hypothesis H.4 (ii), we may write :

$$\hat{E}(\hat{v}_i\hat{v}_j\widehat{\frac{\partial w_j}{\partial x_i}}) = \hat{E}((\hat{v}_i\hat{v}_j - \hat{\pi}_r(\hat{v}_i\hat{v}_j))\widehat{\frac{\partial w_j}{\partial x_i}}$$

and by using the Bramble-Hilbert lemma

$$|\hat{E}(\hat{v}_i\hat{v}_j\widehat{\frac{\partial w_j}{\partial x_i}})| \leq c_1 \, |\hat{v}_i\hat{v}_j|_{r+1,\hat{K}} \left\|\widehat{\frac{\partial w_j}{\partial x_i}}\right\|_{0,\hat{K}}$$

Hence, using (5.23), we get

$$(6.12) \quad |E_K(v_i v_j \frac{\partial w_j}{\partial x_i})| \leq c_2 h^{r+1} |v_i v_j|_{r+1,K} \left\|\frac{\partial w_j}{\partial x_i}\right\|_{0,K}$$

But, using Leibnitz's rule and Hölder's inequality, we obtain

$$(6.13) \quad |v_i v_j|_{r+1,K} \leq c_3 \sum_{s=0}^{r+1} |v_i|_{s,4,K} \, |v_j|_{r+1-s,4,K} \leq$$

$$\leq c_4 \|v_i\|_{r+1,4,K} \, \|v_j\|_{r+1,4,K}$$

The proof of (6.10) is achieved by combining inequalities (6.12) and (6.13).

Consider next the term $E_K(v_i \frac{\partial v_j}{\partial x_i} w_j)$ and assume that $r \geq 1$ (the case $r=0$ is left to the reader). We write :

$$\hat{E}(\hat{v}_i \widehat{\frac{\partial v_j}{\partial x_i}} \hat{w}_j) = \hat{E}(\hat{v}_i \widehat{\frac{\partial v_j}{\partial x_i}} (\hat{w}_j - \hat{\pi}_o \hat{w}_j)) + \hat{E}(\hat{v}_i \widehat{\frac{\partial v_j}{\partial x_i}} \hat{\pi}_o \hat{w}_j)$$

By Hypothesis H.4 (ii), we get

$$\hat{E}(\hat{v}_i \widehat{\frac{\partial v_j}{\partial x_i}} (\hat{w}_j - \hat{\pi}_o \hat{w}_j)) = \hat{E}((\hat{v}_i \widehat{\frac{\partial v_j}{\partial x_i}} - \hat{\pi}_{r-1}(\hat{v}_i \widehat{\frac{\partial v_j}{\partial x_i}}))(\hat{w}_j - \hat{\pi}_o \hat{w}_j))$$

and by the Bramble-Hilbert lemma

$$(6.14) \quad |\hat{E}(\hat{v}_i \widehat{\frac{\partial v_j}{\partial x_i}} (\hat{w}_j - \hat{\pi}_o \hat{w}_j))| \leq c_5 \left|\hat{v}_i \widehat{\frac{\partial v_j}{\partial x_i}}\right|_{r,\hat{K}} |\hat{w}_j|_{1,\hat{K}}$$

Similarly, we get by H.4(ii)

$$\hat{E}(\hat{v}_i \widehat{\frac{\partial v_j}{\partial x_i}} \hat{\pi}_o \hat{w}_j) = \hat{E}((\hat{v}_i \widehat{\frac{\partial v_j}{\partial x_i}} - \hat{\pi}_r(\hat{v}_i \widehat{\frac{\partial v_j}{\partial x_i}}))\hat{\pi}_o \hat{w}_j)$$

and therefore

$$(6.15) \quad |\hat{E}(\hat{v}_i \widehat{\frac{\partial v_j}{\partial x_i}} \hat{\pi}_o \hat{w}_j)| \leq c_6 \left|\hat{v}_i \widehat{\frac{\partial v_j}{\partial x_i}}\right|_{r+1,4/3,\hat{K}} \|\hat{w}_j\|_{0,4,\hat{K}}$$

Thus, it follows from (5.23), (6.14) and (6.15)

$$(6.16) \quad |E_K(v_i \frac{\partial v_j}{\partial x_i} w_j)| \leq c_6 h^{r+1} \{ \left|v_i \frac{\partial v_j}{\partial x_i}\right|_{r,K} |w_j|_{1,K} +$$

$$+ \left|v_i \frac{\partial v_j}{\partial x_i}\right|_{r+1,4/3,K} \|w_j\|_{0,4,K} \}$$

Then, (6.11) is a consequence of (6.16) and

$$\left| v_i \frac{\partial v_j}{\partial x_i} \right|_{r,K} \leq c_8 \| v_i \|_{r,4,K} \left\| \frac{\partial v_j}{\partial x_i} \right\|_{r,4,K} ,$$

$$\left| v_i \frac{\partial v_j}{\partial x_i} \right|_{r+1,4/3,K} \leq c_9 \| v_i \|_{r+1,4,K} \left\| \frac{\partial v_j}{\partial x_i} \right\|_{r+1,K} . \blacksquare$$

Consider next

$$(\vec{f},\vec{w}_h)-(\vec{f},\vec{w}_h)_h = \sum_{i=1}^{N} \sum_{K\in\mathcal{C}_h} E_K(f_i w_i)$$

For estimating A_4, we shall use the following lemma which has been proved in [3, Theorem 4].

<u>Lemma 8</u> : <u>Assume that Hypothesis H.4 (ii) holds for some integer $s=r+k'-1$ with $r\geq 0$. Assume, in addition, that the function $f_i \in W^{r+1,q}(\Omega)$ for some $q\geq 1$ with $r+1-\frac{N}{q}>0$. Then, there exists a constant $C>0$ independent of h and K such that</u>

(6.17) $\quad |E_K(f_i w_i)| \leq Ch^{r+1} \| f_i \|_{r+1,q,K} \| w_i \|_{1,q',K}$

<u>for all $K\in\mathcal{C}_h$ and all $w_i \in W_h$, $\frac{1}{q}+\frac{1}{q'}=1$.</u>

We are now able to prove

<u>Theorem 7</u> : <u>We make the following assumptions</u>

(i) <u>Hypothesis $\widetilde{H.1}$ holds</u> ;

(ii) <u>Hypothesis H.4 holds for some integer $s=r+k'-1$ with $0\leq r\leq k-1$</u>;

(iii) $\vec{f} \in (W^{r+1,q}(\Omega))^N$ <u>with</u> $q\geq 2$, $r+1-\frac{N}{q}>0$ <u>and satisfies condition (2.22)</u> ;

(iv) <u>The solution $(\vec{u},p)$ of (2.19) verifies the smoothness properties (4.9)</u> ;

(v) <u>The triangulation $\mathcal{C}_h$</u> <u>satisfies the uniformity condition (4.33)</u>.

<u>Then, for h small enough, problem (5.8) has a unique solution $\vec{u}_h \in V_h$ and we have the estimate</u>

(6.18) $$\|\vec{u}_h-\vec{u}\| \leq C_1 h^k (|\vec{u}|_{k+1,\Omega}+|p|_{k,\Omega}) + C_2 h^{r+1}(|\vec{u}|_{r+2,\Omega}+\|u\|^2_{r+2,\Omega}+\|\vec{f}\|_{r+1,q,\Omega})$$

<u>where C_1 and C_2 are positive constants independent of h, $\vec{u}$ and p.</u>

<u>Proof</u> : Taking $\vec{v}_h=r_h\vec{u}$ in (6.6), we obtain

$$A_1 \leq (1+2\|\vec{u}\|)\|\vec{u}-r_h\vec{u}\|+\|\vec{u}-r_h\vec{u}\|^2+\|p-\rho_h p\|_{0,\Omega}$$

By applying (2.24), (4.7) and (5.21), we get :

(6.19) $A_1 \leq C_3 h^k(|\vec{u}|_{k+1,\Omega}+|p|_{k,\Omega})+C_4 h^{2r+2}|\vec{u}|^2_{r+2,\Omega}$

Next, using (5.24) with $\vec{v}_h = r_h\vec{u}$ and (5.21), we obtain

(6.20) $A_2 \leq C_5 h^{r+1}|\vec{u}|_{r+2,\Omega}$

Now, using Lemma 7, we get

$$|b(r_h\vec{u},r_h,\vec{u},\vec{w}_h)-b_h(r_h\vec{u},r_h\vec{u},\vec{w}_h)| \leq$$

$$\leq C_6 h^{r+1}\{(\sum_{K\in\mathcal{T}_h}\|r_h\vec{u}\|^4_{r+1,4,K})^{1/2}\ \|\vec{w}_h\| +$$

$$+ (\sum_{K\in\mathcal{T}_h}\|r_h\vec{u}\|^4_{r+1,4,K})^{1/4}(\sum_{K\in\mathcal{T}_h}\|r_h\vec{u}\|^2_{r+2,K})^{1/2}\ \|\vec{w}_h\|_{0,4,\Omega}\}$$

and by using (5.21) and by continuity of the imbedding of $H^1(\Omega)$ into $L^4(\Omega)$

(6.21) $A_3 \leq C_7 h^{r+1}\ \|\vec{u}\|^2_{r+2,\Omega}$.

Finally, using Lemma 8, we obtain

$$|(\vec{f},\vec{w}_h)-(\vec{f},\vec{w}_h)_h| \leq C_8 h^{r+1}\|\vec{f}\|_{r+1,q,\Omega}\ \|\vec{w}_h\|_{1,q,\Omega}$$

and since $q'\leq 2$

(6.22) $A_4 \leq C_9 h^{r+1}\ \|\vec{f}\|_{r+1,q,\Omega}$

Thus, inequality (6.18) follows from (6.5), (6.19),..., (6.22).

<u>Corollary</u> : <u>Assume that the hypotheses of Theorem 7 are satisfied with r=k-1</u>. <u>Then</u>, <u>we have</u> :

(6.23) $\|\tilde{\vec{u}}_h-\vec{u}\| \leq Ch^k(|\vec{u}|_{k+1,\Omega}+|p|_{k,\Omega}+\|\vec{u}\|^2_{k+1,\Omega}+\|\vec{f}\|_{k,q,\Omega})$.

Therefore, the order of convergence in X of the finite element method is not lowered when we use a <u>quadrature formula</u> (5.1) <u>which is exact for all polynomials of degree $\leq$ k+k'-2</u>.

<u>Remark</u> : We want to mention that we need the uniformity condition (4.33) only for proving the convergence of $\tilde{\beta}_h$ to β as h tends to zero and not for deriving the error estimate (6.18). Wether this condition (4.33) is necessary for obtaining (5.30) or not is an open question.

<u>Example 1</u> (continued). We go back to Example 1 which corresponds to the case k=2, k'=3. Thus, in order to get an optimal error estimate in X, it is sufficient to use a quadrature formula (5.1) which is exact for all polynomials of degree $\leq$ 3 and such that $\{\hat{b}_\ell\}_{\ell=1}^I$ contains a P_2-unisolvent subset. This is an important simplification since the exact computation of $b(\vec{u}_h,\vec{u}_h,\vec{v}_h)$ would require the integration of polynomials of degree 8. In particular, we may choose the quadrature formula

$$(6.24)\qquad \int_K \varphi(x)dx \simeq \text{meas}(K)\Big\{\frac{8}{60}\sum_{i=1}^{2}\varphi(a_{i,K})+\frac{3}{60}\sum_{1\leq i<j\leq 3}\varphi(a_{ij,K}) + \frac{27}{60}\varphi(a_{123,K})\Big\}$$

since this formula is exact for all polynomials of degree ≤ 3 and the set $\{a_{i,K}\}_{1\leq i\leq 3} \cup \{a_{ij,K}\}_{1\leq i<j\leq 3}$ is a P_2-unisolvent set. Furthermore, note that in this case, for each finite element K, the interpolation nodes coincide with the quadrature nodes.

6.2. Error estimate in $(L^2(\Omega))^N$

Let us state the theorem first.

Theorem 8 : The assumptions are the same as for theorem 7 with the stronger requirement that hypothesis (ii) of theorem 7 holds for $s=\max\{r+k'-1,k\}$. Assume also $k'\leq k+1$. Then, for h small enough, we have the estimate :

$$(6.25)\qquad \|\tilde{\vec{u}}_h-\vec{u}\|_{0,\Omega} \leq Ch^{k+1} + C'h^{r+2}$$

where $C=C(\vec{u},p)$ and $C'=C'(\vec{u},p)$ are certain constants independent of h.

Proof : We proceed like in section 4.2. Starting from (4.19) and defining $\vec{\varphi}$ by (4.21), we get :

$$(6.26)\qquad |(\tilde{\vec{u}}_h-\vec{u},\vec{g})| \leq |B_1|+\nu|B_2|+|B_3|+|B_4|\ ,\ \text{where :}$$

$$B_1=\nu\, a(\tilde{\vec{u}}_h-\vec{u},\vec{\varphi}-\vec{\varphi}_h)+b(\tilde{\vec{u}}_h-\vec{u},\tilde{\vec{u}}_h,\vec{\varphi}-\vec{\varphi}_h)+b(\vec{u},\tilde{\vec{u}}_h-\vec{u},\vec{\varphi}-\vec{\varphi}_h)+$$
$$-b(\tilde{\vec{u}}_h-\vec{u},\tilde{\vec{u}}_h-\vec{u},\vec{\varphi})-(\chi,\text{div}(\tilde{\vec{u}}_h-\vec{u}))+(p,\text{div}(\vec{\varphi}-\vec{\varphi}_h))$$

$$B_2=a(\tilde{\vec{u}}_h,\vec{\varphi}_h)-a_h(\tilde{\vec{u}}_h,\vec{\varphi}_h)$$

$$B_3=b(\tilde{\vec{u}}_h,\tilde{\vec{u}}_h,\vec{\varphi}_h)-b_h(\tilde{\vec{u}}_h,\tilde{\vec{u}}_h,\vec{\varphi}_h)$$

$$B_4=(\vec{f},\vec{\varphi}_h)-(\vec{f},\vec{\varphi}_h)_h$$

The term B_1 is identical to the term obtained in section 4.2 and the three terms B_2, B_3 and B_4 stem from the use of numerical quadrature. We must estimate these terms for $\vec{\varphi}_h=r_h\vec{\varphi}$. For the first one we get like in (4.30) :

$$(6.27)\qquad |B_1| \leq Ch^{k+1}(\|\vec{\varphi}\|_{2,\Omega}+|\chi|_{1,\Omega})\ ,$$

where $C=C(\vec{u},p)$ is independent of h.

For the term B_3, we can establish an estimate of the form :

$$(6.28)\qquad |B_3| \leq Ch^{r+2}\|\vec{\varphi}\|_{2,\Omega}.$$

We will only sketch the proof of (6.28). We write :

$$B_3 = B_{3,1}+B_{3,2}+B_{3,3}+B_{3,4}\ ,\ \text{where :}$$
$$B_{3,1} = (b-b_h)(r_h\vec{u},r_h\vec{u},\vec{\varphi}_h)$$
$$B_{3,2} = (b-b_h)(\tilde{\vec{u}}_h-r_h\vec{u},r_h\vec{u},\vec{\varphi}_h)$$

$$B_{3,3} = (b-b_h)(r_h\vec{u},\tilde{\vec{u}}_h-r_h\vec{u},\vec{\varphi}_h)$$

$$B_{3,4} = (b-b_h)(\tilde{\vec{u}}_h-r_h\vec{u},\tilde{\vec{u}}_h-r_h\vec{u},\vec{\varphi}_h)$$

We have :

$$(6.29)\qquad B_{3,1} = \frac{1}{2}\sum_{i,j=1}\sum_{K\in\mathcal{C}_h}\{E_K(v_i\frac{\partial v_j}{\partial x_i}\varphi_j)-E_K(v_i\frac{\partial \varphi_j}{\partial x_i}v_j)\},$$

where v_i, φ_i denote the components of $\vec{v}_h=r_h\vec{u}$ and $\vec{\varphi}_h$.

We can write :

$$(6.30)\qquad E_K(v_i\frac{\partial v_j}{\partial x_i}\varphi_j) = E_K(v_i\frac{\partial v_j}{\partial x_i}\Pi_1\varphi_j)+E_K(v_i\frac{\partial v_j}{\partial x_i}(\varphi_j-\Pi_1\varphi_j))$$

Let $z=v_i\frac{\partial v_j}{\partial x_i}\Pi_1\varphi_j$. Since $r+1\leq k\leq s$, we have by H.4 :

$$|\hat{E}(\hat{z})| = |\hat{E}(\hat{z}-\hat{\Pi}_{r+1}\hat{z})| \leq C_1\|\hat{z}-\hat{\Pi}_{r+1}\hat{z}\|_{0,\hat{K}} \leq C_2|\hat{z}|_{r+2,\hat{K}}$$

It follows that :

$$(6.31)\qquad \sum_{K\in\mathcal{C}_h}|E_K(v_i\frac{\partial v_j}{\partial x_i}\Pi_1\varphi_j)| \leq C_3h^{r+2}(\sum_{K\in\mathcal{C}_h}|v_i\frac{\partial v_j}{\partial x_i}\Pi_1\varphi_j|^2_{r+2,K})^{1/2} \leq$$

$$\leq C_3h^{r+2}\{(\sum_K\left|v_i\frac{\partial v_j}{\partial x_i}\right|^2_{r+2,1,K})^{1/2}|\Pi_1\varphi_j|_{0,\infty,K} +$$

$$+(\sum_K\left|v_i\frac{\partial v_j}{\partial x_i}\right|^4_{r+1,4,K})^{1/4}(\sum_K|\Pi_1\varphi_j|^4_{1,4,K})^{1/4}\}$$

But :

$$\left|v_i\frac{\partial v_j}{\partial x_i}\right|_{r+2,1,K} \leq \|v_i\|_{r+2,K}\left\|\frac{\partial v_j}{\partial x_i}\right\|_{r+2,K} \leq \|r_h\vec{u}\|^2_{k+1,K}$$

since $v_i=(r_h\vec{u})_i \in P_k, \subset P_{k+1}$. Hence, by $\widetilde{H}_1$:

$$(\sum_K\left|v_i\frac{\partial v_j}{\partial x_i}\right|^2_{r+2,1,K})^{1/2} \leq C_4\|\vec{u}\|^2_{k+1,\Omega}$$

In the same way :

$$\sum_K(\left|v_i\frac{\partial v_j}{\partial x_i}\right|^4_{r+1,4,K})^{1/4} \leq C_6\|\vec{u}\|^2_{k+1,\Omega}$$

On the other hand :

$$|\Pi_1\varphi_j|_{0,\infty,K} \leq C_7|\vec{\varphi}_h|_{0,\infty,K} \leq C_7|\vec{\varphi}_h|_{0,\infty,\Omega} \leq$$

$$\leq C_8\|\vec{\varphi}_h\|_{1,4,\Omega} \leq C_9\|\vec{\varphi}\|_{1,4,\Omega} \leq C_{10}\|\vec{\varphi}\|_{2,\Omega}$$

by $\widetilde{H}.1$ and the imbedding : $H^2(\Omega)\subset W^{1,4}(\Omega)\subset C^0(\Omega)$.

In the same way, we have :

$$(\sum_K |\Pi_1 \varphi_j|^4_{1,4,K})^{1/4} \leq C_{11} \|\vec{\varphi}\|_{2,\Omega}$$

Taking the foregoing estimates into (6.31), we get :

$$(6.32) \qquad \sum_{K\in\mathcal{C}_h} |E_K(v_i \frac{\partial v_j}{\partial x_i} \Pi_1 \varphi_j)| \leq C_{12} h^{r+2} |\vec{u}|^2_{k+1,\Omega} \|\vec{\varphi}\|_{2,\Omega}$$

Now, we must consider the second term of (6.30). We have :

$$|\hat{E}(\hat{v}_i \widehat{\frac{\partial v_j}{\partial x_i}}(\hat{\varphi}_j - \hat{\Pi}_1 \hat{\varphi}_j)| = |\hat{E}((\hat{v}_i \widehat{\frac{\partial v_j}{\partial x_i}} - \hat{\Pi}_{s-k'}(\hat{v}_i \widehat{\frac{\partial v_j}{\partial x_i}}))(\hat{\varphi}_j - \Pi_1 \hat{\varphi}_j))| \leq$$

$$\leq C_{13} \left| \hat{v}_i \widehat{\frac{\partial v_j}{\partial x_i}} \right|_{s-k'+1,\hat{K}} |\hat{\varphi}_j|_{2,\hat{K}} .$$

Hence, we conclude as before, since $s-k'+1=r\leq k-1$:

$$\sum_{K\in\mathcal{C}_h} |E_K(v_i \frac{\partial v_j}{\partial x_i}(\varphi_j - \Pi_1 \varphi_j))| \leq C_{14} h^{r+2} |\vec{u}|^2_{k,4,\Omega} |\vec{\varphi}\|_{2,\Omega} \leq$$

$$\leq C_{15} h^{r+2} |\vec{u}\|^2_{k+1,\Omega} \|\vec{\varphi}\|_{2,\Omega}$$

which, together with (6.32) yields :

$$\sum_{K\in\mathcal{C}_h} |E_K(v_i \frac{\partial v_j}{\partial x_i} \varphi_j)| \leq C h^{r+2} \|\vec{u}\|^2_{k+1,\Omega} \|\vec{\varphi}\|_{2,\Omega}$$

A similar estimate for the second term in the right handside member of (6.29) is obtained by writing :

$$E(v_i v_j \frac{\partial \varphi_j}{\partial x_i}) = E(v_i v_j \Pi_o(\frac{\partial \varphi_j}{\partial x_i})) + E(v_i v_j (\frac{\partial \varphi_j}{\partial x_i} - \Pi_o(\frac{\partial \varphi_j}{\partial x_i}))$$

The estimates for $B_{3,2}$, $B_{3,3}$ and $B_{3,4}$ are obtained by identical techniques and we leave them to the reader. Finally, estimates for B_2 and B_4 in terms of $\|\vec{\varphi}\|_{2,\Omega}$ have been derived in Ciarlet-Raviart [3], which ends the proof of the theorem.

<u>Example 1</u> (continued)

In the case of example 1, if we use the numerical quadrature formula given at the end of section 6.1, the hypotheses of theorem 8 are satisfied with k=2, s=3, r=1. Hence we get the estimate :

$$\|\tilde{\vec{u}}_h - \vec{u}\|_{0,\Omega} = O(h^3) .$$

6.3. Error estimate for the pressure

The following result holds :

<u>Theorem 9</u> : Let us make the same assumptions as in theorem 7 and assume in addition that hypothesis H.3 holds. Then :

$$(6.34) \qquad |\tilde{p}_h - p\|_{L^2(\Omega)/\mathbb{R}} \leq C h^k + C' h^{r+1} ,$$

where C and C' are constants independent of h.

<u>Proof</u> : The proof is identical to the proof of theorem 5. There appears three additional terms which are identical to the terms A_2, A_3, A_4 of section 6.1 and which have already been estimated.

7. AN EXAMPLE OF A NONCONFORMING METHOD

For simplicity, we have restricted our presentation to the case of conforming finite elements, i.e. to the case $X_h \subset X$. However, all the foregoing results can be extended to nonconforming elements provided these elements satisfy the compatibility condition H.2 of Crouzeix - Raviart [4] . The derivation of the estimates is identical except that we must consider additional terms involving integrals on the faces of each element K ; these terms can be estimated in the same way as in [4] . We will not develop these computations here ; we will only give a simple example for which we refer to Crouzeix - Raviart [4 , example 4].

<u>Example 2</u> : Let K be a N-simplex of $\mathcal{C}_h$ with vertices $a_{i,K}$, $1 \leq i \leq N+1$. Denote by $\alpha_{i,K}$ the centroïd of the (N-1)-dimensional face of K which does not contain $a_{i,K}$.

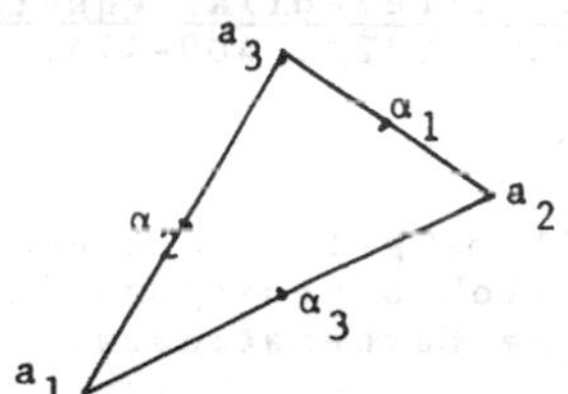

We choose $P_K = P_1$, i.e. k=k'=1 and we define V_h to be the space of all functions $\vec{v}_h$ defined on Ω which are continuous at the points $\alpha_{i,K}$ and whose restriction to each $K \in \mathcal{C}_h$ satisfies : $\vec{v}_h|_K \in (P_K)^N$ and $\operatorname{div} \vec{v}_{h|K} = 0$. The hypotheses H.1, H.2 and H.3 are satisfied (see [4]). On the other hand, the corresponding analogue of theorem 8 shows that hypothesis H.4 must be satisfied with r=0 and s=1. Let $\|\vec{v}_h\| = (\sum_{K \in \mathcal{C}_h} |\vec{v}_h|^2_{1,K})^{1/2}$; then, the following estimates hold :

$$\|\tilde{\vec{u}}_h - \vec{u}\| = O(h) \ , \ \|\tilde{\vec{u}}_h - \vec{u}\|_{0,\Omega} = O(h^2) \ , \ |\tilde{p}_h - p|_{L^2(\Omega)/\mathbb{R}} = O(h) \ . \tag{7.1}$$

Note that we can use for example one of the two following quadrature formulae :

$$I_K(\varphi) = \int_K \varphi(x)dx \sim \text{Meas } K. \varphi(a_{123}), \text{ where } a_{123} \text{ is the} \tag{7.2}$$

center of gravity of K, or :

$$I_K(\varphi) \sim \frac{1}{3} \text{Meas } K \sum_{i=1}^{N+1} \varphi(\alpha_{i,K}) \tag{7.3}$$

Indeed, if we use (7.3) all the integrals are computed exactly except those corresponding to the right handside member $\vec{f}$.

<u>Remark</u> : We have not discussed in this paper the practical solution of the finite element equations. In this respect, we refer to Crouzeix and Raviart [4 , II], where basis functions for the

various spaces V_h are exhibited and to Fortin [5] and Fortin - Peyret - Temam [6] , where various iterative methods are discussed.

REFERENCES

[1] Bramble, J.H. and S.R. Hilbert.

Estimation of linear functionals on Sobolev spaces with applications to Fourier transforms and spline interpolation. SIAM J. Numer. Anal. 7 (1970), 112-124.

[2] Ciarlet, P.G. and P-A. RAVIART.

General Lagrange and Hermite interpolation in $\mathbb{R}^n$ with applications to finite element methods. Arch. Rat. Mech. Anal. 46, (1972), 177-199.

[3] Ciarlet, P.G. and P-A. Raviart.

The combined effect of curved boundaries and numerical integration in isoparametric finite element methods. "The mathematical fundations of the finite element method with applications to partial differential equations" A.K. Aziz ed. Academic press, New-York (1972), 409-474.

[4] Crouzeix, M. and P-A. Raviart.

Conforming and non-conforming finite element methods for solving the stationary Stokes equations (I, II). To appear in RAIRO, Série Mathématiques.

[5] Fortin, M.

Calcul numérique des écoulements des fluides de Bingham et des fluides newtoniens incompressibles par la méthode des éléments finis. Thèse, Paris, 1972.

[6] Fortin, M., R. Peyret et R. Temam.

Résolution numérique des équations de Navier-Stokes pour un fluide incompressible. Journal de mécanique, 10, 3 (1971), 357-390.

[7] Grisvard P.

Alternative de Fredholm relative au problème de Dirichlet dans un polygone ou un polyhèdre. Boll. Un. Mat. Ital. 5 (1972), 132-164.

[8] Kondratiev V.A.

Boundary problems for elliptic equations with conical or angular points. Trans. Moscow Math. Soc. 16 (1967), 227-313.

[9] Ladyzhenskaya, O.A.

The mathematical theory of viscous incompressible flow. Gordon and Breach, 1963.

[10] Lions, J.L.

Quelques méthodes de résolution des problèmes aux limites non linéaires, Dunod, 1969.

[11] Scott, R.

Finite element techniques for curved boundaries.
Ph. D. Dissertation, Mass. Inst. Tech. (1973).

[12] Strang, G. and G.J. Fix

An analysis of the finite element method, Prentice Hall (1973).

[13] Taylor C. and P. Hood

A numerical solution of the Navier-Stokes equations using the finite element technique, Computers and Fluids, 1 (1973), 73-100.

[14] Zlamal M.

Curved elements in the finite element method.
SIAM J. Numer. Anal. 10 (1973), 229-240.

FINITE ELEMENTS METHOD IN AEROSPACE ENGINEERING PROBLEMS

B. FRAEIJS de VEUBEKE

Head, Aerospace Engineering Laboratory, Univ. of Liège, Belgium

SUMMARY

Some key areas of finite element development are briefly reviewed on the basis of 10 years experience in the analysis of aerospace structures. The emphasis is on the practicability of the dual analysis concept for linear elastostatics, elastodynamics and steady state heat flow.

Typical displacement and equilibrium models and test problems are described, that were found to be of practical value and belong to the library of elements currently used in the ASEF and DYNAM programs developped by the Aerospace Laboratory.

The oral presentation will include samples of large scale computations involving static strain energy bounds, eigenvalues (frequencies and critical loads) and panel flutter under thermal constraints.

INTRODUCTION

Past the era of Matrix Structural Analysis, concerned essentially with the topological problems of element interconnexions, the developments of the finite element method have been largely centered on the nature and qualities of finite element models with respect to computational efficiency, ease of stress output interpretation and convergence characteristics. Improvements in mathematical models will not be without interaction with the methods of matrix structural analysis because of the growing need for overall economy as larger and more complicated problems are investigated. The volume of computations required to handle non-linearities, geometrical and material, and structural optimization is such that, in some cases, advanced versions of the Force Method or combined methods may well be preferred to the present, almost universally favored, Displacement or Direct Stiffness method.

MODELLING OF FINITE ELEMENTS

From the basic work of PRAGER and SYNGE it is well known that upper and lower bounds to the strain energy can be obtained from discretizations based on the dual principles of minimum total energy and minimum complementary energy. The application of this idea to finite elements [1, 4] requires properties of interelement connexions known respectively as conformity and diffusitivity.

The possibility of a quantitative assessment of energy convergence by displacement conforming, or (C, C), elements and equilibrium diffusive, or (E, E), elements has certainly weighed heavily in favor of their development and inclusion in the library of ASEF.

For triangular membrane elements and tetraedral 3-dimensional (C, C) elements, complete polynomial expansions of arbitrary degree in the displacement vector

$$u(x) = Q(x)\ q + B(x)\ b \qquad (1)$$

are easily expressed in terms of shaping functions Q(x) related to a set of independent boundary displacements q and a set of "bubble functions" B(x). Conformity requires no more than C_o continuity of displacements and this coincides with nodal identification of the q coordinates.

The Kirchhoff-Love assumption in plate bending and shell theory is responsible for difficulties associated with C_1 continuity, but those can now be revolved, for any polynomial degree, by a subdomain formulation (see Type 15 hereafter) or by explicit formulation of dependency constraints between the q coordinates.

(E, E) elements are obtained from complete polynomial expansions of a stress vector

$$\sigma = S(x)\ s + H(x)\ h \qquad (2)$$

in terms of a set of internal stress redundancies s and body loading modes h, or by a stress function discretization [2, 5, 8, 16]. Diffusitivity follows from either C_o continuity of the stress functions, as in Kirchhoff plate bending, or C_1 continuity, as in the case of the Airy function of membrane elements. In the latter case, the subdomain formulation again resolves the difficulty by virtue of static-geometric analogies [2, 4].

The extension of the use of (C, C) models to elastodynamics is straightforward through the use of the HAMILTON principle and the production of a consistent mass matrix in addition to the stiffness matrix. As shown by GERADIN and TABARROK [9, 10, 19], (E, E) models are also applicable through the discretization of the TOUPIN principle, the dual of Hamilton's principle [4, 7], in which case a consistent inverse mass matrix is produced and the self-stressing states can be statically condensed, leaving a reduced eigenvalue problem. Eigenvalues are, as a rule, underestimated by this process, but an economical algorithm to predict the exact nature of the bound is still lacking.

Similarly steady state heat conduction can be approached by dual variational principles on a "dissipation", or linearized entropy production functional [6] . The properties of conformity and diffisitivity are replaced here by C_o continuity of piecewise differentiable temperature fields and C_o continuity of equilibrated heat fluxes.

A bewildering variety of other models can be constructed, either by relaxing conformity or diffusitivity (the hybrid elements), or by discretizing the more general two-field variational principles [1] (the mixed elements). Such combination of elements do no more generate energy bounds but may well present superior convergence characteristics [13] .
In the hybrid (E, C) the internal assumed stress field is no more connected at the boundary ∂E of the element as it is in (E, E) by the weak displacements

$$q = \int_{\partial E} T^T(x)\, u(x)\, dS \tag{3}$$

which are averages of the unknown displacements, weighted by the surface traction modes. It is connected through a strong assumed displacement field that needs only to be defined at the interfaces. advantages over the (E, E) element may comprize : easier elimination of kinematical modes and increase in nodal valency. The loss of the guarantee in energy bounding seems however a high price to pay; the more so since experiments [5] have shown that an injection of bubble modes of higher degree in (C, C) elements raises, as would be expected, their flexibility to a level comparable to (E, C) elements without losing the bounding property.
A similar remark applies to the dual hybrids (C, E), where the weak surface traction coordinates

$$g = \int_{\partial E} Q^T(x)\, t(x)\, dx \tag{4}$$

are replaced, for connexion purposes, by assumed strong surface traction modes. Injection of bubble stress modes of higher degree in (E, E) models increases their rigidity to a level comparable to the hybrid without loss of the bounding property.
The mixed elements have not been explored to such an extent that conclusions may be derived regarding their merits. We would venture to say that before embarking on such an exploration program, better guidelines are needed from

mathematical studies of convergence. Nor is the field of model development exhausted by the previous classification. Convergence studies based on the patch test [12, 18] will give birth to new finite element models of the non-conforming variety, some of which may prove to be simple and efficient. Quasi-diffusive elements [8] , in which we sacrifice the transmission of some statically zero portion of the surface tractions at an interface, have duals in the static-geometric sense which are non conforming elements passing the patch test (an unpublished result).
Another recent development leading to a new family of elements is the discretization of rotational equilibirum [8] . It enables C_0 continuity to prevail in all cases for stress functions implementing the translational equilibrium equations. The static-geometric duals of such elements are yet to be investigated.

ASSEMBLING FINITE ELEMENTS

(C, C) and (E, C) models are most easily assembled by the direct stiffness method [20] , by passing the need for a topological analysis of the self-stressing states.
(C, E) and (E, E) models can be assembled by a dual type of direct flexibility method [3, 4] , using the local stress function values to generate automatically the self-stressings and applying the complementary energy principle to the whole structure.
However the direct stiffness method is also applicable to (E, E) elements by considering the weak boundary displacements as the connectors and conversely for the (C, C) elements, where weak stress function values can be introduced at the interfaces. In general any assembling software type is applicable to any type of model, the choice is governed by the efficiency in the process and reduction in the size of the final system of equations.

STRESS OUTPUT EVALUATION

This remain a problem, especially with (C, C) and (C, E) elements, where local stress values are known to be unreliable. The strong stress output, obtained through the constitutive equations with Hookean matrix H :

$$\sigma = H \left[D\ Q(x) \right] q + H \left[D\ B(x) \right] b \qquad (5)$$

is preferably replaced by the weak stress information

$$\int_E \left[D\ Q(x) \right]^T \sigma\, dV = K_{qq}\, q + K_{qb}\, b \qquad (6)$$

$$\int_E \left[D\ B(x) \right]^T \sigma\ dV = K_{bq}\ q + K_{bb}\ b$$

which states the weighted averages obtained for the equilibrium equations. The strong information (5) satisfies (6). Often the analyst will not be satisfied by the mere knowledge of the average stresses (6) and will want a smoothing interpolation procedure between the elements without the need for reshuffling the whole stress information. This poses the interesting problem of inverting, so to speak, the Gaussian quadrature procedure. How can one derive from the weak information (6) a set of reliable local estimates and in which local points of the element ?

ELEMENT LIBRARY AND TEST PROBLEMS

The following pages are devoted to a short survey of the finite element models which are operational in the ASEF and DYNAM programs up to I969. Whenever new models are introduced,they are normally tested by comparison with the others in at least one of the test problems described on pages 30,3I and 32.

TYPE 1 **FRAME ELEMENT**

- References : AFFDL-TR-66-199 (1966)
- Assumptions : $u = \alpha_1 + \alpha_2 x$

$$v = \alpha_1' + \alpha_2' x + \alpha_3' x^2 + \alpha_4' x^3$$

$$w = \alpha_1'' + \alpha_2'' x + \alpha''_3 x^2 + \alpha''_4 x^3$$

$$\phi_x = \beta_1 + \beta_2 x$$

- The frame element is a straight prismatic member for which deformation modes in extension, bending in two perpendicular planes and in torsion are assumed. It follows the simplest engineering beam theory.
- The local axes of the element are the inertia axes with the Ox axis oriented from node 1 to node 2 while a third node defines the local x Oz plane of coordinates.

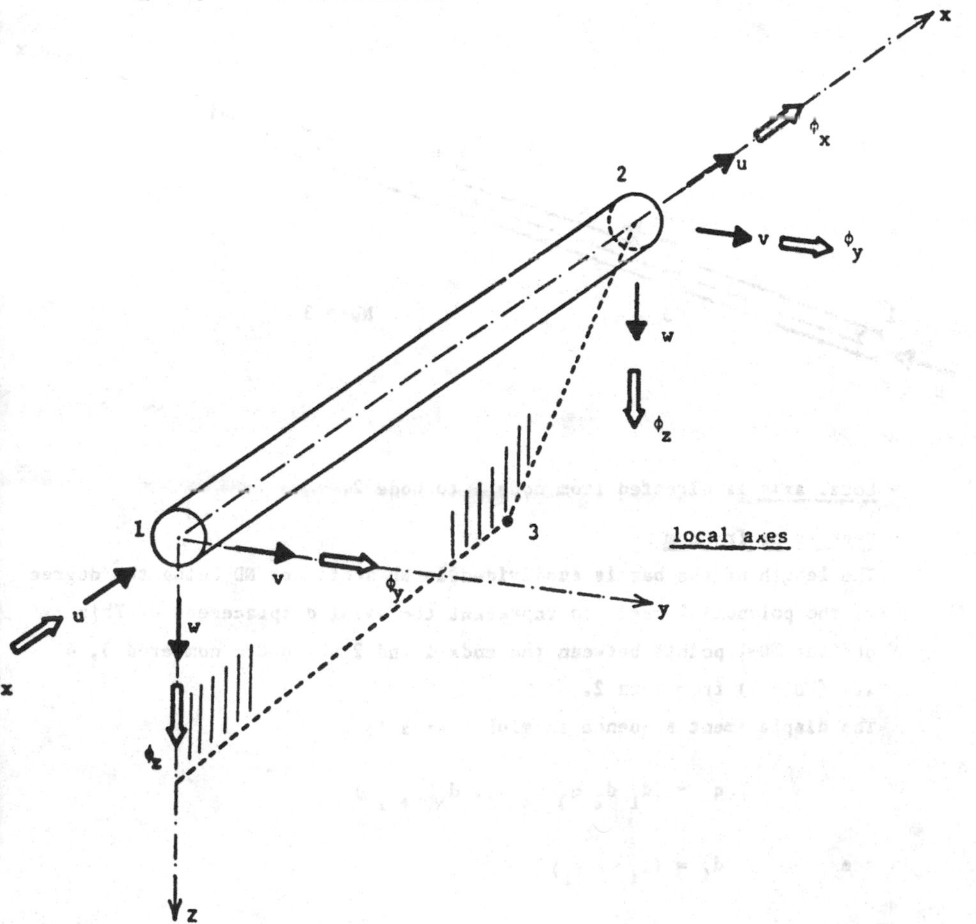

TYPE 2 BAR ELEMENT OF VARIABLE DEGREE

- References : AFFDL-TR-66-I99 (I966)
- Assumption : $u = \alpha_1 + \alpha_2 x + \alpha_3 x^2 + \alpha_4 x^3 \ldots + \alpha_{10} x^9$

(complete polynomial truncated at a specified degree)

- Description

This element has only the axial deformation mode. It is intented to reinforce the conforming membrane elements of types 3, 4, 6 or 20 and the hybrid element of type 14. The degrees of the polynomial approximation for u and that used to represent the axial distribution of the cross section can be fixed independantly to any value between 0 and 9. Analytical integration is always used for obtaining the stiffness matrix.

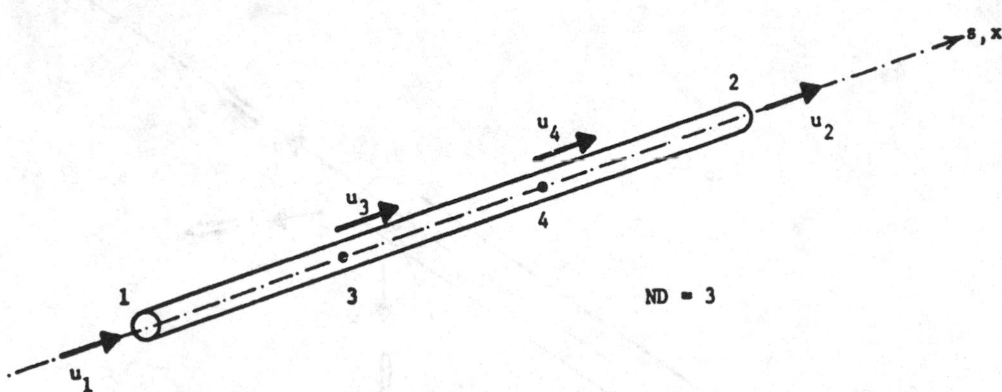

- Local axis is directed from node 1 to node 2.
- Degrees of freedom

The length of the bar is subdivided in ND sections, ND being the degree of the polynomial used to reprasent the axial displacement u. This defines ND-1 points between the ends 1 and 2 which are numbered 3, 4 ... (ND + 1) from 1 to 2.

The displacement sequence in global axes is :

$$q' = (d_1 \; d_2 \; d_3 \; d_4 \; \ldots \; d_{ND+1})$$

where $d_i = (u_i \; v_i \; w_i)$

TYPE 3 **CONFORMING TRIANGULAR MEMBRANE ELEMENT**

- **Reference** : A.9 (internal)
- **Assumption** : $u = \alpha_1 + \alpha_2 x + \alpha_3 y + \alpha_4 x^2 + \alpha_5 xy + \alpha_6 y^2$

$$+ \alpha_7 x^3 + \alpha_8 x^2 y + \alpha_9 xy^2 + \alpha_{10} y^3$$

$$+ \dots + \alpha_{15} y^4 + \dots \dots + \alpha_{21} y^5$$

$$v = \alpha'_1 + \alpha'_2 x + \alpha'_3 y + \alpha'_4 x^2 + \alpha'_5 xy + \alpha'_6 y^2$$

$$+ \alpha'_7 x^3 + \alpha'_8 x^2 y + \alpha'_9 xy^2 + \alpha'_{10} y^3$$

$$+ \dots \alpha'_{15} y^4 + \dots + \alpha'_{21} y^5$$

(complete polynomial in x, y truncated at a specified degree)

- **Description**

This element generalizes the classical triangular membrane element in this sense that it can be of any degree between 1 and 5 along any of the 3 interfaces and inside, independently. The thickness is assumed to vary linearly between the 3 vertices. The Hooke's law modification necessary to use the element by the Southwell analogies as a plate bending element is also provided (in this case the thickness has however to be constant).

- **Local axes and degrees of freedom**

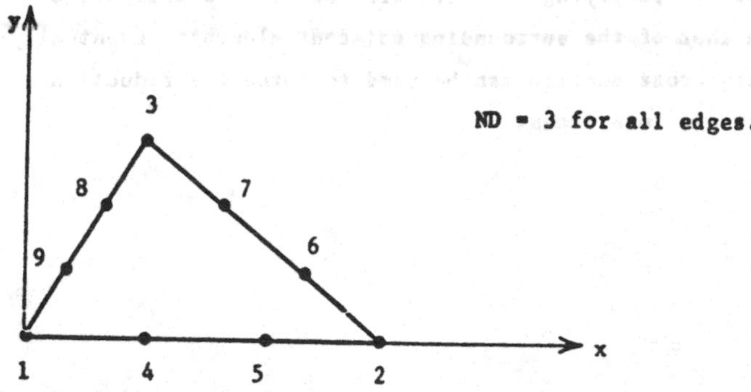

The local axes are directed as indicated above with the axis Ox coinciding with the edge 1-2. They influence only the stress ouput.

Each edge is subdivided in ND equal segments, ND being the degree assigned by the phase 1 to each edge. These segments define a certain number of points along the interfaces which are numbered following the same sense of rotation as for the 3 geometrical nodes 1.2.3. The example given above applies for ND = 3 on all edges. The displacements sequence is :

$$q' = (d_1\ d_2\ d_3\ d_4\ d_5\ \dots\ d_n)$$

where $d_i = (u_i\ v_i\ w_i)$ in global axes. Eventually, if along an interface, only 2 membrane elements are connected (plus eventually a bar of type 2) which are coplanar and not in a plane of coordinates, the phase 1 decides to express the displacements of the interface in special local axes. These axes are defined by the tangent and normal to the interface. Their orientation is given by a reference node printed in the output. If this node is positive the normal is directed in the half plane containing this node. If the reference node is negative the normal is directed in the opposite half plane. The advantage of these special axes is that the out of plane stiffness is automatically zero at the interface points and therefore is automatically fixed by the program. If the 2 membrane elements are "almost" coplanar, the special local axes are selected if the angle is smaller than .01 radiants.

- Bubble functions of displacement

If the degree specified for the element is higher than the degree of the interfaces, bubble functions of displacement are automatically included. This is also the case if the degree is higher than 2 in which case internal degrees of freedom have to be defined. They can be interpreted also as bubble functions. The presence of bubble modes can be forced in various ways : for instance by specifying the variable NDB or by specifying a degree higher than that of the surrounding adjacent elements. Eventually bar elements of zero cross section can be used to force the reduction of degree along certain interfaces.

TYPE 4 **CONFORMING QUADRILATERAL MEMBRANE ELEMENT**

- **Reference :** A.9 (internal)
- **Assumption :** $u = \alpha_1 + \alpha_2 x + \alpha_3 y + \alpha_4 x^2 + \alpha_5 xy + \alpha_6 y^2$

$$+ \alpha_7 x^3 + \alpha_8 x^2 y + \alpha_9 xy^2 + \alpha_{10} y^3$$

$$v = \alpha'_1 + \alpha'_2 x + \alpha'_3 y + \alpha'_4 x^2 + \alpha'_5 xy + \alpha'_6 y^2$$

$$+ \alpha'_7 x^3 + \alpha'_8 x^2 y + \alpha'_9 xy^2 + \alpha'_{10} y^3$$

(complete polynomial in x, y truncated at a specified degree in each triangle independantly)

- **Description**

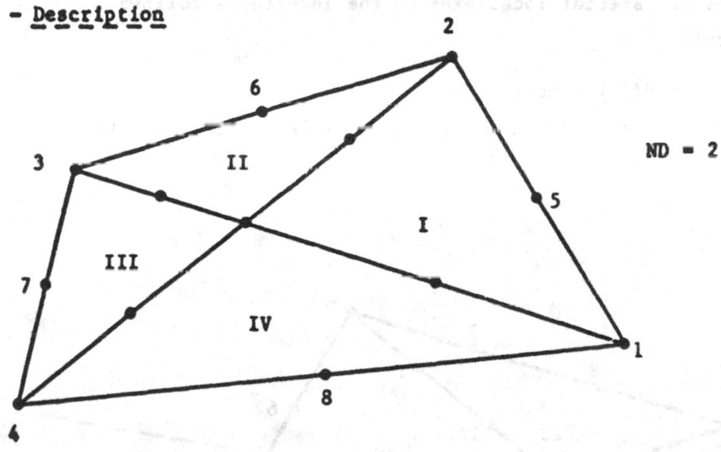

This quadrilateral is a super-element composed of 4 triangular membrane elements of type 3. The internal interfaces are defined by the diagonals of the quadrilateral. The internal degrees of freedom corresponding to the internal interfaces and eventually to internal modes of the triangles are eliminated by condensation. The degrees of the 4 triangles are assumed to be identical and not higher than 3. The reduction of the degree along the external interfaces of the quadrilateral is possible and follows the same rules for the type 3 element. The possibility of using the element as a plate bending element by the Southwell analogies is also provided.

The thickness can vary linearly along each external interface and is defined by the local values at the vertices. The thickness at the diagonal intersection point is interpolated as follows : a linear variation is assumed along the two diagonals. The thickness at the central node is the average of 2 thicknesses so defined at this point. If the 4 vertices of the quadrilateral are not coplanar, a correction of the warping is achieved by defining a mean plane and projecting the 4 nodes in this plane. The importance of the warping in NOT checked.

- Degrees of freedom

The sequence of the generalized displacements is

$$q' = (d_1\ d_2\ d_3\ d_4\ d_5\ d_6\ d_7\ d_8\ \ldots)$$

following the same conventions as for the type 3 element.
The selection of the special local axes on the interfaces follows also the same rules.

- Bubble functions of displacement

Such functions can be introduced following the rules defined for the element of type 3.

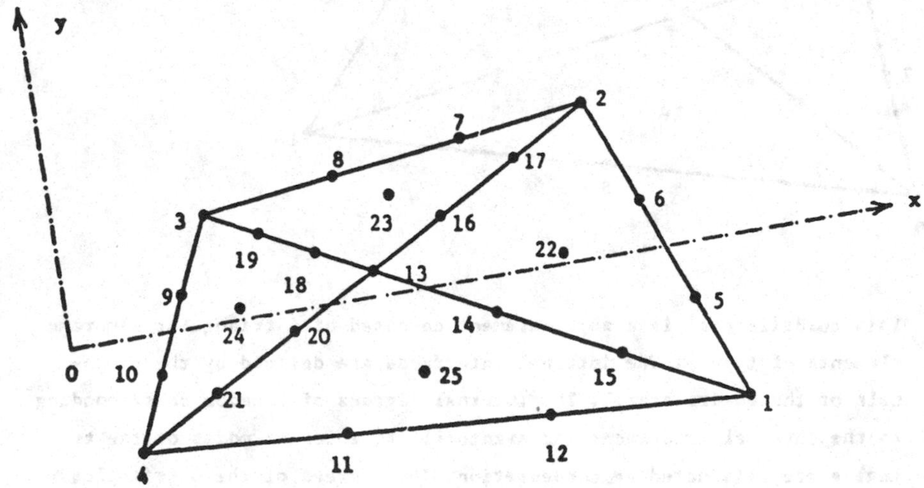

Local axes for stress output and numbering of the reference points for NDT = 3

TYPE 6 SPECIAL BULKHEAD ELEMENT

- Reference : A.7 (internal)

- Assumptions : $u = \alpha_1 + \alpha_2 x + \alpha_3 x^2 + \alpha_4 x^3 + y(\alpha_5 + \alpha_6 x + \alpha_7 x^2 + \alpha_8 x^3)$

$$v = \beta_1 + \beta_2 x + \beta_3 x^2 + \beta_4 x^3 + y(\beta_5 + \beta_6 x + \beta_7 x^2 + \beta_8 x^3)$$

(eventually reduced to 2^d degree along the edge 1-2)

- Description

The special bulkhead element is a kind of frame or spar element designed to reinforce conforming membrane elements for out of plane bending and for which the neutral axis is not in the plane of the membrane. This situation is often met in the idealization of bulkheads in fuselage analysis. The element is a quadrilateral membrane which can be connected with the membrane elements of the fuselage skin only by the edge 1-2 along which it is conforming. The opposite edge is always supposed to be free. The 2 lateral edges 2-3 and 4-1 can be connected with similar elements or with general membrane elements. This connection is stricly conforming only if the lateral edges are perpendicular to the edge 1-2. Otherwise it introduces a slight lack of conformity which, for bulkhead analysis, is not important.

It has the advantage over standard membrane elements (like TYPE 4) of a better representation of the bending modes which include the effects of shear deformation and shortening of the cross section, but with less degrees of freedom. Note that connection is not allowed along the edge 3-4 due to the condensation of the 4 interface degrees of freedom along that edge.

The high of the element can vary linearly and two different reinforcing flanges of linearly varying cross section are provided. The thickness of the web is constant but can be different in extension and in shear to allow a correct representation of the effect of holes in the web. The loading can be achieved, in addition to tip concentrated forces, by a linearly distributed line load applied on the edge 1-2 in the plane of the web. This allows to input the pressurisation of the fuselage with the consistent loads.

- Local axes are oriented with Ox along 1-2

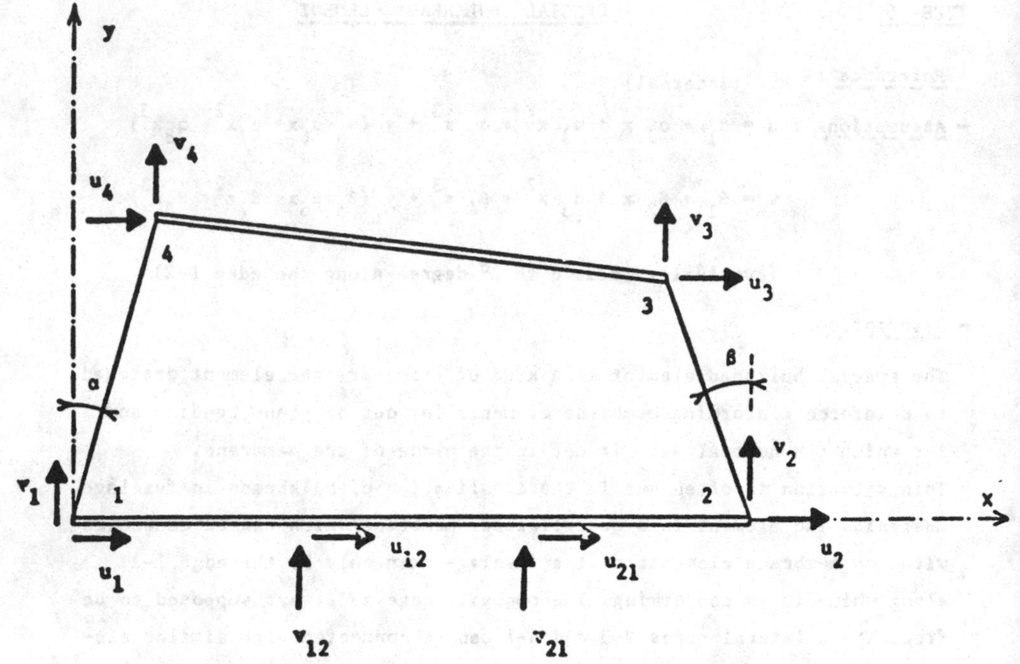

- The angles α and β should be small.

TYPE 7 **FRAME ELEMENT INCLUDING SHEAR DEFORMATION**

- Reference : A.8 (internal)

- Assumptions :

$$u = \alpha_1 + \alpha_2 x + \alpha_3 x^2 + \alpha_4 x^3$$

$$v = \alpha_1' + \alpha_2' x + \alpha_3' x^2 + \alpha_4' x^3$$

$$w = \alpha_1'' + \alpha_2'' x + \alpha_3'' x^2 + \alpha_4'' x^3$$

$$\phi_x = \beta_1 + \beta_2 x + \beta_3 x^2$$

$$\phi_y = \beta_1' + \beta_2' x + \beta_3' x^2$$

$$\phi_z = \beta_1'' + \beta_2'' x + \beta_3'' x^2$$

(eventually the displacements u, v, w are reduced to 2nd degree)

- Description

This element is a straight prismatic member which deforms in extension, bending and torsion. The local axes are the inertia axes of the cross section. As the shear deformation is included in the theory used for bending, the displacements u, v, w are represented by modes independent of those used to describe the rotations. (ϕ_y is not equal to $\frac{\partial w}{\partial x}$, etc...). The difference between the elements of type 1 and type 7 is the same as between the plate bending elements of type 15 (Kirchhoff) and type 8 (Hencky). This element should be used to represent beams reinforcing membrane elements and which have a bending stiffness in the plane of the membranes. The connection can be conforming with membrane elements of 2nd and 3rd degree (Type 3, 4 or 20).

All the characteristics of the cross section can vary linearly along the element neutral axis.

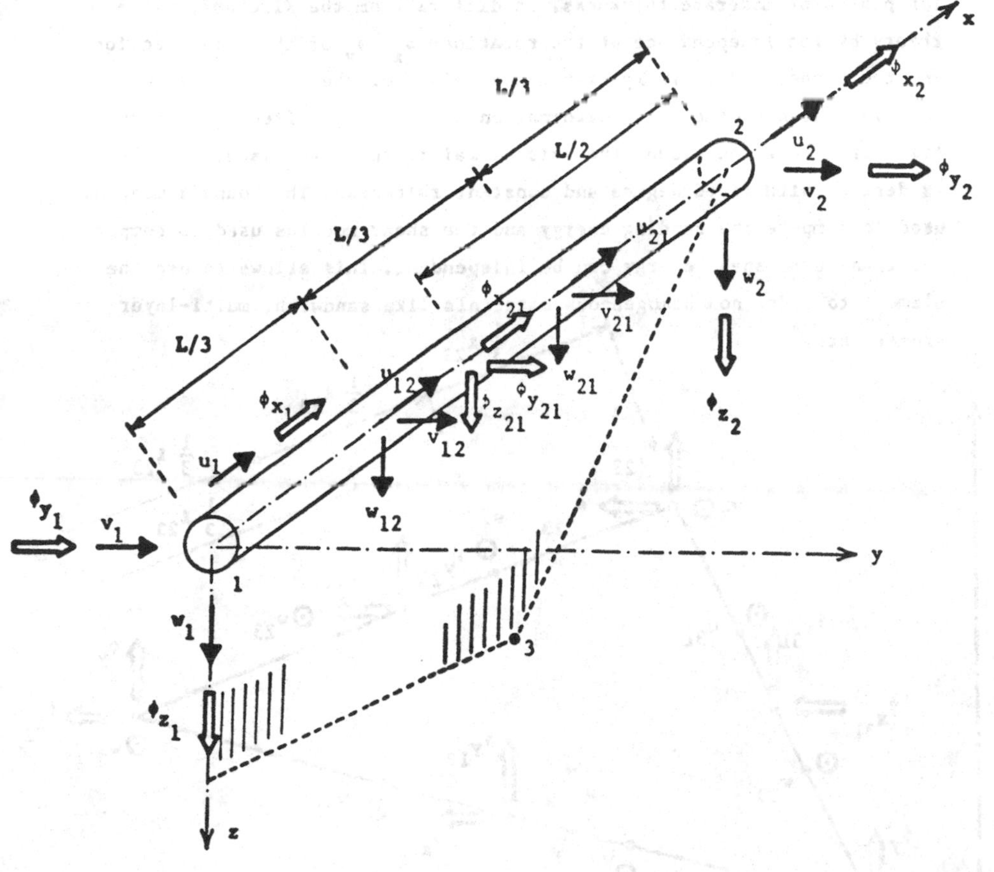

TYPE 8 CONFORMING TRIANGULAR PLATE BENDING ELEMENT OF MODERATE THICKNESS (THEORY OF HENCKY)

- Reference : G.SANDER, Dc.Thesis, Collection des Pub.Fac.Sc.Appl.Lège, N°I5(1969)
- Assumptions : $u = z\,\phi_x\,(x, y)$ $\quad v = z\,\phi_y\,(x, y)$

$$\phi_x = \alpha_1 + \alpha_2 x + \alpha_3 y + \alpha_4 x^2 + \alpha_5 xy + \alpha_6 y^2$$

$$\phi_y = \alpha_1' + \alpha_2' x + \alpha_3' y + \alpha_4' x^2 + \alpha_5' xy + \alpha_6' y^2$$

$$w = \beta_1 + \beta_2 x + \beta_3 y + \beta_4 x^2 + \beta_5 xy + \beta_6 y^2$$

$$\beta_7 x^3 + \beta_8 x^2 y + \beta_9 xy^2 + \beta_{10} y^3$$

- Description

This plate bending element is derived according to the theory of Hencky for plates of moderate thickness. It differs from the Kirchhoff plate theory by the independence of the rotations ϕ_x, ϕ_y of the cross section and the slopes $\partial w/\partial x$, $\partial w/\partial y$ of the mean plane of the plate. It allows to take into account the shear deformation and the edge effect due to the transverse rotation around the axis normal to the mean plane. The element is derived with fixed degree and constant thickness. The Young's modulus used to compute the bending energy and the shear modulus used to compute the transverse shear energy can be independant. This allows to use the element to model non homogeneous materials like sandwich, multi-layer trusses etc.

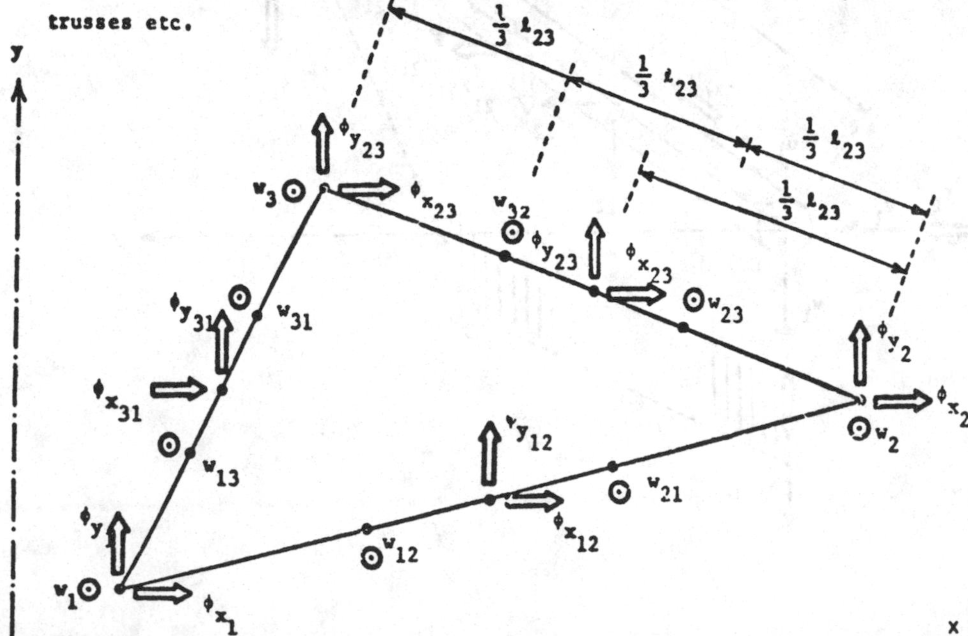

- Degrees of freedom

The element can only be used in the X-Y plane. The sequence of the generalized displacements is, in the global XY axes.

$$q' = (w_1\ \phi_{x1}\ \phi_{y1}\quad w_2\ \phi_{x2}\ \phi_{y2}\quad w_3\ \phi_{x3}\ \phi_{y3}$$

$$w_{12}\ \phi_{x12}\ \phi_{y12}\ w_{21}\ w_{23}\ \phi_{x23}\ \phi_{y23}\ w_{32}\ w_{31}\ \phi_{x31}\ \phi_{y31}\ w_{13})$$

The internal degree of freedom w necessary to derive the element is eliminated by condensation.

To allow a correct representation of the boundary conditions, special axes can be defined at the 6 points where rotations are expressed. Only one set of special axes can be defined per element, by giving their direction cosines in the LOCAL axes. This transformation of coordinates does not necessarily affect all the rotations.

TYPE 9 EQUILIBRIUM QUADRILATERAL PLATE BENDING ELEMENT OF MODERATE THICKNESS (REISSNER THEORY)

- Reference : G.SANDER, Dc.Thesis, Coll.Pub.Fac.Sc.Appl.Liège, N°15 (1969)
- Assumptions : In each triangular region, the bending moment field in the oblique axes defined by the 2 internal interfaces of length a and b is :

$$M_x = \beta_1 + \beta_2 \frac{x}{a} + \beta_3 \frac{y}{b}$$

$$M_y = \beta_4 + \beta_5 \frac{x}{a} + \beta_6 \frac{y}{b}$$

$$M_{xy} = \beta_7 + \beta_8 \frac{x}{a} + \beta_9 \frac{y}{b}$$

A particular solution for constant distributed load p is superimposed

$$p \sin\alpha = -\frac{6}{ab}\,\beta_{10} \qquad (\alpha \text{ is the angle of the oblique axes})$$

- Description

This plate bending element is derived by the equilibrium theory of Reissner for plates of moderate thickness. It differs from the equilibrium formulation of the Kirchhoff theory by the form of the complementary stress energy which includes the contribution of the transverse shear and by the continuity requirements for the surface tractions. In this element the bending and twisting moments are continuous across an interface as well as the shear forces. There are no corner loads.
Although the form of the bending moment field is the same as in the equilibrium Kirchhoff plate bending element of type 13, it is impossible to derive a triangular element free of additional constraints (or kinematic deformation modes)due to the increased number of interface generalized forces. The solution of building a super-element composed of 4 triangles allows to reduce the additional constraints inside the assemblage.
The element is derived with fixed degree and constant thickness.
The Young's modulus can be independent of the transverse shear modulus.

-Degrees of freedom

The element can only be used in the X-Y plane. The sequence of generalized forces is :

$$g' = (M_{n_{12}}\ M_{sn_{12}}\ V_{12}\ M_{n_{21}}\ M_{sn_{21}}\ M_{n_{23}}\ M_{sn_{23}}\ V_{n_{23}}\ M_{n_{32}}\ M_{sn_{32}}\ M_{n_{34}}\ M_{sn_{34}}\ V_{n_{34}}\ M_{n_{43}}\ M_{sn_{43}}\ M_{n_{41}}\ M_{sn_{41}}\ V_{n_{14}}\ M_{n_{14}}\ M_{sn_{14}})$$

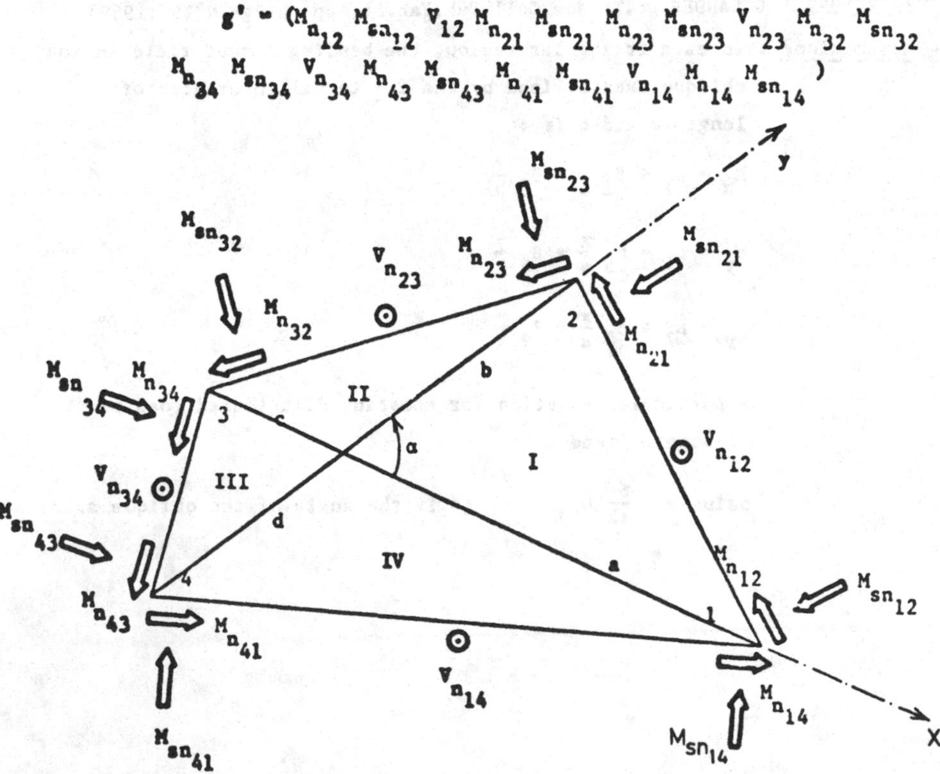

TYPE 11 EQUILIBRIUM BAR ELEMENT WITH CONSTANT SHEAR

- Reference : AFFDL-TR-66-199 (1966)
- Assumption : τ = constant
  or $N(x) = \beta_1 + \beta_2 x$
- Description
  This equilibrium bar element is stressed by a constant longitudinal shear and two tip forces. It is intended to reinforce the equilibrium membrane element of type 12. The section is supposed to be constant.
- Degrees of freedom

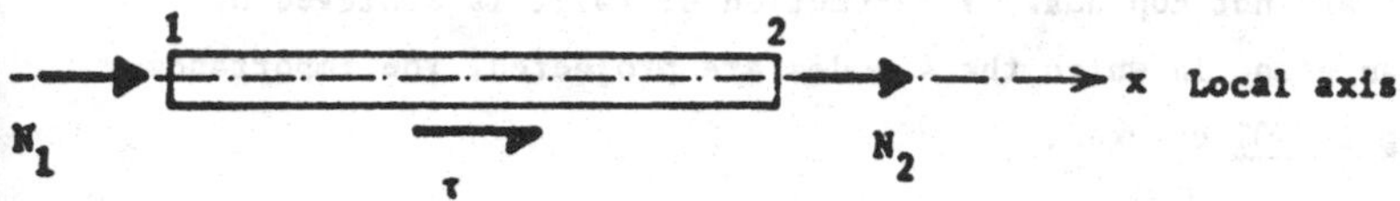

The local axis is oriented from node 1 to node 2 and the generalized forces are N_1, N_2 and τ. $\ell_{12} = N_{12}$. These 3 local forces are expressed in global axes in the sequence

$$g' = (F_{x_1}\ F_{y_1}\ F_{z_1}\ F_{x_2}\ F_{y_2}\ F_{z_2}\ F_{x_{12}}\ F_{y_{12}}\ F_{z_{12}})$$

Eventually, if only 2 membrane elements meet along the interface 1-2 which are coplanar and not in a plane of coordinates the phase 1 decides to keep the local axis for the interface force. The total number of generalized forces remains the same but $F_{y_{12}}$ is replaced by N_{12} while a zero stiffness is given to 2 other components.

TYPE 12 EQUILIBRIUM QUADRILATERAL MEMBRANE ELEMENT WITH CONSTANT STRESSES

- Reference : AFFDL-TR-66-199 (1966)
- Assumptions : In each triangular regions, the stress field in the oblique axes defined by the 2 diagonals is :

$$\sigma_x = \beta_1$$

$$\sigma_y = \beta_2$$

$$\tau_{xy} = \beta_3$$

- <u>Description</u>

This quadrilateral is the simplest equilibrium membrane element. It is subdivided by the diagonals in 4 triangular regions in each of which a constant stress field is assumed. The 12 parameters are reduced to 5 by the constraints of continuity of the normal and tangential surface tractions along the internal interfaces. The element is free of remaining constraints (or kinematical deformation modes). However the connection with other elements is achieved by identifying the simple averages of the displacements along each interface which is equivalent to a pin joint. Therefore special care has to be taken in expressing the boundary conditions to avoid possible mechanism in the structure. Such mechanisms are always avoided if the element is bordered by bar elements of type 11. If the 4 nodes are not coplanar, a correction of twist is achieved by defining a mean plane in which the 4 nodes are projected. The importance of the warping is <u>NOT</u> checked.

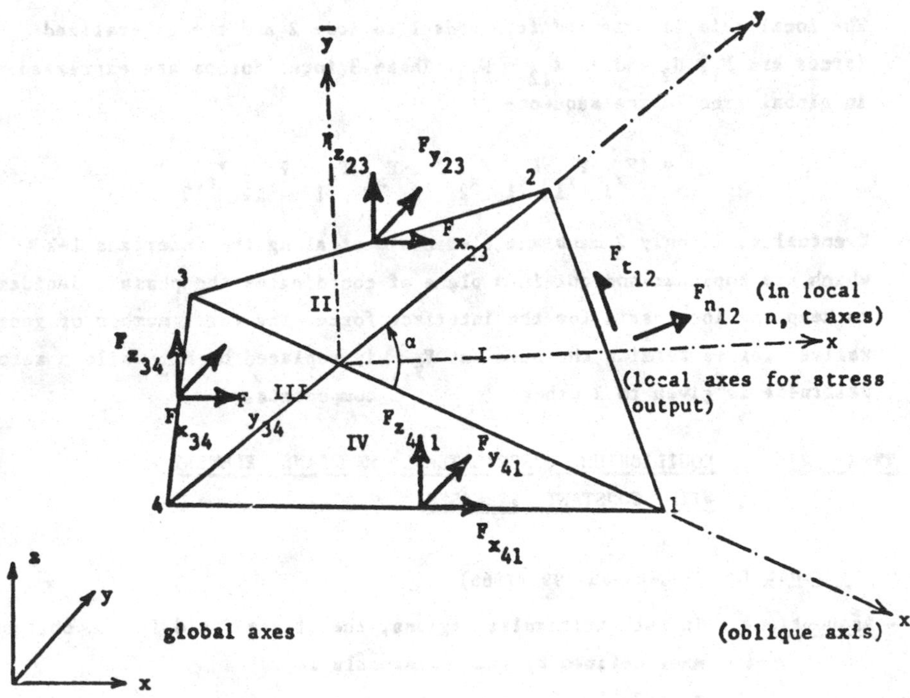

-Degrees of freedom

Along each interface of length ℓ_{ij} the generalized forces are in local cartesian axes normal and tangential to the interface

$$F_{n_{ij}} = \sigma_n \cdot \ell_{ij} \quad \text{and} \quad F_{t_{ij}} = \tau_{sn} \cdot \ell_{ij}$$

They are expressed in global axes in the sequence

$$g' = (F_{x_{12}}\ F_{y_{12}}\ F_{z_{12}}\ F_{x_{23}}\ F_{y_{23}}\ F_{z_{23}}\ F_{x_{34}}\ F_{y_{34}}\ F_{z_{34}}$$

$$F_{x_{41}}\ F_{y_{41}}\ F_{z_{41}})$$

If along an interface there are only 2 adjacent membrane elements which are coplanar and not in a plane of coordinates, the local cartesian axes are kept for the interface and the third component of force is given a zero value.

TYPE 13 KIRCHHOFF EQUILIBRIUM PLATE BENDING TRIANGLE

- References : de Veubeke and Sander, Int.Jl.Sol. Str., 4 (1968)

- Assumption : $M_x = \beta_1 + \beta_2\, x + \beta_3\, y + \beta_{10}\, (1 - x)\, x$

$$M_y = \beta_4 + \beta_5\, x + \beta_6\, y + \beta_{10}\, (1 - y)\, y$$

$$M_{xy} = \beta + \beta_8\, x + \beta_9\, y - \beta_{10}\, xy$$

The parameter β_{10} controls the particular solution under a uniform distributed load.

- Description

This classical equilibrium plate bending element is derived from a linear bending moments field. Such a field satisfies the homogeneous equilibrium equations. A particular solution is superimposed which is in equilibrium with a constant distributed transverse load.

The thickness is assumed to be constant.

- Degrees of freedom

The element can only be used in the X Y plane. The generalized forces which insure the equilibrium along the interfaces (in the sense of Kirchhoff) are : 2 local values of the normal bending moment M_n, the constant value of the normal Kirchhoff shear force $K_n = V_n + \frac{\partial M_{sn}}{\partial s}$ and the 3 corner loads equal to the jump of twisting moment $Z_i = M_{sn_{i+o}} - M_{sn_{i-o}}$.

They are computed in the sequence :

$$g' = (Z_1 \; Z_2 \; Z_3 \; M_{n_{12}} \; K_{n_{12}} \; M_{n_{21}} \; M_{n_{23}} \; K_{n_{23}} \; M_{n_{32}} \; M_{n_{31}} \; K_{n_{31}} \; M_{n_{13}})$$

The internal degree of freedom corresponding to the distributed load is eliminated by condensation.

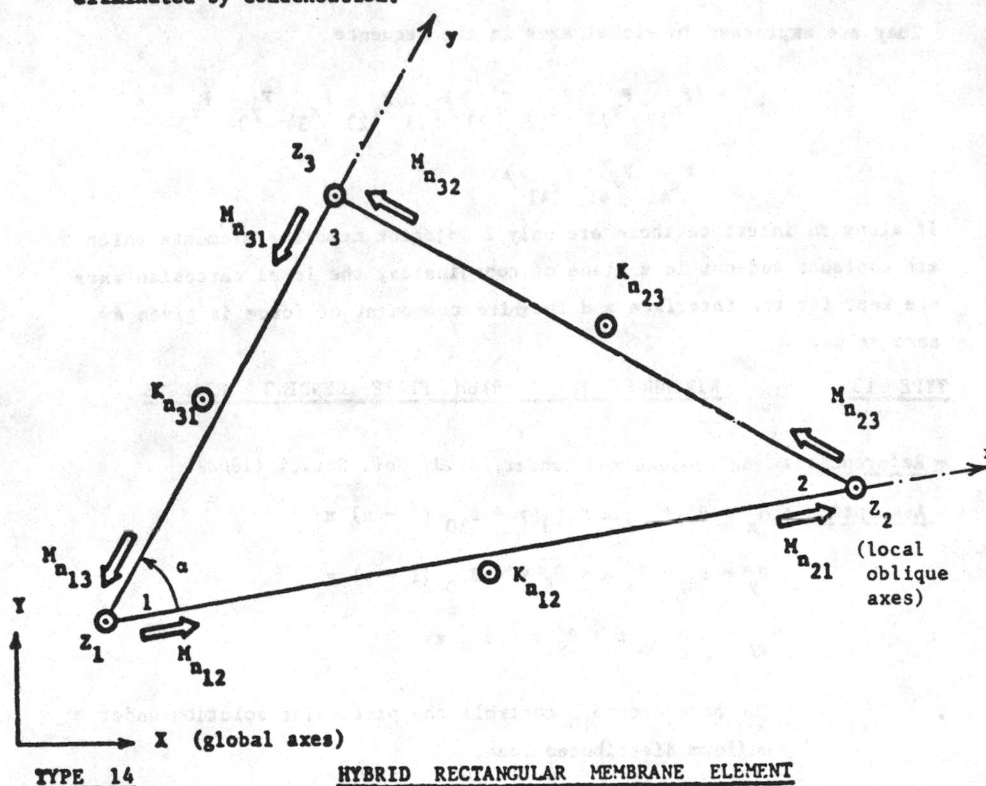

TYPE 14 **HYBRID RECTANGULAR MEMBRANE ELEMENT**

- **Reference** : T.H.PIAN,US-JAPAN Seminar,TOKYO (1969)
- **Assumptions** : 1) $u = \alpha_1 + \alpha_2 s + \alpha_3 s^2 + \alpha_4 s^3 + \alpha_5 s^4 + \alpha_6 s^5 \ldots$

$$v = \alpha_1' + \alpha_2' s + \alpha_3' s^2 + \alpha_4' s^3 + \alpha_5' s^4 + \alpha_6' s^5 \ldots$$

s being a current coordinate tangent to the edges.

2) $\sigma_x = \frac{\partial^2\phi}{\partial y^2}$ $\quad \sigma_y = \frac{\partial^2\phi}{\partial x^2}$ $\quad \tau_{xy} = -\frac{\partial^2\phi}{\partial x\partial y}$

ϕ (x,y) being a complete plynomial in x and y.
The polynomials for u, v, ϕ are truncated at the degrees requested by the user.

- Description

This rectangular membrane element is derived according to the theory of hybrid elements deducible of the Reissner principle and presented in the chapter 2 of the present report. It covers the family of such elements up to the 5th degree for the displacement field assumed along each interface independently and with practically no limitation for the degree of the stress field assumed inside. Numerical difficulties arise however if the degree of the stress field exceeds 8. The nature and the sequence of the generalized displacements defined along the interfaces are such that the element can be joined indifferently to any conforming membrane element of types 3, 4, 6, 20 and to the bar or beam elements of types 2 or 7. It should be noted that no check is incorporated that the element is effectively a plane rectangle. The thickness is supposed constant.

- Degrees of freedom and local axes

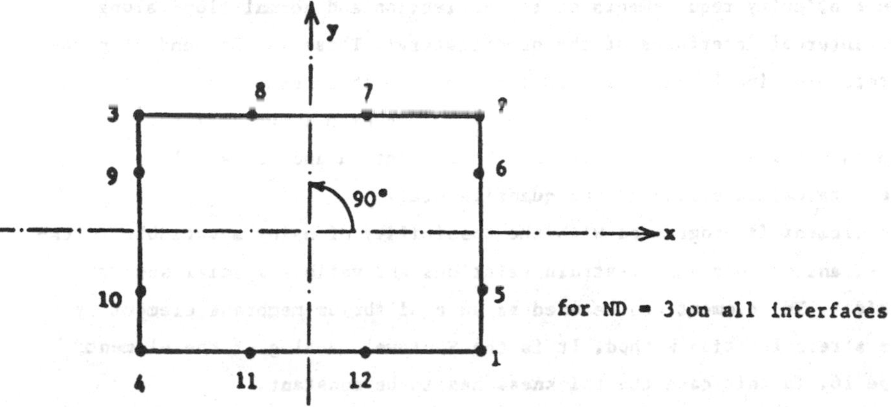

The sequence of the generalized displacements follows the same logic as for the conforming membrane elements of types 3,4 or 20 : the displacements of the vertices are followed by those of points defined on the interfaces taken sequentially turning anticlockwise.

$$q' = (d_1\ d_2\ d_3\ d_4\ d_5\ d_6\ d_7\ \dots\ d_{12})$$

with $d_i = (u_i\ v_i\ w_i)$

The displacements of the vertices are always expressed in global axes while on each individual interface the special local axes defined for the elements of types 3 or 4 can be selected by the phase 1.

TYPE 15 CONFORMING QUADRILATERAL PLATE BENDING ELEMENT (KIRCHHOFF THEORY)

- Reference : de VEUBEKE, Int.Jl.Sol.Str., 4 (1968)

- Assumptions : In each triangular region

$$w = \alpha_1 + \alpha_2 x + \alpha_3 y + \alpha_4 x^2 + \alpha_5 xy + \alpha_6 y^2$$

$$+ \alpha_7 x^3 + \alpha_8 x^2 y + \alpha_9 xy^2 + \alpha_{10} y^3$$

- Description

This plate bending super-element is obtained by assembling the 4 triangular elements defined by the diagonals of the quadrilateral.
In each of these triangles the deflection is represented by a complete cubic. The 40 corresponding parameters are reduced to 16 by expressing the continuity requirements of the deflection and normal slope along the internal interfaces of the quadrilateral. These 16 independent parameters are finally expressed in terms of the 16 generalized displacements (w, $w_{,x}$, $w_{,y}$, at the 3 vertices and $w_{,n}$ along each interface) necessary to insure a strict continuity of the deflection and normal slope along the external interface of the quadrilateral.
The element is programmed with the possibility of using a variable thickness, anisotropic stress-strain relations and various special support options. The element can be used as an equilibrium membrane element by the stress function method. It is the Southwell analog of the element type 16. In this case the thickness has to be constant.

- Degrees of freedom

The element can only be used in the global X-Y plane. The sequence of the 16 generalized displacements is :

$$q' = (w_1 \frac{\partial w}{\partial x_1} \frac{\partial w}{\partial y_2} \quad w_2 \frac{\partial w}{\partial x_2} \frac{\partial w}{\partial y_2} \quad w_3 \frac{\partial w}{\partial x_3} \frac{\partial w}{\partial y_3} \quad w_4 \frac{\partial w}{\partial x_4} \frac{\partial w}{\partial y_4} \frac{\partial w}{\partial n_{12}} \frac{\partial w}{\partial n_{23}} \frac{\partial w}{\partial n_{34}} \frac{\partial w}{\partial n_{41}})$$

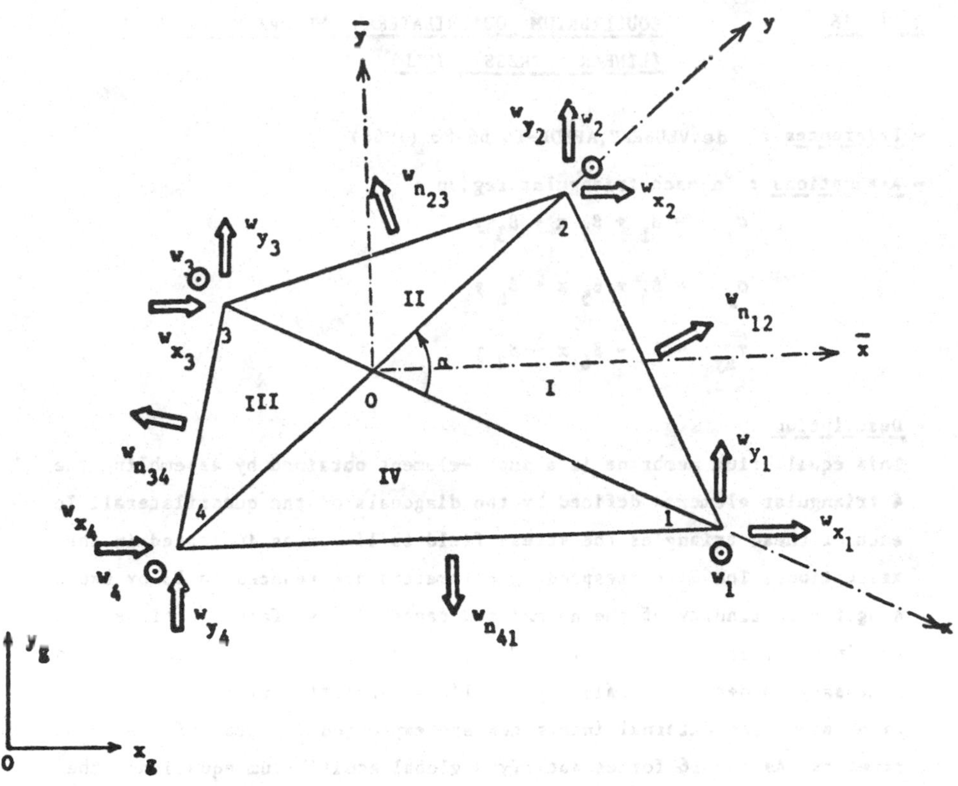

Oxy	**oblique local axes**
$O\bar{x}\,\bar{y}$	**cartesian local axes**
$Ox_g\,y_g$	**global axes**

The local axes $O\bar{x}$ is directed from 0 toward the middle of the edge 12.
The normal slopes $w_{n_{ij}}$ are expressed in the middle of each edge.

- **Special options**

1°/ Variable thickness : the thickness is constant unless the variable
ICHOI = 1 In this case the thickness at point 0 is interpolated from the values defined along the 2 diagonals at this point by a linear variation. The average of the 2 values is assumed. When the thickness is variable all the other special options are ineffective.

2°/ Anisotropy : it is controlled by the variable IANISO. IANISO = 0 corresponds to the isotropic case. Four anisotropic layers can be superimposed to the parent plate. Each of these layer can have an independent thickness t_{ani} and the bending rigidity of each layer is $\frac{1}{12}\,E\,t_{ani}^3$.

TYPE 16 EQUILIBRIUM QUADRILATERAL MEMBRANE ELEMENT (LINEAR STRESS FIELD)

- References : de VEUBEKE, AFFDL-TR-66-80 (1966)
- Assumptions : In each triangular region :

$$\sigma_x = \beta_1 + \beta_2 x + \beta_3 y$$

$$\sigma_y = \beta_4 + \beta_5 x + \beta_6 y$$

$$\tau_{xy} = \beta_7 - \beta_6 x - \beta_2 y$$

- Description

This equilibrium membrane is a super-element obtained by assembling the 4 triangular elements defined by the diagonals of the quadrilateral. In each of these triangles the stress field is linear as indicated in the assumptions. The 21 corresponding parameters are reduced to 13 by expressing the continuity of the normal and tangential surface tractions along the internal interfaces of the quadrilateral. The 16 generalized forces necessary to determine uniquely the linear variation of the surface tractions along the external interfaces are expressed in terms of the 13 parameters. As the 16 forces satisfy 3 global equilibrium equations, the element is free of spurious kinematic modes. The generalized forces are the local values of the surface tractions τ_{sn}, σ_n (times the thickness) at each vertex, along an interface. Note that although expressed at a vertex, they are interface variables.

The element is programmed with the possibility of using a linearly variable thickness.

- Degrees of freedom

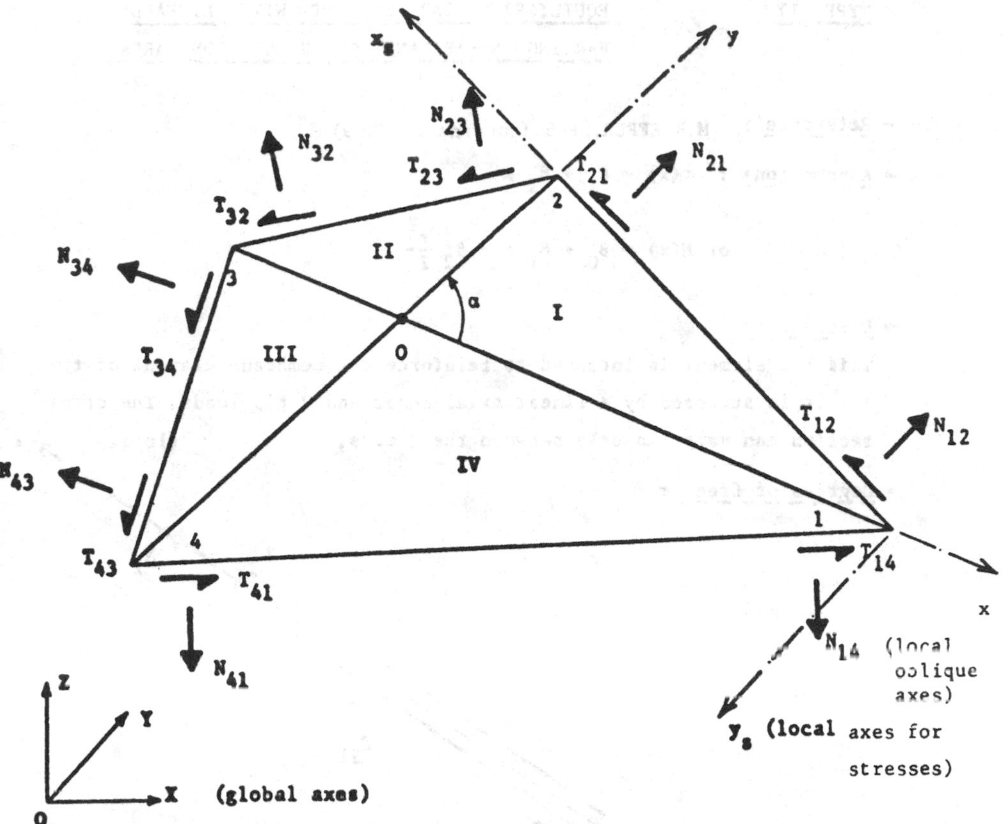

The sequence of the generalized forces in the local axes Oxy is

$$g' = (N_{12}\ T_{12}\ N_{21}\ T_{21}\ N_{23}\ T_{23}\ N_{32}\ T_{32}\ N_{34}\ T_{34}\ N_{43}\ T_{43}\ N_{41}\ T_{41}\ N_{14}\ T_{14}\ )$$

where N_{ij}, T_{ij} are cartesian normal and tangential components of the surface tractions multiplied by the length of the interface. These forces are transformed in global forces

$$g^{:} = (F_{x_{12}}\ F_{y_{12}}\ F_{z_{12}}\ F_{x_{21}}\ F_{y_{21}}\ F_{z_{21}}\ F_{x_{23}}\ \ldots\ F_{z_{14}}\ )$$

Eventually the phase 1 can decide to keep the local n, t axes on an interface in which case the 3rd component of the global forces at each point is given a zero stiffness. This is the case when only 2 membrane elements meet along an interface and are coplanar without being in a plane of coordinates.

TYPE 17 EQUILIBRIUM BAR ELEMENT WITH LINEARLY VARYING SHEAR AND CROSS SECTION AREA

- **Reference** : M.KIEFFER,SF-6 (internal) (1969)
- **Assumptions** : $\tau(x) = \beta_1 + \beta_2 x$

$$\text{or } N(x) = \beta_0 + \beta_1 x + \beta_2 \frac{x^2}{2}$$

- **Description**

This bar element is intended to reinforce the membrane element of type 16. It is stresses by a linear axial shear and 2 tip loads. The cross section can vary linearly between the 2 ends.

(local) x

- **Degrees of freedom**

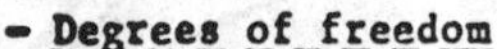

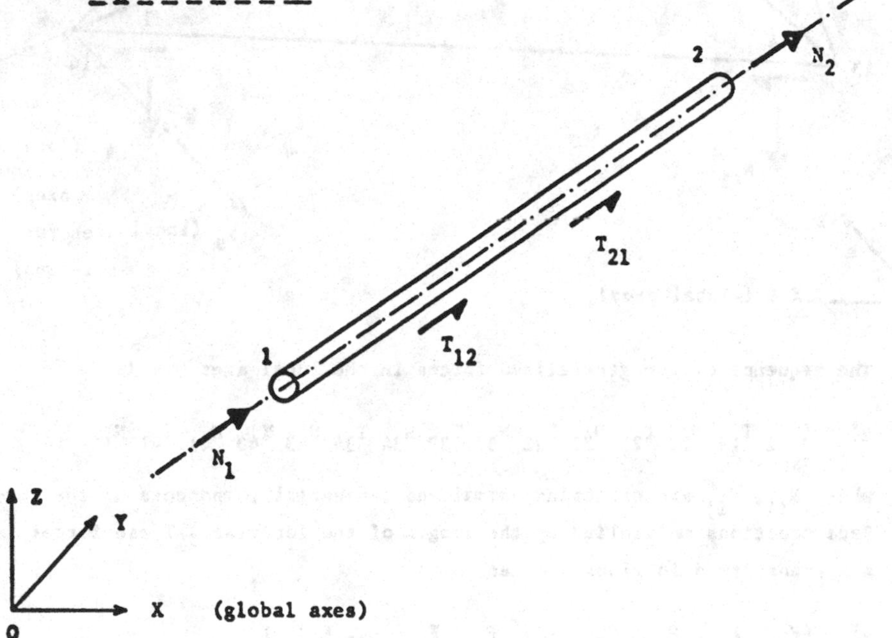

The sequence of the generalized forces in the local axes is

$$g' = (N_1 \; N_2 \;\; T_{12} \; T_{21})$$

where N_i is a tip load and T_{ij} the local value of the shear at an end times the length of the bar.

These forces are expressed in the global axes in the sequence :

$$g' = (F_{x_1}\ F_{y_1}\ F_{z_1}\ F_{x_2}\ F_{y_2}\ F_{z_2}\ T_{x_{12}}\ T_{y_{12}}\ T_{z_{12}}\ T_{x_{21}}\ T_{y_{21}}\ T_{z_{21}})$$

Eventually the forces T_{12} and T_{21} are kept in local axes if this special choice of axes has been decided by the phase 1. In this case, zero stiffness is given to the components $T_{x_{12}}$ $T_{z_{12}}$ and T_{ij} replaces $T_{y_{ij}}$ in the sequence given above.

TYPE 20 CONFORMING PARALLELOGRAM ELEMENT WITH VARIABLE DEGREE AND BUBBLE FUNCTIONS

- **Reference :** A.II (internal)
- **Assumption :** u and v are of the form

$$P_1\ (x, y) + (1 - \frac{x^2}{a^2})\ (1 - \frac{y^2}{b^2})\ P_2\ (x, y)$$

where both functions P_1 and P_2 are

$$P_i = (\alpha_1 + \alpha_2\ x + \alpha_3\ x^2 + \ldots + \alpha_{n+1}\ x^n)(\beta_1 + \beta_2\ y + \beta_3\ y^2 + \ldots + \beta_{n+1}\ y^n)$$

truncated at the degree requested by the user.

- **Description**

This element is a generalization of the classical rectangular membrane elements in this sense that it is extended to variable degree polynomials (from 1 to 9) and that it includes bubble displacement modes of degree independently variable (from 0 to 9).

In this purpose the polynomials used to represent the displacements are split in two parts controlled by the functions P_1 and P_2. P_1 describes the basic field and the interface modes while P_2 represents only bubble displacement modes.

To allow easy comparison with other elements (type 4 or 14) the number of terms retained in the functions P_1 (x, y) corresponds exactly to the number of generalized displacements necessary along the interfaces. This reduction of parameters is obtained by dropping in P_1 the terms of power greater or equal 2 in x AND y and the terms of power greater than n in x OR y, n being the degree of the displacements in the direction of the edges.

The complete form given above is always used for P_2 (x, y).

The thickness is constant and the material isotropic. The element can be used as a plate bending equilibrium element by the Southwell analogies.

- **Degrees of freedom**

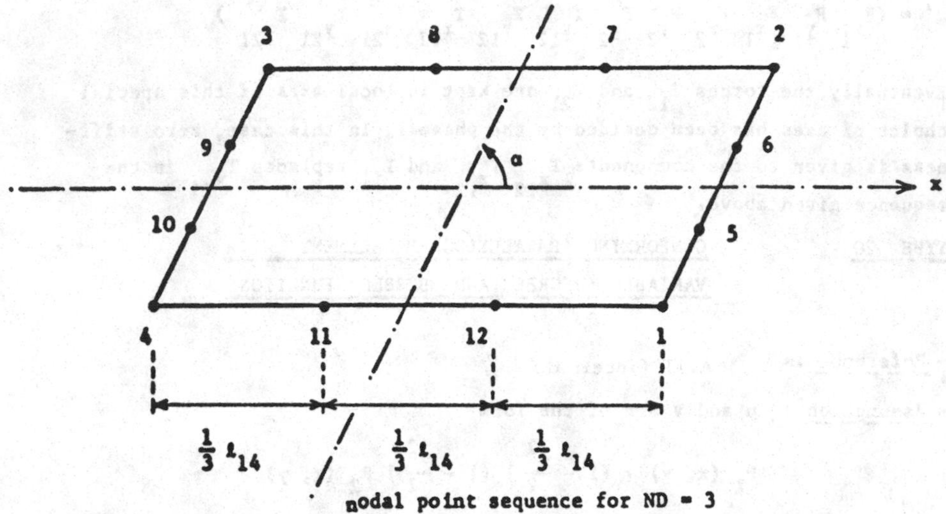

nodal point sequence for ND = 3

The generalized displacements are expressed at equidistant points along the interface, depending of the degree selected . The sequence of the displacements, the conventions for reducing the degree along an interface, the option of local normal-tangent axes are exactly the same as for elements type 4 or 14.

- Stress output

The stresses are computed at reference points which form a regular mesh defined by ND-1 or ITENS and ordered in the sequence illustrated below. The local cartesian axes for stresses have the Ox axis parallel to the edge 4-1.

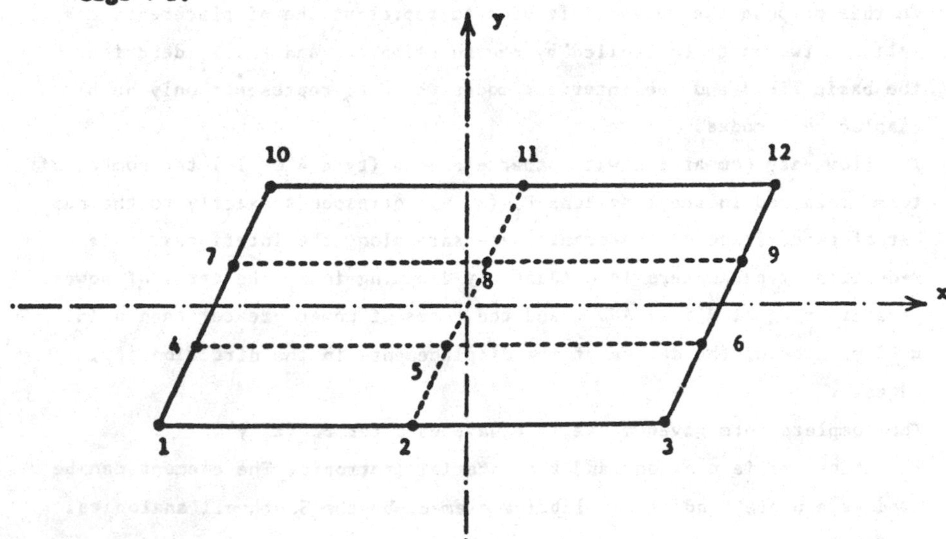

Reference points for stress output : 2nd degree in x and 3rd in y

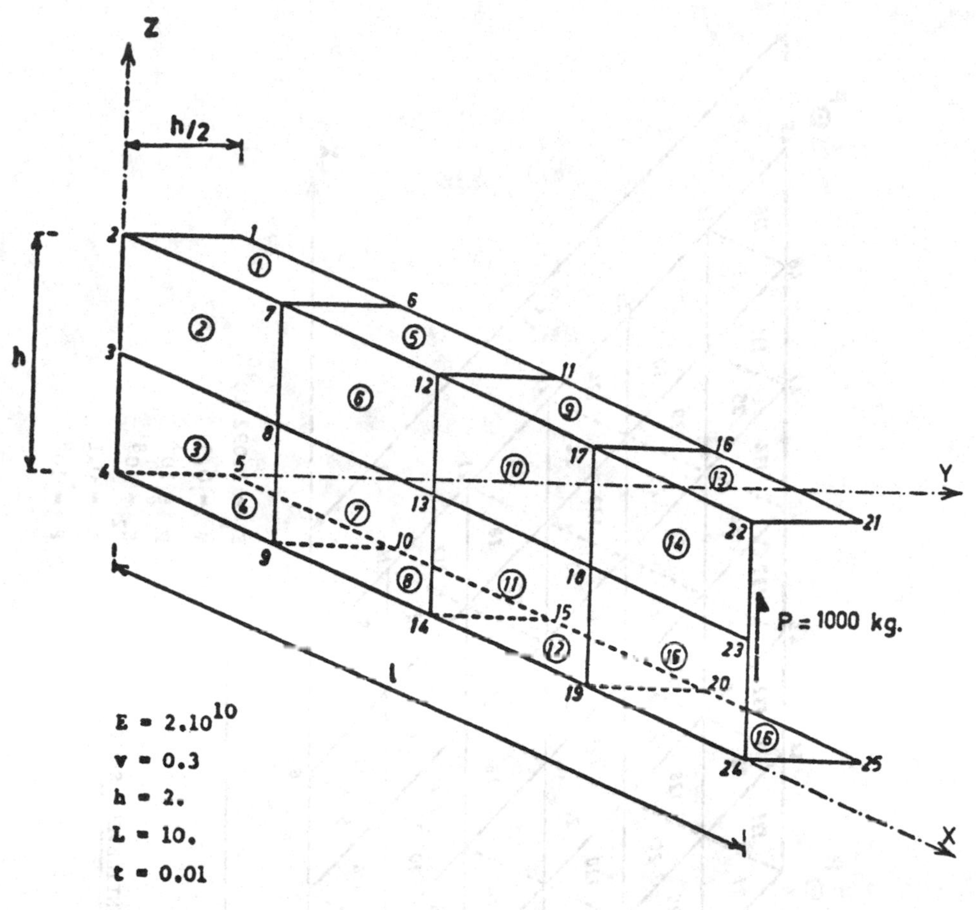

TEST CASE NBR 1 : CANTILEVER U BEAM

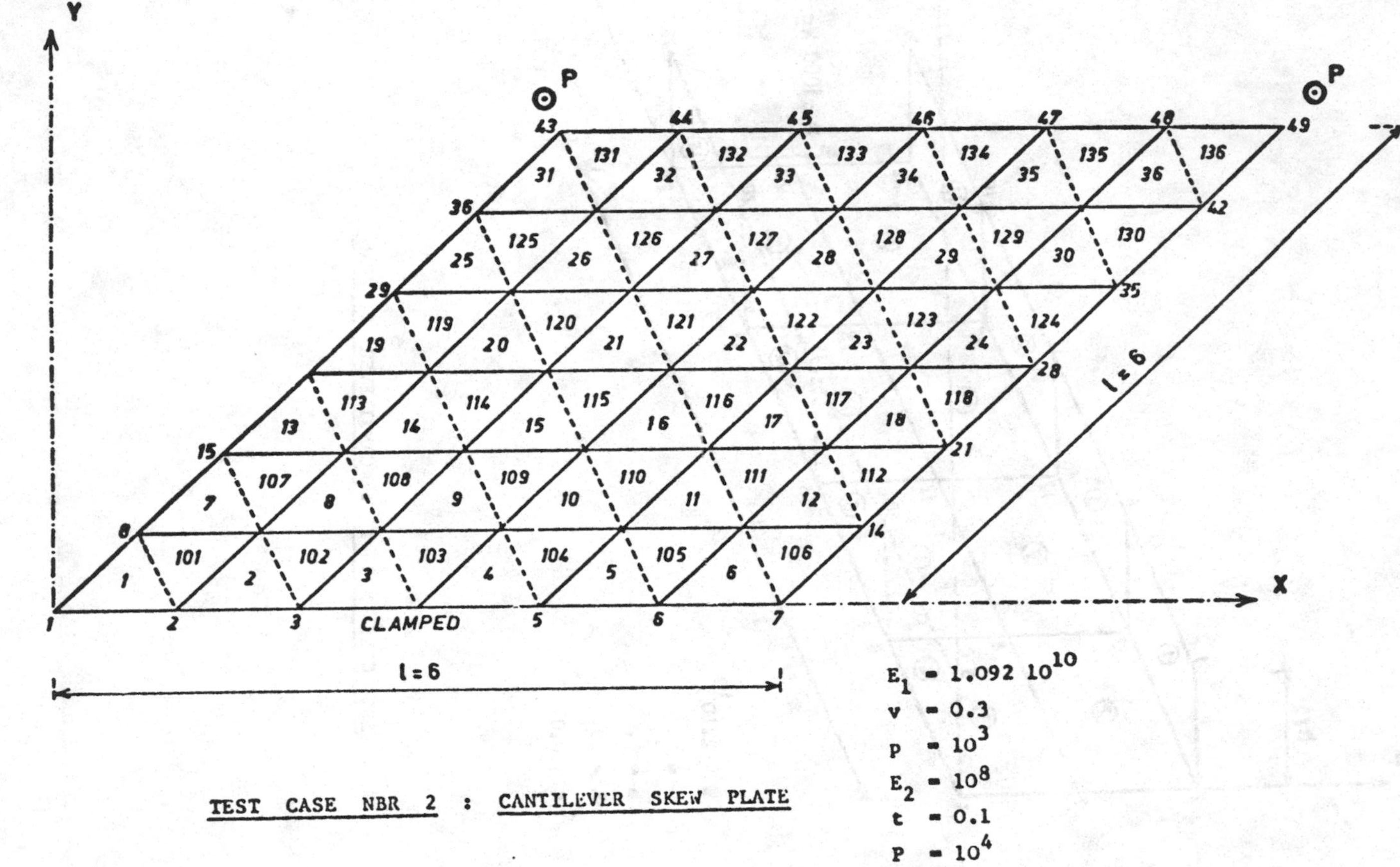

TEST CASE NBR 2 : CANTILEVER SKEW PLATE

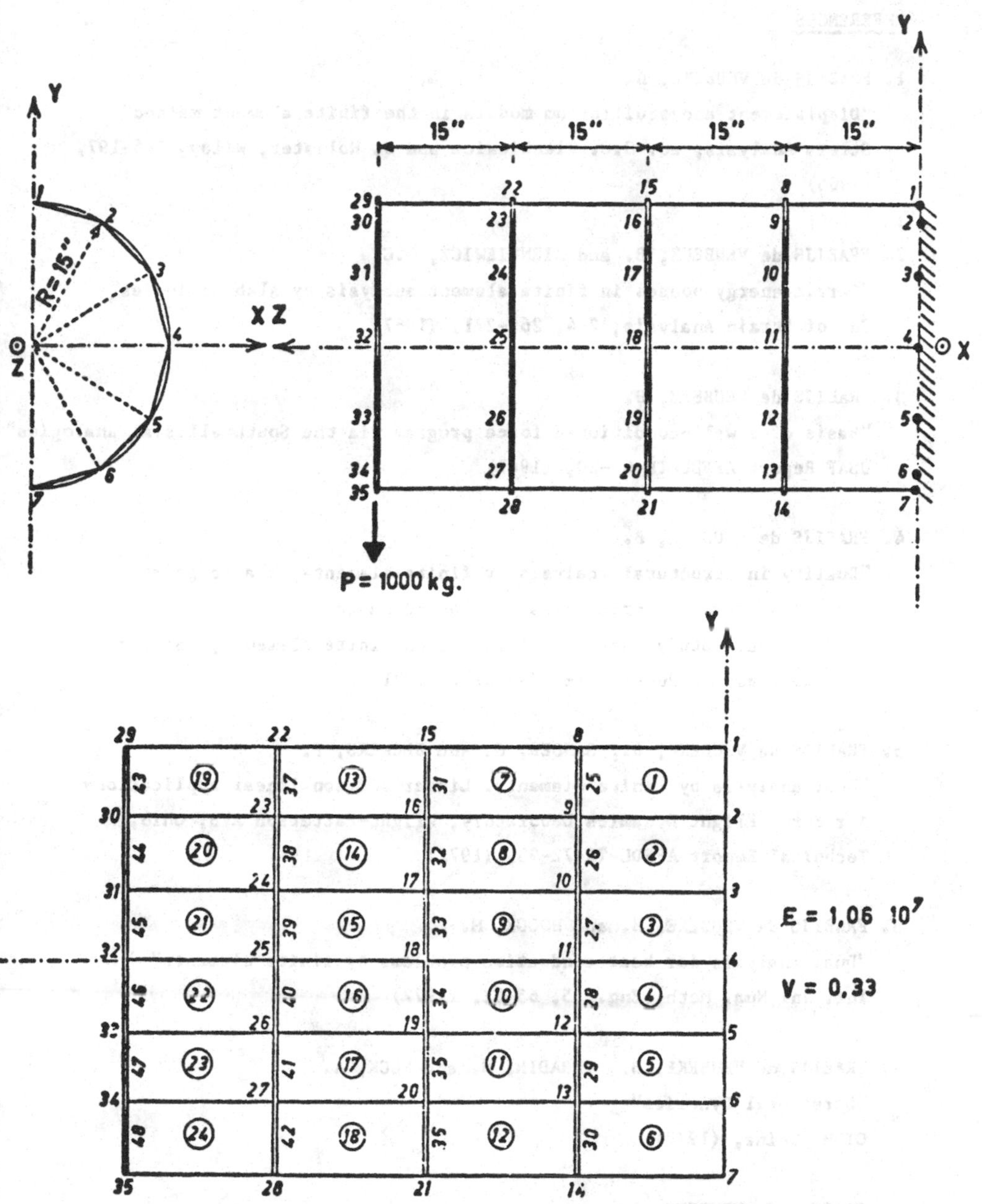

Y
R = 15"
X Z
15"
15"
15"
15"
P = 1000 kg.
E = 1,06 10^7
V = 0,33

REFERENCES

1. FRAEIJS de VEUBEKE, B.
"Displacement and equilibrium models in the finite element method"
Stress Analysis, ed. O.C. Zienkiewicz and G. Holister, Wiley, 145-197, (1965)

2. FRAEIJS de VEUBEKE, B. and ZIENKIEWICZ, O.C.
"Strain energy bounds in finite element analysis by slab analogies"
Jnl of Strain Analysis, 2-4, 265-271, (1967)

3. FRAEIJS de VEUBEKE, B.
"Basis of a well-conditioned force program via the Southwell slab analogies"
USAF Report AFFDL-TR-67-80, (1967)

4. FRAEIJS de VEUBEKE, B.
"Duality in structural analysis by finite elements, static-geometric analogies, the dual principles of elastodynamics"
NATO Advanced Study Institute lectures on finite elements, Univ. of Alabama Press in Huntsville, 299-377, (1971)

5. FRAEIJS de VEUBEKE, B., SANDER, G. and BECKERS, P.
"Dual analysis by finite elements. Linear and non linear applications"
Air Force Flight Dynamics Laboratory, Wright-Patterson AFB, Ohio, Technical Report AFFDL-TR-72-93, (1972)

6. FRAEIJS de VEUBEKE, B. and HOGGE, M.
"Dual analysis for heat conduction problems by finite elements"
Int. Jnl Num. Meth. Eng., 5, 65-82, (1972)

7. FRAEIJS de VEUBEKE, B., GERADIN, M. and HUCK, A.
"Structural Dynamics"
CISM, Udine, (1973)

8. FRAEIJS de VEUBEKE, B.
"Diffusive equilibrium models"
University of Calgary lecture notes, (1973)

9. GERADIN, M.
"Computational efficiency of equilibrium models in eigenvalue analysis"
Proceedings of the IUTAM Symposium on High Speed Computing of Elastic Structures, Congrès et Colloques de l'Université de Liège, Place du XX Août, 16, 4000 LIEGE, 589-623, (1971)

10. GERADIN, M.
"Analyse dynamique duale des structures par la méthode des éléments finis"
Collection des Publications de la Faculté des Sciences Appliquées de l'Université de Liège, 36, 1-173, (1973)

11. IMBERT, J.F., GIRARD, A. and GERADIN, M.
"Modal analysis of a satellite primary structure using a finite element procedure"
Symposium on structures of space vehicles and spacecraft, University College London, (1973)

12. IRONS, B. and RAZZAQUE, A.
"Experiences with the patch test for the convergence of finite elements"
Conference on the mathematical foundations of the finite element theory"
Univ. of Washington (Baltimore), Academic Press, (1972)

13. PIAN, T.M. and PIN TONG
"Basis of finite element methods for solid continua"
Int. Jnl Num. Meth. Eng., 1, 3-28, (1969)

14. SANDER, G., BECKERS, P. and NGUYEN, H.D.
"Digital computation of stresses and deflexions in a box beam"
Collection des Publications de la Faculté des Sciences Appliquées de l'Université de Liège, 4, 87-137, (1967)

15. SANDER, G.
"Dual analysis of a multiweb swept back wing model"
Aircraft Engineering, 6-16, (1968)

16. SANDER, G.
"Application of the dual analysis principle"
Proceedings of the IUTAM Symposium on High Speed Computing of Elastic Structures, Congrès et Colloques de l'Université de Liège, Place du XX Août, 16, 4000 Liège, 167-207, (1971)

17. SANDER, G., BON, C. and GERADIN, M.
"Finite element analysis of supersonic panel flutter"
Int. Jnl Num. Meth. eng., 7-2, (1973)

18. STRANG, G.
"Variational crimes in the finite element method"
Math. Foundations of the finite element method, ed. A.K. AZIZ, Academic Press, (1972)

19. TABARROK, B. and SODHI, D.S.
"The generalization of stress function procedure for dynamic analysis of plates"
Int. Jnl Num. Meth. Eng., 5, 523-542, (1973)

20. TURNER, M.J., MARTIN, H.C. and WEIKEL, R.C.
"Further development and applications of the direct stiffness method"
Matrix methods of structural analysis.
AGARDograph 72, 203-266, Pergamon Press, (1964)

VISCO-PLASTICITY AND PLASTICITY AN ALTERNATIVE FOR FINITE ELEMENT SOLUTION OF MATERIAL NONLINEARITIES

by

O. C. ZIENKIEWICZ
Professor of Civil Engineering, University of Wales, Swansea

and

I. C. CORMEAU
Aspirant F.N.R.S., Université Libre de Bruxelles (now at Swansea)

Summary

In this paper, authors present a formulation and some computational details dealing with a general elastic/visco-plastic material where nonlinear elasticity is admissible and the flow rule and yield condition need not be associated.

If, in a visco-plastic solution method, stationary conditions are reached for the displacements, the solution to an equivalent plasticity problem is obtained. The visco-plastic approach thus provides an alternative technique to solve elasto-plastic problems, and which is found to possess considerable merits vis à vis other iterative processes.

In particular, non-associated flow rules and strain softening can be dealt with in a general purpose program without requiring specific numerical artifices. Further, by providing always an equilibrating solution (within the approximations of the finite element discretisation) and, at displacements stationarity, ensuring a plastically admissible stress distribution, results always give a lower bound to collapse.

The paper includes several examples to illustrate the application of the method to some problems of practical interest.

1. INTRODUCTION

It is now customary to apply finite element techniques to obtain the solution of non-linear material problems (ZIENKIEWICZ[27]). A great variety of specialised numerical models were developed to deal with particular situations such as visco-elasticity (WHITE[19], ZIENKIEWICZ, WATSON and KING[24]), creep (GREENBAUM and RUBINSTEIN[9], SUTHERLAND[17], TREHARNE[18]) or classical elasto-plasticity (ARGYRIS and SHARPF[2], MARCAL and KING[11], NAYAK and ZIENKIEWICZ[12], ZIENKIEWICZ, VALLIAPPAN and KING[25,26]). Not only metals but also polymers, cracking materials, rocks and soils have been idealised by means of several ad hoc models (ZIENKIEWICZ[27]).

The idea of a visco-plastic medium, involving both time and plastic effects is not new (BINGHAM[4], FREUDENTHAL and GEIRINGER[8], REINER[16]). Surprisingly, however, it arose only limited interest among structural analysts and engineers, despite its conceptual simplicity, generality and relative ease of implementation on digital computers.

Early applications of visco-plasticity theory dealt with rigid/visco-perfectly-plastic plates and axisymmetric shells, under linearization assumptions, for static (APPLEBY and PRAGER[1]) and mainly dynamic loadings (WIERZBICKI[21], WIERZBICKI and FLORENCE[22]).

The viscoplastic model does equally well in quasi static situations where the inelastic strains are of the same order as the elastic ones. Closed form solutions exist for simple geometries where the whole material is assumed to be above the static yield limit (WIERZBICKI[20]) and numerical results are reported by CHABOCHE[5] for an elasto-visco-plastic structure subject to time varying thermal gradients.

The formulation and experimental determination of viscoplastic constitutive relations were discussed by ZARKA[23] (microscopic approach - metals), LEMAITRE[10] and PERZYNA[15] (macroscopic approach) among others; these references contain extensive bibliographies on the subject.

Numerical methods for the solution of quasi static elastic/visco-plastic problems of arbitrary geometry were described by NGUYEN and ZARKA[14], ZIENKIEWICZ and CORMEAU[28], but so far only little numerical work has been published.

2. FINITE ELEMENT FORMULATION OF QUASI STATIC SMALL STRAIN ELASTO/VISCO-PLASTICITY

Let a body Ω bounded by a regular surface S be in quasi static equilibrium under body forces $\underset{\sim}{f}$ and surface tractions $\underset{\sim}{t}$, and subject to the boundary conditions for displacements, velocities and surface forces

$$\begin{cases} \underset{\sim}{u} = \underset{\sim}{\bar{u}} \\ \underset{\sim}{v} = 0 \end{cases} \text{on } S_u \qquad \underset{\sim}{t} = \underset{\sim}{\bar{t}} \text{ on } S_t \qquad S = S_u \cup S_t \tag{1}$$

The material is supposed to be capable of transforming a mechanical energy input into both stored and dissipative forms, with possible interaction of externally prescribed thermal effects.

It is well known (ZIENKIEWICZ[27]) that a finite element approximation of a displacement (and velocity) field in Ω, by interpolation in terms of 'nodal' values $\underset{\sim}{\delta}$ such as

$$\begin{aligned} \underset{\sim}{v} = \dot{\underset{\sim}{u}} = \underset{\sim}{N}\, \dot{\underset{\sim}{\delta}} \quad & \text{in } \Omega \\ \underset{\sim}{v} = 0 \quad & \text{on } S_u \end{aligned} \tag{2}$$

leads to a velocity strain distribution in Ω

$$\dot{\underset{\sim}{\varepsilon}} = \left\{ \dot{\varepsilon}_x \; \dot{\varepsilon}_y \; \dot{\varepsilon}_z \; \dot{\gamma}_{yz} \; \dot{\gamma}_{zx} \; \dot{\gamma}_{xy} \right\}^T = \underset{\sim}{B}\, \dot{\underset{\sim}{\delta}} \tag{3}$$

where the matrices $\underset{\sim}{N}$ and $\underset{\sim}{B}$ depend on spatial coordinates $\underset{\sim}{x}$ only if infinitesimal strains are assumed.

With the introduction of stresses conjugate (in the sense of virtual work) to the velocity strains

$$\underset{\sim}{\sigma} = \{\sigma_x \ \sigma_y \ \sigma_z \ \tau_{yz} \ \tau_{zx} \ \tau_{xy}\}^T$$

and of consistent nodal forces $\underset{\sim}{R}$ equivalent to ($\underset{\sim}{t}$, $\underset{\sim}{f}$), the principle of virtual velocities yields the discretised equilibrium equations

$$\underset{\sim}{R} = \int_\Omega \underset{\sim}{B}^T \underset{\sim}{\sigma} \, d\Omega \tag{4a}$$

$$\dot{\underset{\sim}{R}} = \int_\Omega \underset{\sim}{B}^T \dot{\underset{\sim}{\sigma}} \, d\Omega \tag{4b}$$

as long as the changes of geometry are disregarded and assuming that rotations remain small to allow $\dot{\underset{\sim}{\sigma}}$ to be simply taken as

$$\dot{\underset{\sim}{\sigma}} = \frac{\partial \underset{\sim}{\sigma}(\underset{\sim}{x}, t)}{\partial t} \tag{5}$$

With regards to the reversible part of the total behaviour in view of isotropic cases, a specific stored-energy function, depending on the stress invariants, is supposed to represent the mechanical energy that can be released on instantaneous isothermal stress removal

$$\mathcal{A} = \mathcal{A}(\sigma_m, J_2, J_3) \tag{6}$$

where

$$\sigma_m = \frac{1}{3}\sigma_{ii}$$
$$s_{ij} = \sigma_{ij} - \sigma_m$$
$$J_2 = \frac{1}{2} s_{ij} s_{ji}$$
$$J_3 = \frac{1}{3} s_{ij} s_{jk} s_{ki}$$

The rate at which mechanical energy is stored can always be written as

$$\dot{\mathcal{A}} = \underset{\sim}{\sigma}^T \underset{\sim}{M} \dot{\underset{\sim}{\sigma}} \tag{7}$$

where $\underset{\sim}{M}$ is a symmetric, generally stress dependent, matrix given in Appendix I.

Further, it is assumed that the total stress power $\mathcal{P} = \underset{\sim}{\sigma}^T \dot{\underset{\sim}{\varepsilon}}$ can be written as a sum of three independant terms

$$\mathcal{P} = \dot{\mathcal{A}} + \mathcal{P}_\theta + \mathcal{P}_D \tag{8}$$

where $\mathcal{P}_\theta = \underset{\sim}{\sigma}^T \dot{\underset{\sim}{\varepsilon}}^\theta$ denotes the contribution of prescribed thermal effects and $\mathcal{P}_D = \underset{\sim}{\sigma}^T \dot{\underset{\sim}{\varepsilon}}^{vp} \geq 0$ designates the irrecoverable power of dissipation due to viscous and/or creep phenomena. Here, $\underset{\sim}{\varepsilon}^\theta$ and $\underset{\sim}{\varepsilon}^{vp}$ have dimensions of strains and can be considered as internal state variables describing thermal and dissipative effects. The balance equation for the stress power gives

$$\underset{\sim}{\sigma}^T(\dot{\underset{\sim}{\varepsilon}} - \underset{\sim}{M}\dot{\underset{\sim}{\sigma}} - \dot{\underset{\sim}{\varepsilon}}^\theta - \dot{\underset{\sim}{\varepsilon}}^{vp}) = 0 \tag{9}$$

from which the stress velocities are obtained

$$\dot{\underset{\sim}{\sigma}} = \underset{\sim}{M}^{-1}(\dot{\underset{\sim}{\varepsilon}} - \dot{\underset{\sim}{\varepsilon}}^{\theta} - \dot{\underset{\sim}{\varepsilon}}^{vp}) \tag{10}$$

Since dissipative and thermal effects are present, some heat supply per unit volume and unit time and heat flux will exist in Ω and on S to satisfy the principle of conservation of energy; the quasi static hypotheses are therefore extended to the consideration of processes where the retro-action of $\mathcal{P}_D$ onto $\dot{\underset{\sim}{\varepsilon}}^{\theta}$ is negligible, such that $\dot{\underset{\sim}{\varepsilon}}^{\theta}$ remains externally controlled everywhere in Ω at any time.

Combining the local equation (10), the general equilibrium equation (4b) and the strain displacement relation (3) one obtains

$$\dot{\underset{\sim}{R}} = \underset{\sim}{K}_T \dot{\underset{\sim}{\delta}} - \int_{\Omega} \underset{\sim}{B}^T \underset{\sim}{M}^{-1} \dot{\underset{\sim}{\varepsilon}}^{\theta} d\Omega - \int_{\Omega} \underset{\sim}{B}^T \underset{\sim}{M}^{-1} \dot{\underset{\sim}{\varepsilon}}^{vp} d\Omega \tag{11}$$

where $\underset{\sim}{K}_T = \int_{\Omega} \underset{\sim}{B}^T \underset{\sim}{M}^{-1} \underset{\sim}{B} \, d\Omega$ is a stress dependent tangential stiffness matrix. Assuming instantaneous elastic stability, it is possible to solve (11) for the velocities

$$\dot{\underset{\sim}{\delta}} = \underset{\sim}{K}_T^{-1} \left(\dot{\underset{\sim}{R}} + \int_{\Omega} \underset{\sim}{B}^T \underset{\sim}{M}^{-1} \dot{\underset{\sim}{\varepsilon}}^{\theta} d\Omega + \int_{\Omega} \underset{\sim}{B}^T \underset{\sim}{M}^{-1} \dot{\underset{\sim}{\varepsilon}}^{vp} d\Omega \right) \tag{12}$$

A constitutive equation remains to be chosen for $\dot{\underset{\sim}{\varepsilon}}^{vp}$; herein a generalized form of the elastic/visco-plastic model proposed by PERZYNA[15] is adopted since it covers several other models as particular cases. PERZYNA's constitutive equations state that the irrecoverable dissipation occurs only if the stresses exceed the static yield condition

$$\dot{\underset{\sim}{\varepsilon}}^{vp} = \gamma \langle \phi\left(\frac{F}{F_0}\right) \rangle \frac{\partial Q}{\partial \underset{\sim}{\sigma}} \tag{13}$$

where a) γ is a positive, possibly time dependent, fluidity coefficient

b) $\phi(x)$ is a positive scalar-valued monotonic increasing function in the range $x > 0$ such that $\phi^{-1}(x)$ exists and possess similar properties in the same range

c) the notation $\langle \rangle$ stands for

$$\langle \phi(x) \rangle = \phi(x) \quad \text{if} \quad x > 0$$
$$\langle \phi(x) \rangle = 0 \quad \text{if} \quad x \leqslant 0$$

d) $F = \varphi(\underset{\sim}{\sigma}, \underset{\sim}{\varepsilon}^{vp}) - Y(\kappa)$ represents the yield function, being zero when the static yield condition is satisfied.

e) $Y(\kappa)$ is a static yield stress

f) $Q = Q(\underset{\sim}{\sigma}, \underset{\sim}{\varepsilon}^{vp}, \kappa)$ is the visco-plastic potential

g) κ is a hardening parameter, either state or more generally history dependent and whose value is then given by the integration along the path of past states of an evolution equation

$$\dot{\kappa} = \dot{\kappa}(\underset{\sim}{\sigma}, \underset{\sim}{\varepsilon}^{vp}, \kappa)$$

h) F_0 is a positive quantity introduced to make F/F_0 dimensionless to

allow arbitrary forms of the function ϕ .
Specific forms for F, Q and κ were derived by NAYAK and ZIENKIEWICZ[12] for some popular isotropic yield criteria and plastic potentials, in a form convenient to computations and can be found in Appendix II.

In isotropic situations F and Q depend on the stress invariants; as shown in Appendix I, it is also possible to write

$$\dot{\underset{\sim}{\varepsilon}}^{vp} = \gamma \langle \phi(\frac{F}{F_0}) \rangle \frac{\partial Q(\sigma_m, J_2, J_3, \underset{\sim}{\varepsilon}^{vp}, \kappa)}{\partial \underset{\sim}{\sigma}} = \underset{\sim}{\Gamma} \, \underset{\sim}{\sigma} \tag{14}$$

where Γ is another state dependent symmetric matrix which should be at least positive semidefinite since

$$\mathcal{P}_D = \underset{\sim}{\sigma}^T \dot{\underset{\sim}{\varepsilon}}^{vp} = \underset{\sim}{\sigma}^T \underset{\sim}{\Gamma} \, \underset{\sim}{\sigma} \geqslant 0 \qquad \forall \underset{\sim}{\sigma} \neq 0 \tag{15}$$

and that vanishes for any stresses below the current static yield surface $F = 0$.

The mathematical nature of the final problem to be solved can be better appreciated after $\dot{\underset{\sim}{\delta}}$ and $\dot{\underset{\sim}{\varepsilon}}$ have been eliminated between (3, 10, 12, 14)

$$\begin{aligned} \frac{\partial \underset{\sim}{\sigma}(\underset{\sim}{x},t)}{\partial t} &= \dot{\underset{\sim}{\sigma}} = \underset{\sim}{M}^{-1}\left[\underset{\sim}{B}\underset{\sim}{K}_T^{-1}\left(\dot{\underset{\sim}{R}} + \int_\Omega \underset{\sim}{B}^T \underset{\sim}{M}^{-1} \dot{\underset{\sim}{\varepsilon}}^{\theta} d\Omega + \int_\Omega \underset{\sim}{B}^T \underset{\sim}{M}^{-1} \dot{\underset{\sim}{\varepsilon}}^{vp} d\Omega\right) - \dot{\underset{\sim}{\varepsilon}}^{\theta} - \dot{\underset{\sim}{\varepsilon}}^{vp}\right] \\ \frac{\partial \varepsilon^{vp}(\underset{\sim}{x},t)}{\partial t} &= \dot{\underset{\sim}{\varepsilon}}^{vp} = \underset{\sim}{\Gamma}\, \underset{\sim}{\sigma} \\ \frac{\partial \kappa(\underset{\sim}{x},t)}{\partial t} &= \dot{\kappa} = \dot{\kappa}(\underset{\sim}{\sigma}, \underset{\sim}{\varepsilon}^{vp}, \kappa, \underset{\sim}{x}) \end{aligned} \tag{16}$$

thus giving rise to a nonlinear first order system of partial differential equations for the stresses and hidden variables $\underset{\sim}{\varepsilon}^{vp}, \kappa$. In the following sections, simplifications will be achieved by considering linear elasticity and numerical integration.

3. LINEAR ELASTIC/NONLINEAR VISCO-PLASTIC BEHAVIOUR

Isotropic linear elastic properties result from a particular form of the specific stored energy function:

$$\mathcal{A} = \frac{3(1-2\nu)}{2E} \sigma_m^2 + \frac{1+\nu}{E} J_2 \tag{17}$$

where E and ν are Young's modulus and Poisson's ratio respectively. Equation (10) becomes

$$\dot{\underset{\sim}{\sigma}} = \underset{\sim}{D}(\dot{\underset{\sim}{\varepsilon}} - \dot{\underset{\sim}{\varepsilon}}^{\theta} - \dot{\underset{\sim}{\varepsilon}}^{vp}) \tag{18}$$

where $\underset{\sim}{D}$ is the usual elasticity matrix; integration in time gives

$$\underset{\sim}{\sigma} = \underset{\sim}{D}(\underset{\sim}{\varepsilon} - \underset{\sim}{\varepsilon}^{\theta} - \underset{\sim}{\varepsilon}^{vp}) + \underset{\sim}{\sigma}' \tag{19}$$

$\underset{\sim}{\sigma}'$ denoting an arbitrary co-ordinate dependent stress distribution.

The tangential stiffness matrix reduces to the ordinary stiffness matrix

$$\underset{\sim}{K} = \int_\Omega \underset{\sim}{B}^T \underset{\sim}{D}\, \underset{\sim}{B}\, d\Omega \tag{20}$$

which can now be assembled, part inverted and kept in this form once for all times ready for further operations involving $\underset{\sim}{K}^{-1}$.

Initial conditions determining a solution to the initial value problem (16) may consist of an elastic set as follows:

for $\underset{\sim}{\varepsilon}^{\theta_0}, \underset{\sim}{\varepsilon}^{vp_0}, K^{\circ}, \underset{\sim}{R}^{\circ}, \underset{\sim}{\sigma}'$ being given arbitrary values one has

$$\underset{\sim}{\delta}^{\circ} = \underset{\sim}{K}^{-1}\left[\underset{\sim}{R}^{\circ} + \int_{\Omega} \underset{\sim}{B}^T \underset{\sim}{D} \underset{\sim}{\varepsilon}^{\theta_0} d\Omega + \int_{\Omega} \underset{\sim}{B}^T \underset{\sim}{D} \underset{\sim}{\varepsilon}^{vp_0} d\Omega - \int_{\Omega} \underset{\sim}{B}^T \underset{\sim}{\sigma}' d\Omega\right]$$

$$\underset{\sim}{\varepsilon}^{\circ} = \underset{\sim}{B}\, \underset{\sim}{\delta}^{\circ} \tag{21}$$

$$\underset{\sim}{\sigma}^{\circ} = \underset{\sim}{\sigma}' + \underset{\sim}{D}\left(\underset{\sim}{\varepsilon}^{\circ} - \underset{\sim}{\varepsilon}^{\theta_0} - \underset{\sim}{\varepsilon}^{vp_0}\right)$$

$$Y^{\circ} = Y(K^{\circ})$$

4. PARAMETRIC DISPLACEMENT FIELD AND NUMERICAL INTEGRATION

The discretization of the velocity field (2) is generally not sufficient to eliminate fully the space variables $\underset{\sim}{x}$ which are still implicitly presence since $\underset{\sim}{\sigma}$, $\underset{\sim}{\varepsilon}^{vp}$ and K are allowed to vary within every finite element unless simplex constant stress elements are used (ZIENKIEWICZ and CORMEAU[28]).

Even if, at a given stage t^* of the calculations, the analytical form $\underset{\sim}{\sigma}(\underset{\sim}{x}, t^*)$ were known, the exact integration of $\int_{\Omega} \underset{\sim}{B}^T \underset{\sim}{D}\, \dot{\underset{\sim}{\varepsilon}}^{vp} d\Omega$ would remain difficult since the instantaneous visco-plastic boundary crosses some elements; moreover considering the possibly complex form of $\dot{\underset{\sim}{\varepsilon}}^{vp}$, it is concluded that numerical integration will be required, a context in which (iso)parametric elements find their natural justification. These elements, fully described by ZIENKIEWICZ[27] have proved their capabilities in many non-linear problems.

Displacements and velocities are interpolated over an element by means of parametric equations where the parameters ξ and η (2-D problems) are curvilinear co-ordinates ranging from -1 to +1:

$$\underset{\sim}{u} = \sum_i N_i(\xi,\eta)\, \underset{\sim}{u}_i \qquad \text{displacement interpolation} \tag{22a}$$

$$\underset{\sim}{x} = \sum_j N'_j(\xi,\eta)\, \underset{\sim}{x}_j \qquad \text{co-ordinates transformation} \tag{22b}$$

Introducing the Jacobian matrix

$$\underset{\sim}{J} = \begin{bmatrix} \partial x/\partial \xi & \partial x/\partial \eta \\ \partial y/\partial \xi & \partial y/\partial \eta \end{bmatrix} \tag{23}$$

one has for planar cases,

$$d\Omega = dx\,dy = \sum_{i,j} x_i y_j \left(\frac{\partial N'_i}{\partial \xi}\cdot\frac{\partial N'_j}{\partial \eta} - \frac{\partial N'_i}{\partial \eta}\cdot\frac{\partial N'_j}{\partial \xi}\right) d\xi\, d\eta \tag{24a}$$

and for axisymmetric cases, where $x=0$ is the axis of revolution

$$d\Omega = 2\pi x\, dx\, dy = 2\pi \sum_{i,j,k} x_i x_j y_k N_i' \left(\frac{\partial N_j'}{\partial \xi} \cdot \frac{\partial N_k'}{\partial \eta} - \frac{\partial N_j'}{\partial \eta} \cdot \frac{\partial N_k'}{\partial \xi} \right) d\xi\, d\eta \tag{24b}$$

The matrix $\underset{\sim}{B}$ depends on Cartesian derivatives of the displacement interpolation functions N_i and on the radial co-ordinate in axisymmetric cases

$$\frac{\partial N_i}{\partial x} = \frac{1}{\det|\underset{\sim}{J}|} \left[\left(\sum_j y_j \frac{\partial N_j'}{\partial \eta} \right) \frac{\partial N_i}{\partial \xi} - \left(\sum_j y_j \frac{\partial N_j'}{\partial \xi} \right) \frac{\partial N_i}{\partial \eta} \right]$$

$$\frac{\partial N_i}{\partial y} = \frac{1}{\det|\underset{\sim}{J}|} \left[\left(\sum_j x_j \frac{\partial N_j'}{\partial \xi} \right) \frac{\partial N_i}{\partial \eta} - \left(\sum_j x_j \frac{\partial N_j'}{\partial \eta} \right) \frac{\partial N_i}{\partial \xi} \right] \tag{25}$$

$$\frac{N_i}{x} = \frac{N_i}{\sum_j x_j N_j'} \quad (\text{axisym. only})$$

Convergence, with uniform mesh refinement, of the finite element approximations, to the solution of the continuum problem, will occur if the following (sufficient) conditions are met:

a) the approximate displacement field can represent the exact one in the limit; if the constant strain and interelement compatibility criteria are satisfied, this condition is fulfilled provided the exact strain field is bounded in Ω.

b) nodal equilibrium equations are exactly satisfied when constant stresses and body forces prevail in all elements, provided the exact stress field is bounded in Ω.

c) Constitutive relationships are satisfied for all stresses and strains appearing in the discretized equations (16).

Conditions (a) are always satisfied by isoparametric ($N_i' \equiv N_i$) elements and by subparametric elements if linear relations $N_i' = \alpha_{ij} N_j$ exist (ZIENKIEWICZ[27]).

Condition (b) requires an exact integration of

$$\int_\Omega \underset{\sim}{B}^T \underset{\sim}{\sigma}\, d\Omega \quad \int_\Omega \underset{\sim}{B}^T \underset{\sim}{\varepsilon}^{vp} d\Omega \quad \int_\Omega \underset{\sim}{B}^T \underset{\sim}{\varepsilon}^{\theta} d\Omega$$

and of

$$\int_\Omega \underset{\sim}{N}^T \underset{\sim}{f}\, d\Omega$$

if body forces are present,

for constant vectors $\underset{\sim}{\sigma}$, $\underset{\sim}{\varepsilon}^{vp}$, $\underset{\sim}{\varepsilon}^{\theta}$, $\underset{\sim}{f}$. Relevant 'square' Gaussian rules can be found in Appendix III for various 2-D cases.

Condition (c) is related to the convergence properties of the numerical method used to integrate (16) in time.

In order to examine the effect of numerical integration on the discretization, integrals are approximated by the symbolic formula

$$\int_\Omega \psi(\underset{\sim}{x})\, d\Omega = \sum_1^I c_i\, \psi(\underset{\sim}{x}_i) \tag{26a}$$

where I denotes the total number of integrating points in Ω and

$$c_i = \text{integration weight} \times \text{element of volume } \det|\underset{\sim}{J}(\underset{\sim}{x}_i)| \tag{26b}$$

This leads to a further discretization since the approximate fields $\underset{\sim}{\sigma}$, $\underset{\sim}{\varepsilon}^{vp}$, κ depending on $\underset{\sim}{x}$ and t are replaced by a finite number of time dependent values at the integrating points only.

Introducing 'structural' vectors grouping all integrating point quantities such as

$$\underset{\sim}{\Sigma}(t)=\begin{Bmatrix}\underset{\sim}{\sigma}_1\\ \vdots\\ \underset{\sim}{\sigma}_I\end{Bmatrix}\quad \underset{\sim}{\Sigma}'=\begin{Bmatrix}\underset{\sim}{\sigma}'_1\\ \vdots\\ \sigma'_I\end{Bmatrix}\quad \underset{\sim}{\mathbb{E}}(t)=\begin{Bmatrix}\underset{\sim}{\varepsilon}_1\\ \vdots\\ \underset{\sim}{\varepsilon}_I\end{Bmatrix}\quad \underset{\sim}{\mathbb{E}}^{\theta}(t)=\begin{Bmatrix}\varepsilon_1^{\theta}\\ \vdots\\ \varepsilon_I^{\theta}\end{Bmatrix}\quad \underset{\sim}{\mathbb{E}}^{vp}(t)=\begin{Bmatrix}\varepsilon_1^{vp}\\ \vdots\\ \varepsilon_I^{vp}\end{Bmatrix}\quad \underset{\sim}{\mathbb{K}}(t)=\begin{Bmatrix}\kappa_1\\ \vdots\\ \kappa_I\end{Bmatrix} \tag{27}$$

it is possible to rewrite the discretised equations in a compact form:

$$\dot{\underset{\sim}{\mathbb{E}}} = \underset{\sim}{\mathbb{B}}\,\dot{\underset{\sim}{\delta}} \tag{28a}$$

$$\underset{\sim}{R} = \underset{\sim}{\mathbb{B}}^T \underset{\sim}{\mathbb{C}}\,\underset{\sim}{\Sigma}\quad,\quad \dot{\underset{\sim}{R}} = \underset{\sim}{\mathbb{B}}^T \underset{\sim}{\mathbb{C}}\,\dot{\underset{\sim}{\Sigma}} \tag{28b}$$

$$\dot{\underset{\sim}{\mathbb{E}}}^{vp} = \underset{\sim}{\Gamma}\,\underset{\sim}{\Sigma} \tag{28c}$$

$$\underset{\sim}{\Sigma} = \underset{\sim}{\mathbb{D}}\left[\underset{\sim}{\mathbb{E}} - \underset{\sim}{\mathbb{E}}^{\theta} - \underset{\sim}{\mathbb{E}}^{vp}\right] + \underset{\sim}{\Sigma}' \tag{28d}$$

$$\underset{\sim}{K} = \underset{\sim}{\mathbb{B}}^T \underset{\sim}{\mathbb{D}}\,\underset{\sim}{\mathbb{C}}\,\underset{\sim}{\mathbb{B}} \tag{28e}$$

where: $\underset{\sim}{\mathbb{B}}$ is a constant structural strain displacement matrix made of elemental $\underset{\sim}{B}$ matrices computed at the integrating points

$\underset{\sim}{\mathbb{C}}$ is a constant diagonal matrix of c_i coefficients defined in (26)

$\underset{\sim}{\mathbb{D}}$ is a constant symmetric matrix made of $\underset{\sim}{D}$ matrices following each other along the diagonal of $\underset{\sim}{\mathbb{D}}$

$\underset{\sim}{\Gamma}$ is a state dependent symmetric positive semidefinite matrix with structure analogous to that of $\underset{\sim}{\mathbb{D}}$

and such that $\underset{\sim}{\mathbb{C}}\,\underset{\sim}{\mathbb{D}} = \underset{\sim}{\mathbb{D}}\,\underset{\sim}{\mathbb{C}}$ and $\underset{\sim}{\mathbb{C}}\,\underset{\sim}{\Gamma} = \underset{\sim}{\Gamma}\,\underset{\sim}{\mathbb{C}}$

In the case of linear elasticity, Eqns. (16) are replaced by

$$\frac{d\underset{\sim}{\Sigma}}{dt} = \dot{\underset{\sim}{\Sigma}} = \underset{\sim}{S}\,\underset{\sim}{\mathbb{C}}\,\dot{\underset{\sim}{\mathbb{E}}}^{vp} + \dot{\underset{\sim}{\Xi}} \tag{29a}$$

$$\frac{d\underset{\sim}{\mathbb{E}}^{vp}}{dt} = \underset{\sim}{\Gamma}\,\underset{\sim}{\Sigma} \tag{29b}$$

$$\frac{d\underset{\sim}{\mathbb{K}}}{dt} = \dot{\underset{\sim}{\mathbb{K}}}(\underset{\sim}{\Sigma}, \underset{\sim}{\mathbb{E}}^{vp}, \underset{\sim}{\mathbb{K}}) \tag{29c}$$

where

$$\underset{\sim}{S} = \underset{\sim}{\mathbb{D}}\,\underset{\sim}{\mathbb{B}}\,\underset{\sim}{K}^{-1}\underset{\sim}{\mathbb{B}}^T\underset{\sim}{\mathbb{D}} - \underset{\sim}{\mathbb{D}}\,\underset{\sim}{\mathbb{C}}^{-1} \tag{30a}$$

is a constant, symmetric, negative semidefinite matrix and

where $\underset{\sim}{\Xi} = \underset{\sim}{S}\,\underset{\sim}{C}\,\underset{\sim}{E}^{\theta} + \underset{\sim}{D}\,\underset{\sim}{B}\,\underset{\sim}{K}^{-1}\underset{\sim}{R} - \underset{\sim}{D}\,\underset{\sim}{B}\,\underset{\sim}{K}^{-1}\underset{\sim}{B}^{T}\underset{\sim}{C}\,\underset{\sim}{\Sigma}'$ (30b)

is a known, time varying, vector.

For ideal visco-plasticity, Eq. (29c) does not exist and $\underset{\sim}{\Gamma}$ depends solely on $\underset{\sim}{\Sigma}$ so that finally the problem reduces to a nonlinear ordinary differential vector equation

$$\dot{\underset{\sim}{\Sigma}} = \underset{\sim}{A}\,\underset{\sim}{\Sigma} + \dot{\underset{\sim}{\Xi}} \tag{31}$$

where $\underset{\sim}{A} = (\underset{\sim}{S})(\underset{\sim}{C}\,\underset{\sim}{\Gamma})$, though itself non-symmetric, is the product of two symmetric matrices.

Alternatively it is possible to derive a similar expression for weighted visco-plastic strains

$$\underset{\sim}{G} = \underset{\sim}{C}\,\underset{\sim}{E}^{vp} \tag{32a}$$

$$\dot{\underset{\sim}{G}} = \underset{\sim}{A}^{T}\underset{\sim}{G} + \underset{\sim}{C}\,\underset{\sim}{\Gamma}\,\underset{\sim}{\Xi} \tag{32b}$$

but where the stresses are still implicitly present in $\underset{\sim}{A}^{T}$ and $\underset{\sim}{\Gamma}$.

It is seen that the size of the numerical problem is proportional to the number of integrating points in Ω ; it is therefore of prime importance to use the lowest possible order of numerical integration compatible with convergence conditions (b) mentioned earlier in this section if economy requirements are to be met.

5. COMPUTATIONAL STRATEGY

5.1 Basic algorithm

The solution to (29) starting from initial conditions (21) can be obtained by a time marching procedure.

Let an equilibrium situation be known at a time t_n

i.e. $\underset{\sim}{\delta}_n, \underset{\sim}{E}^{vp}_n, \underset{\sim}{E}^{\theta}_n, \underset{\sim}{\Sigma}_n, \underset{\sim}{K}_n, \underset{\sim}{R}_n$

A vector of current pseudo loads is kept permanently up-to-date

$$\underset{\sim}{V}_n = \underset{\sim}{R}_n + \underset{\sim}{B}^{T}\underset{\sim}{C}\,\underset{\sim}{D}\,\underset{\sim}{E}^{\theta}_n + \underset{\sim}{B}^{T}\underset{\sim}{C}\,\underset{\sim}{D}\,\underset{\sim}{E}^{vp}_n - \underset{\sim}{B}^{T}\underset{\sim}{C}\,\underset{\sim}{\Sigma}' \tag{33}$$

Increments of hidden variables and pseudo loads are calculated over a time interval $\Delta t_n = t_{n+1} - t_n$

$$\begin{cases} \Delta \underset{\sim}{E}^{\theta}_n = \dot{\underset{\sim}{E}}^{\theta}_{mean}\,\Delta t_n \\ \underset{\sim}{E}^{\theta}_{n+1} = \underset{\sim}{E}^{\theta}_n + \Delta \underset{\sim}{E}^{\theta}_n \end{cases} \tag{34a}$$

$$\begin{cases} \Delta \underset{\sim}{E}^{vp}_n = \dot{\underset{\sim}{E}}^{vp}_{mean}\,\Delta t_n \\ \underset{\sim}{E}^{vp}_{n+1} = \underset{\sim}{E}^{vp}_n + \Delta \underset{\sim}{E}^{vp}_n \end{cases} \tag{34b}$$

$$\begin{cases} \Delta \underset{\sim}{\mathbb{K}}_n = \dot{\underset{\sim}{\mathbb{K}}}_{mean}\, \Delta t_n \\ \underset{\sim}{\mathbb{K}}_{n+1} = \underset{\sim}{\mathbb{K}}_n + \Delta \underset{\sim}{\mathbb{K}}_n \end{cases} \tag{34c}$$

$$\begin{cases} \Delta \underset{\sim}{R}_n = \dot{\underset{\sim}{R}}_{mean}\, \Delta t_n \\ \underset{\sim}{R}_{n+1} = \underset{\sim}{R}_n + \Delta \underset{\sim}{R}_n \end{cases} \tag{34d}$$

$$\begin{cases} \Delta \underset{\sim}{V}_n = \Delta \underset{\sim}{R}_n + \underset{\sim}{\mathbb{B}}^T \underset{\sim}{\mathbb{C}}\, \underset{\sim}{\mathbb{D}}\, \Delta \underset{\sim}{\mathbb{E}}_n^{\theta} + \underset{\sim}{\mathbb{B}}^T \underset{\sim}{\mathbb{C}}\, \underset{\sim}{\mathbb{D}}\, \Delta \underset{\sim}{\mathbb{E}}_n^{vp} \\ \underset{\sim}{V}_{n+1} = \underset{\sim}{V}_n + \Delta \underset{\sim}{V}_n \end{cases} \tag{34e}$$

and the total displacements, strains and stresses are fully recalculated at time t_{n+1}

$$\underset{\sim}{\delta}_{n+1} = \underset{\sim}{K}^{-1}\, \underset{\sim}{V}_{n+1} \tag{35a}$$

$$\underset{\sim}{\mathbb{E}}_{n+1} = \underset{\sim}{\mathbb{B}}\; \underset{\sim}{\delta}_{n+1} \tag{35b}$$

$$\underset{\sim}{\Sigma}_{n+1} = \underset{\sim}{\mathbb{D}} \left(\underset{\sim}{\mathbb{E}}_{n+1} - \underset{\sim}{\mathbb{E}}^{\theta}_{n+1} - \underset{\sim}{\mathbb{E}}^{vp}_{n+1} \right) + \underset{\sim}{\Sigma}' \tag{35c}$$

so that nodal equilibrium is maintained exactly at all stages of the computations. This procedure is slightly different from that presented earlier by ZIENKIEWICZ and CORMEAU[28] since it avoids the possible accumulation of errors due to the summation of incremental displacements; the proposed process, however, would not apply in the case of nonlinear elastic properties, where $\underset{\sim}{K}_T$ is to be used with incremental displacements only.

5.2 Time intervals selection

Finite time intervals add new errors to the usual finite element space discretization errors. Though a constant time step is the simplest procedure, it is uneconomic near steady state if it is chosen as to give accurate results in early transient stages. A variable interval is desirable, increasing when stresses approach stationary and decreasing when the visco-plastic flow accelerates (when strain softening occurs in highly stressed regions or upon instantaneous load application).

Two empirical criteria were used with success:

Criterion 1: limitation of the incremental visco-plastic strains

$$\Delta t_n \leqslant \min_I \left\{ \tau \frac{\left[2\left(\varepsilon_x^2 + \varepsilon_y^2 + \varepsilon_z^2\right) + \left(\gamma_{yz}^2 + \gamma_{zx}^2 + \gamma_{xy}^2\right) \right]^{1/2}}{\left[2\left(\dot{\varepsilon}_x^{vp^2} + \dot{\varepsilon}_y^{vp^2} + \dot{\varepsilon}_z^{vp^2}\right) + \left(\dot{\gamma}_{yz}^{vp^2} + \dot{\gamma}_{zx}^{vp^2} + \dot{\gamma}_{xy}^{vp^2}\right) \right]^{1/2}} \right\} \qquad n=0,1,2,\dots \tag{36}$$

where $\min_I$ is the minimum taken over all the integrating points in Ω and where τ is a time increment parameter specified by the user. Practical experience indicates the ranges $0.1<\tau<0.15$ for simple problems of contained plastic flow

$0.02<\tau<0.05$ for problems of stress concentrations on structures loaded slightly below their static bearing capacity.

This criterion is well behaved in transient analysis but fails if steady state conditions are reached for stresses and viscoplastic strains; hence the introduction of

Criterion 2: limitation of the growth of successive steps

$$\Delta t_{n+1} \leq k \, \Delta t_n \qquad n=1,2,\cdots \tag{37}$$

In all results presented herein, a value $k=1.5$ was assumed. SUTHERLAND[17] reported the range $1.2 \leq k \leq 2$ in a transient creep analysis.

These two criteria do not offer an absolute safety regarding the propagation of truncation and roundoff errors; for most problems of contained visco-plastic flows, however, a plastically admissible stress vector $\underset{\sim}{\Sigma}$ is generally achieved before significant instabilities manifest themselves.

For visco-plastic laws where the second order derivatives $\ddot{\underset{\sim}{\varepsilon}}^{vp}$ can be computed easily, CHABOCHE[5] reported a more elaborate method based on the second order TAYLOR expansion of the visco-plastic strains;

$$\Delta t = \frac{2\eta^*}{\sup\limits_{\substack{i,j=1,2,3\\ \underset{\sim}{x}\in\Omega}} \left| \dfrac{\ddot{\varepsilon}_{ij}^{vp}(\underset{\sim}{x},t)}{\dot{\varepsilon}_{ij}^{vp}(\underset{\sim}{x},t)} \right|} \tag{38}$$

where η^* is a precision parameter; here the stress velocities $\dot{\underset{\sim}{\sigma}}$ must be calculated at each step.

5.3 Some schemes for integration in the time domain

So far, the mean rates of Eqns. (34) have been left undefined. While exact values can be computed for known quantities $\underset{\sim}{E}^{\theta}$, $\underset{\sim}{R}$ only approximate values can be used for the unknown hidden variables

$$\underset{\sim}{Y} = \left\{ \begin{matrix} \underset{\sim}{E}^{vp} \\ \underset{\sim}{K} \end{matrix} \right\} \tag{39}$$

The simplest, and crudest, approximation is EULER's rule

$$\dot{\underset{\sim}{Y}}_{mean} = \dot{\underset{\sim}{Y}}_n \tag{40}$$

giving a per step truncation error on $\underset{\sim}{Y}$ $O(\Delta t^2)$ and being unstable when the steps exceed a critical value $\Delta t > \Delta t_{crit}$ which is generally stress dependent and difficult to estimate. It was also found that EULER's rule tends to overestimate $\underset{\sim}{E}^{vp}$ and can cause premature collapse of elastic/visco-perfectly-plastic structures loaded below their bearing capacity. Despite these undesirable features,

EULER's rule remains attractive because of its simplicity.

More accurate results can be obtained from the trapezoidal rule

$$\dot{Y}_{mean} = \frac{1}{2}\left(\dot{Y}_{n+1} + \dot{Y}_{n}\right) \tag{41}$$

but since quantities at t_{n+1} cannot be expressed explicitly as functions of quantities at t_n, an iterative scheme must be used:

predictor $$\underset{\sim}{Y}^{(1)}_{n+1} = \underset{\sim}{Y}_n + \Delta t\, \dot{\underset{\sim}{Y}}_n \tag{42a}$$

corrector $$\underset{\sim}{Y}^{(i+1)}_{n+1} = \underset{\sim}{Y}_n + \frac{\Delta t}{2}\left(\dot{\underset{\sim}{Y}}_n + \dot{\underset{\sim}{Y}}^{(i)}_{n+1}\right) \qquad i = 1, 2, \cdots \tag{42b}$$

The predictor and each repetition of the corrector involve a complete resolution (34b-c-e, 35 a-b-c). If iterations converge, the trapezoidal rule (41) is satisfied, providing a per step error on $\underset{\sim}{Y}$ $O(\Delta t^3)$. This is true even when only one cycle of the corrector is performed (HEUN's rule); sincere there is no guarantee that continued iterations would yield more accurate results in the end, HEUN's rule is preferred for reasons of economy.

Convergence of iterations require the time intervals to obey precisely the same condition as necessary for stability of EULER's and HEUN's rules; this could possibly offer a method of error control during the computations.

In a variant of the midpoint rule, averaged values of σ, ε^{vp}, κ are considered:

predictor $$\underset{\sim}{Y}^{(1)}_{n+1} = \underset{\sim}{Y}_n + \Delta t\, \dot{\underset{\sim}{Y}}_n \tag{43a}$$

corrector $$\underset{\sim}{Y}^{(i+1)}_{n+1} = \underset{\sim}{Y}_n + \Delta t\, \dot{\underset{\sim}{Y}}^{(i)}_{\frac{2n+1}{2}} \tag{43b}$$

where $$\dot{\underset{\sim}{Y}}^{(i)}_{\frac{2n+1}{2}} = \dot{\underset{\sim}{Y}}\left(\frac{\sigma_n + \sigma^{(i)}_{n+1}}{2}, \frac{\varepsilon^{vp}_n + \varepsilon^{vp(i)}_{n+1}}{2}, \frac{\kappa_n + \kappa^{(i)}_{n+1}}{2}\right) \tag{43c}$$

Converged iterations do not give a standard numerical integration formula. The converged and one-cycle midpoint rules have both a per step error on $\underset{\sim}{Y}$ $O(\Delta t^3)$ and appear to have a behaviour very similar to their trapezoidal equivalents.

5.4 Storage requirements

The amount of computer resources needed increases when predictor corrector methods are used; particular attention must be paid to integrating points data which are frequently accessed during the computations, whose transfers between central memory and backing store should be optimised (if any) and whose storage requirements are given in TABLE 1.

TABLE 1

Problem type	Algorithm	Time stepping	$\underset{\sim}{E}^{vp}_n$	$\dot{\underset{\sim}{E}}^{vp}_n$	$\underset{\sim}{\Sigma}_n$	$\underset{\sim}{K}_n$	$\dot{\underset{\sim}{K}}_n$	$\underset{\sim}{E}^{vp}_{n+1}$	$\underset{\sim}{K}_{n+1}$	Integrating points Storage	Example (K)
PP	E	C	*							$N x I_e x d\varepsilon$	1.6
IH	E	C	*			*				$N x I_e x (d_\varepsilon +1)$	2
PP	E	V	*	*						$2 x N x I_e x d_\varepsilon$	3.2
IH	E	V	*	*		*	*			$2 x N x I_e x (d_\varepsilon +1)$	4
PP	T	V	*	*				*		$3 x N x I_e x d\varepsilon$	4.8
IH	T	V	*	*		*	*	*	*	$3 x N x I_e x (d_\varepsilon +1)$	6
PP	M	V	*		*			*		$N x I_e x (2d_\varepsilon + d_\sigma)$	4.8
IH	M	V	*		*	*		*	*	$N x I_e x (2d_\varepsilon + d_\sigma +2)$	5.6

PP: perfectly plastic IH: isotropic hardening E: EULER T: Trapezoidal
M: Midpoint C: constant V: variable N: number of elements I_e: nr. integ. points per element d_ε: dimension of $\underset{\sim}{\varepsilon}$ d_σ: dimension of $\underset{\sim}{\sigma}$
Example: 100 quadratic elements, axisymmetric, 2x2 Gaussian integration

6. LIMIT ANALYSIS BY THE VISCO-PLASTIC APPROACH

This section deals with two discretised bodies Ω^{p} and Ω^{vp}, subject to a proportional loading $\lambda \underset{\sim}{R}$ (where λ is the load parameter), and which are identical in all respects except for the constitutive relations of their respective materials.

For Ω^{p} an elastic/perfectly plastic associated behaviour is assumed

$$\dot{\underset{\sim}{\varepsilon}} = \underset{\sim}{D}^{-1} \dot{\underset{\sim}{\sigma}} + \dot{\lambda} \frac{\partial F}{\partial \underset{\sim}{\sigma}} \quad \begin{cases} \dot{\lambda} > 0 \text{ if } F = \varphi(\underset{\sim}{\sigma}) - Y = 0 \text{ and } \dot{F} = \dot{\varphi} = 0 \\ \dot{\lambda} = 0 \text{ if } F < 0 \text{ or } F = 0 \text{ and } \dot{F} < 0 \end{cases}$$

while for Ω^{vp} a corresponding elastic/visco (perfectly) plastic law of the associated type is postulated

$$\dot{\underset{\sim}{\varepsilon}} = \underset{\sim}{D}^{-1} \dot{\underset{\sim}{\sigma}} + \gamma \left\langle \phi\left(\frac{F}{F_0}\right) \right\rangle \frac{\partial F}{\partial \underset{\sim}{\sigma}} \quad \begin{cases} \langle \phi \rangle = \phi \quad \text{if } F > 0 \\ \langle \phi \rangle = 0 \quad \text{if } F \leq 0 \\ \phi \text{ satisfies conditions (b) sub Eq. 13} \\ \gamma > 0 \qquad F_0 > 0 \end{cases}$$

Under the additional assumptions that

$\varphi(\underset{\sim}{\sigma})$ is a homogeneous function of degree $\mu > 0$

$\varphi(\underset{\sim}{\sigma}) - Y = 0$ represents a non-concave surface in the space of $\underset{\sim}{\sigma}$

it is possible to prove two bound theorems:

lower bound theorem

If, under the constant loads $\lambda_L \underset{\sim}{R}$, total stationarity conditions are reached in Ω^{vp} such that $\dot{\underset{\sim}{\Sigma}} = 0$ and $\dot{\underset{\sim}{E}} = 0$, then $\lambda_L \leq \lambda_c^p$ where the latter denotes the perfectly plastic collapse load parameter associated with Ω^p and $\underset{\sim}{R}$.

This is an immediate application of the well known lower bound theorem of DRUCKER, PRAGER and GREENBERG[7], since at total stationarity, $\underset{\sim}{\Sigma}$ is plastically admissible and in equilibrium with $\lambda_L \underset{\sim}{R}$.

upper bound theorem

If, under the constant loads $\lambda_U \underset{\sim}{R}$, partial stationarity conditions are reached in Ω^{vp} such that $\dot{\underset{\sim}{\Sigma}} = 0$ and $\dot{\underset{\sim}{E}}$ = constant $\neq 0$, then $\lambda_c^p < \lambda_U$

The proof relies on the fact that, if $\underset{\sim}{\Sigma}^*$ is an arbitrary plastically admissible 'structural' stress vector, $(\underset{\sim}{\Sigma}^T - \underset{\sim}{\Sigma}^{*T}) \dot{\underset{\sim}{E}} > 0$, and follows lines very similar to those of the lower bound theorem.

These theorems bear out a very useful feature of the visco-plastic approach in limit analysis: whatever constant loads act on a structure, the final viscoplastic results will indicate their position with respect to the corresponding collapse loads. Therefore, the safety of a structure designed to bear specific maximum service loads can be tested by a unique visco-plastic analysis under full loads; this contrasts with the incremental elasto-plastic approach where load increments must be specified ab initio according to some predicted value of λ_c^p , an estimate that is often not available with great accuracy.

7. APPLICATION

As a first example, a rectangular plate of aspect ratio 2/1, unit thickness and initially free of stresses, is clamped to a rigid support and instantaneously cooled the restraint put on shrinkage strains near the fixed edge induces stresses which are assumed to violate the static yield condition of the plate material considered to be in a state of plane stress. Symmetry permits to analyze only a half-plate, as shown on Fig. 1 where the element subdivision is refined in the region of the expected stress concentration.

Elastic and asymptotic elastic/visco-plastic displacement fields are almost identical, except for the stress peak region where a slight increase of displacements, parallel to the support, is observed. The stress reduction is therefore mainly due to relaxation at quasi constant total deformation.

Elastic and asymptotic stress distributions (Fig. 2) show a significant stress variation along the entire bonded edge while the plastic straining

$$\bar{\varepsilon}_p = \int_0^\infty \dot{\kappa}\, dt \qquad (\dot{\kappa} : \text{strain hardening form, Appendix II})$$

remains localised at the corners.

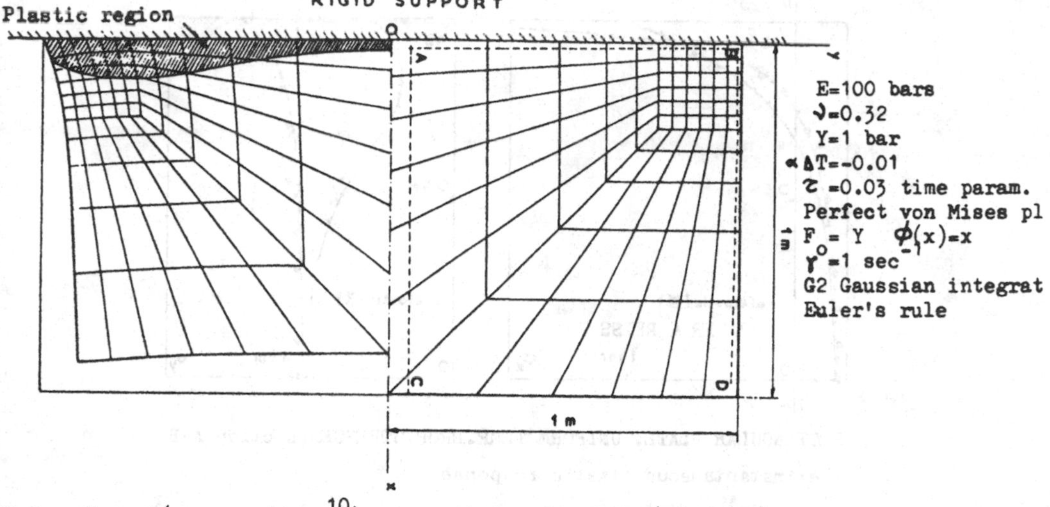

Deformed mesh(exaggeration $\frac{10}{1}$)   Mesh subdivision(96 elts.)

RECTANGULAR VISCO-PLASTIC PLATE. UNIFORM TEMPERATURE DROP

FIG. 1

Another typical application, concerned with limit analysis, is that of the elastic/visco-perfectly-plastic cantilever viewed on Fig. 3, and subject to either an incremental prescribed displacement or an incremented concentrated load. For comparison with bending elasto-plastic beam theory it is useful to introduce the dimensionless variables

$$\lambda = \frac{6\ell}{Y h^2} P \qquad \varphi_1 = \frac{3Eh}{2Y\ell^2} f$$

for which the theoretical load-deflection formula for the mid depth node at the free end is

$$\varphi_1 = \lambda \qquad 0 \leq \lambda \leq 1$$

$$\varphi_1 = \frac{5}{\lambda^2} - \left(\frac{1}{\lambda} + \frac{3}{\lambda^2}\right)\sqrt{3-2\lambda} \qquad 1 \leq \lambda \leq 1.5$$

Fig. 3 also illustrates the time propagation of the visco-plastic boundary when the beam is subject to a single step load increment $\lambda = 1.5$, for which no collapse was encountered.

Fig. 4 shows how various finite element results compare with beam theory. With an incremented load, again, no collapse occurred for $\lambda = 1.5$; EULER's rule failed to converge under $\lambda = 1.51$ after 50 additional time steps but HEUN's rule did reach a fully stationary state for $\lambda = 1.51$ and $\lambda = 1.52$. Incremental displacements give an even better lower bound to collapse, $\lambda_L = 1.55$; in this case, however, smaller time steps were used. There is no doubt about the lower bound character of these last results: stresses are in equilibrium with the concentrated reaction and no longer violate the yield condition when steady state is reached.

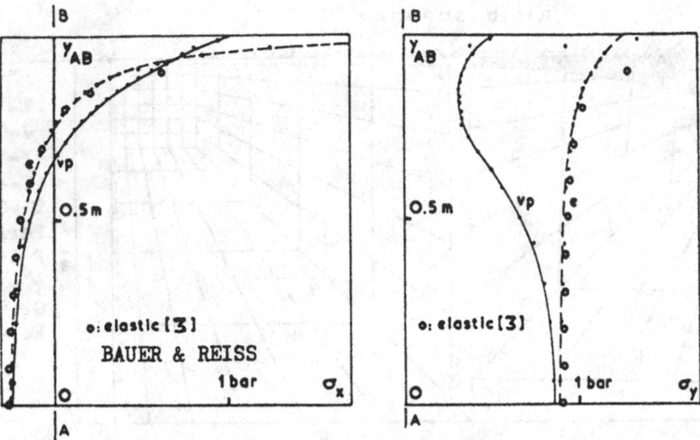

RECTANGULAR PLATE. UNIFORM TEMP.DROP.STRESSES(section A-B)

e:instantaneous elastic response

vp:asymptotic state

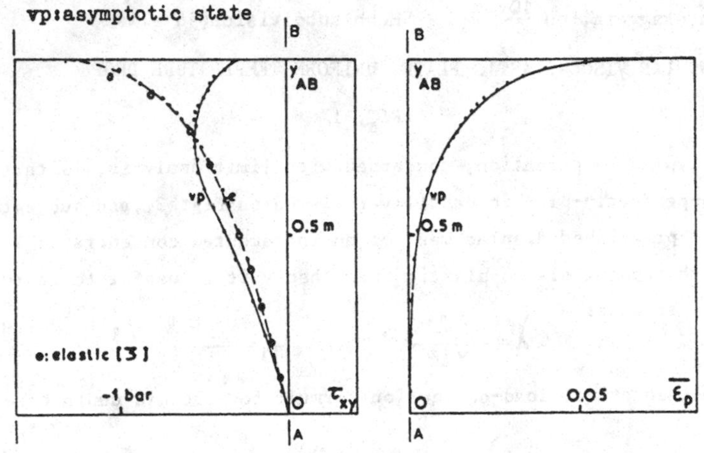

FIG. 2

The negligible difference between the deflections given by a unique algorithm (EULER here) for a load λ = 1.5, applied either in a single step or incrementally, is of prime interest and renews the suggestion that proportional incremental loading is superfluous in visco-plastic limit analysis (unless load-deflection characteristics must be fully determined).

The comparatively poor deflections predicted by the fully integrated (G3) parabolic elements confirm previous tests in favour of the reduced integration technique in isoparametric elements, while the use of more complex cubic elements had no significant effect on the results.

To finish with this problem, Fig. 5 represents the time variable stress distribution, under one step λ = 1.5, in section AA of Fig. 3.

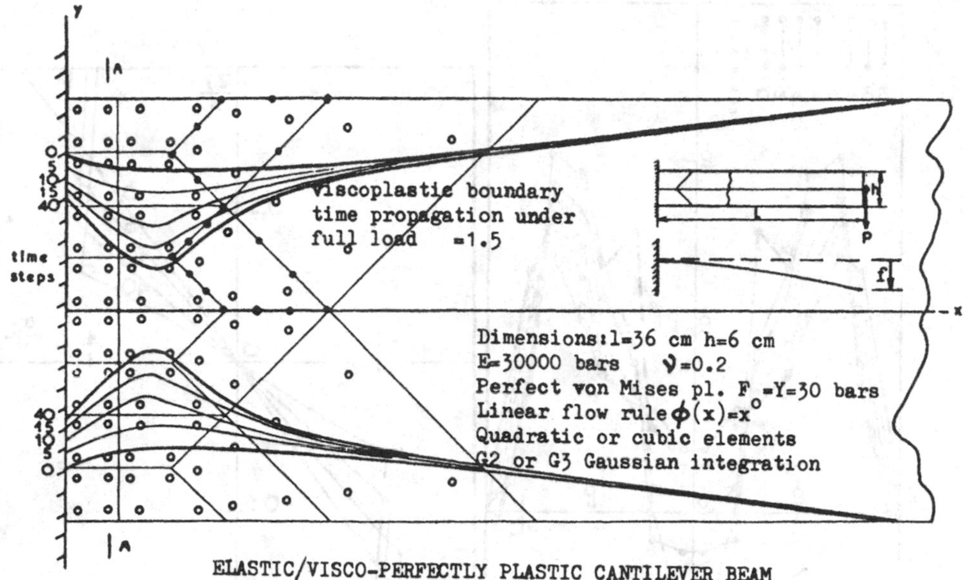

ELASTIC/VISCO-PERFECTLY PLASTIC CANTILEVER BEAM
LOAD OR DISPLACEMENT BOUNDARY CONDITIONS

FIG. 3

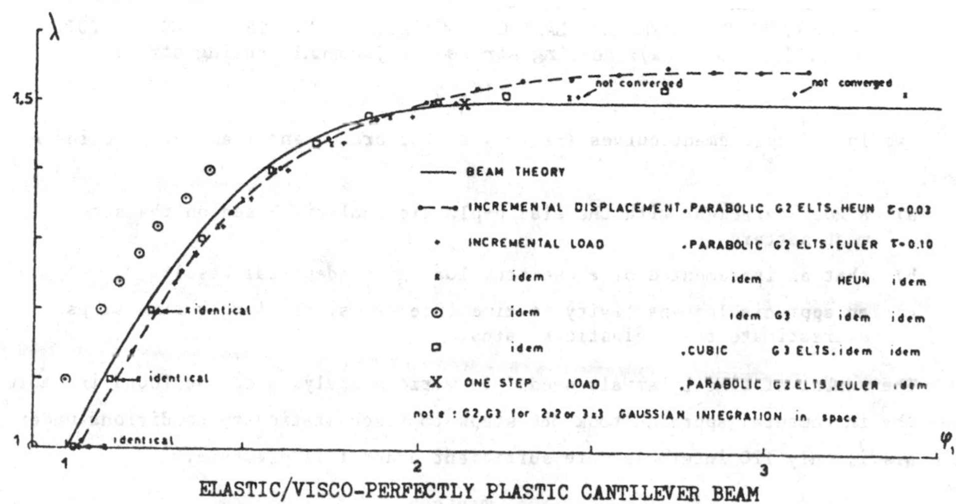

ELASTIC/VISCO-PERFECTLY PLASTIC CANTILEVER BEAM
NON-DIMENSIONAL LOAD-DEFLECTION CURVE AT FREE END.

FIG. 4

The more realistic application which follows consists of an axi-symmetric pressurized thin shell for which experimental (DINNO and GILL[6]) as well as numerical elasto-plastic results (NAYAK and ZIENKIEWICZ)[13] are available. Fig. 6 gives full details about problem specification, together with the localized deformation, at the sphere/branch junction. Quadratic isoparametric elements, 2x2 Gaussian integration and EULER's rule were used once more. The pressure was applied in a single step or incremented.

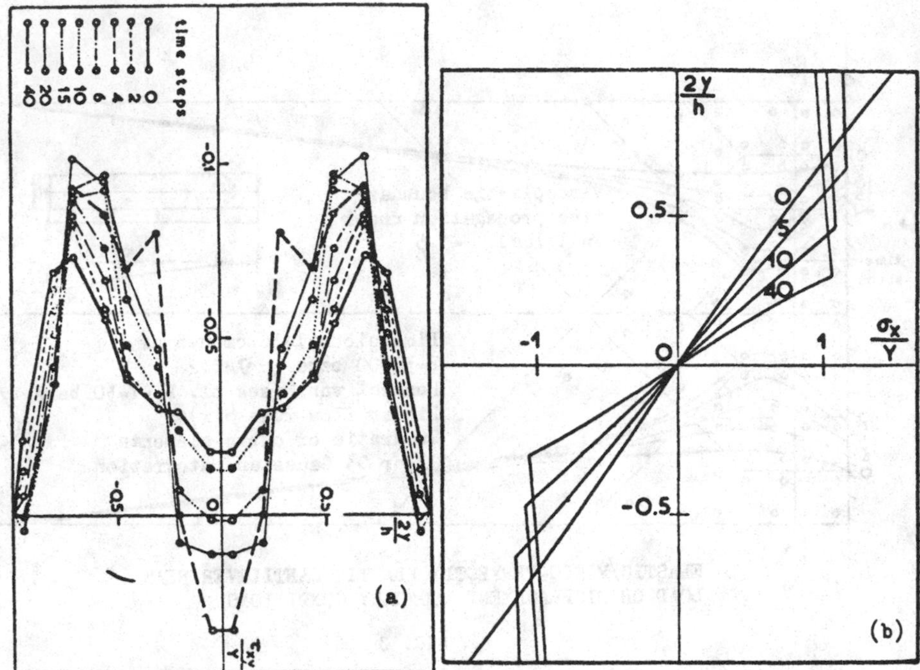

ELASTIC/VISCO-PERFECTLY PLASTIC CANTILEVER BEAM. STRESS REDISTRIBUTION IN SECTION A-A. (a):Shearing stress (b):Normal bending stress.

FIG. 5

Two load/displacement curves (Fig. 7) at the branch end T and at junction A show:

a) a good agreement with the elasto-plastic analysis based on the same mesh pattern

b) that an incremented or a one-step load give identical results

c) an appreciable sensitivity to time interval size: larger time steps overestimate the inelastic strains.

The number of time intervals needed in various analyses can be found in Table 2 When the incremental approach took 386 steps to reach stationary conditions under 1140 p.s.i, only 120 intervals were sufficient under full pressure.

TABLE 2

Incremental	p (psi)	900	950	1000	1020	1040	1060								
τ = 0.15	time steps	4	14	31	5	16	20								
Incremental	p (psi)	900	920	940	960	980	1000	1020	1040	1060	1080	1100	1120	1140	1
τ = 0.03	time steps	10	6	8	7	6	8	8	36	34	76	43	82	62 >	
One step	p (psi)	1140			1180										
τ = 0.03	time steps	120			No convergence after 400 steps										

As a last example, the relaxation of a rock mass around a lined tunnel is analyzed. In this problem, described in Figs. 8 and 9, the rock behaves like an

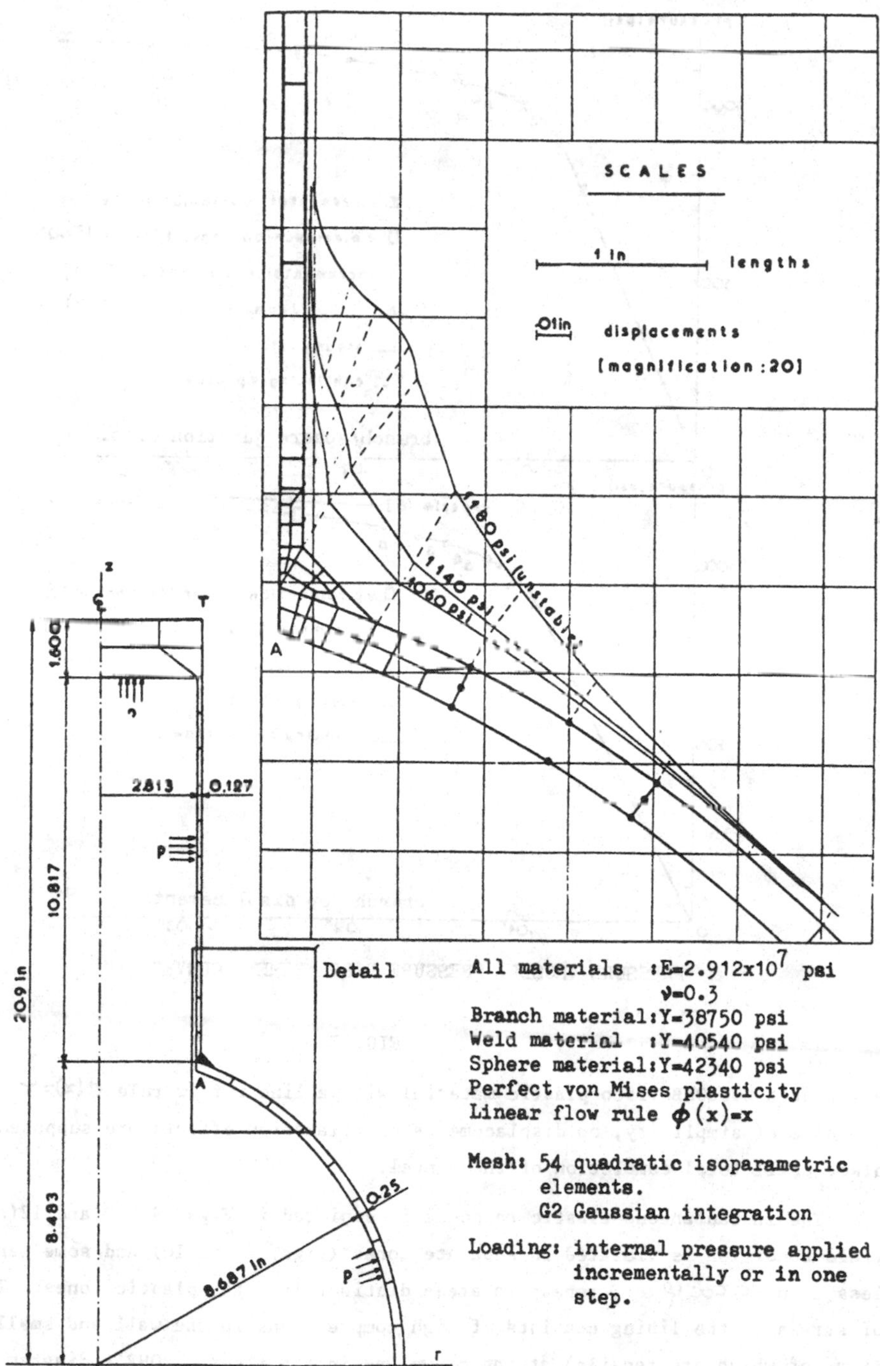

AXISYMMETRIC ELASTIC/VISCO-PERFECTLY PLASTIC PRESSURE VESSEL.

FIG. 6

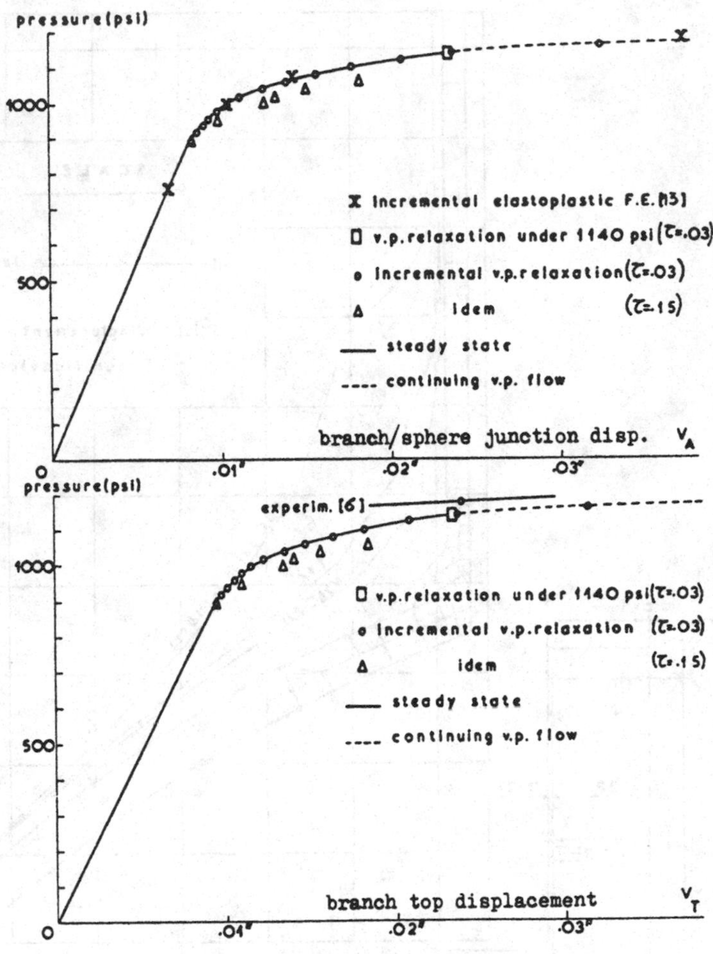

PRESSURE VESSEL: PRESSURE-DISPLACEMENT CURVES

FIG. 7

associated COULOMB visco-plastic material with a linear flow rule $\phi(x)=x$ For the sake of simplicity, no displacements or relaxation effects are supposed to take place until total completion of the tunnel.

The instantaneous elastic response is depicted in Figs. 9, 10 and 12(a). The yield condition is violated in separate zones (Figs. 8 and 10) and some tensions, less than $c \cot \varphi$, appear in areas distinct from the plastic zones. The state of stress in the lining consists of high compressions in the wall and small stresses (some of which are tensile) at the crown and in the floor. MOHR's diagram (Fig. 11) suggests that a considerable proportion of the loads are transmitted to the lining by shearing stresses distributed along the inclined parts of the rock/lining interface.

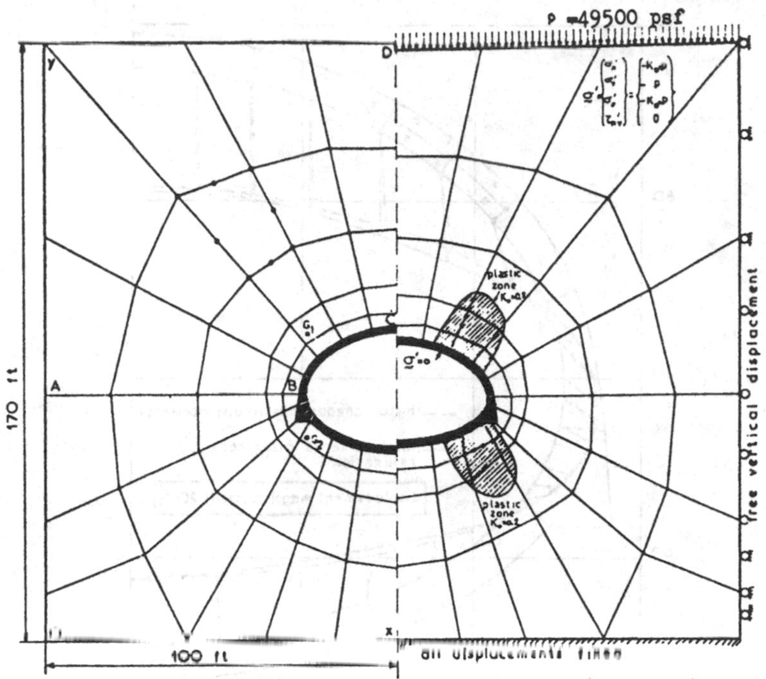

Mesh subdivision(63 quad.els) Deformed mesh(exag.100)
Lining: $E=4.32\times10^{8}$ psf $\nu=0.15$
Rock: $E=0.72\times10^{8}$ psf $\nu=0.20$ $C=14400$ psf $\varphi=\varphi'=30°$
Mohr-Coulomb perfect plasticity(associated); $F_0=C\cos\varphi$; $\phi(x)=x$
Euler's rule; time increment parameter $\tau=0.05$
ROCK RELAXATION AROUND A LINED TUNNEL

FIG. 8

Asymptotic displacements δ_∞ obtained after 27 time intervals are given in Fig. 8 and their inelastic components $\delta_\infty - \delta_0$ show (Fig. 10) a shortening of the upper and lower vaults and an elongation of the lining wall, thus causing a transfer of compressions from wall to vaults. The mechanism of this transfer appears from the orientation of the slip facets families S_1 and S_2 in Fig. 10: MOHR's diagram shows a reduction of the shearing stress and an increase of the normal stress acting upon these facets, a family of which remains parallel to the rock /lining interface.

Finally Fig. 12(b) depicts the asymptotic state of stress in the lining (suppression of lining tensions) as well as shrunken rock tensile zones. Although the present material properties did not cause pronounced plastic flow, the general conclusions drawn here remained valid, with amplification, when the cohesion was reduced, resulting in the expansion of visco-plastic zones and greater stress variations in the lining.

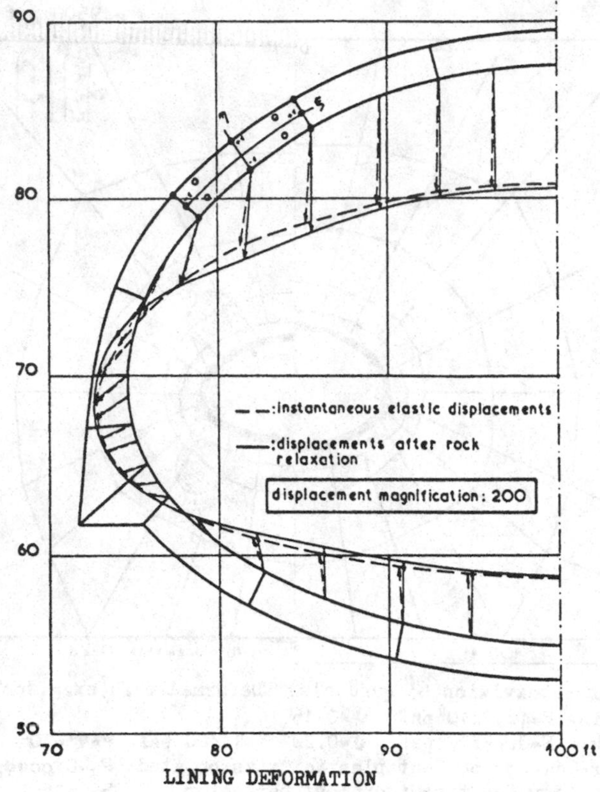

LINING DEFORMATION

FIG. 9

8. CONCLUDING REMARKS

Due to space limitation, only four examples have been presented and discussed. Problems involving non-linear flow rules, isotropic hardening or softening and non-associated viscoplastic laws have been solved without creating any particular difficulty and bear out the versatility of the method in materially non-linear analyses. Though the present formulation deals with isotropic situations, it should be possible to extend it to anisotropic cases such as laminated and joint materials.

The approximations related to the visco-plastic approach (finite element space discretization and numerical integration in the time domain) stand out to be well defined; this contrasts with the elasto-plastic approach, where several computationa artifices such as corrections in plastic stress estimates must be used to restore the stresses to the correct yield surface and where equilibrium must be permanently checked.

However the visco-plastic method was shown to lead ultimately to a non-linear system of first order differential equations, the numerical solution of which can, in principle, be obtained by a great variety of classical procedures.

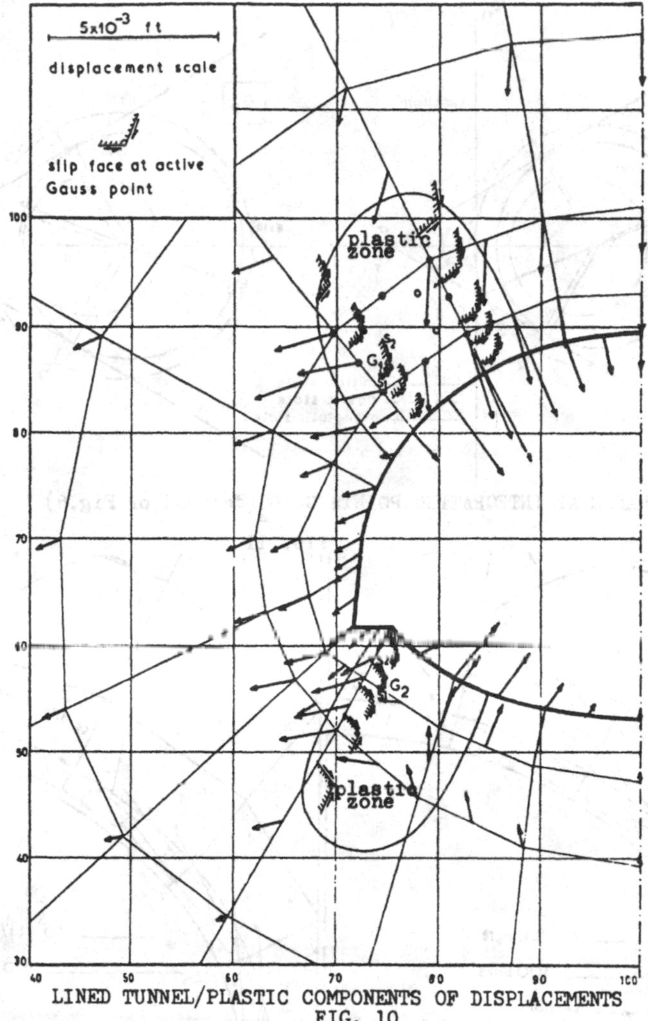

LINED TUNNEL/PLASTIC COMPONENTS OF DISPLACEMENTS
FIG. 10

In practical engineering applications, extreme accuracy is not the goal. An ideal scheme of integration should:

- minimize the number of time intervals for a prescribed accuracy compatible with engineering practice
- prevent the appearance of numerical instabilities or, at least, detect them and take appropriate measures after their detection
- give an estimate of the truncation errors cumulated as the integration proceeds in the time domain
- remain reasonably simple to implement on computers (coding and especially storage requirements)
- be conceived to deal with systems of realistic size (at least 500 simultaneous differential equations)

To the authors' knowledge, such an ideal scheme has not yet been produced in relation to visco-plasticity applications and opens a wide field to future research.

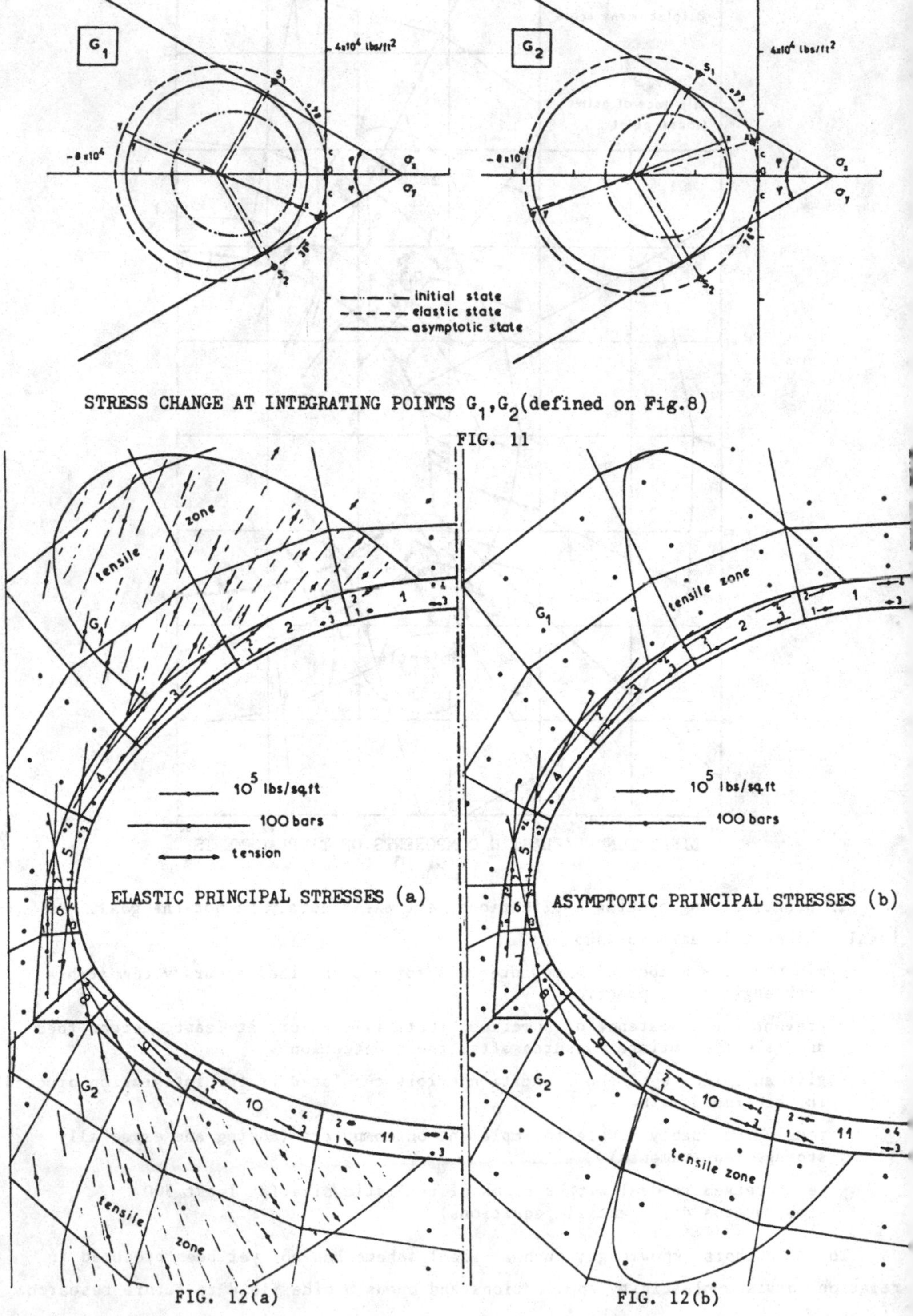

STRESS CHANGE AT INTEGRATING POINTS G_1, G_2 (defined on Fig.8)

FIG. 11

FIG. 12(a)

FIG. 12(b)

APPENDIX I: FUNCTIONS OF STRESS INVARIANTS

Let $\quad \sigma_m = \frac{1}{3}\sigma_{ii} \quad s_{ij} = \sigma_{ij} - \sigma_m \delta_{ij} \quad J_2 = \frac{1}{2} s_{ij} s_{ji} \quad J_3 = \frac{1}{3} s_{ij} s_{jk} s_{ki}$

The derivatives of the stress invariants may be written as

$$\frac{\partial \sigma_m}{\partial \underset{\sim}{\sigma}} = \underset{\sim}{M}_{-1} \underset{\sim}{\sigma} \qquad \frac{\partial J_2}{\partial \underset{\sim}{\sigma}} = \underset{\sim}{M}_{0} \underset{\sim}{\sigma} \qquad \frac{\partial J_3}{\partial \underset{\sim}{\sigma}} = \underset{\sim}{M}_{1} \underset{\sim}{\sigma}$$

where $\quad \underset{\sim}{M}_{-1}, \underset{\sim}{M}_{0}, \underset{\sim}{M}_{1}$ are symmetric matrices

$$\underset{\sim}{M}_{-1} = \frac{1}{9\sigma_m} \left[\begin{array}{ccc|c} 1 & 1 & 1 & \\ 1 & 1 & 1 & 0 \\ 1 & 1 & 1 & \\ \hline & 0 & & 0 \end{array}\right] \qquad \underset{\sim}{M}_{0} = \left[\begin{array}{ccc|ccc} \frac{2}{3} & -\frac{1}{3} & -\frac{1}{3} & & & \\ -\frac{1}{3} & \frac{2}{3} & -\frac{1}{3} & & 0 & \\ -\frac{1}{3} & -\frac{1}{3} & \frac{2}{3} & & & \\ \hline & & & 2 & 0 & 0 \\ & 0 & & 0 & 2 & 0 \\ & & & 0 & 0 & 2 \end{array}\right]$$

$$\underset{\sim}{M}_{1} = \left[\begin{array}{ccc|ccc} -\frac{1}{3}\sigma_m + \frac{7}{9}\sigma_x & \frac{\sigma_z - \sigma_m}{3} & \frac{\sigma_y - \sigma_m}{3} & -\frac{2}{3}\tau_{yz} & \frac{1}{3}\tau_{zx} & \frac{1}{3}\tau_{xy} \\ & -\frac{1}{3}\sigma_m + \frac{7}{9}\sigma_y & \frac{\sigma_x - \sigma_m}{3} & \frac{1}{3}\tau_{yz} & -\frac{2}{3}\tau_{zx} & \frac{1}{3}\tau_{xy} \\ \text{symm.} & & -\frac{1}{3}\sigma_m + \frac{7}{9}\sigma_z & \frac{1}{3}\tau_{yz} & \frac{1}{3}\tau_{zx} & -\frac{2}{3}\tau_{xy} \\ \hline & & & \sigma_m - \sigma_x & \tau_{xy} & \tau_{zx} \\ & \text{symm.} & & & \sigma_m - \sigma_y & \tau_{yz} \\ & & & \text{symm.} & & \sigma_m - \sigma_z \end{array}\right]$$

if $\quad \mathcal{A} = \mathcal{A}(\sigma_m, J_2, J_3)$ one has

$$\begin{aligned} \dot{\mathcal{A}} &= \frac{\partial \mathcal{A}}{\partial \underset{\sim}{\sigma}} \dot{\underset{\sim}{\sigma}} \\ &= \left(\frac{\partial \mathcal{A}}{\partial \sigma_m} \frac{\partial \sigma_m}{\partial \underset{\sim}{\sigma}} + \frac{\partial \mathcal{A}}{\partial J_2} \frac{\partial J_2}{\partial \underset{\sim}{\sigma}} + \frac{\partial \mathcal{A}}{\partial J_3} \frac{\partial J_3}{\partial \underset{\sim}{\sigma}} \right) \dot{\underset{\sim}{\sigma}} \\ &= \underset{\sim}{\sigma}^T \left(\frac{\partial \mathcal{A}}{\partial \sigma_m} \underset{\sim}{M}_{-1} + \frac{\partial \mathcal{A}}{\partial J_2} \underset{\sim}{M}_{0} + \frac{\partial \mathcal{A}}{\partial J_3} \underset{\sim}{M}_{1} \right) \dot{\underset{\sim}{\sigma}} \\ &= \underset{\sim}{\sigma}^T \underset{\sim}{M} \dot{\underset{\sim}{\sigma}} = \dot{\underset{\sim}{\sigma}}^T \underset{\sim}{M} \underset{\sim}{\sigma} \end{aligned}$$

where $\quad \underset{\sim}{M}$ is a symmetric, stress dependent, matrix.

Similarly, $\quad$ if $\quad Q = Q(\sigma_m, J_2, J_3, \underset{\sim}{\varepsilon}^{vp}, \kappa)$ one has

$$\gamma \langle \phi(\tfrac{F}{F_0}) \rangle \frac{\partial Q}{\partial \underset{\sim}{\sigma}} = \underset{\sim}{\Gamma} \underset{\sim}{\sigma}$$

where

$$\underset{\sim}{\Gamma} = \gamma \langle \phi(\tfrac{F}{F_0}) \rangle \left(\frac{\partial Q}{\partial \sigma_m} \underset{\sim}{M}_{-1} + \frac{\partial Q}{\partial J_2} \underset{\sim}{M}_{0} + \frac{\partial Q}{\partial J_3} \underset{\sim}{M}_{1} \right)$$

APPENDIX II: SPECIFIC VISCOPLATICITY FORMS

Together with the notation of Appendix I, let

$$\theta = \frac{1}{3} \arcsin\left[\frac{-3\sqrt{3}}{2} \quad \frac{J_3}{J_2^{3/2}}\right] \qquad -\frac{\pi}{6} < \theta < \frac{\pi}{6} \qquad \varepsilon = \frac{\pi}{180}$$

Yield functions and viscoplastic potentials

Criterion	Yield function	Viscoplastic potential
von Mises	$F = \sqrt{3J_2} - Y(K)$ $\quad F_o = Y(K)$ if $Y \neq 0$ $Y(K)$: uniaxial yield stress	$Q = \sqrt{3J_2}$
Tresca	$F = 2\sqrt{J_2}\cos\theta - Y(K)$ $\quad F_o = Y(K)$ if $Y \neq 0$ $Y(K)$: uniaxial yield stress	$Q = 2\sqrt{J_2}\cos\theta \qquad 0 \leq \lvert\theta\rvert \leq \frac{\pi}{6} - \varepsilon$ $Q = \sqrt{3J_2} \qquad \frac{\pi}{6} - \varepsilon < \lvert\theta\rvert \leq \frac{\pi}{6}$
Drucker-Prager	$F = \frac{2\sqrt{3}\sin\varphi}{3-\sin\varphi}\sigma_m + \sqrt{J_2} - \frac{2\sqrt{3}C\cos\varphi}{3-\sin\varphi}$ $\quad F_o = \frac{2\sqrt{3}C\cos\varphi}{3-\sin\varphi}$ if $C \neq 0$ φ: friction angle C: cohesion	$Q = \frac{2\sqrt{3}\sin\varphi'}{3-\sin\varphi'}\sigma_m + \sqrt{J_2}$ φ': flow function angle
Mohr-Coulomb	$F = \sin\varphi\,\sigma_m + \left(\cos\theta - \frac{1}{\sqrt{3}}\sin\theta\sin\varphi\right)\sqrt{J_2} - C\cos\varphi$ $F_o = C\cos\varphi$ if $C \neq 0$ φ: friction angle C: cohesion	$Q = \sin\varphi'\sigma_m + \left(\cos\theta - \frac{1}{\sqrt{3}}\sin\theta\sin\varphi'\right)\sqrt{J_2} \qquad 0 \leq \lvert\theta\rvert \leq \frac{\pi}{6} - \varepsilon$ $Q = \sin\varphi'\sigma_m + \frac{\sqrt{3}}{2}\left(1 - \frac{1}{3}\sin\varphi'\right)\sqrt{J_2} \qquad \frac{\pi}{6} - \varepsilon < \theta \leq \frac{\pi}{6}$ $Q = \sin\varphi'\sigma_m + \frac{\sqrt{3}}{2}\left(1 + \frac{1}{3}\sin\varphi'\right)\sqrt{J_2} \qquad -\frac{\pi}{6} \leq \theta < -\frac{\pi}{6} + \varepsilon$

Isotropic hardening

$$\dot{K} = \left[\frac{2}{3}\left(\dot{\varepsilon}_x^{vp^2} + \dot{\varepsilon}_y^{vp^2} + \dot{\varepsilon}_z^{vp^2}\right) + \frac{1}{3}\left(\dot{\gamma}_{yz}^{vp^2} + \dot{\gamma}_{zx}^{vp^2} + \dot{\gamma}_{xy}^{vp^2}\right)\right]^{1/2} = \dot{\bar{\varepsilon}}^{vp} \quad \text{for strain hardening}$$

$$\dot{K} = \sigma_x\dot{\varepsilon}_x^{vp} + \sigma_y\dot{\varepsilon}_y^{vp} + \sigma_z\dot{\varepsilon}_z^{vp} + \tau_{yz}\dot{\gamma}_{yz}^{vp} + \tau_{zx}\dot{\gamma}_{zx}^{vp} + \tau_{xy}\dot{\gamma}_{xy}^{vp} \quad \text{for work hardening}$$

APPENDIX III: GAUSSIAN INTEGRATION RULES

Element characteristics			Plane Stress & Plane Strain					Axial symmetry						
displacement and velocity fields N_i	geometrical interpolation N'_i	sketch	$\int_\Omega d\Omega$ exact	$\underset{\sim}{K}$ exact	$\underset{\sim}{K}$ lim ++	$\int_\Omega \underset{\sim}{B}^T \underset{\sim}{\sigma} d\Omega$ $\int_\Omega \underset{\sim}{B}^T \underset{\sim}{D} \underset{\sim}{\varepsilon}^{vp} d\Omega$ $\int_\Omega \underset{\sim}{B}^T \underset{\sim}{D} \underset{\sim}{\varepsilon}^{\theta} d\Omega$ +++	$\int_\Omega \underset{\sim}{N}^T \underset{\sim}{f} d\Omega$ ++++	$\int_\Omega d\Omega$ exact	$\int_\Omega d\Omega$ approx □	$\underset{\sim}{K}$ exact	$\underset{\sim}{K}$ approx	$\underset{\sim}{K}$ limit ++	$\int_\Omega \underset{\sim}{B}^T \underset{\sim}{\sigma} d\Omega$ $\int_\Omega \underset{\sim}{B}^T \underset{\sim}{D} \underset{\sim}{\varepsilon}^{vp} d\Omega$ $\int_\Omega \underset{\sim}{B}^T \underset{\sim}{D} \underset{\sim}{\varepsilon}^{\theta} d\Omega$ +++	$\int_\Omega \underset{\sim}{N}^T \underset{\sim}{f} d\Omega$ □□:
linear $N_i[\xi\eta]$ *	isoparametric ** $N'_i[\xi\eta]$		G1	– +	G2	G1	G2	G2	G1	–	–	G2	G2	G2
	affine**** $N'_i[\xi,\eta]$	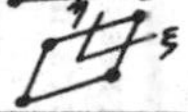	G1	G2	G2	G1	G1	G1	G1	–	G2	G2	G1	G1
quadratic $N_i[\xi^2\eta, \xi\eta^2]$	isoparametric $N'_i[\xi^2\eta, \xi\eta^2]$		G2	–	G3	G2	G3	G3	G2	–	–	G3	G3	G3
	subparametric *** $N'_i[\xi\eta]$		G1	–	G3	G2	G2	G2	G1	–	–	G3	G2	G2
	affine $N'_i[\xi,\eta]$	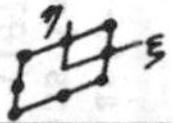	G1	G3	G3	G2	G2	G1	G1	–	G3	G3	G2	G2
cubic $N_i[\xi^3\eta, \xi\eta^3]$	isoparametric $N'_i[\xi^3\eta, \xi\eta^3]$		G3	–	G4	G3	G5	G5	G3	–	–	G4	G5	G5
	subparametric $N'_i[\xi\eta]$		G1	–	G4	G2	G3	G2	G1	–	–	G4	G3	G3
	affine $N'_i[\xi,\eta]$		G1	G4	G4	G2	G2	G1	G1	–	G4	G4	G3	G2

*the higher order terms of the polynomial in ξ, η is bracketed; ** $N'_i \equiv N_i$

***mid-side nodes linearly interpolated between corner nodes; ****constant $|J|$ throughout the element;

+the function is rational and cannot be exactly integrated by Gauss' rule; ++assuming that $|J| \rightarrow$ constant matrix when mesh is refined; +++assuming that $\underset{\sim}{\sigma}, \underset{\sim}{\varepsilon}^{vp}, \underset{\sim}{\varepsilon}^{\theta} \rightarrow$ constant values in every element;
++++assuming that $\underset{\sim}{f} \rightarrow$ constant value in every element; □ neglecting the variation of the radius x inside element
□□ : (++++ and □) simultaneously;

REFERENCES

1. APPLEBY, E. J. and PRAGER, W. 'A problem in visco-plasticity' J. Appl. Mech., 29, 381-384 (1962).

2. ARGYRIS, J. H. and SHARPF, D. W. 'Methods of elasto-plastic analysis'. Symp. on Finite Element Techniques, Stuttgart (1969).

3. BAUER, F. and REISS, E. L. 'On the numerical determination of shrinkage stresses'. A.S.M.E. Trans., J. Appl. Mech., March 1970, 123-27 (1970).

4. BINGHAM, E. C. 'Fluidity and Plasticity' Chapter VIII, 215-218, McGraw-Hill, New York (1922).

5. CHABOCHE, J. L. 'Calcul des déformations visco-plastiques d'une structure soumise à des gradients thermiques évolutifs' Faculté des Sciences d'Orsay. Paris. Thèse (1972).

6. DINNO, K. S. and GILL, S. S. 'An experimental investigation into the plastic behaviour of flush nozzles in spherical pressure vessels' Int. J. Mech. Sci., 7, 817 (1965).

7. DRUCKER, D. C., PRAGER, W. and GREENBERG, H. J. 'Extended limit design theorems for continuous media' Quart. Appl. Math., 9, 381-389 (1952).

8. FREUDENTHAL, A. M. and GEIRINGER, H. 'The mathematical theories of the inelastic continuum' Encyclopedia of Physics, Vol. VI, 229-433 (1958).

9. GREENBAUM, G. A., and RUBINSTEIN, M. F. 'Creep analysis of axisymmetric bodies using finite elements'. Nucl. Eng. and Design, 7, 4, 378-397 (1968).

10. LEMAITRE, J. 'Elasto-visco-plastic constitutive relations for quasi-static structures calculations' ONERA publication TP 1089 - Chatillon (France) (1972).

11. MARCAL, P. V., and KING, I. P. 'Elastic plastic analysis of two dimensional stress systems by the finite element method'. Int. J. Mech. Sci., 9, 143-155 (1967).

12. NAYAK, G. C. and ZIENKIEWICZ, O. C. 'Convenient form of stress invariants for plasticity' Proc. A.S.C.E., 98, ST4, 949-954 (1972).

13. NAYAK, G. C. and ZIENKIEWICZ, O. C. 'Elasto-plastic stress analysis. Generalization for various constitutive relations including strain softening'. Int. J. Num. Meths. in Eng., 5, 113-135 (1972).

14. NGUYEN, Q. S. and ZARKA, J. 'Quelques méthodes de résolution numérique en élastoplasticité classique et en élastoviscoplasticité' Séminaire Plasticité et Viscoplasticité, Ecole Polytechnique, Paris (1972).

15. PERZYNA, P. 'Fundamental problems in viscoplasticity' Advances in Applied Mechanics, 9, 243-377 (1966).

16. REINER, M. 'Rhéologie théorique' Dunod, Paris (1955)

17. SUTHERLAND, W. H. 'AXICRP. Finite element computer code for creep analysis of plane stress, plane strain and axisymmetric bodies' Nucl. Eng. and Design, 11, 269-285 (1970).

18. TREHARNE, G. 'Applications of the finite element method to the stress analysis of materials subject to creep' Ph.D. thesis, University of Wales, Swansea (1971).

19. WHITE, J. L. 'Finite elements in linear viscoelasticity' Proc. 2d. Conf. Matrix Methods Struct. Mech. AFFDL-TR-68-150, pp. 489-516, Wright-Patterson A.F.B., Ohio (1968).

20. WIERZBICKI, T. 'A thick-walled elasto-visco-plastic spherical container under stress and displacement boundary value conditions'. Archiwum Mech. Stos. 2, 15, 297-308 (1963).

21. WIERZBICKI, T. 'Impulsive loading of rigid viscoplastic plates' Int. J. Solids and Struct., 3, 635-647 (1967).

22. WIERZBICKI, T. and FLORENCE, A. L. 'A theoretical and experimental investigation of impulsively loaded clamped circular viscoplastic plates'. Int. J. Solids and Struct., 6, 553-568 (1970).

23. ZARKA, J. 'Généralisation de la théorie du potentiel multiple en viscoplasticité'. J. Mech. Phys. Solids, 20, 179-195 (1972).

24. ZIENKIEWICZ, O. C., WATSON, M. and KING, I. P. 'A numerical method of visco-elastic stress analysis' Int. J. Mech. Sci., 10, 807-827 (1968).

25. ZIENKIEWICZ, O. C. and VALLIAPPAN, S. 'Analysis of real structures for creep, plasticity and other complex constitutive laws'. Int. Conf. on Struct., Sol. Mech., Eng. Design and Civ. Eng. Mat., Southampton (1969).

26. ZIENKIEWICZ, O. C., VALLIAPPAN, S. and KING, I. P. 'Elasto-plastic solutions of engineering problems. Initial stress, finite element approach'. Int. J. Num. Meths. Eng., 1, 75-100 (1969).

27. ZIENKIEWICZ, O. C. 'The finite element method in Engineering science' McGraw-Hill, London (1971).

28. ZIENKIEWICZ, O. C. and CORMEAU, I. C. 'Viscoplasticity solution by finite element process'. Archives of Mechanics, 24, 5-6, 873-888 (1972).

SOME SUPERCONVERGENCE RESULTS FOR AN H^1-GALERKIN PROCEDURE FOR THE HEAT EQUATION

Jim Douglas, Jr., Todd Dupont, and Mary Fanett Wheeler

1. Introduction. We shall consider a Galerkin method based on the use of the inner product in the Sobolev space $H^1(I)$ introduced by Thomée and Wahlbin [4] in a more general setting for approximating the solution of the simple parabolic boundary problem

$$
\begin{aligned}
&\frac{\partial u}{\partial t} - \frac{\partial^2 u}{\partial x^2} = -f(x,t), \quad x \in I = [0,1], \quad t \in J = (0,T], \\
(1.1)\qquad &u(0,t) = u(1,t) = 0, \quad t \in J, \\
&u(x,0) = u_0(x), \quad x \in I.
\end{aligned}
$$

Let $\mathcal{M}$ denote a finite-dimensional subspace of $H^2(I) \cap H_0^1(I)$, and define a map $U : [0,T] \to \mathcal{M}$, with $U(0)$ to be determined later in a rather particular fashion, such that (the inner product being on real $L^2(I)$)

$$
(1.2)\qquad \left(\frac{\partial^2 U}{\partial x \partial t}, \frac{dv}{dx}\right) + \left(\frac{\partial^2 U}{\partial x^2}, \frac{d^2 v}{dx^2}\right) = \left(f, \frac{d^2 v}{dx^2}\right), \quad v \in \mathcal{M}, \quad t \in J.
$$

This map provides the H^1-Galerkin process to be analyzed. Existence and uniqueness of U follows whenever $f \in L^2(I \times J)$, as can be seen by choosing the test function $v = U$.

Sponsored by the United States Army under Contract No. DA-31-124-ARO-D-462 and the National Science Foundation.
University of Wisconsin - Madison Mathematics Research Center Technical Summary Report No. 1382

We shall always assume that we have a family of subspaces, $\mathcal{M} = \mathcal{M}_h$, $0 < h < 1$, satisfying the approximability condition for any function $z \in H^p(I) \cap H_0^1(I)$ given by

$$\inf_{\chi \in \mathcal{M}_h} (\|z-\chi\| + h\|z-\chi\|_1 + h^2\|z-\chi\|_2) \leq C\|z\|_p h^p, \quad 2 \leq p \leq r+1, \tag{1.3}$$

for some integer $r \geq 3$. The norms indicated above are the Sobolev norms

$$\|z\| = \|z\|_0 = \|z\|_{L^2(I)}, \quad \|z\|_k = \|z\|_{H^k(I)}.$$

With no further restriction on the subspace $\mathcal{M}$ it can be shown [4] that

$$\|u - U\|_{L^\infty(H^j)} = \operatorname{ess\,sup}_{0 \leq t \leq T} \|(u-U)(t)\|_{H^j(I)} \leq C(u)h^{r+1-j}, \quad 1 \leq j \leq 2, \tag{1.4}$$

for sufficiently smooth u, provided that $U(0)$ is chosen subject to some rather mild constraints.

The main purpose of this paper is to derive superconvergence estimates at the knots for two particular classes of subspaces. Let $\delta : 0 = x_0 < x_1 < \cdots < x_M = 1$, $0 < h_i = x_i - x_{i-1}$, $\max_i h_i = h$, $I_i = [x_{i-1}, x_i]$.

Denote by $P_r(E)$ the class of functions on I having restrictions to the set $E \subset I$ which agree on E with a polynomial of degree not greater than r. Let

$$\mathcal{M}_k(r, \delta) = \{v \in C^k(I) \mid v \in P_r(I_i),\ i = 1, \ldots, M\}$$

and set

$$\mathcal{M}_k = \{v \in \mathcal{M}_k(r, \delta) \mid v(0) = v(1) = 0\}. \tag{1.5}$$

The two families that will interest us are $\mathcal{M}_1$ and $\mathcal{M}_2$. We shall show in section 3 that, provided $U(0)$ is chosen in a particular way,

(1.6) $$|(u - U)(x_i, t)| \leq C(u)h^{2r-2}, \ \mathcal{M} = \mathcal{M}_1 \text{ or } \mathcal{M}_2,$$

and that

(1.7) $$\left|\frac{\partial}{\partial x}(u - U)(x_i, t)\right| \leq C(u)h^{2r-2}, \ \mathcal{M} = \mathcal{M}_1 .$$

The proofs of these results will be based on a quasi-projection approximation procedure introduced by the authors [1] in order to demonstrate knot superconvergence when the space $\mathcal{M}_0$ is employed in the standard Galerkin method for parabolic equations based on an L^2-inner product rather than the H^1-inner product.

The results of this paper can be extended in several ways. It is clear from the development of section 3 that, if $\bar{x} \in (0, 1)$ is a fixed point such that $\bar{x} = x_{i(\delta)}$ as $h \to 0$, the estimate (1.6) or (1.7) holds at the point $\bar{x}$ whenever the space $\mathcal{M}_k$, $k \geq 1$, is employed in (1.2) after modifying the smoothness constraint at the single knot $\bar{x}$ to be $C^2(I_{i(\delta)} \cup I_{i(\delta)+1})$ or $C^1(I_{i(\delta)} \cup I_{i(\delta)+1})$, respectively. In particular, it follows that the heat flux at the end points $x = 0$ and $x = 1$ always satisfies (1.7) for any choice of k without modification of the space. This is in marked contrast with the situation for the standard Galerkin method using $\mathcal{M}_k$ [2, 5]. It is of interest to discretize (1.2) in time in such a fashion as to preserve the superconvergence associated with the H^1-Galerkin process in the space variable; see

[1] for a collocation-in-time method that can be adapted to the present case in such a way that the estimates at the knot (x_i, t_k) would be of the form $O(h^{2r-2} + (\Delta t)^{2s})$, where piecewise-polynomials of degree s are employed in time. Finally, more general differential operators should be considered, and the authors will return to this question in another paper.

#1382

<u>2. Global Estimates</u>. Let us quickly produce an H^2 estimate similar to that of Thomée-Wahlbin [4]. Let $\zeta = u - U$. Then,

$$\left(\frac{\partial^2\zeta}{\partial x\partial t}, v'\right) + \left(\frac{\partial^2\zeta}{\partial x^2}, v''\right) = 0, \quad v \in \mathcal{M}, \ t \in J. \tag{2.1}$$

Take $v = \frac{\partial\zeta}{\partial t} + \frac{\partial}{\partial t}(\chi-u)$, $\frac{\partial\chi}{\partial t} \in \mathcal{M}$. Then,

$$\left(\frac{\partial^2\zeta}{\partial x\partial t}, \frac{\partial^2\zeta}{\partial x\partial t}\right) + \frac{1}{2}\frac{d}{dt}\left(\frac{\partial^2\zeta}{\partial x^2}, \frac{\partial^2\zeta}{\partial x^2}\right) = \left(\frac{\partial^2\zeta}{\partial x\partial t}, \frac{\partial^2}{\partial x\partial t}(\chi-u)\right) + \left(\frac{\partial^2\zeta}{\partial x^2}, \frac{\partial^3}{\partial x^2\partial t}(\chi-u)\right).$$

It follows easily that

$$\left\|\frac{\partial\zeta}{\partial t}\right\|_{L^2(H^1)} + \|\zeta\|_{L^\infty(H^2)} \le C\left\{\|\zeta(0)\|_2 + \left\|\frac{\partial}{\partial t}(\chi-u)\right\|_{L^2(H^1)} + \left\|\frac{\partial}{\partial t}(\chi-u)\right\|_{L^1(H^2)}\right\} \tag{2.2}$$

Select the initial condition $U(0)$ so that

$$\|\zeta(0)\| + h\|\zeta(0)\|_1 + h^2\|\zeta(0)\|_2 \le C\|u_0\|_{r+1}h^{r+1} \ ; \tag{2.3}$$

this can be done in many ways. In particular, we shall note below that the "biharmonic" projection

$$((U(0) - u_0)'', v'') = 0, \quad v \in \mathcal{M}, \tag{2.4}$$

satisfies (2.3); it will also be the case that the more complicated initial condition (3.5) needed to obtain superconvergence at the knots satisfies an inequality similar to (2.3). It then follows from (2.3) and (1.3) that

$$\|u - U\|_{L^\infty(H^2)} \le C\left(\left\|\frac{\partial u}{\partial t}\right\|_{L^1(H^{r+1})} + \left\|\frac{\partial u}{\partial t}\right\|_{L^2(H^r)} + \|u_0\|_{r+1}\right)h^{r-1}. \tag{2.5}$$

Now, let $W : [0, T] \to \mathcal{M}$ be the biharmonic projection of u. If $\eta = u - W$,

$$(2.6) \qquad (\frac{\partial^2}{\partial x^2}(u - W), v'') = (\frac{\partial^2 \eta}{\partial x^2}, v'') = 0, \ v \in \mathcal{M}, \ t \in J.$$

It is obvious that

$$\|\frac{\partial^2 \eta}{\partial x^2}\| \le \inf_{\chi \in \mathcal{M}} \|\frac{\partial^2 u}{\partial x^2} - \chi''\| \le C\|u\|_{r+1} h^{r-1}.$$

Since $\eta(0) = \eta(1) = 0$, then

$$(2.7) \qquad \|\eta\|_2 \le C\|u\|_{r+1} h^{r-1}, \ t \in J.$$

Let z be the solution of the two point boundary problem $z'' = -\eta$, $x \in I$, $z(0) = z(1) = 0$. Then, by (2.6)

$$(\frac{\partial \eta}{\partial x}, \frac{\partial \eta}{\partial x}) = (\frac{\partial^2 \eta}{\partial x^2}, z'') = (\frac{\partial^2 \eta}{\partial x^2}, z'' - \chi''), \ \chi \in \mathcal{M},$$

and trivial elliptic regularity for z implies that

$$(2.8) \qquad \|\eta\|_1 \le C\|\eta\|_2 h \le C\|u\|_{r+1} h^r, \ t \in J.$$

Let $\psi \in H^s(I)$ and let $\varphi \in H^{s+4}(I)$ be the solution of

$$(2.9) \qquad \begin{aligned} \varphi^{(iv)} &= \psi, \ x \in I, \\ \varphi &= \varphi'' = 0, \ x \in \partial I. \end{aligned}$$

Then, for $0 \le s \le r-3$,

$$(\eta, \psi) = (\frac{\partial^2 \eta}{\partial x^2}, \varphi'') = (\frac{\partial^2 \eta}{\partial x^2}, \varphi'' - \chi'')$$

$$= O(\|\eta\|_2 \|\psi\|_s h^{s+2}).$$

Thus, if we define $H^{-s}(I) = H^s(I)'$ using the norm

$$\|g\|_{-s} = \sup_{0 \neq \psi \in H^s(I)} \frac{(g,\psi)}{\|\psi\|_s},$$

we have shown that

$$\|\eta\|_{-s} \leq C \|u\|_{r+1} h^{r+s+1}, \quad 0 \leq s \leq r-3.$$

An obvious modification of the argument above gives the slight generalization

(2.10) $$\|\eta\|_{-s} \leq C \|u\|_q h^{q+s}, \quad 2 \leq q \leq r+1, \quad -2 \leq s \leq r-3.$$

We can derive an L^2 estimate for the error using the first step of the development of the next section and the bounds on η. If $\xi = U - W$, then

(2.11) $$\left(\frac{\partial^2 \xi}{\partial x \partial t}, v'\right) + \left(\frac{\partial^2 \xi}{\partial x^2}, v''\right) = \left(\frac{\partial^2 \eta}{\partial x \partial t}, v'\right), \quad v \in \mathcal{M}, \quad t \in J.$$

Set $Y_0 = \eta$ and define (mostly for future use) a sequence of projections by the relations

(2.12) $$\left(\frac{\partial^2 Y_\ell}{\partial x^2}, v''\right) = -\left(\frac{\partial^2 Y_{\ell-1}}{\partial x \partial t}, v'\right), \quad v \in \mathcal{M}, \quad t \in J, \quad \ell \geq 1.$$

If we set

(2.13) $$\theta_\ell = (\xi + Y_1 + \cdots + Y_\ell) : [0,T] \to \mathcal{M},$$

then an easy calculation shows that

(2.14) $$\left(\frac{\partial^2 \theta_\ell}{\partial x \partial t}, v'\right) + \left(\frac{\partial^2 \theta_\ell}{\partial x^2}, v''\right) = \left(\frac{\partial^2 Y_\ell}{\partial x \partial t}, v'\right), \quad v \in \mathcal{M}.$$

For the global estimate it is sufficient to look at θ_1. Use the test function $v = \theta_1$ in (2.14) to show that

$$\|\theta_1\|_{L^\infty(H^1)} + \|\theta_1\|_{L^2(H^2)} \leq C\left\{\|\theta_1(0)\|_1 + \left\|\frac{\partial^2 Y_1}{\partial x \partial t}\right\|_{L^2(H^{-1})}\right\}$$

(2.15)

$$\leq C\left\{\|\theta_1(0)\|_1 + \left\|\frac{\partial^2 Y_1}{\partial t}\right\|_{L^2(L^2)}\right\}.$$

It is clear that we need to estimate $\partial Y_1/\partial t$. Since we shall need bounds on $\partial^k Y_\ell/\partial t^k$ later, we shall treat all of them now.

Lemma 1. If $2 \leq q \leq r+1$ and $-2 \leq s \leq r - 2\ell - 3$, then

(2.16)
$$\left\|\frac{\partial^k Y_\ell}{\partial t^k}\right\|_{-s} \leq C\left\|\frac{\partial^{k+\ell} u}{\partial t^{k+\ell}}\right\|_q h^{q+s+2\ell}, \quad t \in J.$$

Proof. The inequalities (2.16) hold for $\ell = 0$, by (2.10). Now,

$$\left(\frac{\partial^2 Y_\ell}{\partial x^2}, \frac{\partial^2 Y_\ell}{\partial x^2}\right) = -\left(\frac{\partial^2 Y_{\ell-1}}{\partial x \partial t}, \frac{\partial Y_\ell}{\partial x}\right) = \left(\frac{\partial Y_{\ell-1}}{\partial t}, \frac{\partial^2 Y_\ell}{\partial x^2}\right),$$

and

$$\|Y_\ell\|_2 \leq C\left\|\frac{\partial Y_{\ell-1}}{\partial t}\right\|.$$

By differentiating (2.12) with respect to t, it follows in like manner that

$$\left\|\frac{\partial^k Y_\ell}{\partial t^k}\right\|_2 \leq C\left\|\frac{\partial^{k+1} Y_{\ell-1}}{\partial t^{k+1}}\right\|.$$

Next, let $\psi \in H^s(I)$ and define φ by (2.9). Then, for any $\chi \in \mathcal{M}$,

$$\left(\frac{\partial^k Y_\ell}{\partial t^k}, \psi\right) = \left(\frac{\partial^{k+2} Y_\ell}{\partial x^2 \partial t^k}, \varphi''\right)$$

$$= -\left(\frac{\partial^{k+2} Y_{\ell-1}}{\partial x \partial t^{k+1}}, \chi'\right) + \left(\frac{\partial^{k+2} Y_\ell}{\partial x^2 \partial t^k}, \varphi'' - \chi''\right)$$

$$= \left(\frac{\partial^{k+2} Y_\ell}{\partial x^2 \partial t^k} - \frac{\partial^{k+1} Y_{\ell-1}}{\partial t^{k+1}}, \varphi'' - \chi''\right) + \left(\frac{\partial^{k+1} Y_{\ell-1}}{\partial t^{k+1}}, \varphi''\right) .$$

By (1.3), there exist $\chi \in \mathcal{M}$ such that

(2.17) $\quad \|\varphi'' - \chi''\| \le C\|\varphi\|_{s+4} h^{s+2} \le C\|\psi\|_s h^{s+2}, \quad s + 4 \le r + 1 .$

For the global L^2 bound we shall need (2.17) only in the case $s = 0$; however, since we really are after the superconvergence results in this paper, we shall not complicate the statements of our results by treating this special case. Now, it follows that

$$\left\|\frac{\partial^k Y_\ell}{\partial t^k}\right\|_{-s} \le C\left\|\frac{\partial^{k+1} Y_{\ell-1}}{\partial t^{k+1}}\right\|_{-s-2} + C\left(\left\|\frac{\partial^k Y_\ell}{\partial t^k}\right\|_2 + \left\|\frac{\partial^{k+1} Y_{\ell-1}}{\partial t^{k+1}}\right\|\right) h^{s+2}$$

$$\le C\left\{\left\|\frac{\partial^{k+1} Y_{\ell-1}}{\partial t^{k+1}}\right\|_{-s-2} + \left\|\frac{\partial^{k+1} Y_{\ell-1}}{\partial t^{k+1}}\right\| h^{s+2}\right\} .$$

The lemma then follows by induction. Note that the maximum exponent on h that can be achieved is $2r - 2$.

Let us apply this lemma to (2.15). First,

$$\left\|\frac{\partial Y_1}{\partial t}\right\|_{L^2(I \times J)} \le C\left\|\frac{\partial^2 u}{\partial t^2}\right\|_{L^2(H^{r-1})} h^{r+1} .$$

Also,

$$\|Y_1(0)\|_1 \le C\|\frac{\partial u}{\partial t}(0)\|_r h^{r+1} ,$$

so that the choice

$$U(0) = W(0) \tag{2.18}$$

is adequate to imply that $\|\theta_1(0)\|_1 \le C\|\partial u/\partial t(0)\|_r h^{r+1}$. Assume more generally that the initial condition is selected so that

$$\|\theta_1(0)\|_1 \le C_0(u)h^{r+1} . \tag{2.19}$$

Then, since

$$\|\eta\|_{L^\infty(H^j)} \le C\|u\|_{L^\infty(H^{r+1})} h^{r+1-j} , \quad 0 \le j \le 2 ,$$

we have shown that

$$\|u - U\|_{L^\infty(H^j)} \le C_0(u)h^{r+1} + C\{\|u\|_{L^\infty(H^{r+1})} + \|\frac{\partial^2 u}{\partial t^2}\|_{L^2(H^{r-1-j})}\}h^{r+1-j}, \quad 0 \le j \le 1 . \tag{2.20}$$

<u>Theorem 1</u>. Let $\mathcal{M} = \mathcal{M}_h$ be selected from a family of subspaces such that (1.3) holds. Then, if $U(0)$ is chosen so that (2.19) is valid, the error in the solution of the H^1-Galerkin process (1.2) satisfies the inequality (2.20). In particular, if $U(0)$ is defined as the biharmonic projection of u_0 , then $C_0(u)$ has the form $O(\|\partial u/\partial t(0)\|_r)$. Moreover, if $U(0)$ is given by (3.4), then $C_0(u)$ has the same form as above for $r = 3$, vanishes for $r = 4$ or 5 , and is given by (3.16) for $r \ge 6$.

The last sentence of the theorem is proved at the end of section 3.

The L^2 estimate above was derived by use of the argument to be used in the next section for obtaining superconvergence; this derivation does not lead to minimal smoothness requirements on the solution u. We shall utilize the following lemma to reduce the smoothness required of u to exactly the same as needed by the standard Galerkin procedure [3].

Lemma 2. Let $\xi : [0,T] \to \mathcal{M}$ satisfy the equation

$$(2.21)\qquad (\frac{\partial^2 \xi}{\partial x \partial t}, v') + (\frac{\partial^2 \xi}{\partial x^2}, v'') = (\rho, v''), \quad v \in \mathcal{M}, \quad t \in J.$$

Then,

$$(2.22)\quad \|\xi\|_{L^\infty(L^2)} \leq C\{\|\xi(0)\| + h\|\xi(0)\|_1 + \|\rho\|_{L^2(H^{-1})} + h\|\rho\|_{L^2(L^2)}\}.$$

Proof. Let $\beta : [0,T] \to \mathcal{M}$ satisfy

$$(2.23)\qquad (\frac{\partial^2 \beta}{\partial x^2}, v'') = (\frac{\partial \xi}{\partial x}, v'), \quad v \in \mathcal{M}.$$

Then,

$$(\frac{\partial^2 \xi}{\partial x^2}, \frac{\partial^2 \beta}{\partial x^2}) = \|\frac{\partial \xi}{\partial x}\|^2 \quad \text{and} \quad (\frac{\partial^2 \xi}{\partial x \partial t}, \frac{\partial \beta}{\partial x}) = \frac{1}{2}\frac{d}{dt}\|\frac{\partial^2 \beta}{\partial x^2}\|^2;$$

thus, the choice $v = \beta$ in (2.21) shows that

$$(2.24)\qquad \frac{1}{2}\frac{d}{dt}\|\frac{\partial^2 \beta}{\partial x^2}\|^2 + \|\frac{\partial \xi}{\partial x}\|^2 = (\rho, \frac{\partial^2 \beta}{\partial x^2}).$$

Next, let $\chi : [0,T] \to \mathcal{M}$ be the projection given by

$$(2.25)\qquad (\rho - \frac{\partial^2 \chi}{\partial x^2}, v'') = 0, \quad v \in \mathcal{M}.$$

Then, for any $v \in \mathcal{M}$,

$$(\rho, \frac{\partial^2\beta}{\partial x^2}) = (\frac{\partial^2\chi}{\partial x^2}, \frac{\partial^2\beta}{\partial x^2}) = (\frac{\partial\xi}{\partial x}, \frac{\partial\chi}{\partial x}) = -(\xi, \frac{\partial^2\chi}{\partial x^2})$$

$$= -(\xi - v'', \frac{\partial^2\chi}{\partial x^2} - \rho) - (\xi, \rho)$$

and

$$(2.26) \qquad |(\rho, \frac{\partial^2\beta}{\partial x^2})| \le C\{h\|\rho\| + \|\rho\|_{-1}\}\|\xi\|_1 .$$

It then follows from (2.24) and (2.26) that

$$\|\beta\|_{L^\infty(H^2)} \le C\{\|\beta(0)\|_2 + \|\rho\|_{L^2(H^{-1})} + h\|\rho\|_{L^2(L^2)}\} .$$

If the right-hand side of (2.23) is integrated by parts, the choice $v = \beta$ implies that

$$(2.27) \qquad \|\beta\|_{L^\infty(H^2)} \le C\{\|\xi(0)\| + \|\rho\|_{L^2(H^{-1})} + h\|\rho\|_{L^2(L^2)}\} .$$

If $v = \xi$ in (2.21),

$$(2.28) \qquad \|\xi\|_{L^\infty(H^1)} \le C\{\|\xi(0)\|_1 + \|\rho\|_{L^2(L^2)}\} .$$

The proof will be accomplished if we show that

$$(2.29) \qquad \|\xi\| \le C\{\|\beta\|_2 + h\|\xi\|_1\} .$$

Since $(\frac{\partial^2\beta}{\partial x^2} + \xi, v'') = 0$ for $v \in \mathcal{M}$, then

$$\|\xi\|^2 = (\xi + \frac{\partial^2\beta}{\partial x^2}, \xi) - (\frac{\partial^2\beta}{\partial x^2}, \xi) = (\xi + \frac{\partial^2\beta}{\partial x^2}, \xi - v'') + \left\|\frac{\partial^2\beta}{\partial x^2}\right\|^2, \quad v \in \mathcal{M} .$$

Hence,

$$\|\xi\|^2 \le (\|\xi\| + \|\frac{\partial^2\beta}{\partial x^2}\|) \inf_{v \in \mathcal{M}} \|\xi - v''\| + \|\frac{\partial^2\beta}{\partial x^2}\|^2 ,$$

and (2.29) follows from (1.3) applied to the function φ given by

$\varphi'' = \xi$ for $\chi \in I$, $\varphi(0) = \varphi(1) = 0$.

Now, apply Lemma 2 to (2.11), after integrating the right-hand side by parts. Then,

$$\begin{aligned} \|\xi\|_{L^\infty(L^2)} &\le C\{\|\xi(0)\| + h\|\xi(0)\|_1 + \|\frac{\partial\eta}{\partial t}\|_{L^2(H^{-1})} + h\|\frac{\partial\eta}{\partial t}\|_{L^2(L^2)}\} \\ &\le C\{\|\xi(0)\| + h\|\xi(0)\|_1 + \|\frac{\partial u}{\partial t}\|_{L^2(H^r)} h^{r+1}\} , \end{aligned} \tag{2.30}$$

by (2.10). If $U(0)$ is chosen by (2.4), then $\xi(0) = 0$. If $U(0)$ is chosen by (3.4), then (3.17) indicates that minimal smoothness is retained when superconvergence is sought for odd r, but a loss equivalent to one space derivative occurs in the even case. The results of the above argument can be stated as follows.

<u>Theorem 2</u>. If $U(0) = W(0)$ or, more generally, if (2.3) is valid, then

$$\|u - U\|_{L^\infty(L^2)} \le C\{\|u\|_{L^\infty(H^{r+1})} + \|\frac{\partial u}{\partial t}\|_{L^2(H^r)}\}h^{r+1} . \tag{2.31}$$

If $U(0)$ is given by (3.4), then (2.31) holds for $r = 3$ and for $r \ge 4$

$$\begin{aligned} \|u - U\|_{L^\infty(L^2)} \le C\{&\|u\|_{L^\infty(H^{r+1})} + \|\frac{\partial u}{\partial t}\|_{L^2(H^r)} \\ &+ \sum_{\ell=1}^{m} \|\frac{\partial^\ell u}{\partial t^\ell}(0)\|_{\max(4, r-2\ell+1)}\}h^{r+1} , \end{aligned} \tag{2.32}$$

where m is defined by (3.3).

The inequalities (2.31) and (2.32) are best possible for odd r in the sense that, when $f = 0$ and u_0 satisfies sufficient compatibility conditions at $x = 0$ and 1, then

$$\|u - U\|_{L^\infty(L^2)} \leq C\|u_0\|_{r+1}h^{r+1} ; \tag{2.33}$$

see [3].

<u>3. Knot Estimates</u>. We are driving at $O(h^{2r-2})$ estimates. From Lemma 1, when r is even,

$$(3.1)\qquad \left\| \frac{\partial Y_{\frac{r}{2}-1}}{\partial t} \right\|_1 \leq C \left\| \frac{\partial^{\frac{r}{2}} u}{\partial t^{\frac{r}{2}}} \right\|_{r+1} h^{2r-2} .$$

For r odd,

$$(3.2)\qquad \left\| \frac{\partial^k Y_{\frac{r-3}{2}}}{\partial t^k} \right\| \leq C \left\| \frac{\partial^{\frac{r-3}{2}+k} u}{\partial t^{\frac{r-3}{2}+k}} \right\|_{r+1} h^{2r-2} .$$

Set

$$m = \frac{r}{2} - 1 , \quad \alpha = \frac{r}{2}, \quad r \text{ even} ,$$

$$(3.3)\qquad m = \frac{r-3}{2} , \quad \alpha = \frac{r-1}{2}, \quad r \text{ odd} ,$$

$$\theta = \theta_m = U - \hat{W}, \quad \hat{W} = W - Y_1 - \cdots - Y_m .$$

Let us require that the initial condition $U(0)$ be chosen so that $\theta(0) = 0$:

$$(3.4)\qquad U(0) = \hat{W}(0) .$$

Note that $\hat{W}(0)$ can be computed from the data of the problem alone; thus, this assignment is implementable, and actually rather easily so for $\mathcal{M} = \mathcal{M}_1$ or $\mathcal{M}_2$.

Choose the test function $v = \partial\theta/\partial t$ in (2.14). For r even, it follows directly that

$$(3.5)\quad \left\|\frac{\partial\theta}{\partial t}\right\|_{L^2(H^1)} + \|\theta\|_{L^\infty(H^2)} \le C\left\|\frac{\partial Y_m}{\partial t}\right\|_{L^2(H^1)} \le C\left\|\frac{\partial^\alpha u}{\partial t^\alpha}\right\|_{L^2(H^{r+1})} h^{2r-2}, \quad r \text{ even}.$$

For r odd, integrate the term on the right-hand side of (2.14) by parts first with respect to x and then, after integrating (2.14) with respect to t, with respect to t. Thus,

$$\left\|\frac{\partial\theta}{\partial t}\right\|_{L^2(H^1)} + \|\theta\|_{L^\infty(H^2)} \le C\left[\left\|\frac{\partial Y_m}{\partial t}\right\|_{L^\infty(L^2)} + \left\|\frac{\partial^2 Y_m}{\partial t^2}\right\|_{L^1(L^2)}\right]$$

$$(3.6)\qquad \le C\left[\left\|\frac{\partial^\alpha u}{\partial t^\alpha}\right\|_{L^\infty(H^{r+1})} + \left\|\frac{\partial^{\alpha+1} u}{\partial t^{\alpha+1}}\right\|_{L^1(H^{r+1})}\right] h^{2r-2}, \quad r \text{ odd}.$$

If

$$(3.7)\qquad \|g\|_{W_1^\infty} = \|g\|_{L^\infty(I\times J)} + \left\|\frac{\partial g}{\partial x}\right\|_{L^\infty(I\times J)},$$

then

$$(3.8)\quad \|\theta\|_{W_1^\infty} \le \begin{cases} C\left\|\dfrac{\partial^\alpha u}{\partial t^\alpha}\right\|_{L^2(H^{r+1})} h^{2r-2}, & r \text{ even}, \\[2ex] C\left(\left\|\dfrac{\partial^\alpha u}{\partial t^\alpha}\right\|_{L^\infty(H^{r+1})} + \left\|\dfrac{\partial^{\alpha+1} u}{\partial t^{\alpha+1}}\right\|_{L^1(H^{r+1})}\right) h^{2r-2}, & r \text{ odd}. \end{cases}$$

We need to determine bounds at the knots for the values of the function and its x-derivative for η, $Y_1, \ldots, Y_m$. We shall treat η first. Let us define two Green's functions as follows:

$$\frac{\partial^4 G_0}{\partial \xi^4}(x_i, \xi) = \delta_{x_i}, \quad \xi \in I,$$

(3.9)

$$G_0(x_i, \xi) = \frac{\partial^2 G_0}{\partial \xi^2}(x_i, \xi) = 0, \quad \xi \in \partial I,$$

and

$$\frac{\partial^4 G_1}{\partial \xi^4}(x_i, \xi) = -\delta'_{x_i}, \quad \xi \in I,$$

(3.10)

$$G_1(x_i, \xi) = \frac{\partial^2 G_1}{\partial \xi^2}(x_i, \xi) = 0, \quad \xi \in \partial I.$$

Note that both are piecewise-cubic functions and that $G_0(x_i, \cdot) \in C^2(I)$ and $G_1(x_i, \cdot) \in C^1(I)$. Moreover, we can require that $\partial^3 G_1(x_i, \xi)/\partial \xi^3$ be continuous. Then, for any $\chi \in \mathcal{M}$,

$$\eta(x_i, t) = (\eta, \frac{\partial^4}{\partial \xi^4} G_0(x_i, \cdot)) = (\frac{\partial^2 \eta}{\partial x^2}, \frac{\partial^2}{\partial \xi^2} G_0(x_i, \cdot) - \chi'')$$

$$= O(\|\eta\|_2 \, \|\frac{\partial^2}{\partial \xi^2} G_0(x_i, \cdot) - \chi''\|)$$

$$= O(\|u\|_{r+1} h^{r-1} \, \|\frac{\partial^2}{\partial \xi^2} G_0(x_i, \cdot) - \chi''\|).$$

It is at this point that we need to select $\mathcal{M} = \mathcal{M}_1$ or $\mathcal{M}_2$, since we can approximate $\partial^2 G_0/\partial \xi^2$ well in either case. Indeed,

$$\text{(3.11)} \qquad \inf_{\chi \in \mathcal{M}_k} \|\frac{\partial^2}{\partial \xi^2} G_j(x_i, \cdot) - \chi''\| \le C h^{r-1}, \quad r \ge 3,$$

for $k = 1$ or 2 when $j = 0$ and for $k = 1$ when $j = 1$. Thus,

$$|\eta(x_i, t)| \le C \|u\|_{L^\infty(H^{r+1})} h^{2r-2} \tag{3.12}$$

when $\mathcal{M} = \mathcal{M}_1$ or $\mathcal{M}_2$. The function G_1 can be used in like manner to show that

$$\left|\frac{\partial\eta}{\partial x}(x_i, t)\right| \le C \|u\|_{L^\infty(H^{r+1})} h^{2r-2} \tag{3.13}$$

for $\mathcal{M} = \mathcal{M}_1$, $r \ge 3$. Note that for the very simple case of the heat operator, $G_0 \in \mathcal{M}_2$ and $G_1 \in \mathcal{M}_1$; hence, the infima above are zero.

Consider the functions Y_ℓ. If a bound on $Y_\ell(x_i, t)$ is to be obtained, it necessitates redoing the duality argument considering the space

$$\hat{H}^s = [H^s(0, x_i) \otimes H^s(x_i, 1)] \otimes \mathbb{R}, \quad s \ge 0,$$

equipped with the norm

$$|||(\psi, q)|||_s^2 = \|\psi\|^2_{H^s(0,x_i)} + \|\psi\|^2_{H^s(x_i,1)} + q^2 .$$

If bounds are desired on both $Y_\ell(x_i, t)$ and $\partial Y_\ell/\partial x(x_i, t)$, the space

$$\tilde{H}^s = [H^s(0, x_i) \otimes H^s(x_i, 1)] \otimes \mathbb{R}^2, \quad s \ge 0,$$

equipped with the norm

$$|||(\psi, q)|||_s^2 = \|\psi\|^2_{H^s(0,x_i)} + \|\psi\|^2_{H^s(x_i,1)} + q_0^2 + q_1^2$$

should be studied. In either case we consider the duality

$$[g, (\psi, q)] = (g, \psi) + \begin{cases} g(x_i)q, & (\psi, q) \in \hat{H}^s, \\ g(x_i)q_0 + g'(x_i)q_1, & (\psi, q) \in \tilde{H}^s, \end{cases}$$

for functions $g \in H^2(I)$, and define

$$|||g|||_{-s} = \sup_{(\psi, q) \neq 0} \frac{[g, (\psi, q)]}{|||(\psi, q)|||_s}, \quad g \in H^2(I).$$

It is clear that $|||g|||_{-s}$ dominates $g(x_i)$ for $\hat{H}^s$ and both $g(x_i)$ and $g'(x_i)$ for $\tilde{H}^s$.

The definition of φ given by (2.9) has to be changed as follows. For the space $\hat{H}^s$, let $\varphi \in C^2(I)$ satisfy

$$\varphi^{(iv)} = \psi, \quad x \in I\backslash\{x_i\},$$

$$\varphi = \varphi'' = 0, \quad x \in \partial I,$$

$$\varphi'''(x_i + 0) - \varphi'''(x_i - 0) = q = q_0.$$

For the space $\tilde{H}^s$, let $\varphi \in C^1(I)$ satisfy the above plus the relation

$$\varphi''(x_i + 0) - \varphi''(x_i - 0) = -q_1.$$

It then follows that

$$[Y_\ell, (\psi, q)] = (\frac{\partial^2 Y_\ell}{\partial x^2}, \varphi'')$$

in either case. When $\mathcal{M} = \mathcal{M}_2$, φ'' can be approximated as before when $(\psi, q) \in \hat{H}^s$. When $\mathcal{M} = \mathcal{M}_1$, φ'' can be handled when $(\psi, q) \in \tilde{H}^s$. Thus, we can carry out the argument leading to Lemma 1 to see that

$$|||\frac{\partial^k Y_\ell}{\partial t^k}|||_{-s} \leq C\|\frac{\partial^{k+\ell} u}{\partial t^{k+\ell}}\|_q h^{q+s+2\ell}, \quad 2 \leq q \leq r+1, \quad 0 \leq s \leq r - 2\ell - 3, \quad t \in J.$$

Also, it follows that

$$|||\frac{\partial Y_m}{\partial t}|||_0 \leq C\|\frac{\partial^\alpha u}{\partial t^\alpha}\|_{r+1} h^{2r-2}, \quad r \text{ even}.$$

Thus, we see that

$$(3.14)\quad \begin{aligned} |Y_\ell(x_i,t)| &\le C \sum_{k=1}^{\alpha} \left\|\frac{\partial^k u}{\partial t^k}\right\|_{L^\infty(H^{r+1})} h^{2r-2}, \ 1 \le \ell \le m,\ \mathcal{M} = \mathcal{M}_1 \text{ or } \mathcal{M}_2, \\ \left|\frac{\partial Y_\ell}{\partial x}(x_i,t)\right| &\le C \sum_{k=1}^{\alpha} \left\|\frac{\partial^k u}{\partial t^k}\right\|_{L^\infty(H^{r+1})} h^{2r-2}, \ 1 \le \ell \le m,\ \mathcal{M} = \mathcal{M}_1 . \end{aligned}$$

Let

$$(3.15)\quad Q(u) = \sum_{k=0}^{\alpha} \left\|\frac{\partial^k u}{\partial t^k}\right\|_{L^\infty(H^{r+1})} + (1-(-1)^r)\left\|\frac{\partial^{\alpha+1} u}{\partial t^{\alpha+1}}\right\|_{L^1(H^{r+1})} .$$

The above bounds can be combined to complete the proof of the following theorem.

<u>Theorem 3</u>. Let $U(0) = \hat{W}(0)$ and let $\bar{x} = x_{i(\delta)}$ as $h \to 0$. Then,

$$|(u-U)(\bar{x},t)| \le CQ(u)h^{2r-2}, \quad \mathcal{M} = \mathcal{M}_1 \text{ or } \mathcal{M}_2,$$

$$\left|\frac{\partial}{\partial x}(u-U)(\bar{x},t)\right| \le CQ(u)h^{2r-2}, \quad \mathcal{M} = \mathcal{M}_1 .$$

In the case $\mathcal{M} = \mathcal{M}_1$ this represents a superconvergence result for the derivative for $r \ge 3$; in either case superconvergence occurs for the knot values for $r \ge 4$.

We have left to make some small remarks to complete the proof of the last sentences of Theorems 1 and 2. We need a bound of the form

$$\|\theta_1(0)\|_1 = \|(Y_2 + \cdots + Y_m)(0)\|_1 \le C_0(u)h^{r+1}, \quad r \ge 6 .$$

It follows easily from Lemma 1, (3.1), and (3.2) that

$$\|(Y_2 + \cdots + Y_m)(0)\|_1 \le C \sum_{\ell=2}^{m} \left\|\frac{\partial^\ell u}{\partial t^\ell}(0)\right\|_{r-2\ell+2} h^{r+1} ;$$

i.e.,

(3.16)
$$C_0(u) = C \sum_{\ell=2}^{m} \left\| \frac{\partial^\ell u}{\partial t^\ell}(0) \right\|_{r-2\ell+2} .$$

It also follows that, for the choice $U(0) = \hat{W}(0)$,

(3.17)
$$\|\xi(0)\| + h\|\xi(0)\|_1 \leq C \sum_{\ell=1}^{m} \left\| \frac{\partial^\ell u}{\partial t^\ell}(0) \right\|_{\max(4, r-2\ell+1)} h^{r+1} .$$

REFERENCES

1. J. Douglas, Jr., T. Dupont, and M. F. Wheeler, A quasi-projection approximation method applied to Galerkin procedures for parabolic and hyperbolic equations, to appear.

2. J. Douglas, Jr., T. Dupont, and M. F. Wheeler, A Galerkin procedure for approximating the flux on the boundary for elliptic and parabolic boundary value problems, MRC report #1381 and to appear.

3. T. Dupont, Some L^2 error estimates for parabolic Galerkin methods, The Mathematical Foundations of the Finite Element Method with Applications to Partial Differential Equations, A. K. Aziz (ed.), Academic Press, New York, 1972.

4. V. Thomée and L. Wahlbin, to appear.

5. M. F. Wheeler, A Galerkin procedure for estimating the flux for two point boundary value problems, to appear in SIAM J. Numer. Anal.

AR 70-31 Unclassified

Security Classification

DOCUMENT CONTROL DATA - R & D	
(Security classification of title, body of abstract and indexing annotation must be entered when the overall report is classified)	
1. ORIGINATING ACTIVITY (Corporate author) Mathematics Research Center University of Wisconsin, Madison, Wis. 53706	2a. REPORT SECURITY CLASSIFICATION Unclassified 2b. GROUP None
3. REPORT TITLE SOME SUPERCONVERGENCE RESULTS FOR AN H^1-GALERKIN PROCEDURE FOR THE HEAT EQUATION	
4. DESCRIPTIVE NOTES (Type of report and inclusive dates) Summary Report: no specific reporting period.	
5. AUTHOR(S) (First name, middle initial, last name) Jim Douglas, Jr., Todd Dupont, and Mary Fanett Wheeler	

6. REPORT DATE	7a. TOTAL NO. OF PAGES	7b. NO. OF REFS
	22	5

8a. CONTRACT OR GRANT NO. Contract No. DA-31-124-ARO-D-462 b. PROJECT NO. None c. d.	9a. ORIGINATOR'S REPORT NUMBER(S) 1382 9b. OTHER REPORT NO(S) (Any other numbers that may be assigned this report) None
10. DISTRIBUTION STATEMENT Distribution of this document is unlimited.	
11. SUPPLEMENTARY NOTES None	12. SPONSORING MILITARY ACTIVITY Army Research Office-Durham, N.C.

13. ABSTRACT

Thomée and Wahlbin have introduced a Galerkin method for the heat equation in a single space variable based on the H^1-inner product and have obtained H^2 and H^1 estimates for the error. An L^2 estimate is given here. The main object is to show knot superconvergence phenomena when the subspace is a piecewise-polynomial space. For C^2-piecewise-polynomials of degree r, the error in the knot values is $O(h^{2r-2})$; for the C^1 case, both knot values and knot first x-derivatives are approximated to within $O(h^{2r-2})$.

DD FORM 1 NOV 65 1473

Unclassified

Security Classification

AGO 5698A

Mathematics Research Center UNCLASSIFIED

SOME SUPERCONVERGENCE RESULTS FOR AN H^1-GALERKIN PROCEDURE FOR THE HEAT EQUATION

Galerkin methods
superconvergence

Jim Douglas, Jr., Todd Dupont, and Mary Fanett Wheeler

MRC Report No. 1382 AD ______ 22 pp.

Contract No. DA-31-124-ARO-D-462

The main object is to show knot superconvergence phenomena when the subspace is a piecewise-polynomial space. For C^2-piecewise-polynomials of degree r, the error in the knot values is $O(h^{2r-2})$; for the C^1 case, both knot values and knot first x-derivatives are approximated to within $O(h^{2r-2})$.

Mathematics Research Center UNCLASSIFIED

SOME SUPERCONVERGENCE RESULTS FOR AN H^1-GALERKIN PROCEDURE FOR THE HEAT EQUATION

Galerkin methods
superconvergence

Jim Douglas, Jr., Todd Dupont, and Mary Fanett Wheeler

MRC Report No. 1382 AD ______ 22 pp.

Contract No. DA-31-124-ARO-D-462

The main object is to show knot superconvergence phenomena when the subspace is a piecewise-polynomial space. For C^2-piecewise-polynomials of degree r, the error in the knot values is $O(h^{2r-2})$; for the C^1 case, both knot values and knot first x-derivatives are approximated to within $O(h^{2r-2})$.

Mathematics Research Center UNCLASSIFIED

SOME SUPERCONVERGENCE RESULTS FOR AN H^1-GALERKIN PROCEDURE FOR THE HEAT EQUATION

Galerkin methods
superconvergence

Jim Douglas, Jr., Todd Dupont, and Mary Fanett Wheeler

MRC Report No. 1382 AD ______ 22 pp.

Contract No. DA-31-124-ARO-D-462

The main object is to show knot superconvergence phenomena when the subspace is a piecewise-polynomial space. For C^2-piecewise-polynomials of degree r, the error in the knot values is $O(h^{2r-2})$; for the C^1 case, both knot values and knot first x-derivatives are approximated to within $O(h^{2r-2})$.

Mathematics Research Center UNCLASSIFIED

SOME SUPERCONVERGENCE RESULTS FOR AN H^1-GALERKIN PROCEDURE FOR THE HEAT EQUATION

Galerkin methods
superconvergence

Jim Douglas, Jr., Todd Dupont, and Mary Fanett Wheeler

MRC Report No. 1382 AD ______ 22 pp.

Contract No. DA-31-124-ARO-D-462

The main object is to show knot superconvergence phenomena when the subspace is a piecewise-polynomial space. For C^2-piecewise-polynomials of degree r, the error in the knot values is $O(h^{2r-2})$; for the C^1 case, both knot values and knot first x-derivatives are approximated to within $O(h^{2r-2})$.

APPLICATION DE LA METHODE DES ELEMENTS FINIS
- UN PROCEDE DE SOUS-ASSEMBLAGE -

J.M. BOISSERIE
Ingénieur Chercheur à Electricité de France

Une des idées les plus utiles au calcul automatique des solutions d'équations aux dérivées partielles est celle de la décomposition du domaine Ω de frontière Γ en sous-domaines élémentaires. La reconstitution de Ω aboutit à poser un système d'équations à grand nombre de variables que beaucoup de praticiens traitent comme un tout après avoir choisi une méthode itérative ou une méthode directe.

Il existe cependant une autre façon de faire. Le domaine Ω est reconstitué par étapes, c'est ce qu'on appelle le sous-assemblage [Réf. 1,2,3]. A la place de l'unique et grand système d'équations posées, se trouve une suite de systèmes satellites complètement découplés et coordonnés par un système principal de taille et de largeur de bande réduite. Généralement, ce procédé est un cas particulier des méthodes directes. Pourtant le système principal est susceptible d'être résolu itérativement.

Ce procédé est rendu possible parce que la signification de l'opération de reconstitution du domaine Ω est tout à fait indépendante des frontières $\gamma^{(e)}$ des sous-domaines ou des domaines élémentaires. Ce procédé est naturel. Il facilite l'utilisation de la machine à calculer. Les mémoires lentes de l'ordinateur conservent les résultats des calculs relatifs au sous-domaines déjà traités. La mémoire rapide ne contient que ce qui est nécessaire au traitement d'un seul sous-domaine. Le découplage des différents systèmes satellites ralentit la propagation du bruit numérique. Enfin, les procédures de découpages, pourvu qu'elles soient adaptées à l'algorithme de résolution, trouvent leur efficacité.

Nous allons présenter un sous-assemblage très simple qui est à la base d'un des codes de calcul utilisé à la Direction des Etudes et Recherches d'Electricité de France pour les problèmes d'équations aux dérivées partielles du second ordre elliptiques et auto-adjointes. Les sous-domaines sont des files simples d'éléments discrétisés de façon analogue et dont la forme est quadrangulaire curviligne pour les problèmes à deux dimensions et hexaédrale curviligne dans le cas de trois. Le sous-domaine est appelé réglette. Le nom symbolique du code est RULE.

L'aspect modulaire du sous-assemblage a pour conséquences de simplifier à l'extrême la structure du système principal et des systèmes satellites qui est tri-diagonale par blocs identiques. L'algorithme de Gauss par blocs est adaptée à leur résolution.

1 - NOTION DE REGLETTE

Soit Ω le domaine considéré et $\Gamma = \partial\Omega$ sa frontière. A la suite de la décomposition apparaissent des domaines élémentaires ou éléments finis $\omega^{(e)}$ de frontière $\gamma^{(e)}$ et nous avons :

1,1)

$$\text{a)}\quad \bigcup \bar{\omega}^{(e)} = \bar{\Omega}$$

$$\text{b)}\quad \bigcap \omega^{(e)} = \emptyset$$

$$\text{c)}\quad \bigcup \gamma^{(e)} = \Gamma + \Gamma_{aux}$$

Γ_{aux} est donc l'ensemble des frontières nouvelles qui apparaissent après la décomposition de Ω .

Dans tout ce qui suit nous n'examinerons que les situations bi-dimensionnelles. La généralisation à trois dimensions est en effet immédiate. D'autre part nous imposerons toujours sur Γ_{aux} la condition de Dirichlet. Cela est effectivement rendu possible par la nature des problèmes traités : celui du Potentiel et de l'Elasticité en formulation déplacement.

Enfin les éléments finis utilisés ont une discrétisation particulière [Réf. 4]. Sur la figure 1) est représenté un des ces éléments et ses quatre côtés $\gamma_{①}$, $\gamma_{②}$, $\gamma_{③}$, $\gamma_{④}$. Les points de discrétisation qui le décrivent peuvent être répartis en cinq ensembles que nous désignerons par S_i avec $1 \leqslant i \leqslant 5$.

Nous avons :

2,1)

$$S_i \quad 1 \leqslant i \leqslant 4 \qquad S_i \subset \gamma_{ⓘ}$$

$$i = 5 \qquad S_5 \subset \omega$$

Nous disons que cet élément est "écorné" parce que

$$S_i \cap S_j = \emptyset \quad \forall\, i \neq j \qquad 1 \leqslant i,j \leqslant 5$$

Aucun point de discrétisation n'appartient simultanément à deux S_i. Si nous repérons les éléments par (e) les notations $\omega^{(e)}$ et $S_i^{(e)}$ ont une signification évidente.

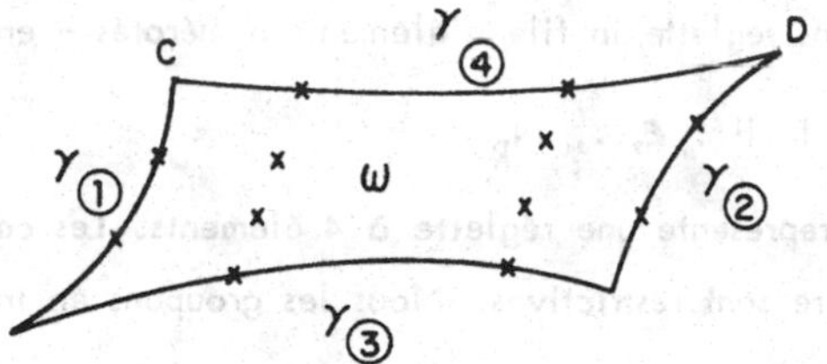

FIGURE 1

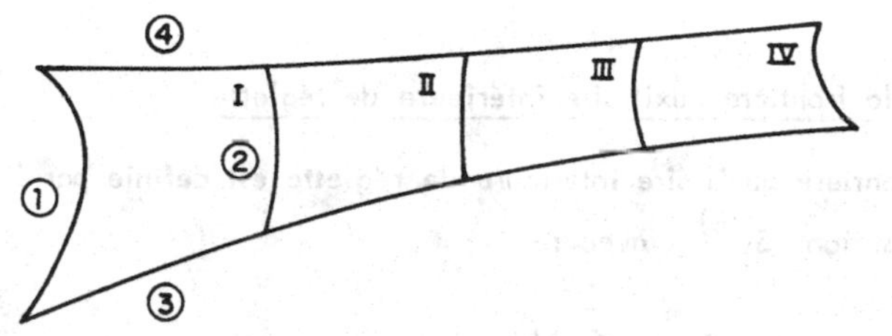

FIGURE 2

Nous appelons réglette la file d'éléments numérotés – en chiffres romains – :

$$I, II ., e, ... N_R$$

La figure 2 représente une réglette à 4 éléments. Les conditions de voisinage entre éléments et frontière sont restrictives. Nous les groupons en trois rubriques :

1) Conditions de recouvrement de la frontière donnée

N_E réglettes suffisent à couvrir Ω .

La première réglette touche Γ par toutes les faces ③ des éléments qui la composent. La dernière réglette touche Γ par toutes les faces ④ des éléments qui la composent.

Enfin toutes les réglettes recouvrent Γ par la face ① de leur premier élément et par la face ② du $N_R$ième élément.

Toutes ces conditions font que le domaine Ω est topologiquement équivalent à un carré.

2) Définition de la frontière auxiliaire intérieure de réglette

La frontière auxiliaire intérieure de réglette est définie par l'ensemble des points de discrétisation $S_1^{(e)}$ avec :

$$2 \leqslant e \leqslant N_R$$

et $S_2^{(e)}$ avec

$$1 \leqslant e \leqslant N_R - 1$$

Le but du sous-assemblage est d'éliminer les inconnues relatives à cette frontière.

3) Définition de la frontière auxiliaire extérieure de réglette

Les ensembles de points de discrétisation $S_3^{(e)}$ et $S_4^{(e)}$ avec $1 \leqslant e \leqslant NR$ discrétisent la frontière auxiliaire extérieure de réglette. Rappelons que pour la première et la dernière des N_E réglettes, la frontière Γ est confondue avec une partie de leur frontière auxiliaire extérieure.

2 - ASSEMBLAGE D'UNE REGLETTE ET SYSTEMES SATELLITES

Le code RULE résout des équations de type elliptique et auto-adjoint :

1,2_a) $\mathcal{L}(u) - f = 0$ dans Ω

1,2_b) $B(u) - g = 0$ sur Γ

où u est fonction inconnue.

Il existe donc une autre façon de poser le problème :

2,2) $$\mathrm{Min}_V \left\{ J(V) = \int_\Omega F(V, V_x, V_y \ldots)\, d\Omega \right\}$$

les conditions 1,2_b) étant satisfaites.

Pour résoudre (2,2), on exprime que la variation δJ de J, lorsque la solution u est incrémentée de δu, est nulle. L'expression de δJ est :

3,2) $$\delta J = \iint_\Omega \delta u \, \big[F \big]_u + \int_\Gamma \delta u \, (F_{u_x}\, dy - F_{u_y}\, dx) = \delta J_1 + \delta J_2$$

avec $\big[F \big]_u = \mathcal{L}(u) - f$

et

$$F_{u_x}\, dx - F_{u_y}\, dy = h(u)\, ds_\Gamma$$

Lorsque F est donné, il est possible de calculer h(u). La condition h(u) = 0 est appelée la condition naturelle du problème (2,2). Cette relation est satisfaite sur tout le pourtour si on minimise J(V) sans aucune contrainte.

Ω est décomposé en une suite de domaines $\omega^{(e)}$ et on a :

4,2) $$\delta J_2 = \int_\Gamma \delta u\, h(u)\, ds_\Gamma + \int_{\Gamma_{aux}} \delta u\, h(u)\, ds_{\Gamma_{aux}}$$

Comme Γ_{aux} est frontière entre deux éléments - et deux seulement si les éléments sont "écornés" -, les contributions à δJ_2 de deux éléments contigus par l'intermédiaire de leur frontière commune doivent être de somme nulle. En notant Γ^*_{aux}

cet élément de frontière commune aux éléments (e) et (e') on a :

5,2) $$\int_{\Gamma^*_{aux}} \delta u \,(h_{(e)}(u) + h_{(e')}(u)\,)\, ds_{\Gamma^*_{aux}} = 0$$

la relation 5,2) valant pour tous les δu "raisonnables" on a :

6,2) $$h_{(e)}(u) + h_{(e')}(u) = 0$$

sur tous les points de la frontière commune Γ^*_{aux} et en particulier sur les points de discrétisation $S_i^{(e)}$. La relation 6,2) est la condition d'assemblage.

<u>REMARQUE</u> : Le fait que les éléments soient "écornés" exclut de la frontière discrétisée les coins où la fonction inconnue perd de la "régularité".

La discrétisation par éléments finis que nous employons dans RULE joue un double rôle. Le premier est celui de l'interpolation. Lorsque toutes les conditions aux limites $g(x)$ sont connues sur la frontière $\gamma_{(e)}$ u est calculé par interpolation sur ω_e ou $S_5^{(e)}$. Le second est de produire la correspondance discrétisée entre $h(u)$ et u en tous les points :

7,2) $$\gamma^{(e)} \cap \Gamma_{aux}$$

Nous notons cette correspondance :

8,2) $$h_i^{(e)} = R_{ij}^{(e)} \; g_j^{(e)}$$

L'ensemble des $R_{ij}^{(e)}$ à e fixé, avec $1 \leqslant i,j \leqslant 5$ est souvent appelé matrice de rigidité de l'élément parce que dans le problème de l'élasticité $h_i^{(e)}$ est une contrainte superficielle et $g_j^{(e)}$ un déplacement.

Trois cas sont à distinguer :

a) Si $S_j^{(e)}$ est sur la frontière auxiliaire <u>extérieure</u> ou <u>intérieure</u> de réglette, g_j est la valeur de la fonction inconnue puisque la condition de Dirichlet est imposée sur Γ_{aux}.

b) Si $S_j^{(e)}$ est sur la frontière Γ de Ω, les conditions aux limites sont données et très généralement elles sont du type mêlé. Les g_j sont les véritables données de frontière du problème.

c) Si $S_i^{(e)}$ est l'intérieur d'un élément. C'est le cas $i = 5$. Les g_5 sont les seconds membres f des équations à résoudre. Lorsque l'équation est homogène les g_5 sont nuls et les termes $R_{i5}^{(e)}$ ne sont pas calculés.

Dans le premier de ces trois cas, les valeurs des $g_i = u_i$ ne sont pas initialement connues. Dans le cas de la méthode de sous-assemblage de RULE elles sont fournies au fur et à mesure de la résolution.

Nous sommes maintenant en mesure de poser le système d'équation satellite qui exprime la continuité de la réglette (équation 6,2) sur les faces appartenant à la frontière auxiliaire <u>intérieure</u> de réglette.

Ces équations figurent dans le tableau I.

Les inconnues sont l'ensemble complet des valeurs de u_i aux points de discrétisation de la frontière auxiliaire intérieure U_{int}

$$U_{int} = \left\{ u_2^{e} \right\} = \left\{ u_1^{e'} \right\}$$

avec $1 < e < N_{R-1}$ et $2 < e' < N_R$

L'opérateur linéaire du premier membre dans l'équation du tableau I est de nature tri-diagonale par blocs. C'est une matrice dont le rang est égal au nombre d'éléments de U_{int}, à savoir :

$$(N_R - 1) \times \text{dimension de } S_2^{e} \text{ ou } S_1^{e'}$$

Associée à un problème de même nature numérique que le problème général, cette matrice est positive et inversible. Les seconds membres ne sont pas constitués par un seul vecteur mais par une suite de matrices B_k qui opèrent sur :

a) des valeurs initialement inconnues sur les faces ③ et ④ qui constituent la frontière auxiliaire extérieure, en général.

b) le vecteur des valeurs g_i sur la portion de Γ recouverte par la réglette.

c) le vecteur des valeurs f_i donné à l'intérieur de Ω .

Si nous désignons par G_k les valeurs de g_i ordonnées comme le montre le tableau I , la forme des équations d'assemblage de la réglette est :

9,2) $$A\ U_{int} = \sum_{k=1}^{k=4} B_k\ G_k$$

En multipliant les deux membres de cette relation par A^{-1} nous établissons une correspondance entre les valeurs de U_{int} et celles des G_k, relation qui est :

10,2) $$U_{int} = \sum_{k=1}^{k=4} O_k\ G_k$$

Cette relation va être celle qui permet la construction de la matrice de rigidité de la réglette.

3 - MATRICE DE RIGIDITE D'UNE REGLETTE ET SYSTEME PRINCIPAL

Nous venons de voir comment assurer la recomposition d'une réglette. Mais le but de l'algorithme est de reconstituer le domaine entier Ω en posant le système d'équations principal. Cela est possible parce que la relation de voisinage des réglettes entre elles est analogue à celle des éléments entre eux dans cette réglette. Donc le système d'équations principal va avoir la même structure que les systèmes satellites déjà présentés et attachés à chaque réglette.

Si nous examinons le tableau I, nous voyons que les premiers membres du système d'équation satellite ne fait intervenir que des $R_{ij}^{(e)}$ avec :

$$1 \leqslant i \quad \text{et} \quad j \leqslant 2$$

c'est-à-dire que les S_j et S_i correspondants appartiennent tous à la frontière auxiliaire <u>intérieure</u> de réglette.

Le système d'équations principal fait jouer aux frontières auxiliaires <u>extérieures</u> de réglette le rôle joué dans les systèmes satellites par les frontières auxiliaires <u>intérieures</u>. Nous allons construire les opérateurs

$$T_{ij}^{(r)} \qquad 3 \leqslant i \leqslant 4 \qquad \text{et} \qquad 1 \leqslant j \leqslant 4$$

$$1 \leqslant r \leqslant N_E \quad \text{nombre de réglettes}$$

attachés à chaque réglette, qui vont permettre de poser le système d'équations principal.

En utilisant la définition des $R_{ij}^{(e)}$ nous pouvons construire la relation discrète entre :

a) les valeurs des h_3 et h_4 sur la frontière auxiliaire extérieure,

b) l'ensemble $U_{int} \cup G_k$.

Cette relation figure au tableau II et attire les commentaires suivants :

a) le tableau résulte de la seule définition des $R_{3j}^{(e)}$. Ceux-ci y figurent tous.

b) la même définition est celle de $T_{4j}^{(r)}$ et fait intervenir tous les $R_{4j}^{(e)}$.

c) les opérandes des différentes matrices sont définis et <u>rangés</u> de façon identique à ce qui figure au tableau I.

La matrice de rigidité de la réglette sera définie comme la relation discrétisée entre les valeurs de h(u) prises sur la frontière auxiliaire <u>extérieure</u> de réglette et :

a) les valeurs de u_i sur les faces ③ et ④ qui constituent pour chaque réglette sa frontière extérieure.

b) les valeurs de g_i sur la partie Γ recouverte par la frontière de la réglette.

c) les valeurs de f_i données à l'intérieur de la réglette - la frontière auxiliaire intérieure étant exclue -

On aura donc une relation tout à fait analogue à 9,2)

1,3) $$T_{3j}^{(r)} = TA\ U_{int} + \sum_{k=1}^{k=4} TB_k\ G_k$$

Mais nous pouvons éliminer U_{int} en tenant compte de 10,2).

Il vient :

2,3) $$T_{3j}^{(r)} = \left\{ TA \times O_k + TB_k \right\} G_k$$

Il est alors possible de construire le système d'équations principal qui se déduit du systèmes satellites :

- en remplaçant N_R par N_E
- en remplaçant les $R_{ij}^{(e)}$ avec $1 \leqslant i,j \leqslant 2$ par les

$$T_{ij}^{(r)} \text{ avec } 3 \leqslant i,j \leqslant 4$$

Les seconds membres du système d'équations principal ne font plus intervenir que les valeurs connues des g sur Γ et des f sur Ω.

La fin de l'algorithme - souvent appelé la redescente - consiste à déterminer les U_{int} par utilisation de 10,2). Après que ces derniers aient été calculés, la propriété d'interpolation des éléments permet d'avoir le champ inconnu en tous les points de discrétisation.

Dans le cas du programme tri-dimensionnel le sous-assemblage se fait lui-même par étape. Les éléments sont d'abord assemblés en réglette du premier type. Les réglettes sont elles-mêmes associées en réglettes du second type qui par un troisième assemblage reconstituent le domaine Ω.

4 - APPLICATIONS

Les applications du code RULE ont été assez nombreuses. La comparaison avec l'expérience et avec les résultats d'autres codes de calcul a été faite.

A) Calculs élastiques

Le code RULE a été écrit en vue de calculs de béton précontraint dans la filière française (MAGNOX). Le béton est un matériau non linéaire. Il y avait à prévoir une méthode incrémentale de calcul.

De cette sorte d'étude il reste un exemple qui montre bien l'intérêt d'éléments à frontière curviligne. Sur la figure 3) sont représentées les lignes "iso-valeur" de la contrainte circonférencielle dans le cas de deux caissons en béton précontraint soumis à la pression de service. Le premier est l'ouvrage réel. Il a un gousset de raccordement entre le fond et le cylindre. Il figure à gauche de la figure 3). Le nombre d'éléments utilisés est de 608. Chaque élément a 64 degrés de liberté. Le second résultat figure à droite de la figure 3). Il s'agit d'un ouvrage fictif dont le raccordement jupe-dalle est réalisé par un arc de conique. Le nombre d'éléments utilisé est beaucoup moins grand. Il y en a 100. Les résultats sont aussi réguliers que dans le cas précédent.

Les caractéristiques de ces deux calculs figurent dans le tableau III.

B) Calculs de potentiel

Un autre problème dont nous montrons le résultat est du type potentiel. Le résultat cherché est celui de l'intégrale du flux du gradient autour d'une cavité. La moitié du domaine est discrétisé. Le maillage est représenté sur la figure 4 . C'est un problème mêlé.

Conditions aux limites :

BC	Neumann
CD	Dirichlet
DE	Dirichlet
EF	Neumann
FA	Dirichlet

Sur le segment AB , 2 conditions sont possibles Neumann ou Dirichlet. L'étude a consisté à comparer les résultats de plusieurs découpages. Une erreur de calcul inférieure à 10^{-3} était le but à atteindre.

TABLEAU IV

Nombre de degrés de liberté par élément	N_R	N_E	Cas 1	Cas 2
21	7	35	0.37792	0.38087
21	9	35	0.37788	0.38067
21	11	35	0.37785	0.38029
32	6	35	0.37797	0.38042
32	6	25	0.37789	0.38048
45*	5	25	0.37793	0.38036

Les lignes iso-valeurs du potentiel sont représentées sur les figures 5 et 6. Les difficultés de cette étude proviennent du voisinage de AB où les lignes iso-potentielles ont une courbure très variable.

C) La version tri-dimensionnelle de RULE

Cette version permet dans l'état de la programmation actuel de sous-assembler en deux étapes 16 éléments hexaédriques à 96 degrés de liberté.

La largeur de bande maximale du système principal est de 576. C'est actuellement le seuil critique. Les autres seuils critiques sont la taille des systèmes satellites et la capacité des mémoires lentes.

Le sous-domaine de type réglette a, au plus, 1272 degrés de liberté. Le système satellite de premier niveau a un rang au plus égal à 168. Le temps de traitement d'un tel sous-assemblage est de l'ordre de 80 secondes en CDC 6600.

Il n'y a pas à l'heure actuelle de traceurs de résultats associés à cette version.

---

* La description de ce calcul est la seule qui figure au tableau III.

CONCLUSION

Le code RULE a permis de poser et de résoudre la plupart des problèmes pesés par la programmation de l'idée du sous-assemblage. La simplicité de la notion de réglette était nécessaire pour réduire l'effort de programmation et surtout de maintenance. Des situations à grand nombre de variables ont permis de s'assurer de la stabilité des algorithmes mis en jeu.

BIBLIOGRAPHIE

[1] ARGYRIS : Recent advances in matrix methods of structural analysis Pergamon Press - 1964.

[2] SCHREM ROY : An automatic system for kinematic analysis ASKA High Speed compreting of elastic structures Proc of Symposium IUTAM - August 1970.

[3] WILLIAMS : Comparison between sparse stiffness matrix and substructures methods - Int Journal for Numerical Methods in Engineering 5-3 p.383.

[4] BOISSERIE : Generation of Two- and Three-dimensional finite elemnts International Journal for Numerical Methods in Engineering - Vol. 3 327-347.

TABLEAU I

SOUS-ASSEMBLAGE D'UNE REGLETTE A 4 ELEMENTS DANS R_2

U_{inter} = − faces ③ − faces ④ − ensembles ⑤ − faces Γ

A (U_{inter})

(1) (2) 22+11	(2) 12	0
(2) 21	(2)(3) 22+11	(3) 12
0	(3) 21	(3)(4) 22+11

= −

B_1 (faces ③)

(1) 23	(2) 13	0	0
0	(2) 23	(3) 13	0
0	0	(3) 23	(4) 13

−

B_2 (faces ④)

(1) 24	(2) 14	0	0
0	(2) 24	(3) 14	0
0	0	(3) 24	(4) 14

−

B_3 (ensembles ⑤)

(1) 25	(2) 15	0	0
0	(2) 25	(3) 15	0
0	0	(3) 25	(4) 15

−

B_4 (faces Γ)

(1) 21	0
0	0
0	(4) 12

Premiers membres

Seconds membres

Les opérateurs $R^{(e)}_{iJ}$ sont représentés (e) iJ

TABLEAU II

MATRICE DE RIGIDITE D'UNE REGLETTE A 4 ELEMENTS DANS R_2

U_{inter} = + faces ③ + faces ④ + ensembles ⑤ + faces Γ

TA (U_{inter})

1 32	0	0
2 31	2 32	0
0	3 31	3 32
0	0	4 31

TB_1 (faces ③)

(1) 33	0	0	0
0	(2) 33	0	0
0	0	(3) 33	0
0	0	0	(4) 33

TB_2 (faces ④)

(1) 34	0	0	0
0	(2) 34	0	0
0	0	(3) 34	0
0	0	0	(4) 34

TB_3 (ensembles ⑤)

(1) 35	0	0	0
0	(2) 35	0	0
0	0	(3) 35	0
0	0	0	(4) 35

TB_4 (faces Γ)

(1) 31	0
0	0
0	0
0	(4) 32

Les opérateurs $R^{(e)}_{iJ}$ sont représentés $\begin{smallmatrix}(e)\\ iJ\end{smallmatrix}$

TABLEAU III

TITRE DU CALCUL	Nombre de réglettes	Nombre d' éléments	Nombre de points	SYSTEMES SATELLITES		SYSTEME PRINCIPAL	
				premiers membres	nombre de seconds membres	ordre	largeur bande
Calcul élastique axi-symétrique Eléments quadrangles	76	76 x 8 = 603 éléments à 64 degrés de liberté	14928	75 systèmes d'ordre 64	144	4800	192
Calcul élastique axi-symétrique éléments curvilignes	20	20 x 5 = 100 éléments à 64 degrés de liberté	2500	20 systèmes d'ordre 32	96	760	120
Problème potentiel	25	25 x 5 = 125 éléments à 45 degrés de liberté	4525	25 systèmes d'ordre 20	60	600	75

Figure 3

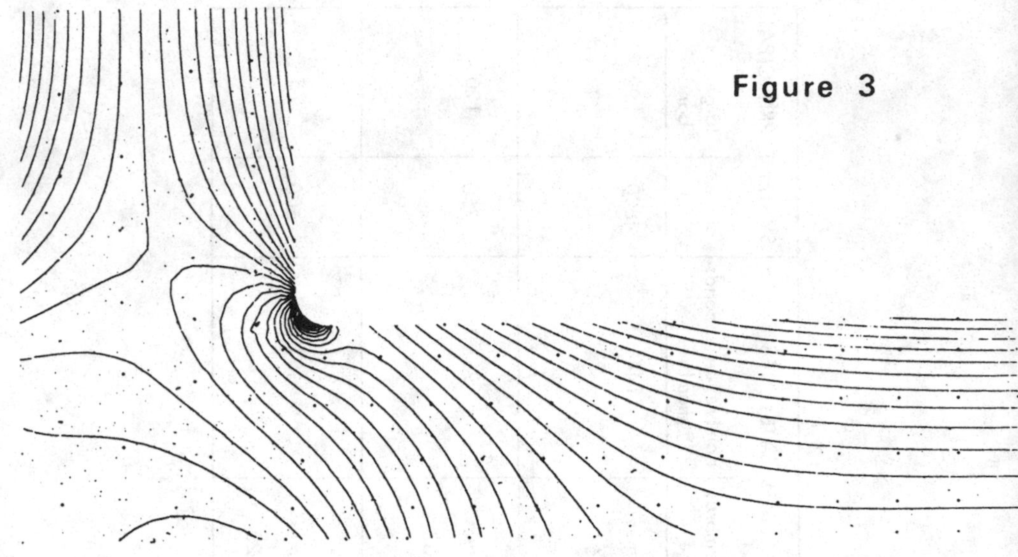

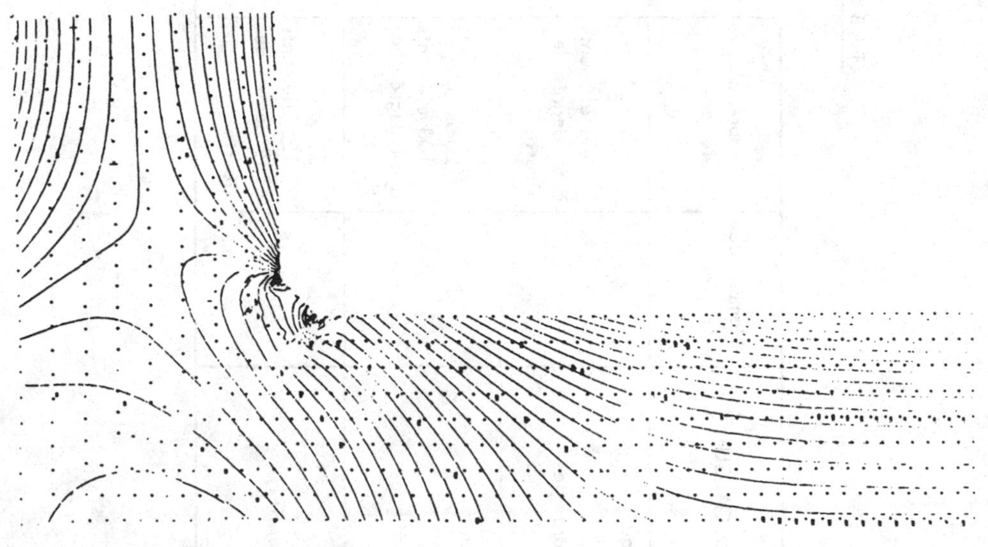

Figure 4

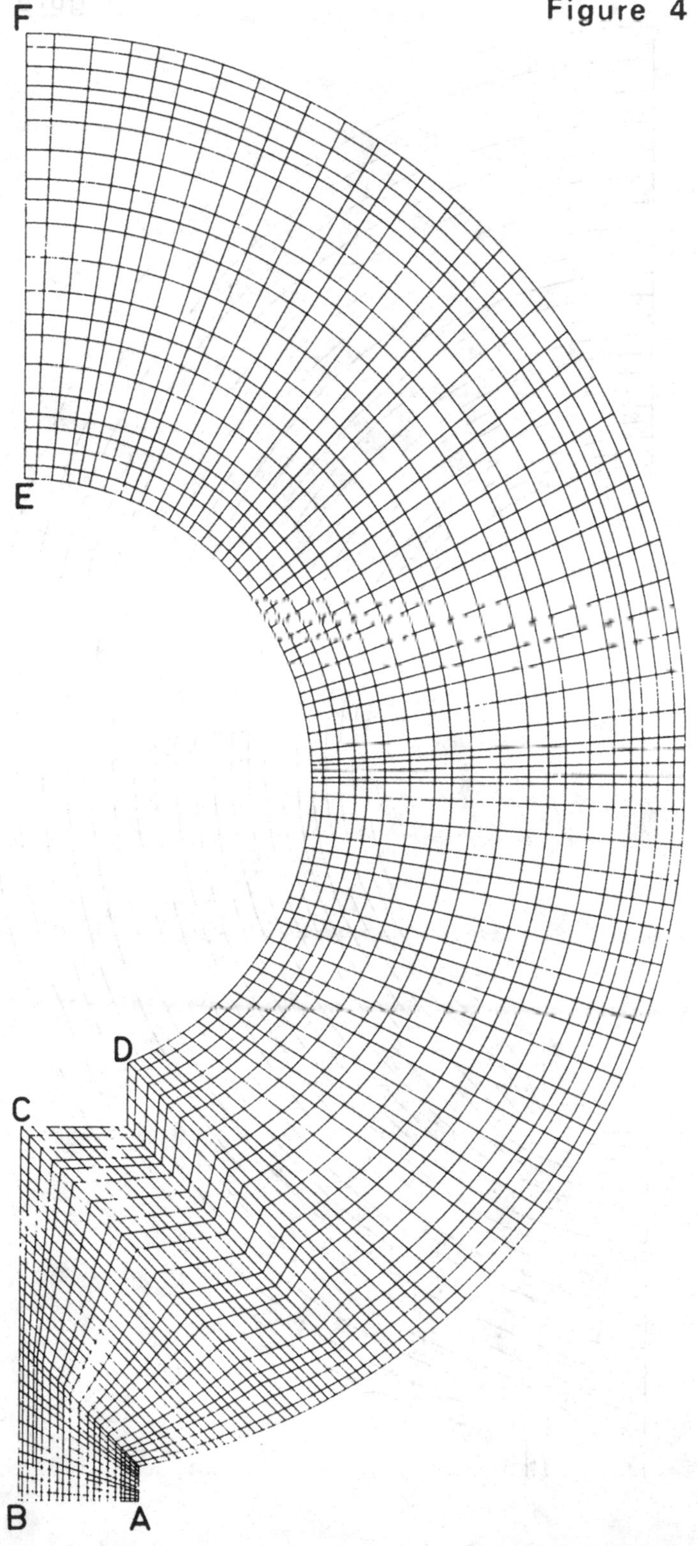

Figure 5

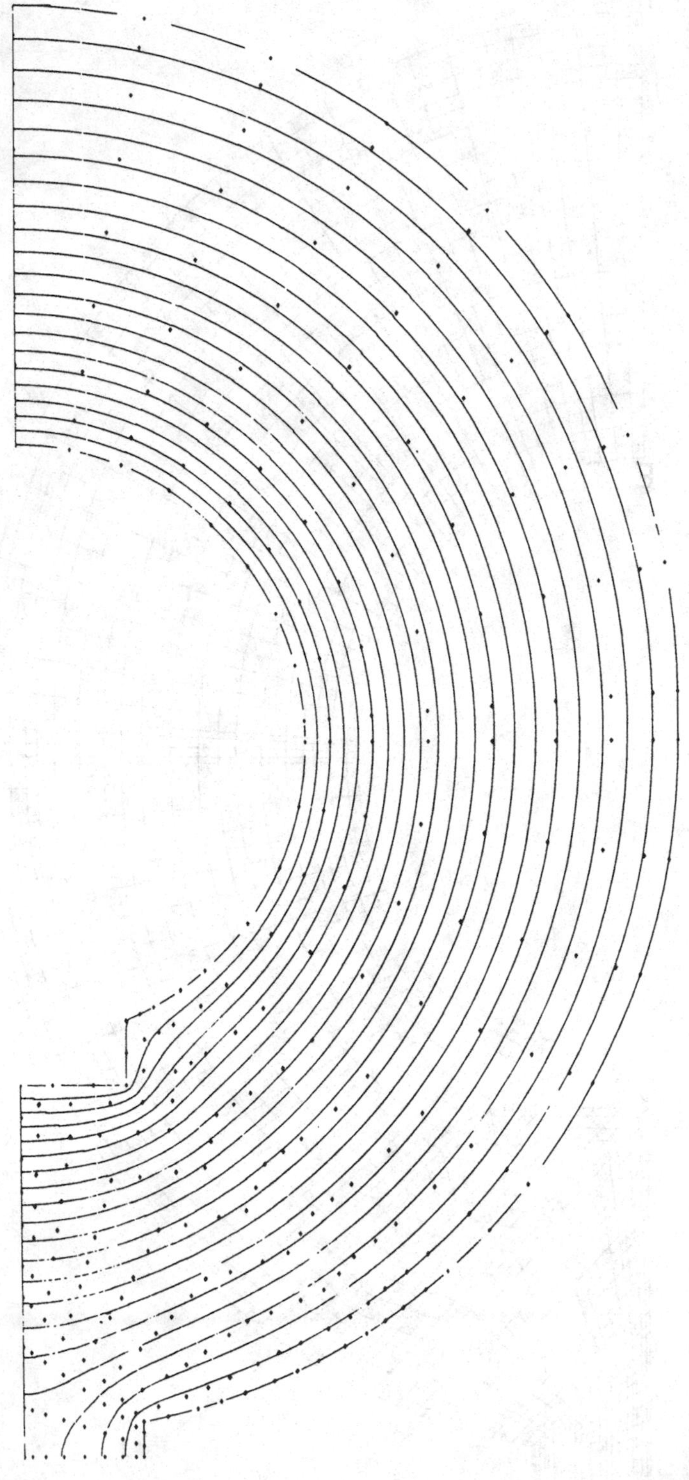

Figure 6

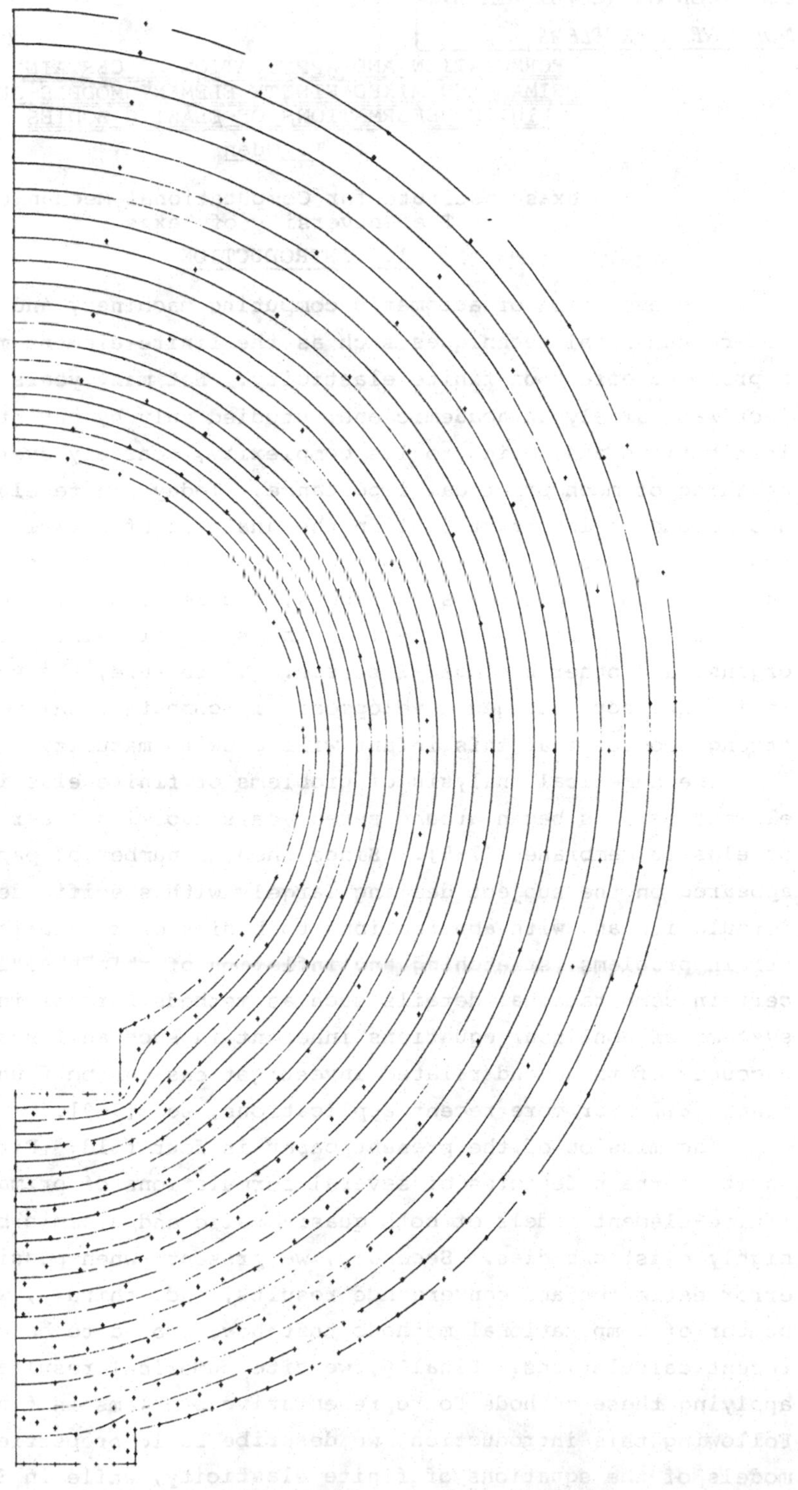

PROBLEMES NON-LINEAIRES

NON-LINEAR PROBLEMS

FORMULATION AND APPLICATION OF CERTAIN PRIMAL AND MIXED FINITE ELEMENT MODELS OF FINITE DEFORMATIONS OF ELASTIC BODIES

J. T. Oden

Texas Institute for Computational Mechanics
The University of Texas

1. INTRODUCTION

The evolution of automatic computing machinery and the advent of modern numerical techniques such as the finite-element method have had a profound effect on finite elasticity. Not many years ago the subject was largely an academic one, studied only by purists at a few institutions and, owing to its complexity, scarcely ever applied to anything of much practical importance. Today finite elasticity theory has become an important tool in the analysis of a variety of complex systems, including air cushions and bags, flexible storage tanks bearing pads, shock absorbers, balloons, deceleration systems, membranes, inflatable structures, as well as the study of veins, arteries, human organs, and other biological tissue. To be sure, the subject is still in its infancy, but new developments in computational methods give strong promise that this infant will grow to maturity.

The numerical analysis of problems of finite elasticity by finite element methods began around seven years ago with a series of studies of elastic membranes [1-5]. Since then, a number of papers have appeared on the subject dealing largely with specific details of the formulation and with applications to bodies of revolution, plane strain problems, stretching and inflation of thin sheets, and with certain computational details such as methods for solving the large systems of nonlinear equations inherent in such analyses. Summary accounts of these and related investigations can be found in the monograph [6]. For more recent applications, see [7-9].

The mission of the present paper is four fold: First, we summarize certain features of several formulations of primal and mixed finite-element models of both quasi-static and dynamic behavior of highly elastic bodies. Secondly, we present; when possible, certain error estimates and convergence results, and, thirdly, we discuss a number of computational methods that have proved to be effective in recent calculations. Finally, we cite numerical results obtained by applying these methods to representative problems in finite elasticity. Following this introduction, we describe basic properties of Galerkin models of the equations of finite elasticity, while in Section 3 we describe in some detail properties of a one-dimensional model. Under appropriate assumptions, we are able to prove convergence of primal and a mixed approximation. We also introduce these notations of consistency and stability of the finite element approximation. In Section 4 we comment on several computational methods, with emphasis on incremental loading methods for quasistatic problems. We also introduce here a finite-element-based, Lax-Wendroff type scheme for shock wave calculations. In the fifth section we cite numerical examples which include nonlinear elastostatics problems, stability and post-buckling behavior, large-amplitude transient motions, and shock waves.

2. GALERKIN APPROXIMATIONS IN FINITE ELASTICITY

The motion of a hyperelastic body Ω is governed by the system of nonlinear equations (see, e.g. [10,11])

$$\nabla_{x} \cdot S(u(x,t)) + \rho F = \rho a \quad \text{in } \Omega$$

$$S(u(x,t)) \cdot n = T \; , \quad x \epsilon \; \partial\Omega_1 \; , \quad t \geq 0$$

$$u(x,t) = g(x,t), \quad x \epsilon \; \partial\Omega_2, \quad t \geq 0 \tag{2.1}$$

Here ∇_x is the material gradient, $x = (x^1, x^2, x^3)$ describes labels of a material point $x \epsilon \Omega$, $S(u(x,t))$ is a nonlinear operator on the displacement vector $u(x,t)$ which represents the first Piola-Kirchhoff stress tensor, F is the body force, ρ the initial mass density, and $a = \partial^2 u(x,t)/\partial t^2 \equiv \ddot{u} \equiv D_t^2 u$ the acceleration. It is understood that $\nabla_x \cdot S \equiv \text{div } S$. The boundary $\partial\Omega$ is the sum of two parts, $\partial\Omega_1$ and $\partial\Omega_2$, on which the stress vector $S \cdot n$, n being a unit normal to $\partial\Omega$, is prescribed as T and the displacement is prescribed as g, respectively. For such hyperelastic bodies, the stress S is derivable from a potential function W, referred to as the strain energy for unit initial volume, in the sense that

$$S = \partial_{\gamma} W \cdot F \; ; \quad F = I + H \; ; \quad H = \nabla_x \otimes u \tag{2.2}$$

where $\gamma \equiv (H + H^T + H^T H)/2$ is the strain tensor and H is the displacement gradient.

Let $A(x)$, $B(x)$ be second-order tensors and $a(x)$, $b(x)$ be vectors defined over Ω. We define inner products according to

$$\langle A, B \rangle = \int_{\Omega} \text{tr } A \cdot B d\Omega \; , \quad (a,b) = \int_{\Omega} a \cdot b d\Omega \tag{2.3}$$

Here tr denotes the trace of the traction $A \cdot B$ and Lebesque integration is implied. The completions of the space of second-order tensors in the norm induced by $<\cdot,\cdot>$ and the space of vectors in the norm associated with $(\cdot,\cdot)$ are Hilbert spaces, denoted $J(\Omega)$ and $L_2(\Omega)$ respectively. The completion in the norm $(\cdot,\cdot)^{1/2}$ of the space of vector-valued functions which vanish on $\partial\Omega$, is denoted $\underset{\sim}{L}{}_2^{01}(\Omega)$.

Let $\underset{\sim}{v}(x)$ be an arbitrary vector in $L_2^{01}(\Omega)$. Then, upon taking the inner product of (2.1) with $\underset{\sim}{v}(\underset{\sim}{x})$ and using the Green-Gauss Theorem, we obtain from (2.1) the nonlinear variational problem: find $\underset{\sim}{u}\,\varepsilon\, L_2^{01}(\Omega)\times(0,t^*]$ such that

$$(\rho\underset{\sim}{a},\underset{\sim}{v}) + <\underset{\sim}{S}(\underset{\sim}{u}),\nabla_x \otimes \underset{\sim}{v}> = \ell(\underset{\sim}{v}) \quad \forall\ \underset{\sim}{v}\,\varepsilon\, L_2^{01}(\Omega)$$

and $t\ \varepsilon\ [0,t^*]$, wherein (2.4)

$$\ell(\underset{\sim}{v}) = (\rho\underset{\sim}{F},\underset{\sim}{v}) + \int_{\partial\Omega_2} \underset{\sim}{T}\cdot\underset{\sim}{v}\ ds \tag{2.5}$$

Moreover, $\underset{\sim}{u}$ is also subject to the initial conditions,

$$(\underset{\sim}{u}(\cdot,o)-\underset{\sim}{u}_o(\cdot),\underset{\sim}{v}) = 0\ ;\ (\dot{\underset{\sim}{u}}(\cdot,o)-\underset{\sim}{v}_o(\cdot),\underset{\sim}{v}) = 0 \quad \forall\ \underset{\sim}{v}\,\varepsilon\, L_2^{01}(\Omega). \tag{2.6}$$

Let $\underset{\sim}{g}_i(\underset{\sim}{x})$ be a basis of $\underset{\sim}{L}_2(\Omega)$; then each $\underset{\sim}{v}$ in $\underset{\sim}{L}_2(\Omega)$ is of the form $\underset{\sim}{v}(\underset{\sim}{x})=\Sigma v^i(\underset{\sim}{x})\underset{\sim}{g}_i(\underset{\sim}{x})$, $v^i(\underset{\sim}{x})\,\varepsilon\, L_2(\Omega)$. Let $\overline{W}{}_m^{01}(\Omega)$ be the Sobolev space of functions whose derivatives of order m are in $L_2(\Omega)$. We now construct a subspace $S_h^k(\Omega)$ of $W_m^{01}(\Omega)$, of finite dimension G, by identifying a collection of G linearly independent functions $\phi_1(\underset{\sim}{x}),\phi_2(\underset{\sim}{x}),\ldots,\phi_G(\underset{\sim}{x})$. The identification of these basis functions defines an $L_2(\Omega)$--orthogonal projection Π_h of $W_m^{01}(\Omega)$ into $S_h^k(\Omega)$ such that the image of any $\underset{\sim}{v}(\underset{\sim}{x})\,\varepsilon\, W_m^{01}(\Omega)$ under Π_h^k is of the form

$$\Pi_h\underset{\sim}{v}(\underset{\sim}{x}) = \sum_{\alpha=1}^{G} (\underset{\sim}{v},\underset{\sim}{\phi}^\alpha)_o\phi_\alpha(\underset{\sim}{x}) \equiv V(\underset{\sim}{x}) \tag{2.7}$$

where $(v_1,v_2)_o \equiv \int_\Omega v_1v_2 d\Omega$ and $\underset{\sim}{\phi}^\alpha(\underset{\sim}{x}) \equiv \sum_\beta^G (\phi_\alpha,\phi_\beta)_0^{-1}\phi_\beta(\underset{\sim}{x})$.

The subspace $S_h^k(\Omega)$ is assumed to have the following properties:

(i) There exists a constant C_o independent of h and v such that

$$||\Pi_h v||_m \leq C_o||v||_m \qquad \forall\ h \tag{2.8}$$

wherein $||v||_m^2 = ||v||^2_{W_2^m(\Omega)} \equiv \int_\Omega \sum_{|\underset{\sim}{\alpha}|\leq m} ||D_{\underset{\sim}{\alpha}} v||_o d\Omega$, $\underset{\sim}{\alpha}$ being a multi-index: $\underset{\sim}{\alpha} = (\alpha_1,\alpha_2,\alpha_3)$; α_i = integer ≥ 0, $|\underset{\sim}{\alpha}| \equiv \alpha_1,\alpha_2,\alpha_3$;

$D_{\underset{\sim}{\alpha}} v \equiv \partial^{|\underset{\sim}{\alpha}|} v / \partial x_1^{\alpha_1} \, \partial x_2^{\alpha_2} \, \partial x_3^{\alpha_3}$.

(ii) If $p(\underset{\sim}{x})$ is a polynomial of degree $\leq k$,

$$\Pi_h p(\underset{\sim}{x}) = p(\underset{\sim}{x}) \tag{2.9}$$

(iii) For any r such that $0 \leq r \leq k$, there exists a constant $C > 0$ such that

$$||(I-\Pi_h)v||_s \leq Ch^{k+1-s}|v|_{k+1} \tag{2.10}$$

wherein $|v|^2_{k+1} = \int_\Omega \Big(\sum_{|\underset{\sim}{\alpha}|=k+1}^{G} D_{\underset{\sim}{\alpha}} v\Big)^2 d\Omega$. In all of these relations, h is a real number, generally selected so that $0 \leq h \leq 1$ (i.e., h is a <u>mesh parameter</u>).

Let E be the real numbers and let $[0,T] \subseteq E$ be a finite time interval. Let $B[0,T]$ be a linear space of functions defined on $[0,T]$ (generally we take $B[0,T] = C^r[0,T]$, r=0,1,2,or3). The space $S_h^k(\Omega,[0,T]) = S_h^k(\Omega) \times B[0,T]$ is termed the space of semidiscrete Galerkin functions. Galerkin's method amounts to seeking among the elements in $S_h^k(\Omega,[0,T])$ the function(s)

$$\underset{\sim}{U}(\underset{\sim}{x},t) = \sum_{i=1}^{3} \sum_{\alpha=1}^{G} \underset{\sim}{g}_i(\underset{\sim}{x},t)\, A^{i\alpha}(t)\,\phi_\alpha(\underset{\sim}{x}) \tag{2.11}$$

which satisfy (2.4) for $\dot{\underset{\sim}{v}} \in S_h^k(\Omega)$:

$$(\rho D_t^2 \underset{\sim}{U}, \underset{\sim}{V}) + \langle \underset{\sim}{S}(\underset{\sim}{U}), \underset{\sim}{\nabla}_x \otimes \underset{\sim}{V} \rangle = \ell(\underset{\sim}{V}) \quad \forall\, \underset{\sim}{V} \in S_h^k(\Omega)$$

$$(\underset{\sim}{U}(\cdot,0) - \underset{\sim}{u}_o(\cdot), \underset{\sim}{V}) = 0\ ; \ (D_t \underset{\sim}{U}(\cdot,0) - \underset{\sim}{v}_o(\cdot), \underset{\sim}{V}) = 0 \tag{2.12}$$

Here $D_t^2 \underset{\sim}{U} = \underset{\sim}{a}$ and $\underset{\sim}{g}_i(x,t) = \Sigma F^m_{\cdot i}(x,t)\underset{\sim}{g}_m(x,0)$. Upon introducing (2.8) into (2.9), we obtain a large system of nonlinear differential equations in the coefficients $A^{i\alpha}(t)$:

$$\sum_{i,\alpha} M^j_{i\alpha\beta} \ddot{A}^{i\alpha}(t) + \langle \underset{\sim}{S}\big(\sum_{i,\alpha} \underset{\sim}{g}_i A^{i\alpha}(t)\phi_\alpha\big)_{\bullet}, \frac{\partial}{\partial x_j}\phi_\beta \rangle = \overline{F}^j_{\cdot\beta}(t)$$

$$\sum_{i,\alpha} (\underset{\sim}{g}_i \phi_\alpha, \underset{\sim}{g}^j \phi_\beta)_{\bullet} \dot{A}^{i\alpha}(0) = (\underset{\sim}{u}_o, \underset{\sim}{g}^j \phi_\beta)_{\bullet};$$

$$\sum_{i,\alpha} (\underset{\sim}{g}_i \phi_\alpha, \underset{\sim}{g}^j \phi_\beta)_{\bullet} A^{i\alpha}(0) = (\underset{\sim}{v}_o, \underset{\sim}{g}^j \phi_\beta)_{\bullet} \tag{2.13}$$

Here $M^j_{i\alpha\beta}$ and $F^j_{\cdot\beta}$ denote the mass matrix and the generalized forces,

$$M^j_{i\alpha\beta} = (\rho \underset{\sim}{g}_i \phi_\alpha, \underset{\sim}{g}^j \phi_\beta)_{\bullet}\ ; \ \overline{F}^j_{\cdot\beta}(t) = \ell(\underset{\sim}{g}^j \phi_\beta)_{\bullet} \tag{2.14}$$

with $i,j = 1,2,3$; $\alpha,\beta = 1,2,\ldots,G$.

Finite Element Formulations. The finite-element concept provides for a direct and systematic application of the Galerkin method to arbitrary domains Ω which, in general, leads to well-conditioned systems of equations. We partition Ω into E subdomains (finite elements) so that

$$\bar{\Omega} = \bigcup_{e=1}^{E} \bar{\Omega}_e \; ; \; \Omega_e \cap \Omega_f = \phi, \; e \neq f \tag{2.15}$$

On each element e we introduce a system of local interpolation functions $\chi_{\underset{\sim}{N}}^{e\alpha}(\underset{\sim}{x})$ such that

$$D_{\underset{\sim}{\beta}} \chi_{\underset{\sim}{N}}^{e\alpha}(\underset{\sim}{x}^M) = \delta_N^M \delta_{\underset{\sim}{\beta}}^{\alpha} \; ; \; \chi_{\underset{\sim}{N}}^{e\alpha}(\underset{\sim}{x}) \equiv 0 \text{ for } \underset{\sim}{x} \notin \bar{\Omega}_e \tag{2.16}$$

here $\underset{\sim}{x}^M$ denotes one of N_e prescribed nodes in $\bar{\Omega}_e$ $(M,N=1,2,\ldots,N_e)$. Global "coordinate" functions $\phi_{\underset{\sim}{\Delta}}^{\alpha}(\underset{\sim}{x})$ are then given by

$$\phi_{\underset{\sim}{\Delta}}^{\alpha}(\underset{\sim}{x}) = \bigcup_{e=1}^{E} \sum_{N}^{N_e} \overset{(e)}{\Omega}{}_{\Delta}^{N} \chi_{N}^{e\alpha}(\underset{\sim}{x}) \tag{2.17}$$

where $\overset{(e)}{\Omega}{}_{\Delta}^{N}$ is a Boolean transformation: $\overset{(e)}{\Omega}{}_{\Delta}^{N}=1$ if node N of $\bar{\Omega}_e$ coincides with $\underset{\sim}{x}^{\Delta} \in \Omega$ and is zero if otherwise.

The local functions defined in (2.16) generally are in $S_h^k(\bar{\Omega}_e)$ with $h = \text{dia}\,\bar{\Omega}_e$ [see (2.6)-(2.8)]. Property $(2.16)_2$ is responsible for the banded character of $\langle \underset{\sim}{S}(A^{i\alpha}), \partial_j \phi_\beta \rangle$ in linear problems, and makes it possible to formulate a local Galerkin approximation of the type (2.10) for each independent element. For example, suppose $|\alpha| = 0$ in (2.12) (i.e., only values are prescribed at nodes) and $\phi_\alpha(\underset{\sim}{x}) \equiv \bigcup_e \sum_N \overset{(e)}{\Omega}{}_{\alpha}^{N} \chi_N^e(\underset{\sim}{x})$. Also let $\underset{\sim}{g}_i(\underset{\sim}{x},t) = \underset{\sim}{i}_i (\underset{\sim}{i}_i \cdot \underset{\sim}{i}_j = \delta_{ij})$. Then, for each finite element we have the local equations,

$$\sum_N m_{NM}^{(e)} \ddot{a}_{iN}^{(e)}(t) + \langle \underset{\sim}{S}(\sum_i \sum_N a_{jN}^{(e)}(t) \underset{\sim}{i}_j \chi_N^e(\cdot)), \partial_i \chi_M^e(\cdot) \rangle_e = f_{iN}^e(t) \tag{2.18}$$

where $\langle \cdot,\cdot \rangle_e$ is the inner product in (2.3) obtained using restructions of the arguments to $\bar{\Omega}_e$ and

$$m_{NM}^{(e)} = (\rho \chi_N^e, \chi_M^e) \; ; \; f_{iN}^e = \mathcal{L}(\underset{\sim}{i}_i \chi_N^e) \; ; \; a_{iN}^{(e)} = \sum_\alpha \overset{(e)}{\Omega}{}_{N}^{\alpha} A_{i\alpha} \tag{2.19}$$

The global equations are obtained by "connecting the elements together" using (2.15) and the fact that $\bar{F}_{i\alpha}(t)$, the global generalized force, is precisely $\sum_e^E \sum_N \overset{(e)}{\Omega}{}_{\alpha}^{N} f_{iN}^e(t)$. See [6,12] for additional details.

It is well-known that finite-element interpolants can be easily constructed so that (2.6) and (2.8) are satisfied, with h defined as $h = \max_e \{h_1, h_2, \cdots, h_e\}$, h_e=diameter $\bar{\Omega}_e$. Indeed, Ciarlet and Raviart [13], in extending work of Fried [14], have shown that for a wide class of elements (2.8) can be replaced by

$$||(I-\Pi_k)v||_s \leq C\frac{h^{k+1}}{\rho^s} |v|_{k+1} \tag{2.20}$$

where if ρ_e is the diameter of the largest sphere that can be inscribed in an element $\bar{\Omega}_e$, $\rho=\min_e \{\rho_e\}$. Often $\rho=\nu h$ for ν = constant>0, so that (2.20) reduces to (2.10).

3. ACCURACY AND CONVERGENCE STUDIES

In this article we shall investigate several special forms of the Galkerin approximation (2.9). In some cases we construct estimates of accuracy and prove convergence. In particular, we consider incompressible, homogeneous, isotropic, hyperelastic bodies for which the strain energy function W is of the form

$$W = W(I_1, I_2) \qquad I_3=1 \tag{3.1}$$

where I_i are the principal invariants of the deformation tensor $\underset{\sim}{G} = \underset{\sim}{I} + 2\underset{\sim}{\gamma}$ [see (2.2)]; i.e., using the summation convention

$$I_1 = 3 + 2\gamma^r_r \ ; \ I_2 = 3 + 4\gamma^r_r + 2(\gamma^r_r\gamma^s_s - \gamma^r_s\gamma^s_r) \ ; \ I_3 = |\delta^r_s + 2\gamma^r_s| \tag{3.2}$$

where $\gamma^r_s = g^{rm}\gamma_{ms}$, γ_{ms} are the covariant components of $\underset{\sim}{\gamma}$, and g^{rm} are the covariant components of the metric tensor associated with x^i at t=0.

Among forms of $W(I_1, I_2)$ in use in the characterization of natural and synthetic rubbers, we mention as examples the Mooney form,

$$W = M_1(I_1-3) + M_2(I_2-3) \tag{3.3$_1$}$$

the Hart-Smith form

$$W = C\{\int \exp [k_1(I_1-3)^2]dI_1 + k_2 \ln \frac{I_2}{3}\} \tag{3.3$_2$}$$

and the Biderman form

$$W = B_1(I_1-3) + B_2(I_1-3)^2 + B_3(I_1-3)^3 + B_4(I_2-3) \tag{3.3$_3$}$$

Here M_1, M_2, C, k_1, k_2, and B_i are material constants. Numerous other examples are cited in [6].

Owing to the incompressibility constraint, $(3.1)_2$, the stress tensor $\underset{\sim}{S}$ of (2.2) is given by,

$$\underset{\sim}{S} = \underset{\sim}{\Sigma} \cdot \underset{\sim}{F} \; ; \; \underset{\sim}{\Sigma} = \partial_{\underset{\sim}{\gamma}} W \; ; \; \sigma^{ij} = \sum_{\alpha=1}^{2} \frac{\partial W}{\partial I_\alpha} \cdot \frac{\partial I_\alpha}{\partial \gamma_{ij}} + h \frac{\partial I_3}{\partial \gamma_{ij}} \tag{3.4}$$

where in σ^{ij} are components of $\underset{\sim}{\Sigma}$ and the Lagrange multiplier h is called the hydrostatic pressure (see [6,pp.236-242]).

<u>3.1 Nonlinear Quasistatic Two-Point BVP</u>. As a first simple case, we consider the stretching of a long, thin cylindrical rod of incompressible, hyperelastic material, fixed at $x^1=0$, subjected to a static tensile force at its free end of p, and to a force per unit length of f. Assuming that the transverse normal stresses are negligible, the hydrostatic pressure can be eliminated ab initio and the longitudinal Piola-Kirchhoff stress is found to be

$$S(\lambda) = 2(1-\lambda^{-3})(\lambda \frac{\partial W}{\partial I_1} + \frac{\partial W}{\partial I_2}) \tag{3.5}$$

where λ is the longitudinal extension ratio; i.e., if u(x) is the longitudinal displacement and $u' = du/dx$, then $\lambda = 1 + u'$.

Denote $D \equiv d/dx$. We shall use the notation $S(\lambda)$ and $S(Du)$ interchangeably, even though $S(\lambda) = S(1+Du)$. Likewise, for one-dimensional problems of this type, $\langle A,B \rangle = (A,B)_o$. The weak form of this boundary-value problem is then: find u such that

$$(S(Du), Dv)_o = \ell(v), \quad \forall\, v \in H^1(0,L) \tag{3.6}$$

whereas the associated Galerkin problem is find $U \in S_h^k\ (0,L)$ such that

$$(S(DU),DV)_o = \ell(V), \qquad \forall\, V \in S_h^k(0,L) \tag{3.7}$$

Denoting $\Lambda=1+DU$, we easily arrive at the orthogonality condition

$$(S(\lambda) - S(\Lambda), DV)_o = 0 \;, \quad \forall\, V \in S_h^k(0,L) \tag{3.8}$$

by setting v=V in (3.6) and subtracting (3.7).

Assuming $S(\lambda) \in C^1$, we have

$$S(\lambda) = S(\Lambda) + S^1(\bar{\lambda})e_\lambda \; ; \quad \bar{\lambda} = \lambda + \theta(\lambda-\Lambda) \; ; \quad e_\lambda = \lambda - \Lambda \tag{3.9}$$

with $0 \leq \theta \leq 1$, $S'(\bar{\lambda}) \equiv dS(\bar{\lambda})/d\lambda$. Hence

$$(S(\lambda) - S(\Lambda), \lambda-\Lambda)_o = (S'(\bar{\lambda})e_\lambda, e_\lambda) \tag{3.10}$$

For most hyperelastic materials, there are numbers μ_o, $\mu_1 > 0$ such that $\mu_o \leq S'(\bar{\lambda}) \leq \mu_1$ for every $\lambda > \lambda_c$, where λ_c is some critical extension ratio > 0. Assuming this is the case,

$$\mu_o||e_\lambda||_o^2 \leq (S'(\bar{\lambda})e_\lambda, \lambda-\Lambda+\Pi_h\lambda-\Pi_h\lambda)$$

$$= (S'(\lambda)e_\lambda, E_\lambda) \leq \mu_1||e_\lambda||_o \; ||E_\lambda||_o$$

where $E_\lambda = \lambda - \Pi_h\lambda = 1+u'=\Pi_h 1-\Pi_h u'=(I-\Pi_h)Du=E_{u'}$, and $e_\lambda=\lambda-\Lambda=D(u-U)=De_u$. Consequently

$$||De_u||_o \leq \frac{\mu_1}{\mu_o} ||E_{u'}||_o \tag{3.11}$$

We summarize these results in the following theorem:

<u>Theorem 3.1</u> Let the first Piola-Kirchhoff stress $S(\lambda)$ in a homogeneous rod of isotropic hyperelastic material be such that constants μ_o, $\mu_1 > o$ exist so that

$$0 < \mu_o \leq \frac{dS(\lambda)}{d\lambda} \leq \mu_1 \tag{3.12}$$

$\forall \lambda \in [\lambda_c, \infty]$. Let U denote the Galerkin approximation of the solution u of (3.6) and $e_u = u-U$ be the error. Then (3.11) holds. Moreover, if $U \in S_h^k(O,L)$ for which (2.6)-(2.8) hold, then

$$||De_u||_o \leq kh^k|u|_{k+1} \; ; \quad ||e_u||_o \leq kh^{k+1}|u|_{k+1} \tag{3.13}$$

where k is a constant independent of h.

The results of (3.13) follow from (2.8) and (3.11) together with the observation that $||e_u||_1 \geq c||De_u||_o$ and $||e_u||_o \leq hc_1||De_u||_o$ for the simple case under consideration. Thus, if polynomials of order k are used in constructing $S_h^k(O,L)$, the approximation is convergent and $||De_u||_o = O(h^k)$, $||e_u||_o = O(h^{k+1})$.

<u>Remark</u>: Observe that $\ddot{u} - \frac{1}{\rho} DS(u_x) = \ddot{u} - \frac{1}{\rho}\frac{dS}{d\lambda} u_{xx}$. Hence

$$C(Du) \equiv \sqrt{\frac{1}{\rho}\frac{dS}{d\lambda}} \tag{3.14}$$

is the intrinsic wave speed in the material. When S(Du) is such that S'(Du) exists ∀ Du and (3.12) holds, disturbances in the body travel with real and finite wave speeds. When this occurs, we shall say that S(Du) satisfies the <u>wave condition</u>.

<u>3.2. Stretching of a Rod of Mooney Material</u>. More precise results can be obtained if specific forms of $W(I_1,I_2)$ are identified. To illustrate, suppose the material is of the Mooney type [see (3.3),]. Then it can be shown that

$$S(\lambda) = 2(1-\lambda^{-3})(\lambda M_1 + M_2); \quad h = -\lambda^{-1}[M_1 + \lambda^{-1}M_2(1+\lambda^3) \tag{3.15}$$

so that

$$\frac{dS}{d\lambda} = 2M_1(1+2\lambda^{-3}) + 6M_2\lambda^{-4} \tag{3.16}$$

For stretching of the rod, $\lambda \geq \lambda_c = 1$; hence, S satisfies the wave condition and, in fact,

$$0 < 2M_1 \leq \frac{dS}{d\lambda} \leq 6(M_1+M_2) \tag{3.17}$$

Thus

$$||De_u||_o \leq 3(1+M_1/M_2)||E_{u'}||_o \tag{3.18}$$

<u>Convergence of the Hydrostatic Pressure</u>. The approximation H(x) of the hydrostatic pressure h(x) also converges, and, in fact from (3.15)

$$||h-H||_o \leq ||M_1 + \{\lambda^2(1-\frac{e_\lambda}{\lambda}) + \frac{2\lambda e_\lambda - e_\lambda^2}{\lambda^2(1-e_\lambda/\lambda)}\} M_2||_o \times ||e_\lambda\lambda^{-2}(1-e_\lambda/\lambda)^{-1}||_o \tag{3.19}$$

Here $e_\lambda = \lambda - \Lambda = Du - DU = De_u$, which is bounded above by the interpolation error DE_u in (3.11).

<u>3.3 Mixed Finite Element Models</u>. In the linear theory it is known that [15] improvements in the accuracy of approximations of derivatives can be obtained by using mixed models in which two or more dependent variables are approximated simultaneously. We shall explore certain properties of a mixed nonlinear formulation here. In particular, consider the following canonical form of the basic nonlinear quasistatic two-point boundary-value problem

$$\begin{aligned} v(x) &\equiv S(Du) \; ; \quad u(o) = 0 \\ Dv(x) &= -f \; ; \quad v(L) = P/A_o \end{aligned} \tag{3.20}$$

These equations corresponds to the longitudinal deformations of a thin rod of initial cross-sectional area A_o and length L fixed at x = 0 and subjected to a force P at x = L. Independent approximations are now made of the displacement u and the stress v. Now the Kirchhoff stress $S(D_u)$ is considered to be a mapping from a Space U into V, with $u(x) \varepsilon U$ and $v(x) \varepsilon V$. Let $S_h^k(O.L)$ be a finite-dimensional subspace of U and let $T_\ell^m(O,L)$ be a finite-dimensional subspace of V. Then, if $\Pi_h : U \to S_h^k(O,L)$ and $P_\ell : V \to T_\ell^m(O,L)$ are orthogonal projections into these subspaces, the projections of arbitrary elements $u \varepsilon U$ and $v \varepsilon V$ are

$$\Pi_h u = \sum_{\alpha=1}^{G} (u,\phi^\alpha)_O \phi_\alpha(x) \;;\; P_\ell v = \sum_{\Delta=1}^{H} (v,\omega^\Delta)_O \omega_\Delta(x) \qquad (3.21)$$

where $\{\phi_\alpha\}_{\alpha=1}^G$ and $\{\omega_\Delta\}_{\Delta=1}^H$ are bases of $S_h^k(O,L)$ and $T_\ell^m(O,L)$ respectively, each generated using appropriate finite-element models. Let u* and v* be the actual solution of (3.20). The finite-element appropriate solutions are the elements $U^* \varepsilon S_h^k(O,L)$ and $V^* \varepsilon T_\ell^m(O,L)$ such that

$$P_\ell(V^* - S(U^*)) = 0 \;, \text{ and } \Pi_h(DV^* + f) = 0 \qquad (3.22)$$

with $V^*(L) = P/A_O$, $U^*(o) = 0$ (say).

<u>Lemma 3.1</u>. Let (3.22) hold and denote

$$e_u = u^* - U^* \;;\; e_v = v^* - V^* \;;\; E_u = u^* - \Pi_h u^*$$
$$E_v = v^* - P_\ell v^* \;;\; \varepsilon_u = U^* - \Pi_h u^* \;;\; \varepsilon_v = V^* - P_\ell v^* \qquad (3.23)$$

Then the following hold:

$$P_\ell(S(u_x^*) - S(U_x^*)) + e_v = E_v \qquad (3.24)$$

$$\Pi_h De_v = 0 \qquad (3.25)$$

<u>Proof:</u> (3.24) is obtained by adding and substracting $P_\ell v^* + v^* + P_\ell S(u^*)$ in (3.22), whereas (3.23) follows from (3.20) and (3.22) upon replacing $\Pi_h f$ by $-\Pi_h Dv^*$. In (3.23) e_u, e_v are <u>approximation errors</u> associated with u and v; E_u, E_v are <u>interpolation errors</u>, and ε_u, ε_v are termed <u>projection errors</u>, respectively.

Let $u \epsilon U$ and $v \epsilon V$. We shall term (3.22) a <u>consistent</u> Galerkin approximation of (3.20) if

$$\lim_{\ell\to 0} L_\ell(v) = 0 \text{ and } \lim_{h,\ell\to 0} M_{h\ell}(u,v) = 0 \qquad (3.26)$$

where $L_h(v)$ and $M_{h\ell}(u,v)$ are the lack-of-consistency functions

$$L_\ell(v) \equiv (Dv,v) - (DP_\ell v,v) \;;\; M_{h\ell}(u,v) \equiv (S(Du),v) - (S(D\Pi_h u,P_\ell v) \qquad (3.27)$$

A simple calculation reveals that

$$L_\ell(v) \le ||v||_o\,||DE_v||_o \text{ and } M_{h\ell}(u,v) \le ||v||_o\,||S(Du) - S(D\Pi_h u)||_o + ||S(D\Pi_h u)||_o||E_v||_o \quad (3.28)$$

While several different defintions of stability suggest themselves at this juncture, we shall choose to refer to the Galerkin approximation (3.22) as <u>stable</u> whenever constants $\alpha,\beta > 0$ exist such that

$$||\Pi_h DP_\ell S'(Du)\Pi_h u||_o \ge \alpha||\Pi_h u||_o \text{ and } ||P_\ell S'(Du)P_\ell v||_o \ge \beta||P_\ell v||_o \quad (3.29)$$

for every $u\varepsilon U$ and $v\varepsilon V$. This may be a rather strong requirement for stability.

<u>Theorem 3.2</u>. Let the Piola-Kirchhoff stress $S(Du)$ satisfy the wave condition and let the subspaces $S_h^k(O,L)$ and $T_\ell^m(O,L)$ be such that (2.6) - (2.8) are satisfied and $||DE_v||_o$ and $||DE_u||_o$ vanish as $h, \ell \to 0$. Then the Galerkin approximation is consistent.

<u>Proof</u>: This is obvious. Simply set $S(Du) - S(D\Pi_h u) = S'(D\bar{u})DE_u$ in (3.28) and use (3.14). It then follows that L_h, $M_{\ell h} \to 0$ as $h,\ell\to 0$

<u>Theorem 3.3</u>. Let the conditions of Theorem 3.2 hold and let the Galerkin scheme be stable in the sense of (3.29). Then it is convergent in the sense that $||De_u||_o$ vanish as $h,\ell\to 0$.

<u>Proof</u>: According to the triangle inequality,

$$||De_u||_o \le ||DE_u||_o + ||D\varepsilon_u||_o \quad (3.30)$$

Since $S(Du\lambda)$ obeys the wave condition, (3.24) yields

$$P_\ell S'(\bar{\lambda})De_u = E_v - e_v = \varepsilon_v = P_\ell S'(\bar{\lambda})D(\varepsilon_u - E_u) \quad (3.31)$$

Hence,

$$\Pi_h DP_\ell S'(\bar{\lambda})D\varepsilon_u = \Pi_h DP_\ell S'(\bar{\lambda})DE_u + \Pi_h D\varepsilon_u \quad (3.32)$$

However, $\Pi_h D\varepsilon_u = \Pi_h DE_v$, in accordance with (3.25). Since, by hypothesis, (3.29) holds, we have

$$||D\varepsilon_u||_o \le \frac{1}{\alpha}\,||\Pi_h DP_\ell S'(\bar{\lambda})||_o\,||DE_u||_o + \frac{1}{\alpha}\,||\Pi_h DE_v||_o$$

Combining this with (3.30) and (3.31) gives

$$||De_u||_o \leq (1 + \frac{1}{\alpha} ||\Pi_h DP_\ell S'(\bar{\lambda})||_o) ||DE_u||_o + \frac{1}{\alpha} ||DE_v||_o \qquad (3.33)$$

and

$$||e_v||_o \leq ||E_v||_o + c||De_u||_o \qquad (3.34)$$

Since $S(\bar{\lambda})$ satisfies the wave condition, $DP_\ell S'$ is bounded. Consequently, both De_u and e_v are bounded above by $||DE_u||_o$, $||DE_v||_o$ and $||E_v||_o$, which vanish as $h, \ell \to 0$.

3.4. Time-Dependent Problems. In the case of time dependent problems we shall use the combined finite-difference/finite-element approximation

$$\rho (\delta_t^2 U^i, V)_o + (S(DU^i), DV)_o = \ell(V^i) \qquad (3.35)$$

$V \epsilon S_h^k(O,L)$, wherein δ_t^2 is a second-order central difference operator and $U^i = U(x, i\Delta t)$; $0 = t_o < t < \ldots < t_R = T$; $t_{i+1} - t_i = \Delta t$. If the exact solution $u \epsilon C^3[o,T]$, then

$$\rho (\delta_t^2 u^i, v)_o + (S(Du^i), Dv)_o = \ell(v^i) + \rho (\omega^i \Delta t, v) \qquad (3.36)$$

where ω^i is a bounded function of t. The following lemmas are proved in [15]:

Lemma 3.2. Let (3.35) and (3.36) hold and let S(u) satisfy the wave condition. Then

$$\rho(\delta_t^2 \varepsilon^i, \varepsilon^i) + \alpha_o ||D\varepsilon^i||_o^2 \leq \rho_o(\delta_t^2 E^i, \varepsilon^i) + \alpha_1 h^2 + \alpha_2 (\Delta t)^2 \qquad (3.37)$$

and

$$\rho(\delta_t^2 e^i, \varepsilon^i) \leq \beta_o ||DE^i||_o^2 + \beta_1 ||D\varepsilon^i||_o^2 + \beta_2 (\Delta t)^2 \qquad (3.38)$$

wherein α_i, β_i are constants > 0 and independent of Δt and h and $e^i = u(x, i\Delta t) - U(x, i\Delta t)$, $E^i = u(x, i\Delta t) - \Pi_h u(x, i\Delta t)$, $\varepsilon^i = U(x, i\Delta t) - \Pi_h u(x, i\Delta t)$.

Theorem 3.4. Let (3.35) and (3.36) hold and let S(u) satisfy the wave condition. Then the finite-element/difference approximation error e(x,t) is such that for sufficiently small h and Δt,

$$||De^i||_o = O(\Delta t + h) \qquad (3.39)$$

Proof: This result is obtained immediately from (3.37) and (3.38) by observing that $\rho(\delta_t^2 \varepsilon, \varepsilon) - \rho(\delta_t^2 E, \varepsilon) = -\rho(\delta_t^2 e, \varepsilon)$ in (3.37) and then using (3.38). Since the α_i, β_i are arbitrary, find constants k_1 and k_2 such that $||De^i||_o^2 \leq k_1 h^2 + k_2 \Delta t^2$, from which (3.39) follows.

The question of numerical stability, of course, arises here. In [15] it is shown that the approximation (3.35) is stable in energy whenever $(h/\Delta t) > \nu_i C^i_{max}/\sqrt{2}$, where $C^i_{max} = \max[S'(U^i_x)/\rho_o]^{1/2}$, $i = 1,2$, with $\nu_1 = 2/\sqrt{3}$ and $\nu_2 = 2$. The case involving ν_1 pertains to the use of the consistent mass matrix of (2.14) in the calculations, whereas ν_2 corresponds to the case in which masses are lumped. We describe some specific numerical results in Section 5 that were obtained using approximations of the type described here.

3.5 Shock Waves in Elastic Rods. Consider once again the one-dimensional hyperelastic rod problem and again denote by $\lambda(x,t)$ the longitudinal extension ratio, $\lambda = 1 + Du$. Since $C(\lambda) \equiv \left(\frac{1}{\rho}\partial S/\partial\lambda\right)^{1/2}$ is the intrinsic material (acoustical) wave speed, and since $D\ddot{u} = \ddot{\lambda}$, we have the equation

$$\ddot{\lambda} - D[C^2(\lambda)D\lambda] = 0 \tag{3.40}$$

This alternate form of the wave equation is useful in studying shock waves in nonlinear materials. Whenever $\dot{\lambda} \in C^3$, the expansions

$$\begin{aligned} q^{n+1}(x) &= q^n(x) + \frac{\Delta t}{\rho}D^2 S(\lambda^n(x)) + \frac{\Delta t^2}{2\rho}D^2[S'(\lambda^n(x)q^n(x)] + O(\Delta t^3) \\ \lambda^{n+1}(x) &= \lambda^n(x) + \frac{\Delta t}{\rho}q^n(x) + \frac{\Delta t^2}{2\rho}D^2 S(\lambda^n(x)) + O(\Delta t^3) \end{aligned} \tag{3.41}$$

can be used to develop a finite-element based-Lax-Wendroff type integration scheme. In (3.41), $q(x,t) = \dot{\lambda}(x,t)$ and $\lambda^n(x) \equiv \lambda(x,n\Delta t)$ where $0 \leq t_1 \leq t_2 \leq \cdots \leq t_R = T$ and $\Delta t = t_{i+1} - t_i$. We describe such a scheme in the next section and cite some numerical results obtained using it in Section 5.

4. COMPUTATIONAL METHODS FOR NONLINEAR SYSTEMS OF EQUATIONS

In this section we shall describe a number of computational methods that have proved to be effective in the solution of the large systems of nonlinear equations associated with the models described previously. We begin with the description of methods for systems of nonlinear algebraic equations encountered in static problems.

4.1 Incremental Loading/Newton-Raphson Method. The idea of transforming a system of nonlinear algebraic equations into an equivalent system of ordinary differential equations and then solving them by by numerical integration, was introduced independently by Lahaye [16], Davidenko [17], and Goldberg and Richard [18], and a brief history of the method can be found in [19] and [6]. We shall outline one form of the method developed in [6] and [20] which has been used to solve very large systems having multiple roots [21].

For nonlinear problems, the finite-element method described in §3 leads, for quasi-static problems, to a system of n nonlinear equations of the form

$$f(x,p) = 0 \tag{4.1}$$

wherein f is an n-vector of nonlinear equations in the n unknown generalized displacement $x = (x_1, \cdots, x_n)^T$ and a parameter p representing the applied load. By assuming that x and p are functions of a parameter s, we can compute

$$\dot{f} = \frac{df}{ds} = 0 = \frac{\partial f(x,p)}{\partial x}\dot{x} + \frac{\partial f(x,p)}{\partial p}\dot{p} \tag{4.2}$$

Thus (4.1) is transformed into the system of differential equations

$$J(x,p)\dot{x} + g(x,p)\dot{p} = 0 \tag{4.3}$$

where $J(x,p) \equiv \partial f(x,p)/\partial x$ is the Jacobian matrix and $g(x,p) \equiv \frac{\partial f(x,p)}{\partial p}$ is a "load-correction" vector.

We now proceed to integrate (4.3) numerically. While a number of sophisticated numerical schemes could be used, numerical experiments have repeatedly indicated that, for large systems, none have any definite advantages over the standard Euler technique, provided a corrector of some type is introduced to reduce errors at the end of each increment Δs. Hence, suppose $s \in [0,1]$ and introduce the partition $0 = s_0 < s_1 < \ldots < s_n = 1$, $s_{i+1} - s_i = \Delta s$. Denoting $x^r = x(s_r)$, $p^r = p(s_r)$, and $\Delta p^r = p^{r+1} - p^r$, we arrive at the recurrance relation

$$J(x^r,p^r)(x^{r+1} - x^r) + g(x^r,p^r)\Delta p^r = 0 \tag{4.4}$$

Ordinarily we set $\Delta p^r = \Delta s$ and prescribe the load increments Δp^r hence the term "incremental loading." However, it is sometimes convenient (in fact, necessary) to treat Δp^r as an unknown. Then we append to (4.4) the approximation

$$(\Delta x^{r-1})^T \Delta x^r + \Delta p^{r-1} \Delta p^r = \Delta s^2 \tag{4.5}$$

of the arc length $ds^2 = dx^T dx + dp^2$ in E^{n+1}. Here $\Delta x^r = x^{r+1} - \Delta x^r$.

We now propose to reduce the accumulated round-off error at the end of each load increment using Newton-Rapshom iterations such that

$$\underset{\sim}{x}^{r,m+1} = \underset{\sim}{x}^{r,m} - \underset{\sim}{J}^{-1}(\underset{\sim}{x}^{r,m},p^r)\underset{\sim}{f}(\underset{\sim}{x}^r,p^r) \tag{4.6}$$

where the starting value is $\underset{\sim}{x}^{r,o}=\underset{\sim}{x}^r$ and m=0,1,2,...,k. The number k is determined by prescribing initially an exceptable error E such that $[(\underset{\sim}{x}^{r,m})^T(\underset{\sim}{x}^{r,m})]^{1/2} = ||\underset{\sim}{x}^{r,m}||_{E^n} \leq \varepsilon$ for m > k. Ortega and **Rhein**-boldt [19] prove a version of the following theorem

<u>Theorem 4.1</u> (Cf[19]). Consider the system of equations (2.1) where $\underset{\sim}{f}: D \subseteq E^n \times [0,1] \to E^n$. Let $\underset{\sim}{f}$ be differentiable with respect to $\underset{\sim}{x}$ and let its derivative $\underset{\sim}{J}(x,p) = \partial \underset{\sim}{f}/\partial \underset{\sim}{x}$ be continuous and non-singular on Dx[0,1] for all s ε [0,1] and assume a solution $\underset{\sim}{x}(s)$ [or $\underset{\sim}{x}(p(s))$] exists. Then there exists a partition of [0,1] and integers $k_1,k_2,\ldots$ such that the sequence $\{\underset{\sim}{x}^{r,m}\}$, m=0,...,$k_r$-1 remains in D and, after N load increments, $\lim_{m\to\infty} \underset{\sim}{x}^{N,m} = \underset{\sim}{x}(1)$.

In applications, the major problem with this method is its inability to handle, without major modifications, cases in which J(x,p) is discontinuous or singular. Such cases are encountered frequently in nonlinear elasticity in the form of bifurcations and limit points on the equilibrium path Γ: $\underset{\sim}{x} = \underset{\sim}{x}(p)$.

<u>4.2. Stability, Bifurcations, and Limit Points</u>. We consider a modification of the procedure described above which can be used to determine limit points and points of bifurcation and to carry the solution beyond these along stable equilibrium paths.

Ideally, at critical points $\underset{\sim}{x}_c$ such that det $\underset{\sim}{J}(\underset{\sim}{x}_c,p_c) = 0$, we introcuce a change of variables $\underset{\sim}{x} = \underset{\sim}{A}\underset{\sim}{y}$ such that the matrix

$$\underset{\sim}{H} = \underset{\sim}{A}^T\underset{\sim}{J}(\underset{\sim}{x}_c,p)\underset{\sim}{A} \tag{4.7}$$

is diagonal and of rank r < n, with zeros in the last n-r entries. Let $\underset{\sim}{y} = (\underset{\sim}{y}_1,\underset{\sim}{y}_2)^T$, $\underset{\sim}{y}_1$ being the first r rows of $\underset{\sim}{y}$, and let $\underset{\sim}{z}_o$ be an arbitrary r-vector of constants. We set $\bar{\underset{\sim}{x}} = \underset{\sim}{A}(\underset{\sim}{z}_o,\underset{\sim}{y}_2)$, holding p constant. This moves the solution off an equilibrium path Γ but in a direction tangent to Γ at the critical point $\underset{\sim}{x}_c$. Holding $\bar{\underset{\sim}{x}}$ constant, we iterate on p until $\underset{\sim}{f}(\underset{\sim}{x},p^*) = \underset{\sim}{0}$ (approximately). If $p^* > p_c$, the postcritical equilibrium path is stable. If $p^* < p_c$, it is unstable, whereas if p*=p, the test fails, a new $\underset{\sim}{z}_1$ is selected ($|\underset{\sim}{z}_1| > |\underset{\sim}{z}_o|$) and the process is repeated. Once a postcritical equilibrium path is reached, the incremental loading process is continued with prescribed load increments Δp such that Δp > o if

$p^* < p_c$ and $\Delta p < 0$ if $p^* < p_c$.

To determine x_c with sufficient accuracy, we employ a procedure described by Gallagher [22], and evaluate the sign of the determinant of $J(x,p)$ at each load increment. This is a numerically sensitive undertaking. Generally J must be appropriately scaled, and x_c is only estimated by linear or quadratic interpolation. However, the test is necessary since bifurcation points can be inadvertently by-passed in the incremental loading process.

The elaborate procedure for post-critical analysis just described is generally too slow and expensive for the practical study of large scale nonlinear problems. An alternative that has been used effectively is described in [9]. In this process, each bifurcation point (i.e., each critical point through which two or more stable equilibrium paths cross) is interpreted as a limit point (i.e., a critical point involving only one equilibrium path) of a perturbed system obtained by introducing imperfections into the original system of equations. These imperfections are generally in the form of perturbations in either the stiffness coefficients, the location of loads, or both, and are represented by an imperfection parameter ζ. The incremental scheme is based on the observation that for small ζ, the post-critical equilibrium path of the imperfect system approaches asymptotically that of the "perfect" system and bifurcation points in the perfect system are reduced to limit points in the imperfect system. Thus, we proceed with the usual incremental loading Newton-Raphson technique, checking det J as described previously, until a critical point $x^r = x_c$ is reached. The system at x^{r-1} is perturbed, and the equilibrium path of the perturbed system is traced beyond x_c. Newton-Raphson iterations (with $\zeta=0$) then return the system to the correct equilibrium path and the incremental loading process is re-initiated. Examples of postbuckling problems solved in this way are given in the next section.

4.3 Explicit Integration Procedures. Instead of numerically integrating (4.3), which requires an implicit integration scheme, we can construct the system of differential equations

$$\dot{x} + Cf(x,p) = 0 \tag{4.8}$$

where C is a damping matrix, and $x(0)$ is usually 0. Then the solution x^* of (4.1) is the steady-state solution of (4.8), provided (4.8) is a stable dynamical system. The damping matrix C can generally be selected so that (4.8) is stable. Taking C to be the diagonal matrix

$\underset{\sim}{cI}$, one choice of an explicit integration scheme for (4.8) is

$$\underset{\sim}{x}^{r+1} = \underset{\sim}{x}^{r} + \Delta s \; c \; \underset{\sim}{f}(\underset{\sim}{x}^{r},p) \tag{4.9}$$

$\Delta s = s_{r+1} - s_r$, $s \in [0,1]$. Since p is new held constant, $\underset{\sim}{x}(s)$ may not intersect with an equilibrium path at any points other than s=0 and s=1. We cite an example problem solved using this method in the next section.

4.4 Simple Explicit Scheme for Transient Response. We now turn to the elastodynamics problem (2.9), which, for the present, can be thought of as a system of second-order nonlinear differential equations of the form

$$\begin{aligned} \underset{\sim}{M}\ddot{\underset{\sim}{x}} + \underset{\sim}{f}(\underset{\sim}{x},p) &= \underset{\sim}{0} \\ \underset{\sim}{x}(0) = \underset{\sim}{x}_o \;;\; \dot{\underset{\sim}{x}}(o) &= \underset{\sim}{v}_o \end{aligned} \tag{4.10}$$

Here $\underset{\sim}{M}$ is the mass matrix described in (2.14). We describe some results in the next secion obtained using the following scheme: The matrix $\underset{\sim}{M}$ is replaced by a "lumped" mass matrix $m\underset{\sim}{I}$. It can be shown that this does not deteriorate the accuracy of the approximation for sufficiently smooth $\underset{\sim}{x}(t)$ and it leads to a better definition of wave fronts. This step also makes it particularly easy to solve (4.10) using explicit schemes. Next, we replace (4.10) by the equivalent system

$$\begin{aligned} \dot{\underset{\sim}{v}} &= \frac{-1}{m}\underset{\sim}{f}(\underset{\sim}{x},p) \;,\quad \underset{\sim}{v}(0) = \underset{\sim}{v}_o \\ \dot{\underset{\sim}{x}} &= \underset{\sim}{v} \;,\quad \underset{\sim}{x}(0) = \underset{\sim}{x}_o \end{aligned} \tag{4.11}$$

which we approximate using the divided central difference scheme

$$\begin{aligned} \underset{\sim}{v}^{r+\frac{1}{2}} &= \underset{\sim}{v}^{r-\frac{1}{2}} - \frac{\Delta t}{m}\,\underset{\sim}{f}(\underset{\sim}{x}^r,p) \\ \underset{\sim}{x}^{r+1} &= \underset{\sim}{x}^{r} + \Delta t\;\underset{\sim}{v}^{r+\frac{1}{2}} \end{aligned} \tag{4.12}$$

This scheme is easily programmed and has yielded surprisingly good results for some large problems.

4.4. A Finite-Element Based Lax-Wendroff-Type Scheme for Shock Waves in Elastic Materials. Consider two finite-element subspaces $S_h^k(\Omega)$ and $R_\ell^m(\Omega)$ with bases $\{\phi_\alpha(x)\}_{\alpha=1}^{G}$ and $\{\psi_\Delta^h(x)\}_{\Delta=1}^{H}$, respectively, $(\Omega = [0,L])$. Suppose

$$G_{\alpha\beta} = (\phi_\alpha, \phi_\beta) \quad ; \quad H_{\Delta\Gamma} = (\psi_\Delta, \psi_\Gamma)$$

$$\Lambda(x,t) = \sum_\alpha A^\alpha(t)\phi_\alpha(x) \quad ; \quad Q(x,t) = \sum_\alpha B^\Delta(t)\psi_\Delta(x) \tag{4.13}$$

If Λ and Q are finite-element approximations of λ and q of (3.41), a finite-element/Lax-Wendroff scheme is obtained by introducing (4.13) into (3.41) and equating the projections of the residuals in $S_h^k(\Omega)$ and $R_\ell^m(\Omega)$ to zero:

$$\sum_\Gamma H_{\Delta\Gamma}B^{\Gamma(n+1)} = \sum_\Gamma H_{\Delta\Gamma}B^{\Gamma(n+1)} = \sum_\Gamma\{H_{\Delta\Gamma} - \frac{\Delta t^2}{2\rho}(DS'(\Lambda^n)\psi_\Gamma, D\psi_\Delta)\}\, B^{\Gamma(n)}$$

$$- \frac{\Delta t}{\rho}\sum_\alpha (S'(\Lambda^n)D\phi_\alpha,\, D\psi_\Delta)A^{\alpha(n)} + \ell_2^n$$

$$\sum_\beta G_{\alpha\beta}A^{\beta(n+1)} = \sum_\beta\{G_{\alpha\beta} - \frac{\Delta t^2}{\rho}(S'(\Lambda^n)D\phi_\alpha,\, D\phi_\beta)\}A^{\alpha(n)} + \frac{\Delta t}{\rho}\sum_\Delta(\psi_\Delta, \psi_\alpha)B^{\Delta(n)}$$

$$+ \ell_2^n \tag{4.14}$$

Here $A^{\alpha(n)} = A^\alpha(n\Delta t)$, etc. and ℓ_1^n, ℓ_2^n are terms contributed by (known) generalized forces. In general, we replace $G_{\alpha\beta}$ and $H_{\Delta\Gamma}$ in (4.14) by "lumped" matrices so as to produce an explicit integration scheme.

5. SOME NUMERICAL RESULTS

We conclude this investigation by citing numerical results obtained by applying the methods described previously to a number of representative problems.

5.1. Large Deformation of an Elastic Frame. As a first example, we comment on the numerical analysis of large deformations and postbuckling behaviour of a Hookean two-bar frame shown in Fig. 1, subjected to a vertical load $\bar{P}$. If $u = \bar{u}/b$ and $v = \bar{v}/b$ are non-dimensionalized horizontal and vertical displacements of the center node and $P = \bar{P}d^3/a_oEb^3$ is a non-dimensional load, a_o being the initial bar area and E the modulus, then the system is described by the equations [20]

$$(v-\mu)(v^2-2\mu v + u^2) = P \quad ; \quad u[u^2 - (2\mu v - 2(2-v^2))] = 0 \tag{5.1}$$

where $\mu = c/b$. For $\mu < \sqrt{2}$, limit-point behaviour is encountered since $u = 0\ \forall\ P$. For $\mu \geq \sqrt{2}$, bifurcations in the equilibrium path exist, as indicated in Fig. 1. Figure 2 shows numerical solutions obtained using the uncremental-loading/Newton Raphson procedure described in Section 4.1, together with a postbuckling analysis of the type mentioned in Section 4.2, for the cases $\mu = 1.0$ and $\mu = 1.5$. Good agreement is obtained.

5.2. Biaxial Strip Problem. The stretching of a rectangular strip has become a standard test problem for computational methods in nonlinear elasticity. In Figure 3 we illustrated results obtained using the explicit time-integration technique described in §4.2 on the finite element model of a strip of Mooney material, initially 8.0 in. square, 0.05 in. thick, $M_1 = 24.0$ and $M_2 = 1.5$ lbs. per sq. in., for various values of damping: $c = .001$ to $.0001$. Another version of basically the same problem was described in [24]. Again very rapid solution times were obtained.

5.3. Stability and Postbuckling Behavior. For completeness, we cite in Figures 4-6 some recent results obtained in [9] on stability and postbuckling behavior of hyperelastic bodies at finite strain. The bodies considered are neo-Hookean ($C_2 = 0$) with $C_1 = 24$ lbs. per sq. in., all 1/3 in. thick. In Figure 4, a 2.0 x 8.0 in. body is subjected to an axial load in the x_2-direction with the surfaces $x_2 = 0$ fixed and $x_2 = L$ fixed against rotation. The finite element model consists of 64 triangular elements and 72 unknown nodal displacements. The resulting 72 nonlinear equilibrium equations, which are sixth-degree polynomials, were solved by the method of incremental loading with Newton-Raphson corrections. The load was applied in increments of $\Delta P = 0.4$ lbs. The determinant of the stability matrix changed from a positive to negative value at the seventh increment of load ($P = 2.8$ lbs.) indicating that a bifurcation point occurred within the increment. The incremental solution was restarted at a load of $P = 2.4$ lbs, with load increments $\Delta P = 0.05$ lbs, for which case the Newton-Raphson technique failed to converge at a load of 2.65 lbs. Hence, the critical load P^c was isolated to the range $2.60 < P^c < 2.65$ lbs. This agrees well with the critical load which is $P^c = \pi^2 EI/L^2 = 2.35$ lbs., if the modulus of elasticity is approximated by $E = 6C_1$ and the moment of inertia I and length L were evaluated in the deformed state near the critical load. Before buckling, the vertical center line remained vertical, and the vertical displacements were linear. The vertical displacement at buckling was 0.51 in. or 6.4 percent of the original height, with a maximum change in width of 0.07 in. or 3.5 percent of the original width. Figure 4 shows the column at state of zero load, the deformed shape at the critical load, and the postbuckled shape. After the first critical load was determined, a small horizontal load ($\rho = 0.15$ lbs.) was applied at the top ($x_2 = L$) of the column to give the system an initial deformation. While holding the horizontal load constant, the vertical load was again increased from zero to the critical by the incremental technique. For this case the equilibrium path of the imperfect system was stable to a load of 3.60 lbs. where limit-point type buckling was indicated. Holding the vertical load constant at 3.0 lbs., the horizontal load was incremented to zero to project to the postbuckled path of the perfect system. The motion followed by the structure in removal of the horizontalload is shown by line segment I-J in Figure 5. With the system now presumably on the postbuckled path of the perfect system, the vertical load was increased from 3.0 lbs. to the second critical load of $3.75 \text{ lbs.} < P^c < 3.80 \text{ lbs.}$ where limit-point type buckling was experienced. The first two increasing load increments from point J (Figure 5) indicates that the system has not returned to a point of complete relative minimum of the total potential energy. This action is attributed to the weak condition of the system. The postbuckled path of the perfect system from point K to the second critical point at point L does appear to be of correct form in that it follows nearly parallel to the imperfect system.

A second example is indicated in Figure 6. Here we see an arch-type structure modelled with 72 triangular elements and 110 degrees-of-freedom. A load was applied along the axis of symmetry in increments of 0.2 lbs., and the bifurcation point was passed in the increment from 1.4 to 1.6 lbs. This is shown graphically in Figure 6. The incremental solution was restarted at a load of P = 1.4 lbs. with the load increment $\delta P = 0.02$ lbs. In this particular case, the incremental solution did actually pick up the postbuckled path at a load of P = 1.50 lbs. Geometric deformations were measured rapidly from this point (Figure 6), and the critical load P^c was isolated to the interval $1.515 \text{ lbs} < P^c < 1.520 \text{ lbs}$. Successive plots of the deformed structure with increasing load (Figure 7) are interesting in that they show the step-wise transition to a buckled mode. It is noted that one of the members reverses curvature, which is typical of this type structure. A small couple was applied at the vertex of the structure and the load was increased to the critical. The critical load of the imperfect system was found to be $1.00 < P^c < 1.05$ lb. The critical load of the perturbed system occurs well below that of the perfect system, which indicates that the perfect system exhibits unstable symmetric bifurcation. This, of course, is typical of this type structure.

<u>5.4. Nonlinear Elastodynamics-Shock Evaluation</u>. We consider a thin rod of Mooney material (M_1 = 24.0 psi, M_2 = 1.5 psi) with the following undeformed characteristics: length = 3.0 in., cross-sectional

area = 0.0314 in^2, mass density = 10^{-4} $lb.sec^2/in.^4$. For the finite element model, we take 60 evenly spaced elements, so that h = 0.05 in. and N_0 = 61, and we consider a concentrated, time-dependent load which varies sinusoidally is applied at the free end; a complete loading cycle occurs in 0.002 seconds. It is clear from the computed response shown in Figure 8 that shocks develop quickly for this kind of loading. Unlike the response for the tensile step load where the unloading wave is produced by simply removing the load, the sinusoidal load actually "pushes" the end of the rod: The instant the load starts to decrease is the moment when the first wavelet is generated which propagates faster than the preceding one. Thus, at some time subsequent to when the compression cycle starts, a compression shock forms in the rod.

A comparison between two integration, velocity-centered central differences and the finite-element/Lax-Wendroff scheme, is also shown in Figure 9 for the sinusoidal loading. In this case, it is clear that the internal energy behind the compression shock renders the central difference scheme unacceptable. It is interesting to note, however, that the tension cycle evidently "absorbs" the large oscillations preceding it and again produces a smooth wave front. The detailed response to this loading is shown in Figure 10. From the response shown, we notive several interesting features of non-linear wave motion. First, the compressive shock wave is reflected from the wall as a compressive shock wave by almost doubling the compressive stress, but the tension part of the stress wave is re-flected with only a small increase in stress. Secondly, at t = 4.7 milliseconds, twc compressive shocks are to collide, with relatively little deterioration, possibly owing to the fact that mechanical work of the external forces is continuously supplied to the system. In addition, where we compare the response at t = 3 milliseconds to that at t = 5 milliseconds, we find that it approximately repeats itself, again indicating relatively little deterioration. Finally, we note that, as in the development of shocks from Lipschitz con-tinuous data, the shock forms subsequent to initiation of the compressive cycle. Thus we are led to examine the positive slope characteristics in the X-t plane to see if they preduct t_{CR} for this type of loading. Figure 11 shows that if we assume straight compression characteristics of positive slope, the cusp of the corresponding envelope in the X-t plane does, in fact, give a good estimate of the t_{CR} observed in the stress-time plots.

Acknowledgement. Portions of this work were sponsored by the U.S. Air Force Office of Scientific Research under Contract F44620-69-C-0124 to the University of Alabama in Huntsville. The work reported on nonlinear elastodynamics was completed with the assistance of Mr. R.B. Fost under the support of a grant, GK-39071, from the U.S. National Science Foundation to the University of Texas at Austin.

6. REFERENCES

1. Oden J.T. Int'l Congress on Large-Span Shells, Leningrad, 1966.

2. Oden, J.T. and Sato, T. Int'l. J. of Solids and Structures, 1, 471-488, 1967.

3. Oden, J.T. and Kubitza, W.K. Proceedings, Int'l. Coll. on Pneumatic Structures, Stuttgart, 82-107, 1967.

4. Becker, E.B. "A Numerical Solution of a Class of Problems of Finite Elastic Deformation", PhD Dissertation, The University of California, Berkeley, 1961.

5. Oden, J.T. J. St. Div., ASCE, 93, No. ST3, 235-255, 1967.

6. Oden, J.T. Finite Elements of Nonlinear Continua, McGraw-Hill, New York, 1972.

7. Oden, J.T. J. Comp. Structures, 2, No. 7, 175-194, 1973.

8. Oden, J.T. Nonlinear Elasticity, Edited by W. Dickey, Academic Press, New York, (To appear).

9. Sandidge, D. and Oden, J.T. Proceedings, Midwestern Conf. Appl'd. Mech., Pittsburg, 1973.

10. Truesdell, C. and Noll, W. Encyclopedia of Physics, Edited by S. Fluggee, III/3, Springer-Verlag, New York, 1965.

11. Green, A.E. and Adkins, J.E. Large Elastic Deformations, Second Edition, Clarendon Press, Oxford Press, 1972.

12. Oden, J.T. Mechanics Today-1973, Edited by S. Nemmet-Nasser, Pergamoon Press, Oxford, (To appear).

13. Ciarlet, P.G. and Ciarlet, P.A. Arch. Rat. Mech. and Anal, 46, 3, 177-199, 1972.

14. Fried, I. "Discretization and Round-Off Error in the Finite Element Method Analysis of Elliptic Boundary-Value Problems and Eigenvalue Problems," PhD Dissertation, Massachusetts Institute of Technology, Cambridge, 1971.

15. Oden, J.T. and Fost, R.B. Int'l. J. Num. Meth. Engr'g., 6, 357-365, 1973.

16. Lahaye, E. Acad. Royal Belgian Bull. Cl. Sc., 5, 805-822, 1948.

17. Davidenko, D. Dokl. Akad. Nauk. USSR, 88, 601-604, 1953.

18. Goldberg, J. and Richard, J. Struct. Div. ASCE, 89, 333-351, 1963.

19. Ortega, J.M. and Rheinboldt, W.D. Iterative Solution of Nonlinear Equations in Several Variables, Academic Press, New York, 235, 1970.

20. Oden, J.T. (NATO) Lectures on Finite Element Methods in Continuum Mechanics, Edited by J.T. Oden and E. Arantes e Oliveira, The UAH Press, Huntsville, 1972.

21. Oden, J.T. J. Comp. Structures,

22. Gallagher, R.H. Nat'l Sym. Comp. Struct'l Anal. and Designs, Washington, D.C., 1972, (See also J. Comp. Struct.

23. Oden, J.T. and Key, J.E. Int'l J. Num. Meth. in Engr'g. (To appear).

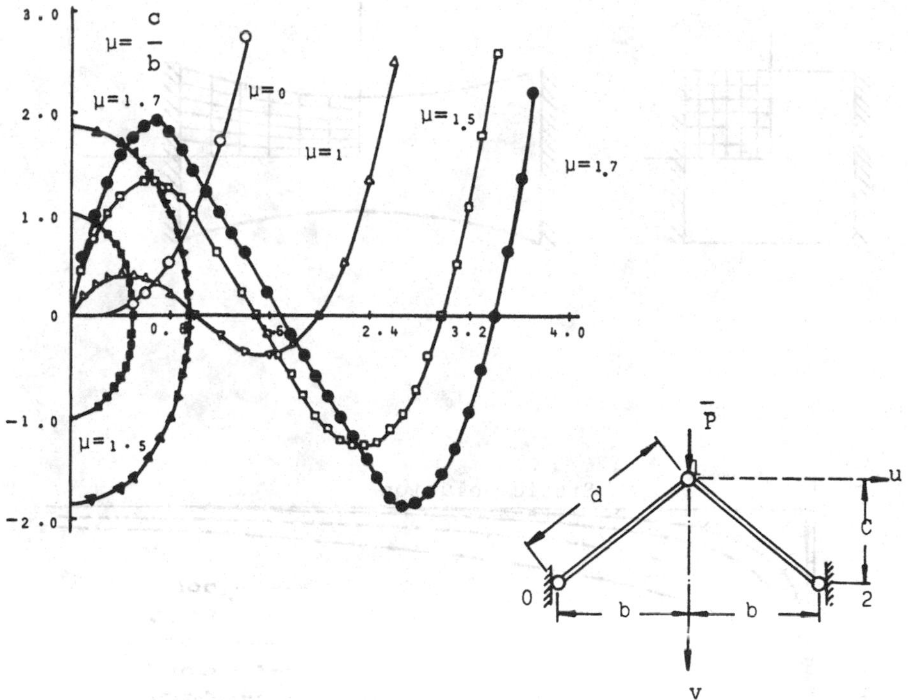

Figure 1. Nonlinear Response of a Two-Bar Frame.

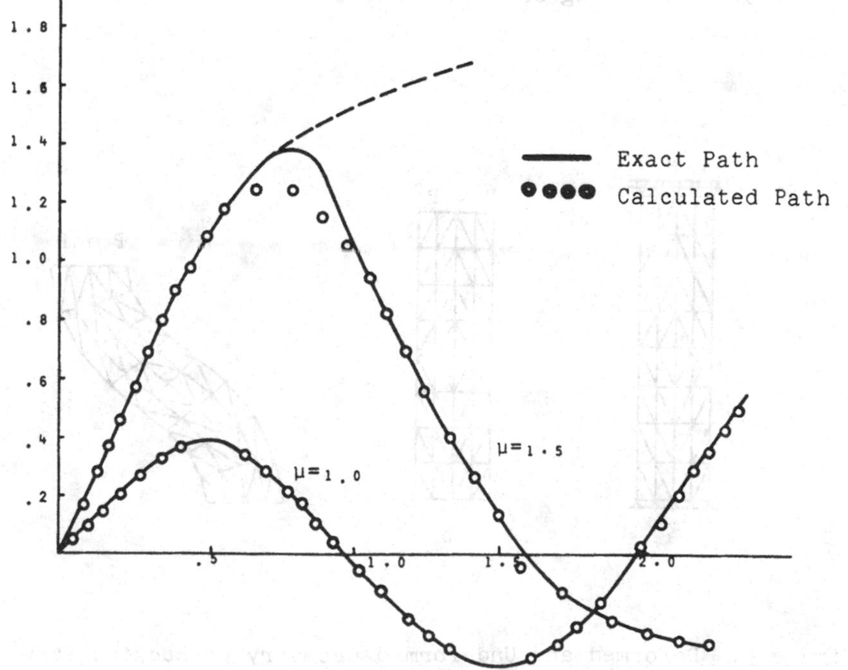

Figure 2. Analysis of a Two-Bar Frame.

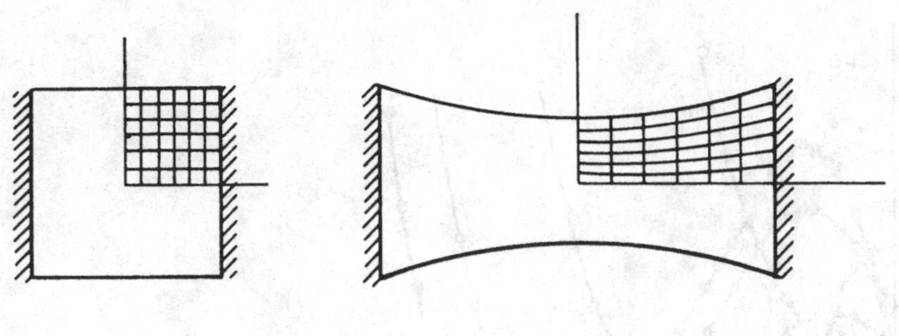

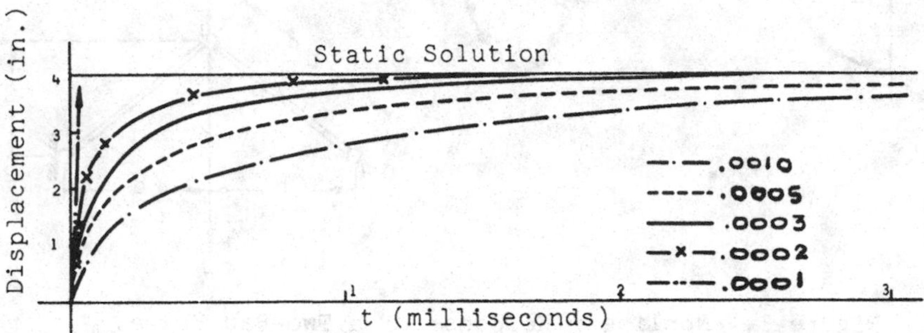

Figure 3. Stretching of a Thin Strip

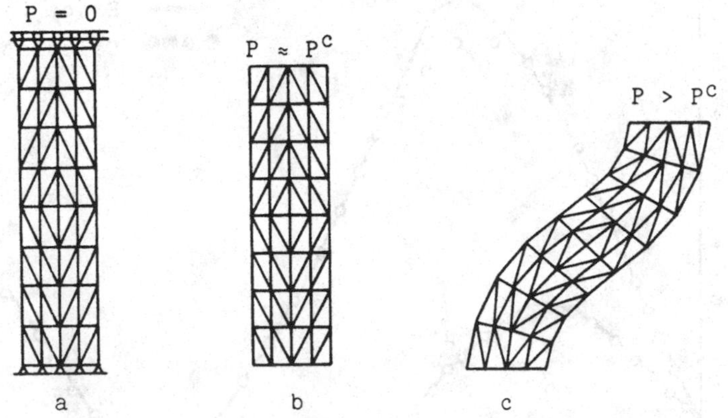

Figure 4. Deformed and Undeformed Geometry of Buckled Structure.

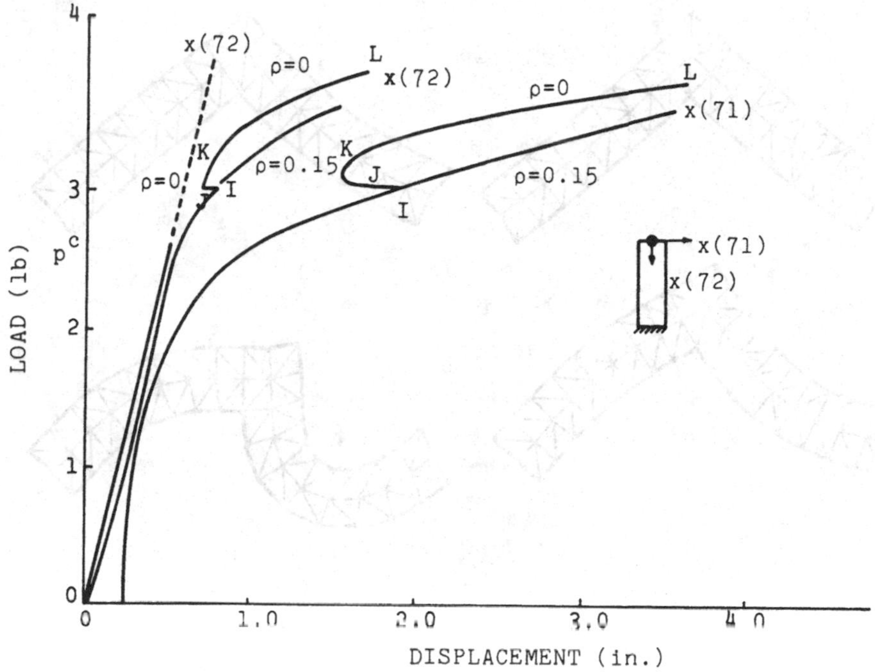

Figure 5. Load-displacement Curves.

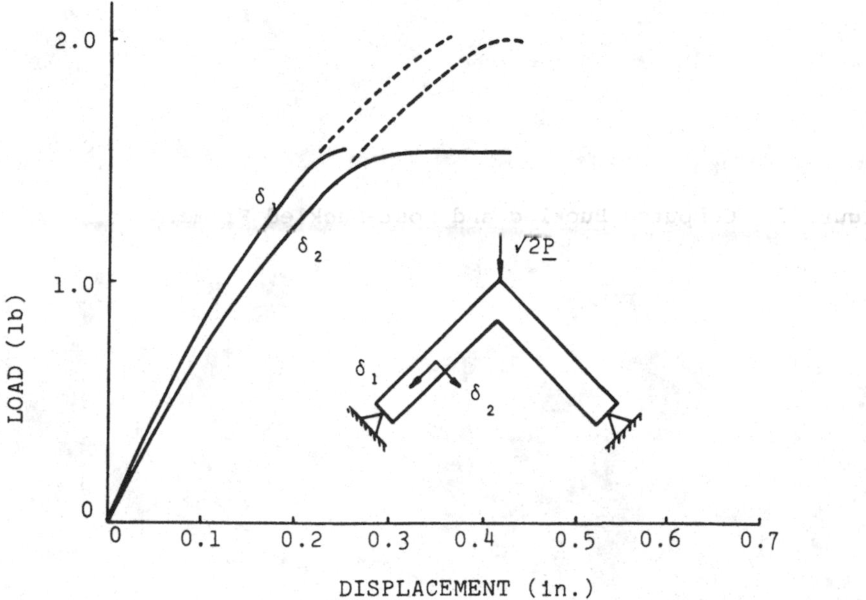

Figure 6. Frame Instability at Finite Strain.

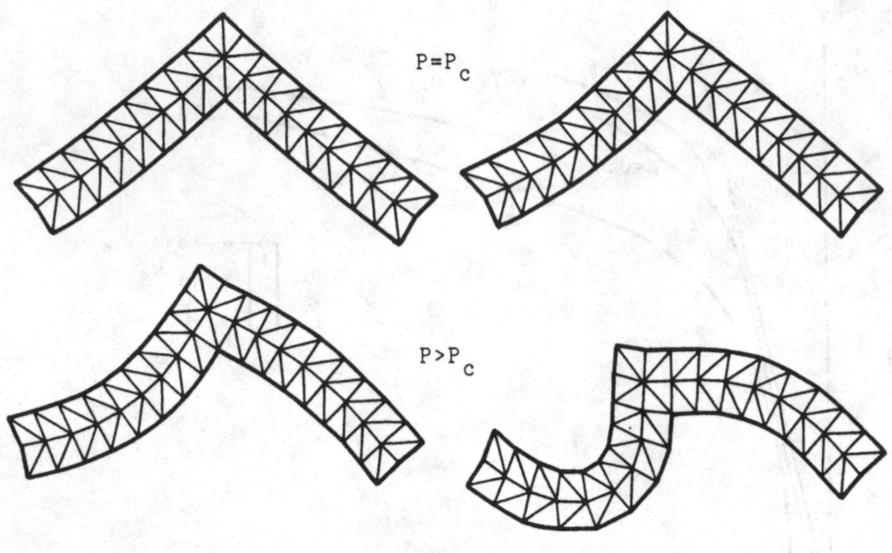

Figure 7. Computed Buckled and Post-Buckled Frame.

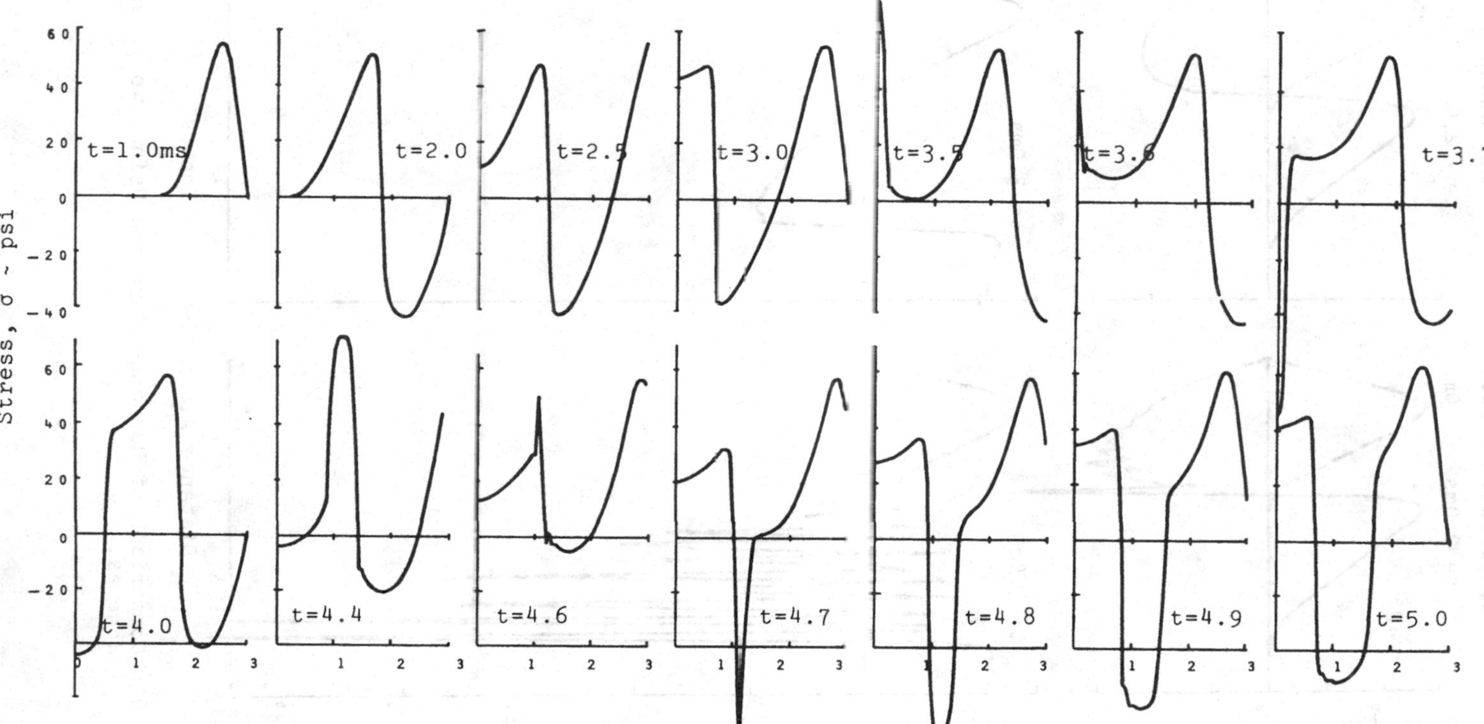

Figure 8. Time history of stress wave response to sinusoidal end load.

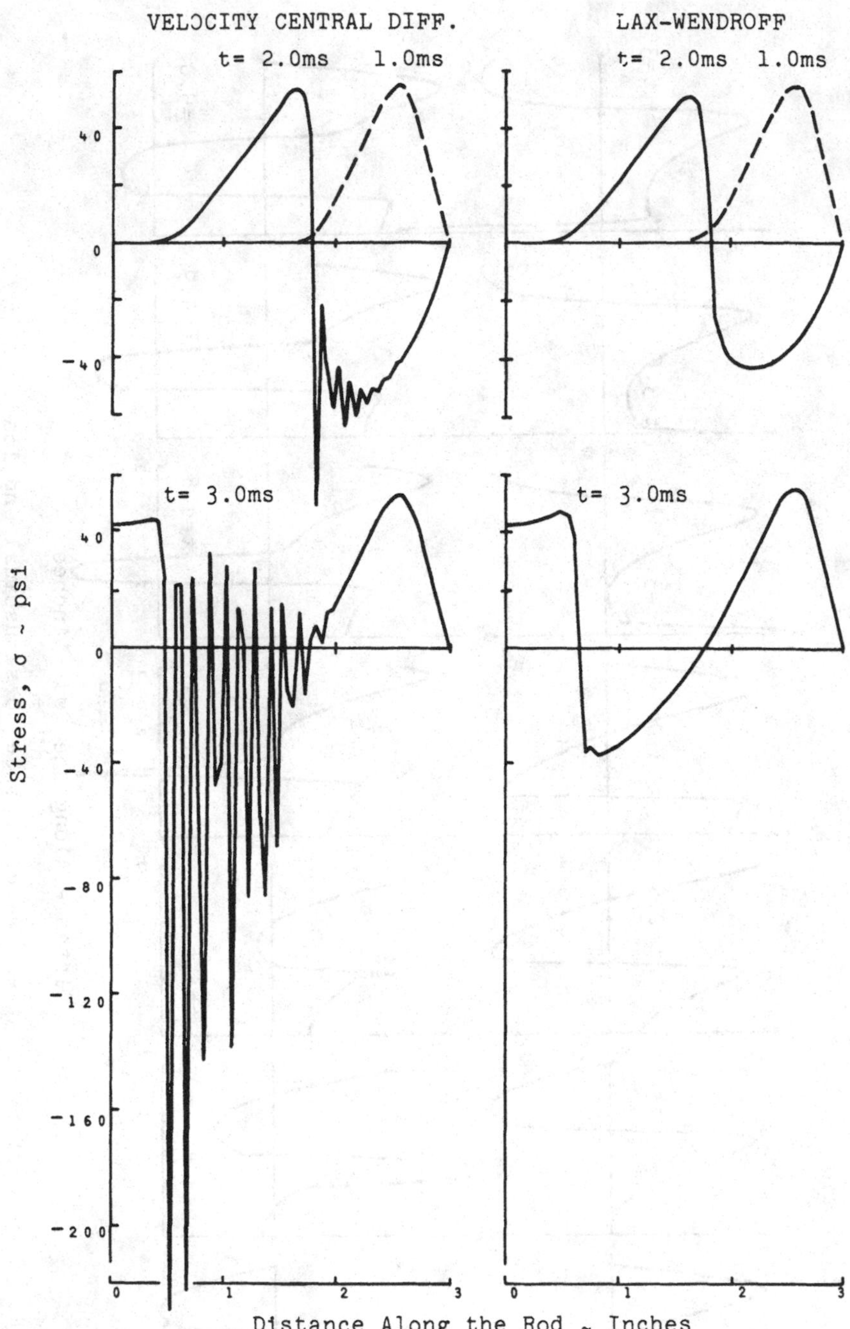

Figure 9. Comparison of Response Computed Using Two Integration Schemes.

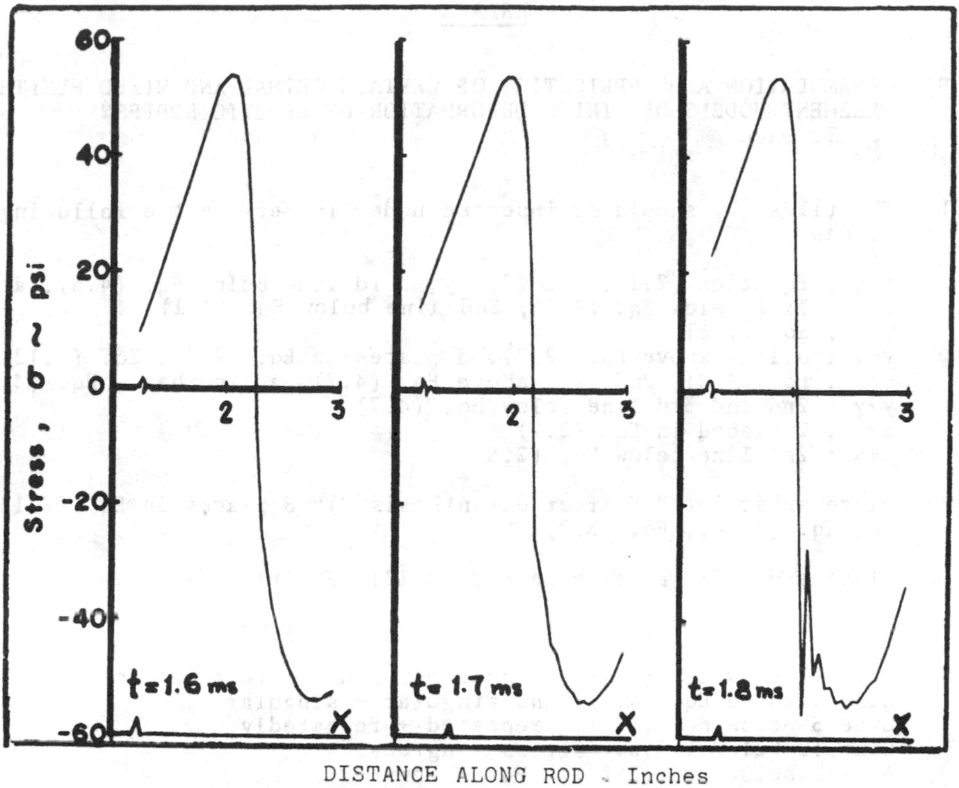

Stress, σ ~ psi

60 40 20 0 -20 -40 -60

2 3 2 3 2 3

t=1.6 ms X t= 1.7 ms X t=1.8 ms X

DISTANCE ALONG ROD - Inches

Figure 10. Change in Stress During Shock Formation.

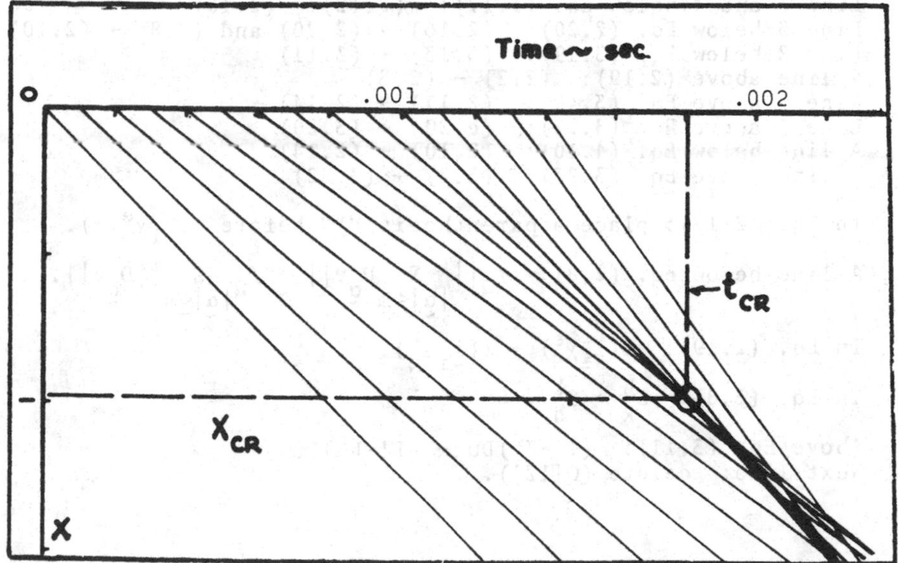

Figure 11. Computed Characteristic Field

ERRATA

For "FORMULATION AND APPLICATION OF CERTAIN PRIMAL AND MIXED FINITE ELEMENT MODELS OF FINITE DEFORMATION OF ELASTIC BODIES"
By J. T. Oden

1. The tilda (~) should be inserted under letters in the following places:

   $x \to \underset{\sim}{x}$; Equation (2.1), Eq. (2.16), 3 rd line below Eq. (4.6), a line below Eq. (4.8), 2nd line below Eq. (4.1)
   $u \to \underset{\sim}{u}$; Eq. (2.6)
   $v \to \underset{\sim}{v}$; a line above Eq. (2.7), 3 places in Eq. (2.7), Eq. (2.12)
   $o \to \underset{\sim}{o}$; Eq. (4.2), 2nd line above Eq. (4.7), a line below Eq. (4.8)
   $y \to \underset{\sim}{y}$; 2nd and 3rd line below Eq. (4.7)
   $\phi \to \underset{\sim}{\phi}$; 2 placed in Eq. (2.7)
   $\alpha \to \underset{\sim}{\alpha}$; 2nd line below Eq. (2.8).

2. Place subscript "o" after parenthesis ")" 8 places in Eq. (2.13) and Eq. (2.14), Eq. (3.7).

3. Place a dot "•" after F in Eq. (2.13), $\bar{F}^{j}{}_{\beta}(t) \to \bar{F}^{\bullet j}{}_{\beta}(t)$.

4. Place a bar on first Ωe in Eq. (2.15), $\Omega e \to \bar{\Omega} e$.

5. A line below Eq. (2.15): interpoltaion → interpolation
   Line 9 above Eq. (4.7): nonsingular → singular
   Line 5 below Eq. (4.3): repeated → repeatedly
   Line 19 below § 5.3: agress → agrees
   A line below Eq. (3.29): For → for
   Line 29 above § 5.4: were → where
   Line 13 above § 5.4: measured → were measured.

6. Line 3 and 4 below Eq. (2.17): (2.12) → (2.16)
   Line 3 below Eq. (2.20): (2.16) → (2.20) and (2.8) → (2.10)
   Line 2 below Eq. (3.19): (3.13) → (3.11)
   A line above (2.19): (2.2) → (2.3)
   Line 9 above Eq. (3.40): (2.11) → (2.14)
   Line 3 above Eq. (3.22): (e.20) → (3.20)
   A line below Eq. (4.10): (2.10) → (2.14)
   A line above Eq. (3.23): (3.2) → (3.22)

7. In Eq. (2.18): place a parenthesis ")" before $,\partial_i \chi^e_M(\cdot)$.

8. A line below Eq. (2.8): $\int_\Omega || \sum_{|\underset{\sim}{\alpha}| \le m} D_{\underset{\sim}{\alpha}} v|| \to \int_\Omega \sum_{|\underset{\sim}{\alpha}| \le m} ||D_{\underset{\sim}{\alpha}} v||$.

9. In Eq. (2.19): $1(\underset{\sim}{i}_i \chi^e_N) \to \ell(\underset{\sim}{i}_i \chi^e_N)$.

10. In Eq. (3.8): $S^h_k \to S^k_h$.

11. Above Eq. (3.11): (I'=Πh)Du → (I'-Πh)Du
    Next line: delete (Q[12]).

Errata

In Eq. (3.21) and Eq. (3.24): $P \to P_\ell$
In Eq. (3.23): $e \to e_u$ and $\varepsilon_v = V^*-P_\ell V^* \to \varepsilon_v = V^*-P_\ell v^*$

Line 2 above Eq. (3.26): $u\ U \to u\varepsilon U$ and $v\ V \to v\varepsilon V$.

In Eq. (3.27): $M_{h\ell}(u,v) = \to M_{h\ell}(u,v) \equiv$.

In Eq. (3.28): take off a dot "•" in front of S(Du)

In Eq. (3.29): place β after "$\geq$" .

Take off "o" from ρ_o i.e. $\rho_o \to \rho$ in Eq. (3.35) and Eq. (3.36).
Take off parenthesis "(" i.e., $\delta_t^2(\to \delta_t^2$.
Take off comma from $t_o < t, <$ ... 2nd line below Eq. (3.35).

Place a minus "-" before $\rho(\delta_t^2 e,\varepsilon)$ at 2nd line below Eq. (3.39).

Line 10 above § 3.5, $d_i,\beta_i \to \alpha_i,\beta_i$ and $K_1,K_2 \to k_1,k_2$.
Line 2 below § 3.5, $C^2(\lambda) = \frac{1}{\rho} d\sigma/\partial\lambda \to C(\lambda) = \sqrt{\frac{1}{\rho}\partial\sigma/\partial\lambda}$.

In Eq. (3.40), $\lambda = D \to \ddot{X} - D$.

In Eq. (3.41), 2 places: $O(\Delta t^3) \to O(\Delta t^3)$.

Change ρ to p in Eq. (4.3); and a line below Eq. (4.3) in 4 places.

Line below Eq. (4.9): $\Delta s + s_{r+1}-s_r$, $s \in [0,1] \to \Delta s = s_{r+1}-s_r$, $s \in [0,1]$

Line 3 above Eq. (5.1); $P = Pd^3/a_o Eb^3 \to P = \overline{P}d^3/a_o Eb^3$.
Line 6 below Eq. (5.1); $\mu = 1.2 \to \mu = 1.5$.

Line 8 below § 5.2: c = .001 to .0010 $\to$ c = .001 to .0001.
On the same page at Line 6 from the bottom: 4a $\to$ 4.

Line 6 from the top of § 5.4; load shown $\to$ load is shown.
On the same page at Line 11 from the top: (Figure 5 $\to$ (Figure 5).

In the Figure 1., take off Q and place a bar on P. i.e. $P \to \overline{P}$.

Line 2 above (2.18): $g_i(\underset{\sim}{x},t) = \underset{\sim}{i}_i \cdot \underset{\sim}{i}_j = \delta_{ij} \to g_i(\underset{\sim}{x},t) = \underset{\sim}{i}_i,\ \underset{\sim}{i}_i \cdot \underset{\sim}{i}_j = \delta_{ij}$
Place superscript "i" on V in Eq. (3.30): $\ell(v) \to \ell(v^i)$

$0 \to \underset{\sim}{o}$ in Equation (4.3).

METHODES NUMERIQUES POUR LE PROJET D'APPAREILLAGES INDUSTRIELS AVANCES

par S. ALBERTONI

Université de Pavia et ARS SpA, Milano

Introduction

Il est bien connu que, grâce soit au développement rapide des techniques numériques aptes à résoudre des problèmes technologiques compliqués, grâce soit au développement de la technologie (soft-ware et hard ware) des calculateurs modernes, il est devenu possible, à présent, de donner des réponses valables, du point de vue numérique, pour le projet, la conduite et le contrôle d'une série d'appareillages très importants auprès de différents secteurs de l'industrie.

Plus précisement, c'est la stimulation qui se rattache aux exigences de l'industrie moderne, qui marquent de plus en plus clairement la pression de la compétition, où bien c'est la nécessité d'une réalisation technologiquement avancée pour de buts spéciaux, qui s'imposent au techniciens pour des solutions décidément lointaines des solutions classiques. D'ici la nécessité de la mise au point de modèles mathématiques d'apparats technologiques qui s'approchent de la réalité physique bien d'avantage par rapport aux rapprochements habituels de routine. Cela entraîne la nécessité aussi d'avoir à la disposition des méthodes de calcul convenables à la structure sophistiquée des modèles qu'on vient de mentionner soit du point de vue de la précision que de la fiabilité. En particulier ces exigences se sont révélées dans les derniers temps auprès du secteur des modèles fluido-dynamiques et de l'échange thermique. Ces questions là sont en effet de plus en plus importantes pour l'analyse de chaque type de processus avancé puisque, par exemple dans le génie chimique, souvent c'est bien à partir d'ici, et non pas tellement de l'aspect pu rement chimique du problème, où l'on doit combattre, à travers une analyse détaillée des phénomènes de transport, la bataille du rendement et de la fiabilité.

Malheureusement lorsqu'on parle de méthodes de calcul concernant les modèles concrets, on ne connait pas assez, du point de vue de la fiabilité, le choix des méthodes générales optimales; c'est toutefois bien là la nature du problème-même, ainsi que l'espérience du génie et de la mathématique expérimentale qui, à la fin, en impose sur la méthodologie des considérations techniques générales, ces dernières étant toujours, bien naturellement, très importantes pour une vue d'ensemble des choses.

Il suffit de mentionner les difficultés, toujours à l'égard du cas concret, qui naissent des conditions aux limites, de la nature spécifique des non-linéairités, du type d'accouplement entre les différentes équations, et encore, du degré d'information que l'on peut obtenir à propos du comportement "a priori" de la solution, même si approximatif, et enfin de la difficulté à prevoir en avance l'épesseur du réseau d'après lequel dépend, naturellement, tout solution précise. Il suit de là que l'on a préferé dans cette communication, puisque l'analyse théorique concernant ces difficultés n'était pas tellement significative, de se réferer à un certain nombre de cas concrets, développés numériquement auprès de l'ARS dans le but d'obtenir des solutions pour des projets d'appareillages qu'ont été réalisés par la suite.

1. Modèle pour le contrôle thermique d'un réacteur de polymérisation

a) Description du problème

On a étudié le comportement thermo-fluido-dynamique d'un réacteur tubulaire de polymérisation à flux continu en régime stationnaire. Un mélange partiellement polymérisé entre dans la partie supérieure du réacteur, et après avoir été complètement polymérisé, on le prélève de la section inférieure en sortie du réacteur. La réaction de polymérisation est exothermique et dépend fortement de la température à laquelle la réaction a lieu. Le poids moléculaire moyen du produit obtenu est inver sement proportionnel à la temperature de réaction.

Le but de cette étude a été de vérifier s'il est possible d'obtenir un contrôle thermique du réacteur satisfaisant à l'aide de convenables distributions de températures sur la paroi externe du réacteur. L'output du modèle consiste donc dans la détermination des fonctions ($\vec{v}$, p) (champ de mouvement), C_i (i = 1, 2; concentration des deux espèces polymériques), T (champ thermique).

b) Modèle mathématique

La géométrie du système est de type axial-symétrique (r, z) (Fig. 1.1). Les équations qui décrivent l'état du système sont constituées par des équations habituelles de conservation de la masse, du moment, de l'énergie et de l'espèce chimique, les quelles, en termes des variables ψ (fonction de courant) et ω (tourbillon) ont la forme suivante:

$$(1.1)\quad \underbrace{-\frac{\partial}{\partial r}\left(\frac{\omega}{r}\frac{\partial\psi}{\partial z}\right)+\frac{\partial}{\partial z}\left(\frac{\omega}{r}\frac{\partial\psi}{\partial r}\right)}_{\text{termes de convection}}\underbrace{-\frac{\partial}{\partial r}\left[\frac{1}{r}\frac{\partial}{\partial r}(\mu\omega r)\right]-\frac{\partial^2}{\partial z^2}(\mu\omega)}_{\text{termes de diffusion}}=\underbrace{-\frac{\partial}{\partial r}(\rho g)}_{\text{source}}$$

$$\underbrace{-\frac{\partial}{\partial r}\left(\frac{1}{r\rho}\frac{\partial\psi}{\partial r}\right)-\frac{\partial}{\partial z}\left(\frac{1}{r\rho}\frac{\partial\psi}{\partial z}\right)}_{\text{termes de diffusion}}=\underbrace{\omega}_{\text{source}}$$

$$\underbrace{-\frac{\partial}{\partial r}\left(c_p T\frac{\partial\psi}{\partial z}\right)+\frac{\partial}{\partial z}\left(c_p T\frac{\partial\psi}{\partial r}\right)}_{\text{termes de convection}}\underbrace{-\frac{\partial}{\partial r}\left(kr\frac{\partial T}{\partial r}\right)-\frac{\partial}{\partial z}\left(kr\frac{\partial T}{\partial z}\right)}_{\text{termes de diffusion}}=\underbrace{\rho K c r \Delta H}_{\text{source}}$$

$$\underbrace{-\frac{\partial}{\partial r}\left(c\frac{\partial\psi}{\partial z}\right)+\frac{\partial}{\partial z}\left(c\frac{\partial\psi}{\partial r}\right)}_{\text{termes de convection}}\underbrace{-\frac{\partial}{\partial r}\left(r\rho D\frac{\partial c}{\partial r}\right)-\frac{\partial}{\partial z}\left(r\rho D\frac{\partial c}{\partial z}\right)}_{\text{termes de diffusion}}=\underbrace{-\rho K r c}_{\text{source}}$$

où: $\rho u = -\frac{1}{r}\frac{\partial\psi}{\partial z}$ $\qquad \rho v = \frac{1}{r}\frac{\partial\psi}{\partial r}$

$$\omega = \frac{\partial u}{\partial z} - \frac{\partial v}{\partial r}$$

u, v composants selon r, z de la vitesse v
ρ densité
μ viscosité dynamique
C_p chaleur spécifique
T température
K constante cinétique
k conductibilité thermique
ΔH chaleur de réaction
C fraction de la masse du monomère
D coefficient de diffusion

A' ces équations il faut joindre l'équation d'état (1.5) et la dependence (1.6) de la viscosité par rapport à la variable T, c (loi rhéologique) et la dependence (1.7) de la constante cinétique de la variable T.

$$(1.5) \quad \rho = \rho(c, T) = 1 \Big/ \left[\frac{c + \alpha T}{\alpha_1} + \frac{(1-c)(1+\beta T)}{\beta_1} \right]$$

$$(1.6) \quad \mu = \mu(c, T) = \eta \exp\left[\eta_1 \big/ (\eta_2 c^2 + \eta_3) + \delta_1 \big/ (T + 273) \right]$$

$$(1.7) \quad K = K(T) = \gamma_1 \exp\left[-\gamma_2 \big/ (T + 273) \right]$$

$\alpha, \alpha_1, \beta, \beta_1, \eta, \eta_1, \eta_2, \eta_3, \delta_1, \gamma_1, \gamma_2$ sont des coefficients numériques.

Les conditions aux limites, associées au système (1.1) - (1.7) et se référant à la Fig. 1.1 sont:

$$r = 0 \quad \psi = 0 \; ; \quad \frac{\omega}{r} = \left(\frac{\omega}{r}\right)_{r+\Delta r} - r\Delta r \left(\frac{\omega}{r}\right)_{r+\Delta r} \; , \quad \frac{\partial c}{\partial r} = \frac{\partial T}{\partial r} = 0$$

$$z = 0 \quad \psi = \psi_i(r) \; ; \; \frac{\omega}{r} = \Omega_i \; ; \; c = c_i \; ; \; T = T_i \quad \text{(assignées)}$$

$$z = H \qquad \frac{\partial \psi}{\partial z} = \frac{\partial (\omega/r)}{\partial z} = \frac{\partial c}{\partial z} = \frac{\partial T}{\partial z} = 0$$

$$r=R \qquad \psi=\psi_i(R)\,; \quad \frac{\omega}{r}=-\frac{3\left[\psi(R-\Delta r)-\psi(R)\right]}{\rho R^2 \Delta r^2}+\left(\frac{\omega}{r}\right)_{R-\Delta r}$$

$$\frac{\partial c}{\partial r}=0 \qquad T=T_w(z)$$ (distribution assignée de la température à la paroi)

c) Méthode de solution

Le système (1.1) - (1.7), avec les conditions (1.8) a été discrétisé en utilisant les différences en contrevent dans les termes de convection, tandis que les différences centrales ont été utilisées pour les termes de diffusion. On a ainsi obtenu un système d'équations algébriques non-linéaires ayant la forme suivante (Fig. 1):

$$(1.9) \qquad \varphi_{i,j}=C_{1\,i,j}\,\varphi_{i+1,j}+C_{2\,i,j}\,\varphi_{i,j+1}+C_{3\,i,j}\,\varphi_{i-1,j}+C_{4\,i,j}\,\varphi_{i,j-1}+S_{i,j}$$

où φ peut représenter la fonction de courant, le tourbillon, la température et la concentration.

Le système algébrique (1.9) a été résolu itérativement à l'aide de la méthode de Gauss-Seidel.

Etant donnée la très forte dépendence de la température pour ce qui concerne la viscosité et la vitesse de réaction on a dû introduire de convenables techniques de sous-relaxation pour obtenir la convergence de la solution numérique.

d) Résultats obtenus

La première application de la méthode de calcul a été réalisée sur un réacteur à dimensions industrielles ayant la distribution de température sur la paroi comme d'après la Fig. 1.2. Les résultats obtenus pour la distribution de ψ ,T , c, sont reportés en Fig. 1.2, 1.3.

On peut remarquer l'existence d'une zone de recirculation près de l'axe dans la zone de sortie du réacteur.

En correspondance de cette zone il y a un maximum dans la distribution de température dont la valeur rélative est égale à celle que l'on obtiendrait dans un réacteur adiabatique.

La concentration varie réguilièrement dans la couche qui adère à la paroi, tandis qu'elle est remarquablement différente près de l'axe par l'effet de l'augmentation de température qui se produit dans cet endroit.

Dans le but de diminuer la variation de température à l'intérieur du réacteur, on a pris en considération une distribution de température de la paroi linéairement croissante, ayante une dérivée axiale mineure (Fig. 1.4 - ligne b).

D'après les résultats obtenus on peut remarquer que la région de flux est partagée en deux parties ayant un comportement différent. La première partie, près de la paroi, est caractérisée par une viscosité élevée, une vitesse d'écoulement plus petite et une efficience en la polymérisation du monomère, elle-aussi mineure. En diminuant la température de la paroi on a causé donc la croissance d'une couche de fluide presque stagnante qui adhère à la paroi externe. Presque tout le fluide est obligé d'écouler près de l'axe avec un temps de séjour insuffisant pour une complète polymérisation du monomère.

On a pris en considération d'autres distributions de température de la paroi sans obtenir des résultats qui diffèrent sensiblement de ceux que l'on vient de décrire. Une amélioration remarquable a été toutefois obtenue en considérant un réacteur avec un diamètre 6 fois inférieur. D'après la distribution de température de la paroi reportée en Fig. 1.4, 1.5, les résultats obtenus montrent comment, dans ce cas, l'augmentation de température dans la zone centrale du réacteur est très limitée et, par consequent, la concentration du monomère prende le comportement regulier désiré.

2. Ultracentrifuge[(x)]

a) Description du problème

On a étudié le comportement fluidodynamique et thermique, en cond_ tions stationnaires, d'une ultracentrifuge constituée par un corps annulaire axial-symétrique fermé à l'extremité par deux couvercles. Le mouvement de convection à l'intérieur de l'ultracentrifuge est provoqu par une différence ΔT de température appliquée entre les deux couvercles (Fig. 2.1).

On n'a pas considéré la présence de l'alimentation et du prélèvement du mélange dont les composants, ayant un poids moléculaire différent, veulent se séparer par effet de l'ultracentrifugation. On veut déterminer: les fonctions $\vec{V}$, p (champ de mouvement), T (champ thermiq

Le but principale de l'étude a été celui de déterminer l'extensio des couches limites dans la région la plus intéressée à la recirculati ainsi que les caractéristiques des composantes de la vitesse.

b) Modèle mathématique

La géométrie du système est de nouveau axial-symétrique (r, z). Contrairement au cas précedent, et à cause du mouvement de rotation, o a considéré aussi la composante selon θ de la vitesse. Les équations qui décrivent le système sont celles de conservation de la masse, du moment et de l'énergie.

Elles ont été décrites par un système de rotation, avec la vitesse angulaire de l'ultracentrifuge, et en outre elles ont été linéairis par rapport à la solution obtenue en absence de gradient thermique im posé entre les plats.

Les équations considérées sont donc:

$$\frac{1}{r}\frac{\partial}{\partial r}\left(r\rho_0 u\right)+\frac{\partial}{\partial z}\left(\rho_0 w\right)=0 \tag{2.1}$$

(x) - Travail executé sous contract avec le CNEM (Comitato Nazionale per l'Energia Nucleare), Roma.

(2.2) $$\mu \frac{\partial}{\partial r}\left[\frac{1}{r}\frac{\partial}{\partial r}(r u)\right] + \mu \frac{\partial^2 u}{\partial z^2} = \frac{\partial p'}{\partial r} - \omega^2 \rho' r + 2\omega \rho_o v$$

termes de diffusion — source

(2.3) $$\mu \frac{\partial}{\partial r}\left[\frac{1}{r}\frac{\partial}{\partial r}(r v)\right] + \mu \frac{\partial^2 v}{\partial z^2} = 2\omega \rho_o u$$

termes de diffusion — source

(2.4) $$\frac{\mu}{r}\frac{\partial}{\partial r}\left[r \frac{\partial w}{\partial r}\right] + \mu \frac{\partial^2 w}{\partial z^2} = \frac{\partial p'}{\partial z}$$

termes de diffusion — source

(2.5) $$C_v \rho_o\left[w \frac{\partial T'}{\partial z} + u \frac{\partial T'}{\partial r}\right] - \frac{k}{r}\frac{\partial}{\partial r}\left(r \frac{\partial T'}{\partial r}\right) - k \frac{\partial^2 T'}{\partial z^2} = \omega^2 r \rho_o u$$

termes de convection — termes de diffusion — source

où: $p = p_o + p'$; $\rho = \rho_o + \rho'$; $T = T_o + T'$

u, v, w — composantes de la vitesse selon r, θ, z.

p_o, ρ_o, T_o — pression, densité, température de l'état statique ($\Delta T = 0$)

μ — viscosité

C_v — chaleur spécifique

k — conductibilité thermique

ω — vitesse angulaire

u_o, v_o, w_o — vitesse de référence

Comme équation d'état, pour l'achèvement du système, on a supposé que:

(2.6) $$\rho' = - \rho_o \frac{T'}{T_o}$$

les conditions aux limites associées sont:

$$\left.\begin{array}{l} r = R_1 \\ r = R \end{array}\right\} \quad u = v = w = 0 \quad ; \quad \frac{\partial T'}{\partial r} = 0$$

$$(2.7) \qquad z = 0 \qquad u = v = w = 0 \quad ; \quad T' = T_0 + \frac{\Delta T}{2}$$

$$z = H \qquad u = v = w = 0 \quad ; \quad T' = T_0 - \frac{\Delta T}{2}$$

c) Méthode de solution

Le système d'équations (2.1) - (2.6) avec les conditions aux limites (2.7) a été résolu en conservant les variables naturelles u, v, w, p', T'.

Comme réseau d'intégration on a considéré le réseau montré en Fig. 2.1, où les composantes radiales et axiales sont déplacées d'un demi-pas par rapport au point central où l'on calcule la pression et la température.

Le procédé adopté pour atteindre la solution présente les phases suivantes:

1) Le équations sont discrétisées avec les différences centrales et les différences en contrevent, pour les termes de convection de l'équation (2.5).

2) L'équation (2.3) pour la vitesse azimutale est eliminée en la résolvant par rapport à la composante radiale et en la substituant dans la (2.2).

3) Pour chaque cellule de calcul on décrit les 4 équations du moment pour les points $(i-\frac{1}{2}, j)$, $(i+\frac{1}{2}, j)$, $(i, j-\frac{1}{2})$, $(i, j+\frac{1}{2})$ qui entourent le point générique (i, j).

4) En supposant que les valeurs des différentes variables dans les cellules près l'une de l'autre soient connues, et en substituant ces 4 équations dans l'équation de continuité, on obtient une seule équation linéaire qui donne $p'_{i,j}$.

5) En substituant la valeur $p'_{i,j}$ dans les 4 équations du moment, employées on obtient les valeurs des 4 vitesses relatives.

6) L'équation de la température a été résolue, cellule par cellule, à l'aide de la méthode de Gauss-Seidel.

7) Le procédé est repété itérativement pour toutes les cellules qui recouvrent le domaine d'intégration, jusqu'à obtenir la convergence de la solution numérique.

d) Résultats

Le modèle mathématique a été appliqué à une centrifuge tournante à haute vitesse angulaire, avec le rapport $\frac{H}{R}$ = 10. Les résultats obtenus, concernant la vitesse axiale et azimutale, ainsi que la température (en forme adimensionelle), sont montrés en Fig. 2.2, 2.3 et 2.4.

Dans la première figure on reporte le comportement de la vitesse axiale en fonction de la coordonnée radiale en correspondance de 3 différentes valeurs de la coordonnée axiale. Par effet de la rotation et de la différence de température imposée entre les couvercles, il se produit un mouvement de recirculation qui interfère sur toute la région d'intégration.

On peut constater aussi comment la couche limite dynamique près de la paroi externe ait une extension très petite par rapport au rayon de la centrifuge.

Dans la deuxième figure sont reportés les comportements radiaux de la vitesse azimutale et de la température, rélatifs aux mêmes valeurs de la coordonnée axiale.

Dans la zone centrale, la vitesse azimutale augmente lineairement avec r dans la région où la vitesse axiale reste pratiquement constante. En s'approchant de la paroi latérale la v présente un minimum et un maximum associés au correspondant comportement de w.

L'examen du comportement de la température montre l'importance des termes de convection, qui détruisent la symétrie par rapport au plan moyen de la centrifuge.

3. Distribution de la charge dans un échangeur de chaleur

a) Description du problème

On a étudié le champ de mouvement dans le circuit principal d'un échangeur cylindrique à faiseaux de tuyaux (Fig. 3.1). L'entrée et le prélévement du fluide ont lieu sur toute la paroi latérale limitrophe de l'échangeur.

A l'intérieur de l'échangeur, outre la présence du faiseau de tuyaux, il y a une série de grilles radiales ayant la fonction d'uniformer la distribution de la charge. Le modèle mathématique doit donner le distributions de $\vec{V}$, P (champ de mouvement).

b) Modèle mathématique

L'effet qui est dû à la présence du faiseau de tuyaux dans l'échangeur, a été simulé en supposant que le fluide principal soit dépourvu de la viscosité et que les pertes de la charge en direction radiale et axiale, soient données par des coefficients différentsentr'eux et connu

La présence des grilles a été simulé en introduisant des pertes de charge localisées.

Pour ces hypothèses, les équations qui décrivent le champ de mouvement sont les suivantes:

$$\frac{1}{r}\frac{\partial(ru)}{\partial r} + \frac{\partial v}{\partial z} = 0 \qquad (3.1)$$

$$(3.2)\qquad \frac{\partial u}{\partial t} + u\frac{\partial u}{\partial r} + v\frac{\partial u}{\partial z} = -\frac{1}{\rho}\frac{\partial P}{\partial r} - \frac{K_r}{\rho}\eta^2 u|u|^m$$

termes de convection — sources

$$(3.3)\qquad \frac{\partial v}{\partial t} + u\frac{\partial v}{\partial r} + v\frac{\partial v}{\partial z} = -\frac{1}{\rho}\frac{\partial P}{\partial z} - \frac{K_z}{\rho}\eta^2 v|v|^n - \frac{\xi_G v|v|}{2}$$

termes de convection — sources

où

u, v composantes de la vitesse

P pression

$K_r\eta^2$, $K_z\eta^2$ coéfficients pour le calcul de la perte de charge

ξ_G coéfficient de la perte localisée par les grilles

ρ densité apparante $= \rho_{fluide} \cdot \frac{V_{fluide}}{V_{tot}}$

Les conditions aux limites sont les suivantes

$z = 0$	$0 \leq r \leq R$	$v = 0$
$z = H$	$0 \leq r \leq R$	$v = 0$
$r = 0$	$0 \leq z \leq H$	$u = 0$
$r = R$	$0 \leq z \leq h_1$ $h_2 \leq z \leq h_3$ $h_4 \leq z \leq H$	$u = 0$
$r = R$	$h_1 \leq z \leq h_2$ $h_3 \leq z \leq h_4$	$U = U_i(z)$ assignée $\frac{\partial u}{\partial r} = 0$

c) Méthode de solution

Les équations ont été discrétisées en employant le réseau décrit dans le paragraphe précédent.

Les équations ont été résolues en utilisant la methode Marker et Cell (MAC).

Les termes de convection ont été discrétisés en utilisant des différences en contrevent.

L'équation de Poisson pour la pression a été résolue en inversant directement la matrice des coéfficients, à l'aide de l'algorithme tri-diagonal à blocs.

La solution stationnaire a été obtenue comme limite asymptotique de la solution transitoire.

d) Résultats obtenus

Un example de distribution de la charge est reporté en Fig. 3.2. On peut remarquer que dans la région centrale de l'échangeur, la direction du flux coïncide avec la direction axiale, les composantes radiales dues à la sortie et à l'entrée étant presentes seulement tout près de ces dernières entrées.

BIBLIOGRAPHIE

Problème 1

G. Astarita, R. Sala, A. Tozzi, F. Valz Gris
"Styrène polymerization reactor", ARS RT70/35 (1970)

G. Astarita, R. Sala, A. Tozzi, F. Valz Gris
"A parametric study for styrene polymerization reactors having cylindrical and annular geometry", ARS RT71/5 (1971)

A. D. Gosman, W. M. Pun, A. K. Runchal, D. B. Spalding, M. Wolfshtein
"Heat and Mass Transfer in Recirculating Flows", Academic Press, London (1969)

Problème 2

L. S. Caretto, A. D. Gosman, D. B. Spalding
"Removal of an instability in a free convection problem", EF/TN/A/35 (1971)

R. Sala, A. Tozzi, F. Valz Gris
"Soluzione numerica del campo di moto delle ultracentrifughe a controllo termico", ARS RT 72/40 (1972)

R. Sala, A. Tozzi
"Comportamento fluidodinamico delle ultracentrifughe a controllo termico"
ARS RT 72/38

Problème 3

F. H. Harlow, J. E. Welch
"Numerical calculation of time-dependent viscous incompressible flow of fluid with free surface", Phys. Fluids 8, 2182 (1965)

L. Biasi, A. Colombo, A. Tozzi
"Codice per la soluzione di problemi di fluidodinamica in uno scambiatore di calore" ARS RT 73/11 (1973)

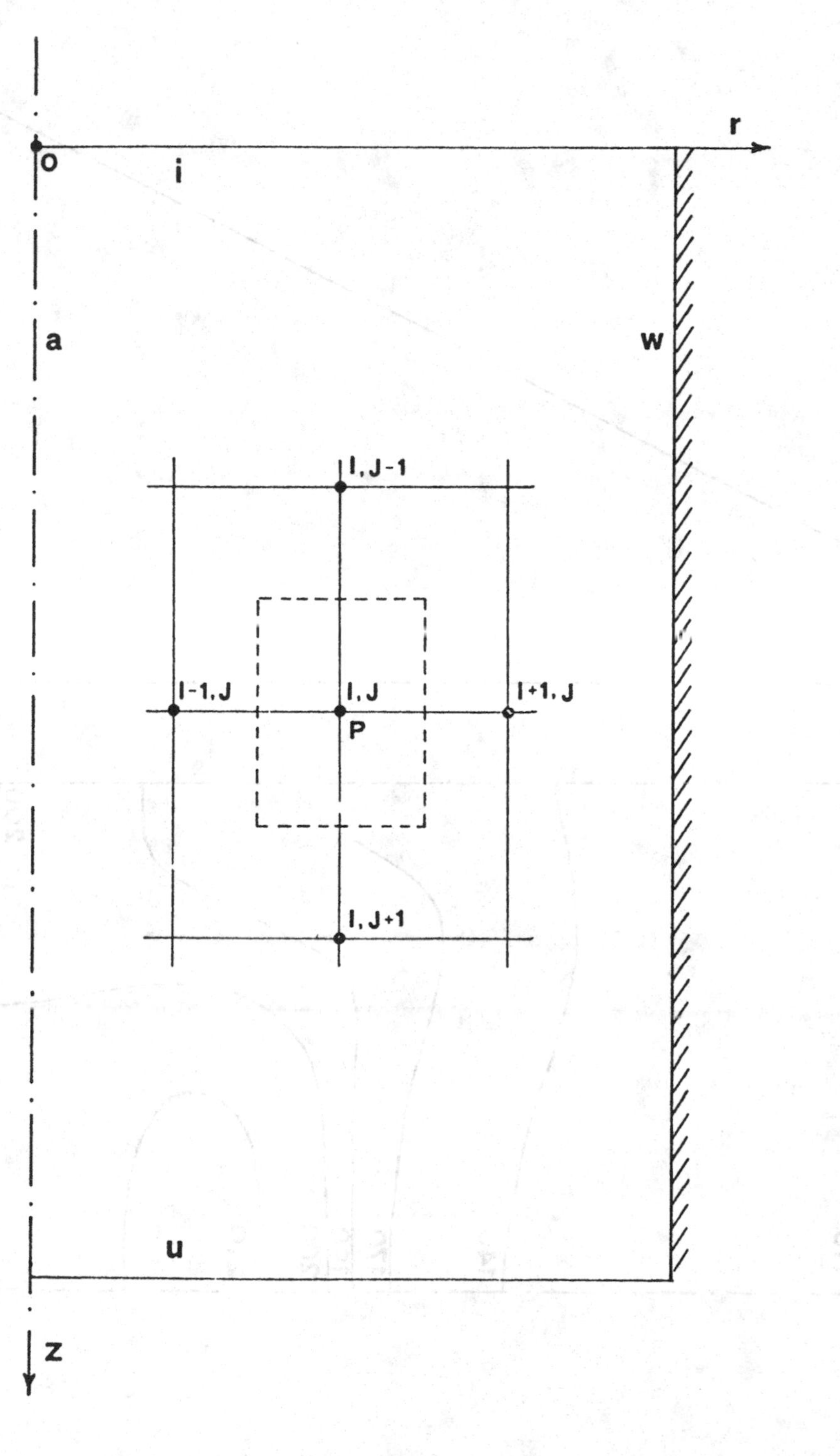

Fig. 1, 1

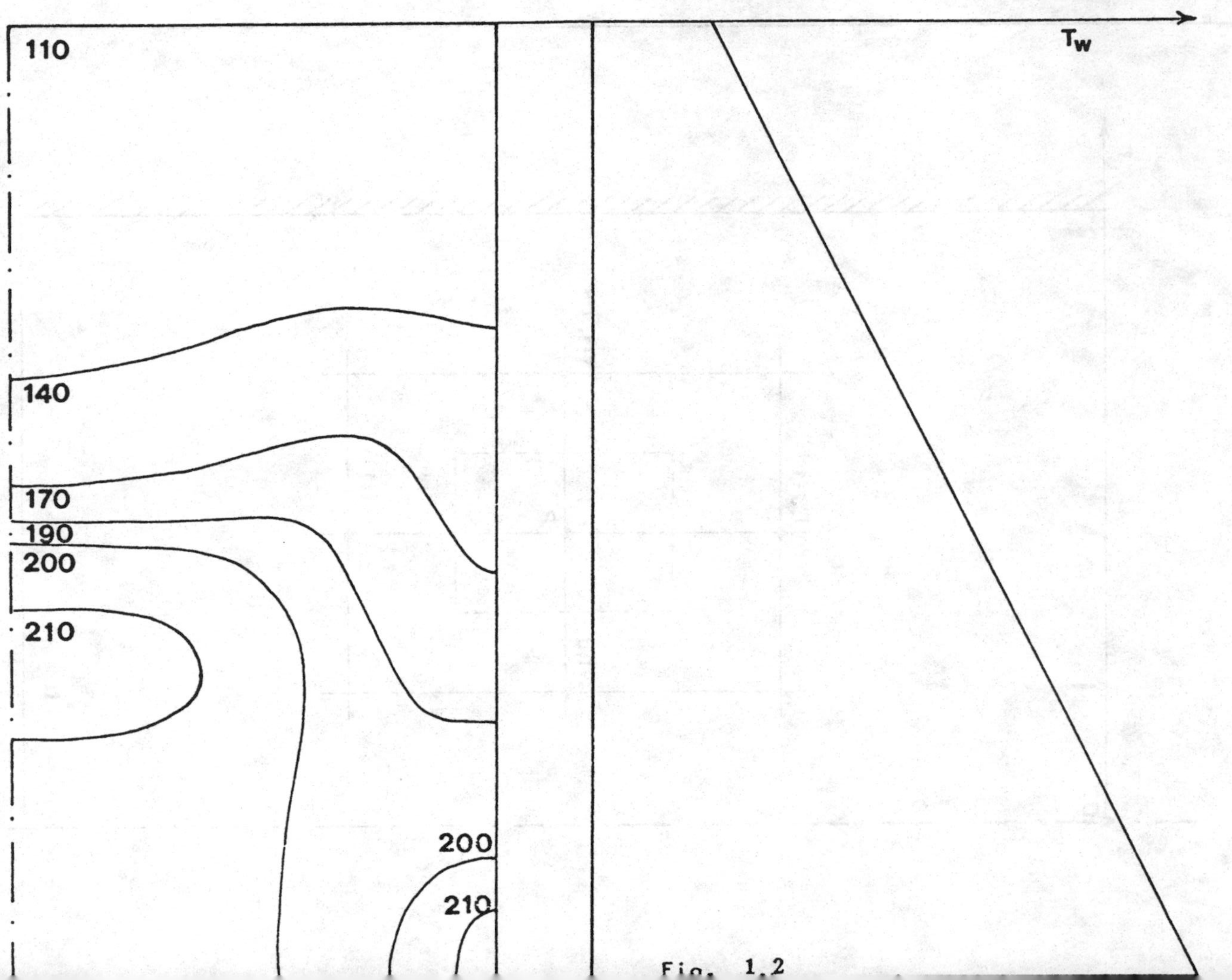

Fig. 1.2

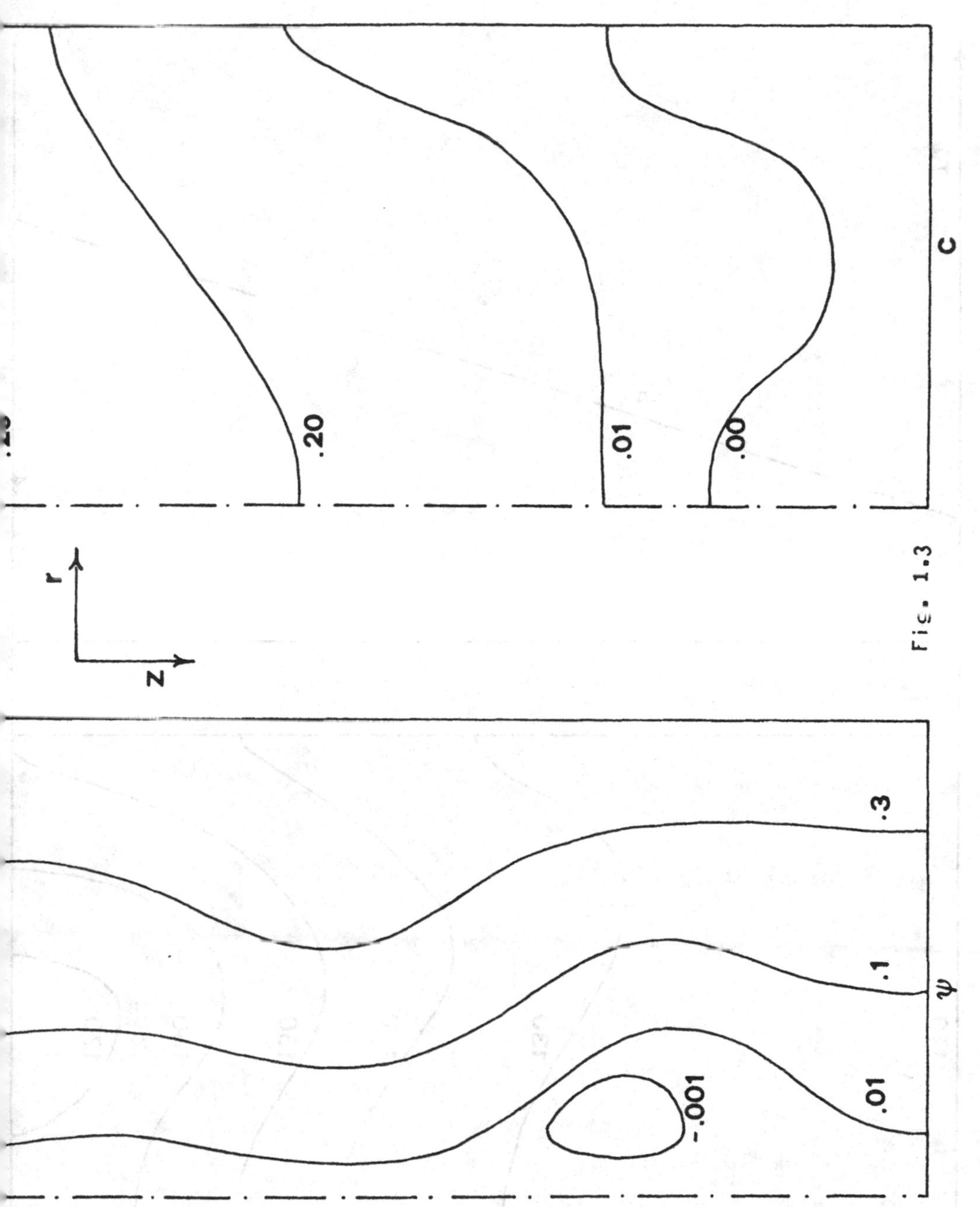

Fig. 1.3

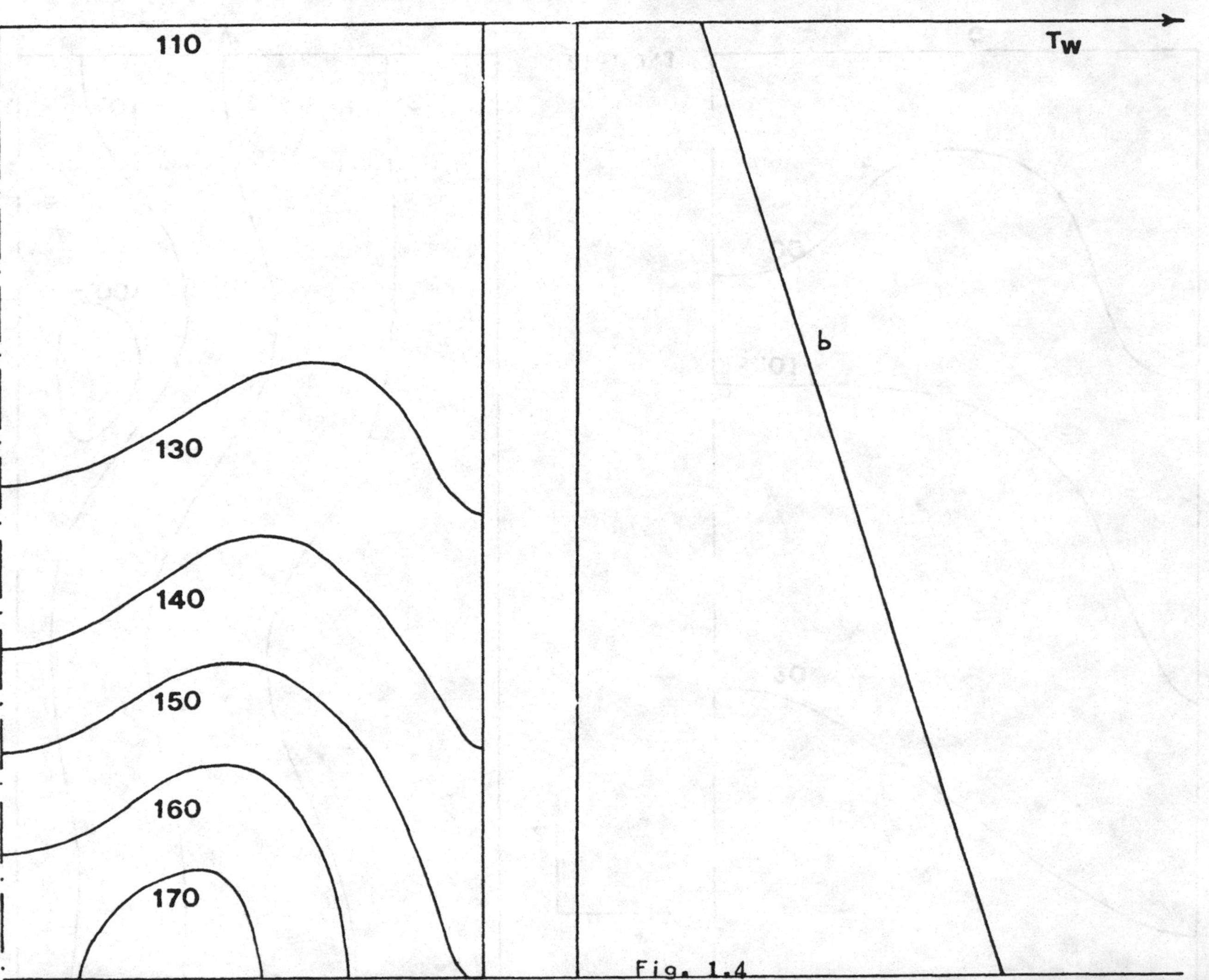

Fig. 1.4

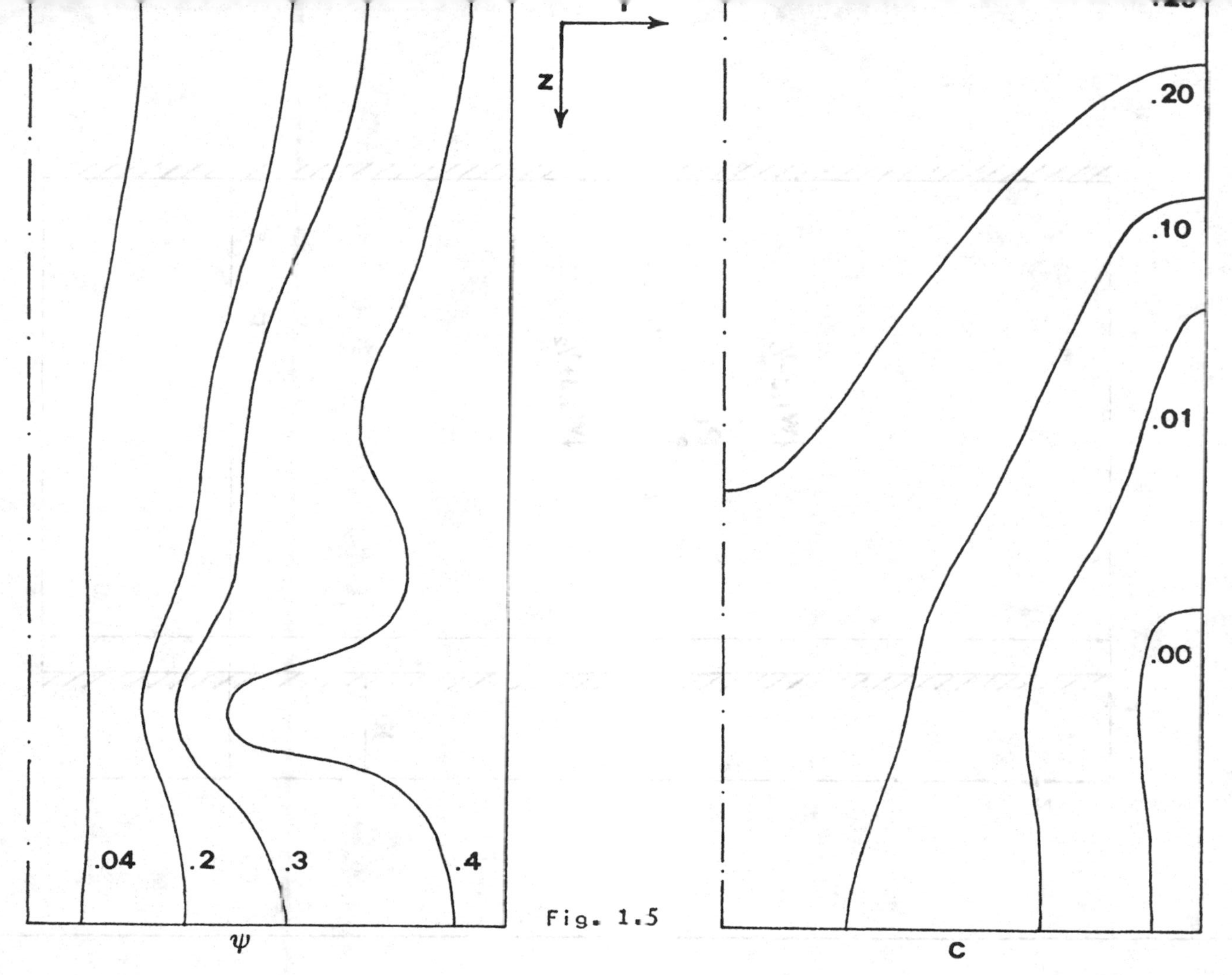

Fig. 1.5

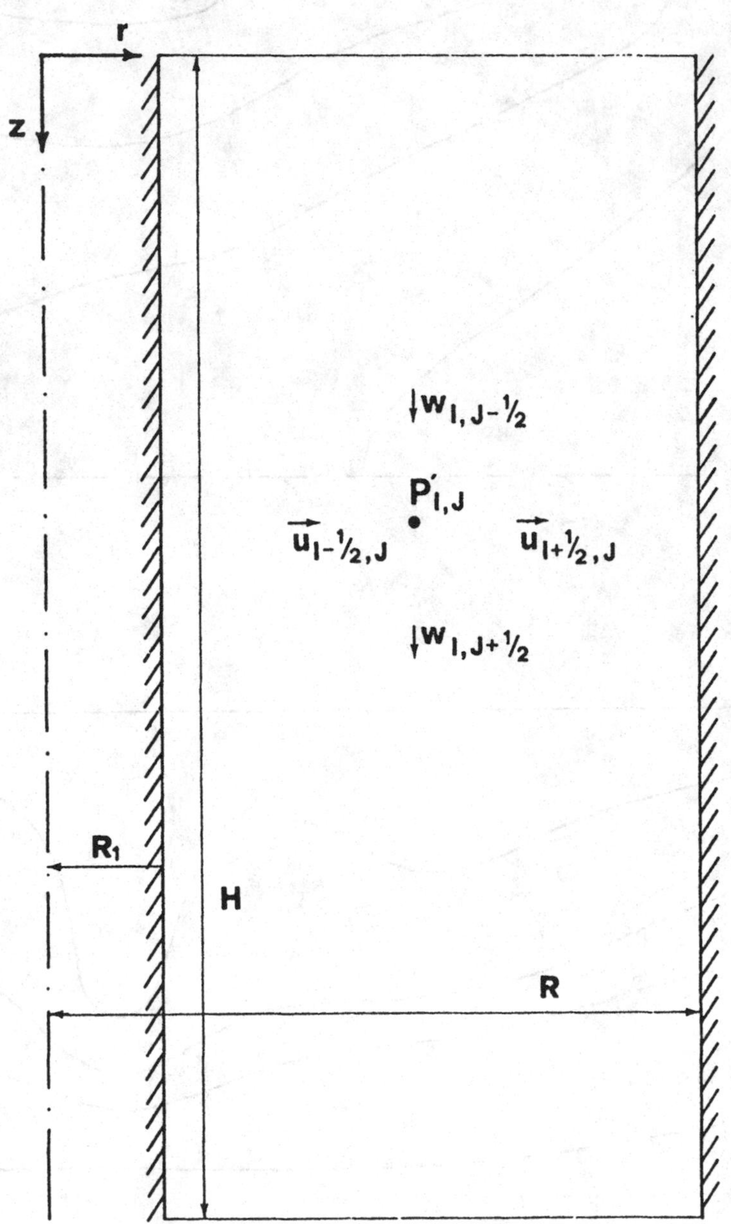

Fig. 2.1

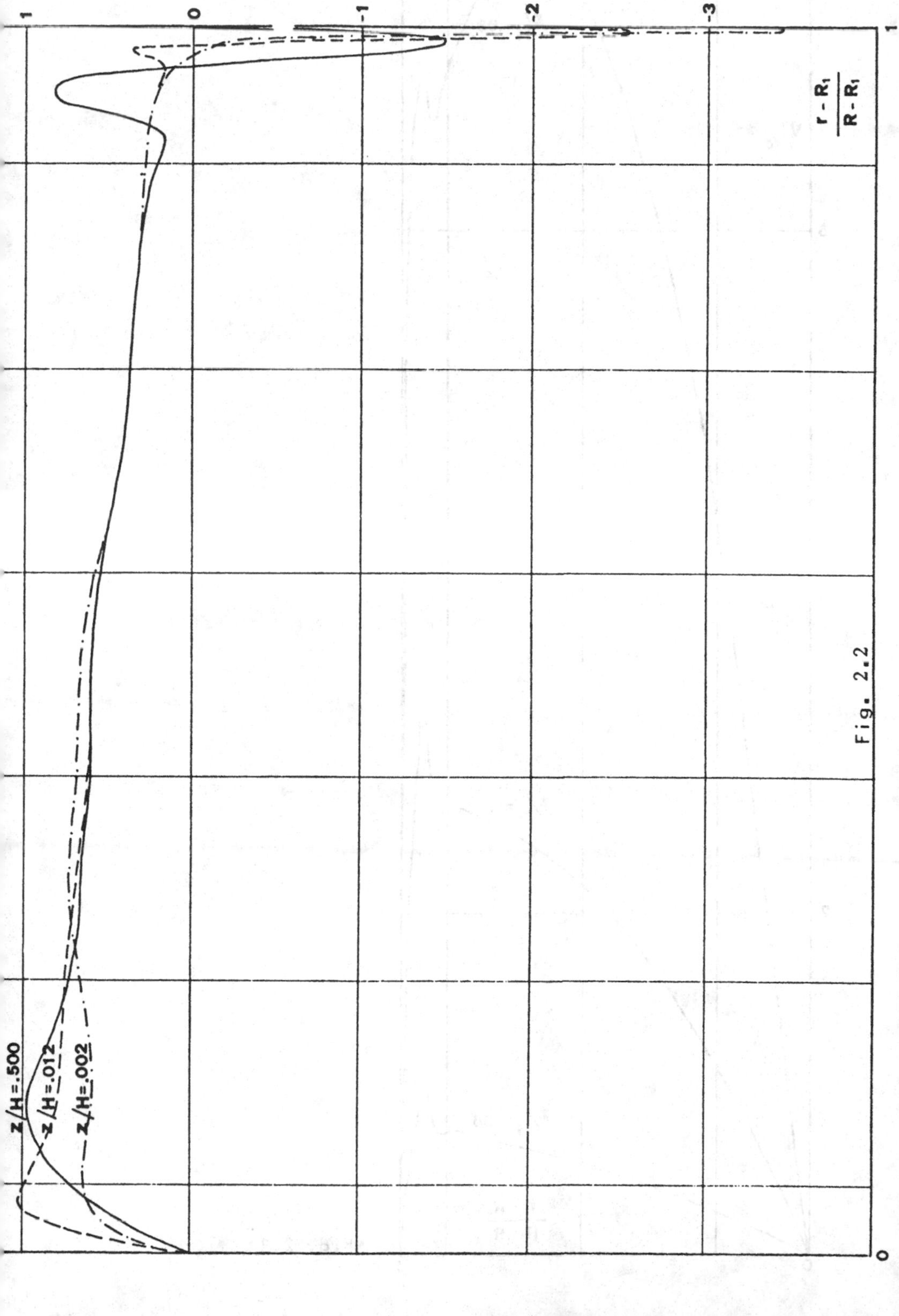

$z/H = .500$

$z/H = .012$

$z/H = .002$

$\frac{r - R_1}{R - R_1}$

Fig. 2.2

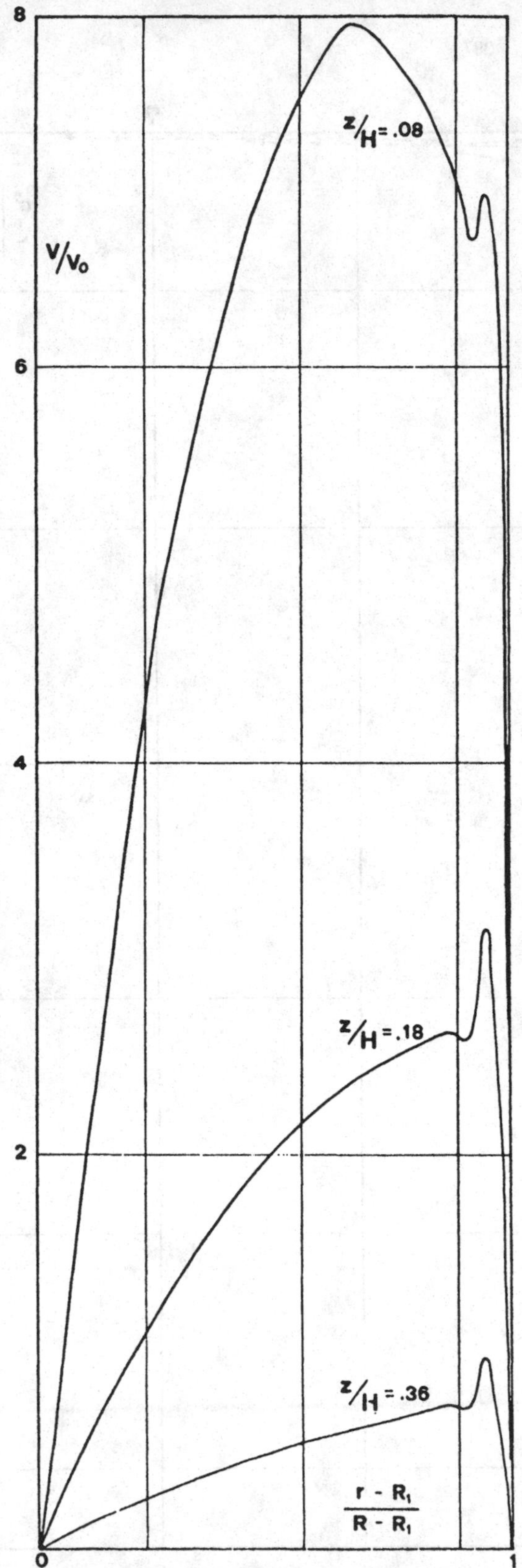

Fig. 2.3

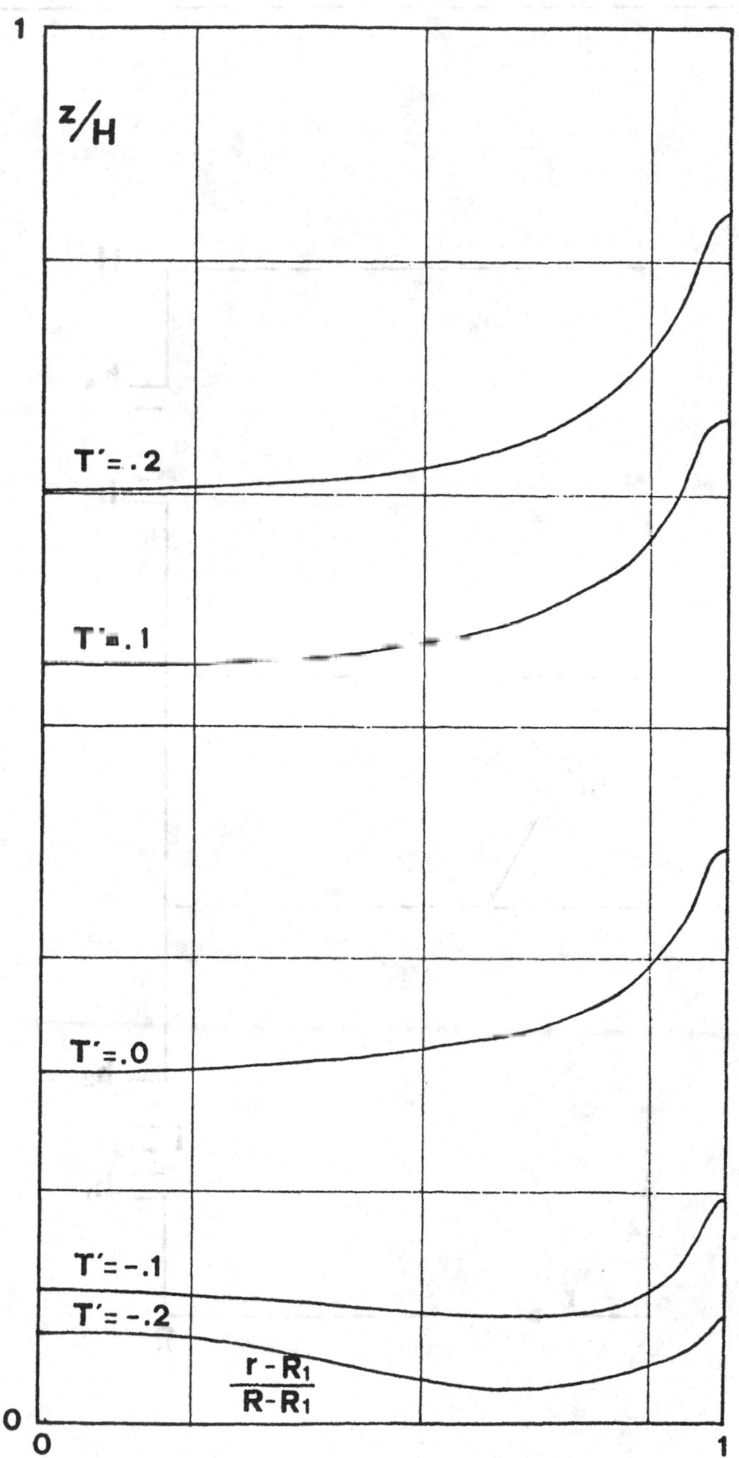

Fig. 2.4

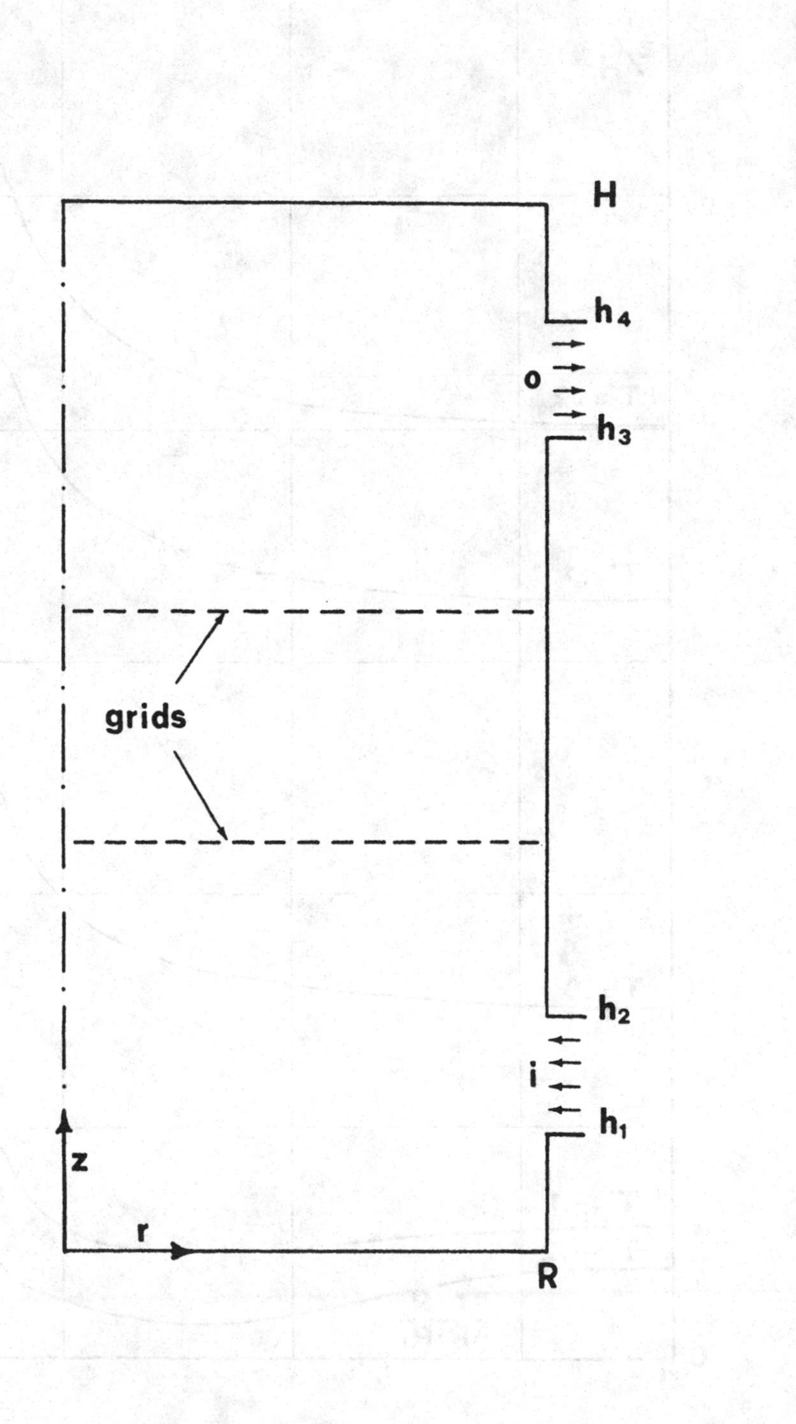

Fig. 3.1

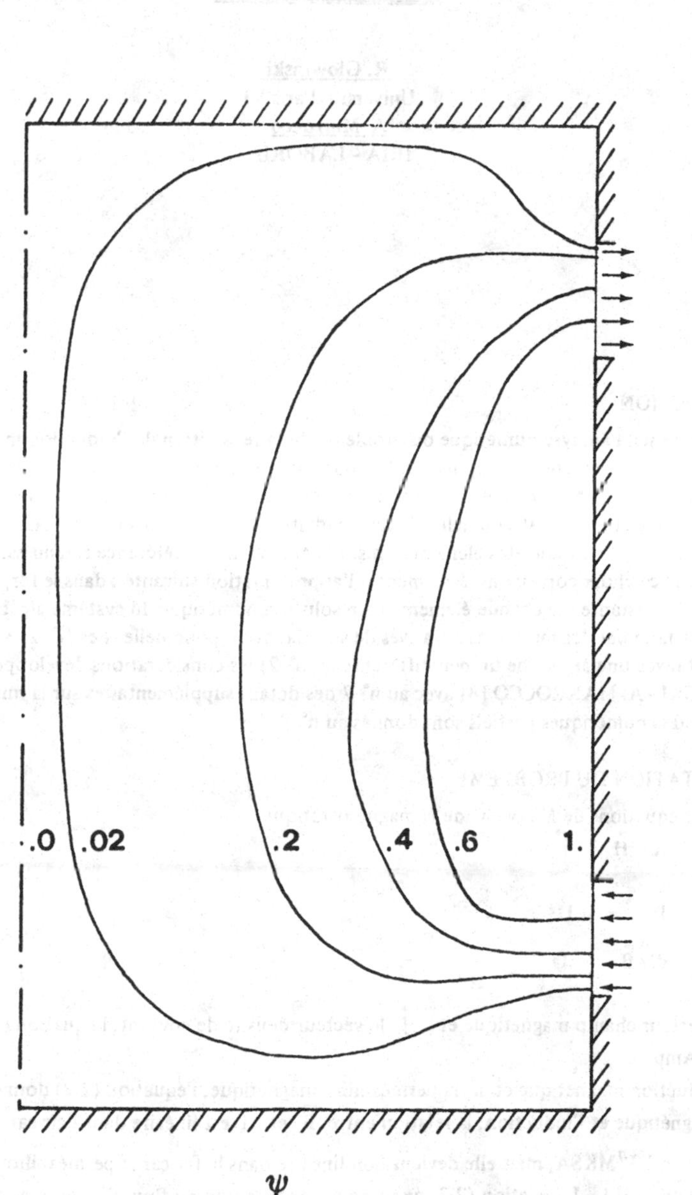

Fig. 3.2

ETUDE NUMÉRIQUE DU CHAMP MAGNÉTIQUE DANS UN ALTERNATEUR TÉTRAPOLAIRE PAR LA MÉTHODE DES ÉLÉMENTS FINIS

R. Glowinski
Université Paris VI
A. Marrocco
IRIA - LABORIA

I - INTRODUCTION

Nous présentons ici, l'analyse numérique du problème de la répartition de l'induction magnétique dans une machine tournante (alternateur tétrapolaire). L'étude est faite pour une coupe transversale médiane de la machine, ce qui ramène le problème, qui en toute généralité est tridimensionnel, à un problème bidimensionnel. Le phénomène étudié est stationnaire. L'approximation des équations pour le calcul effectif par ordinateur a été faite par la technique des éléments finis. L'élément fini de référence retenu est l'élément triangulaire de degré 1 ; ce choix correspond également à l'approximation suivante : dans le fer, la perméabilité magétique sera constante sur chaque élément. La résolution numérique du système algébrique non linéaire résultant a été faite par des méthodes itératives de surrélaxation ponctuelle. Les N°s 2, 3, 4, 5, 6 reprennent succintement (avec une approche un peu différente au n° 2) les considérations développées dans R. GLOWINSKI - A. MARROCCO [8] avec au n° 7 des détails supplémentaires sur la mise en œuvre pratique; des résultats numériques partiels sont donnés au n° 8.

II - PRÉSENTATION DU PROBLEME

Rappelons les équations de Maxwell de la magnétostatique

(2-1) $\qquad \text{rot}\ \vec{H} = \vec{j}$

(2-2) $\qquad \vec{B} = \mu \vec{H}$

(2-3) $\qquad \text{div}\ \vec{B} = O$

$\vec{H}$ est le vecteur champ magnétique et $\vec{j}$ le vecteur densité de courant; l'équation (2-1) est la relation de Maxwell-Ampère.

$\vec{B}$ est l'induction magnétique et μ la perméabilité magnétique; l'équation (2-2) donne la relation entre le champ magnétique et l'induction; la relation entre $\vec{B}$ et $\vec{H}$ est linéaire dans l'air car

$\mu = \mu_o = 4\pi\ 10^{-7}$MKSA, mais elle devient non linéaire dans le fer car la perméabilité μ est elle -même une fonction de $|\vec{H}|$. La relation (2-3) exprime la conservation du flux d'induction.

La relation (2-3) permet d'introduire le potentiel vecteur $\vec{A} = (A_1, A_2, A_3)$ lié à $\vec{B}$ par

(2-4) $\qquad \vec{B} = \text{rot } \vec{A}$

Si nous utilisons (2-4), les relations (2-1), (2-2), (2-3) deviennent

(2-5) $\qquad \text{rot}(\nu \text{ rot } \vec{A}) = \vec{j} \qquad \text{avec} \qquad \nu = \frac{1}{\mu}$

Le problème étudié est bidimensionnel; certaines considérations physiques permettent de choisir dans ce cas particulier, le potentiel vecteur $\vec{A}$ comme un vecteur n'ayant qu'une composante non nulle A_3 (le courant $\vec{j}$ est aussi donné sous la forme $\vec{j} = (0, 0, j_3)$, si bien que l'équation (2-5) s'écrit dans ce cas

(2-6) $\qquad -\sum_{i=1} \frac{\partial}{\partial x_i} \left(\nu \frac{\partial A_3}{\partial x_i}\right) = j_3$

REMARQUE 2-1

La relation (2-4) ne détermine pas uniquement $\vec{A}$; pour avoir cette unicité il suffit par exemple [cf.0] d'imposer une valeur à div $\vec{A}$ (par ex. div $\vec{A} = 0$ se trouve implicitement vérifié par notre choix du potentiel vecteur;

L'équation (2-5) ou (2-6) est valable théoriquement dans tout le plan. D'un point de vue pratique, on se limite à un domaine borné. La figure 1 indique le domaine retenu; nous avons considéré une «zône de garde» à l'extérieur du stator, constituée par de l'air évidemment. Sur le bord extérieur de cette bande nous imposons la condition $A_3 = 0$. Cette condition entraîne en particulier que toutes les lignes de champ (ou d'induction) sont contenues dans le domaine considéré; et donc que le phénomène magnétique se trouve confiné au domaine choisi. Les résultats numériques obtenus montrent en fait que l'on aurait pu imposer cette condition $A_3 = 0$ sur le bord du stator. Cette condition aux limites entraîne l'unicité du potentiel vecteur comme nous le verrons en III et IV.

REMARQUE 2-2

La machine effectivement étudiée est un alternateur tétrapolaire; si l'on tient compte des conditions d'antipériodicité, il suffit de n'étudier qu'un quart de la machine. L'étude théorique va être faite sur le domaine entier, il faudra évidemment modifier légèrement le cadre fonctionnel si on veut prendre en compte ces conditions d'antipériodicité.

REMARQUE 2-3

Pour le problème bi-dimensionnel étudié, les lignes d'induction dans la machine sont données par les lignes équipotentielles (ou lignes de niveau) de la fonction $A_3(x_1, x_2)$

III - LE MODELE MATHEMATIQUE

II.1. Equations aux dérivées partielles

Le domaine Ω considéré est un cercle dont le bord est noté Γ.

La détermination du champ magnétique (ou de l'induction magnétique) dans Ω, se ramène dans la cas présent, à la résolution de l'équation aux dérivées partielles

3-1) $\qquad -\frac{\partial}{\partial x_1}\left[\nu(x,A)\frac{\partial A}{\partial x_1}\right] - \frac{\partial}{\partial x_2}\left[\nu(x,A)\frac{\partial A}{\partial x_2}\right] = j \text{ dans } \Omega$

ou $x = (x_1, x_2)$

avec les conditions aux limites

3-2) $\qquad A = 0 \text{ sur } \Gamma$

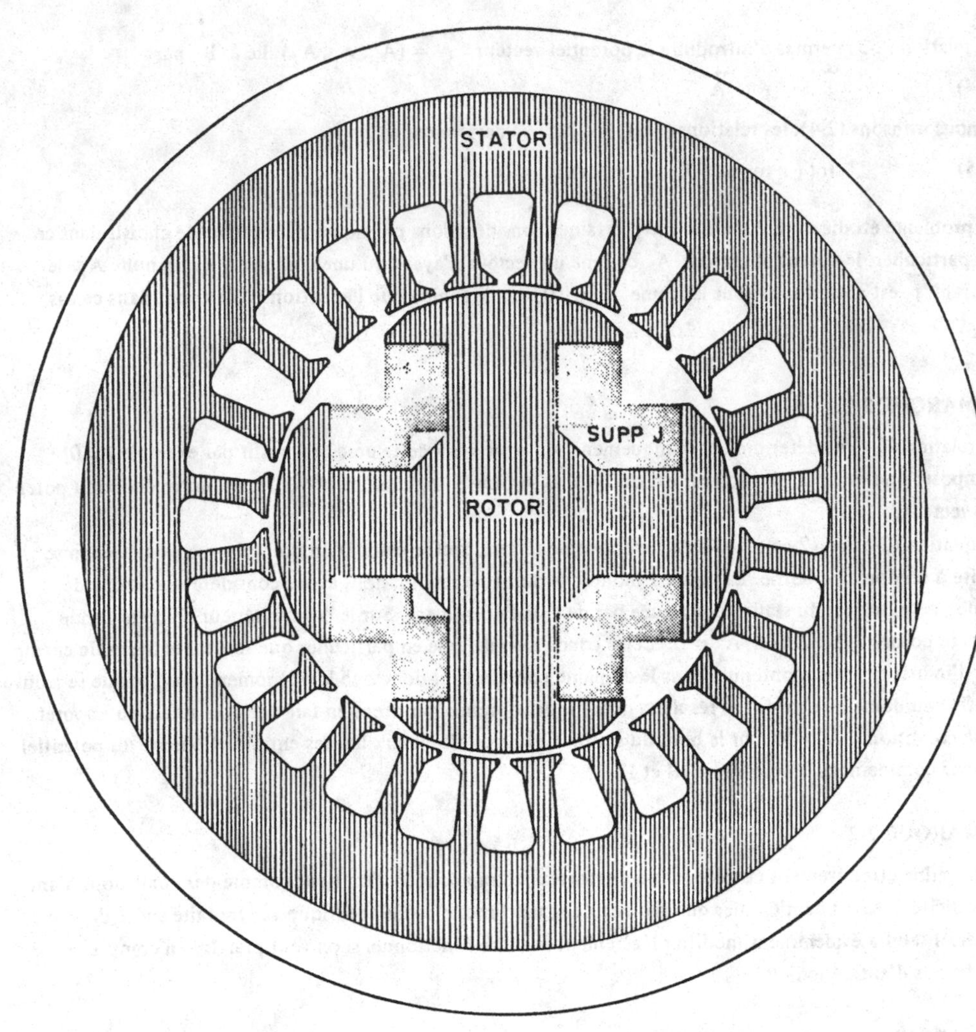

Fig. 1

Nous avons indiqué la dépendance de ν par rapport à la variable d'espace x et A

$\nu(x, A) = \nu_0 = \frac{1}{\mu_0}$ si x est dans l'air

mais ν dépend non linéairement de l'induction, et donc de A par (2-4) lorsque x est dans le fer.

III-2. **Fonctionnelle d'énergie**

Il y a équivalence entre la résolution de (3-1), (3-2) et la minimisation (sur un espace à préciser) de la fonctionnelle d'énergie (cf. [1] [2])

(3-3) $$\mathfrak{F}(A) = \int_\Omega \left[\int_0^{|\vec{B}|} \nu(x,b)\, b\, db \right] dx - \int_\Omega j\, A\, dx$$

ou rappelons-le

(3-4) $$\vec{B} = \text{rot}\, \vec{A} \qquad \text{avec } \vec{A} = (0, 0, A)$$

L'équation d'Euler du problème de calcul des variations redonne (3-1)

Pour le fer nous tirons la fonction ν des caractéristiques magnétiques du stator du rotor et nous l'exprimons comme fonction de $|\vec{B}|^2$. Ceci va simplifier l'écriture de la fonctionnelle d'énergie (3-3), qui devient, si on note ψ la primitive de ν considérée comme fonction de $|\vec{B}|^2$ qui s'annule pour la valeur 0,

(3-5) $$\mathfrak{F}(A) = \frac{1}{2} \int_\Omega \psi(x, |\vec{B}|^2)\, dx - \int_\Omega j\, A\, dx$$

soit aussi

(3-6) $$\mathfrak{F}(A) = \frac{1}{2} \int_\Omega \psi(x, |\text{rot}\, \vec{A}|^2)\, dx - \int_\Omega j\, A\, dx$$

ou encore

(3-7) $$\mathfrak{F}(A) = \frac{1}{2} \int_\Omega \psi(x, |\text{grad}\, A|^2)\, dx - \int_\Omega j\, A\, dx$$

puisque dans le cas bidimensionnel on a

$$|\vec{B}| = |\text{rot}\, \vec{A}| = |\text{grad}\, A|$$

III.3. **Approximation de ν**

L'inverse de la perméabilité magnétique peut s'écrire

$\nu = \nu_0\, \nu_r$ ou $\nu_0 = \frac{1}{4\pi 10^{-7}}$ MKSA

et ν_r est la valeur relative par rapport à l'air; nous avons

$$0 < \nu_r \leq 1$$

Dans le fer, nous approchons ν_r par une fonction strictement croissante de $|\vec{B}|^2$ de la forme

(3-8) $$\nu_r(|\vec{B}|^2) = \alpha + (1 - \alpha) \frac{(|\vec{B}|^2)^4}{(|B|^2)^4 + \beta}$$

Voir sur les figures [2, 3] l'approximation réalisée. Cette approximation a été réalisée par une méthode des moindres carrés et a donné pour valeur des paramètres

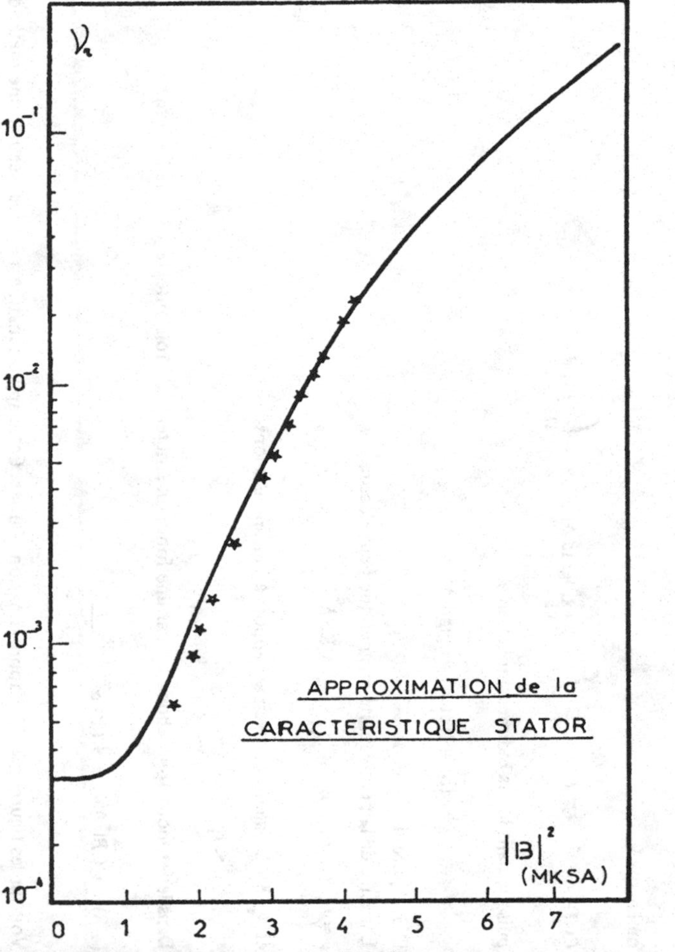

ν
10⁻¹
10⁻²
10⁻³
10⁻⁴
0 1 2 3 4 5 6 7
|B|²
(MKSA)
APPROXIMATION de la
CARACTERISTIQUE STATOR

Fig. 2

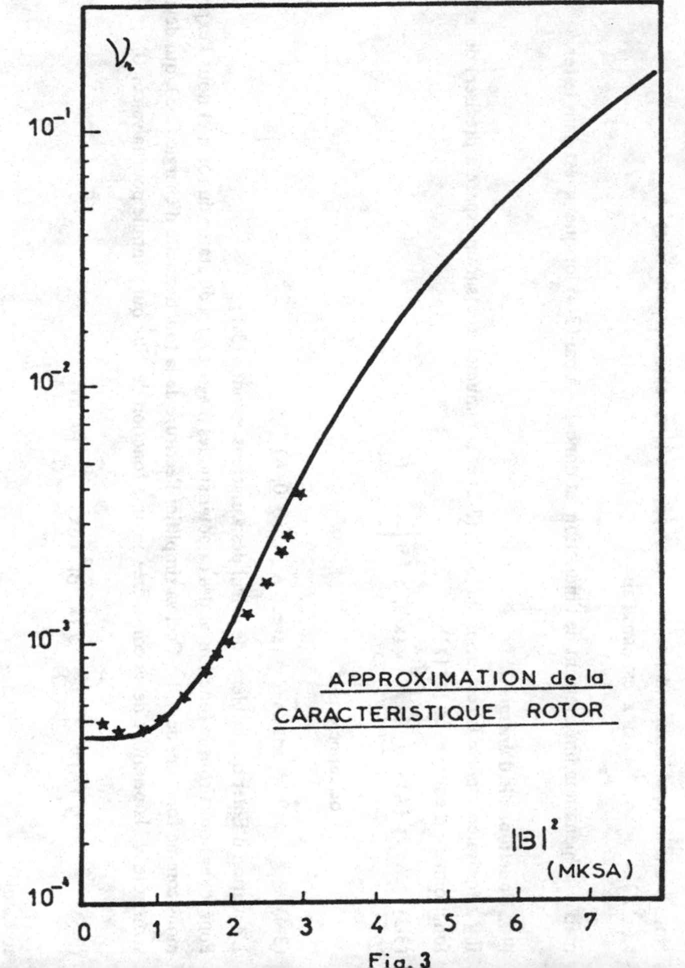

ν
10⁻¹
10⁻²
10⁻³
10⁻⁴
0 1 2 3 4 5 6 7
|B|²
(MKSA)
APPROXIMATION de la
CARACTERISTIQUE ROTOR

Fig. 3

(3-9) $\begin{cases} \alpha = 4,5 \quad 10^{-4} \\ \beta = 2,2 \quad 10^{4} \end{cases}$ dans le rotor

(3-10) $\begin{cases} \alpha = 3 \quad 10^{-4} \\ \beta = 1,6 \quad 10^{4} \end{cases}$ dans le stator

On n'a pas tenu compte de l'effet d'hystérésis qui conduirait à des représentations multivoques pour ν_r

Nous avons dans tout le domaine Ω

(3-11) $\quad 0 < \epsilon \leqslant \nu_r \leqslant 1$

IV - ETUDE THEORIQUE DU PROBLEME

IV.1. Formulation précise du problème

On cherche $A \in H_0^1(\Omega)$ solution de

(4-1) $\quad \mathfrak{F}(A) \leqslant \mathfrak{F}(\nu) \qquad \forall \nu \in H_0^1(\Omega)$

ou $\mathfrak{F}$ est donné par

(4-2) $$\mathfrak{F}(A) = \frac{1}{2}\int_\Omega \psi(x, |\text{grad } A|^2)\, dx - \int_\Omega j\, A\, dx$$

avec ψ défini en III.2

(4-3) $$\begin{cases} H_0^1(\Omega) = \{ \nu, |\nu, \frac{\partial \nu}{\partial x_i} \in L^2(\Omega), \ i = 1,2 \ , \ \nu|_\Gamma = 0 \} \\ \|\nu\|_{H_0^1(\Omega)} = (\int_\Omega |\text{grad } \nu|^2 \, dx)^{1/2} \end{cases}$$

IV.2. Résultat d'existence et d'unicité

THÉOREME 4-1 – Le problème de minimisation (4-1) admet une solution et une seule.

Démonstration

On fait un changement d'unité tel que $\nu = \nu_r$

• la fonction $\xi \to \psi(x, \xi)$ est contractante, $\forall x \in \Omega$ d'après (3-11), cela entraîne que $\mathfrak{F}$ est fortement continue sur $H_0^1(\Omega)$

• la fonction $\xi \to \frac{\partial \psi}{\partial \xi}(x, \xi)$ est strictement monotone croissante, la fonction $\mathfrak{F}$ est donc strictement convexe

* d'après 3-11 on a

$$\int_\Omega \psi(x, |\text{grad } \vartheta|^2)\, dx \geqslant \epsilon \int |\text{grad } \vartheta|^2 \, dx = \epsilon \, \|\vartheta\|^2_{H_0^1(\Omega)}$$

donc $\lim\limits_{\|\vartheta\| \to \infty} \mathfrak{F}(\vartheta) = +\infty$

De ces propriétés on déduit par un raisonnement classique d'analyse convexe (cf. [3]) l'existence et l'unicité d'une solution pour (4-1)

IV.3. Relation entre le problème aux limites (3-1), (3-2) et le problème (4-1)

THÉOREME 4-2

A solution de (4-1) est solution unique de (3-1) (3-2) dans $H_0^1(\Omega)$

Démonstration

$\mathfrak{J}$ est différentiable au sens de GATEAUX sur $H^1_0(\Omega)$ c'est-à-dire (cf.[4]) $\forall u \in H^1_0(\Omega)$ il existe $\mathfrak{J}'(u) \in H^{-1}(\Omega)$ (dual topologique de $H^1_0(\Omega)$) tel que $\forall \vartheta \in H^1_0(\Omega)$ on a

(4-4) $$\lim_{\substack{t \to 0 \\ t \neq 0}} \frac{\mathfrak{J}(u + t\vartheta) - \mathfrak{J}(u)}{t} = (\mathfrak{J}'(u), \vartheta)$$

Donc si A est solution de (4-1) on a

(4-5) $$\frac{\mathfrak{J}(A + t\vartheta) - \mathfrak{J}(A)}{t} \geq 0 \qquad \forall t > 0, \quad \forall \vartheta \in H^1_0(\Omega)$$

D'où à la limite

(4-6) $(\mathfrak{J}'(A), \vartheta) \geq 0 \qquad \forall \vartheta \in H^1_0(\Omega)$

En prenant $t < 0$ on trouve

(4-7) $(\mathfrak{J}'(A), \vartheta) \leq 0 \qquad \forall \vartheta \in H^1_0(\Omega)$

Ce qui donne

(4-8) $(\mathfrak{J}'(A), \vartheta) = 0 \qquad \forall \vartheta \in H^1_0(\Omega)$

d'où

(4-9) $\mathfrak{J}'(A) = 0$

Les formes explicites de (4-8) et (4-9) sont données respectivement par (4-10) et (4-11)

(4-10) $$\int_\Omega \nu(x, A) \operatorname{grad} A . \operatorname{grad} \vartheta \, dx - \int_\Omega j \vartheta \, dx = 0 \qquad \forall \vartheta \in H^1_0(\Omega)$$

(4-11) $$\begin{cases} -\sum_{i=1}^{2} \frac{\partial}{\partial x_i} \left(\nu(x, A) \frac{\partial A}{\partial x_i} \right) - j = 0 \\ A|_\Gamma = 0 \end{cases}$$

A est donc bien solution de (3-1), (3-2). $\mathfrak{J}$ étant strictement convexe sur $H^1_0(\Omega)$, la relation (4-9) caractérise complètement A.

V - APPROXIMATION PAR ÉLÉMENTS FINIS

V.1. Triangulation de Ω et notations

On se donne une triangulation $\mathfrak{T}_h$ de Ω (h égal au plus grand côté de tous les triangles par exemple)

(5-1) $$\bigcup_{T \in \mathfrak{T}_h} T \subset \bar{\Omega}$$

Avec les propriétés habituelles si T_1 et $T_2 \in \mathfrak{T}_h$

(5-2) $$\begin{cases} \text{ou } T_1 \cap T_2 = \phi \\ \text{ou } T_1 \text{ et } T_2 \text{ ont un côté commun} \\ \text{ou } T_1 \text{ et } T_2 \text{ ont un sommet commun} \end{cases}$$

Les interfaces air-fer coïncident au mieux avec des côtés de triangles

Notations

(5-3) $\Omega_h = \overset{\circ}{\bigcup_{T\in \mathcal{T}_h} T}$, $\Gamma_h = \partial\Omega_h$

(5-4) $\omega_h = \{ P \mid P \in \Omega_h ,\ P \text{ sommet de } T \in \mathcal{T}_h \}$

(5-5) $\gamma_h = \{ P \mid P \in \Gamma_h ,\ P \text{ sommet de } T \in \mathcal{T}_h \}$

(5-6) $\overline{\omega}_h = \omega_h + \gamma_h$

V.2. Approximation de $H^1_0(\Omega)$

Pour chaque nœud $M \in \omega_h$ (5-4) on définit la fonction W_h^M de la façon suivante

(5-7) $$\begin{cases} W_h^M (P) = \begin{matrix} 1 \text{ si } P = M \\ 0 \text{ si } P \neq M \end{matrix} \\ W_h^M \quad \text{affiné sur chaque triangle} \\ W_h^M = 0 \quad \text{sur } \Omega - \Omega_h \end{cases}$$

Les fonctions $W_h^M(x)$ ainsi définies sont continues sur $\overline{\Omega}$, elles sont dans $H^1_0(\Omega)$ et linéairement indépendantes

(5-8) V_{oh} est l'espace engendré par les W_h^M pour $M \in \omega_h$

Tout élément ϑ_h de V_{oh} est complètement déterminé par les valeurs prises sur ω_h. En supposant les éléments de W_h ordonnés et indexés par i pour $i = 1, 2 \dots N_h = \text{Card}(\omega_h) = \dim V_{oh}$ on notera

(5-9) $\vartheta_i = \vartheta_h(M_i) \qquad i = 1, 2 \dots N_h$

REMARQUE 5-1

La restriction de $\vartheta_h \in V_{oh}$ à un triangle est affiné, cela entraîne que le gradient de ϑ_h est constant sur chaque triangle de même ν (2-5) qui est une fonction de $|\text{grad}\,\vartheta_h|^2$ sera constant sur chaque triangle. Un élément $\vartheta_h \in V_{oh}$ s'exprime explicitement de la façon suivante

(5-10) $$\vartheta_h(x,y) = \sum_{T\in \mathcal{T}_h} \frac{1}{2\Delta(T)} \left(\sum_{j=1}^{3} (p_j^T + q_j^T x + r_j^T y)\, \vartheta_j^T \right) \Theta_h^T (x, y)$$

ou $\Delta(T)$ représente la surface du triangle T

Θ_h^T est la fonction caractéristique du triangle T

p_j^T, q_j^T, r_j^T, sont des fonctions des coordonnées des sommets du triangle T

ϑ_j^T est la valeur de la fonction au sommet j du triangle T

V.3. Formulation du problème approché

L'analogue discret du problème (4-1) est

(5-11) trouver $A_h \in V_{oh}$ tel que

$\mathcal{J}(A_h) \leq \mathcal{J}(\vartheta_h) \qquad \forall \vartheta_h \in V_{oh}$

ou $\mathcal{J}$ est toujours donné par (4-2)

THÉOREME 5-1

Le problème d'optimisation (5-11) admet une solution et une seule caractérisée par

(5-12) $$\frac{\partial \mathcal{J}}{\partial \vartheta_i}(A_h) = o \qquad i = 1, 2 \ldots N_h$$

On peut montrer le résultat suivant

THÉOREME 5-2

Si i) $\Omega - \Omega_h \to o$ lorsque $h \to o$

ii) les angles de tous les triangles $T \in \mathcal{C}_h$ sont bornés inférieurement, uniformément en h par $\Theta_o > o$ on a

(5-12) $$\lim_{h \to o} A_h = A \text{ dans } \overset{1}{H_o}(\Omega) \text{ fort}$$

A solution de (4-1)

Le problème de l'estimation de l'erreur d'approximation en fonction de h est lié à celui de la régularité de la solution A de (4-1) qui est un problème ouvert à notre connaissance.

VI - RÉSOLUTION NUMÉRIQUE

Le problème approché (5-11) peut se mettre sous la forme variationnelle équivalente

(6-1) $$\begin{cases} \int_\Omega \nu(x, A_h) \operatorname{grad} A_h \operatorname{grad} \vartheta_h \, dx = \int_\Omega j\, \vartheta_h \, dx & \forall \vartheta_h \in V_{oh} \\ A_h \in V_{oh} \end{cases}$$

VI.1. Linéarisation

Dans ces conditions, il est très naturel pour résoudre (5-11) de songer à utiliser l'algorithme suivant qui ramène la résolution du problème approché à celle d'une suite de problèmes linéaires (à coefficients variables avec x et n les inconnues étant bien entendu les valeurs nodales A_i^{n+1})

(6-2) A_h^o donné dans V_{oh}

A_h^n connu, on calcule A_h^{n+1} par

(6-3) $$\begin{cases} \int_\Omega \nu(x, A_h^n) \operatorname{grad} A_h^{n+1} \operatorname{grad} \vartheta_h \, dx = \int_\Omega j\, \vartheta_h \, dx & \forall \vartheta_h \in V_{oh} \\ A_h^{n+1} \in V_{oh} \end{cases}$$

Une variante de cet algorithme est la suivante : au lieu de résoudre complètement le problème linéaire 6-3, on se contente d'effectuer un balayage de type surrélaxation ponctuelle limité à un seul cycle.

Pour ces deux algorithmes, il n'y a convergence que pour des valeurs de j (densité de courant d'excitation) assez petites ($j \leqslant 0.5$ A/mm²).

La divergence pour j plus grand étant visiblement liée à la variation trop rapide d'une itération à l'autre du coefficient $x \rightsquigarrow \nu(x, A_h^n)$, il a donc fallu mettre en œuvre des algorithmes tenant plus implicitement compte de cette variation.

VI.2. Résolution par surrelaxation ponctuelle non linéaire

On utilise le formalisme du paragraphe V, on notera

$N = N_h = \dim V_{oh}$ et $\vartheta_h = (\vartheta_1, \vartheta_2 \ldots \vartheta_N)$, d'où pour le système non linéaire la formulation équivalente

(6-4) $$\frac{\partial \mathfrak{J}}{\partial \vartheta_i}(A_1, A_2, \ldots A_N) = o \qquad i = 1, 2 \ldots N$$

VI.2-1 **Description de l'algorithme SNL1**

(6-5) A_h^o donné dans V_{oh} ($A_h^o = o$ par exemple)

A_h^n connu, on calcule A_h^{n+1} coordonnée par coordonnée par

(6-6) $$\begin{cases} \dfrac{\partial \mathfrak{J}}{\partial \vartheta_i}(A_1^{n+1}, \ldots A_{i-1}^{n+1}, \overline{A_i^{n+1}}, A_{i+1}^n \ldots A_N^n) = o \\ A_i^{n+1} = A_i^n + \omega\,(\overline{A_i^{n+1}} - A_i^n) \qquad o < \omega < \omega_M \leqslant 2 \\ i = 1, 2, \ldots N \end{cases}$$

VI.2-2 **Convergence de l'algorithme SNL1**

Proposition 6-1. Pour ω_M suffisamment petit, la suite A_h^n définie par (6-5), (6-6) converge vers la solution A_h du système (6-4)

Démonstration

L'application $\vartheta_h \to \mathfrak{J}(\vartheta_h)$ est C^∞ de $\mathbb{R}^N$ dans $\mathbb{R}$ et strictement convexe; par ailleurs (3-11) entraîne également que la matrice hessienne

$$\vartheta_h \to \left\| \frac{\partial^2 \mathfrak{J}}{\partial \vartheta_i \partial \vartheta_j}(\vartheta_h) \right\| \quad \text{est définie positive}$$

Il résulte alors de S. SCHECHTER ([5],[6],[7]), l'existence de ω_M, $o < \omega_M \leqslant 2$ pour lequel il y a convergence de SNL1.

VI.2-3 **Description de l'algorithme SNL2**

(6-7) A_h^0 donné dans V_{oh} ($A_h^o = o$ par exemple)

A_h^n connu, on calcule A_h^{n+1} coordonnée par coordonnée par

(6-8) $$\begin{cases} \dfrac{\partial \mathfrak{J}}{\partial \vartheta_i}(A_1^{n+1}, \ldots A_{i-1}^{n+1}, A_i^{n+1}, A_{i+1}^n, \ldots A_N^n) = (1-\omega)\dfrac{\partial \mathfrak{J}}{\partial \vartheta_i}(A_1^{n+1}, \ldots A_{i-1}^{n+1}, A_i^n, A_{i+1}^n, \ldots A_N^n) \\ o < \omega \leqslant \omega_M \leqslant 2 \qquad \text{pour } i = 1, 2 \ldots N \end{cases}$$

Le problème de la convergence de l'algorithme SNL2 semble ouvert sauf bien entendu, pour $\omega = 1$ car SNL1 $\equiv$ SNL2. Pour notre problème précis les deux algorithmes SNL1 et SNL2 ont donné des résultats équivalents du point de rapidité.

VI.2-4 **Compléments et remarques sur SNL1 et SNL2 – Algorithme EGSN**

L'utilisation de SNL1 et SNL2 conduit à résoudre une suite d'équations non linéaires à une variable pour déterminer $\overline{A_i^{n+1}}$ et A_i^{n+1} par (6-6) et (6-8) respectivement. Dans ces conditions, il est très naturel d'utiliser la méthode de Newton à une variable et ceci conduit de façon évidente à considérer les variantes des algorithmes SNL1 et SNL2 dans lesquelles on prend respectivement pour $\overline{A_i^{n+1}}$ et A_i^{n+1} le premier itéré de Newton avec initialisation par A_i^n. On vérifiera que ceci conduit, en fait au même algorithme dont la forme explicite est donnée par

(6-9) A_h^o donné dans V_{oh} ($A_h^o = o$ par exemple)

A_h^n connu, on calcule A_h^{n+1} coordonnée par coordonnée par

DOMAINE TRIANGULATION CHOISIE Fig. 4

$$(6\text{-}10)\quad \left\{ \begin{array}{l} A_i^{n+1} = A_i^n - \omega \dfrac{\dfrac{\partial \mathfrak{F}}{\partial \vartheta_i}(A_1^{n+1}, \ldots A_{i-1}^{n+1}, A_i^n, A_{i+1}^n, \ldots A_N^n)}{\dfrac{\partial^2 \mathfrak{F}}{\partial \vartheta_i^2}(A_1^{n+1}, \ldots A_{i-1}^{n+1}, A_i^n, A_{i+1}^n, \ldots A_N^n)} \\ 0 < \omega < \omega_M \leq 2 \\ \text{pour } i = 1, 2 \ldots \ N \end{array} \right.$$

On démontre dans S. SCHECHTER (loc. cit.) qui compte tenu des propriétés de $\mathfrak{F}$ déjà énoncées, il y a convergence pour ω_M suffisamment petit de la suite A_h^n définie par l'algorithme (6-9) (6-10), algorithme que nous noterons EGSN (Extrapolated - Gauss - Seidel - Newton)

VII - QUELQUES REMARQUES SUR LA MISE EN ŒUVRE

Nous devons effectuer une triangulation d'un cercle (domaine Ω); il n'y aurait vraiment aucune difficulté, s'il n'y avait à l'intérieur, des frontières naturelles à respecter, constituées par les interfaces air-fer (voir fig.1). Pour la génération de la triangulation nous avons tenu compte de la répétition de la géométrie (24 dans la partie stator et 4 dans la région rotor) et il a suffit de découper en triangles un secteur de couronne de 15° pour la partie stator et un quart de cercle pour la partie rotor, il a ensuite fallu faire des répétitions. Il a donc été nécessaire d'entrer les données topologiques (numéro du nœud de la triangulation correspondant au $k^{ième}$ sommet, $k = 1, 2, 3$, du triangle considéré ; les sommets sont toujours numérotés dans un sens déterminé, celui adopté est le sens trigonométrique) pour 305 triangles ce qui fait 915 nombres entiers. Le calcul des coordonnées de certains nœuds de la triangulation a dû être fait avec précision cela pour approcher au mieux la géométrie de la machine.

La discrétisation du domaine adoptée a conduit au découpage de celui-ci en 3.240 triangles. Le nombre total de nœuds est 1.645 avec 1.597 nœuds intérieurs. La numérotation des triangles n'a pas été quelconque; on doit connaître les triangles se trouvant dans le fer (stator ou rotor), ainsi que ceux qui sont supports du courant d'excitation (voir fig.4. triangulation 1/4 du domaine).

On remarque au milieu de l'entrefer une ligne sur laquelle les nœuds sont espacés régulièrement; nous appelons cette ligne «ligne de rotation».

La disposition régulière des nœuds sur cette ligne permet une rotation discrète de pas 1°30' du rotor (ou plus précisément de la région rotor) par rapport au stator ; il suffit pour cela de recalculer les coordonnées des nœuds qui ont été tranformés par cette rotation et de modifier en conséquence la topologie au voisinage de la ligne de rotation. Nous obtenons ainsi 10 positions relatives rotor/stator différentes.

Le calcul des surfaces des triangles par produit vectoriel permet de déceler des erreurs grossières de triangulation, mais ce n'est pas un moyen efficace de vérification; un moyen plus sûr et plus direct est le tracé automatique (par l'intermédiaire d'un traceur BENSON par exemple) de cette triangulation.

Ce procédé n'est cependant pas infaillible. Par exemple (Fig. 5) les triangles ABC et BAD d'une part, et ABC et BCD d'autre part, donneront le même tracé ; les premiers font partie d'une triangulation régulière, les seconds non. Ainsi lorsque la triangulation se fait en partie (ou entièrement) manuellement, il est pratiquement nécessaire de recourir au procédé suivant pour être certain du non chevauchement de triangles. Un triangle ABC étant donné, on trace effectivement par le BENSON un triangle A'B'C' homothétique de ABC et intérieur à celui-ci. (Fig. 6).

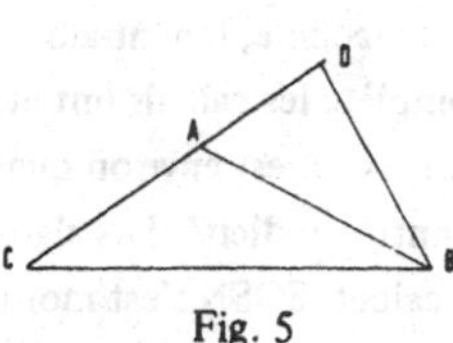

Fig. 5

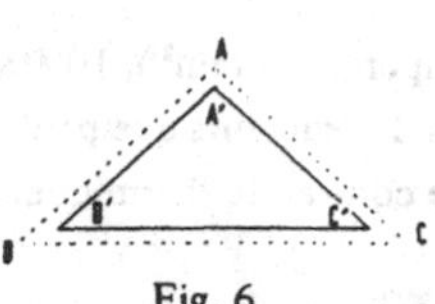

Fig. 6

Chaque triangle est ainsi individualisé, et au premier coup d'œil sur l'ensemble du tracé, on se trouve renseigné sur la validité de la triangulation.

Pour l'utilisation des algorithmes SNL1, SNL2 et EGSN il est utile d'avoir calculé une fois pour toute, pour chaque nœud I

* le nombre M. de trianglesayant le nœud I pour sommet,
* le numéro du $\ell^{ième}$ triangle associé au nœud I $\quad 1 \leqslant \ell \leqslant M$,
* dans ce $\ell^{ième}$ triangle associé au nœud I, à quel sommet 1, 2 ou 3 correspond le nœud I.

Il faut aussi connaître pour chaque triangle de la triangulation, la surface de celui-ci, ainsi que les termes (combinaisons des p_j, q_j, r_j intervenant dans 5-10) utilisés pour le calcul de $|\text{grad } A|^2$ et pour $\frac{\partial}{\partial A_I} |\text{grad} A|^2$

Prise en considération des conditions d'anti-périodicité

Le découpage en triangles est le même que pour le domaine entier. Pour une certaine position du rotor par rapport au stator le domaine Ω' est un quart de cercle (Fig. 7)

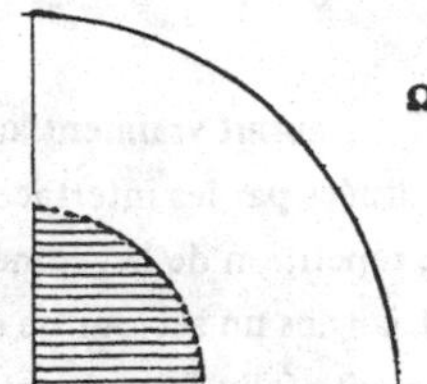

Fig. 7

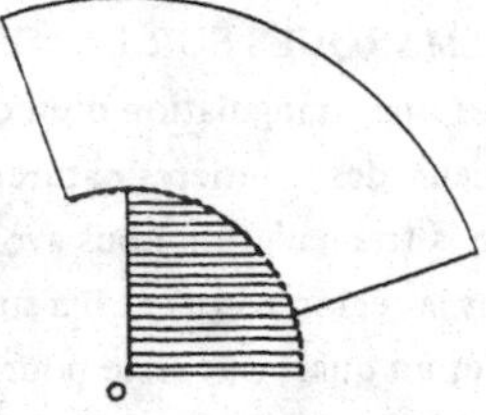

Fig. 8

Pour retrouver les 10 positions différentes du rotor par rapport au stator, on fait glisser la région stator sur la ligne de rotation (Fig. 8), mais alors ici le nombre de nœuds intérieurs, le nombre total de nœuds, ainsi que le nombre de nœuds pour lesquels il faut tenir compte de la condition d'anti-périodicité varient avec chaque position. Nous nous trouvons ici devant un problème de topologie assez difficile. Nous pensons avoir réduit considérablement les difficultés en procédant de la façon suivante.

La numérotation des triangles et des nœuds de la région stator est faite indépendamment de celle des triangles et nœuds de la région rotor ; la topologie de chaque région reste donc fixe quelle que soit la position relative rotor/stator. Nous sommes ainsi pratiquement en présence de deux domaines indépendants; la liaison est faite lors de la résolution en «recollant» les équations aux nœuds communs de la ligne de rotation, et en tenant compte de la condition d'anti-périodicité pour les autres nœuds de cette ligne.

Pour la région rotor, la discrétisation est faite par 296 triangles et 187 nœuds. Il y a 516 triangles et 304 nœuds dans la région stator.

On aurait pu, bien entendu, conserver le domaine Ω' à sa forme initiale (un quart de cercle), et changer la géométrie intérieure, cela ne simplifie pas le problème, car il faut à chaque position rotor/stator générer une nouvelle triangulation.

VIII - RÉSULTATS NUMÉRIQUES

Les algorithmes SNL1 ((6-5), (6-6)), SNL2 ((6-7), (6-8)) et EGSN ((6-9), (6-10)) ont tous trois été testés numériquement.

Des essais ont été faits aussi bien sur la structure complète que sur un quart de machine, tenant alors compte des conditions d'anti-périodicité. Même dans le cas d'étude de la structure complète les calculs ont été faits sur ordinateur CII 10.070 sans utilisation de mémoires auxiliaires ; le temps de calcul est environ quatre fois celui utilisé pour la résolution sur un quart de machine avec les conditions d'antipériodicité. Les algorithmes SNL1 et SNL2 ont donné des résultats équivalents du point de vue temps de calcul, EGSN s'est montré beaucoup plus efficace.

VIII.1 Valeurs de différents paramètres

Les valeurs des densités de courant retenues sont 0,5 ; 2 ; 5 ; 7,5 ; 10 (en ampères par mm^2), 10 étant la valeur limite acceptable physiquement en raison de phénomènes thermiques destructeurs que peut entraîner un trop fort courant. Les méthodes présentées ne sont pas limitées par cette contrainte thermique. Le problème a été aussi résolu pour $J = 20$ et $J = 100$.

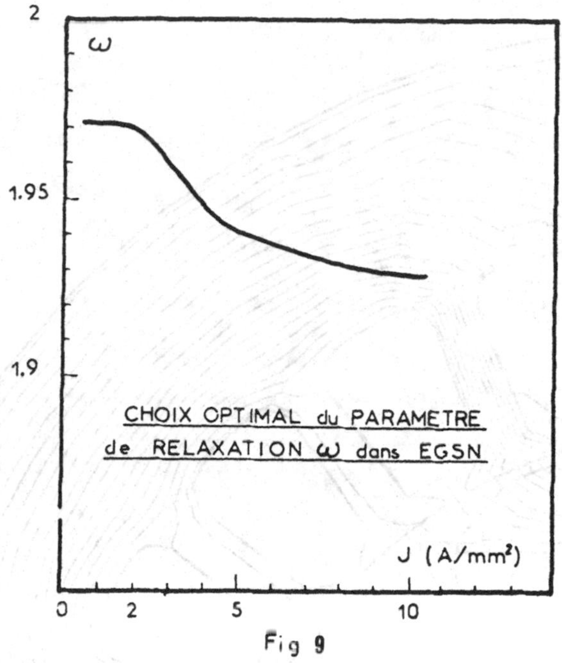
ω
2
1.95
1.9
CHOIX OPTIMAL du PARAMETRE
de RELAXATION ω dans EGSN
J (A/mm²)
0
2
5
10

Fig 9

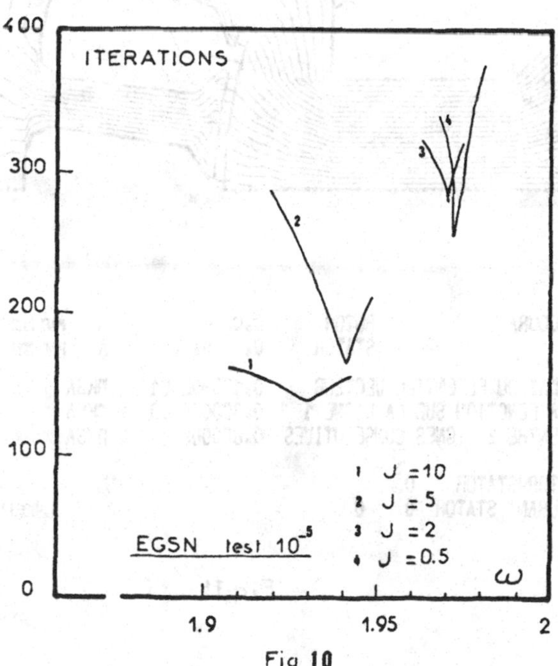
ITERATIONS
400
300
200
100
0
1 J = 10
2 J = 5
3 J = 2
4 J = 0.5
EGSN test 10⁻⁵
ω
1.9
1.95
2

Fig 10

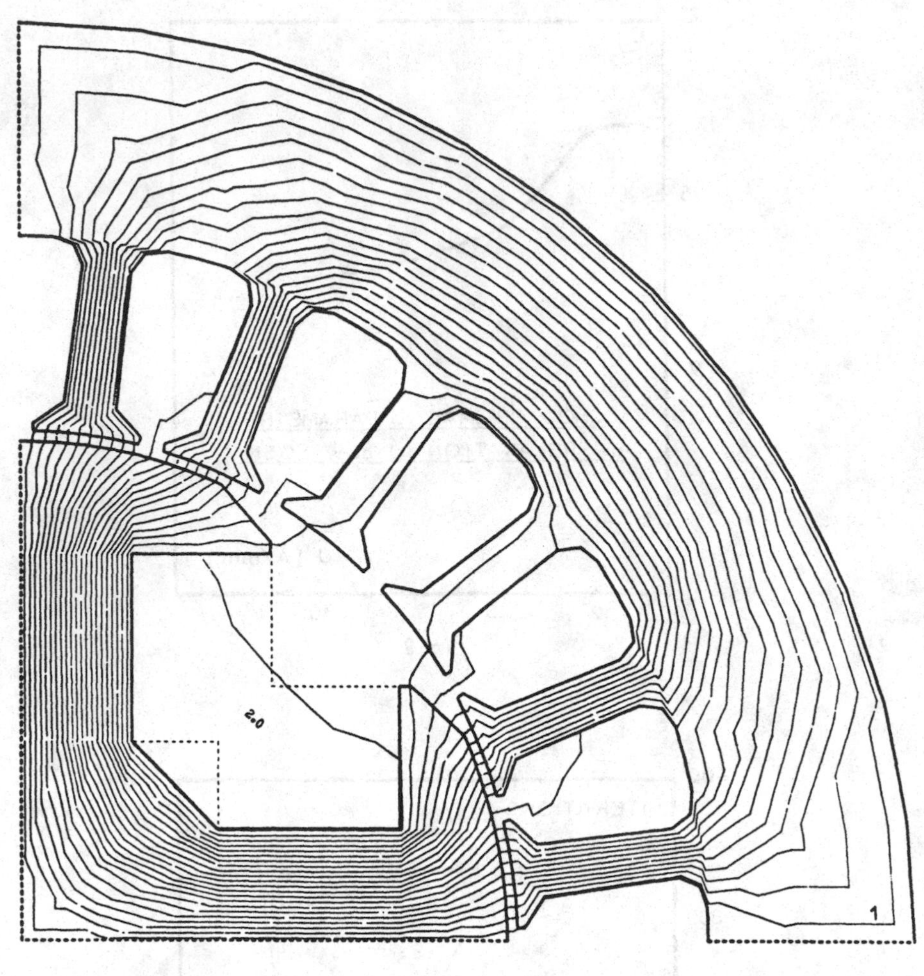

DENSITE DE COURANT	ROTOR	2.0	A PAR MM2
	STATOR	0. 0.	A PAR MM2

VALEUR ABS-MAX DU POTENTIEL VECTEUR	0.13090E-01	MKSA
VALEUR DE LA FONCTION SUR LA LIGNE 1	0.30000E-03	MKSA
DIFFERENCE ENTRE 2 LIGNES CONSECUTIVES	0.60000E-03	MKSA

POSITION ROTOR-STATOR 0
POSITION COURANT STATOR 0 0

LABORIA A.MARROCCO

Fig 11

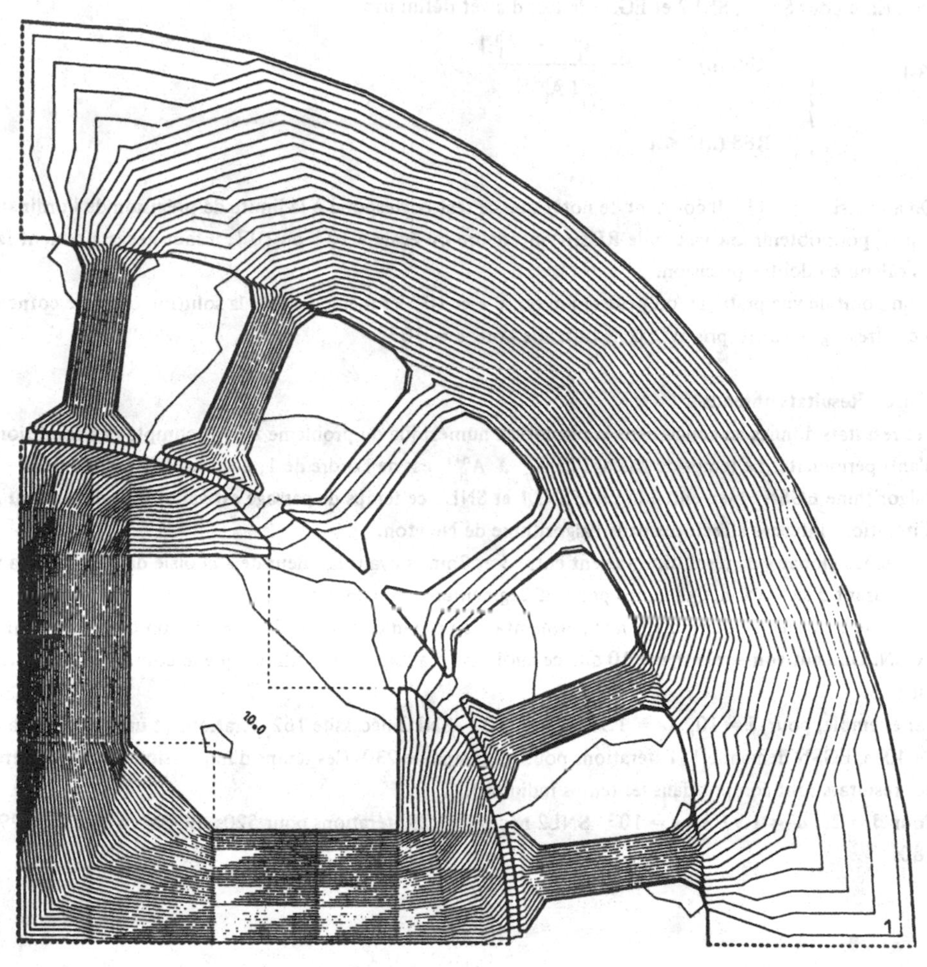

DENSITE DE COURANT	ROTOR	10.0	A	PAR MM2
	STATOR	0. 0.	A	PAR MM2

VALEUR ABS-MAX DU POTENTIEL VECTEUR 0.24332E-01 MKSA
VALEUR DE LA FONCTION SUR LA LIGNE 1 0.30000E-03 MKSA
DIFFERENCE ENTRE 2 LIGNES CONSECUTIVES 0.60000E-03 MKSA

POSITION ROTOR-STATOR 0
POSITION COURANT STATOR 0 0

LABORIA A.MARROCCO

Fig 12

On utilise pour SNL1, SNL2 et EGSN le test d'arrêt défini par

(8-1)
$$\begin{cases} RES(n) = \dfrac{\sum_{i=1}^{N} |A_i^{n+1} - A_i^n|}{\sum_{i=1}^{N} |A_i^{n+1}|} \\ RES(n) \leq \epsilon \end{cases}$$

On a choisi $\epsilon = 10^{-5}$. Il convient de noter que ce test correspond à la limite de précision de l'ordinateur utilisé, pour obtenir une valeur de RES(n) inférieure ou égale à 10^{-6} ou 10^{-7}, il faut nécessairement faire les calculs en double précision.

D'un point de vue pratique, on peut se limiter à $\epsilon = 10^{-4}$ et même 5.10^{-4}, la solution obtenue coïncide à 3 chiffres significatifs, pris avec celle obtenue avec $\epsilon = 10^{-5}$.

VIII.2 **Résultats obtenus**

Les résultats donnés ici concernent la résolution numérique du problème tenant compte des conditions d'anti-périodicité. Le temps de passage de A_h^n à A_h^{n+1} est de l'ordre de 1, 2 s sur CII 10.070 pour l'algorithme EGSN ; bien entendu pour SNL1 et SNL2 ce temps de passage est variable et dépend du nomb d'itérations internes effectuées dans l'algorithme de Newton.

Les temps globaux de résolution varient entre 3 et 7mm suivant la valeur de ϵ choisie dans (8-1) et la valeur du courant d'excitation. Ces temps peuvent augmenter si le paramètre de relaxation ω est mal choisi.

La figure 9 donne la détermination expérimentale du paramètre optimal de relaxation pour l'algorithme EGSN. On peut voir sur la figure 10 que ce choix est d'autant plus critique que le courant d'excitation est petit.

Par exemple, pour $J = 10$, $\omega = 1.92$ et $\epsilon = 10^{-5}$, SNL2 nécessite 162 itérations et un temps de calcul de 404s, EGSN demande 151 itérations pour un temps de 230s (les temps d'impression et d'interprétation des résultats sont compris dans les temps indiqués).

Pour $J = 2$, $\omega = 1.97$ et $\epsilon = 10^{-5}$ SNL2 nécessite 229 itérations pour 520s, EGSN en demande 290 pou 380s.

BIBLIOGRAPHIE

0 – **G. Bruhat** - Electricité

1 – **P. Silvester - M.V.K. Chari** - Analysis of turboalternator magnetic field by finite elements
IEEE. PAS 90 N°2 454-464 1971

2 – **P. Silvester - M.V.K. Chari** - Finite element analysis of magnetically saturated D.C. machines
IEEE. PAS 2.362-2.372 Oct. 1971

3 – **J.L. Lions** - Contrôle optimal de systèmes gouvernés par des équations aux dérivées partielles
DUNOD. Paris 1968

4 – **J. Cea** - Optimisation - DUNOD. Paris 1971

5 – **S. Schechter** - Iteration method for non linear problems
TRANS. A.M.S. 104 p. 179-189 1962

6 – **S. Schechter** - Relaxation methods for convex problems
SIAM J. on numerical analysis 5 p. 601-612

7 – **S. Schechter** - Minimisation of convex function by relaxation
INTEGER AND NON LINEAR PROGRAMMING
ABADIE-EDITOR North Holland 1970 p. 177-189

8 – **R. Glowinski - A. Marrocco** - Analyse numérique du champ magnétique d'un alternateur par éléments finis et surrelaxation ponctuelle non linéaire
Computer methods in applied - mechanics and engineering 1973

≈≈≈≈≈≈

UNE NOUVELLE METHODE D'ANALYSE NUMERIQUE DES PROBLEMES DE FILTRATION DANS LES MATERIAUX POREUX

par C. BAIOCCHI (Pavia, Italie)

I - DESCRIPTION DU PROBLEME PHYSIQUE

On considère une classe de problèmes de filtration dont un cas typique peut être schématisé sous la forme suivante : sur une base imperméable deux bassins d'eau, de niveaux différents, sont en communication à travers une digue en matériau poreux; l'eau filtre du niveau le plus élevé au niveau le moins élevé; et on veut déterminer la "partie mouillée" de la digue ainsi que les grandeurs physiques (telles que vitesse, débit, etc..) associées au mouvement.

II - TRADUCTION EN PROBLEME MATHEMATIQUE DE FRONTIERE LIBRE (Cf [13], [15]).

Supposons la digue infiniment étendue et à section constante (de façon à étudier un problème bidimensionnel); en absence de capillarité pour un fluxe stationnaire,irrotationnel, incompressible, la loi de Darcy assure que le mouvement de l'eau dans la digue est lié à un potentiel de vitesse; plus précisément, si Ω est la partie mouillée de la digue D, et si $p(x,y)$ est la pression au point (x,y) de Ω (x axe horizontal, y axe vertical) on a que la vitesse est proportionnelle au gradient de $y + \frac{p(x,y)}{\gamma}$ le coefficient $k(x,y)$ étant un coefficient de perméabilité; et la fonction $u(x,y) = y + \frac{p(x,y)}{\gamma}$ (qui est une hauteur piézométrique) satisfait, grâce à l'incomprimibilité :

$$\text{div } k \text{ grad } u = 0 \quad \text{dans } \Omega \tag{1}$$

A cette équation aux dérivées partielles on doit ajouter des conditions aux limites qui sont de deux types; du type Neumann

$$\frac{\partial u}{\partial n} = 0 \quad \text{le long des ligues de courants} \tag{2}$$

($\frac{\partial}{\partial n}$ désignant la dérivée normale; en particulier (2) doit être imposée le long de la base imperméable et le long de la "ligne libre", $\partial\Omega - \partial D$) et de type Dirichlet

$$p(x,y) = 0 \Longrightarrow u(x,y) = y \quad \text{pour les points } \partial\Omega \text{ à contact avec l'air} \tag{3}$$

$$u(x,y) = y_1 \quad \text{sur la partie } \partial\Omega \text{ à contact avec le premier bassin.} \tag{4}$$

(5) $u(x,y) = y_2$ sur la partie de $\partial\Omega$ à contact avec le deuxième bassin.

(y_1, y_2 désignant les hauteurs des deux bassins).

Il s'agit d'un classique problème à frontière libre : sur le domaine inconnu Ω on doit résoudre un problème aux limites (2) ... (5) pour l'équation (1), avec condition surhabondantes ((2) et (3)) sur la partie inconnue $\partial\Omega - \partial D$ de la frontière de Ω.

III - ESQUISSE DES METHODES NUMERIQUES TRADITIONNELLES

Une idée classique pour la résolution numérique de problèmes à frontière libre est la suivante (Cf [10] pour une vue d'ensemble; Cf aussi [14] et sa bibliographie pour le problème considéré ici) : on fixe une courbe $y = \varphi_0(x)$ comme première approximation de la frontière libre; dans la correspondante approximation Ω_0 de la partie mouillée de D on résoud un problème mêlé pour l'équation (1) en imposant le long de $y = \varphi_0(x)$ une seulement des deux conditions (2) et (3); puis l'on modifie φ_0 de façon que l'autre condition soit remplie, en obtenant ainsi une nouvelle courbe $\varphi_1(x)$; on itère le procédé $\varphi_0 \to \varphi_1$ pour passer à une nouvelle courbe φ_2 et ainsi de suite. Par exemple si le problème mêlé que l'on résoud correspond à imposer le long de $y = \varphi_0(x)$ la condition de Neumann (2), on obtiendra $\varphi_1(x)$ par la formule $\varphi_1(x) = u_0(x, \varphi_0(x))$ (u_0 étant la solution du problème mêlé); et la solution du problème à frontière libre est un point fixe pour la transformation $\varphi_0 \to \varphi_1$.

Toutefois on doit remarquer que : a) du point de vue théorique on ne sait pas justifier ces procédés (on ne connaît ni existence et unicité de la solution, ni stabilité, convergence, majoration de l'erreur etc... pour les solutions approchées);

b) du point de vue numérique le procédé est très lourd, dès que l'on doit résoudre une famille de problèmes mêlés, sur des domaines qui varient à chaque étape en fonction de la solution de l'itération précédente.

IV - REDUCTION A INEQUATIONS VARIATIONNELLES

Dans une étude théorique du problème j'ai montre (Cf [1]) que, dans le cas le plus simple où $k(x,y) = 1$ et D est un rectangle, $D =]0,a[\times]0,y_1[$ (cas correspondant à une digue homogène, à base horizontale, à parois verticales, d'épaisseur a) on peut ramener le problème à une inéquation variationnelle, quitte à remplacer l'inconnue $u(x,y)$ définie dans Ω par une primitive de $u(x,y)$ convenablement prolongée hors de Ω.

Précisément si l'on pose, pour $(x,y) \in D$:

(6) $$w(x,y) = \int_y^{y_1} [\hat{u}(x,t)-t]\,dt$$

où $\hat{u}$ est la fonction qui prolonge u à y hors de Ω, on peut montrer que w satisfait les relations :

(7) $$w \geq 0 \quad ; \quad \Delta w \leq 1 \quad ; \quad w(1-\Delta w) = 0 \quad \text{dans } D$$

et on peut évaluer une fonction $g(x,y)$ définie sur ∂D telle que

(8) $$w_{|\partial D} = g$$

(g dépendant des données $\underline{a}$, y_1, y_2).

Si l'on pose alors ($H^1(D)$ désignant l'usuel espace de Sobolev) :

(9) $$K = \{v \in H^1(D) \mid v \geq 0 \quad ; \quad v_{|\partial D} = g\}$$

on peut traduire (7) et (8) sous la forme d'inéquation variationnelle :

(10) $$\begin{cases} w \in K \quad ; \quad \forall\, v \in K : \\ \int_D \nabla w \cdot \nabla(v-w)\,dx\,dy \geq \int_D (w-v)\,dx\,dy \end{cases}$$

où équivalemment, dans le problème de minimum :

(11) w minimise sur K la fonctionnelle $\frac{1}{2}\int_D |\nabla v|^2\,dx\,dy + \int_D v\,dx\,dy$

Vice versa, connaissant w, on remonte à Ω,u par les formules :

(12) $$\Omega = \{(x,y) \in D \mid w(x,y) > 0\}$$

(13) $$u(x,y) = y - w_y(x,y) \quad \text{dans } \Omega$$

et, à partir d'ici et des résultats connus sur les inéquations du type (10) on obtient un Théorème d'existence et unicité pour le problème à frontière libre (pour les détails Cf toujours [1]).

Successivement, dans une série de travaux (Cf [2], [3], [4], [5], [8], [8], [16]) ce résultat a été adapté à des problèmes de filtration plus compliqués (perméabilité variable, géométrie plus générale, présence de plusieurs liquides immiscibles ...) et à des problèmes à frontière libre de nature différente (écoulement subsonique autour d'un profil, problème de Stefan ...; Cf [4],[6],[11]).

Tout en restant dans les problèmes de filtration il faut remarquer que, en général, on doit étudier non plus <u>une</u> inéquation variationnelle (telle que (10)) mais <u>une famille</u> d'inéquations dépendante d'un ou plusieurs paramètres (ayant eux aussi un intérêt physique : par exemple le débit et l'abscisse initiale de la ligne d'émergence, qui, dans le cas simple précédent sont connus a priori).

V - RESOLUTION NUMERIQUE

La résolution numérique d'inéquation telles que (10) (dans le cas général on doit ajouter un algorithme pour la détermination des paramètres) n'offre pas de difficultés : on connait (Cf par exemple [12]) de nombreux procédés de discrétisation parfaitement justifiés du point de vue théorique et efficient du point de vue pratique (en général, après discrétisation, on parvient à des problèmes de programmation quadratique). Par exemple (Cf [9],[2] pour les détails) en discrétisant en différences finies on remplacera le convexe K par une famille $\{K_h\}_h$ (h pas de discrétisation) de convexes constitués par fonctions constantes par morceaux, qui sont non négatives et qui, sur le "bord discret" de D prennent des valeurs g_h discrétisantes la fonction g; on tombe sur le système (qui est la discrétisation de (7),(8) ; Δ_h est la discrétisation à 5 points de Δ) :

$$\begin{cases} w_h \geq 0 \quad ; \Delta_h \, w_h \leq 1 \; ; \quad w_h(1-\Delta_h \, w_h) = 0 \\ \text{dans } \ell' \text{ "intérieur discret" de D} \end{cases}$$

$$w_h = g_h \quad \text{sur le "bord discret" de D ,}$$

système qui peut, par exemple, être résolu en adaptant l'algorithme de S.O.R.

On remarquera finalement que les résultats classiques sur les inéquations assurent que $w_h \to w$ dans H^1 discret, mais que la "vraie" inconnue du problème est non pas w mais l'ensemble Ω; or si l'on pose (analoguement à (12)) :

$$\Omega_h = \{(x,y) \in D \mid w_h(x,y) > 0\}$$

la convergence de w_h à w dans H^1 discret n'assure pas la "convergence" de Ω_h à Ω. En effet on peut montrer (Cf [4]) que Ω_h converge vers Ω au sens suivant

$$\Omega = \text{intérieur } (\lim_{h\to 0}{}' \Omega_h) .$$

BIBLIOGRAPHIE

[1] C. BAIOCCHI , Su un problema di frontiera libera connesso a questioni di idraulica. Ann. di Mat. pura e appl. (IV) vol. XCII,(1972), 107-127; note aux C.R. Acad. Sc. Paris, t.273 (1971), 1215-1217.

[2] C. BAIOCCHI, V.COMINCIOLI, L.GUERRI, G.VOLPI. Free boundary problems in the theory of fluid flow through porous media : a numerical approach. Calcolo X(1973) 1-86.

[3] C. BAIOCCHI, V.COMINCIOLI, E.MAGENES, G.A.POZZI; Free boundary problems in the theory of fluid flow through porous media : existence and uniqueness theorems. Ann. di Mat. XCVII (1973) 1.82.

[4] C. BAIOCCHI, E.MAGENES, Problemi di frontiera libera in idraulica. A paraitre aux "Atti del Convegno Internazionale : Metodi valutativi nella fisica matematica" 15-20 dicembre 1972. Academia Nazionale dei Lincei. Roma

[5] V. BENCI, Su un problema di filtrazione attraverso un mezzo poroso. A praraitre aux Annli di Mat. pura e appl.

[6] H. BREZIS, G.DUVAUT, Ecoulement avec sillage autour d'un profil symétrique sans incidence. C.R. Ac. Sc. Paris 276 (1973)

[7] H. BREZIS, G.STAMPACCHIA, Une nouvelle méthode pour l'étude d'écoulements stationnaires. C.R. Acad. Sc. Paris 276(1973).

[8] V. COMINCIOLI, A theoretical and numerical approach to some free boundary problems. A paraitre aux Annali di Mat. Pura e appl.

[9] V.COMINCIOLI , L.GUERRI, G.VOLPI, Analisi numerica di un prohlema di frontiera libera connesso col moto di un fluido attraverso un mezzo poroso. Publication 17 du Laboratorio di Analisi Numerica C.N.R. Pavia (1971).

[10] C.W. CRYER, On the approximate solution of free boundary problems using finite differences. J. Assoc. Comput. Mach., 17, N. 3(1970),397-411.

[11] G. DUVAUT, Résolution d'un problème de Stéfan (fusion d'un bloc à zéro degrès). C.R. Ac. Sc. Paris 276 (1973).

[12] R. GLOWINSKI, J.L. LIONS, R. TREMOLIERES, Résolution numérique des inéquations de la Mécanique et de la Physique. A paraitre, Dunod Paris.

[13] M.E. HARR, Grounwater and seepage. New York ; Mc Graw-Hill 1962

[14] E. MAGENES, Su alcuni problemi ellittici di frontiera libera connessi con il comportamento dei fluidi nei mezzi porosi. Symposia Math. Roma, 1972.

[15] M. MUSKAT, The flow of homogenous fluids through porous media. New York : Mc Graw-Hill 1937

[16] A. TORELLI, Su un problema di filtrazione da un canale. A paraitre.

CIRCUITS ET TRANSISTORS
NETWORKS AND SEMI-CONDUCTORS

NUMERICAL METHODS FOR STIFF SYSTEMS OF DIFFERENTIAL EQUATIONS RELATED WITH TRANSISTORS, TUNNEL DIODES, ETC.

by

Willard L. Miranker
IBM Research Center

and

Frank Hoppensteadt
New York University

1. INTRODUCTION

The models of circuits which contain elements such as transistors or tunnel diodes are differential equations as is well known. Because of the high speed of performance of these circuit elements, the range of the parameter values and of the device characteristics of current interest in the corresponding differential equations result in solutions with an extreme range of behavior. These solutions may be composed of slowly varying components, highly damped components, highly oscillatory components, and combinations of some or all of these. This variation in behavior of the solutions is characterized by the term stiffness. In Section 2 we will describe a simple circuit model for a tunnel diode and we show how this range of solutions does arise.

The numerical solution of stiff differential equations meets with difficulties because of the extremes in the range of behavior of the solutions. In recent years a number of numerical methods for stiff differential equations have been devised. (cf. G. G. Bjurel (1970).) Some of these methods have been applied successfully to certain classe of stiff differential equations. Nevertheless it is still not known how to deal effectively with this computational problem in general. Especially difficult is the class of differential equations which con tain highly oscillatory components in its solutions.

In previous studies (cf. W. L. Miranker (1973) and W. L. Miranker and J. P. Morreeuw (1973))one of us has pointed out the relationship between stiff differential equations and differential equations subject to singular perturbations, and has exploited this relationship to develope numerical methods for the solution of stiff equations. In this study we will enlarge on this point of view to develope numerical methods which can deal with the full range of behavior in solutions just described. To do this requires that a uniform method be develope for characterizing the solutions of singular perturbation problems throughout the full range of indicated solution behavior. As is well known (cf. J. Cole (1968) and A. H. Nayfeh (1973)) the choice of asymptotic techniques used to obtain descriptions of solutions of differential equations depends on the nature of the solution (e.g. strong ly damped or highly oscillatory).

In Section 3 we show how the multitime technique of asymptotic expansions may be combined with the method of averaging of Bogoliubov to produce a procedure for deriving the asymptotic form of solutions of singularly perturbed differential equations over the full indicated range of solution behavior. We do this for the simple model problem

$$\varepsilon \frac{du}{dt} = (A_0 + \varepsilon A_1)u \tag{1.1}$$

and we include the proof of validity of the expansion to within $O(\varepsilon^2)$. We make these limitations for the sake of clarity of presentation and because this much of the asymptotic development is adequate for the specification of the numerical method. We emphasize that this asymptotic theory (and the numerical method) may be carried over to non-linear problems and to all orders, but we defer this treatment to another study.

In the singular limit, highly oscillatory solutions may converge to invariant manifolds of dimension greater than one. Thus the meaningfulness of describing such a trajectory by a set of its values on the points of a time mesh is lost. Indeed this suggests the reasons for the lack of effectiveness of existing numerical methods for such problems. To remedy this difficulty we introduce in Section 4 a new numerical solution concept for differential equations. We accept a quantity as an approximation to the solution at a point in time if the quantity approximates any value which the solution assumes on a neighborhood of that point in time, the size of the neighborhood being arbitrary but positive. With this numerical solution concept we then construct a numerical method based on the asymptotic theory introduced in Section 3. We illustrate the numerical method by means of calculations based on several sample problems.

2. A CIRCUIT MODEL AND STIFF BEHAVIOR

In this section we will discuss a model for a tunnel diode circuit and show how various solution classes with extreme behavior arise.

A simple circuit representing a tunnel diode is given schematically in figure 2.1a

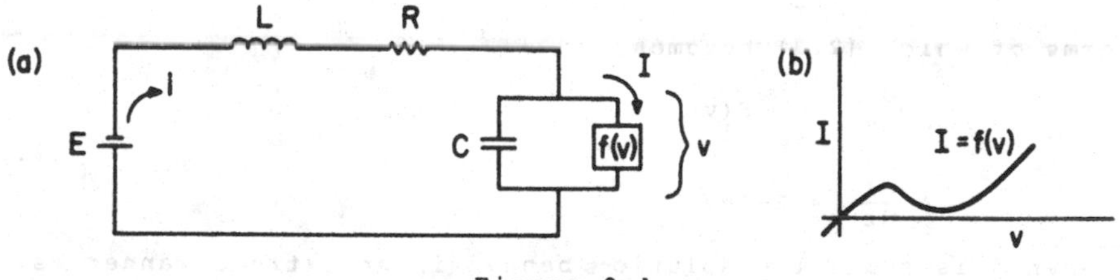

Figure 2.1

The current through the non-linear element is given by $I=f(v)$, where the tunnel diode characteristic, $f(v)$, is the S shaped graph as indicated in figure 2.1b. The differential equations describing this circuit are

$$\begin{aligned} C\frac{dv}{dt} &= i - f(v) \\ L\frac{di}{dt} &= E - Ri - v \end{aligned} \tag{2.1}$$

For certain ranges of values of the parameters, the simple model (2.1) is a stiff system whose solutions exhibit a variety of extreme behavior. We will now give an indication of this behavior.

Introduce the new variables

$$x = \frac{R}{L} t, \ \varepsilon = \frac{CR^2}{L}, \quad I = Ri, \ F(v) = Rf(v) \tag{2.2}$$

in (2.1). We get

$$\begin{aligned} \varepsilon \frac{dv}{dx} &= I - F(v) \\ \frac{dI}{dx} &= E - v - I \end{aligned} \tag{2.3}$$

When ε is small this system is stiff and solutions move alternately through regions of slow change and rapid change. A typical family of solutions in this case is schematized in figure 2.2a.

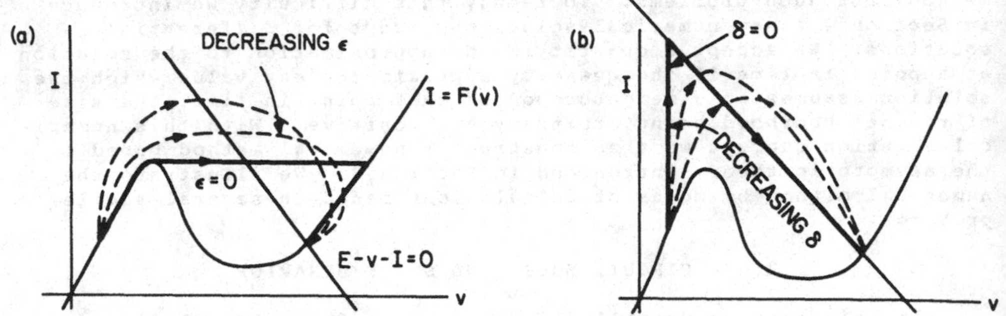

Figure 2.2

Alternatively we may introduce the variables

$$z = \frac{t}{RC} \qquad \delta = 1/\varepsilon , \tag{2.4}$$

in terms of which (2.3) becomes

$$\begin{aligned} \frac{dv}{dz} &= I - F(v) \\ \delta \frac{dI}{dz} &= E - I - v. \end{aligned} \tag{2.5}$$

When δ is small the solutions behave in an extreme manner as schematized in figure 2.2b.

A different form of extreme behavior of solutions of (2.3) for certain other ranges of parameter values may be seen by introducing the variable

$$y = t/\sqrt{LC} \tag{2.6}$$

and writing the system (2.3) as a single equation

$$\frac{d^2v}{dy^2} + \omega^2 v = K(v, \frac{dv}{dy}) \tag{2.7}$$

where

$$K = (\omega^2-1)v - Rf(v) - (R\sqrt{\frac{C}{L}} + \sqrt{\frac{L}{C}}\; f'(v))\frac{dv}{dy} + E. \tag{2.8}$$

In this case there are one and sometimes two periodic solutions of (1.9) as illustrated in figure 2.3.

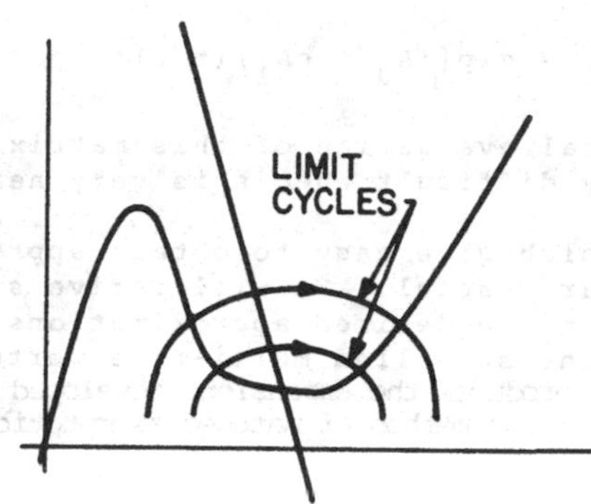

Figure 2.3

The frequency of these limit cycles is approximately

$$\omega^2 = C(L-R^2) \tag{2.9}$$

in the t-time scale. Thus for certain values of C, L and R there are oscillatory solutions with possibly high frequency.

Detailed studies of the solutions of the tunnel diode equations were made by one of us giving precise characterizations of the solution classes just displayed. The methods used were typical asymptotic expansion techniques involving time stretching, matching, use of the so called secularity condition etc. We refer to W. L. Miranker (1962 a,b) for details.

3. ASYMPTOTIC ANALYSIS

From consideration of the circuit example in Section 2, we are led to study stiff systems of ordinary differential equations whose solutions exhibit abrupt excursions both in the sense of rapid damping and in the sense of rapid oscillations and of course mixtures of the two.

In this section we will consider a simple prototype of such systems and develope a technique for approximating its solution. We have restricted our development to this sample problem to illustrate the method in a clear manner. We emphasize that the development may be carried over to non-linear problems but we defer this treatment to another study.

3.1 The Two Time Approach

Consider the following system of differential equations

$$\varepsilon \frac{du}{dt} = (A_0 + \varepsilon A_1)u \tag{3.1}$$

where u is an n-vector, A_0 and A_1 are nxn matrices and ε is a small parameter. We seek to approximate the solution of the initial value problem for (3.1) on a fixed time interval, $0 \leq t \leq T$. The fundamental matrix of this system may be represented in the form

$$\psi(t,\varepsilon) = \exp[(A_0 + \varepsilon A_1)(t/\varepsilon)]. \tag{3.2}$$

However, the numerical evaluation of this matrix over the interval $0 \leq t \leq T$ is usually difficult when ε is very near zero.

Thus methods which give easy to obtain approximations to the fundamental matrix are useful. We will derive such a method which we will use to obtain the desired approximations. In addition our method illustrates the so called multi-time perturbation method. Moreover our method produces the expansions developed by two other widely used perturbation techniques : the method of matched asymptotic expansions and the method of averaging.

When a new time scale $\tau = t/\varepsilon$ is introduced, (3.1) becomes

$$du/d\tau = (A_0 + \varepsilon A_1)u \tag{3.3}$$

and the fundamental matrix becomes

$$\psi(\tau,\varepsilon) = \exp[A_0\tau + A_1\ \varepsilon\tau]. \tag{3.4}$$

While this change of variables apparently makes the problem into one whose solution depends smoothly on the parameter ε near $\varepsilon = 0$, the standard Taylor series approach for constructing approximations to the solution gives a result valid only on bounded τ intervals. However, the problem (3.3) is to be considered on the large interval $0 \leq \tau \leq T/\varepsilon$.

The matrix ψ may be considered to be a function of the two time scales, t and τ:

$$\psi = \exp\ [A_0\tau + A_1 t]. \tag{3.5}$$

This motivates us to seek approximations to the solution of (3.3) in the form of a general two-time expansion

$$u = \sum_{r=0}^{\infty} u_r(t,\tau)\ \varepsilon^r. \tag{3.6}$$

This will be a useful series for purposes of approximation, if we hav

$$u_r(t,t/\varepsilon)\ \varepsilon^r = o(\varepsilon^{r-1}), \quad r = 1,2,..., \tag{3.7}$$

as $\varepsilon \to 0$, uniformly for $0 \leq t \leq T$. With (3.7) valid we say that (3.6) is an asymptotic expansion with asymptotic scale ε^r. A suffic condition for (3.7) is that

$$u_r(t,\tau) = o(\tau) \tag{3.8}$$

as $\tau \to \infty$ for $r = 1,2,\ldots$.

The expansion resulting from this prescription of form (3.6)-(3.8) of the solution will be derived below. It is possible to obtain more information from the expansion by placing a stronger condition on the coefficients than (3.8). In particular we will determine conditions on A_0 and A_1 so that the requirement

$$u_r(t,\tau) = o(\tau e^{A_0\tau}) \tag{3.9}$$

as $\tau \to \infty$ for $r = 1,2,\ldots$, can be used to obtain a valid expansion.

Now, if A_0 is an oscillatory matrix (all eigenvalues have zero real part), then conditions (3.8) and (3.9) are equivalent. If A_0 is a stable matrix (all eigenvalues have negative real parts), then condition (3.9) is more restrictive than (3.8). In the stable case it may not be possible to obtain an expansion of the solution of (3.3) in the form (3.6) whose coefficients satisfy (3.9). However, we will describe another restriction on the problem which when used with (3.9) guarantees that the solution of (3.3) can be approximately solved in the form (3.6). This approximation technique proceeds via the two-time approach. This result is valid when the eigenvalues of A_0 lie in the stable half plane; therefore, it contains both the stable and oscillatory cases. In the stable case, the expansion found by this method reduces to the one which would be obtained by the method of matched asymptotic expansions. In the oscillatory case, this result reduces to an expansion equivalent to the one obtained by the Bogoliubov method of averaging.

3.2 Formal Expansion Procedure

We consider the initial value problem for the system (3.3) and we write the initial conditions in the form

$$u(0) = \sum_{r=0}^{\infty} a_r \varepsilon^r \tag{3.10}$$

To simplify computation let

$$v(t,\tau) = e^{-A_0\tau} u(t,\tau). \tag{3.11}$$

Since v is considered as a function of the two variables τ and $t=\varepsilon\tau$

$$\frac{dv\,(\varepsilon\tau,\tau)}{d\tau} = \varepsilon\frac{\partial v(t,\tau)}{\partial t} + \frac{\partial v(t,\tau)}{\partial \tau} . \tag{3.12}$$

Then (3.3) becomes the following equation for v:

$$\varepsilon\frac{\partial v}{\partial t} + \frac{\partial v}{\partial \tau} = \varepsilon B(\tau)v, \quad v(0) = \sum_{r=0}^{\infty} a_r \varepsilon^r \tag{3.13}$$

where

$$B(\tau) = e^{-A_0\tau} A_1 e^{A_0\tau} . \tag{3.14}$$

We seek a solution in the form (3.6) which becomes

$$v = \sum_{r=0}^{\infty} v_r(t,\tau)\varepsilon^r \tag{3.15}$$

subject to the condition (3.9) on the u_r. In terms of the v_r, the latter becomes

$$v_r(t,\tau) = o(\tau) \text{ as } \tau \to \infty, \quad r = 0,1,\dots . \tag{3.16}$$

Substituting (3.15) into (3.13) and equating coefficients of the like powers of ε gives

$$\frac{\partial v_r}{\partial \tau} = B(\tau)v_{r-1} - \frac{\partial v_{r-1}}{\partial t}, \quad v_r(0,0) = a_r, \; r = 0,1,\dots \tag{3.17}$$

Here $v_{-1} \equiv 0$.

The problem (3.17) is underdetermined. The equation (3.17) for v_r can be integrated to give

$$v_r(t,\tau) = \tilde{v}_r(t) + \int_0^\tau [B(\sigma)v_{r-1}(t,\sigma) - \frac{\partial v_{r-1}(t,\sigma)}{\partial t}]d\sigma, \; r=0,1,\dots \tag{3.18}$$

where

$$\tilde{v}_r(0) = a_r . \tag{3.19}$$

Except for (3.19), $\tilde{v}_r(t)$ is arbitrary. Differentiating (3.18) with respect to t gives

$$\frac{\partial v_r}{\partial t} = \frac{\partial \tilde{v}_r}{\partial t} + \int_0^\tau [B(\sigma) \frac{\partial v_{r-1}}{\partial t} - \frac{\partial^2 v_{r-1}}{\partial t^2}]d\sigma . \tag{3.20}$$

Combining this with (3.18) gives

$$v_r(t,\tau) = \tilde{v}_r(t) + \int_0^\tau B(\sigma)d\sigma\, \tilde{v}_{r-1}(t) - \tau \frac{d\tilde{v}_{r-1}}{dt} + \int_0^\tau R_{r-1}(t,\sigma)d\sigma \tag{3.21}$$

where

$$R_r(t,\sigma) = -\int_0^\sigma [B(\sigma) \frac{\partial v_{r-1}(t,\sigma')}{\partial t} - \frac{\partial^2 v_{r-1}(t,\sigma')}{\partial t^2}]d\sigma'$$

$$+ B(\sigma) \int_0^\sigma [B(\sigma')v_{r-1}(t,\sigma') - \frac{\partial v_{r-1}(t,\sigma')}{\partial t}]d\sigma'. \tag{3.22}$$

(3.21) and (3.22) hold for r=0,1,..., where $\tilde{v}_{-1} \equiv R_{-1} \equiv R_0 \equiv 0$. Let us impose the growth condition (3.16) in (3.21). To do this, divide (3.21) by τ and take the limit as $\tau \to \infty$. This results in the following condition for $\tilde{v}_r$.

$$\frac{d\tilde{v}_r}{d\tau} = (\lim_{\tau\to\infty} \frac{1}{\tau}\int_0^\tau B(\sigma)d\sigma)\tilde{v}_r + \lim_{\tau\to\infty} (\frac{1}{\tau}\int_0^\tau R_r(t,\sigma)d\sigma), r=0,1,\dots \tag{3.23}$$

When these limits exist, (3.23) along with (3.19) determine $\tilde{v}_r$, r=0,1,... .

This approach depends critically on the existence of the limits in (3.23). The development will be simplified using the notation

$$\bar{f} = \lim_{\tau\to\infty} \frac{1}{\tau} \int_0^\tau f(x)dx. \tag{3.24}$$

If $\bar{f}$ exists we will call it the average of f. In terms of this notation (3.23) becomes

$$\frac{d\tilde{v}_r}{dt} = \bar{B}\,\tilde{v}_r + \bar{R}_r(t),\ \tilde{v}_r(0) = a_r,\quad r=0,1,\ldots, \tag{3.25}$$

provided the averages exist.

We turn now to the question of the existence of the averages which appear in (3.25).

<u>Remark</u>: We content ourselves here with a study of $\bar{B}$ and $\bar{R}_1$ since the existence of these two averages provides us with the existence of the approximation $v_0 + \varepsilon v_1$ to v. This approximation is adequate for our computational purposes. Note that $v_0(t,\tau) \equiv v_0(t) \equiv \tilde{v}_0(t)$.

3.3 <u>Existence of the Average, $\bar{B}$</u>

The example $A_0 = \begin{pmatrix}-1 & 0\\ 0 & -2\end{pmatrix}$, $A_1 = \begin{pmatrix}0 & 0\\ 1 & 0\end{pmatrix}$ shows that $\bar{B}$ may not exist.

<u>Restriction</u>: We assume in this analysis that the matrix A_0 has simple elementary divisors. In which case we may assume without loss of generality that A_0 is a diagonal matrix. We denote the elements of A_0 and A_1 respectively by

$$A_0 = (\lambda_i\,\delta_{ij}) \text{ and } A_1 = (a^1_{ij}). \tag{3.26}$$

Then

$$\frac{1}{\tau}\int_0^\tau e^{-A_0\sigma} A_1 e^{A_0\sigma} = (a^1_{ij}\, f_{ij}) \tag{3.27}$$

where

$$f_{ij} = \begin{cases} \dfrac{e^{(\lambda_j-\lambda_i)\tau} - 1}{\tau(\lambda_j-\lambda_i)}, & \lambda_i \neq \lambda_j \\[2ex] 1, & \lambda_i = \lambda_j. \end{cases} \tag{3.28}$$

This computation demonstrates the following theorem.

<u>Theorem 3.1</u>: $\bar{B}$ exists if and only if $a^1_{ij} = 0$ whenever $\mathrm{Re}(\lambda_j-\lambda_i)>0$.

<u>Remark 3.1</u>: We henceforth assume that the hypothesis of Theorem 3.1 holds.

The computation also has the following corollary.

<u>Corollary 3.1</u>:

i) If $\bar{B}$ exists then $\bar{B}_{ij} = a^1_{ij}\,\delta(\lambda_i, \lambda_j)$, where δ is the Kronecker delta.

ii) If the eigenvalues of A_0 are distinct then $\bar{B} = (a^1_{ij}\,\delta_{ij})$.

iii) If A_0 and A_1 are normal matrices then $\bar{B}$ exists and is conjugate to A_1.

iv) If A_0 and A_1 commute then $\bar{B}$ exists and is conjugate to A_1.

v) If A_1 is diagonal then $\bar{B} = A_1$.

vi) If $A_0 = \lambda I$ then $\bar{B} = A_1$.

vii) Let $\bar{B}$ exist and suppose that $\lambda_1 = \lambda_2 = \ldots = \lambda_m = 0$ and and $\lambda_{m+i} \neq 0$, $i=1, \ldots, n-m$. Let A^1_{11} be the mxm principle submatrix of A_1. Then the mxm principle submatrix of $\bar{B}$ is A^1_{11} while $\bar{B}_{ij} = 0$ for $j > m$ and $i \leq m$ and for $j \leq m$ and $i > m$.

In terms of a block decomposition of A_1 and $\bar{B}$ this result may be represented by:

$$A_1 = \begin{bmatrix} A^1_{11} & A^1_{12} \\ A^1_{21} & A^1_{22} \end{bmatrix} \Rightarrow \bar{B} = \begin{bmatrix} A^1_{11} & 0 \\ 0 & \bar{A}^1_{22} \end{bmatrix}$$

where $\bar{A}^1_{22}$ is unspecified but assumed to exist.

<u>Proof</u>: (iii) and (iv) follow since A_0 and A_1 are simultaneously diagonalizable in these cases. All other statements are immediate.

3.4 Existence of the Average $\bar{R}_1$.

The following theorem characterizes the existence of $\bar{R}_1$.

<u>Theorem 3.2</u>: If $\bar{B}$ exists then $\bar{R}_1$ exists.

<u>Proof</u>: The proof is based on theorem 3.1 and the following computation: Let

$$\rho(\sigma) = \int_0^\sigma (B(\sigma')-\bar{B})d\sigma' \quad . \tag{3.29}$$

Then from (3.22) we have

$$R_1(t,\sigma) = (B(\sigma)\,\rho(\sigma) - \rho(\sigma)\bar{B})e^{\bar{B}t}\, v_0(0) \tag{3.30}$$

where we have used $\frac{d\tilde{v}_0}{dt} = \bar{B}\,\tilde{v}_0$ which follows from (3.25).

We first show the existence of $\bar{\rho}$. The ij-th element of ρ is from (3.28)

$$(\rho)_{ij} = \left(a^1_{ij} \cdot \begin{cases} \dfrac{e^{(\lambda_j-\lambda_i)\sigma} - 1}{\lambda_j-\lambda_i}, & \lambda_i \neq \lambda_j \\ \sigma, & \lambda_i = \lambda_j \end{cases} \right) - \left(\begin{matrix} 0 & , \lambda_i \neq \lambda_j \\ \sigma a^1_{ij} & , \lambda_i = \lambda_j \end{matrix} \right)$$

$$= \left(\begin{matrix} a^1_{ij} \dfrac{e^{(\lambda_j-\lambda_i)\sigma} - 1}{\lambda_j-\lambda_i} & , \lambda_i \neq \lambda_j \\ 0 & , \lambda_i = \lambda_j \end{matrix} \right).$$

Then

$$\frac{1}{\tau}\int_0^\tau \rho(\sigma)d\sigma = \begin{pmatrix} \frac{a^1_{ij}}{\lambda_j-\lambda_i}\left[\frac{1}{\tau}\int_0^\tau e^{(\lambda_j-\lambda_i)\sigma}d\sigma-1\right], & \lambda_i \neq \lambda_j \\ 0 & , \lambda_i = \lambda_j \end{pmatrix}. \tag{3.31}$$

The limit of (3.31), as $\tau \to \infty$ exists if an only if $a^1_{ij} = 0$ whenever $\mathrm{Re}(\lambda_j-\lambda_i)>0$. In this case we have

$$\bar{\rho} = \begin{pmatrix} \frac{-a^1_{ij}}{\lambda_j-\lambda_i} & , \quad \lambda_i \neq \lambda_j \\ 0 & , \quad \lambda_i = \lambda_j \end{pmatrix}, \tag{3.32}$$

demonstrating the existence of $\bar{\rho}$.

We now show the existence of the average $\overline{B\rho}$. We have

$$(B\rho)_{ij} = \sum_{k=1}^n B_{ik}\rho_{kj} = \sum_{k=1}^n a^1_{ik} e^{(\lambda_k-\lambda_i)\sigma}(\sigma\, a^1_{kj} f_{kj} - \sigma\, \bar{B}_{kj})$$

$$= \sum_{\substack{k=1\\ \lambda_j\neq\lambda_k}}^n a^1_{ik} a^1_{kj} \frac{e^{(\lambda_j-\lambda_i)\sigma} - e^{(\lambda_k-\lambda_i)\sigma}}{\lambda_j-\lambda_k} + \sum_{\substack{k=1\\ \lambda_j=\lambda_k}}^n (\sigma a^1_{ik} a^1_{kj} - \sigma a^1_{ik}\bar{B}_{kj})$$

$$= \sum_{\substack{k=1\\ \lambda_j\neq\lambda_k}}^n a^1_{ik} a^1_{kj} \frac{e^{(\lambda_j-\lambda_i)\sigma} - e^{(\lambda_k-\lambda_i)\sigma}}{\lambda_j-\lambda_k}$$

$$= \sum_{\substack{k=1\\ \lambda_j\neq\lambda_k}}^n a^1_{ik} e^{(\lambda_k-\lambda_i)\sigma} a^1_{kj} \frac{e^{(\lambda_j-\lambda_k)\sigma}-1}{\lambda_j-\lambda_k} . \tag{3.33}$$

If the real part of any exponent appearing in this expression is positive, then by hypothesis the corresponding element of A_1 appearing in front of that exponential term vanishes. Thus the sum appearing here contains only exponentials with exponents with non-positive real part. Thus $B\rho$ exists.

This completes the proof of the theorem.

<u>Remark 3.2:</u> We may show that

$$(\overline{B\rho} - \bar{\rho}\,\bar{B})_{ij} = \sum_{\substack{k=1\\ \lambda_i\neq\lambda_k}}^n \frac{a^1_{ik}\bar{B}_{kj}}{\lambda_k-\lambda_i} . \tag{3.34}$$

3.5 Estimate of the Remainder

As we remarked above, we will restrict ourselves to estimate the deviation of the approximation $v_o + \varepsilon v_1$ from v.

Let

$$w = v - v_o - \varepsilon v_1 \, . \tag{3.35}$$

We will derive a differential equation for w, solve this equation and estimate its solution.

Using $\frac{dv}{d\tau} = \varepsilon B(\tau)v$ (cf. (3.13)) and $\frac{dv_o}{dt} = \bar{B}v_o$ (cf. (3.21) and (3.25)), we differentiate (3.35) to obtain

$$\begin{aligned} \frac{dw(\varepsilon\tau,\tau)}{d\tau} &= \varepsilon Bv(\varepsilon\tau,\tau) - \varepsilon\bar{B}v_o(\varepsilon\tau) - \varepsilon \frac{dv_1(\varepsilon\tau,\tau)}{d\tau} \\ &= \varepsilon B(w+v_o+\varepsilon v_1) - \varepsilon\bar{B}v_o(\varepsilon\tau) - \varepsilon \frac{dv_1(\varepsilon\tau,\tau)}{d\tau} \, . \end{aligned} \tag{3.36}$$

Let

$$C(\sigma) = B(\sigma)\rho(\sigma) - \rho(\sigma)\bar{B}. \tag{3.37}$$

Then from (3.25) and (3.30) we obtain

$$\frac{d\tilde{v}_1(t)}{dt} = \bar{B}\tilde{v}_1 + \bar{C}v_o(t) \quad . \tag{3.38}$$

From (3.18) and (3.29) we have

$$v_1(t,\tau) = \tilde{v}_1(t) + \rho(\tau)\, v_o(t). \tag{3.39}$$

Differentiating this relation with respect to τ gives

$$\frac{dv_1(\varepsilon\tau,\tau)}{d\tau} = \varepsilon \frac{d\tilde{v}_1(\varepsilon\tau)}{dt} + (B(\tau) - \bar{B})v_o(\varepsilon\tau) + \varepsilon\rho(\tau)\bar{B}v_o(\varepsilon\tau). \tag{3.40}$$

Combining this with (3.38) gives us an expression for $dv_1(\varepsilon\tau,\tau)/d\tau$ which when inserted into (3.36) gives us the following differential equation for w.

$$\begin{aligned} \frac{d}{d\tau} w(\varepsilon\tau,\tau) &= \varepsilon B(w+v_o+\varepsilon v_1) - \varepsilon\bar{B}v_o - \varepsilon^2\bar{B}\tilde{v}_1 - \varepsilon^2\bar{C}v_o \\ &\quad - \varepsilon(B-\bar{B})v_o + \varepsilon^2\rho\bar{B}v_o \quad . \end{aligned} \tag{3.41}$$

Note that $\bar{C}$ is given by (3.34). Using (3.37) and (3.39), (3.41) becomes

$$\frac{d}{d\tau} w(\varepsilon\tau,\tau) = \varepsilon Bw + \varepsilon^2 \, [(B-\bar{B})\tilde{v}_1 + (C-\bar{C})\tilde{v}_o] \, . \tag{3.42}$$

To estimate w we first introduce the fundamental matrix Ψ defined by

$$\frac{d\Psi}{d\tau} = \varepsilon B\Psi, \quad \Psi(0) = I. \tag{3.43}$$

Note that

$$\frac{d}{d\tau}(\Psi^{-1}) = -\varepsilon\Psi^{-1}B. \qquad (3.44)$$

Let B^* denote the complex conjugate of B and B^T its transpose. Then

$$\frac{d}{d\tau}||\Psi||^2 \equiv \frac{d}{d\tau}(\Psi^T\Psi^*) = \varepsilon\,\Psi^T(B^T + B^*)\Psi^*. \qquad (3.45)$$

Then since $B^T + B^*$ is Hermitian, there exists K (e.g. the magnitude of the largest eigenvalue of $B^T + B^*$) such that

$$\frac{d}{d\tau}||\Psi||^2 \leq \varepsilon\,K\,||\Psi||^2. \qquad (3.46)$$

Then

$$||\Psi||^2 \leq e^{\varepsilon K\tau}. \qquad (3.47)$$

By our hypothesis (cf. Remark 3.1), $B(\tau)$ is a bounded function of τ for $\tau \geq 0$. Thus K is independent of τ and (3.47) shows that $||\Psi||^2$ is bounded uniformly for τ restricted to an interval of the form, $0 \leq \tau \leq T/\varepsilon$.

Now we solve (3.42) and write

$$w(\varepsilon\tau,\tau) = \Psi(\tau)[a_2\varepsilon^2+\dots] + \\ + \varepsilon^2\int_0^\tau \Psi(\tau)\Psi^{-1}(\sigma)[(B-\bar{B})\tilde{v}_1(\varepsilon\sigma)+(C-\bar{C})\tilde{v}_o(\varepsilon\sigma)]d\sigma. \qquad (3.48)$$

In (3.48) write $(B-\bar{B})$ as $\frac{d}{d\sigma}\int_0^\sigma (B-\bar{B})d\sigma'$ and $(C-\bar{C})$ as $\frac{d}{d\sigma}\int_0^\sigma (C-\bar{C})d\sigma'$. Then use the formula $(FGH)' = FGH' + FG'H + F'GH$ to integrate by parts the integral with respect to σ. Using (3.29) and (3.44) in what results, we obtain finally

$$w(\varepsilon\tau,\tau) = \varepsilon^2\{\Psi(\tau)\,O(1) + \rho(\tau)\tilde{v}_1(\varepsilon\tau) + \int_0^\tau (C-\bar{C})d\sigma'\,\tilde{v}_o(\varepsilon\tau) \\ + \varepsilon\int_0^\tau \Psi(\tau)\Psi^{-1}(\sigma)[B(\sigma)\int_0^\sigma (C-\bar{C})d\sigma'\tilde{v}_o(\varepsilon\sigma)-\rho(\sigma)\frac{d}{dt}\tilde{v}_1(\varepsilon\sigma) \\ + B\rho(\sigma)\tilde{v}_1(\varepsilon\sigma) - \int_0^\sigma (C-\bar{C})d\sigma'\,\bar{B}\tilde{v}_o(\varepsilon\sigma)]d\sigma\}. \qquad (3.49)$$

We have remarked that $||\Psi||$ is bounded uniformly on the interval $0 \leq \tau \leq T/\varepsilon$ and that B is bounded for $\tau \geq 0$ (cf (3.47) f.f.). The functions $v_o(\varepsilon\sigma)$ and $v_1(\varepsilon\tau)$ appearing in (3.49) are defined as continuous functions and their arguments range over the bounded interval $0 \leq \varepsilon\tau \leq T$. Thus these functions may be uniformly bounded. The quantities $\rho(\sigma)$ and $\int_0^\sigma (C-\bar{C})d\sigma'$ appearing in (3.49) exist as bounded functions for $0 \leq \sigma < \infty$ since they are continuous functions

When the eigenvalues of A_0 have negative real parts, so that our method reproduces the results of the matched asymptotic expansion technique, δ may also be taken to be zero.

4.2 The Algorithm

For the sake of simplicity we take the leading term, $u_o(t,\tau)$ of the expansion (3.6) as an approximation to the solution of the initial value problem (3.1) and (3.10). From (3.11) and (3.18)

$$u_o(t,\tau) = \Phi(\tau)\tilde{v}_o(t) . \tag{4.1}$$

$\Phi(\tau)$ is the fundamental matrix given by

$$\Phi_\tau = A_0\Phi, \ \Phi(0) = I, \tag{4.2}$$

while from (3.25)

$$\frac{d\tilde{v}_o}{dt} = \bar{B}\,\tilde{v}_o, \ \tilde{v}_o(0) = a_o. \tag{4.3}$$

From (3.14)

$$\bar{B} = \lim_{\tau\to\infty} \frac{1}{\tau} \int_o^\tau \Phi^{-1}(\sigma)A_1\ \Phi(\sigma)d\sigma . \tag{4.4}$$

We describe the algorithm for replacing a_o the approximation to u(0) by U(h) the approximation to u(h) (in the sense of the solution concept in section 4.1 above). The algorithm is to be repeated approximating u(t) at u(2h), ..., u(nh) successively.

Algorithm

i) Solve (4.2) on a mesh of increment k in the τ scale by some self starting numerical method, obtaining the sequence $\Phi(jk)$, j=0, ..., N.

ii) Using the values $\Phi(jk)$ obtained in (i), approximate $\bar{B}$ by truncating the limit of integration τ and replacing the integral in (4.4) by a quadrature formula, say

$$\bar{B} = \frac{1}{N} \sum_{j=0}^{N} C_k\ \Phi^{-1}(jk)\ A_1\ \Phi(jk).$$

The integer N is determined by a numerical criterion which assures that the elements of the matrix $\bar{B}$ are calculated to some desired accuracy.

iii) With $\bar{B}$ (approximately) determined in (ii), solve (3.3) for $\tilde{v}_o(h)$ by some self starting numerical method.

iv) Compute $u_o(h,Nk) = \Phi(Nk)\tilde{v}_o(h)$ and take this as the approximation to u(h).

Refinement: The method may be refined by adding an approximation of $\varepsilon v_1(h,h/\varepsilon)$ to $\tilde{v}_o(h)$ prior to multiplication by $\Phi(Nk)$ (step (iv)). This approximation in turn is determined from a numerical solution of the equations defining $v_1(t,\tau)$; viz.

which are bounded at infinity (cf.(3.29)). Thus (3.49) yields :

$$\max_{0 \le \tau \le T/\varepsilon} |w(\varepsilon\tau,\tau)| \le \text{const}\ \varepsilon^2, \qquad (3.50)$$

our desired estimate.

4. THE NUMERICAL APPROXIMATION

4.1 Solution Concept

From our consideration of the circuit equations in section 2 and/or the form (3.5) of the fundamental matrix, we see that the solution of the initial value problem may describe a trajectory with components which are, slowly varying, highly damped, highly oscillatory or a combination of all of these. The usual notion of a numerical approximation to a trajectory is untenable for problems with this range of behavior in its solution. In the highly oscillatory case the solution may come as close as we may measure to any specified precision to a manifold of dimension greater than one. (Consider the example $A_0 = \begin{bmatrix} 0 & -1 \\ 1 & 0 \end{bmatrix}$ and $A_1 = \begin{bmatrix} -1 & 0 \\ 0 & -1 \end{bmatrix}$. As $\varepsilon \to 0$ the solution converges (in an approximate sense) to the "cone" obtained by rotating the curve $||u(0)||e^{-t}$ about the t axis.) Thus the meaningfulness of describing a trajectory by a set of its values on the points of a mesh $\{jh | j=0,1,\ldots,[T/h]\}$ is lost.

A variety of alternate numerical solution concepts may be formulated. Consider the following one.

Solution concept: Given $\varepsilon > 0$ and $\delta > 0$ we say that $U(t)$ is an (ε,δ) (numerical) approximation to $u(t)$ if there exists τ with $|\tau| \le \delta$ such that

$$|U(t) - u(t+\tau)| \le \varepsilon.$$

Of course $\delta = 0$ for the classical concept of (numerical) approximation. In figure 4.1 an example of this approximation is given

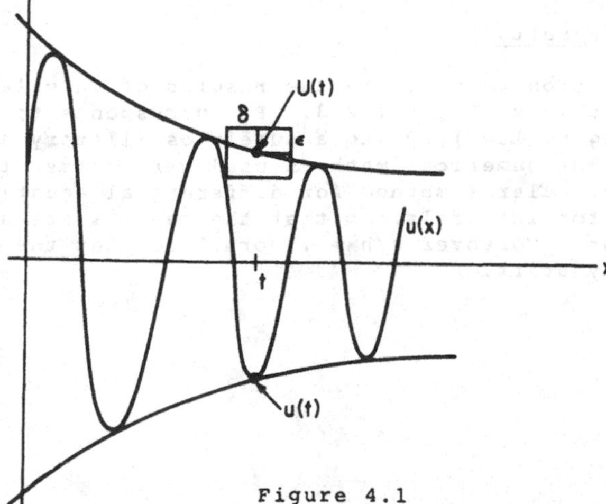

Figure 4.1

$$v_1(t,\tau) = \tilde{v}_1(t) - \tau\bar{B} - \int_0^\tau B(\sigma)d\sigma\ \tilde{v}_0(t)$$

$$\frac{d\tilde{v}_1}{dt} = \bar{B}\tilde{v}_1 + \bar{R}_1(t) \qquad (4.5)$$

$$\bar{R}_1(t) = (\overline{B\rho} - \overline{\rho B})v_0(t).$$

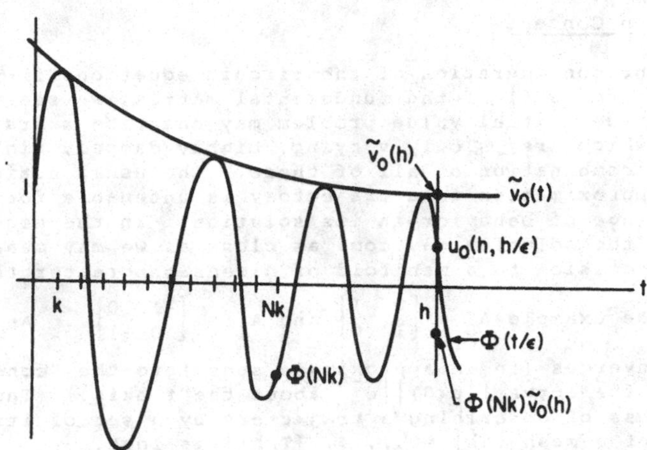

Figure 4.2

In figure 4.2 we schematize the computation. Of course in practice ε will be extremely small so that unlike the schematic an enormous number of oscillations of Φ will occur in the t interval [0,h]. Notice how far the computed answer $\Phi(Nk)\tilde{v}_0(h)$ may be from the classical approximation to the solution, $u_0(h,h/\varepsilon)$. The fundamental matrix $\Phi(\tau)$ is composed of modes corresponding to the eigenvalues of A_0. Since A_0 is not an unstable matrix, the profile for (a component) of Φ will after some moderate number of cycles settle down to an (almost) periodic function. Thus the set of mesh points $\{jk|k=0,\ldots,N\}$ may be expected to extend over just these cycles (approximately).

4.3 Numerical Results

In this section we tabulate the results of calculations with three sample problems, P_i, i=1,2,3. P_1 corresponds to a damped case (A_0 has real eigenvalues), P_2 to a purely oscillatory A_0 and P_3 to a mixed case. The numerical methods used were chosen to be the most elementary (e.g. Euler's method for differential equations and Simpson's rule for integrals) so that the results are accurate only to a few percent. Moreover ε/h = .1 or .2 so that the examples are not particularly stiff.

TABLES

Problem P_1 (damped case)

$$A_o = \begin{bmatrix} 0 & 0 \\ 0 & -1 \end{bmatrix} \qquad A_1 = \begin{bmatrix} -1 & 1 \\ 0 & 0 \end{bmatrix} \qquad \begin{aligned} \varepsilon &= .01 \\ h &= .05 \\ k &= .05 \end{aligned}$$

t	$\tilde{u}_o$		$\Phi(kN)\tilde{u}_o$	
0	1.00	1.00	1.00	1.00
.05	.953	1.	.953	0.0
.10	.908	1.	.906	0.0
.15	.865	1.	.862	0.0
.20	.824	1.	.820	0.0
.25	.785	1.	.780	0.0

Problem P_2 (oscillatory case)

$$A_o = \begin{bmatrix} 0 & -1 \\ 1 & 0 \end{bmatrix} \qquad A_1 = \begin{bmatrix} -2 & 0 \\ 0 & 0 \end{bmatrix} \qquad \begin{aligned} \varepsilon &= .001 \\ h &= .01 \\ k &= .05 \end{aligned}$$

t	$\tilde{u}_o$		$\Phi(kN)\tilde{u}_o$	
0	0.5	0.5	0.5	0.5
.01	.495	.495	.325	.605
.02	.490	.490	.184	.669
.03	.485	.485	.007	.687
.04	.480	.481	-.167	.660
.05	.475	.476	-.327	.589

Problem P_3 (mixed case)

$$A_o = \begin{bmatrix} 0 & 0 & 0 & 0 \\ 0 & -1 & 0 & 0 \\ 0 & 0 & 0 & -1 \\ 0 & 0 & 1 & 0 \end{bmatrix} \qquad A_1 = \begin{bmatrix} 1 & 1 & 1 & 0 \\ 0 & 1 & 0 & 0 \\ 1 & 1 & 1 & 0 \\ 0 & 0 & 0 & 1 \end{bmatrix} \qquad \begin{aligned} \varepsilon &= .01 \\ h &= .05 \\ k &= .05 \end{aligned}$$

t	$\tilde{u}_o$				$\Phi(kN)\tilde{u}_o$			
0	1.0	1.0	1.0	1.0	1.0	1.0	1.0	1.0
.05	1.05	1.05	1.06	1.04	1.05	0.0	-1.45	.327
.10	1.11	1.11	1.12	1.09	1.10	0.0	.534	-1.46
.15	1.17	1.16	1.18	1.14	1.17	0.0	.997	1.31
.20	1.23	1.22	1.24	1.19	1.22	0.0	-1.72	.149
.25	1.29	1.28	1.31	1.24	1.28	0.0	.846	-1.60

REFERENCES

G. G. Bjurel et al, Survey of stiff ordinary differential equations, Report NA70.11 (1970), Dept. of Inf. Proc., The Royal Inst. Tech., Stockholm.

J. Cole, Perturbation Methods in Applied Mathematics, Blaisdell (1968)

W. L. Miranker, Singular perturbation analysis of the differential equations of a tunnel diode circuit, Quart. of Appl. Math XX (1962) 279-299.

W. L. Miranker, The occurrence of limit cycles in the equations of a tunnel diode circuit, IRE Trans. on Circuit Theory (1962) 316-320.

W. L. Miranker, Numerical methods of boundary layer type for stiff systems of ordinary differential equations, Computing, 11, (1973)

W. L. Miranker and J. P. Morreeuw, Semi-analytic numerical studies of turning points arising in stiff boundary value problems, IBM Research Center Report RC 4458, (1973).

A. H. Nayfeh, Perturbation Methods, Wiley (1973).

SUPPLEMENTARY BIBLIOGRAPHY

F. Hoppensteadt, Properties of solutions of ordinary differential equations with small parameters, Comm. Pure and Appl. Math. XXIV (1971) 807-840.

J. A. Morrison, Comparison of the modified method of averaging and the two variable expansion procedure, SIAM Rev. 8 (1966) 66-85.

V. M. Volosov, Averaging in systems of ordinary differential equations Russian Math Surveys 17 (1962) 1-126.

CONCEPTION, SIMULATION, OPTIMISATION D'UN FILTRE A L'AIDE D'UN ORDINATEUR

Agnès GUERARD,
Centre National d'Etudes des Télécommunications

INTRODUCTION

Dans le cadre très général de l'analyse et de la synthèse de réseaux électroniques, nous proposons ici un algorithme qui a pour but de linéariser le déphasage de la réponse d'un filtre en ajustant les valeurs des éléments de façon à minimiser l'amplitude de la variation du temps de propagation de groupe dans une certaine bande de fréquences, en général la bande passante du filtre en question.

Rappelons brièvement qu'un filtre analogique est un quadripôle composé de cellules élémentaires. Certaines de ces cellules sont des résonateurs qui rejettent chacun une fréquence. L'ensemble constitue un filtre qui ne laisse passer qu'une bande de fréquence.

Il existe des programmes de synthèse directe qui permettent de calculer les valeurs des éléments et des programmes d'analyse qui permettent de simuler le comportement de la réponse en amplitude. Le programme réalisé ici permet d'optimiser le comportement de la réponse en phase.

II - METHODE PROPOSEE

A - ELEMENTS DU PROBLEME

1°

$$s = \begin{vmatrix} \sigma_1 \\ \sigma_2 \\ \vdots \\ \sigma_n \end{vmatrix} \qquad s \in K = [a_1, b_1] \times [a_2, b_2] \times \ldots \times [a_n, b_n]$$

s est le vecteur des paramètres de base, composants du réseau, sur lesquels se fait la recherche d'un optimum. Ces paramètres sont au nombre de n et varient dans un domaine K qui est, en général, un produit d'intervalles.

2° Pour toute fréquence $f = \dfrac{\omega}{2\pi}$, $C^k(s,\omega)$ est la matrice de chaîne du $k^{\text{ième}}$ quadripôle élémentaire constituant le réseau, composée de 4 nombres complexes.

$$C^k(s,\omega) = \begin{vmatrix} \alpha_1^k(s,\omega) + j\alpha_2^k(s,\omega) & \beta_1^k(s,\omega) + j\beta_2^k(s,\omega) \\ \gamma_1^k(s,\omega) + j\gamma_2^k(s,\omega) & \delta_1^k(s,\omega) + j\delta_2^k(s,\omega) \end{vmatrix}$$

C^k est une fonction de $\mathbb{R}^{n+1} \longrightarrow \mathbb{R}^8$

$\prod_{\mathbb{C}^2}$ désignant le produit de matrices complexes carrées d'ordre 2, C est la fonction de $\mathbb{R}^{n+1} \longrightarrow \mathbb{R}^8$ définie par :

$$C(s, \omega) = \prod_{k=1}^{m}{}_{\mathbb{C}^2} \quad C^k(s, \omega)$$

m désigne le nombre de quadripôles élémentaires qui constituent le filtre : ils sont supposés être associés en cascade.

3° Pour une fréquence donnée, posons $A = C(s, \omega) = \begin{vmatrix} \Gamma_{11} & \Gamma_{12} \\ \Gamma_{21} & \Gamma_{21} \end{vmatrix}$

Alors l'amplitude a et le déphasage φ de la réponse sont donnés par la relation ci-dessous :

$$e^{a+j\varphi} = \frac{1}{2\sqrt{R_0 R_n}} \left(\Gamma_{11} R_n + \Gamma_{12} + \Gamma_{21} \; R_0 R_n + \Gamma_{22} \; R_0 \right)$$

R_0 et R_n étant les résistances d'entrée et de sortie appliquées au quadripôle.

On en déduit :

$$\varphi = \psi \text{ (A)} \quad \text{où} \quad \psi : \mathbb{R}^8 \longrightarrow \mathbb{R}$$

4° Remarque :

Une application linéaire de $\mathbb{C}^2 \rightarrow \mathbb{C}^2$, représentée par un système linéaire complexe d'ordre 2 :

$$\begin{vmatrix} \xi_1 + j\,\xi_2 \\ \eta_1 + j\,\eta_2 \end{vmatrix} = \begin{vmatrix} \alpha_1 + j\,\alpha_2 & \beta_1 + j\,\beta_2 \\ \gamma_1 + j\,\gamma_2 & \delta_1 + j\,\delta_2 \end{vmatrix} \begin{vmatrix} \sigma_1 + j\,\sigma_2 \\ \tau_1 + j\,\tau_2 \end{vmatrix}$$

peut être considérée comme une application linéaire de $\mathbb{R}^4 \longrightarrow \mathbb{R}^4$ et représentée par le système ci-dessous :

$$\begin{vmatrix} \xi_1 \\ \xi_2 \\ \eta_1 \\ \eta_2 \end{vmatrix} = \begin{vmatrix} \alpha_1 & -\alpha_2 & \beta_1 & -\beta_2 \\ \alpha_2 & \alpha_1 & \beta_2 & \beta_1 \\ \gamma_1 & -\gamma_2 & \delta_1 & -\delta_2 \\ \gamma_2 & \gamma_1 & \delta_2 & \delta_1 \end{vmatrix} \begin{vmatrix} \sigma_1 \\ \sigma_2 \\ \tau_1 \\ \tau_2 \end{vmatrix}$$

B - PROBLEME

On cherche dans le domaine K de variation des paramètres s, domaine qui a été déterminé par exemple par un programme de simulation de façon que le gabarit en amplitude y soit toujours respecté, le point pour lequel la phase est "la plus linéaire possible" dans la bande passante.

Sur un ensemble de fréquences $(\omega_l)_{\ l = 1 \text{ à } L}$ convenablement réparties dans la bande passante, la linéarité du déphasage est caractérisée par le coefficient de corrélation.

$$\rho^2 = \frac{\left(\sum_{l=1}^{L} (\varphi_l - \bar{\varphi})(\omega_l - \bar{\omega})\right)^2}{\sum_{l=1}^{L} (\varphi_l - \bar{\varphi})^2 \times \sum_{l=1}^{L} (\omega_l - \bar{\omega})^2}$$

Ce coefficient doit être le plus proche possible de la valeur 1.

Ce problème consiste donc à minimiser $1-\rho^2$ pour $s \in K$, sous les contraintes :

$$\left.\begin{aligned} \varphi_l &= \psi(A_l) \\ A_l &= C(s, \omega_l) \end{aligned}\right\} \forall l \in \{1, 2, \ldots, L\}$$

C - RESOLUTION

On introduit les multiplicateurs :

$$\mu_1, \mu_2, \ldots\ldots, \mu_L$$

$$R_1, R_2, \ldots\ldots, R_l$$

et le Hamiltonnien :

$$\lambda(s\ ; \mu_1, \mu_2, \ldots, \mu_L, R_1, R_2, \ldots, R_L) =$$

$$1-\rho^2 + \sum_{l=1}^{L} \mu_l (\varphi_l - \psi(A_l)) + \sum_{l=1}^{L} R_l^* (A_l - C(s, \omega_l))$$

Remarque :

On note $R_l * (A_l - C(s, \omega_l))$ le produit scalaire de R_l et de $(A_l - C(s,\omega_l))$ considérés comme des vecteurs de $\mathbb{R}^8$.

Minimiser $1 - \rho^2$ sous les contraintes indiquées revient à minimiser λ pour $s \in K$.

On doit donc chercher un point $s^* \in K$ tel que :

$$\frac{\partial \lambda}{\partial \varphi_l}(s^*) = 0 \qquad \text{et} \qquad \frac{\partial \lambda}{\partial A_l}(s^*) = 0, \ \forall l$$

Mais $\dfrac{\partial \lambda}{\partial \varphi_l} = - \dfrac{\partial \rho^2}{\partial \varphi_l} + \mu_l$ et $\dfrac{\partial \lambda}{\partial A_l} = \mu_l \dfrac{\partial \psi}{\partial A_l} + R_l$

Au point s^* on doit donc avoir :

$$\mu_l = \frac{\partial \rho^2}{\partial \varphi_l} \quad \text{et} \quad R_l = \mu_l \frac{\partial \psi}{\partial A_l}, \quad \forall l$$

D'autre part, si on se trouve en un point s relativement proche de s^*, on peut écrire :

$$\Delta \lambda = \sum_{i=1}^{n} \frac{\partial \lambda}{\partial \sigma_i} \Delta \sigma_i$$

A l'optimum, $\lambda^* = 0$, et :

$$-\lambda = \sum_{i=1}^{n} \frac{\partial \lambda}{\partial \sigma_i} (\sigma_i^* - \sigma_i)$$

D - ALGORITHME

1° - Choisir $s^{(0)}$, point de départ.

2° - A l'étape k, $s^{(k)}$ étant supposé connu, L analyses du système pour les différentes valeurs $(\omega_l)_{l=1 \text{ à } L}$ fournissent φ_l et A_l, pour $l = 1$ à L.

On en déduit :

$$\mu_l^{(k)} = \frac{\partial \rho^2}{\partial \varphi_l} \quad \text{et} \quad R_l^{(k)} = \mu_l \frac{\partial \varphi}{\partial A_l}, \text{ pour } l = 1 \text{ à } L$$

$$\text{et} \quad \lambda^{(k)} = \lambda\,(s^{(k)}\,;\mu_1^{(k)},\ldots,\mu_L^{(k)}\,;R_1^{(k)},\ldots,R_L^{(k)})$$

3° - Le point $s^{(k+1)}$ est la projection sur le domaine admissible K du point $s'^{(k+1)}$ obtenu en modifiant une seule des composantes de $s^{(k)}$:

$$\sigma_i'^{(k+1)} - \sigma_i^{(k)} = \frac{-\lambda^{(k)}}{\partial\lambda/\partial\sigma_i}$$

l'indice i de la composante modifiée est augmenté, modulo n, de 1 à chaque itération.

4° - Le processus est itéré jusqu'à ce que soit atteinte une précision relative raisonnable pour les valeurs des composants, suivant la nature du problème traité, ou bien lorsque le point courant $s^{(k)}$ se trouve à un sommet du domaine K.

Note :

Au cours des premières itérations, et si le domaine K est vaste, il convient d'appliquer un cœfficient de sous-relaxation :

$$\sigma_i'^{(k+1)} - \sigma_i^{(k)} = -\alpha \frac{\lambda^{(k)}}{\partial\lambda/\partial\sigma_i}, \quad \alpha < 1$$

pour éviter un éloignement du point optimum.

III - APPLICATION

Considérons par exemple le quadripôle dont le schéma équivalent est ci-dessous :

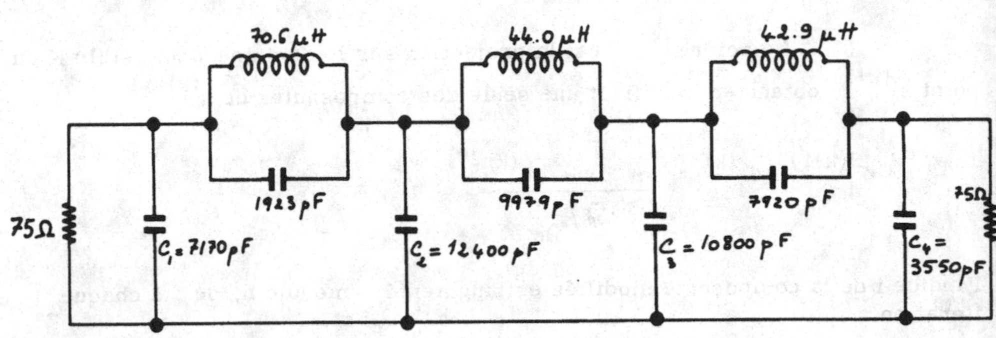

C'est un filtre passe-bas dont la bande passante est 0-200 KHz. On cherche donc à maximiser le coefficient de corrélation ρ^2 dans la bande 0-200 KHz en faisant varier uniquement les capacités C_1, C_2, C_3 et C_4.

RESULTATS

A/ ΔC_{max} = 2000 pF

s^2	C_1	C_2	C_3	C_4
0.964	7170	12400	10800	3550
0.965	9170	-	-	-
0.968	-	10400	-	-
0.972	-	-	8988	-
0.974	-	-	-	5550
0.975	-	-	8800	-

$B/\Delta C_{max}$ = 5000 pF

s^2	C_1	C_2	C_3	C_4
0.964	7170	12400	10800	3550
0.967	12023	-	-	-
0.970	-	10660	-	-
0.974	-	-	8927	-
0.9768	-	-	-	5284
0.9769	12170	-	-	-
0.979	-	9750	-	-
0.981	-	-	8116	-
0.983	-	-	-	6635

Bibliographie

J. CEA

Optimisation, théorie et algorithmes, Dunod 1971.

P. ALLEMANDOU

Calcul des filtres en tenant compte des pertes des composants dissipatif
Câbles et transmissions, 25, n° 2, avril 1971.

A. GUERARD et A. JOLIVET

Conception assistée des filtres par ordinateur. Annales des Télécommunications tome 27, n° 12, janvier-février 1972.

Y. BENIGUEL - A. GLOWINSKI - A. GUERARD

Conception, simulation, optimisation de filtres par ordinateur. L'Echo des Recherches, n° 71, janvier 1973.

COMPUTING METHODS IN SEMICONDUCTOR PROBLEMS

by

Martin Reiser

IBM Research Laboratory
San Jose, California

1. INTRODUCTION

The fast rate of progress in semiconductor technology has led to structures and dimensions, where the traditional analytical approximation models are no longer adequate. What is needed is a two- or even three-dimensional solution of the full set of nonlinear partial differential equations, which is known as diffusion model. The success of treating two-dimensional problems analytically was rather limited [Fulkerson 68, Lewis 70] and one has to revert to numerical methods to obtain solutions for the complicated geometries of modern devices. In recent years, suitable computer programs for one- and two-dimensional analyses have begun to close the gap between the simple models and the needs of the device designer. A rapidly growing literature documents the increasing influence of computing in this field.

The object of this paper is to survey numerical solution methods for semiconductor device problems. For an area of research which is still in a relatively early stage as far as rapid progress is concerned, such a survey cannot be fully objective and personal judgement plays an important role. The findings, therefore, are all subject to discussion and revision. Results are quoted according to their relevance to numerical methods. Emphasis is on two-dimensional solutions of the device problem. The references are not fully comprehensive, especially not in one-dimensional solutions.

The history of numerical methods in semiconductor problems started with the pioneering work of H. K. Gummel about a decade ago. His sequential iteration method is still widely used today. First transient solutions were attempted in the area of Gunn diodes as early as 1966 [McCumber 66]. For p-n junctions and Read-Diode oscillators such solutions followed in late 1968 [DeMari] and early 1969 [Scharfetter]. In the latter publication D. L. Scharfetter and H. K. Gummel introduced the best suited finite-difference approximation. Among the later publications of one-dimensional results [DeMari 68, Caughey 69, Gokhale 70, Arandjelovic 70, Hachtel 72, Seidman 72, Petersen 73] the method of G. D. Hachtel, R. C. Roy and J. W. Cooley deserves special attention because of its efficiency and generality. One-dimensional numerical analysis plays an important role in many areas but its most significant contribution was for the bipolar transistor.

Two-dimensional solutions appeared in the literature in late 1969 [Kennedey, Slotboom]. The first two-dimensional version of Gummel's method was described by J. W. Slotboom. Around the same time, the simpler zero-current or capacitance problem was successfully solved by numerical methods [Dubock 69, Wasserstrom 70]. The most important incentive, however, came from the development of the modern short channel field-effect transistor in the mid-sixties. Unlike the bipolar transistor, this device is based on two-dimensional flow patterns. The scope of the traditional regional modes for this device is quite limited and failed to answer many vitally important questions. The urgent need for better models justified the large-scale use of digital computing and the field-effect transistor has become the first device extensively investigated by two-dimensional numerical analysis [Loeb 69, Kennedey 69,-71, Kim 70, Reiser 70,-71,-72, Vandorpe 71,-72, Heydemann 71, Jutzi 72, Ruch 72, Himsworth 72, Mock 73]. Some attempts were made to reduce the amount of computing by substituting a two-dimensional potential solution in the regional model [Loeb 69, Amelio 72] or by simplifying the geometry [Kim 70]. These attempts to avoid a full solution, however, were not too successful. Understandably, the d.c. problem was tackled first. It was, however, shown that getting a complete transient solution is not necessarily more demanding than the d.c. problem [Reiser 71,-72] and a complete d.c.-, a.c.- and transient analysis of Schottky-gate field-effect transistors was achieved [Reiser 73].

Two-dimensional analysis played a less significant role in other areas of device technology. Only few results, for example, were published for the bipolar transistor although the need for understanding parasitic effects (such as current spreading) seems to have led to a revival of two-dimensional analysis in this field [Heimeier 73, Slotboom 73]. Other two-dimensional results were obtained for Gunn diodes [Katakoa 70, Yanai 70, Suzuki 72, Reiser 71] to handle questions about domain nucleation and stabilization.

2. THE PHYSICAL MODEL

The basic physical model for the charge transport in semiconductors has remained essentially unchanged since the pioneering work of Shockley and Schottky in the fifties. Its success in understanding and quantitatively describing semiconductor devices was so great that it is now generally accepted without further discussion. This is dangerous in physical sciences and technology is, indeed, rapidly progressing into dimensions where the model can no longer be taken for granted.

In this section, we present the equations which are known as diffusion model. A short discussion of the basic assumptions underlying the diffusion model is also given.

2.1 The Diffusion Model

In suitably normalized form, the equations are:

(1) Continuity Equation

$$\frac{\partial n}{\partial t} = \nabla \cdot \vec{J}_n + R_n \quad , \tag{1}$$

$$\frac{\partial p}{\partial t} = - \nabla \cdot \vec{J}_p + R_p \quad . \tag{2}$$

(2) Transport Equation

$$\vec{J}_n = n\mu_n \vec{E} + D_n \cdot \nabla_n \quad , \tag{3}$$

$$\vec{J}_p = p\mu_p \vec{E} - D_p \cdot \nabla_p \quad . \tag{4}$$

(3) Poisson's Equation

$$-\nabla^2\psi = N + p - n \quad , \tag{5}$$

$$\vec{E} = -\nabla\psi \quad . \tag{6}$$

The meaning of the symbols is:

n: electron density, p: hole density, $\vec{J}$: current density, R: recombination rate, μ: mobility, D: diffusivity, $\vec{E}$: electrical field, ψ: potential field, and N: the ionized impurity density.

The subscript n refers to electrons, p to holes.

Additional <u>state equations</u> describe properties of different materials. The following assumptions are typically made:

(1) $R_n = R_p = R(n,p)$ according to the Shockley-Read-Hall model.

(2) Global validity of Einstein's relation, i.e., $D = \mu$ and empirical formulas for the dependence of the mobility on the electrical field-strength E, i.e.,

$$\vec{J}_n = \mu_n(E)[\vec{E} + \nabla n] \quad . \tag{7}$$

(3) All impurities ionized, i.e., $N = N(\vec{x})$ with $\vec{x}$ the position vector.

The mathematical description is completed by specification of a domain, three boundary conditions for n, p and ψ and an initial condition in the case of the time dependent problem. The boundary usually consists of several segments, i.e., contacts and insulated surfaces where

(1) ψ, n and p have fixed prescribed values in the case of <u>ohmic contacts</u>.

(2) ψ given and normal components of $\vec{J}_n$ and $\vec{J}_p$ zero in the case of <u>insulated surfaces</u>.

The following transformation of variables is often found:

$$n = e^{\psi+\phi_n} \quad , \tag{8}$$

$$p = e^{-\psi+\phi_p} \tag{9}$$

with ϕ called pseudo Fermi-potentials. Equation (7) becomes

$$\vec{J}_n = \mu_n n \nabla\phi_n = \mu_n e^{\psi+\phi_n} \nabla\phi_n \tag{10}$$

and similarly for $\vec{J}_p$. It is also customary to introduce the logarithmic variables $\Phi_n = \exp(\phi_n)$ and $\Phi_p = \exp(\phi_p)$ yielding the form

$$\vec{J}_n = \mu_n e^{\psi} \nabla\Phi_n . \tag{11}$$

In the zero-current or equilibrium case it is $\phi = 0$ and equations (8) and (9) revert to the well known relations

$$n = e^{\psi} \quad , \tag{12}$$

$$p = e^{-\psi} \quad . \tag{13}$$

Combining Poisson's equation (5) with (12) and (13) gives the so-called Shockley-Poisson equation

$$-\nabla^2\psi = N + e^{-\psi} - e^{\psi} \tag{14}$$

which describes the zero-current case.

2.2 Limits of the Diffusion Model

The diffusion model can be derived from the Boltzmann's equation by a set of assumptions, namely:

(1) The distribution can be fully characterized by the mean velocity $\vec{v}$ (or equivalently the second and all higher moments have negligible relaxation time). The problem can then be described by the first two moment equations.

(2) Neglect of $\partial\vec{v}/\partial t$ and of the Bernoulli term in the first moment equation (or momentum balance) to get

$$n\vec{v} = -J_n = -n\mu\vec{E} - D\nabla n \quad . \tag{15}$$

(3) Neglect of magnetic forces and static treatment of the electric fields.

Most serious is assumption (1) and its consequences, i.e., no thermal forces and no explicit energy balance equation.

The electrical field-strength is not a good description of the physical state and equation (7) may lead to serious contradictions. This becomes apparent in regions where large density gradients are balanced by correspondingly high fields so that no current flow results. In such areas, equation (7) would produce unphysical "hot-electron" effects. This problem has led to serious difficulties in the analysis of the insulated-gate field-effect transistor. A better form based on the assumption of additivity of the forces is [Reiser 71]

$$\vec{J}_n = n\mu(F)\vec{F} \tag{16}$$

with $\vec{F} = \vec{E} + \nabla \log (n)$ and $\mu(F)$ the same form as $\mu(E)$ in equation (7).

2.3 Special Aspects of Various Devices

Not all terms and equations of the diffusion model (1) to (6) are always relevant and simpler models which are computationally less demanding may be adequate. The following is a short discussion of the properties of various important devices:

(1) The bipolar transistor is based on injection of minority carriers and thus the full set of equations is relevant. The solution depends critically on the recombination and diffusion term and a density-dependent diffusivity may even be required to account for degeneracy in high injection levels [Hachtel 72]. A one-dimensional analysis is sufficient in most cases.

(2) The field-effect transistor is a majority-carrier device and therefore neglect or approximative treatment of the minority carriers are usually justified. Recombination effects can be neglected, even if minority carriers are taken into account. The solution is insensitive to changes in the diffusion term.

The proper nonlinear drift term, however, is important. The shortcomings of drift equation (7) are especially apparent in the current channel of the insulated gate field-effect transistor and use of the more appropriate form (16) is strongly indicated. The field-effect transistor requires a two-dimensional solution.

(3) Gunn-effect devices. In the case of "two-valley" semiconductors such as GaAs, the solution is totally dominated by the nonlinear drift law which has a range of negative differential conductance. Minority carriers (i.e., holes) can be neglected. The proper form of the state dependent diffusion term is unknown and many authors use a constant diffusivity. Often no steady-state solution exists and therefore a transient analysis is always required.

3. NUMERICAL SOLUTION

The set of equations known as diffusion model are nonlinear partial differential equations of the parabolic type or of the elliptic type in the case of the d.c. problem. All numerical solutions of these equations described so far in the literature fall into the class of finite-difference methods on rectangular grids with low order centered difference approximations (so-called five-point formulas). The problem then is one of:

(1) choosing optimal finite difference expressions, and

(2) solving the resultant system of algebraic equations efficiently.

The need for efficiency is absolutely predominant since especially in the two-dimensional case the demand on computing and the resulting costs may well be prohibitive for any extensive use of numerical analysis.

The following well known properties of the solution are typical for an ill-conditioned system and make a numerical solution accordingly difficult:

(1) Over short distances, the density variables may vary over several orders of magnitude.

(2) The solution, especially the location of space charge areas is very sensitive to changes in the boundary conditions (i.e., the applied voltages).

(3) Important macroscopic quantities such as the device current are defined over differentials of the solution.

3.1 Mesh and Finite-Difference Approximation

Regular rectangular grids are a preferred choice for the solution of two-dimensional plane problems as they lead to simple finite-difference formulas and to sparse matrices with only few non-zero diagonals (a regular mesh is one where no grid line ends in the interior of the domain). To save mesh points in the uninteresting neutral areas nonuniform mesh spacings are often used. Regular nonuniform grids, however, also have drawbacks which in certain cases may even offset their advantages, i.e., (1) reduced order of accuracy, (2) numerically degenerate long-shaped rectangles in certain areas, and (3) computational overhead in the equation setup.

There is a great deal of freedom in choosing finite-difference approximations to the original equations. Two requirements are important, viz.,

(1) Consistency, i.e., the finite difference equation converges to the differential equation if the mesh is refined.

(2) The conservation property of the continuity equation has its discrete analogue.

The second condition turns out to be necessary in order to obtain a uniquely defined device current [Reiser 71]. Centered difference formulas are the simplest class satisfying both conditions. We subsequently give several examples as found in the literature. For notational convenience a one-dimensional uniform grid with spacings h is assumed. The generalization to two space-dimensions is usually straightforward. Moreover, we give the examples for the electron current only and omit the subscript n. The basic centered difference approximation of the divergence term is

$$\nabla\cdot\vec{J}|_{x=ih} = [\hat{J}_{i+1/2} - \hat{J}_{i-1/2}]/h + O(h^2) \quad . \tag{17}$$

The various methods published differ in the approximations $\hat{J}$ of the current density, i.e., in basic variables n [Katakoa 70, Reiser 71, Suzuki 72]

$$\mathfrak{J}_{i+1/2} = \frac{n_{i+1} + n_i}{2} \mu_{i+1/2} \frac{\psi_i - \psi_{i+1}}{h} + D_{i+1/2} \frac{n_{i+1} - n_i}{h} \quad , \tag{18}$$

or in logarithmic variables Φ [Slotboom 69]

$$\mathfrak{J}_{i+1/2} = \mu_{i+1/2} e^{\psi_{i+1/2}} \frac{\Phi_{i+1} - \Phi_i}{h} \tag{19}$$

where $\exp(\psi_{i+1/2})$ may be approximated by grid values by $1/2[\exp(\psi_i) + \exp(\psi_{i+1})]$ or $\exp(\frac{1}{2} \psi_i + \psi_{i+1})$ or better by [Mock 73] $[\exp(\psi_{i+1}) - \exp(\psi_i)]/h$. Some position-dependent scaling is required as Φ may become very large and, in fact, even exceed the range of floating point numbers of many present-day computers. A particularly simple form is obtained if the density function itself is used for scaling, in which case equation (19) becomes [Vandorpe 71]:

$$\mathfrak{J}_{i+1/2} = \mu_{i+1/2} e^{(\psi_i + \psi_{i+1})/2} \left[\frac{n_{i+1} e^{-\psi_{i+1}} - n_i e^{-\psi_i}}{h} \right] . \tag{20}$$

As first observed by D. L. Scharfetter and H. K. Gummel all the above formulas may lead to gross errors in case of large voltage drops $|\nabla\psi| = |\psi_{i+1} - \psi_i|$ over a single mesh cell. This can easily be seen in equation (18) which in case of zero-current condition, cannot be satisfied by both n_i and n_{i+1} positive whenever $|\nabla\psi| > 2$, which is obviously an unphysical situation. As reported recently, the same type of error is associated with equations (19) and (20) [Mock 73]. A serious restriction of the mesh size may result in case of high bias voltages. A scheme which avoids this problem may be obtained by assuming J and E constant over the mesh cell and integrating the transport equation $J\mu^{-1} = nE + dn/dx$ yielding

$$\mathfrak{J}_{i+1/2} = -\mu_{i+1/2} \frac{\Delta\psi}{h} \left[\frac{n_{i+1}}{1 - \exp(\Delta\psi)} + \frac{n_i}{1 - \exp(-\Delta\psi)} \right] . \tag{21}$$

For $|\Delta\psi| << 1$, equation (21) reverts to the standard centered difference formula (18), whereas for $|\Delta\psi| >> 1$ a pure drift current of the form

$$\hat{J}_{i+1/2} = \begin{cases} \mu_{i+1/2} \frac{\Delta\psi}{h} n_{i+1} & \text{if} \quad \Delta\psi > 0 \\ \mu_{i+1/2} \frac{\Delta\psi}{h} n_i & \text{if} \quad \Delta\psi < 0 \end{cases} \tag{22}$$

is obtained. The superiority of this Scharfetter-Gummel scheme was recently demonstrated theoretically [Mock, to appear].

The discretization of Poisson's equation offers no problems. Standard five-point formulas [Varga 62] are most widely used. Care has to be taken that the discretization of the boundary conditions does not violate the current conservation property. Techniques for treating boundary conditions are well known (viz., the so-called phantom-point method) and need not be discussed in detail.

3.2 D.C. Problem

In case of the d.c. problem, the time derivatives in equations (1) and (2) are put to zero. In discretized form a set of nonlinear algebraic equations results which may be symbolically written as

$$A(\underset{\sim}{\psi})\underset{\sim}{n} = -\underset{\sim}{R} \tag{23}$$

$$B(\underset{\sim}{\psi})\underset{\sim}{p} = \underset{\sim}{R} \tag{24}$$

$$L\underset{\sim}{\psi} = \underset{\sim}{N} + \underset{\sim}{p} - \underset{\sim}{n} \tag{25}$$

where $\underset{\sim}{n}$, $\underset{\sim}{p}$, $\underset{\sim}{\psi}$, $\underset{\sim}{R}$ and $\underset{\sim}{N}$ are the vectors of grid values, and $A(\underset{\sim}{\psi})$, $B(\underset{\sim}{\psi})$ and L are band matrices (three-diagonal in the one-dimensional case, five-diagonal in the two-dimensional case). The proper form of $A(\underset{\sim}{\psi})$ and $B(\underset{\sim}{\psi})$ is defined by the finite-difference formulas used, i.e., in the case of the standard centered difference formula (18) $A(\psi)$ becomes

$$h^2A(\underline{\psi}) = h^2[a_{ij}(\underline{\psi})] = \begin{cases} D_{i+1/2} + \mu_{i+1/2}\frac{1}{2}(\psi_i - \psi_{i+1}) & \text{if } j=i+1 \\ -(D_{i+1/2} + D_{i-1/2}) + \frac{1}{2}\mu_{i+1/2}(\psi_i - \psi_{i+1}) & \\ \quad - \frac{1}{2}\mu_{i-1/2}(\psi_{i-1} - \psi_i) & \text{if } j=i \\ D_{i-1/2} - \mu_{i-1/2}(\psi_{i-1} - \psi_i) & \text{if } j=i-1 \\ 0 & \text{otherwise} \end{cases} \tag{26}$$

where in case of field-dependent μ and D it is $\mu_{i+1/2} = \mu(\psi_i - \psi_{i+1})$ etc.

Two methods have been in use to solve this system, namely:

(1) sequential iteration or Gummel's method,

(2) Newton's method.

Methods of the first kind are simple but have only a first order rate of convergence whereas Newton's method requires a more complicated equation setup but promise second-order convergence.

Sequential iteration is the most widely used method. It is based on the fact that the discretized continuity equation is linear in the density variables n and p or Φ_n and Φ_p (but not in ϕ_n and ϕ_p). This suggests the following algorithm:

Step 1:

Compute mobility and recombination rate for current values of $\underline{\psi}^k$, $\underline{n}^k$ and $\underline{p}^k$:

$$\underline{\mu}^k = \mu(\underline{\psi}^k) \quad , \quad \underline{R}^k = R(n^k, p^k)$$

Step 2:

For ψ^k fixed compute $\underline{n}^{k+1}$ and p^{k+1} such that the continuity equations are satisfied, i.e.

$$A(\underset{\sim}{\psi}^k)\underset{\sim}{n}^{k+1} = -\underset{\sim}{R}^k \quad , \quad B(\underset{\sim}{\psi}^k)\underset{\sim}{p}^{k+1} = \underset{\sim}{R}^k$$

Step 3:

Compute updated potential values $\underset{\sim}{\psi}^{k+1}$ as a function of the newly computed $\underset{\sim}{n}^{k+1}$ and $\underset{\sim}{p}^{k+1}$.

Steps 1 to 3 are repeated until the desired convergence is achieved (or divergence becomes apparent). Note that both Step 2 and Step 3 lead to systems of linear equations which in the two-dimensional case are of five-diagonal form and may be solved conveniently by standard iterative methods [Varga 62]. Logarithmic density variables Φ_n and Φ_p may substitute for n and p.

Many variations of this algorithm have been used. They differ mainly in the following:

(1) The density state variables, i.e., basic variables n and p [Dubock 70, Vandorpe 71], logarithmic variables Φ_n and Φ_p [Slotboom 69, Heydeman 71, Heimeier 73] or other [Mock 73].

(2) The finite-difference formulas (see section 31).

(3) The methods used in Step 3 (see discussion below).

(4) The methods for solving the systems of linear equations in Steps 2 and 3, i.e., point relaxation (SOR) [Slotboom 69, Dubock 70], line relaxation (LSOR) [Vandorpe 71, Heydemann 71, Mock 73], Douglas Racheford methods (ADI) [Vandorpe 72, Mock 73], or Stone's method (SIP) [Heimeier 73, Mock 73]. LSOR is particularly well suited for the insulated gate field-effect transistor whereas SIP is best if different device geometries are to be analyzed.

The simplest way to treat Step 3 would be simply to solve the Poisson's equation $-\nabla^2\psi^{k+1} = N + p - n$. This formula, however, was never actually used as it would lead to slow convergence. Most widely employed is the method of the original publication [Gummel 64], i.e.,

$$\nabla^2\psi^{k+1} + (n + p)[\psi^{k+1} - \psi^k] + N + p - n = 0 \quad . \tag{27}$$

This formula is derived by linearization of the nonlinear potential equation $-\nabla^2\psi + \Phi_p \exp(-\psi) - \Phi_n \exp(\psi) = 0$ around the current estimate ψ^k. A different approach to accelerating is the following two-stage iterative process:

$$\psi^{k+1} = \psi^k + \alpha^k[\overline{\psi}^{k+1} - \psi^k] + \beta^k[\psi^k - \psi^{k-1}] \tag{28}$$

where $\overline{\psi}^{k+1}$ is defined by $-\nabla^2\overline{\psi}^{k+1} = N + p - n$ and α^k and β^k are acceleration parameters for which appropriate Chebychev sequences can be constructed [Mock 73].

A mathematical analysis of the asymptotic rate of convergence was recently achieved under some simplifying assumptions [Mock 72]. Convergence problems are predicted for forward bias condition and high recombination rates. Some variations of the sequential iteration procedure avoiding these convergence problems were subsequently described [Seidmann 72]. The idea is to treat a linearized part of the recombination rate computation in Step 2 rather than in Step 1. Note, however, that the analysis which is based on a perturbation argument says nothing about the global convergence behavior. Unfortunately, the information about this most important question is only fragmentary. Figures from 20 to 200 overall iterations are found in the literature. Generally, convergence is slower:

(1) the more charge is stored in the device (i.e., the higher N);

(2) the higher the applied voltages;

(3) the higher the recombination rate.

Arriving at a suitable initial guess of the solution is a nontrivial problem. In case of large voltages, the full voltage drop may have to be applied in small steps at a time. It may even be necessary to build up the doping level slowly in order to avoid convergence problems.

<u>Newton's method</u> has so far been used in one-dimensional problems only [Scharfetter 69, Gaughey 69, Hachtel 72]. The difficulty with two-dimensional problems is the fact that now the Poisson and continuity equation have to be solved simultaneously, thus leading to a larger system of equations with more than five non-zero diagonals. If for simplicity holes are neglected, the equations take the form

$$F(\underset{\sim}{x}) = \begin{pmatrix} A(\underset{\sim}{\psi}) & 0 \\ I & L \end{pmatrix} \begin{pmatrix} \underset{\sim}{n} \\ \underset{\sim}{\psi} \end{pmatrix} - \begin{pmatrix} 0 \\ \underset{\sim}{N} \end{pmatrix} = 0 \quad , \tag{29}$$

where $\underset{\sim}{x}$ is the combined vector of mesh values, i.e., $\underset{\sim}{x}^T = (\underset{\sim}{n},\underset{\sim}{\psi})$ and I is the identity matrix. Then, Newton's method is:

$$\underset{\sim}{x}^{k+1} = \underset{\sim}{x}^k - J^{-1}(\underset{\sim}{x}^k)\, F(\underset{\sim}{x}^k) \tag{30}$$

or more conveniently for numerical computations:

$$J\underset{\sim}{x}^{k+1} = J(\underset{\sim}{x}^k)\underset{\sim}{x}^k - F(\underset{\sim}{x}^k) \tag{31}$$

where $J(x)$ is the Jacobian (i.e., $J_{ij} = \partial F_i/\partial x_j$). Since A and L are five-diagonal matrices, J has the structure

$$J = \begin{pmatrix} A & A' \\ I & L \end{pmatrix} \tag{32}$$

where $A, A' = \partial A(\underset{\sim}{\psi})/\partial\underset{\sim}{\psi}$ and L are all five-diagonal submatrices. Classical methods, such as SOR, are not suitable for solving this system of linear equations since J has more than five non-zero diagonals. Stone's method [Stone 68], however, is exactly tailored to such "coupled systems" and allows for a efficient solution. Promising results with this Newton-Stone's method have already been achieved [Hachtel, private comm.].

3.3 The Transient Problem

Finite difference schemes of the Crank-Nicholson type [Richtmeyer 57] are the simplest method for solving the transient problem. In case of electrons in the absence of holes, the discretized continuity equation takes the form:

$$\frac{\underset{\sim}{n}^{k+1} - \underset{\sim}{n}^k}{\Delta t} = \alpha A(\underset{\sim}{\psi}^{k+1})\underset{\sim}{n}^{k+1} + (1-\alpha)A(\psi^k)n^k \tag{33}$$

with an error term of the order $O(\Delta t^2, h^2)$ in case of $\alpha = 1/2$, $O(\Delta t, h^2)$ otherwise. In case of $\alpha = 0$ one speaks of an <u>explicit scheme</u>, $\alpha > 0$ are <u>implicit schemes</u>. As is well known, the explicit scheme, which is computationally very simple (no systems of equations) has a strong tendency towards instability and may require prohibitively small time steps, limited by the following stability condition [Reiser 72]:

$$\Delta t \leq \min \left\{ \frac{h^2}{2D}, \frac{2D}{v_{max}^2} \right\} \tag{34}$$

where $v_{max} = \max(\mu\vec{E})$ is the maximum drift velocity which in the case of field-dependent mobility is always finite and well known. Implicit schemes, which avoid this stability problem, lead to nonlinear systems of equations similar to those of the d.c. problem and which have to be solved for every time step. This is feasible in the one-dimensional case but may lead to an excessive amount of computing in the two-dimensional case. Therefore, despite the small Δt, explicit schemes were used for Gunn diode analysis. A compromise between the speed of the explicit method and the stability of the implicit method is the <u>half-implicit</u> method of M. Reiser. This method is based on the same principle as the sequential iteration, i.e., the fact that the continuity equation is linear in n, provided ψ is held fixed. This leads to the following algorithm for carrying out one time step:

<u>Step 1</u>:

Compute $\underset{\sim}{\psi}^k$ for given $\underset{\sim}{n}^k$ according to $L\underset{\sim}{\psi}^k = \underset{\sim}{N} - \underset{\sim}{n}^k$.

<u>Step 2</u>:

Compute new density from the system of linear equations

$$\frac{\underset{\sim}{n}^{k+1} - \underset{\sim}{n}^k}{\Delta t} = \frac{1}{2} A(\underset{\sim}{\psi}^k)\underset{\sim}{n}^{k+1} + \frac{1}{2} A(\underset{\sim}{\psi}^k)\underset{\sim}{n}^k \quad . \tag{35}$$

Both the above steps require the solution of five-diagonal systems of linear equations. Very efficient direct methods exist for the Poisson problem of Step 1

[Hockney 70] which should be utilized whenever possible. Standard iterative methods are appropriate for Step 2.

The instability giving rise to condition (34) is totally avoided by the half-implicit method. It was, however, found that decoupling of continuity and Poisson's equation introduced stability problems of a different kind, leading to the following restriction on Δt [Reiser 73]:

$$\Delta t < \frac{1}{\mu N} \quad . \tag{36}$$

Note that unlike equation (34), the above stability condition is independent of the space increment h. Also the behavior of the unstable solution is quite different from the exponential growth pattern of the diffusion (or linear) instability, i.e., it exhibits stationary standing waves in the density function. These oscillations preferably in neutral areas do not grow as time goes on but prevent the solution from reaching a steady-state. The stability condition (36) restricts the applicability of the half-implicit method to small doping levels $N < 10^{17} cm^{-3}$, as they are typical in Schottky-gate field-effect transistors and Gunn-effect devices. Where applicable, however, it is an efficient method and, owing to the increased stability, faster than the explicit method.

The transient solution is the most general one and a computer program for a transient analysis provides answers to the following problem areas:

(1) large signal responses;

(2) small signal analysis by means of Fourier analysis of step responses;

(3) steady-state or d.c. analysis.

To compute d.c. solutions one starts from a suitable initial condition and proceeds until a steady-state is reached. Unlike in the case of sequential iteration, this initial solution is completely uncritical and $\underset{\sim}{n}^{o} = \underset{\sim}{N}$ has proven to be a good choice. Furthermore, the method is very insensitive to large voltage steps and viewed as an iterative d.c. method, has a linear rate of convergence. It is therefore comparable in efficiency to the sequential iteration method but has the important advantage of giving additional information about important time-constants of the device as a by-product of each d.c. computation.

3.4 On the Problem of Accuracy

In many publications the adjective "accurate" appears in the title but they generally fall short of convincingly demonstrating its justification. The mathematical theory is still far from producing error bounds for a given mesh and even the somewhat weaker question of convergence of a given finite-difference scheme (i.e., whether the solution of the difference converges to the solution of the partial differential equation) generally remains unsolved. Some progress towards a mathematical treatment of the convergence problem has been made recently [Mock, to appear]. Bounds on the error in the total device current, introduced by an imperfect potential solution $\hat{\psi}$ were found. The assumptions are (1) $D = \mu =$ constant, (2) $\hat{n}$ and $\hat{p}$ such that the continuity equations are fulfilled <u>exactly</u> [i.e., $\nabla\cdot(\nabla\hat{n} - \hat{n}\nabla\hat{\psi}) = 0$], and (3) the current $\hat{I}$ is computed as a suitable average of the currents through the ohmic contacts. Then the error $|I - \hat{I}|$ is found to be bounded by

$$|I - \hat{I}| \le C_1 \sqrt{\hat{I}}\; ||\psi_{res}|| \tag{37}$$

where C_1 is a suitable constant, $||\cdot||$ is a norm and $\psi_{res} = \nabla^2\hat{\psi} + N + \hat{p} - \hat{n}$ are the potential residuals. Note that this result is obtained by purely analytical means for the general two-dimensional case with mixed boundary conditions. In one space dimension, equation (37) may be sharpened and applied to particular finite difference schemes. It is found that standard centered difference formulas for the Poisson problem together with Scharfetter-Gummel type formulas for the continuity equation yield an error $O(h^2)$ in the computed device current. Other schemes are shown to have larger error, i.e., of the form $O(h)$. This important theoretical result supports the earlier finding that th Scharfetter-Gummel formula is better than other common discretization schemes.

In the absence of a rigorous mathematical theory, numerical experiments are the only means of investigating the properties of numerical methods. The following should always be performed and the results disclosed in the publications:

(1) observation of the solution as the mesh is refined;

(2) convergence properties of the iterative equation solvers;

(3) check on the independence of the device current of the integration paths;

(4) single and double precision computations.

With regard to point 3, for example, it is generally found that a large portion of the required iterations is spent to slow and minute changes in the field variables in order to get a path independent current.

Round-off errors are an additional source of inaccuracy. Although there is generally no error build-up in the iterative equation solvers for the systems of linear equations arising, the finite precision arithmetic may lead to serious accuracy problems, especially in the case of fine meshes. Double precision computations are advisable when economically feasible. In the case of Scharfetter-Gummel formulas, special attention should be paid to the evaluation of exponential terms in the denominators. It is an advantage to test the value of $|\Delta\psi|$ and revert to a standard finite-difference formula in case of $|\Delta\psi| \ll 1$. Such a procedure is not only more efficient but reduces serious cancellation problems in computation of the terms $[1 - \exp(\Delta\psi)]$ and $[1 - \exp(-\Delta\psi)]$.

3.5 The Systems Aspect of Computer Programs for Device Analysis

Computer programs which embody the numerical methods described above usually represent a long programming effort in the neighborhood between one to five man-years. The ideal program has:

(1) a user oriented input language;

(2) a numerically stable equation solver which requires no extra information;

(3) a graphical result display and storage of already computed results in libraries

(4) programs for handling such result libraries.

Experience shows that the auxiliary components (1), (3) and (4) are a significant part of the whole programming effort, especially if graphical output is desired.

It is most desirable to have at least some primitive form of a graphical output. The simplest, fastest and least expensive means are chain-printer plots. The resolution of such plots is adequate for debugging and gross characterization of the solution. More sophisticated is the use of plotters or CRT displays. Perspective drawings or contour maps have both been used successfully. For tutorial purposes, movie pictures were made by several authors, i.e., [Slotboom, Hachtel] for steady-state solutions and [Reiser] for transient solutions. The most elaborate system described so far makes use of an interactive CRT terminal for result evaluation and history file handling [Reiser 72].

None of the computer programs known so far is general enough to handle several devices. They are all more or less ad-hoc (i.e., for one case only) solutions and running the programs usually requires supervision by the authors. There is still a long way to general purpose simualtion packages for a two-dimensional analysis like in common use for one-dimensional problems.

4. CONCLUSION

In about one decade, numerical device models have become an important tool for research and development of semiconductor devices. In the one-dimensional case, a conclusive state is reached. Scharfetter-Gummel finite-difference formulas paired with Newton's method have proven to be accurate, stable and efficient. Elaborate program packages with automatic control of the discretization prarameters such as mesh size have been implemented and extensively used for design of the bipolar transistor. Besides these d.c. programs, a.c. and transient solutions have been obtained for various devices. The computing capacity necessary for any desired one-dimensional solution is now freely available and procuring such solutions may be considered a routine task.

The situation in the two-dimensional case is far from such a definitive state. Computing costs are still a limiting factor to the proliferation of programs and the search for the best methods is in full progress. The only device, so far, where a two-dimensional analysis has played an important role is the short channel field-effect transistors. Finite difference methods using centered difference formulas on rectangular meshes are common to all the published results. Understandably, the d.c. problem is being most intensively investigated and the relatively simple and slow sequential iteration procedure is the main method for solving the systems of nonlinear equations. The Newton-Stone method is an interesting alternative and may very well prove similarly superior as in the one-dimensional case. Transient solutions have been obtained for low-doped devices but the simple schemes used are not capable of solving the general case. There is no way in sight to avoid this difficulty without exceeding reasonable bounds on the demand on computing.

The finite-difference methods used in semiconductor device analysis are rather primitive if measured by the standards of other fields in computational physics such as structural mechanics or fluid dynamics. <u>The finite-element method</u>, for example, has led to significant progress in the solution of more-dimensional boundary and initial value problems, the main advantage being

(1) the use of a triangular grid which allows arbitrary local refinement;

(2) variable order of accuracy of the discretized equations.

Application of the finite element method to the semiconductor problem is an open area for future research.

The trend in semiconductor technology is towards integration of full circuits on a single chip of semiconductor material. Analysis, so far, is limited to single devices only. It is clear that the numerical analysis and optimization of a full circuit would be the ultimate goal. In general, this would require a three-dimensional transient solution. Such a solution is not yet economically feasible and would approach the limits of the fastest computers. Some limited progress in applying numerical analysis to more complicated structures can be expected for charge coupled devices [Amelio 72] and CMOS memory cells which allow for a two-dimensional analysis.

As the limitations of the traditional diffusion model have now become apparent, a revival of the search for improved models will have to take place. Progress may be expected along two lines, viz.,

(1) improved "hydrodynamic" models based on moment equations (i.e., energy-balance model instead of diffusion model [Cheung 72]);

(2) spatially non-homogeneous solutions of the Boltzmann equation by Monte-Carlo or iterative methods.

The first approach, i.e., supplementing the diffusion model by the energy balance model goes hand in hand with a theoretical determination of the new energy transfer coefficients which enter into the model but at the time being are not accessible by experimental methods. The computational complexity of the energy-balance model is not seriously greater than that of the diffusion model. It might even be conjectured that the energy-balance model may lead to better conditioned equations.

The second approach, i.e., a microscopic model for the charge transport is computationally very demanding and reaches the limit of today's fastest computer. Such models are a combination of particle models, as is common in plasma physics and of Monte-Carlo methods. The idea of the method is to observe the time evolution of an ensemble of particles. At discrete points in time, the self-consistent field is computed and then the particles are moved and scattered for another time increment according to conventional Monte-Carlo procedures. Some first results in this direction are already available, i.e., a full microscopic simulation of a GaAs sample in one space dimension [Lebwohl 71] and results for two-dimensional problems under the simplifying assumptions of (1) a fixed (i.e., non-self-consistent) field [Ruch 72] and (2) a simplified law of motion in conjunction with a self-consistent field [Hockney 72]. Owing to the tremendous computing power required it is not likely that such models will supplant the "hydrodynamic" models in the near future. They are, however, a great scientific advance and will furnish important reference solutions against which simpler models can be validated.

ACKNOWLEDGMENT

The views expressed in this paper are the essence of many discussions with eminent scientists in the field of semiconductor technology and computing, most notably Prof. E. Baumann, Prof. Dejon, Prof. R. W. Hockney, Prof. Thomas, Dr. P.

Gueret, Dr. G. D. Hachtel, Dr. W. Jutzi, Dr. P. Wolf and J. W. Slotboom. The author is grateful for the assistance of all these people. He would also like to thank Mrs. Bruellmann for careful manuscipt reading.

REFERENCES

Amelio, G. F.: Computer modelling of charge-coupled device characteristics, The Bell Sys. Tech. J., 51, 705-730 (1972).

Arandjelovic, V.: Accurate numerical steady-state solutions for a diffused one-dimensional junction diode, Solid State Electron., 13, 865-871 (1970).

Caughey, M.: Simulation of UHF transistor small-signal behavior to 10 GHz for circuit modelling, Proc. Second Biennial Cornell E. E. Conf., IEEE Catalog No. 69 C 65-CORN (1969).

Cheung, P. S. and Hearn, C. J.: Energy balance model for Gunn-domains, Electron. Lett., 8, 79-81 (January 1972).

De Mari, A.: An accurate numerical steady-state one-dimensional solution of the p-n junction, Solid State Electron., 11, 33-58 (January 1968).

De Mari, A.: An accurate numerical one-dimensional solution of the p-n junction under arbitrary transient conditions, Solid State Electron., 11, 1021-1053 (November 1968).

Dubock, P.: Numerical analysis of forward and reverse bias potential distribution in a two-dimensional p-n junction with applications to capacitance calculations, Electron. Lett., 5, 236-238 (May 1969).

Dubock, P.: D.C. numerical model for arbitrarily biased bipolar transistors in two dimensions, Electron. Lett., 6, 53-55 (February 1970).

Fawcett, W., Boardman, A. D., and Swain, S.: Monte Carlo determination of electron transport properties in gallium arsenide, J. Phys. Chem. Solids, 31, 1963-1990 (July 1970).

Fulkerson, D. E.: A two-dimensional model for the calculation of common-emitter current gains of lateral p-n-p transistors, Solid State Electron., 11, 821-826 (August 1968).

Gummel, H. K.: A self-consistent iterative scheme for one-dimensional steady-state transistor calculations, IEEE Trans. Electron Devices, ED-11, 455-465 (October 1964).

Gokhale, B. V.: Numerical solutions for a one-dimensional silicon n-p-n transistor, IEEE Trans. Electron Devices, ED-17, 594-602 (August 1970).

Hachtel, G. D., Joy, R. C., and Cooley, J. W.: A new efficient one-dimensional analysis program for junction device modelling, Proc. of the IEEE, 60 (January 1972).

Heimeier, H. H.: A two-dimensional numerical analysis of a silicon N-P-N transistor, IEEE Trans. Electron Devices, ED-20 (August 1973).

Heydemann, M.: Methode numérique d'étude des structures M.O.S.T., Electron. Lett., 6, 735-737 (May 1971).

Himsworth, B.: A two-dimensional analysis of gallium-arsenide junction field-effect transistors with long and short channels, Solid-State Electron., 15, 1353-1361 (1972).

Hockney, R. W.: A fast solution of Poisson's equation using Fourier analysis, J. ACM, 12, 95-113 (January 1965).

Hockney, R. W.: The potential calculation and some applications, Meth. in Comp. Phys., 9, 135-211 (1970).

Hockney, R. W. and Reiser, M.: Two-dimensional particle models in semiconductors device analysis, IBM Res. Report, RZ482 (February 1972).

Hutzi, W. and Reiser, M.: Threshold voltage of normally off MESFET's, IEEE Trans. Electron Devices, ED-19, 514-522 (March 1972).

Katakoa, S., Tanteno, H., and Hawashima, M.: Two-dimensional computer analysis of dielectric-surface-loaded GaAs bulk element, Electron. Lett., 6, 169-171 (March 1970).

Kennedey, D. P. and O'Brien, R.: Electric current saturation in a junction field-effect transistor, Solid State Electron, 12, 829-830 (August 1969).

Kennedey, D. P. and O'Brien, R. R.: Computer-aided two-dimensional analysis of the junction field-effect transistor, IBM J. Res. Develop., 14, 95-116 (March 1971).

Kennedey, D. P. and O'Brien, R. R.: Two-dimensional analysis of J.F.E.T. structure containing a low-conductivity substrate, Electron. Lett., 7, 714-716 (December 1971).

Kilpatrick, J. A. and Ryan, W. D.: Two-dimensional analysis of lateral-base transistors, zelectron. Lett., 7, 226-227 (May 1971).

Kim, C. and Yang, E. S.: An analysis of current saturation mechanism of junction field-effect transistors, IEEE Trans. Electron Devices, E-17, 120-127 (February 1970).

Lebwohl, P. A. and Price, P. J.: Direct microscopic simulation of Gunn-domain phenomena, Applied Phys. Lett., 19, 530-532 (December 1971).

Lewis, J. A.: The flat plate problem for a semiconductor, Bell Syst. Tech. J., 49, 1484-1490 (September 1970).

Loeb, H. W., Andrew, R., and Love, W.: Application of two-dimensional solution of the Shockley-Poisson equation to inversion-layer MOST devices, Electron. Lett., 4, 352-354 (August 1969).

McCumber, D.E. and Chynoweth, A. G.: Theory of negative-conductance amplification and of Gunn instabilities in two-valley semiconductors, IEEE Trans. Electron Devices, ED-13, 4-21 (January 1966).

Mock, M.S.: On the convergence of Gummel's numerical algorithm, Solid-State Electron., 15, 1-4 (January 1972).

Mock, M. S.: A two-dimensional mathematical model of the insulated field-effect transistor, Solid State Electron., 16, 601-609 (1973).

Mock, M.S.: On the computation of semiconductor device current characteristics by finite difference methods, to appear.

Mock, M. S., On equations describing steady-state carrier distributions in a semiconductor device, to appear.

Petersen, O. G., Rikoski, R. A., and Cowles, W. W.: Numerical method for the solution of the transient behavior of bipolar semiconductor devices, Solid State Electron., 16, 239-251 (1973).

Reiser, M.: Two-dimensional anslysis of substrate effects in junction F.E.T.s, Electron. Lett., 6, 493-494 (August 1970).

Reiser, M.: Difference methods for the solution of the time-dependent semiconductor flow equations, Electron. Lett., 7, 353-355 (June 1971).

Reiser, M.: Zweidimensionale Lösung der instationären Halbleitertransportgleichungen für Feldeffekt-Transistoren, Ph.D. Thesis, Swiss Federal Institute of Technology (ETH) Zurich (July 1971).

Reiser, M. and Wolf, P.: Computer study of submersion F.E.T.s, Electron. Lett., 8, 254-256 (April 1972).

Reiser, M.: Large-scale numerical simulation in semiconductor device modelling, Computer Methods in Appl. Mech. and Eng., I, 17-39 (April 1973).

Reiser, M.: A two-dimensional numerical FET model for dc, ac, and large signal analysis, IEEE Trans. Electron Devices, 20, 35-45 (January 1973).

Reiser, M.: On the stability of finite difference schemes in transient semiconductor problems, Computer Meth. in Appl. Mech. and Eng., 2, 65-68 (1973).

Richtmeyer, R. D. and Morton, K. W.: Difference methods for initial value problems, New York, Wiley-Interscience (1957).

Ruch, J.G.: Electron dynamics in short channel field-effect transistors, IEEE Trans. Electron Devices, 19, 652-654 (May 1972).

Scharfetter, D. L. and Gummel, H. K.: Large-signal analysis of a silicon read diode oscillator, IEEE Trans. Electron Devices, 16, 64-77 (January 1969).

Seidman, T. I. and Choo, S. C.: Iterative scheme for computer simulation of semiconductor devices, Solid-State Electrons., 15, 1229-1235 (1972).

Slotboom, J. W.: Iterative scheme for one- and two-dimensional dc- transistor simulation, Electron. Lett., 5, 677-678 (December 1969).

Slotboom, J. W.: Computer aided two-dimensional analysis of bipolar transistor, IEEE Trans. Electron Devices, ED-20 (August 1973).

Stone, H. L.: Iterative solution of implicit approximations of multi-dimensional partial differential equations, SIAM J. Numer. Anal., 5, 530-558 (September 1968).

Stratton, R.: Semiconductor flow equations (diffusion and degeneracy), IEEE Trans. Electron Devices, ED-19, 1288-1292 (December 1972).

Suzuki, N., Yanai, H., and Ikoma, T.: Simple analysis and computer simulation of lateral spreading of space charge in bulk GaAs, IEEE Trans. Electron Devices, 19, 364-375 (March 1972).

Vandorpe, D. and Xuong, N. H.: Mathematical two-dimensional model of semiconductor devices, Electron. Lett., 7, 47-50 (January 1971).

Vandorpe, D., Barel, J., Merckel, G., and Saintot, P.: An accurate two-dimensional numerical analysis of the MOS transistor, Solid State Electron., 15, 547-557 (1972).

Varga, R. S.: Matrix iterative analysis, New Jersey, Prentice Hall, Inc., (1962).

Wasserstrom, E. and McKenna, J.: The potential due to a charged metallic strip on a semiconductor surface, Bell Syst. Tech. J., 49, 853-877 (May 1970).

Yanai, H., Suzuki, N., Sugeta, T., and Tainimoto, M.: Effect of electrode structure on dipole-domain formation, Proc. of the Third Intern. Symp. on GaAs and Rel. Compounds, the Inst. of Phys., London and Bristol, 153-162 (1970).

SIMULATION NUMERIQUE DE LA FABRICATION ET DU COMPORTEMENT DES DISPOSITIFS SEMICONDUCTEURS

D. VANDORPE

Institut de Physique Nucléaire de Lyon - 43, Bd du 11 novembre 1918
69 - VILLEURBANNE

L'évolution extrêmement rapide de la technologie des semi-conducteurs a entraîné une modification radicale de la manière de concevoir et de réaliser les circuits électroniques. Vu la complexité et le coût élevé des réalisations les concepteurs sont maintenant amenés à utiliser de façon courante les outils de la conception assistée par ordinateurs pour la simulation de leurs circuits avant réalisation.

Il est bien évident que la qualité d'une simulation sur ordinateur dépend essentiellement de la qualité des modèles utilisés, c'est ce qui a amené les électroniciens à développer une importante recherche dans le domaine des "Modèles Mathématiques".

Par ailleurs la réduction importante de la taille des dispositifs dans les circuits intégrés a accru fortement l'influence d'effets précédemment négligés (surface, bords des diverses zones des dispositifs, ...) aussi il est indispensable de tenir compte de ces phénomènes qui deviennent prépondérants pour certaines structures ce qui amène à affiner les modèles et à les rendre beaucoup plus complexes.

Le travail présenté ici a été commencé à l'Institut de Mathématiques Appliquées de Grenoble et financé en partie par la Délégation Générale à la Recherche Scientifique et Technique (contrat D. G. R. S. T. n° 67 00 864) et le Commissariat à l'Energie Atomique (contrat C. E. A. / GR - 751. 066).

Enfin on a toujours cherché à relier simplement la technologie et les processus de fabrication avec les modèles de composants. La simulation réalisée dans le cadre de cette étude apporte de nombreux éléments de réponse à ce problème. Elle permet en outre :

- de mieux comprendre certains phénomènes physiques fondamentaux,
- de relier les performances du dispositif à ses caractéristiques technologiques,
- d'aborder l'optimisation des dispositifs eux-mêmes.

On a vu apparaître ces dernières années de nombreuses études sur la simulation du comportement des dispositifs, unidimensionnelles tout d'abord, étudiant diodes et transistors bipolaires en fonctionnement statique (5, 9, 24) et dynamique (6, 30) puis bidimensionnelles statiques (2, 10, 22, 25) et même bidimensionnelles dynamiques pour des dispositifs particuliers (18). Toutes ces études reposent en général sur les mêmes hypothèses physiques fondamentales nécessaires à la mise en équation du problème. Elles nécessitent par ailleurs la connaissance préalable du profil de dopage du semi-conducteur qui intervient comme donnée numérique. Malheureusement la mesure expérimentale de ces profils est difficile et relativement imprécise si l'on cherche à connaître le dopage en fonction de la profondeur exclusivement, elle devient quasiment impossible si l'on désire un profil bidimensionnel réel.

Pour résoudre ce problème on a donc été amené à réaliser également une simulation numérique du processus technologique de fabrication des dispositifs (12, 15, 16, 27).

On présente ci-après les principaux problèmes rencontrés dans cette étude et la manière dont ils ont été résolus.

I - ETUDE NUMERIQUE DE LA DIFFUSION D'IMPURETES DANS UN SEMI-CONDUCTEUR.

I.1. - Système d'équations

Compte-tenu des divers mécanismes physiques de diffusion des impuretés dans le silicium et de leurs interactions possibles (15) on peut écrire (après normalisation des diverses fonctions) pour chaque type d'impuretés les équations

(1) $$\vec{J} = - D \ \overrightarrow{\text{grad}} \ (C) - \mu C . \vec{E} . Z$$

(2) $$\frac{\partial C}{\partial t} = - \text{div} \ (\vec{J})$$

où : $\vec{J}$ est le flux d'impuretés,

C la concentration,

E le champ électrique,

μ la mobilité de l'impureté,

Z la charge électrique de l'impureté,

D le coefficient de diffusion.

La réalisation d'un transistor par exemple nécessite la diffusion simultanée de deux types d'impuretés (donneurs et accepteurs notés C_A et C_D). Une fois introduites dans le réseau cristallin les impuretés s'ionisent et créent des charges libres. Pour évaluer le champ électrique E qui intervient dans le mécanisme de diffusion, il conviendrait donc de résoudre l'équation de Poisson et d'évaluer les courants des porteurs libres ce qui nous aménerait à analyser un modèle de conduction en transitoire à dopage variable en fonction du temps.

Cette façon d'aborder le problème serait sans doute envisageable sur un modèle à une variable géométrique mais semble irréaliste sur un modèle à deux variables géométriques, essentiellement en raison du temps de calcul nécessaire pour une telle étude.

On fait donc une hypothèse physique complèmentaire en admettant que la charge d'espace est nulle et que le système est à l'équilibre thermodynamique ce qui permet d'obtenir le système suivant :

(3) $$\frac{\partial C_D}{\partial t} = \frac{\partial}{\partial x}\left[D_D\left(h_D \frac{\partial C_D}{\partial x} - (h_D - 1)\frac{\partial C_A}{\partial x}\right)\right]$$

(4) $$\frac{\partial C_A}{\partial t} = \frac{\partial}{\partial x}\Big[D_A\left(h_A \frac{\partial C_A}{\partial x} - (h_A - 1)\frac{\partial C_D}{\partial x}\right)$$

Sur un modèle unidimensionnel et sur un modèle bidimensionnel :

(5) $$\frac{\partial C_D}{\partial t} = \frac{\partial}{\partial x}\left[D_D\left(h_D \frac{\partial C_D}{\partial x} - (h_D - 1)\frac{\partial C_A}{\partial x}\right)\right] + \frac{\partial}{\partial y}\left[D_D\left(h_D \frac{\partial C_D}{\partial y} - (h_D - 1)\frac{\partial C_A}{\partial y}\right)\right]$$

(6) $$\frac{\partial C_A}{\partial t} = \frac{\partial}{\partial x}\left[D_A \left(h_A \frac{\partial C_A}{\partial x} - (h_A - 1) \frac{\partial C_D}{\partial x}\right)\right] + \frac{\partial}{\partial y}\left[\left(D_A \left(h_A \frac{\partial C_A}{\partial y} - (h_A - 1) \frac{\partial C_D}{\partial y}\right)\right]$$

où x et y sont les variables géométriques,

t le temps,

les quantités h_A et h_D sont des fonctions de C_A et C_D.

(7) $$h_D = 1 + \frac{C_D}{2\,n_i}\;\frac{1}{\sqrt{\left(\frac{C_D - C_A}{2\,n_i}\right)^2 + 1}}$$

(8) $$h_A = 1 + \frac{C_A}{2\,n_i}\;\frac{1}{\sqrt{\left(\frac{C_D - C_A}{2\,n_i}\right)^2 + 1}}$$

n_i étant la concentration d'électrons libres dans le semi-conducteur intrinsèque ($n_i > 0$)

De même les coefficients de diffusion D_A et D_D varient en fonction de C_A et C_D d'après les lois :

(9) $$D_D = D_{\circ D}\,\frac{2 + \beta\left[\frac{C_D}{n_i} + 1\right]}{2 +}$$

(10) $$D_A = D_{\circ A}\,\frac{2 + \beta'\left[\frac{n_i}{C_A + n_i}\right]}{2 + {}'}$$

$D_{\circ A}$, $D_{\circ D}$ sont les valeurs des coefficients pour le semi-conducteur intrinsèque, β et β' sont des coefficients qui caractérisent le processus de diffusion de l'impureté considérée.

Toutes ces qualités sont strictement positives de même que les fonctions inconnues C_A et C_D .

I. 2. - Conditions aux limites

La fabrication des dispositifs se fait en plusieurs phases successives, les unes dites de prédépôt ou à faible température, on fait circuler un gaz porteur d'impuretés qui restent en surface du dispositif, les autres dites de redistribution qui se font à température élevée pour permettre aux impuretés de diffuser dans le volume. Les phases de redistribution sont accompagnées d'une oxydation en surface ce qui va poser un problème particulier dû à la présence de deux milieux différents (oxyde et silicium) les équations dans l'oxyde étant légèrement différentes. Par ailleurs, la position de la frontière géométrique ainsi que l'épaisseur totale varient au cours du temps.

Les conditions aux limites à prendre en compte sont alors les suivantes :

I. 2. 1. - Modèle unidimensionnel

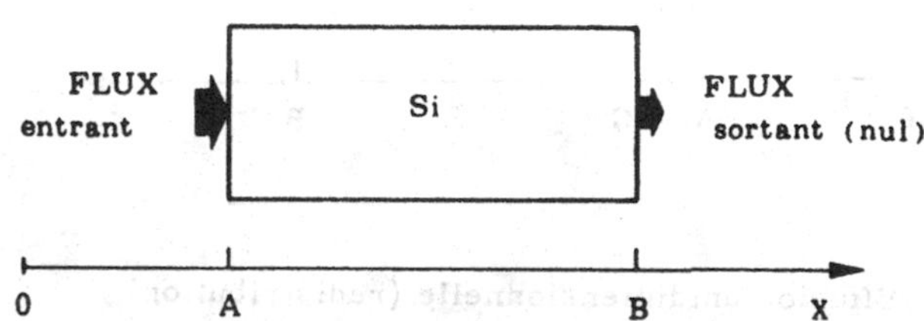

FIGURE 1 - Diffusion unidimensionnelle (prédépôt)

Dans le cas d'un prédépôt, on suppose que le flux sortant est nul, soit :

$$\frac{\partial C_D}{\partial x}(B) = \frac{\partial C_A}{\partial x}(B) = 0 \qquad (11)$$

On connaît les flux entrant en surface :

$$J_D = \alpha(C_\circ - C_D(A)) \qquad (12)$$

ou $J_A = \alpha\,(C_\circ - C_A(A))$

On ne prédépose en effet qu'une impureté à la fois.

α et $C_\circ$ sont des constantes positives.

On pourrait bien sûr prendre en considération dans le modèle toute autre condition aux limites qu'elle soit de type Dirichlet ou Neumann sans avoir à modifier sensiblement les programmes numériques.

La solution initiale utilisée sera soit le résultat d'une phase antérieure, soit une répartition uniforme (cas du premier pré-dépôt) pour la redistribution, on néglige l'influence du champ électrique dans l'oxyde et les valeurs des coefficients de diffusion sont différentes.

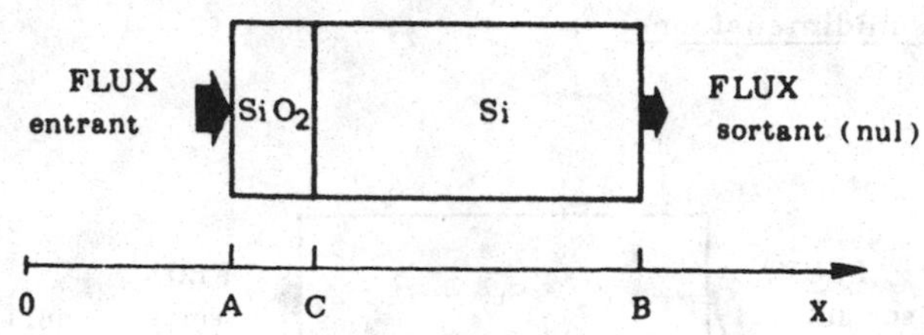

FIGURE 2 - Diffusion unidimensionnelle (redistribution)

Les conditions aux limites en A (t) et B sont les mêmes que pour le prédépôt (aux valeurs numériques près).

Les équations à l'interface Si SiO_2 sont :

$$\frac{C_{Si}}{C_{SiO_2}} = m$$

m : étant une constante positive (coefficient de ségrégation).

$$C_{SiO_2}\left(\gamma - \frac{1}{m}\right) V(t) = D_{SiO_2}\frac{\partial C_{SiO_2}}{\partial x} - D_{Si}\frac{\partial C_{Si}}{\partial x} \tag{13}$$

étant le rapport entre l'épaisseur de silicium oxydé et celle de silice créé

V (t) la vitesse d'oxydation.

On tient compte par ailleurs du déplacement géométrique des points

A et C , B étant supposé fixe.

La solution initiale est le résultat d'une phase antérieure.

I. 2. 2. - Modèle bidimensionnel

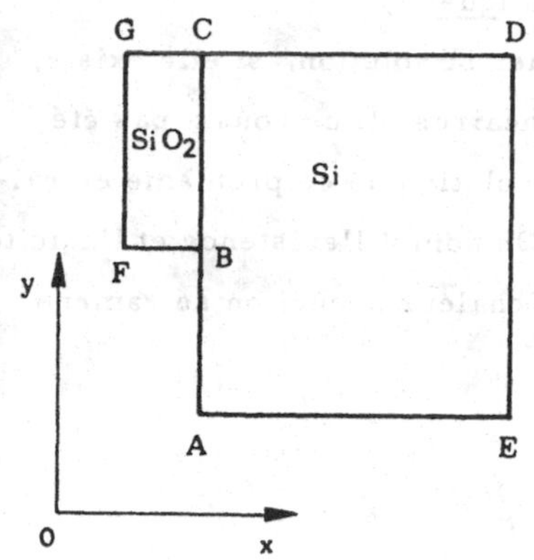

FIGURE 3 - Modèle bidimensionnel de diffusion (prédépôt)

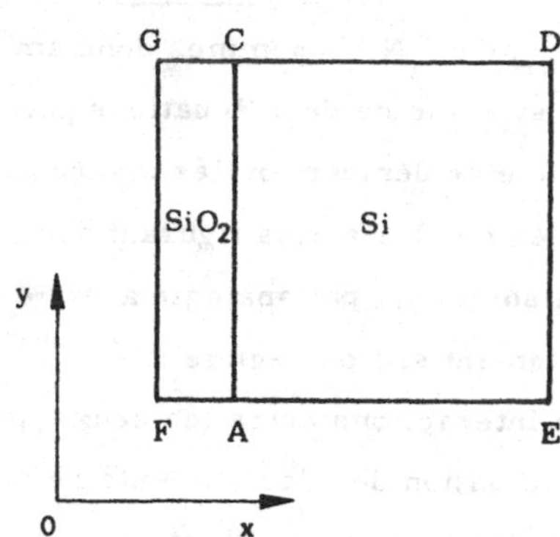

FIGURE 4 - Modèle bidimensionnel de diffusion (redistribution)

Nous faisons les mêmes hypothèses que pour le modèle unidimensionnel. Cependant dans cette étude, on devrait tenir compte de la présence d'oxyde même pour le prédépôt (en dehors de la "fenêtre" par laquelle s'effectue la diffusion). Cette présence n'ayant qu'une influence relativement faible nous n'en avons pas tenu compte rigoureusement et étudions uniquement le rectangle A C D E en supposant que, le long de B C , il n'y a pas d'échanges avec l'extérieur.

On a donc :

sur B C et D E $\quad \dfrac{\partial C}{\partial x} = 0$

sur C D et A E $\quad \dfrac{\partial C}{\partial y} = 0$

sur A B $\quad J_n = f(C)$

où J_n est la composante normale du flux d'impuretés. On a pris pour J_n la même fonction f que précédemment soit :

$$f(C) = \alpha (C_\circ - C) \tag{14}$$

Pour la redistribution les conditions aux limites sont identiques à celles du prédépôt (aux valeurs des constantes près) et on ne tient plus compte de l'existence de la fenêtre de diffusion en supposant que la vitesse de croissance d'oxyde est indépendante de Y et que l'épaisseur d'oxyde est nulle au début de la phase de redistribution. L'équation d'interface est la même que celle écrite précédemment sur le modèle unidimensionnel.

I. 3. - Position du problème mathématique

Nous sommes donc amenés à rechercher la solution, si elle existe, d'un système de deux équations paraboliques non linéaires. Il ne nous a pas été possible de démontrer l'existence et l'unicité de la solution de ce problème en raison des non linéarités figurant dans les équations. On admet l'existence et l'unicité de la solution, par analogie avec le problème de la chaleur auquel on se ramène exactement si l'on néglige :

- les interactions entre les deux types d'impuretés,
- la variation des "coefficients de diffusion",
- les effets du champ électrique.

Ce système étant impossible à intégrer formellement, on remplace le problème continu par un problème discret en utilisant pour ce faire une méthode de différences finies. Il conviendrait alors de démontrer que la limite, quand les grandeurs des pas de discrétisation tendent vers zéro, de la solution du problème discret tend vers la solution du problème continu. Cette démonstration n'a pu être faite. Nous sommes conduits à admettre ce résultat, après avoir vérifié en faisant plusieurs essais numériques sur le même cas, avec des valeurs de pas différentes que la solution trouvée ne dépend pas du maillage choisi.

I. 4. - Méthodes numériques de traitement

Pour tenir compte correctement des variations des phénomènes de diffusion dans l'espace et le temps, nous sommes amenés à utiliser des pas de discrétisation variables en X , Y , T.

On écrit chacune des deux équations à traiter sous la forme (en bidimensionnel) :

(15) $$L(u) = \frac{\partial u}{\partial t} - \frac{\partial}{\partial x}\left(a \frac{\partial u}{\partial x}\right) - \frac{\partial}{\partial y}\left(a \frac{\partial u}{y}\right) - b = 0$$

où a et b sont des fonctions de x et t dans lesquelles on fait entrer tous les termes non linéaires et ceux dépendant de la seconde impureté, séparant ainsi le système complet en deux sous-systèmes où l'on considère qu'il n'y a qu'une fonction inconnue C_A ou C_D.

On approxime les dérivées de u par une méthode classique de différences finies (7, 29).

Pour des raisons de stabilité (11) nous avons choisi une méthode purement implicite.

Cette façon de faire, nous amène alors à utiliser un processus de calcul itératif basé sur la méthode du point fixe. Ceci n'est pas un inconvénient car, en raison de la non linéarité du problème, cette solution se serait imposée naturellement. Par contre, un avantage important de ces choix réside dans le fait que les matrices des systèmes d'équations linéaires rencontrés dans le processus de calcul sont :

- tridiagonales pour le modèle unidimensionnel,
- tridiagonales par bloc pour le modèle bidimensionnel,

ce qui simplifie grandement les calculs nécessaires à la résolution des systèmes. On précisera ultérieurement les méthodes de calcul utilisées.

I. 5. - Algorithme et programmes

La méthode exposée ci-dessus a été programmée pour les deux modèles uni et bidimensionnels. L'algorithme général est identique dans les deux cas :

1) - Entrée des données et initialisation.
2) - Calcul du pas en temps. Calcul éventuel de l'épaisseur d'oxyde créée.
3) - Calcul des coefficients de diffusion.
4) - Résolution des deux systèmes d'équations.
5) - Test convergence et retour éventuel en 3.
6) - Test final, retour éventuel en 2.

Les programmes sont écrits en Fortran IV et utilisés sur matériel IBM 360 50 et 67 . Ils sont relativement courts (1000 cartes environ pour le modèle bidimensionnel sous système CP/CMS) et rapides. Le calcul pour un intervalle de temps nécessite 90 à 30 itérations pour le modèle bidimensionnel et de 15 à 3 itérations pour le modèle unidimensionnel.

Un modèle de tracé automatique fournit à l'utilisateur une représentation graphique des résultats.

I. 6. - Résultats obtenus

On donne à titre d'exemple sur la figure 5 le résultat de la simulation bidimensionnelle de la fabrication d'un transistor bipolaire sur du silicium. L'analyse physique de tels résultats a déjà été entreprise (11) et les conclusions que l'on en tire sont très intéressantes pour les électroniciens, tant pour la compréhension physique des phénomènes que pour l'amélioration de la technologie et l'optimisation

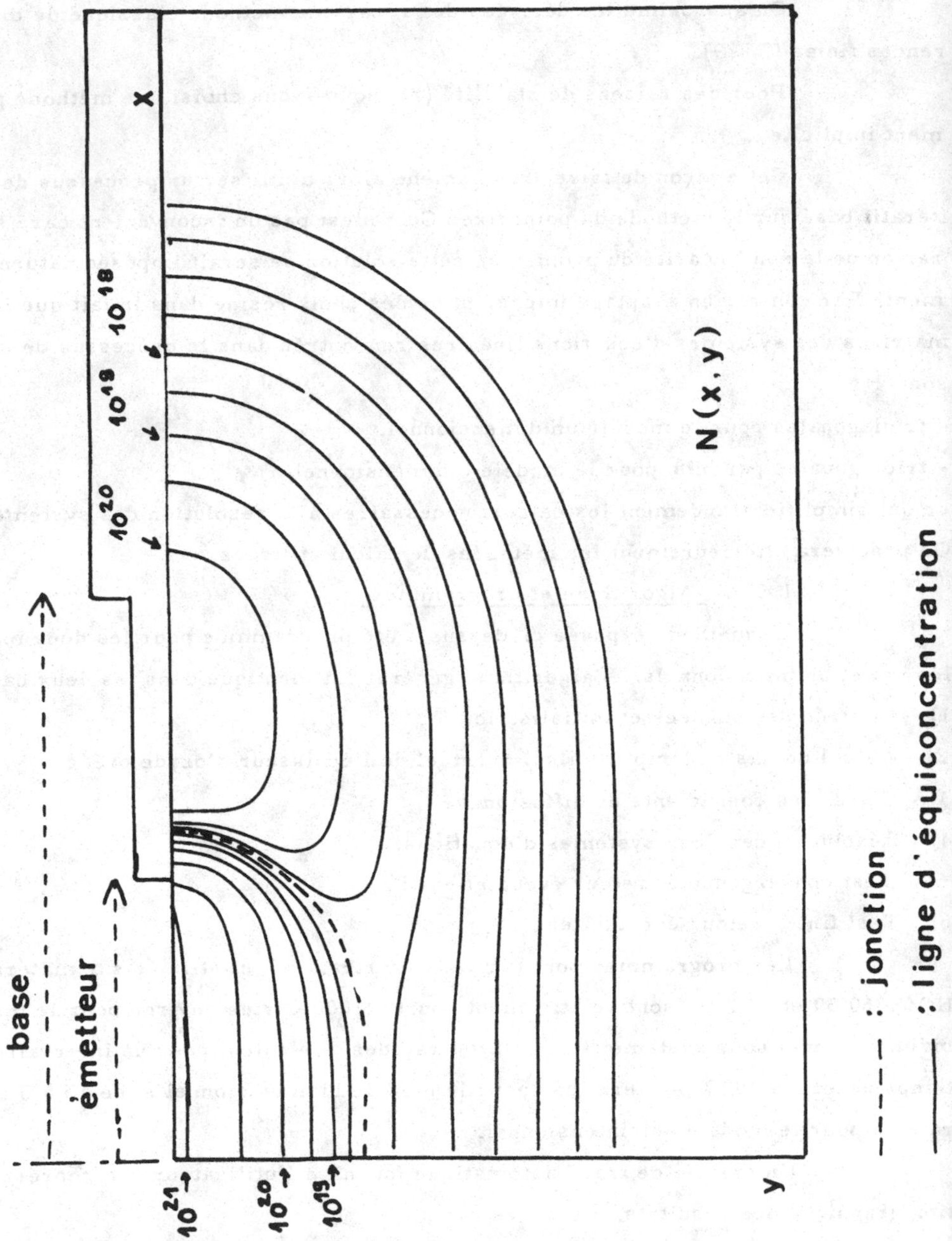

FIGURE 5 - Simulation de la fabrication d'un transistor

des dispositifs. Signalons simplement à ce propos que les programmes DIFFUSI sont utilisés de façon courante dans plusieurs laboratoires.

II - ETUDE NUMERIQUE DU FONCTIONNEMENT DE CERTAINS DISPOSITIFS SEMICONDUCTEURS

L'étude numérique des phénomènes de conduction dans les dispositifs semiconducteurs présentée ici résulte de considérations classiques de physique du solide. On peut montrer que sous certaines hypothèses raisonnables, généralement vérifiées on peut écrire le système d'équations.

$$\vec{j}_n = q\mu_n\, n\, \vec{e} + q\, d_n\, \vec{grad}\,(n) \tag{16}$$

$$\vec{j}_p = q\mu_p\, p\, \vec{e} - q\, d_p\, \vec{grad}\,(p) \tag{17}$$

$$\frac{\partial p}{\partial t} = -R - \frac{1}{q}\ \mathrm{div}\,(\vec{j}_p) \tag{18}$$

$$\frac{\partial n}{\partial t} = -R + \frac{1}{q}\ \mathrm{div}\,(\vec{j}_n) \tag{19}$$

$$\mathrm{div}\,(\vec{e}) = \frac{q}{\varepsilon}\,(n - p - \mathrm{dop}) \tag{20}$$

Les symboles utilisés étant définis dans la table ci-dessous

On transforme ce système d'équations en définisant un nouveau système d'unités pour obtenir :

$$\vec{J}_p = -\frac{1}{\gamma_p}\left(\vec{grad}\,(P) + P\ \vec{grad}\,(\Psi)\right) \tag{21}$$

$$\vec{J}_n = \frac{1}{\gamma_n}\left(\vec{grad}\,(N) - N\ \vec{grad}\,(\Psi)\right) \tag{22}$$

$$\frac{P}{T} = -U - \mathrm{div}\,(\vec{J}_p) \tag{23}$$

$$\frac{N}{T} = -U + \mathrm{div}\,(\vec{J}_n) \tag{24}$$

$$\nabla^2\Psi = N - P - DOP \tag{25}$$

Les inconnues principales seront N, P, Ψ , on supposera connaître les expressions analytiques de γ_n, γ_p , U en fonction de N, P, Ψ et de leurs dérivées. La fonction DOP est connue (en général numériquement) en fonction des variables géométriques.

TABLE 1 - LISTE DES SYMBOLES

Symbole		Grandeur représentée
non normalisé	normalisé	
x, y	X, Y	Variables géométriques
t	T	temps
n	N	concentration d'électrons libres
p	P	concentration de trous
$\vec{j}_t$	$\vec{J}_t$	densité de courant externe
$\vec{j}_n$	$\vec{J}_n$	densité de courant d'électrons
$\vec{j}_p$	$\vec{J}_p$	densité de courant de trous
$\vec{e}$	$\vec{E}$	champ électrique
v	Ψ	potentiel électrostatique
μ_n	γ_n^{-1}	mobilité des électrons
μ_p	γ_p^{-1}	mobilité des trous
d_n	D_n	coefficient de diffusion des électrons
d_p	D_p	coefficient de diffusion des trous
dop	DOP	dopage du semiconducteur
R	U	bilan génération - recombinaison
τ_p	TAUP	durée de vie des trous
τ_n	TAUN	durée de vie des électrons
q		charge de l'électron

N et P sont des fonctions strictement positives de même que γ_n et γ_p.

2.1. - Conditions aux limites

On a étudié ce problème sur des modèles géométriques à une puis à deux dimensions. L'analyse unidimensionnelle a été faite en régime statique et en régime dynamique, en tenant compte éventuellement de phénomènes particuliers tels la génération par effet d'avalanche (13) ou par effets des rayonnements (18) l'analyse bidimensionnelle a été réalisée uniquement en régime statique.

2.1.1. - Conditions aux limites sur le modèle unidimensionnel statique

Sur ce modèle on ne peut étudier que des dispositifs ou les effets de surface sont négligeables tels la jonction PN et le transistor bipolaire.

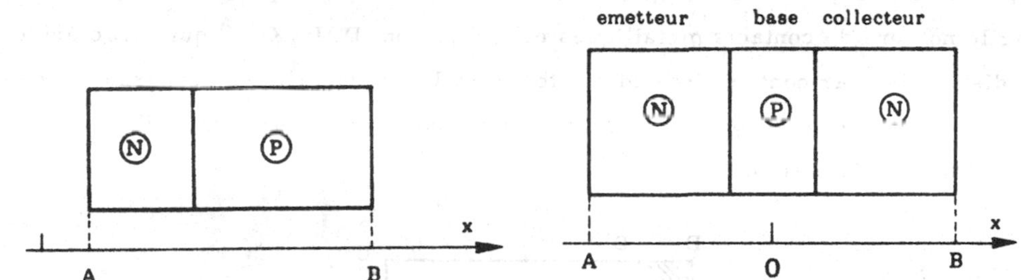

FIGURE 6 - Modèle unidimensionnel de jonction PN

FIGURE 7 - Modèle unidimensionnel de transistor NPN

Aux deux limites A et B on a alors des conditions de type Dirichlet sur les trois inconnues N, P, Ψ car les points A et B représentent les contacts métalliques sur lesquels on suppose vérifier les conditions de neutralité électrique.

Pour le transistor bipolaire il faut tenir compte du contact de base ce qui est impossible de façon rigoureuse. On peut résoudre partiellement cette difficulté en fixant l'origine des potentiels (qui sont définis à une constante additive près) par une hypothèse physique complémentaire donnant la valeur de $\Psi_{(o)}$.

2.1.2. - Conditions aux limites sur le modèle unidimensionnel dynamique

Pour l'étude dynamique de ce problème il s'avère que le choix des variables principales doit être modifié et que l'on a intérêt à étudier les fonctions N, P, E les conditions aux limites sur N et P étant comme précédemment de type Dirichlet, les conditions aux limites sur E étant par contre de type Neumann.

(26) $$\frac{\partial E(A, T)}{\partial X} = \frac{\partial E(B, T)}{\partial X} = 0 \qquad \forall \; T$$

Les conditions initiales étant alors soit le résultat d'un calcul en statique, soit le résultat d'un précédent calcul en dynamique quand on désire poursuivre une simulation.

On doit par ailleurs imposer en outre la contrainte due au circuit extérieur sous la forme :

(27) $$f\left(\left(\Psi_B(T) - \Psi_A(T) \right),\; J_t(T) \right) = 0$$

2.1.3. - Conditions aux limites sur le modèle bidimensionnel statique

Nous ne donnons ici que les conditions aux limites sur le modèle de jonction PN représenté en figure 8. En effet les divers dispositifs ne diffèrent que par le nombre de contacts métalliques et la fonction DOP (X, Y) qui caractérise le dispositif. Par contre, on étudiera toujours les dispositifs en supposant l'existence d'une couche d'oxyde en surface, cette couche étant surmontée d'une électrode métallique (anneau de garde).

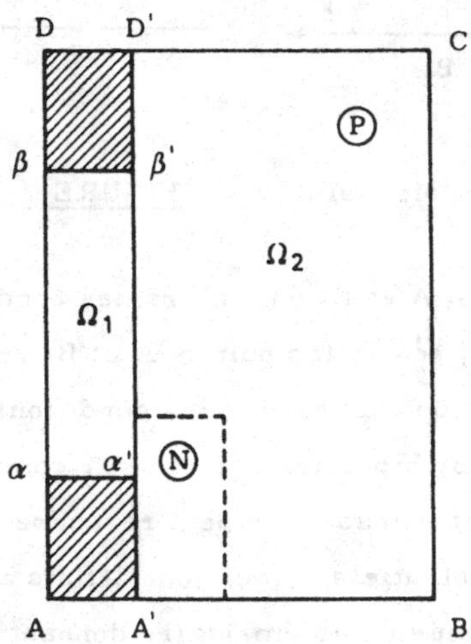

FIGURE 8 - Modèle géométrique de jonction PN

Sur le modèle les parties hachurées correspondent à l'emplacement des contacts métalliques. On étudie les deux fonctions N et P sur le rectangle A' B C D' et la fonction sur le rectangle A B C D. C'est-à-dire que pour chaque dispositif les fonctions N et P ne sont définies que sur le rectangle représentant le semi-conducteur (Ω_2) alors que le potentiel est étudié dans le semi-conducteur et dans l'oxyde ($\Omega_1 \cup \Omega_2$).

Pour les contacts métalliques tels AA'$\alpha\alpha'$ on a $\Psi(X, Y) = \Psi_1$

et sur A'α' $\quad P(X_1, Y) = P_1$

$N(X_1, Y) = N_1$

et D D'$\beta\beta$' on a $\quad \Psi(X, Y) = \Psi_2$

et sur D ' $\quad P(X_1, Y) = P_2$

$N(X_1, Y) = N_2$

Pour l'électrode de garde $\alpha\beta$ on a $\quad \Psi(X_o, Y) = \Psi_3$

Pour les fonctions du dispositif on a :

sur A' B et D' C $\quad \dfrac{\partial \Psi}{\partial y} = \dfrac{\partial N}{\partial y} = \dfrac{\partial P}{\partial y} = 0$

sur B C $\quad \dfrac{\partial \Psi}{\partial x} = \dfrac{\partial N}{\partial x} = \dfrac{\partial P}{\partial x} = 0$

et sur une interface tel $\alpha'\beta'$ on a les relations :

(28) $$\frac{1}{\gamma_n}\left(\frac{\partial N}{\partial x} - N\frac{\partial \Psi}{\partial x}\right) = \frac{1}{\gamma_p}\left(\frac{\partial P}{\partial x} + P\frac{\partial \Psi}{\partial x}\right) = f(N, P)$$

(29) $$C\,\frac{\partial \Psi_-}{\partial x} - \frac{\partial \Psi_+}{\partial x} = g(\Psi)$$

où les fonctions f et g représentent les phénomènes d'interface et C est une constante.

Dans les essais numériques effectués on a pris :

(30) $$f(N, P) = \frac{A}{P + N}\,(PN - 1)$$

(31) $$g(\Psi) = B\,(\Psi - \Psi_o)$$

où A, B, Ψ_o sont des constantes positives. On a donc un problème mixte à résoudre.

2. 2. - <u>Existence et unicité de la solution</u>

Il ne nous a pas été possible de démontrer l'existence et l'unicité de la solution de ce problème non linéaire.

On a pu alors obtenir quelques résultats très parcellaires d'une telle démonstration (25) mais les hypothèses qu'il est alors nécessaire de faire sont si restrictives que la portée de ces démonstrations reste très limitée.

Nous supposons donc que la solution du problème existe et est unique avant de mettre en oeuvre une méthode numérique pour en trouver une solution approchée discrète.

2.3. - Méthodes numériques de traitement

Pour chacun des modèles réalisés on a employé une méthode de point fixe de type itératif après avoir discrétisé le problème par une méthode de différences finies appropriée. Le choix de la méthode de point fixe itératif s'imposait en effet assez naturellement en raison des non linéarités du problème à traiter. Par ailleurs on peut remarquer, sur le système à intégrer, que si l'on suppose connaître ψ, alors on peut étudier séparément les problèmes en N et P définis par les équations (22) et (24) d'une part, (21) et (23) d'autre part. Par contre si l'on suppose connaître N et P on peut alors résoudre le problème en ψ défini par l'équation (25). Cette séparation en trois problèmes plus simples à traiter simplifiera notablement le traitement et s'insérera très facilement dans la méthode de point fixe choisie également en raison de ce découpage.

2.3.1. - Modèle unidimensionnel statique

On a repris pour ce problème l'algorithme proposé par Gummel[9] et amélioré par De Mari[5] en lui apportant des simplifications importantes[24].

Le système d'équations s'écrit alors :

$$J_p(X) = -\frac{1}{\gamma_p}\frac{dP(X)}{dX} + P(X)\frac{d\psi}{dX} \tag{32}$$

$$J_n(X) = \frac{1}{\gamma_n}\frac{dN(X)}{dX} - N(X)\frac{d\psi}{dX} \tag{33}$$

$$\frac{dJ_n(X)}{dX} = U \tag{34}$$

$$\frac{dJ_p(X)}{dX} = -U \tag{35}$$

$$\frac{d^2\psi}{dX^2} = N(X) - P(X) - DOP \tag{36}$$

où l'on connaît $\gamma_n(X)$, $\gamma_p(X)$ et DOP (X).

Une des principales difficultés numériques de ce problème provient du fait que les expressions (32) et (33) font intervenir les différences de quantités très grandes devant J_p et J_n comme une évaluation grossièrement approchée le mont[re]. On a alors intérêt, pour faire apparaître un terme calculable de façon précise à i[...]

troduire les variables intermédiaires λ et μ définies par :

$$(37) \qquad N = \lambda \, e^{\Psi}$$

$$(38) \qquad P = \mu \, e^{-\Psi}$$

On peut ensuite intégrer les équations (32) et (33) transformées par ce changement de variables et l'on a pour une fonction PN, par exemple :

$$(39) \qquad \lambda(X) = -\int_X^B \gamma_n(t) \, J_n(t) \, e^{-\Psi(t)} \, dt + \lambda(B)$$

Cette expression étant calculable car, compte-tenu des conditions aux limites et de l'équation (34), on a :

$$(40) \qquad J_n(X) = \int_A^X U(t)\,dt + \frac{\lambda(B) - \lambda(A)}{\int_A^B \gamma_n(t) \, e^{-\Psi(t)} \, dt} - \frac{\int_A^B \gamma_n(t) \, e^{-\Psi(t)} \left[\int_A^t U(y)\,dy\right] dt}{\int_A^B \gamma_n(t) \, e^{-\Psi(t)} \, dt}$$

On voit apparaître dans ces expressions une autre difficulté due à la présence des termes tels e^{Ψ} ou $e^{-\Psi}$. En effet pour des polarisations appliquées de l'ordre de 10 volts Ψ varie de 0 à 4000 environ. Par ailleurs les ordres de grandeur des quantités N et P varient de l'ordre de 10^{-10} à 10^{6} ce qui montre bien que les quantités λ, μ et e^{Ψ} ou $e^{-\Psi}$ sont impossibles à calculer sur ordinateur.

On résoud ici ce problème en exprimant les équations de type (39) à l'aide des quantités N et P pour obtenir :

$$(41) \qquad N(X) = e^{-\Psi(X)} \left[\int_X^B \gamma_n \, J_n(t) \, e^{-\Psi(t)} - N(B) \, e^{-\Psi(B)} \right]$$

et on évaluera les expressions de type $\int_X^B \gamma_n \, e^{-\Psi(t)} \, dt$ en introduisant des fonctions telles :

$$(42) \qquad F_n(X) = \int_X^B \gamma_n \, e^{\Psi(X) - \Psi(t)} \, dt = e^{(X)} \int_X^B {}_n \, e^{-\Psi(t)} dt$$

ce qui permettra ensuite de faire apparaître dans les expressions donnant N (X) des produits tels $e^{\Psi(X)} \; e^{-\Psi(X)} = 1$.

On aura donc cette fois des quantités calculables sur ordinateur de façon simple, ceci quelque soit la valeur de la polarisation appliquée.

En outre, en reportant les valeurs obtenues dans les expressions type 41 on obtient immédiatement la valeur de N et P ou plus précisément λ et μ qui sont les inconnues que l'on cherche à déterminer . La détermination de Ψ se fera ensuite à partir de l'équation :

$$\frac{d^2\Psi}{dx^2} = \lambda e^{\Psi} - \mu e^{-\Psi} - DOP \tag{43}$$

que l'on discrétisera par une méthode de différences finies après avoir utilisé un processus de quasi linéarisation en posant, à la k + lième itération :

$$\Psi_{k+1} = \Psi_k + \alpha_k \tag{44}$$

pour obtenir :

$$\frac{d^2\alpha_k}{dx^2} - \alpha_k\,(\lambda e^{\Psi_k} + \mu e^{-\Psi_k}) = \lambda e^{\Psi_k} - \mu e^{-\Psi_k} - DOP - \frac{d^2\Psi_k}{dx^2} \tag{45}$$

On utilise alors l'algorithme général suivant :

1) - Détermination d'une fonction Ψ_o (x) de départ (à partir de considérations physiques).
2) - Calcul de λ et μ à partir de Ψ on en tire N et P.
3) - Calcul de Ψ à partir de λ et μ .
4) - Test convergence et retour éventuel en 2.
5) - Edition des résultats.

Des programmes correspondant aux divers dispositifs ont été écrits à partir de cette méthode. Ils sont écrits en FORTRAN IV et comportent 5 à 600 cartes. Ils sont très rapides et d'un emploi aisé. Ils sont d'ailleurs utilisés de façon courante dans plusieurs laboratoires de constructeurs et d'universités.

Cependant, sous certaines conditions, des difficultés de convergence peuvent apparaître. Une condition de convergence a pu être mise en évidence par Mock[(14)] et des solutions à ce problème qui avait été constaté expérimentalement ont été proposés ce qui permet d'obtenir la solution dans tous les cas (21, 27).

2.3.2. - Modèle unidimensionnel dynamique

Dans le cas d'une étude dynamique on se rend compte immédiatement que le choix de la variable ψ se révèle très maladroit. En effet il est indispensable de tenir compte de l'équation d'évolution du champ électrique (équation de Maxwell).

$$(46) \qquad \frac{\partial E(X, T)}{\partial T} = J_t(T) - (J_n(X, T) + J_p(X, T))$$

et donc de choisir E comme fonction inconnue, les équations donnant N et P s'écrivant en ce cas :

$$(47) \qquad \frac{\partial N}{\partial T} = \frac{\partial J_n}{\partial X} - U$$

$$(48) \qquad \frac{\partial P}{\partial T} = - \frac{\partial J_p}{\partial X} - U$$

Expressions dans lesquelles on remplace $\frac{\partial J_n}{\partial X}$, $\frac{\partial J_p}{\partial X}$, J_n, J_p et U par leurs valeurs en fonction de N, P et E.

Dans ce modèle unidimensionnel dynamique on a pu tenir compte de phénomènes particuliers et fort importants de par leurs applications pratiques tels les effets de génération par avalanche (13) et effets de rayonnements (8) qui sont des phénomènes essentiellement transitoires qui modifient entièrement le comportement du dispositif en des intervalles de temps très brefs (quelques nanosecondes).

Ce modèle utilise les mêmes techniques de discrétisation que celles évoquées précédemment et nous employons toujours une méthode de discrétisation, par rapport au temps, purement implicite ainsi qu'une quasi-linéarisation systématique pour éliminer les non-linéarités qui apparaissent dans les diverses expressions. Ce qui nous amène de nouveau à devoir résoudre des systèmes d'équations linéaires dont la matrice est tridiagonale en utilisant encore la séparation du problème en deux sous-problèmes liés, l'un donnant E, l'autre N et P.

L'algorithme général est alors le suivant :

1) - Initialisation à partir du modèle statique.
2) - Evaluation du pas en temps et incrémentation du temps.
3) - Evaluation éventuelle du courant extérieur.
4) - Calcul de U en tenant compte éventuellement de la génération par avalanche et par effets ionisants.
5) - Calcul des corrections sur E, N, P.
6) - Test convergence et retour éventuel en 4 ou 3 selon le signal appliqué.

7) - Test fin et retour éventuel en 2.

8) - Edition des résultats.

Un certain nombre de problèmes restant à préciser et en particulier la génération automatique des pas de discrétisation en X et en temps qui se fait en fonction des résultats obtenus dans le calcul (13) pour réaliser le meilleur compromis possible entre l'accroissement de l'erreur, due à des pas trop grands et la durée du temps de calcul nécessaire, due à des pas trop petits.

Des programmes de simulation ont été écrits à partir de cette méthode. On montre à titre d'exemple (figure 9) les résultats obtenus dans la simulation d'une diode hyperfréquence en fonctionnement TRAPATT .

L'emploi de ces programmes est très simple. Le coût de la simulation dépend par contre énormément des phénomènes simulés variant de quelques secondes C. P. U. pour un fonctionnement normal à plus de 20 minutes pour simuler une période de fonctionnement hyperfréquence en raison de l'extrême rapidité des phénomènes (le temps correspondant à une exploitation sur matériel CDC 6600).

Cependant la richesse des informations fournies permet d'expliquer des phénomènes jusqu'alors peu clairs et justifie le coût de telles simulations (8).

2. 3. 3. - Modèle bidimensionnel statique

Compte-tenu du changement de variables donné par les équations (37) et (38) le système d'équations à intégrer d'écrit :

$$\frac{\partial}{\partial x}\left(\frac{1}{\gamma_n} e^{\psi} \frac{\partial \lambda}{\partial x}\right) + \frac{\partial}{\partial y}\left(\frac{1}{\gamma_n} e^{\psi} \frac{\partial \lambda}{\partial y}\right) = U \tag{49}$$

$$\frac{\partial}{\partial x}\left(\frac{1}{\gamma_p} e^{-\psi} \frac{\partial \mu}{\partial x}\right) + \frac{\partial}{\partial y}\left(\frac{1}{\gamma_p}\left(\frac{1}{\gamma_p} e^{-\psi} \frac{\partial \mu}{\partial y}\right) = U \tag{50}$$

$$\frac{\partial^2 \psi}{\partial x^2} + \frac{\partial^2 \psi}{\partial y^2} = \lambda e^{\psi} - \mu e^{-\psi} - DOP \tag{51}$$

On discrétise chacune des équations par une méthode de différences finies spécialement adaptée à ce type d'équation elliptique auto-adjointe (29), soit si l'on appelle r_{ij} le domaine rectangulaire entourant le point i, j défini par

$$(x, y) \in r_{ij} \quad x_i - \frac{h_{i-1}}{2} < x < x_i + \frac{h_i}{2} \quad \text{et}$$

$$y_j + \frac{m_{j-1}}{2} < y < y_j + \frac{m_j}{2}$$

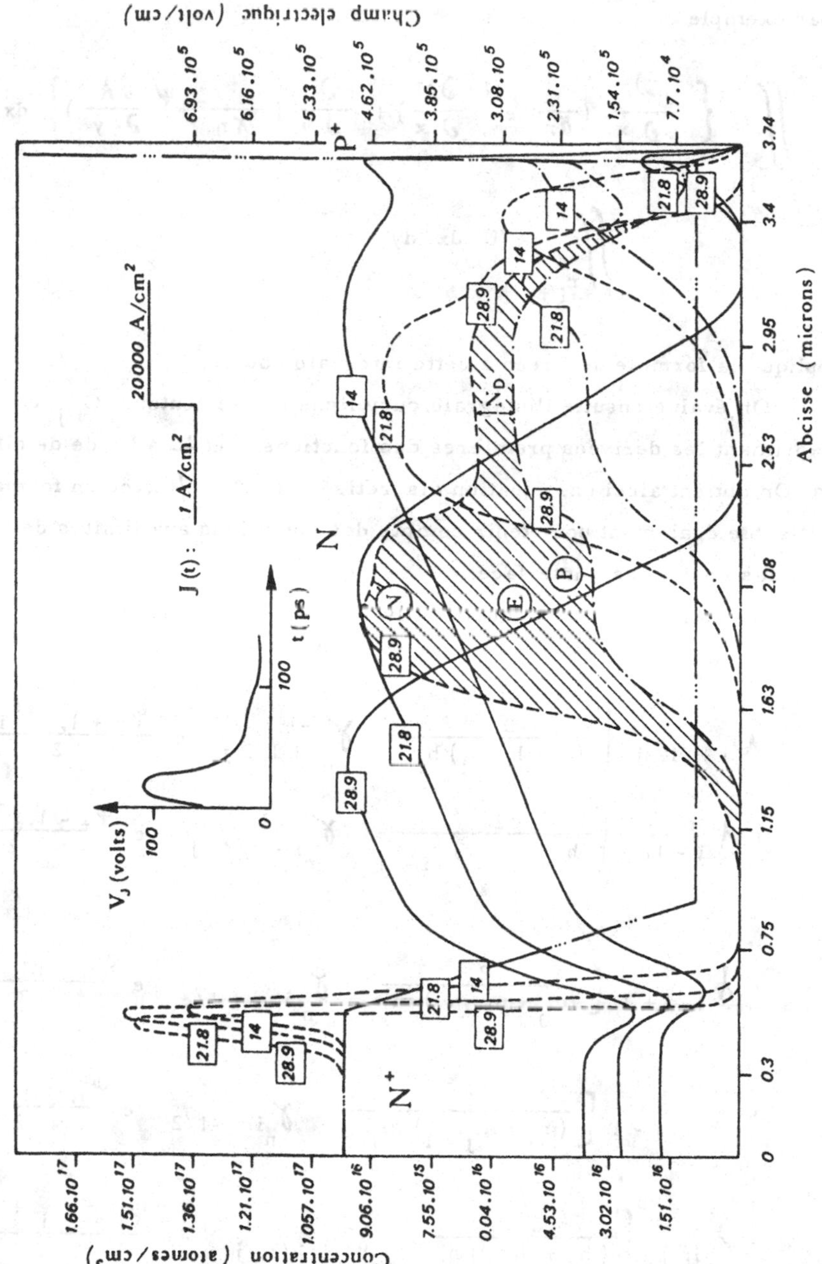

'IGURE 9 - Simulation d'une diode hyperfréquence

on pose par exemple :

(52) $$\iint_{r_{ij}} \left\{ \frac{\partial}{\partial x} \left(\frac{1}{\gamma_n} e^{\psi} \frac{\partial \lambda}{\partial x} \right) + \frac{\partial}{\partial y} \left(\frac{1}{\gamma_n} e^{\psi} \frac{\partial \lambda}{\partial y} \right) \right\} dx\, dy$$

$$= \iint_{r_{ij}} U \; dx \; dy$$

et l'on applique la formule de Green à cette intégrale double.

On évalue ensuite l'intégrale curviligne sur le contour C_{ij} du domai r_{ij} en exprimant les dérivées premières des fonctions λ et μ à l'aide de différences finies. On obtient ainsi une équation discrétisée en λ et μ avec un formalisme qui est utilisable également pour tenir compte des conditions aux limites de type Neumann et des conditions d'interface.

On obtient ainsi des équations linéaires en λ_{ij} et μ_{ij} à l'excepti du terme U_{ij} telle :

(53) $$\lambda_{i+1,\, j} \left[\frac{2}{(h_i + h_{i-1})\, h_i} \gamma_n^{-1}{}_{i+1/2\, j} \; e^{\frac{\psi_{i+1,j} + \psi_{ij}}{2}} \right]$$

$$+ \lambda_{i-1,\, j} \left[\frac{2}{(h_i + h_{i-1})\, h_{i-1}} \gamma_n^{-1}{}_{i-1/2,\, j} \; e^{\frac{\psi_{i-1,j} + \psi_{i,j}}{2}} \right.$$

$$+ \lambda_{i,\, j+1} \left[\frac{2}{(m_j + m_{j-1})\, m_j} \gamma_{n\; i,\, j+1/2} \; e^{\frac{\psi_{i,\, j+1} + \psi_{i,j}}{2}} \right.$$

$$+ \lambda_{i,\, j-1} \left[\frac{2}{(m_j + m_{j-1})\, m_{j-1}} \gamma_{n\; i,\, j-1/2} \; e^{\frac{\psi_{i,\, j-1} + \psi_{i,j}}{2}} \right.$$

$$- \lambda_{i,\, j} \left[\frac{2}{(h_i + h_{i-1})\, h_i} \gamma_{n\; i+1/2,\, j} \; e^{\frac{\psi_{i+1,\, j} + \psi_{i,\, j}}{2}} \right.$$

$$+ \frac{2}{(h_i + h_{i-1})\, h_{i-1}} \gamma_{n\; i-1/2\, j} \; e^{\frac{\psi_{i-1,\, j} + \psi_{i,\, j}}{2}}$$

$$+ \frac{2}{(m_j + m_{j-1})\, m_j} \gamma_{n\; i,\, j+1/2} \; e^{\frac{\psi_{i,\, j+1} + \psi_{i,\, j}}{2}}$$

$$+ \frac{2}{(m_j + m_{j-1})\, m_{j-1}} \; \gamma_{n\, i, j-1/2} \; e^{\frac{\Psi_{i, j-1} + \Psi_{i, j}}{2}} \Big] = U_{i, j}$$

Expressions qui sont utilisables directement uniquement dans le cas des très faibles polarisations et que l'on transforme comme indiqué pour le modèle unidimensionnel de façon à faire apparaître les quantités N et P qui restent d'un ordre de grandeur calculable sur ordinateur et en faisant apparaître uniquement des exponentielles $e^{\Psi_{i, j} - \Psi_{i-1, j}}$ par exemple. Cette discrétisation pose cependant un certain nombre de problèmes liés essentiellement à la précision des résultats obtenus et à l'erreur de discrétisation commise. En effet on a utilisé, pour évaluer l'intégrale double le théorème de Green et l'on fait donc apparaître :

(54) $$\int_{c_{ij}} \left(\frac{1}{\gamma_n} \; e^{\Psi} \frac{\partial \lambda}{\partial x} \right) dy - \left(\frac{1}{\gamma_n} \; e^{\Psi} \frac{\partial \lambda}{\partial y} \right) dx$$

que l'on évalue sur chacun des quatre segments constituant le contour en posant pour l'un d'entre eux par exemple $x = x_i + \frac{h(i)}{2}$; $y_j - \frac{m_{j-1}}{2} \leqslant y \leqslant y_j + \frac{m_{j+1}}{2}$ que l'intégrale curviligne sur ce segment est égale à :

(55) $$\frac{m_{(j)} + m_{(j-1)}}{2} \; \frac{1}{\gamma_{n\, i+1/2, j}} \; e^{\Psi_{i+1/2, j}} \; \frac{\lambda_{i+1, j} - \lambda_{i, j}}{h(i)}$$

alors qu'on aurait dû écrire que cette intégrale en application du théorème de la moyenne est égale à :

(56) $$\frac{m_{(j)} + m_{(j-1)}}{2} \left(\frac{1}{\gamma_n} \; e^{\Psi} \; \frac{\partial \lambda}{\partial x} \right)_{P_o}$$

la fonction $\frac{1}{\gamma_n} \; e^{\Psi} \frac{\partial \lambda}{\partial x}$ étant calculée en un point P_o du segment. On voit apparaître ici une des principales causes d'erreur qui est liée à l'évaluation numérique de e^{Ψ} en un point d'un segment alors que l'on ne connaît les valeurs de qu'aux extrémités de ce segment. Cette constatation impose des contraintes assez strictes sur le maillage (25). Un moyen d'améliorer ce processus consiste à calculer $\int e^{\Psi}$ sur le segment et d'en évaluer la valeur moyenne en supposant une variation linéaire de Ψ le long du segment (10). Cette façon de faire permet d'obtenir des résultats plus acceptables. Il serait préférable d'envisager un lissage très précis de la fonction Ψ ; malheureusement cette solution a coût prohibitif en raison du grand nombre d'itérations nécessaires. Il a par ailleurs été exposé (1) une modification des équations discrétisées pour éviter le calcul systématique de termes exponentiels. Malheureusement cette amélioration ne peut s'appliquer qu'aux faibles polarisations.

La discrétisation de l'équation en ψ se fera en utilisant la même méthode de discrétisation que précédemment ce qui permet de traiter aisément la condition d'interface. On utilise pour cette équation le processus de quasi-linéarisation évoqué précédemment.

L'algorithme général est alors :

1) - Détermination de vecteurs de départ N_o, P_o, ψ_o.
2) - Calcul de la correction sur ψ, λ et μ fixés.
3) - Calcul de la correction sur λ et μ, ψ fixé.
4) - Test convergence et retour éventuel en 2.
5) - Edition des résultats.

Contrairement aux modèles unidimensionnels on devra cette fois utiliser des méthodes indirectes pour résoudre les systèmes d'équations linéaires rencontrés à chaque itération, en raison essentiellement du nombre de points de discrétisation (on prend couramment pour ce problème de 3 à 5000 points). En conservant l'algorithme ci-dessus on a utilisé principalement trois méthodes :

- relaxation par points,
- relaxation par blocs (lignes ou colonnes),
- méthode des directions alternées (Peaceman - Rachford).

La méthode de relaxation par points a été immédiatement abandonnée en raison de sa lenteur de convergence (3 à 4 fois moins vite que les deux autres). Les méthodes de relaxation par blocs et de directions alternées se sont révélées quasiment équivalente, mais s'il a été possible d'évaluer des coefficients de sur-relaxation efficaces et d'apporter une réduction du temps de moitié environ par diverses améliorations de la méthode L. S. O. R. (25) il n'a guère été possible d'accélérer la méthode de Peaceman-Rachford de façon sensible sur ce problème.

On peut aussi penser, accélérer la convergence du processus, modifiant l'algorithme proposé en se contentant par exemple de p balayages complets des lignes du maillage pour l'équation en ψ suivis de q balayages sur les équations en λ et μ et itération de ce processus plutôt que d'attendre la convergence de la méthode indirecte de résolution sur chacun des systèmes linéaires. Cette façon de faire s'est révélée très efficace et il est même très intéressant de faire croître le nombre de balayages au cours du calcul en se contentant d'un seul balayage au début du processus.

Une autre méthode, basée sur une idée exposée par Stone (23), a été utilisée (10), elle semble également très efficace mais sa sensibilité aux paramètres d'accélération la rend d'un emploi relativement délicat. Le gain de temps de calcul reste néanmoins appréciable.

On peut enfin penser que l'application de méthodes d'éléments finis à ce problème devrait permettre une amélioration sensible des performances des programmes et permettre d'aborder dans des conditions réalistes l'étude d'un modèle bidimensionnel dynamique, ce qui est inenvisageable actuellement vu le coût de l'analyse statique. Des études sur l'application de ces méthodes à ce problème sont en cours à l'heure actuelle. Un autre avantage que devraient apporter ces méthodes résiderait dans le fait que l'on pourra s'affranchir de l'obligation des maillages rectangulaires dus aux méthodes de différences finies qui se révèlent trop coûteux pour l'analyse de certains types de dispositifs.

Il reste enfin sur ce modèle un dernier problème à résoudre : celui du calcul des courants. En effet ceux-ci n'apparaissent pas explicitement dans les calculs et il convient de les évaluer à partir des trois inconnues principales λ, μ, ψ.

On a vu que l'on a par exemple :

$$\vec{J}_p = - \frac{1}{\gamma_p} \quad e^{-\psi} \ \overrightarrow{\text{grad}} \ (\mu) \tag{57}$$

expression qui ne serait calculable que pour les très faibles valeurs de polarisation (pour pouvoir exprimer $e^{-\psi}$ et $\overrightarrow{\text{grad}}\ (\mu)$) et qui nécessiterait l'évaluation numérique des dérivées de λ et μ.

Cette façon de faire entraînerait une très forte imprécision dans l'évaluation du courant.

On préférera, pour chacune des composantes des courants J_n et J_p, utiliser une intégration de l'équation (57) entre deux bornes quelconques A et B telle qu'elle a été réalisée pour le modèle unidimensionnel statique ce qui donne par exemple, si l'on intègre entre deux points Y et Y + h , l'équation donnant la composante en Y de J_p soit Y_p.

$$Y_p \ (Y + h) = \frac{P\,(Y) \quad e^{\psi(Y) \ - \ \psi(Y + h)} \ - \ P\,(Y + h)}{h \ \gamma_p \displaystyle\int_Y^{Y + h} e^{\psi(t) \ - \ \psi(Y+h)} \, dt} \tag{58}$$

On retrouve une fois encore la difficulté due à l'évaluation numérique de termes tels $\int e^{\Psi}$ sur un segment quand on ne connaît que les valeurs de aux extrémités. Cette fois cependant on pourra se permettre un lissage de la fonction Ψ car celui-ci ne devra se faire qu'à l'édition des résultats (20). Cette façon de procéder donne des résultats relativement satisfaisants alors que la solution précédemment proposée (25) et reprise par ailleurs (10) amène à des variations sensibles de la valeur calculée du courant en fonction du maillage choisi. Ce point est cependant extrêmement important car c'est uniquement à partir du calcul des densités de courants que l'on peut réaliser une comparaison entre les résultats de la simulation numérique et l'expérience physique.

Des programmes de simulation ont été écrits à partir des méthodes exposées ci-dessus. Il sont sensiblement plus importants que ceux des modèles unidimensionnels (2500 cartes FORTRAN IV environ) et nécessitent une taille mémoire de l'ordre de 300 K octets.

Le temps nécessaire à la simulation d'un dispositif varie de quelques secondes à quelques minutes (2 à 3) sur matériel IBM 360/91, selon le dispositif étudié et la polarisation appliquée. On montre sur la figure 10 à titre d'exemple les résultats obtenus dans la simulation d'un transistor M.O.S. en régime de perçage

Les premières analyses physiques qui ont été faites des résultats obtenus (3, 20, 26) montrent une bonne concordance avec l'expérience et les résultats que l'on pouvait prévoir qualitativement. Il semble que ces programmes devraient se révéler dans un proche avenir un moyen nouveau et très puissant d'analyse physique.

III - CONCLUSION

Bien que de nombreux problèmes mathématiques aient dû être laissés en suspens dans cette étude, tels :

- démonstration de l'existence et de l'unicité de la solution du problème posé,
- démonstration de la convergence de la solution du problème discret vers la solution du problème posé,
- démonstration de la convergence du processus itératif,
- détermination des coefficients optimaux d'accélération.

On a pu montrer par ce travail l'apport extrêmement riche que peut constituer l'application de méthodes numériques de calcul dans le domaine particulier des dispositifs semi-conducteurs.

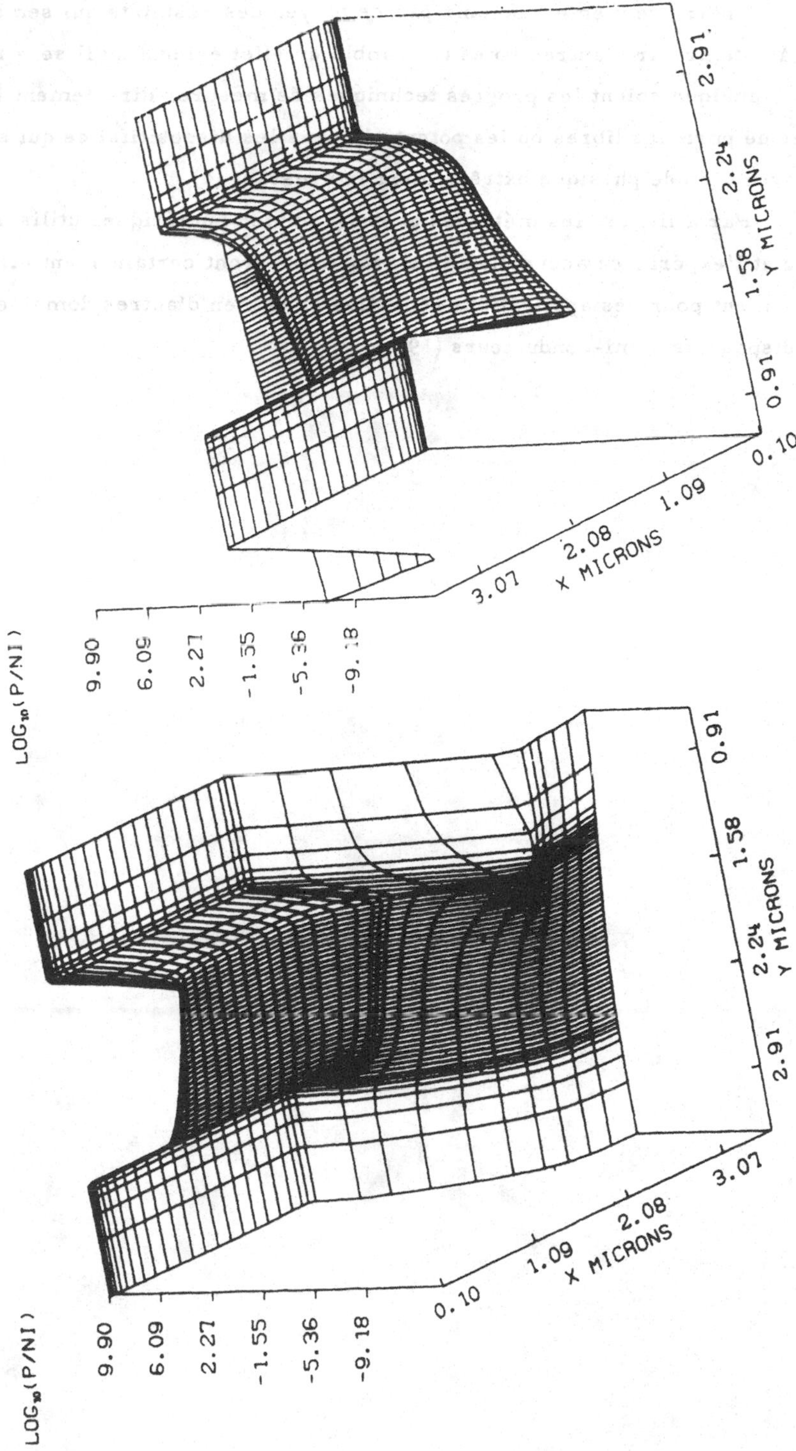

FIGURE 10 - Etude de perçage sur un transistor M.O.S.

On arrive même à obtenir par ce moyen des résultats qui semblent im possibles à obtenir par d'autres voies (il semble en effet évident qu'il sera toujours impossible, quelque soient les progrès techniques de mesurer directement les concentrations de porteurs libres ou les potentiels dans les dispositifs) ce qui se révèl être un moyen d'étude physique extrêmement intéressant (4).

Par ailleurs, les méthodes et programmes numériques utilisés pour cette étude et l'expérience accumulée à ce propos pourront certainement être emplc yés efficacement pour des applications nouvelles dans bien d'autres domaines que celui des dispositifs semi-conducteurs (19).

BIBLIOGRAPHIE

(1) ANDREW R.
Improved formulation of Gummel's algorithm for solving the 2-dimensional current-flow equations in semiconductor devices.
Electronics letters vol. 8 n° 22 536-538 (1972)

(2) BARRON M. B.
Computer aided analysis of I. G. F. E. T.
Techn. Report n° 5501-1 Stanford Labs (1969)

(3) BOREL J., HAJ-SAID F., MERCKEL G., SAINTOT P., VANDORPE D.
A two-dimensionnal analysis of a lateral transistor
E. S. S. D. E. R. C. Munich (1973)

(4) BOREL J., MAFFEI A., MERCKEL G., MONNIER J., SAINTOT P., STERN M., VANDORPE D.
Connection between technology and models using computer analysis.
I. E. E. E. int. Solid state circuits conference. Philadelphie (1973)

(5) DE MARI A.
An accurate numerical steady-state one dimensional solution of the PN junction.
Solid State Electronics vol. 11 p. 33-58 (1968)

(6) DE MARI A.
An accurate one-dimensional solution of the PN junction under arbitrary transient conditions.
Solid state Electronics vol. 11 pp 1021-1053 (1968)

(7) DOUGLAS J.
Survey of numerical methods for parabolic differential equations.
Advances in computers vol. 2 p. 1 Academic press New-York (1961)

(8) GAILLARD R.
Photocourants induits par une impulsion de rayonnements dans les dispositifs semi-conducteurs.
Thèse d'état Lyon (1973)

(9) GUMMEL H. K.
A self consistent iterative scheme for one-dimensional steady-state transistor calculations.
I. E. E. E. Trans. on E. D. E. D. 11 455 (1964)

(10) HEYDEMANN M.
Résolution numérique des équations bidimensionnelles de transport dans les semi-conducteurs.
Thèse Ing. Doct. Paris-Sud (1972)

(11) KELLER J.B.
Résolution d'équations paraboliques aux dérivées partielles ("Méthodes mathématiques pour calculateurs arithmétiques")
Dunod Paris (1965)

(12) KENNEDY D.P., MURLEY P.C.,
Calculations of impurity atom diffusion through a narrow diffusion mas opening.
I.B.M. Jnal 10 pp. 6-12 (1966)

(13) LIONS J.L., MAGENES E.
Problèmes aux limites non homogènes et applications (vol. 1)
Dunod Paris (1968)

(14) MAFFEI A.,
Modèle mathématique unidimensionnel transitoire du fonctionnement des diodes à avalanche.
Thèse de 3ème cycle Lyon (1972)

(15) MOCK M.S.
On the convergence of Gummel's numerical algorithm
Solid State Electronics vol. 15 pp. 1-4 (1972)

(16) MONNIER J.
Simulation numérique de la diffusion d'impuretés dans un semi-conducteur. Application au cas du bore dans le silicium.
Thèse Ing. Doct. Grenoble (1971)

(17) MONNIER J., MAFFEI A., STERN M., VANDORPE D.
Numerical analysis of simultaneous diffusion of several impurities in silicon and silicon dioxide.
Electronics letters 8 pp. 517-518 (1972)

(18) REISER M.
A two-dimensional numerical FET model for DC, AC and large-signal analysis.
I.E.E.E. Trans. on E.D. E.D. 20 pp. 35-45 (1973)

(19) ROUX J.P., TOURNEUR J.L., VANDORPE D.
GENEPI, Générateur de programmes d'intégration.
Rapport D.G.R.S.T. 72.7.0434 (1973)

(20) SAINTOT P.
Analyse bidimensionnelle du transistor M.O.S.
Thèse 3ème cycle Grenoble (1973)

(21) SEIDMANN T.I., CHOO S.C.,
Iterative scheme for computer simulation of semiconductor devices.
Solid State Electronics vol. 15 pp. 1229-1235 (1972)

(22) SLOTBOOM J.W.
Iterative scheme for 1 and 2 dimensional D.C. transistor simulation.
Electronics Letters vol. 5 n° 26 pp, 677-678 (1969)

(23) STONE H. L.
Iterative solution of implicit approximation of multidimensional partial differential equations.
S. I. A. M. Jnal Numer. Anal. vol. 5 n° 3 pp. 530-558 (1968)

(24) VANDORPE D.
Etude d'un modèle mathématique de certains dispositifs semiconducteurs
Ingénieur Docteur Grenoble (1969)

(25) VANDORPE D.
Etude mathématique de la fabrication et du fonctionnement des dispositifs semiconducteurs.
Thèse d'état Lyon (1971)

(26) VANDORPE D., BOREL J., MERCKEL G, SAINTOT P.
An accurate two-dimensional numerical analysis of the M. O. S. transistor
Solid State Electronics vol. 5 pp. 547-557 (1972)

(27) VANDORPE D., MONNIER J.
Two-dimensional analysis of planar diffusion.
Electronics Letters vol. 8 n° 23 pp. 554-555 (1972)

(28) VANDORPE D., XUONG N. H.,
Modèle bidimensionnel de semiconducteurs, effets d'avalanche
Ann. du colloque Int. de microélectronique avancée CHIRON Paris (1970)

(29) VARGA R.
Matrix iterative analysis
Prentice Hall (1962)

(30) XUONG N. H.
Etude du régime transitoire d'un modèle mathématique de jonction PN
Thèse 3ème cycle Grenoble (1969)

Lecture Notes in Economics and Mathematical Systems

Vol. 48: M. Constam, FORTRAN für Anfänger. VI, 148 Seiten. 1973. DM 16,–

Vol. 65: W. Everling, Exercises in Computer Systems Analysis. VIII, 184 pages. 1972. DM 18,–

Vol. 68: J. Loeckx, Computability and Decidability. An Introduction for Students of Computer Science. VI, 76 pages. 1972. DM 16,–

Vol. 75: GI-Gesellschaft für Informatik e. V. Bericht Nr. 3. 1. Fachtagung über Programmiersprachen. München, 9.–11. März 1971. Herausgegeben im Auftrag der Gesellschaft für Informatik von H. Langmaack und M. Paul. VII, 280 Seiten. 1972. DM 24,–

Vol. 78: GI-Gesellschaft für Informatik e. V. 2. Jahrestagung, Karlsruhe, 2.–4. Oktober 1972. Herausgegeben im Auftrag der Gesellschaft für Informatik von P. Deussen. XI, 576 Seiten. 1973. DM 36,–

Vol. 81: Advanced Course on Software Engineering. Edited by F. L. Bauer. XII, 545 pages. 1973. DM 32,–

Vol. 83: NTG/GI-Gesellschaft für Informatik, Nachrichtentechnische Gesellschaft. Fachtagung „Cognitive Verfahren und Systeme“, Hamburg, 11.–13. April 1973. Herausgegeben im Auftrag der NTG/GI von Th. Einsele, W. Giloi und H.-H. Nagel. VIII, 373 Seiten. 1973. DM 28,–

Lecture Notes in Computer Science

Vol. 1: GI-Gesellschaft für Informatik e.V. 3. Jahrestagung, Hamburg, 8.–10. Oktober 1973. Herausgegeben im Auftrag der Gesellschaft für Informatik von W. Brauer. XI, 508 Seiten. 1973. DM 32,–

Vol. 2: GI-Gesellschaft für Informatik e. V. 1. Fachtagung über Automatentheorie und Formale Sprachen, Bonn, 9.–12. Juli 1973. Herausgegeben im Auftrag der Gesellschaft für Informatik von K.-H. Böhling und K. Indermark. VII, 322 Seiten. 1973. DM 26,–

Vol. 3: 5th Conference on Optimization Techniques, Part I. (Series: I.F.I.P. TC7 Optimization Conferences.) Edited by R. Conti and A. Ruberti. XIII, 565 pages. 1973. DM 38,–

Vol. 4: 5th Conference on Optimization Techniques, Part II. (Series: I.F.I.P. TC7 Optimization Conferences.) Edited by R. Conti and A. Ruberti. XIII, 389 pages. 1973. DM 28,–

Vol. 5: International Symposium on Theoretical Programming. Edited by A. Ershov and V. A. Nepomniaschy. VI, 407 pages. 1974. DM 30,–

Vol. 6: B. T. Smith, J. M. Boyle, B. S. Garbow, Y. Ikebe, V. C. Klema, and C. B. Moler, Matrix Eigensystem Routines – EISPACK Guide. X, 387 pages. 1974. DM 28,–

Vol. 7: 3. Fachtagung über Programmiersprachen, Kiel, 5.–7. März 1974. Herausgegeben von B. Schlender und W. Frielinghaus. VI, 225 Seiten. 1974. DM 20,–

Vol. 8: GI-NTG Fachtagung über Struktur und Betrieb von Rechensystemen, Braunschweig, 20.–22. März 1974. Herausgegeben im Auftrag der GI und der NTG von H.-O. Leilich. VI, 340 Seiten. 1974. DM 26,–

Vol. 9: GI-BIFOA Internationale Fachtagung: Informationszentren in Wirtschaft und Verwaltung. Köln, 17./18. Sept. 1973. Herausgegeben im Auftrag der GI und dem BIFOA von P. Schmitz. VI, 259 Seiten. 1974. DM 22,–

Vol. 10: Computing Methods in Applied Sciences and Engineering, Part 1. International Symposium, Versailles, December 17–21, 1973. Edited by R. Glowinski and J. L. Lions. X, 497 pages. 1974. DM 34,–

Vol. 11: Computing Methods in Applied Sciences and Engineering, Part 2. International Symposium, Versailles, December 17–21, 1973. Edited by R. Glowinski and J. L. Lions. X, 434 pages. 1974. DM 30,–

Lecture Notes in Computer Science

Vol. 1: GI-Gesellschaft für Informatik e.V. 3. Jahrestagung, Hamburg, 8.–10. Oktober 1973. Herausgegeben im Auftrag der Gesellschaft für Informatik von W. Brauer. XI, 508 Seiten. 1973. DM 32,–

Vol. 2: GI-Gesellschaft für Informatik e.V. 1. Fachtagung über Automatentheorie und Formale Sprachen, Bonn, 9.–12. Juli 1973. Herausgegeben im Auftrag der Gesellschaft für Informatik von K.-H. Böhling und K. Indermark. VII, 322 Seiten. 1973. DM 26,–

Vol. 3: 5th Conference on Optimization Techniques, Part I. (Series: I.F.I.P. TC7 Optimization Conferences.) Edited by R. Conti and A. Ruberti. XIII, 565 pages. 1973. DM 38,–

Vol. 4: 5th Conference on Optimization Techniques, Part II. (Series: I.F.I.P. TC7 Optimization Conferences.) Edited by R. Conti and A. Ruberti. XIII, 389 pages. 1973. DM 28,–

Vol. 5: International Symposium on Theoretical Programming. Edited by A. Ershov and V. A. Nepomniaschy. VI, 407 pages. 1974. DM 30,–

Vol. 6: B. T. Smith, J. M. Boyle, B. S. Garbow, Y. Ikebe, V. C. Klema, and C. B. Moler, Matrix Eigensystem Routines – EISPACK Guide. X, 387 pages. 1974. DM 28,–

Vol. 7: 3. Fachtagung über Programmiersprachen, Kiel, 5.–7. März 1974. Herausgegeben von B. Schlender und W. Frielinghaus. VI, 225 Seiten. 1974. DM 20,–

Vol. 8: GI-NTG Fachtagung über Struktur und Betrieb von Rechensystemen, Braunschweig, 20.–22. März 1974. Herausgegeben im Auftrag der GI und der NTG von H.-O. Leilich. VI, 340 Seiten. 1974. DM 26,–

Vol. 9: GI-BIFOA Internationale Fachtagung: Informationszentren in Wirtschaft und Verwaltung. Köln, 17./18. Sept. 1973. Herausgegeben im Auftrag der GI und dem BIFOA von P. Schmitz. VI, 259 Seiten. 1974. DM 22,–

Vol. 10: Computing Methods in Applied Sciences and Engineering, Part 1. International Symposium, Versailles, December 17–21, 1973. Edited by R. Glowinski and J. L. Lions. X, 497 pages. 1974. DM 34,–

Vol. 11: Computing Methods in Applied Sciences and Engineering, Part 2. International Symposium, Versailles, December 17–21, 1973. Edited by R. Glowinski and J. L. Lions. X, 434 pages. 1974. DM 30,–